ASIAN RELIGIONS
IN AMERICA

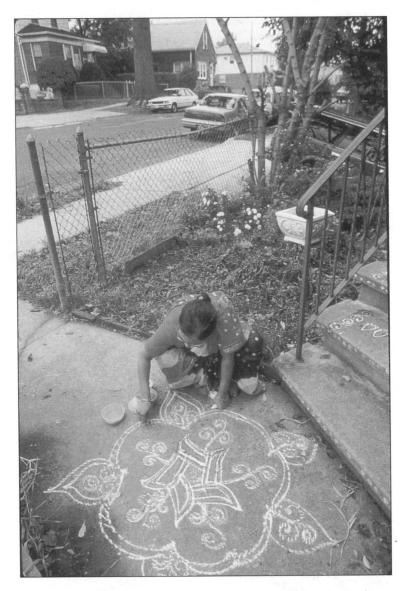

An Indian immigrant paints a Rangoli design on her front stoop in Flushing, New York. Traditionally made of dyed rice flour, these Rangoli paintings are intended to welcome the gods and bring the family good fortune. Copyright © Audrey Gottlieb. Used by permission.

ASIAN RELIGIONS IN AMERICA

A Documentary History

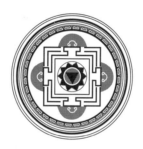

Edited by

THOMAS A. TWEED
STEPHEN PROTHERO

New York   Oxford
OXFORD UNIVERSITY PRESS
1999

Oxford University Press

Oxford   New York
Athens   Auckland   Bangkok   Bogotá   Buenos Aires   Calcutta
Cape Town   Chennai   Dar es Salaam   Delhi   Florence   Hong Kong   Istanbul
Karachi   Kuala Lumpur   Madrid   Melbourne   Mexico City   Mumbai
Nairobi   Paris   São Paulo   Singapore   Taipei   Tokyo   Toronto   Warsaw

and associated companies in
Berlin   Ibadan

Published by Oxford University Press, Inc.
198 Madison Avenue, New York, New York 10016
http://www.oup-usa.org

Library of Congress Cataloging-in-Publication Data
Tweed, Thomas A.
   Asian religions in America : a documentary history / by Thomas A.
Tweed and Stephen Prothero.
      p.   cm.
   Includes bibliographical references and index.
   ISBN 0-19-511338-1 (cloth).—ISBN 0-19-511339-X
(pbk.)
      1. United States—Religion—Sources. 2. Asia—Religion—Sources.
I. Prothero, Stephen R. II. Title
BL2525.T83 1998
200'.973—dc21   98-17674
                                                              CIP

9 8 7 6 5 4 3 2
Printed in the United States of America
on acid-free paper

to William R. Hutchison

CONTENTS

Contents

Contents

Contents

Contents

PREFACE

All books are collaborations among authors, living and dead. Dead authors live on not only in their works, but also in the works of others. Their words transmigrate into epigrams, their books into footnotes, their arguments into occasions for the arguments of others. Sometimes their words find new life in documentary histories like this one, where they mingle with the words of the living, and conspire once again to create a book.

Asian religions in America did not yet exist as a subfield when we met as graduate students at Harvard University in the 1980s. But when each of us cast about for a dissertation topic and reeled in American Buddhism, we were not without collaborators. As far back as the 1930s, Frederic Carpenter wrote *Emerson and Asia*, Arthur Christy *The Orient in American Transcendentalism*, and Wendell Thomas *Hinduism Invades America* (which isn't quite as nasty as it sounds). The investigation of Asian religions in America, such as it was, lay dormant until the 1960s, when the eastward turn in American religion and culture prompted a few sociologists and historians to explore the antecedents. More synthetic studies—Carl T. Jackson's *The Oriental Religions and American Thought* (1981) and Rick Fields's *How the Swans Came to the Lake* (1981)—appeared shortly before we began our graduate work, and shortly thereafter scholars like John Fenton, Raymond Brady Williams, and others produced works devoted to the religious experiences of the new immigrants from Asia.

Today Asian religions in America is emerging as a subfield inside both American religious history and comparative religion. There are now dozens of scholars bringing the insights of history, sociology, anthropology, art history, women's studies, area studies, literary criticism, cultural geography, and religious studies to bear on the subject, which mischievously refuses to respect traditional disciplinary boundaries. Books have appeared on California's Sikhs, American Vedanta, world religions in Atlanta, women in American Buddhism, Asian Americans and the Supreme Court, Chinese-American literature, Asian philosophy in American art, and Buddhism in American poetry. As a result, it is becoming difficult to write a textbook on either religion in America or the religions of Asia without acknowledging that Asian religious traditions aren't just for Asians (or Asia) any more.

In a Supreme Court decision excerpted in this book, Justice William Douglas wrote that the United States was no longer merely a nation of Protestants, Catholics, and Jews. It had become as well "a nation of Buddhists, Confucianists, and Taoists." Our aim in writing this book has been to map the shifting landscape of that nation of religions by documenting the breadth and depth of the American encounter with the religious traditions of Asia. In so doing, we hope to further establish the subfield of Asian religions in America as an important area for both teaching and research.

As we sought assistance in preparing this volume we looked not only to other books but also to colleagues. Robert Ellwood helped get the prospectus off the ground with a number of early suggestions. We later shared the details of our project (in various stages and states of repair) with dozens of scholars, who recommended hundreds of additional entries and, unfortunately, only a handful of deletions. These scholars include John Berthrong, Alfred Bloom, Roger Daniels, Diana Eck, David Eckel, Carl Ernst, John Fenton, Peter Gregory, Brian Hatcher, John Stratton Hawley, Alan Hodder, Victor Hori, Mark Juergensmeyer, Vinay Lal, Bruce Lawrence, Roger Lipsey, Donald Lopez, Jan Nattier, Paul Numrich, Crystal Parikh, Christopher Parr, Charles Prebish, Christopher Queen, Louis Ruprecht, Jr., James Sanford, Jane Singh, Kenneth Tanaka, Timothy Tseng, Richard Seager, Joanne Waghorne, Catherine Wessinger, Raymond Brady Williams, and the anonymous reviewers for Oxford University Press.

Help poured in too from a variety of museums, historical societies, and other institutions: the Religion in Urban America Program at the University of Illinois at Chicago; the Bank of Stockton in Stockton, California; the Haggin Museum, also in Stockton; Boston University's Special Collections; Honolulu's Buddhist Studies Center Press; the Buddhist Churches of America in San Francisco; the Plumas County Museum in Quincy, California; the Nyack Library in Nyack, New York; and Harvard University's Pluralism Project.

Our students pitched in too. For the past few years, we have taught these materials in our own courses in Asian religions and U.S. religion, and in more specialized seminars in Asian religions in America. Our undergraduate and graduate students don't pull punches; they have been some of our best critics. At the University of North Carolina, Chapel Hill, Susan Bales, Phillip Hassett, Sean McCloud, Jennifer Saunders, and Jennifer Wojcikowski were particularly helpful. Polly Trout assisted at Boston University. We also benefited from financial assistance provided by a Collaborative Research Grant from the American Academy of Religion, and by our home institutions of B.U. and U.N.C., Chapel Hill. Our editor at Oxford University Press, Robert Miller, deftly steered the book to publication, as did his assistants, Liam Dalzell, Jeffrey Broesche, and Eric Chinski. Our wives, Margaret McNamee and Edye Nesmith, tolerated our long hours and read and criticized our drafts. Our children—Kevin and Bryn McNamee-Tweed and Molly and Lucy Prothero—waited patiently for the next turn on the computer, or on the phone.

While we have relied in preparing this book on the insights of earlier books and the advice of many scholars and practitioners, we have leaned most heavily on the hundred-plus writers whose words follow our headnotes. Our words are in the minority in this book, which largely allows other authors to speak for themselves, to narrate their stories in their own voices, without annotations or corrections.

When we began working on this book, we knew our authors had tales to tell, but we had no idea how many and varied their stories were. As we conclude our work, we are left with an overwhelming sense of the vastness of this subfield, and of our own inabilities to plumb its depths or track its outer dimensions. This book easily could have swelled to multiple volumes, and it might have gone in a variety of different directions. As editors we made countless agonizing choices. All too often, including one entry meant excluding another. Mark Twain bumped the travelogue of robber baron Andrew Carnegie. Gary Snyder elbowed out fellow poet and Dharma brother Allen Ginsberg. A Vietnamese temple controversy in Los Angeles edged out a similar case in Miami. And in perhaps the unkindest cut of all, Ruth Fuller Sasaki's inclusion necessitated the exclusion of her husband, the Zen master Sokei-an. One expert in religion and literature suggested we include entries by Irving Babbitt, Rabindranath Tagore, Ezra Pound, Eugene O'Neill, Ernest Fenollosa, and Lafcadio Hearn, as well as works by Charles Lanman and James Woods (T. S. Eliot's Sanskrit professors at Harvard). We couldn't find room for any one of them.

Other editors would have crafted a different book. Scholars primarily interested in the experiences of Asian immigrants might have excised works by European-American converts in order to create the space needed to tell a richer and more nuanced immigration narrative. Readers with historical interests may decide that in our efforts to highlight the new Asian immigration we have devoted too much of our book to post-1965 developments. On the other hand, readers with contemporary concerns may decide we have lavished too much attention on dead men and women—the Emersons and Canavarros of our tale.

It has become something of a cliché over the last decade to note how diverse religion in America is (and was). But, as this book demonstrates, America's Buddhisms, Hinduisms, and Sikhisms are no less varied and complex. The stories that emerge in this book are peopled by a vast cast of actors: gurus and roshis, sympathizers and converts, Chinese Americans and African Americans, women and men, children and adults, Confucians and Jains, poets and lawmakers, musicians and monks, priests and presidents, New Englanders and Californians, and immigrants new and old. Each of these actors has her own motivations, his own questions, her own stories to tell. Those stories are played out on a stage that stretches from Japan to Hawaii to California to Cape Cod. They also extend, as this book documents, from 1784 to the present, and, as we will be the first to acknowledge, far beyond the reaches of this book and the collective imagination of its editors.

This history can be read in many different ways. If you are not familiar with Asian religions, you might want to start with the "Introduction to Asian Religions." That essay provides a relatively quick overview of the key beliefs and practices of the major religious traditions of Asia: Hinduism, Buddhism, Jainism, Sikhism, Shinto, Confucianism, and Taoism. It also highlights the diversity within those traditions by discussing, for example, the three main schools of Buddhism and the multiple expressions of Hinduism. After perusing this overview, you might want to know more. If so, we suggest you consult one of the suggested texts on Asian religions listed in "Further Reading."

Readers already familiar with Asian religious traditions but unacquainted with American religious history might want to work through this book with the help of a survey of American religion or a text on world religions in America. Catherine Albanese's *America: Religion and Religions*, Jacob Neusner's *World Religions in America*, and Diana Eck's CD-ROM, *On Common Ground: World Religions in America* might help.

If you decide to read this book, mystery-novel-style, from beginning to end—from the first stirring of interest in Asian religions in the late eighteenth century to the blooming, buzzing confusion of the contemporary period—you should be rewarded with a sense of the grand historical sweep of the story of Asian religions in the United States. With this approach, you can track shifts in American attitudes toward Asian religions from the era of Benjamin Franklin's Oriental Tale (1788) to Gary Snyder's "Smokey the Bear Sutra" (1969), and shifts in rites from the popular Chinese piety outlined in "Pagan Temples in San Francisco" (1892) to a contemporary marriage ceremony at Pittsburgh's Sri Venkateshwara Temple.

Another approach is to read for a story line of your own choosing. If, for example, you want to see how the Buddhist tradition developed in the United States, you might start with treatments of Buddhism in compendia like Hannah Adams's *Dictionary of All Religions* (1817) and James Freeman Clarke's *Ten Great Religions* (1871). You could then move on to Henry David Thoreau's *A Week on the Concord and Merrimack Rivers* (1849) and John Cage's "Lecture on Nothing" (1961). You might also consider works by Asian-American Buddhists and non-Asian-American converts and sympathizers: the letter of the pioneering Japanese Buddhist missionary Shuei Sonoda (1899), the conversion narrative of Theosophist Henry Steel Olcott (1900), and the instructions of Vietnamese Buddhist Thich Nhat Hanh in *The Miracle of Mindfulness* (1975). Hinduism and Sikhism also can be tracked in this way.

But perhaps you're interested in a different narrative. Rather than looking at a particular religious tradition, you might want to focus on one group of actors. If you are interested in Chinese Americans, you might start with the 1876 *San Francisco Chronicle* interview with Fung Chee Pang, a Confucian brought to the United States by Chinatown business leaders for the purpose of getting up a revival of the sage learning of Confucius. If you want to learn about Japanese Americans, you might start with documents related to the World War II internment camps: Roosevelt's Executive Order 9066, the poems of Zen master Nyogen Senzaki from the Heart Mountain camp, and the memoir of Shigeo Kikuchi about the capture and internment of her husband, a Jodo Shinshu priest. You could then move back in time to the writing of Zen pioneer Soyen Shaku, and forward to entries on contemporary Nichiren and Jodo Shinshu Buddhism.

Readers interested in Americans' literary encounter with Asian religion will also find a lot to work with here—poems by Ralph Waldo Emerson, Bret Harte, Walt Whitman, and T.S. Eliot, and excerpts from novels like *Dharma Bums* (1958) and *The Kitchen God's Wife* (1991)—while readers concerned about the role of women in this story can look at entries by (and about) female scholars, teachers, and followers.

Perhaps it's a question rather than a topic that motivates you. How have Asian-born teachers marketed their beliefs and practices to American consumers?

Why have non-Asian Americans left behind Protestantism, Catholicism, or Judaism for Hinduism, Sikhism, or Buddhism? For answers to these questions you can consult entries written by or about swamis, masters, priests, and monks—and an array of autobiographical entries by converts. How has the recent popularity of Asian religions, particularly Taoism, Zen, and Tibetan Buddhism, affected (for better or for worse) the way those religions are understood? On this question, *The Tao of Pooh* (1982) and Phil Jackson's "If You Meet the Buddha in the Lane, Feed Him the Ball" (1995) might be instructive. How have Christians responded to practitioners of Asian religions in their midst? For utterly contrasting views, you might compare E. Stanley Jones's empathetic *The Christ of the Indian Road* (1925) with Walter Martin's censorious *Kingdom of the Cults* (1985).

There is also ample documentation here to begin to investigate Asian religions and the law—the "supply side" of our story. Bills such as the Chinese Exclusion Act of 1882 and the Asian Exclusion Act of 1924 don't make for great reading, but their words carry weight, so we reprint selections from them here. We have included too a number of contemporary Supreme Court decisions that continue to have important ramifications for Asian immigrants, Asian Americans, and non-Asian-American converts alike.

Many readers will be interested primarily in contemporary developments: sex scandals, the rise of American-born and women leaders, the dynamics of new religious movements (NRMs), temple zoning controversies, intergenerational tensions, and interreligious dialogue. They will want to turn right away to the last and longest section of the book: "Passages, 1965 to the Present."

Even if you come to this volume with concerns from the present, it's our bet you'll be drawn back to the past, since in this book, as in the cosmos according to the Buddha, everything is intriguingly intertwined. Members of Los Angeles's Hsi Lai Temple, who following a visit from Vice President Gore became embroiled in an embarrassing fund-raising scandal, play out their lives in a landscape shaped not only by the attitudes and actions of their Vietnamese Buddhist and evangelical Protestant neighbors but also by the assimilative hopes of Frederick Douglass's "Our Composite Nationality" speech, the poignant echoes of the anti-Chinese legislation of the 1880s and 1920s, and the cultural reverberations of films like *Little Buddha* (1993) and songs like "Bodhisattva Vow" (1994).

GENERAL INTRODUCTION[1]

Thomas A. Tweed

In the 1990s, Bart, the animated star of "The Simpsons" television series, meditated cross-legged in one episode and encountered Hindu devotees of Ganesha at the convenience store in another. The Asian guru perched on the mountain awaiting inquirers had become a ubiquitous caricature in entertainment and advertising: in one commercial Michael Jordan of the Chicago Bulls climbed a mountain to seek out an Asian holy man, who advised him to drink Gatorade. At your local mall you could buy Samsara perfume and a Nirvana CD. Movie theaters across the country showed films featuring Tibetan Buddhism, including *Little Buddha*, *Kundun*, and *Seven Years in Tibet*; and *Time* magazine tried to understand "America's Fascination with Buddhism" in a cover story that analyzed these films and other recent signs of interest. At the same time, composers and painters confessed Hindu, Taoist, and Buddhist influence and affiliation. So did icons of popular American culture—movie stars, rock singers, and sports heroes. At bookstores readers could peruse accomplished translations of Asian sacred texts and purchase popular accounts of meditation and yoga. Sitting at the computer, Americans could enter the "cybersangha" by joining a Buddhist on-line discussion group or seek advice electronically about their meditation practice at "cybermonk." They could visit Sikh and Jain homepages and take virtual tours of Hindu temples. They might even change religious affiliation on-line: one web page instructed, "Click here to become a Hindu." Curled in bed, Americans could tutor themselves in *The Tao of Golf* and *The Zen of Recovery*. On street corners, they might encounter Hare Krishnas distributing almost free copies of the Bhagavad Gita. At the therapist's (and who didn't need therapy after all this?) they might be encouraged to try Buddhist mindfulness practice to reduce stress. Most important, in their neighborhoods Americans of European and African descent might encounter Asian Americans in the more than 1,500 Buddhist centers and 400 Hindu communities, and in the new Jain temples and Sikh *gurdwaras*—as the Vice President of the United States did when he visited Hsi Lai, a Chinese Buddhist temple in southern California. Americans also might meet recent Asian immigrants at work, the PTA, the supermarket, or the youth soccer fields. If anyone remained unsure about Asia's influence, they might be convinced by cover stories in *Newsweek* and *Time* that announced that the post-1965 Asian immigrants were changing America's cultural terrain.[2]

Even if the 1960s brought many of these changes, America's encounter with Asia and its religions began much earlier, as this book demonstrates. Columbus had imagined the New World as part of Asia, where he originally was headed when he cast off. However, for most of the colonial period European settlers, native peoples, and African slaves paid little attention to that part of the world. In the first period explored in this volume (1784–1840) that changed as systematic trade with China and India opened in 1784. Suddenly, all along the East Coast—from Salem to Charleston—ships unloaded artifacts, and sometimes people, from Asia. Around the same time translations and interpretations of Asian religions began to appear more frequently in magazines and books, many by those who had lived or traveled in Asia: for example, Amasa Delano published his *Narrative of Voyages and Travels* in 1817. In that same decade, American Protestants began to evangelize in Asian lands. With more information available to Americans and immigrants arriving from Asia, a new period in the engagement with Asian religions opened in the 1840s. Led by Romantic writers and liberal ministers, as well as by foreign missionaries and European scholars, some Americans began to form their first clear impressions of these religious traditions. This period of encounters (from 1840 to 1924) also saw Asian immigrants arrive in significant numbers: the Chinese landed first, then the Japanese, Asian Indians, and others. By the end of the nineteenth century, the unthinkable also had happened—some European Americans had begun to convert to Hinduism and Buddhism.

That personal interest waned after World War I, around the same time the new immigration law of 1924 prohibited Asians from entering America. Asian Americans already in the country continued to practice their religions, of course, but it was not easy in that hostile cultural climate. At the same time, European Americans seemed less interested in the religions of Asia. That began to change in the 1950s, as Asians like D. T. Suzuki influenced American intellectuals and artists, and some American soldiers encountered Buddhism and Confucianism in Korea. However, the major shift happened in the next period, after 1965. In that year Congress revised the immigration laws, opening passage for many more Asians. At the same time, cultural changes in America inclined many to seek alternatives to Western traditions, and some of the disillusioned found their way to Asian religious communities. By the end of the twentieth century, Asian religions had become an undeniable presence in America.

Although some books and articles have begun to trace these developments, much of the history of Asian religions in America has been overlooked and underappreciated. Many Americans still imagine their nation as Christian, or perhaps Jewish and Christian, but the increasing presence of Hindus, Muslims, and Buddhists—along with Sikhs, Baha'is, Confucians, Zoroastrians, and Jains—challenges those assumptions. America is not just multicultural and multiethnic; it is multireligious too. An important part of the nation's religious diversity comes from Asia, and in this book we provide the first historical overview of Asian religions in the United States, using more than one hundred primary documents to tell the story.[3]

By *Asian* religions, we mean religions *of* Asia, not religions *in* Asia. For the sake of coherence—and space—we focus on religious traditions that originated

in South and East Asia. Religions that arose in India (Hinduism, Buddhism, Jainism, and Sikhism) and those that have roots in China and Japan (Confucianism, Taoism, and Shinto) appear here. Islam, by contrast, does not. Although Muslims predominate today in several Asian nations, Islam arose in the Middle East and inherited much from Judaism and Christianity, the other monotheistic faiths that began in that region. While Judaism, Christianity, and Islam are now all in Asia—there are, for example, Muslims in China, Jews in India, and Christians in Korea—they did not originate there. So at least for our purposes they do not count as Asian religions.

A wide range of characters play a role in this story. Asian immigrants are central figures, and we include entries by Chinese, Japanese, Indians, Thais, Koreans, Sri Lankans, and Vietnamese. Asian religious leaders, and their American followers, also have shaped American culture and established religious organizations. Some of those transplanted institutions have attracted mostly followers of Asian descent. Some movements like the International Society for Krishna Consciousness (Hindu), Soka Gakkai International (Buddhist), and the Healthy, Happy, Holy Organization (Sikh) have been founded more recently (although they boast an ancient heritage), and these have drawn mostly non-Asian converts. European-American and African-American converts have announced their allegiance to various Asian religions, and some have even established movements of their own. They tell their stories here too. Before and after Americans began to turn to Asia for spiritual uplift in the middle of the nineteenth century, others had journeyed there and sent back more or less hostile reports: travelers, colonizers, and missionaries typically depicted Asians and their religions as superstitious, backward, and repressive. They focused on the exotic—for example, Indian hook swinging and widow burning—to the delight of their American readers (and to the horror of those Asians who noticed or cared). Missionaries have been especially important interpreters of Asian religions for many Americans. Some Christians and Jews in America engaged in other kinds of encounters, with other aims, as ecumenical movements and dialogue groups began to emerge in the twentieth century. Finally, Asian religions have entered American culture, popular and elite. Here we include selections from many intellectuals and artists who have represented Asian religions, from Ralph Waldo Emerson and Mark Twain to Amy Tan and the Beastie Boys.

These diverse characters confronted a variety of issues. Like immigrants from Europe and elsewhere, Asian Americans have debated how to negotiate sometimes conflicting allegiances to the new land and the old. How much should they resist—or accommodate—American culture? Should Sikh children insist on their right to wear the traditional *kirpan* or dagger in public schools that have metal detectors and weapons regulations? In a nation with a tradition of civil religion and a calendar filled with nationalist celebrations, how do nontheistic Buddhists respond to God references in presidential inaugurations or Memorial Day parades? How comfortable should Asian immigrants get in America? If they came as refugees, like the Vietnamese, should they hope for an eventual return? If they arrived voluntarily, like Asian Indians, how often should they visit their homeland and how fully should they maintain the ancient customs? Finally, as with all immigrants in American history, peoples who have emigrated from Asia have been troubled by intergenerational differences. What should parents, and grandparents, do about their children's loss of traditional values and modifications of religious practice? For their part, the children of immigrants often must deal with the sense of being between two worlds, and not fully of either, as several entries in this book illustrate. Consider the teenage Sikh who asks why her parents treat girls more protectively than other American parents treat their children, or the Thai Buddhist who wonders why his youth group can't have a DJ at the temple dance.

Missionaries also face a range of issues, and those issues are remarkably similar both for American Christians who have evangelized in Asia and Asian religious leaders who have brought their message to the West. Adoniram Judson, the first American Protestant missionary in a Buddhist country, and M. L. Gordon, who evangelized the Japanese later in the nineteenth century, had much in common with Swami Vivekananda, founder of the Ramakrishna movement in America, and Shunryu Suzuki-roshi, who headed the San Francisco Zen Center. Each asked, How do I effectively transmit the religion? How much should missionaries bend beliefs and practices to accommodate the host culture? For example, if Jains are offended by Christians' consumption of meat, and their disregard for animal life, should the Christians who evangelize them in India revise their views and practices? Should Hindu teachers in America demand Indian-style dress and diet, or even the traditional practice of arranged marriage? Or, to consider an issue that Suzuki-roshi confronted, how should Zen teachers deal with the American emphasis on individualism? Because many Americans cherish autonomy, should Zen teachers make them bow more, to cultivate humility, or less, to accommodate their values?

Americans who do not embrace Asian faiths have had their own issues to consider. Christians and Jews have been forced to decide what they believe about other religions: Does one tradition exhaust religious truth? Does one complete the partial truths of the others? Or are there nuggets of truth in all the world's faiths? Some Americans, like the twentieth-century evangelical theologian Carl Henry, have concluded that Jesus is the only sure path to salvation and truth. More moderate Christians and Jews have advanced various forms of a fulfillment model, proposing that their tradition fulfills the limited truths of other faiths. At the most liberal extremes—Unitarian-Universalism, for instance—Americans celebrate truth outside the Judeo-Christian heritage, even incorporating scriptures and practices from other traditions into their religious life. How these Christians and Jews, and those who follow no faith, have assessed Asian religions also has had implications for how they have treated their followers. Everyone in a pluralistic society, and especially those of the predominant faith, confronts the same question: How will I act toward the others around me? Should I ignore them? Should I convert them, exclude them, or engage them?[4]

Americans who have formally embraced an Asian religion face issues that are familiar to converts in other cultural contexts: What does it mean to convert? For interpreters of conversion—and that is what we all become as we read the conversion narratives in this volume—questions arise about why the follower turned to the new tradition. Was it some deficiency or deprivation? To use economic metaphors, was it a "demand-side" response to a widely shared spiritual crisis, or were "supply-side" factors (the increased availability of teachers, translations, and temples) at work? Or was it, as most converts report, the intrinsic value of the new tradition that attracted them? For the converts themselves, however, these issues are, on the whole, unimportant. They worry instead about the meaning of their new religious identity, asking, for example, How can I be a Hindu and an American? How much of my former Jewish faith should I retain and how much of Tibetan Buddhist culture should I adopt? Can I still celebrate Passover? Now that I have become a Sikh, how will my family react when I visit at Christmas wearing the traditional turban? Should I chant in Sanskrit or English? Do I meditate on a *zafu* or a chair? Must I accept rebirth and avoid meat? And what of those who are drawn to an Asian tradition, and maybe even practice it, but do not formally affiliate? These sympathizers might practice Buddhist Insight Meditation during the week and attend the Methodist church on Sunday. How should they make sense of their hybrid religious identity? When asked about their faith, should they say they are Methodist, Buddhist, or something else?[5]

We could multiply examples, but we trust that we have made our point—that the issues Americans confront are as varied as the people themselves, and no single plot emerges from the history of Asian religions in America. Rather, that history unfolds in multiple plots, with the story (and periodization) shifting as the narrator's focus moves from one group (and one issue) to another. There are many characters and issues, and no single story to tell.

Still, historical narratives, like fictional ones, have themes or motifs that give them order. Historians cannot randomly list a series of events; they must put them in a meaningful sequence and interpret the changes over time. As we faced the challenge of telling the complicated story of Asian religions in America through documents, we found that spatial motifs illumined much of that history, and so the book's section titles and section introductions draw on images connected with perceptions of place and movements through space. In particular, we appeal to three spatial themes to tell the story: mapping, meeting, and migration.[6]

MAPPING

When you think of mapping you probably imagine a visual representation of a place, and Americans have mapped Asia in just that way, preparing and consulting representations of the continent's geography. But the term also can be understood more metaphorically. In one sense religion itself is a spatial practice, a cultural process whereby individuals and groups map, construct, and inhabit worlds of meaning. But here we use the term in yet another way. *Mapping* refers to the ways that individuals and groups orient themselves in the natural landscape and social terrain, transforming both in the process.[7]

Americans have always made cognitive maps, imaginative representations of home, neighborhood, nation, and world. Many of the documents in this volume are attempts to imaginatively map the religious world. Travelers and colonizers sometimes did that quite literally, but in a broader sense many interpreters have attempted to orient themselves in relation to Asia, and, after the 1850s, the Asians in their midst. Hannah Adams's *Dictionary of All Religions*, which first appeared in 1784, is such a spiritual cartography. Adams describes the religious world, as well as her sources allowed, and she confronts a "harsh and dreadful truth": most of the world is not Christian. Even though she lived in a small Protestant town southwest of Boston, Adams's world expanded enormously as she read geography texts and travel narratives in booksellers' shops and private libraries. In turn, she mapped the world in new ways.[8]

Mapping refers, however, not only to visual and mental maps, but also to the ways Americans have transformed the built environment. By the last quarter of the nineteenth century Chinese immigrants had transformed the cityscape in San Francisco, as the entry on "Pagan Temples" indicates. The first Chinese temple opened in 1853, and four decades later there were fifteen in the city. Japanese Buddhists also built and renovated temples, first in Hawaii and later in towns up and down the West Coast; and Stockton, California, was transformed in 1915 when Indian Sikhs moved their place of worship from a small renovated home temple to a new *gurdwara* built on an adjacent lot. This process continued among Asian Americans, but temple building increased dramatically after 1965, as religious communities across the nation raised funds to renovate homes and churches or build new sacred architecture, usually in traditional styles but sometimes in hybrid forms that mixed motifs from the homeland with designs from the new land. We consider some of those religious centers in this book: Sri Venkateswara Temple in Pittsburgh and Dharma Vijaya Buddhist Vihara in Los Angeles, Sri Ganesha Temple in Nashville and the Jain temple of Metropolitan Chicago, Yogaville's Light of Truth Universal Shrine in Virginia and Hsi Lai Temple in Southern California. Grand religious architecture like Hsi Lai, the largest Buddhist temple in the western hemisphere, might attract attention, but many smaller centers also dot the American landscape.

MEETING

At those sacred buildings, and at many other places at home and abroad, peoples have encountered each other and Asian religions, and *meeting* is a second theme we draw on to narrate the history of Asian traditions in the United States. At various contact zones, sites in the social and geographical landscape, peoples have met to negotiate power and construct meaning. Both the sites of contact and the types of contact have varied widely. These meetings have been literary (reading popular books on yoga), artifactual (viewing a Chinese sculpture of Kuan Yin in a museum), and interpersonal (encountering a Jain parent at the PTA). Many contacts have crossed religious boundaries; others have been among adherents of the same religion, for example, when Buddhists from every major branch of the tradition have convened at the Buddhist Sangha Council of Southern California. Some contacts have prompted conversions and alliances; others have led to oppression and violence, in America and Asia.[9]

Americans who have journeyed abroad have encountered Asian religions, as Ernest Fenollosa did during his years of teaching in Japan and Elijah Bridgman did in the mission field in China. In the process, interpretations formed and re-formed, but those meetings involved power as well as meaning. One side typically left the contact zone with more economic, political, or social power, as when the art interpreter Fenollosa carried home Japanese art treasures and missionaries like Bridgman represented American "interests" in China—or when American soldiers encountered Asian religions in battlefields in Japan, Korea, and Vietnam.

Americans have encountered each other, and Asian religions, in the United States too, and in a variety of social spaces. Those spaces include the usual religious sites, like Buddhist or Hindu temples, or halls of great symbolic importance, like the meeting place of Chicago's World's Parliament of Religions in 1893. But Americans also have had literary and artifactual encounters in libraries, museums, and homes. Classrooms, work places, and recreational centers have functioned as sites of interpersonal contact and exchange. Consider just two social sites of contact in America, the legal system and popular culture.

As many of the entries in this volume show, Asian religions—especially Zen Buddhism, Vedanta Hinduism, and philosophical Taoism—have penetrated American popular culture. Starting with the Oriental tale and domestic furnishings in the late eighteenth century, this cultural exchange expanded in the nineteenth century and exploded in the twentieth. Americans have met Asian religions in fiction, art, music, health care, therapy, fashion, publishing, the decorative arts, sports, advertising, film, and television. This cultural presence is extensive, especially after 1965. Among the most interesting examples of cultural contact and exchange are the popular books on Taoism and Buddhism sold in bookstores across America. We offer a selection from the best-selling *Tao of Pooh*, but there are many other books in the genre. If we limit the search to books with titles like "Tao of" and "Zen and," and do not include translations of sacred texts or scholarly works, *Books in Print* lists more than sixty works on Taoism and almost two hundred on Zen. These popular prescriptive books deal with almost all dimensions of human life, from the *Tao of Management* to *Zen and the Art of Changing Diapers*. Of course, the treatment of Buddhism and Taoism in these works often is superficial, even annoying or silly, but these popular books have mediated literary encounters with Asian religions.[10]

The legal system has been an even more important contact zone for Asian Americans, and for members of some Asian-inspired new religious movements as well. National and local laws have shaped Asian Americans' experience, often in destructive ways. Most Americans have imagined their nation as a refuge for immigrants, but Asians have not always been welcomed. The First Amendment to the United States Constitution guarantees freedom of religion and a legal separation of church and state, but followers of Asian religions have not always been free to practice their faiths. Racial and religious differences have set Asians apart, and have inspired hatred and prejudice. Asians were made ineligible for citizenship by the 1790 law that limited naturalization to "white" persons, a statute that Congress nullified only in 1952 with the McCarran-Walter Act. The U.S. government treated the Japanese, including some who had been in the country for two generations, as aliens during World War II, and they segregated them in camps when President Franklin D. Roosevelt signed Executive Order 9066 in 1942. Starting with the 1882 Chinese Exclusion Act, laws also kept Asians from entering the nation. The immigration law of 1924 restricted immigration on the basis of a national quota system that, in effect, excluded Asians. Only with the revision of the immigration laws in 1965 did the legal situation change appreciably for Asian immigrants. But everything has not been rosy since. In town after town, Asians trying to build a new place of worship or renovate a home temple have encountered hostility from their neighbors. By reprinting legal decisions, presidential edicts, and immigration acts—as well as three entries written from or about the internment camps—we have tried to illustrate the centrality of the legal system as a site where Americans have met each other, often with harsh consequences for Asian Americans.[11]

MIGRATION

Even if they often have been buffeted about by America's legal system, Asian-American immigrants and their descendants have been an important presence since the 1850s, and *migration* is a third spatial theme in our story. Of course, migration is an important theme not only for the story of Asian religions; it has significance for the whole of U.S. history. Americans, as one historian observed, have been "a people in movement through space." From the emigrations of "Native" Americans from Asia thousands of years ago to the arrival of Cambodian refugees in the late twentieth century, intracontinental and intercontinental movements have shaped American society and culture.[12]

Asians have been arriving in the United States since the nineteenth century, and their numbers and visibility increased dramatically in the twentieth. In 1906, after laws had already restricted Chinese immigration, the U.S. Bureau of the Census counted 62 Chinese temples and 141 shrines in twelve states. The Japanese Pure Land Buddhists already had at least 3,165 official members in twelve organizations, and many more who maintained home shrines and affiliated loosely with Buddhism and Shinto. Although some Asian Indians were admitted to the United States in 1820, they came in significant numbers only in the late 1890s, just as the Japanese were arriving. Almost 3,000 Asian Indians entered America in 1907 and 1908, most of them Sikhs. Many Chinese and Japanese emigrated to Hawaii in the nineteenth century, and at least half of the Koreans who moved there to work on the sugar plantations between 1903 and 1905 were Buddhists. By the first decade of the twentieth century, then, Asians clustered in towns in the American West and Hawaii, but restrictive immigration laws slowed the growth of Asian-American communities for decades after that.[13]

Only after the passing of the Hart-Celler Act of 1965, with its revision of the national quota system established by the 1924 law, did Asian migration increase dramatically. In 1940, Europeans had accounted for 70 percent of immigrants; fifty years later that proportion had shrunk to 15 percent. At the same time, the Asian presence grew: Asians accounted for 37 percent of the total immigration between

1960 and 1989. As a result, the Asian-origin population doubled during the 1980s, rising to more than 7.2 million. By 1990 Asians constituted 3 percent of the U.S. population, and, with Asians continuing to arrive in large numbers each year, demographers predicted the number would rise to 10 percent by 2050.[14]

Those post-1965 Asian immigrants have come from a variety of nations and practiced a number of religions. Approximately half have been Christians: most Filipinos are Catholic, and the majority of Korean immigrants are Protestant. Many Muslims have arrived too, some of them from Asian lands like Pakistan and Indonesia. Still, many of the new immigrants follow one of the religions that originated in Asia. In the 1990s, there were more than 815,447 people of Asian Indian descent in the United States, and as many as 650,000 of them practiced Hinduism. More than 100,000 were Sikhs or Jains. Hundreds of thousands of the new immigrants also have been Buddhists, including Mahayana Buddhists from Vietnam and China and Theravadins from Thailand and Sri Lanka. Estimates of the number of American Buddhists—of European, African, and Asian descent—vary from 401,000 to 4 million, with most observers putting the figure at between 1 and 2 million. Considering only followers of Asian descent, one scholar estimated that there were 500,000 to 750,000 Theravada Buddhists from Laos, Kampuchea, Thailand, Sri Lanka, and Myanmar. A significant proportion of the 1,645,472 Chinese reported in the 1990 U.S. Census were influenced by Buddhism, Confucianism, and Taoism, although it is impossible to say how many; and between 60 and 80 percent of the 593,213 Vietnamese, most of whom have arrived since the fall of Saigon in 1975, claim Buddhist heritage.[15]

These transnational migrations—together with the effects of American conversions and the diffusion of Asian influences—have made the cultures of the United States more diverse than ever. Almost from the first settlements, this land has been religiously and ethnically diverse, with Africans, Natives, and Europeans in contact. After the passage of the First Amendment, the diversity increased, as old denominations split and new religions formed, and immigrants from Europe transformed U.S. society. By the end of the nineteenth century more forms of Christianity and Judaism flourished in America than anywhere else in the world. By the end of the twentieth century, however, a new global diversity had taken hold. Americans had mapped Asia and met its peoples and religions earlier, as the documents in this volume clearly show, but after the 1960s diversity had become not just one feature of the American religious landscape; it was the major one.

The religious world that Hannah Adams tried to map in the eighteenth century had arrived in America by the end of the twentieth. Pluralism had intensified in ways that she hardly could have imagined. Within a short drive from her hometown south of Boston, for example, now stands Sri Lakshmi Temple for Asian Indian Hindus, New England Center of Tao for Euro-American practitioners, Glory Buddhist Temple for Cambodian Buddhists, New England Sikh Study Circle for Panjabi Sikhs, the Jain Center of Greater Boston, and many other religious buildings where Baháís, Zoroastrians, and Muslims worship. This diversity is not confined to New England, however; it extends across the nation. Muslims will soon surpass Jews as the second largest religious tradition in the

United States, and Hindus and Buddhists together could soon outnumber Jews as well. By most counts, in America in the 1990s there were more Buddhists than Quakers, more Muslims than Episcopalians, more Hindus than Disciples of Christ. Columbus might not have found Asia, but five hundred years later Asia certainly had discovered America. In a land transformed by meeting and migration, Americans were struggling to remap the world—and reimagine the nation.[16]

NOTES

1. Portions of the General Introduction were published previously in Thomas A. Tweed, "Asian Religions in America: Reflections on an Emerging Subfield," in Walter H. Conser Jr. and Sumner B. Twiss, eds., *Religious Diversity and American Religious History: Studies in Traditions and Cultures* (Athens and London: University of Georgia Press, 1997), 189–217. Used by permission of the University of Georgia Press.

2. Leland T. Lewis, *The Tao of Golf* (Saratoga, Calif.: R & E Publishers, 1992). Mel Ash, *Zen of Recovery* (New York: J.P. Tarcher, 1993). David Van Biema, "Buddhism in America," *Time,* 13 October 1997, 72–81. Richard Corliss, "Zen and the Art of Moviemaking," *Time,* 13 October 1997, 82–83. Bruce Handy, "A Conversation Runs Through It: Brad Pitt on Buddhism, Fame, and Argentine Girls," *Time,* 13 October 1997, 84. On *Little Buddha* see Helen Tworkov, "Projecting the Buddha: On the Set with Bertolucci," *Tricycle: The Buddhist Review* (Summer 1993): 22–29. Celebrities who have confessed interest in or affiliation with Buddhism include Richard Gere, Patrick Duffy, Phil Jackson, Herbie Hancock, Adam Yauch, Tina Turner, and Steven Seagal. Seagal was even identified in 1997 as the reincarnated Tulku of the Nyingma lineage of Tibetan Buddhism. On celebrity Buddhist interest see also "In with the Om Crowd," *New York* 27, 6 June 1994, 30–34. On the "cybersangha" see Gary L. Ray, "A Resource Roundup for the Cybersangha," *Tricycle: The Buddhist Review* 3 (Summer 1994): 60–63. *Cybermonk* is a service of Zen Mountain Monastery's Dharma Telecommunications in Mt. Tremper, New York, and users can reach the on-line Zen practice advisors at: cybermonk@mhv.net. *Hinduism Today,* the Honolulu-based periodical, maintains the web page inviting browsers to "Click Here to Become a Hindu" (http://hoohana.aloha.net). The estimates of Hindu and Buddhist centers in the United States are based on several sources. One helpful source is Diana Eck, *On Common Ground,* CD-Rom (New York: Columbia University Press, 1997). *Hinduism Today* regularly publishes lists of Hindu centers in North America. Many, though not nearly all, of the Buddhist centers are listed in Don Morreale, *Buddhist America: Centers, Retreats, Practices* (Sante Fe: John Muir Publications, 1988). The estimate for Buddhist centers was confirmed in a telephone interview with the president of the Buddhist Sangha Council of Southern California and president of the College of Buddhist Studies in Los Angeles, who has been involved in a study that aims to identify all Buddhist centers in the United States: Telephone interview, Dr. H. Ratanasara, 23 January 1997. On Vice President Albert Gore's visit to Hsi Lai Temple in Hacienda Heights, California, on 29 April 1996, and the scandal about Democratic Party fund raising that followed, see Christopher Drew and Don Van Natta Jr., "Gore Temple Visit Had Hint of Goal," *New York Times,* 12 June 1997, A1, A15. On Hsi Lai Temple see Irene Lin, "Journey to the Far West: Chinese Buddhism in America," *Amerasia Journal* 22 (1996): 107–32. For some of the print coverage of immigrants see "The New Face of America: How Immigrants Are Shaping the World's First Multicultural Society," *Time: Special Issue* (Fall 1993); Jerry Adler, "The New Immigrants," *Newsweek,* 7 July 1980, 26-31. On converts see "Buddhism in America," *New York Times Magazine,* 3 June 1979, 28–30, 93–99; "More Drawn to the No-frills Spirituality," *USA Today,* 10 August 1994, 1D–2D; "800,000 Hands Clapping," *Newsweek,* 13 June 1994, 46–47.

3. For assessments and citations of the scholarly work done on Asian religions in the United States, see the following: Carl T. Jackson, "The Influence of Asia upon American Thought: A Bibliographical Essay," *American Studies International* 23 (April 1983): 3–31; Thomas A. Tweed, "Asian Religions in the United States: Reflections on an Emerging Subfield," in Walter H. Conser Jr. and Sumner B. Twiss, eds., *Religious Diversity and American Religious History: Studies in Traditions and Cultures* (Athens: University of Georgia Press, 1997), 189–217; and John Y. Fenton, *South Asian Religions in the Americas: An Annotated Bibliography of Immigrant Religious Traditions* (Westport, Conn.: Greenwood, 1995).

4. Carl F. H. Henry, "Supplementary Note: On Finding Christ in Nonbiblical Religions," in *God, Revelation, and Authority,* (Waco, Texas: Word, 1976–83), vol. 6: 360–69. For an official Roman Catholic view see Vatican II's *Nostra Aetate*: Pope Paul VI, *Declaration on the Relation of the Church to Non-Christian Religions,* Proclaimed by His Holiness, Pope Paul VI on October 28, 1965 (Boston: The Daughters of St. Paul, 1965). For Unitarian-Universalist views see their 1984 "Statement of Principles," reprinted in a pamphlet by Jack Mendelsohn, *Meet the Unitarian Universalists* (Boston: Unitarian Universalist Association, 1993). For a helpful typology of attitudes and approaches toward other religions see J. A. Dinoia, "The Doctrines of a Religious Community about Other Religions," *Religious Studies* 18 (1982): 293–307.

5. On the use of the term *sympathizers* see Thomas A. Tweed, *The American Encounter with Buddhism, 1844–1912: Victorian Culture and the Limits of Dissent* (Bloomington: Indiana University Press, 1992), 42–43.

6. On the usefulness of *place*—and mapping, meeting, and migration—as a theme for narrating Latino religious history and a motif for retelling U.S. religious history see Thomas A. Tweed, *Our Lady of the Exile: Diasporic Religion at a Cuban Catholic Shrine in Miami* (New York and Oxford: Oxford University Press, 1997), 134–38. On the problem of narrating American religious history see Thomas A. Tweed, "Introduction," in Thomas A. Tweed, ed., *Retelling U.S. Religious History* (Berkeley: University of California Press, 1997), 1–23.

7. Extending the theorizing of Jonathan Z. Smith and Charles H. Long, Tweed defines religion as a spatial practice and a form of mapping in *Our Lady of the Exile*, 91–98. Jonathan Z. Smith, *Map Is Not Territory: Studies in the History of Religions* (Chicago: University of Chicago Press, 1978), 291; Charles H. Long, *Significations: Signs, Symbols, and Images in the Interpretation of Religion* (Philadelphia: Fortress, 1986), 7.

8. Hannah Adams, *A Dictionary of All Religions and Religious Denominations*, 4th ed., reprint, Classics in Religious Studies Series, Introduction by Thomas A. Tweed (1817; Atlanta: Scholars Press, 1992), 375.

9. This view of *meeting* has been shaped by a number of historical, ethnographic, and theoretical studies, including the work of Mary Louise Pratt, who introduced the term *contact zones* in *Imperial Eyes: Travel Writing and Transculturation* (London and New York: Routledge, 1992).

10. *Books in Print, 1996–97,* (New Providence, N.J.: R.R. Bowker, 1996); Bob Mesing, *Tao of Management* (New York: Bantam, 1992); Sarah Arsone, *Zen and the Art of Changing Diapers* (Ventura, Calif.: Printwheel, 1991).

11. Many relevant laws and court decisions, as well as American responses to them, are collected in Philip S. Foner and Daniel Rosenberg, eds., *Racism, Dissent and Asian Americans from 1850 to the Present: A Documentary History* (Westport, Conn.: Greenwood, 1993). Thomas Pearson also has talked about the legal system as a "contact zone." See Thomas Pearson, "Santería in the Contact Zone," *Excursus: A Review of Religious Studies* 7 (Fall 1994): 5–14.

12. Sidney E. Mead, *The Lively Experiment: The Shaping of American Christianity* (New York: Harper and Row, 1963), 7.

13. The information in this paragraph, and the following ones, comes from a variety of primary and secondary sources, including John Y. Fenton, "Hinduism," in Charles H. Lippy

and Peter W. Williams, eds., *Encyclopedia of the American Religious Experience* (New York: Scribner's, 1988), and Thomas A. Tweed, "Buddhists," in David Levinson and Melvin Ember, eds., *American Immigrant Cultures* (New York: Macmillan, 1997). Statistics were taken from the U.S. Bureau of the Census. On the 1906 figures see U.S. Bureau of the Census, *Religious Bodies: 1906*, Parts 1 and 2 (Washington, D.C.: Government Printing Office, 1910).

14. Peter Kivisto, "Religion and the New Immigrants," in William H. Swatos, Jr., ed., *A Future for Religion?: New Paradigms for Social Analysis* (Newbury Park, Calif., and London: Sage, 1993), 92–108. The demographic predictions appeared in "The New Face of America," *Time*, 15.

15. Tweed, "Buddhists." The estimate of the number of Theravadins in the United States comes from Paul Numrich, *Old Wisdom in the New World: Americanization in Two Immigrant Theravada Buddhist Temples* (Knoxville: University of Tennessee Press, 1996), xix.

16. For a listing and description of the religious centers in the Boston area see Diana Eck, ed., *World Religions in Boston: A Guide to Communities and Resources* (Cambridge, Mass.: The Pluralism Project, Harvard University, n.d.). The comparisons of religious affiliation rates are based on those reported by the National Survey of Religious Identification by the Graduate School of the City University of New York: Barry A. Kosmin and Seymour P. Lachman, *One Nation Under God: Religion in Contemporary Society* (New York: Harmony Books, 1993). Most other estimates report an even higher proportion of affiliation with Asian religions in the United States.

INTRODUCTION TO
ASIAN RELIGIONS

If you are unfamiliar with Asian religions, you might consult one of the historical surveys or reference works listed in the bibliography. Many volumes have been written on this vast topic, and we could not hope to cover it exhaustively here. Still, some readers might welcome a brief overview of the Asian peoples and religions we introduce in this documentary history.

From the earliest American encounters with Asia, diverse religions and peoples have been lumped together in the popular imagination. As one scholar has noted, "Throughout their history in this country, Asians have been struggling in different ways to help America accept and appreciate its [Asia's] diversity." The same has happened with their religions. Nineteenth-century interpreters regularly confused Hinduism and Buddhism, and fused all traditions outside Christianity and Judaism into one "Oriental religion." Almost everyone in America did this before 1840, and many did so years later. Even sophisticated interpreters made these mistakes, and they persisted into the next century. For example, only a very small proportion of the "Hindoos" who emigrated from India during the first decades of the twentieth century actually practiced Hinduism, even though that was how American journalists often portrayed them at that time. Ten percent of those Indian immigrants were Muslims, and most were Sikhs.[1]

If we are to avoid similar mistakes, it is crucial to distinguish the multiple ethnic (and national) groups of Asia on the one hand and the many religious traditions of Asia on the other. Among the immigrants from Asia ten groups have been most influential, numerically and culturally, in the United States: Chinese, Japanese, Indians, Sri Lankans, Koreans, Filipinos, Laotians, Thais, Cambodians, and Vietnamese. These immigrants affiliated with a range of religions when they arrived, including Hinduism, Buddhism, Islam, Sikhism, Zoroastrianism, Jainism, Shinto, and Christianity. Although most immigrants from Thailand are Buddhists and most from the Philippines are Catholics, there is no exact correspondence between nationality and religion. In many cases, the situation is quite complex, as it is among Asian Indians and, to add another example, Vietnamese. Although Roman Catholics constitute approximately 10 percent of the Vietnamese population, they are disproportionately represented among emigrants to America. Estimates suggest that between 29 and 40 percent of Vietnamese refugees in the United States affiliate with Catholicism. Most Vietnamese in the homeland and in the diaspora, however, are Buddhists. To make it more complicated, some describe themselves as Taoist and Confucian, and influences from those traditions also have shaped the native and transplanted cultures.[2]

Diversity also characterizes each of the religious traditions themselves. Consider first the religions that originated in India.

RELIGIONS OF INDIA

Hinduism

The notion of a unified tradition called "Hinduism" arose, to a great extent, as an imaginative construct of Western interpreters, especially during the eighteenth and nineteenth centuries. There are multiple forms of Hinduism, which vary significantly according to differences in ethnicity, nationality, class, region, and historical period. Still, there are family resemblances, common features that occur among many, if not all, of the 80 percent of India's 800 million people who might be identified as Hindus.

Traditionally, Hindus have suggested that all humans have four basic aims in life: wealth (*artha*), pleasure or happiness (*kama*), duty or virtue (*dharma*), and liberation from the cycles of existence (*moksha*). The first two aims—wealth and pleasure—are easiest for Western readers to understand. But what do Hindus mean by *dharma* and *moksha*?

As with all religions, there are moral and ritual duties that all Hindus must meet, but a person's obligations also are determined by other factors, most notably one's caste and stage of life. The caste system, a network of inherited social groupings, is breaking down in contemporary Indian cities, although it survives in some rural areas. That system of classifying members of Indian society identifies thousands of distinct groups and subgroups, each associated with particular occupations and regions. But Indian tradition distinguished four main social groupings (*varnas*): priests (*brahman*); rulers and warriors (*kshatriya*); commoners such as farmers, merchants, and traders (*vaishya*); and servants (*shudra*). A person's *dharma* or duty, then, depends on caste obligations to some extent. It also depends on the person's stage of life (*ashrama*), since different obligations are associated with each. The duties of a student, the first stage of life, are not the same as those of a householder, the second stage, when one's primary responsibility is to care for the home and family. In the third stage, that of a forest dweller, the person retires from the chores of family life, traditionally to a forest to meditate on spiritual matters. Finally, even if few actually do this, one might become a wandering ascetic, one who has renounced the world and all its moral and ritual obligations.

Wealth, pleasure, and duty are not the final goal. Many devotionally inclined Hindus imagine humans' ultimate aim as the "enjoyment" of or union with a personal god. On the other hand, many Hindu ascetics suggest that humans want *moksha* most of all. *Moksha* (literally "liberation") means release from the cycles of existence, which they understand in impersonal terms as the absorption of the self (*atman*) in the absolute (*Brahman*). In the Indian world view—shared by most Buddhists, Jains, and Sikhs too—all life moves through endless cycles of birth, death, and rebirth (*samsara*). One's place is determined by *karma*, the moral law of cause and effect. A nineteenth-century German philosopher said that you are what you eat; the doctrine of karma suggests that you are what you do. Every deed has moral consequences, in this life and the next. It is not as if a divine law-giver is punishing some and rewarding others. Karma operates more impersonally (and automatically) than that. Good actions bring good effects; bad actions bring bad effects.

Doing one's moral and ritual duties, according to the obligations of caste and life stage, is a prerequisite, a necessary but not sufficient condition for reaching final release or moksha, and the path to final release can vary, according to most Hindus. Employing a scheme used in the classic Hindu text, the *Bhagavad Gita*, and which elite nineteenth-century Hindus later refined as an apologetic device, many Hindus have identified three alternative strategies or paths to liberation (*margas*). *Karmamarga*, the path of action, requires that the devotee perform all the usual moral and ritual duties outlined in the Vedas and other sacred texts. Some Indians, including the social reformer and political leader Mohandas Gandhi (1869–1948), also have drawn on the teachings of the *Bhagavad Gita* to imagine this path of action as the selfless performance of one's obligations. In that understanding of *karmamarga* one does good deeds without concern for their personal consequences.

Jñanamarga, the second path, does not seek knowledge as technical mastery or factual accumulation; rather, the path of knowledge seeks spiritual wisdom, mystical insight into reality as it is. This is usually achieved through a series of religious disciplines. The Upanishads, part of the ancient Hindu texts called the Vedas, teach that a person's soul or self (*atman*) is identical with ultimate reality (*Brahman*). Realizing this, according to the path of knowledge, is the key to finding liberation. Building on this view, the Vedanta Hindu tradition emerged in India after 200 CE. It was more fully articulated around 800 CE by Shankara, who sought direct consciousness of the true self through concentration. This concentration, he argued, leads to a state of consciousness, *samadhi*, in which one sees reality as it is, beyond the illusion of usual perception. Followers of the way of knowledge also turn to *yoga* as a process that brings union of atman and Brahman, of self and ultimate reality. Yoga commonly refers to acts of meditation, concentration, or self-denial, as well as to exercises involving controlling the breath or moving the body. A number of systems of yoga developed in India, including the eight-stage system developed by Patanjali whereby the follower uses focused concentration to disentangle matter from spirit and unite the human self and the divine spirit, and *kunadalini yoga*, a process that aims to awaken the latent spiritual power residing at the base of the spine.

Followers of the other main religious path in Hinduism, *bhaktimarga* or the path of devotion, place their hopes for liberation in the power of a personal god. If most forms of *jnanamarga* understand ultimate reality as impersonal and view the religious goal as union with the absolute, *bhaktas*, or followers of the way of devotion, emphasize veneration of a deity and aim at union with that god or goddess. They venerate many gods, although there are three main deities, and three corresponding types of devotional Hinduism: Shiva, the god who destroys the cycles of existence (Shaivism); Vishnu, the preserver of the cycles of existence (Vaishnavism); and the Goddess (Shaktism).

The followers of these three forms of devotional Hinduism—Shaivas, Vaishnavas, and Shaktas—engage in a number of ritual practices: reciting the deity's name (*namajapa*), congregational singing (*samkirtana bhajana*), oblations and fire sacrifices (*homa, yajna*), and pilgrimage (*tirthayatra*). Especially important are rituals of image worship (*puja*) in the home or the temple, where devotees offer hospitality to the god by presenting flowers or food.

All these forms of Hinduism—karmamarga, jnanamarga, and bhaktimarga—have found expression among the approximately 650,000 Hindus in the United States, but American Hinduism is still more complex than that. Gerald James Larson, a scholar of Indian religion and observer of its American expressions, has identified five major forms of Hinduism in the United States. First, many American Hindus follow a devotional path (*bhakti*) that closely resembles traditional practices in India, even if temple symbols and rituals have changed somewhat in the diaspora. In India, temples are dedicated to a particular god or goddess, and they also enshrine his or her divine consorts and manifestations. But many of the almost fifty major Hindu temples built in America are more religiously eclectic. To accommodate the regional, linguistic, ethnic, and religious diversity of Asian-Indian devotees in America, they often enshrine many unrelated deities. For example, the Hindu temple in Flushing, New York, one of the first two to be consecrated in the United States, was erected to honor the god Ganesha, the elephant-headed Lord of auspicious occasions, but additional shrines for devotees of Vishnu and Shiva were added to accommodate the religious needs of the diverse Indian immigrants in the region.[3]

Second, some professional Indian men in America do not affiliate with any religion; they are, according to Larson, "secular Hindus". In other words, if you interrogated them in a telephone survey, they might tell you they are not religious at all. Still, Larson suggests, they have been shaped by Hindu cultures. Other Asian-Indian immigrants might acknowledge that they are religious, but defining their affiliation might be more difficult. They draw on a range of religious practices that originate in their native caste or region, even if they do not affiliate formally with any particular institutional branch of Hinduism. These are, in Larson's language, "non-sectarian Hindus." A fourth type of Hindu adherent in the United States formally identifies with one of the reform groups that arose before and after Indian independence in 1947, such as the Ramakrishna Mission, which Vivekananda founded in 1897 to promote Vedanta philosophy and advocate social reform. Finally, small numbers of Asian Indians—and larger numbers of American converts—have joined the new guru-centered religious movements that Hindu missionaries have carried to the West, including the International Society for Krishna Consciousness (or Hare Krishnas).

Buddhism

A similar complexity characterizes Buddhism in Asia and the United States. This pan-Asian religion that originated in India took on many different forms as it spread. Sometimes the differences among Buddhists seem so great that an out-sider might wonder whether they practice the same religious tradition. All they seem to have in common is that they take the life and teachings of the founder, Siddhartha Gautama (563–483 BCE), as normative in some way.[4]

Whatever their differences, most Buddhists agree to trust—or "take refuge in"—the "Three Jewels": (1) the founder, whom followers revere as "the Awakened One" (*buddha*); (2) his exemplary teachings and experience (*dharma*, not to be confused with the Hindu term for duty); and (3) the religious commu-nity he founded (*sangha*). According to Buddhist tradition, the Buddha presented some of his most important teachings in his first sermon at Deer Park in Sarnath, India. There he talked about the Four Noble Truths: the truth of suffering, the truth of the origin of suffering, the truth of the ending of suffering, and the truth of the path that leads to elimination of suffering. He taught that all humans suf-fer, and they do so because they desire. They desire, in turn, because they fail to understand the nature of things (all things, including the self, are without sub-stantial or enduring reality). But there is a way out, a path to *nirvana*, the elimi-nation of suffering and release from the endless cycles of rebirth (*samsara*). Buddhists can follow the "noble eightfold path." In simplest terms, that path to liberation involves morality, wisdom, and concentration.

If Buddhists agree to revere the Three Jewels—Buddha, his teachings, and his community—they also have disagreed among themselves in important ways. Divisions among Buddhists began as early as one hundred years after the Buddha's death. Although the diversity within the tradition is more rich than this scheme can convey, Buddhists have identified three major forms of the religion, or three Buddhist "vehicles": *Theravada*, *Mahayana*, and *Vajrayana*.

Theravada Buddhism (literally "Teachings of the Elders") described a gradual path of individual religious striving. The original Buddhist community was made up of monks who renounced the world, with lay supporters of various degrees of dedication offering contributions. Following that early model, lay Theravada Buddhists, or those who are not monks, have followed the moral and religious teachings of the Buddha, but they have not engaged in the same renunciations that lead more directly to nirvana, although they do gain "merit" by supporting the monks and nuns (for example, by providing food and clothing). That, lay Theravadin Buddhists believe, might help them achieve a better rebirth in the next life. This form of Buddhism has had great influence in Southeast Asian coun-tries such as Sri Lanka (formerly Ceylon), Myanmar (formerly Burma), Thailand, Kampuchea (formerly Cambodia), and Laos.

Mahayana (literally "Great Vehicle") Buddhists dismissed their opponents from other Buddhist sects or movements, including the Theravadins, as the "lesser vehicle". Their "great vehicle" emphasized the active virtue of compassion as well as the reflective virtue of wisdom, which was so highly valued by Theravadins. The ideal for Theravada Buddhists was the *arhat*, one who is free from all impu-rities through the realization of nirvana and, so, free from all subsequent rebirth. Mahayanists, even lay followers, aimed higher. They sought to *become* a Buddha, one who achieves full enlightenment for the sake of all beings and embodies com-passion as well as wisdom. This emphasis on the path of the *bodhisattva* (future

Buddha)—and not the path of the *shravaka* (future arhat)—has distinguished the Mahayana sects that have predominated in East Asian nations such as China, Korea, and Japan.

A third major division within Buddhism, *Vajrayana* ("Diamond Vehicle"), emphasized that the religious path could be briefer, even in this lifetime. It suggested that this world of rebirth and suffering (*samsara*) is ultimately identical to the final state of liberation and bliss (*nirvana*), at least for those spiritually advanced persons who could see reality as it ultimately is. Vajrayanists reconceived of the religious goal in texts called *tantras*, and in their practices followers used sacred syllables (*mantras*) and cosmic paintings (*mandalas*). As with the other two forms of Buddhism, this Vajrayana or Tantric tradition had Indian roots, but it has predominated in Tibet and Mongolia.

By the 1970s almost the full range of Buddhist traditions had found a place in the U.S. religious landscape. Whereas in Asia one Buddhist vehicle or another tended to dominate in a region, in the United States myriad Buddhist traditions were brought together. Vajrayana Buddhism was represented among the 1,970 Tibetans living in the United States in 1995, and by the more numerous European-American and African-American converts to Tibetan forms of Buddhism, but few Asian Americans have arrived from nations where Vajrayana predominates. Theravada and Mahayana Buddhism have had much greater influence among immigrants. Southeast Asians who arrived in significant numbers during and after the 1960s have transplanted forms of Theravada Buddhism, and American converts have been drawn to forms of meditation carried to the United States from Southeast Asia. East Asian immigrants and teachers from China and Japan have brought forms of Mahayana, especially Zen Buddhism, Nichiren Buddhism, and Pure Land Buddhism. Zen originated in China (where it is called *Ch'an*), as Taoism and Buddhism blended into a tradition that emphasizes meditation and the study of *koan*, or religious riddles. In Japan, Nichiren (1222–82) founded a sect of Buddhism that later inspired new religious movements such as Soka Gakkai. Nichiren-inspired Buddhism has focused attention on one sacred text, the Lotus Sutra. The heart of the sect's religious practice involves chanting "hail to the wonderful law of the lotus" before the *gohonzon*, a scroll depicting Nichiren's sacred calligraphy. Other Buddhists, including the Japanese members of the Buddhist Churches of America, have been Pure Land Buddhists. They focus their devotion on Amida Buddha, the Buddha who presides over the Western paradise and brings his faithful devotees to that "pure land." Although rebirth there does not constitute nirvana, or the final religious goal, from that Western paradise it is much easier to achieve.

Jainism

If Hinduism and Buddhism have been the Asian religions with the most influence in the United States (and so require the fullest explanation), others have had an impact too. One of those, Jainism, arose in India around the same time as Buddhism, and shared much with that religion and with Hinduism too. The early history of Jainism remains obscured, but that Indian religion probably was founded in the sixth century BCE by Vardhamana Mahavira. Jains accept, with modifications, traditional Indian views of rebirth and karma, and they too strive for *moksha*, liberation from the cycles of birth and rebirth.[5]

Jains are probably best known for their emphasis on *ahimsa*, or noninjury. They hold that because all living beings have *jiva*, or soul-substance, humans should refrain from all forms of violence, physical and emotional. That is why Sushil Kumar Muni, a Jain monk who arrived in America in 1975 (the second Jain monk to settle in the United States), wore the traditional mask over his mouth to keep from inhaling insects and carried a brush to sweep insects from his path. This Jain emphasis on nonviolence influenced religions and cultures in India from King Ashoka (c. 265–38 BCE) to Mahatma Gandhi. It has influenced the United States too. Without the criss-crossing influence of the Jain principle of nonviolence—from India to Henry David Thoreau to Gandhi to Martin Luther King and others—the civil rights movement in America might have taken a very different course.

But Jainism's American presence has been broader than that. According to a directory published by the Jain Center of Greater Boston, 75,000 of the world's 4 million Jains live in North America. (The vast majority remain in India, mostly in four western and north central Indian states.) That Jain center in Boston was one of the first to be established in the United States, in 1973, and others have followed. Jains in Boston and elsewhere have revised traditional practice in some ways because of the smaller numbers of followers in most U.S. temples. For example, Jains in India are divided into several subgroups. Especially important is the ancient division among those who argue nudity is required as an ascetic practice for monks (the *Digambara*) and those who claim that wearing a single garment is a sufficient symbol of the monks' detachment from the body and the world (the *Shvetambara*). In American Jain temples those traditional divisions have largely disappeared, as Jains of all kinds have gathered together for worship.[6]

Sikhism

Sikhism, which was founded in the Punjab region of northern India in the sixteenth century by Guru Nanak (1469–1539), also has a presence in America. This religion shares some features with devotional Hinduism and monotheistic Islam, but followers emphasize its distinctiveness. Sikhs stress devotion to the one transcendent and invisible God, the *Sat Nam* (True Name). They also revere a lineage of sixteenth- and seventeenth-century gurus and a sacred book, the *Adi Granth*, which contains the guru's teachings. Sikh men in India stand out because they wear the five identifying symbols of the tradition, known as the five K's: *kes* (uncut hair), *kangha* (comb), *kara* (steel wrist bangle), *kirpan* (short dagger), and *kacch* (undershorts). Each symbolizes a Sikh value: undershorts represent purity; the long hair, comb, and bangle symbolize unity; the sword signals the devotee's willingness to defend the faith. If these symbols (especially the long hair tied in turbans) set them apart, Sikhs also share many beliefs with the Hindus around them—and not only the emphasis on gurus or religious teachers. Sikhs also accept the view that life proceeds through a series of cycles of birth and rebirth, which are determined by karma. They agree too that the world is veiled in *maya*, or illusion, and that *dharma*, or fulfilling one's moral duty, is the way to gain spiritual merit. They do not advocate any form of yoga, however, preferring instead meditation, communal worship (*kirtan*), and concentration on the divine name as means of achieving the highest religious state, *Sachkhand*, the "realm of truth."

Although their numbers have never been large in America, Sikhs have found a place in the nation's religious landscape. Indian immigrants, most of them from the Punjab, arrived by the thousands during the first decade of the twentieth century, and by the end of the century Sikh *gurdwaras* or places of worship had been built from New York to California. This Indian religion also has attracted several thousand American converts, including those who have joined the Healthy-Happy-Holy Organization (3HO), founded in Los Angeles in 1969 by Yogi Bhajan, a Sikh from Delhi.

RELIGIONS OF EAST ASIA

One Indian religion, Buddhism, had great cultural influence in China, and from there it shaped religion and culture in Korea, Vietnam, and Japan as well. Several other religions originated in East Asia. Among the most important are Confucianism and Taoism in China and Shinto in Japan. These faiths interacted in East Asia to produce hybrid traditions and cultures. Among East Asian immigrants to the United States it can be difficult to disentangle these multiple religious influences, and the impact of folk traditions and new religions as well. One scholar has estimated that half of the 2,794,130 Americans of East Asian descent in the United States in 1990 maintained some link to the traditional religions of China, Korea, and Japan. That figure might be inflated, but it is undeniable that these traditions have shaped Asian-American religious life since the middle of the nineteenth century and have influenced American culture since the opening of the China trade in 1784.[7]

Shinto

The ancient indigenous religious practices of Japan gradually came to be recognized and organized as a distinct religion after the entry of religions from China, especially Buddhism. For most of its history, Shinto, or "the way of the *kami*," focused on local gods, shrines, and celebrations. The term *kami* refers to sacred or divine presences that appear in several forms: as mythological deities of heaven and earth; as local forces of nature such as sacred mountains, rivers, and trees; or even as human beings, including the emperor himself. Most Shinto rituals are aligned closely with the seasons—for example, spring, fall, and the new year—when local followers participate in annual festivals at the nearby shrine, although they approach shrines at other times too, calling the *kami*'s attention by clapping their hands twice, to petition them for personal favors. The religion, which had always been linked with both nature and the nation, became in practice the state religion after the Meiji Restoration in 1868. That intimate link between religion and the state, which had consequences in World War II, was severed after 1945 as the emperor announced (to the astonishment of the Japanese people) that he was not divine, and the new American-influenced constitution disestablished Shinto.

In Japan, Shinto intertwined with Buddhism (and Taoism), as many Japanese were married by Shinto priests and buried by Buddhists, and in the United States it has been a part of the religious life of many Japanese Americans since the 1890s. The tradition has gone largely unnoticed in the United States, except when it became associated in the American imagination with the martial impulses of the Japanese during World War II. There are some Shinto shrines in the United States; among the most notable is the Tsubaki Grand Shrine in Stockton, California. Even if Shinto shrines have been less numerous and visible than Buddhist temples, Japan's indigenous tradition has had subtle but enduring influence on the religious practice of Japanese Americans.

Confucianism and Taoism

Two other East Asian religions have had more influence. Confucianism is a philosophical and religious tradition that originated in China and went on to shape all East Asian religions and cultures. It has its roots in the teachings of Confucius (551–479 BCE), whom many have revered as a great sage, a model of the "noble person" (*chun-tzu*). Although other texts came to have authority too, and the tradition absorbed influences from Taoism and Buddhism, most Confucians recognize the centrality of the five classic books: the *Analects* of Confucius (*Lun Yu*), the *Mencius* (*Meng-tzu*), the *Book of History* (*Shu-ching*), the *Book of Poetry* (*Shih-ching*), and *Book of Changes* (*I-ching*). Confucius, and many in the schools of thought that followed him, focused on moral and political questions, asking how individuals should act and how society should function. The sage emphasized the practice of moral virtues, especially humaneness (*jen*) and filial piety (*hsiao*); and in dealings between family members, friends, and ruler and subject these moral virtues must be applied. In a Confucian worldview the family is central, and the ancestor veneration that is so important in China and elsewhere in East Asia is really an application of the Confucian moral principle of filial piety: you should treat family members properly, in life and after death. Confucius held that proper ritual action was as important as sound moral action, and the tradition developed religious as well as philosophical forms, honoring the founder in temples and conducting rites in Chinese civil religion. Confucian ethics of harmony and decorum also shaped the Japanese constitution of 604, and spread in Japan during the Tokugawa period (1600–1868). The tradition shaped Korean culture too. Confucianism's impact in America, as in East Asia, primarily has been as a system of moral values for Chinese, Korean, and Japanese immigrants and their descendants, although some American intellectuals influenced by the Enlightenment found themselves drawn to it.

Taoism also originated in China. As with Confucianism, scholars have debated how to define the tradition, or even whether it represents a single tradition at all. Most agree, however, that it developed as both a philosophical and religious system in China, and from there spread throughout East Asia. As a philosophical school, Taoism arose in China during the Warring States period (481–221 BCE). It emphasized the importance of acting in accordance with the *Tao*—the Way, or natural process—rather than blindly following social norms or individual interests. By the early Han dynasty (206 BCE–220 CE), it also had come to be associated with theories of the cosmos, the cult of immortality, and the ideal of religious transcendence. It developed as an organized religion, with a line of ordained priests, later in the Han period. That religion focused on finding immortality—overcoming death and joining the Taoist pantheon of immortals. Both the philosophical and religious forms of Taoism look to Lao-Tzu as founder, although scholars are not sure whether a historical person of that name actually existed. In any case, Taoist tradition venerates Lao-Tzu as the author of a text produced in the mid-fourth century BCE, *The Book of the Way and Its Power* (*Tao-te ching*), one of the foremost Taoist classics.

In California and Hawaii, traditional Chinese temples, and homes shrines as well, combined Taoist and Buddhist symbols. Some of those temples survive, and new temples and centers have flourished, such as Massachusetts's New England Center of Tao, which attracts mostly European Americans. In America, while Confucianism attracted the attention of some elites as early as the 1780s, Taoism's cultural influence has been most profound since the 1960s, and it has appeared in a few principal forms. First, the Taoist tradition has shaped systems of physical and mental cultivation called Tai Chi and Chi Kung, which aim to strengthen the life-breath or inner energy called *chi*. Tai Chi is a system of exercise with roots in twelfth-century China; Chi Kung uses fixed and moving postures of meditation to circulate *chi*—and achieve longevity and health. Second, Taoism, together with Zen Buddhism, has influenced forms of the martial arts that have attracted American practitioners, from children to the elderly. Finally, Taoism has been filtered into popular culture in books that apply its principles to the problems of daily living. In these texts the term *Taoism* has been applied to a wide range of beliefs and practices, many of which the ordained leaders of religious Taoism would not recognize as part of their tradition. As with the popularizations of other Asian religions, however, that does not prevent these interpretations from having wide appeal and great influence in the United States.

T.A.T.

NOTES

1. Ronald Takaki, *Strangers from a Different Shore: A History of Asian Americans* (New York: Penguin Books, 1989), 473. Takaki, *Strangers*, 295.

2. Paul James Rutledge, *The Vietnamese Experience in America* (Bloomington: Indiana University Press, 1992), 47–49.

3. Gerald James Larson, "Hinduism in India and America," in Jacob Neusner, ed., *World Religions in America: An Introduction* (Louisville, Ky.: Westminster/John Knox, 1994), 177–202. Larson's five types are: (1) devotional (bhakti); (2) secular Hinduism; (3) nonsectarian Hinduism; (4) reformist-nationalist neo-Hinduism; and (5) guru-internationalist-missionizing neo-Hinduism.

4. Dating the life of the historical Buddha is difficult. Different Buddhists have offered different dates. Traditionally, those in Sri Lanka and Southeast Asia list the life of the Buddha from 624 to 544 BCE; East Asian Buddhists usually give a later date, 449 to 368. Modern scholars usually give the date I use here, although many also suggest a later date. Everyone agrees, however, that the Buddha lived for eighty years.

5. In fact, classical Hinduism appears to have taken its views of karma, rebirth, and moksha (which are not found in the Vedas) from indigenous traditions in India, including Jainism.

6. The estimate of Jains in North America is found on the web page of the Jain Center of Greater Boston: "The Jain Center of Greater Boston," 2 July 1997, maintained by Veeral Shah, http//web.mit.edu/veeral/www/jcgb.html. The section on "The Jain Directory" suggests that the 1992 version listed about 16,000 Jains in North America, but "there are now about 75,000 Jains in North America. . . . "

7. Robert S. Ellwood estimated that half of East Asian Americans maintain links with the traditional religions, in "East Asian Religions in Today's America," in Neusner, ed., *World Religions in America*, 223.

P A R T   I

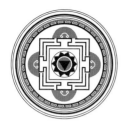

ORIENTATIONS,
1784 to 1840

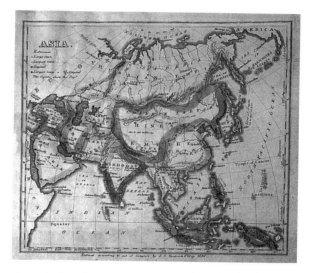

An early American attempt to map the Asian landscape, from the Reverend C. A. Goodrich's *Outlines of Modern Geography* (1826).

In 1784 Jedidiah Morse, a Congregationalist minister and founder of American geography, published *Geography Made Easy*. Whether or not geography was as easy as Morse had suggested, some literate Americans in the former British colonies began to get a sense for the vast global landscape. Also in 1784, Hannah Adams, a liberal opponent of Morse, published the first edition of her influential survey of the religious world, and Sir William Jones and twelve other British gentlemen in colonized India established the Asiatik Society of Bengal, whose publications would provide literate Americans with the results of the first Western scholarship about Asia. Most important, in 1784 the *Empress of China* set sail from New York harbor for Canton, and the *United States* anchored off Pondicherry, thereby initiating systematic trade with China and India. So began this period when Americans oriented themselves in the widening religious world.

At the start of this period Americans began to write Oriental tales, stories set in the exotic East, the nation's first genre of religious fiction. Several decades later, beginning in the 1810s, conservative Protestants like the Baptist David Benedict and the Congregationalist Charles A. Goodrich published book-length interpretations of Asian religions. But Unitarians, the liberal Congregationalists who rejected the doctrines of Calvinism, and deists, Enlightenment rationalists who excised the supernatural from religion, were the most sympathetic interpreters in this period, even if no American would convert until the next. Among the Unitarian interpreters of Asia were Hannah Adams and Joseph Priestley, who wrote one of the first systematic comparisons of world religions published in America, *A Comparison of the Institutions of Moses with Those of the Hindoos and other Ancient Nations* (1799). Unitarian magazines, like the *Christian Disciple* (1813–23) and its successor the *Christian Examiner* (1824–69), published interpretations of Asian religions in this period, as did the *Monthly Anthology* (1803–11) and the *North American Review* (1815–1940). Among American deists who read about Asia were Benjamin Franklin, John Adams, and Thomas Jefferson, although President Adams probably had the most serious interest. Franklin tried his hand at writing an Oriental tale in 1788. Adams and Jefferson, like Franklin and most rationalists of the period, especially admired the naturalistic philosophy and ethical emphasis of Confucianism. In that Chinese tradition they found a historical instance of the "natural religion" they had sought, a tradition free from the intolerance and superstition they saw in the supernaturalist traditions of the West.

Americans at home also could encounter Asian religions in the reports sent back by European colonial representatives in Asia, and the journal published by the Asiatik Society of Bengal, *Asiatik Researches* (1788–1839). Hannah Adams read *Asiatik Researches*, and so did other intellectuals at home. Still other American readers encountered reprints from *Asiatik Researches* in American or European magazines, like the *Edinburgh Review* (1802–30). Western scholarship about Asia continued to develop in the years ahead, and three decades after the founding of the Asiatik Society of Bengal a French university established the first chairs in Sanskrit and Chinese. Americans would not follow European scholars' lead until the next period, when a few Bostonians would establish the American Oriental Society in 1842. Even before then, however, many American readers were influenced by the emerging European scholarship.

This period of orientations also saw the first face-to-face meetings with Asia and Asians, led by those who were involved in international trade. The effects of those contacts were immediate and enduring all along the eastern seaboard, as elite Americans decorated their homes with artifacts from Asia, especially China. In one of those seaports, Salem, men who had traveled to Asia founded the East India Marine Society in 1789. And as entries from a member's diary show, the Society's parades and museum offered residents who could not travel abroad a glimpse of things Asian.

Americans who did journey abroad, travelers and missionaries, encountered followers of Asian religions directly, and they sent back reports for readers at home. Using the available sources to guide their interpretations, travelers like Amasa Delano wrote accounts of their journeys and the peoples and religions they met. While the travelers had been motivated by curiosity or lured by profit, other Americans began to go abroad to save souls. Roman Catholics had sponsored missions in Asia since the first contacts in the late medieval period, and they began systematic efforts to convert the "heathen" after the Portuguese reached India in 1498. For the next two and a half centuries, Catholic missionaries sent back descriptions of the religions they encountered in China, Japan, India, and elsewhere. Those accounts provided Europeans with enduring impressions of those traditions, and Catholic missionaries continued to be quoted in American books and magazines into the middle of the nineteenth century. European Protestant missionaries got a later start, in the first decade of the eighteenth century, but their efforts continued with vigor for two centuries. The Danes, Germans, and English sent back reports from India and elsewhere, and some of those missionary narratives reached American audiences. Sparked by evangelical fervor and inspired by European examples, in the 1810s American Protestants sent their own missionaries to Asia, first to India and Burma. In 1830, they began to preach the gospel in China, following paths that the British had cleared. The *Missionary Herald* and similar magazines printed reports from the mission fields, interpreting the Asian religions missionaries encountered and exhorting American readers to support the cause. As you might expect, the tone of most of those letters and articles was not very sympathetic. Filled with pity and driven by conviction, most Protestant missionaries of this period left home to save the unconverted heathens, who, they believed, otherwise were condemned to eternal torment. It is not surprising, then, that their reports from the mission field emphasized Asians' impoverished religious condition—and the need for continued evangelization.

If some Americans at home had literary and artifactual encounters with Asia, and sailors and missionaries met others abroad, few had interpersonal contacts with Asians on American soil before 1840. Legends assert that the Chinese discovered the West Coast of North America in 459, but reliable historical evidence suggests that the first Asians landed in the late eighteenth century. One report claims that three Chinese crewmen (Ashing, Achun, and Accum) from the ship *Pallas* were stranded in Baltimore harbor in 1785, and in the next decade a few Chinese merchants, carpenters, and servants arrived in Philadelphia. Two other Chinese servants sailed into San Francisco Bay on 2 February 1848 (the first Asian settlers on record) but only forty-three Chinese immigrants lived in America before 1850. This was a period, then, of mapping, and some initial meetings. Asian migration would become important only after the 1840s.

As Americans mapped the religious world during this opening period, they divided it (in descending order of value) into Christian, Jewish, Mahometan (Muslim), and pagan. The category *pagan*, or *heathen*, included an enormous variety of religions, including the indigenous traditions of Africa and the Americas. It also included the religions that originated in Asia, and Hindus and Confucians appeared prominently on most Americans' map of the religious world. Buddhism's Indian origin and Asian history remained unclear to most interpreters; Taoism, Shinto, Sikhism, and Jainism were even more remote, only barely visible in the religious landscape.
T.A.T.

CHAPTER 1

Views from Abroad

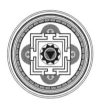

AMASA DELANO, *A NARRATIVE OF VOYAGES AND TRAVELS* (1817)

Travel accounts shaped Americans' views of Asian religions, and Amasa Delano (1763–1823), a ship captain from Massachusetts, published an important one in 1817. A distant ancestor of President Franklin Delano Roosevelt, Delano came from an old New England family, with roots that stretched back to a French Protestant who joined the British Puritans in Holland and arrived in America in 1621. In 1787 Delano took command of a ship bound for Portugal. On the return voyage, the ship was wrecked off Cape Cod, and he came home to financial difficulties. To make ends meet he accepted a job as second officer of the *Massachusetts*, a new ship built for the China trade. From 1790 to 1810 Delano was almost always at sea. He spent the last years of his life in obscurity, although he now is remembered as the author of one of America's earliest and richest travel narratives. *A Narrative* records his impressions of the cultures and religions he encountered. It was informed by his own journal and some of the standard printed sources of the day: encyclopedia entries, travel reports, and the translations and commentaries of British Orientalists such as Sir William Jones. In this selection Delano recalls his journey to India in 1794. He highlights the exotic: Hindus bathing in the holy Ganges River and widows burning with their husbands' corpses (called *sati* or suttee). He also criticizes the caste system, which outraged many Westerners. In turn, many Indians were outraged by Western interpretations, like this one, which distorted and overemphasized these Hindu practices.

. . . It is a common opinion among the natives that the water of the Ganges and of its branches washes away sins. They throw the bodies of their deceased friends

Amasa Delano, *A Narrative of Voyages and Travels in the Northern and Southern Hemispheres* (Boston: E. G. House, 1817), 242–46.

into the river, and even put them into the water to die, when the physicians have despaired of effecting a cure. I have often seen them bring their fathers, brothers, and sons, when they were about dying, to the river on their backs: plaster the mouth, nose, eyes, and ears with mud; and leave them to be carried away by the tide. I have stayed at the bank to watch the conduct of the victims afterwards, and have seen them blow the mud from their mouths and noses; lie still till the water began to rise upon them; turn over upon their faces; crawl upon their hands and knees to the market place; lie down again upon their backs; and cry out for alms or assistance. They were shunned, their cries were disregarded, and they were considered as losing their cast for having refused the blessing of dying in the Ganges according to the custom and faith of their religion. The power of the clergy over the popular faith is so great, that it is extremely difficult to regain one's standing in a cast, after it is lost by any of the higher forms of impiety. The penance for such an one is so severe that an outcast is seldom restored to favour. The nearest friends will never show them affection or regard while they continue under disgrace. Outcasts are often punished in the following manner. Two hooks are put into the back; these are fastened to the end of a pole which is suspended in the middle about fifteen feet high; a rope is attached to the other end of the pole; drawing this rope raises the victim, who has a basket of flowers in his hands; these he is obliged to scatter upon the heads of the people below, as he is carried round upon the end of the pole, which is fixed upon a pivot, and makes a full circle. They perform some prescribed service by a chant during the punishment. The same custom prevails on the coast of Coromandel. Such is the power of this religion over the faith and feelings of the people. It would be gratifying to us, if no tortures in the persecutions carried on by Christians could be found to compare with this in cruelty. But while the excesses of the dominicans, the barbarities of the inquisition, and the mutual destruction too often effected between opposing sects of protestants, make us ashamed of many nominal Christians, we still remember the purity and benevolence of the religion whose laws are violated whenever its disciples indulge such passions and cruelties.

I have seen one woman burnt with her deceased husband. This practice, which is constantly diminishing, seems to have arisen from several causes. The most natural one is that of attachment to the husband, and of grief at the loss which may easily seem at first to be inconsolable. Another reason is the assurance, given by their religion, that the wife, who proves her fidelity by this extreme suffering, shall live with her husband in paradise forever. It is also an idea, handed down by tradition, that as the ashes of the parties are mingled, when their bodies are burned together, so their souls shall be united in affection and happiness for eternity. Wives in India, and under the laws and religion of the Gentoos, are considered as entirely at the command of the husbands, and as included in them, in the same manner that the term mankind includes all women as well as all men. On this principle, the wife is to die when the husband does. Some have supposed that the jealousy of the husband extends beyond the grave, and that the wife is to be burnt to gratify this passion. But such a reason is not consistent with the general character of the Hindoos, and is too vile to be admitted without far stronger evidence that has been offered to support it.

When the husband dies, it is common to inquire of the oldest wife, if she wishes to burn herself with his body. If she refuses, the next is asked; and so through the whole number. Whatever might once be thought of a refusal, it is not now considered as a crime, although to make the sacrifice is an honour, and a great distinction. The laws both of the Christians and the Mahometans have tended powerfully to diminish the custom, and a premium must be paid in order to gain permission to be burnt. This premium is high, and often cannot be paid. When a widow is about to offer herself with the body of her deceased husband, the funeral pile is prepared; the wood is split very fine, and I believe is wet with spirits of some kind to make it burn easily and rapidly; a bed of this is raised six feet square, and two feet thick; the corpse is brought and laid upon it; a priest leads the widow, who steps upon the pile, and lays herself down by her husband, putting her arms around his neck; and his arms are laid so as to embrace her. Two bamboo poles are then fastened into the ground, and are bent over the bodies, crossing each other, the ends being held by two priests. The pile is kindled in several places at once, the fire burns rapidly, and the poles are pressed down upon the bodies till the widow is suffocated and ceases to move. During this ceremony, the priests chant hymns and prayers; and sometimes the voice of the victim is heard for a moment mingling its tones of faith and triumph with the notes of the priests. The bodies are burnt to ashes, and these are preserved; a preservation however which must be temporary, and which is every year of less and less importance.

The cast of bramins once consisted of the most harmless beings in the world. According to their ancient rules, they take the life of no creature; they eat no animal food; they are very superstitious; they worship idols, and particularly some kinds of cattle; a white cow is perfectly sacred in their eyes. A bramin will brush the earth before he sits down, and pray that as he has been merciful to the ant, the Deity may be merciful to him.

The Hindoos have always been divided into four casts, which never intermarry. The *soodra* is the lowest cast, and includes menial servants. The next is the *byse,* consisting of the merchants of all ranks. The third is the *ketri,* or the military tribe. The kings and rulers belong to this cast. The last and highest is the cast of the *bramins.* The sooddras are from the feet; the byses from the belly; the ketris from the heart; and the bramins from the head of Brama. Notwithstanding the ancient purity and benevolence of the bramins, they are now often immoral, ignorant, and cruel. Many of them do honour to their cast, but like all other classes of privileged men, there are many also extremely corrupt. The learning of India is confined to them, and they have the same divisions and theories, on subjects of literature and science, which prevail among Europeans. I have been told by learned men that the Greeks borrowed much of their philosophy from the Bramins. Although I dislike to quote from any book much, yet this is a subject with which I have no acquaintance, and must therefore use the language of others. In the article brachmans, the Endinburg Encyclopedia says, "It is now pretty well ascertained, that the arithmetical characters now employed in Europe are of Indian, and not of Arabian origin as was long supposed." "We find regular systems of logic and metaphysics with all the niceties, distinctions, and classifications, which are to be found among the Grecian dialecticians; and it is doubtful whether Aristotle, the father of logic, did not derive both his materials and arrangement from India. A Mahometan historian, as quoted by Sir William Jones, records a curious anecdote corroborative of this conjecture. He mentions that Callisthenes procured a regular treatise on logic in the Panjab, and transmitted it to Aristotle; and perhaps curiosity may yet be gratified by discovering, that the Grecian philosopher did not invent, but translate and compile a system of dialectics. One thing is certain, that there is scarcely a notion, which has been advanced by metaphysicians, in ancient or modern times, but may be found asserted and illustrated in some of the braminical writings. We meet with materialists, atomists, pantheists, and intellectualists, if we may so denominate the followers of the subtle and ingenious system of Berkeley. There can be little doubt that Pythagoras borrowed most of his mystical phylosophy, his notions respecting the transmigration of the soul, and the unlawfulness of eating animal food, from the ancient Bramins; for we find all these things particularly explained and enforced by the modern Bramins. They still abstain from all kinds of animal food, except that in some provinces they eat a little fish, but so disguised with rice and condiments, as scarcely to be discerned. The most sacred of all their animals is the cow, and to touch its flesh in the way of food is regarded as the highest pollution, and involves a forfeiture of cast, even in the case of those who have been involuntarily guilty of this offence. Hence the tyrant Tippoo forcibly converted a great many of his Hindoo subjects to the Mussulman religion by sprinkling them with cow broth. By these means they were forever rendered unclean in the eyes of their countrymen and were glad to seek an asylum from reproach by embracing Mehometanism."

The casts regard their laws so much that it is difficult to get them to do any thing out of their order. No man will do any kind of labour, which does not belong to his cast. A military man considers himself as disgraced by any other employment. When the sepoys, who are of the military cast, were with us on the coast of New Guinea, I could not get a musket from them, although on any other occasion they would have trembled at my frown, and would have done any thing sooner than disobey a regular order. I have seen one seized, and flogged at the gang-way for stealing a ball of twine from the sail maker, and when he was asked what he had to say in his own defence, he said with a boast that he was of the thief-cast.

Those, who go amongst them to convert them to Christianity, err when they begin with the outcasts. This is sure to disgust all the natives, who have not forfeited their casts, and those principles and hopes are identified with a religion which makes them sacred. If the higher casts could be affected, the lower ones would follow. But all plans for this object must be extremely slow in their operations.

CHRISTIAN DISCIPLE, AN ACCOUNT OF THE SIKHS IN INDIA (1814)

Although Hinduism and Buddhism were better known among nineteenth-century Americans, another Indian religion, Sikhism, also commanded the attention of American writers. More than a century before Sikh immigrants in California established the first *gurdwara* (temple) in America (in Stockton in 1912), readers of the Unitarian periodical *The Christian Disciple* encountered the tradition, or at least Western representations of it. The anonymous author of "Documents Relating to the Seeks" draws on British accounts printed in *Asiatik Researches* and the *Edinburgh Review*, both important sources of information about Asia for Unitarians and other American readers during this early period. The writer presumes the reader shares his or her concern for the success of Christian foreign missions. That explains why this mostly sympathetic account, which emphasizes Sikhism's parallels with Christianity, assures pious readers that efforts to evangelize "the natives in that part of the world will not be in vain."

To those who wish the propagation of Christianity throughout the world, it must be gratifying to hear of any facts or circumstances favorable to that object. The particulars we are about to state will be collected partly from a paper in the *Asiatik Researches*, written by Charles Wilkins, Esq. in 1781, and partly from the *Edinburgh Review* of a sketch of the Sikhs, written by Lt. Col. Malcolm, published in London 1812. In the former work the people are called Seeks; in the latter, Sikhs. The two authors likewise differ in spelling the name of the founder of this sect. Mr. Wilkins calls him Naneek Sah; Col. Malcolm, "Nanae Shah." He "was born in the year of Christ 1469."

Mr. Wilkins informs that he attended public worship at the College of this sect. After some description of the hall in which they met, he proceeds thus; "The congregation arranged themselves upon the carpet on each side of the hall so as to leave a space before the altar from end to end. The great book, desk and all, was brought with some little ceremony from the altar, and placed at the opposite extremity of the hall. An old man with a reverend silver beard, kneeled down before the desk with his face towards the altar; and on one side of him sat a man with a small drum, and two or three with cymbals. The book was now opened, and the old man began to chant to the time of the drum and the cymbals; and at the conclusion of every verse, most of the congregation joined chorus in a response, with countenances exhibiting great marks of joy. The subject was a hymn in praise of the *unity*, the *omnipresence* and *omnipotence* of the Deity. I was singularly delighted with the gestures of the old man. I never saw a countenance so expressive of infelt joy. The hymn being concluded, which consisted of about twenty verses, the whole congregation got up and presented their faces with joined hands towards the altar, in the attitude of prayer. A young man now stood forth, and with a loud and distinct accent solemnly pronounced a long prayer, or kind of liturgy; at certain periods of which all the people joined in a general response, saying *Wa Gooroo!*

They prayed against temptation; for grace to do good; for the general good of mankind; a particular blessing to the Seeks; and for the safety of those who at that time were on their travels. This prayer was followed by a short blessing from the old man, and an invitation to the assembly to partake of a friendly feast."

"Important Documents Relating to the Seeks in India," *Christian Disciple* 2.9 (1814): 269–71.

By conversing with the Seeks Mr. Wilkins was informed, that the sacred book, written by the founder of the sect, "teaches that there is but one God, omnipotent and omnipresent; filling all space and pervading all matter; and that he is to be worshipped and invoked; that there will be a day of retribution, when virtue will be rewarded and vice punished; that it not only commands toleration, but forbids disputes with those of another persuasion; that it forbids murder, theft, and such other deeds as are, by the majority of mankind, esteemed crimes in society; and inculcates the practice of the virtues; but particularly an universal philanthropy, and a general hospitality to strangers. This is all my short visit would permit me to learn of this book. It is a folio volume, containing about four or five hundred pages."

In the Edinburgh Review of Col. Malcolm's "Sketch of the Sikhs," this people are represented as a "great nation in India" which "occupy a grand division of its territory"—"by far the most valuable part of that extensive territory which constituted the Mogul empire in its proudest days."

Nanac, the founder of the Sikhs, "endeavored to conciliate both Hindoos and Moslems to his doctrine, by persuading them to reject those parts of their respective beliefs and usages, which he contended were unworthy of that God whom they both adored."

This reformer also "endeavored with all the power of his genius, to impress both Hindoos and Muhammedans with a love of toleration and an abhorrence of war; and his life was as peaceable as his doctrine." "In a period of two centuries the doctrines of Nanac extended their dominion in peace; nor was it till cruelties had been exercised upon them by the Mahomedans that his followers betook themselves to measures of revenge or defence."

After the disciples of Nanac had suffered these cruelties from the Mahomedans, Guru Govind arose, as the leader of this once pacific people. He gave them a new character, "not by making any material alteration in the tenets of Nanac, but by establishing institutions and usages which, by abolishing all distinction of castes, destroyed at one blow a system of polity that from being interwoven with the religion of a weak and bigotted race, fixed the rule of its priests upon a basis that had withstood the shock of ages." By the distinction of castes a great portion of the Hindoos were kept in a state of servility and suffering. The plan adopted by Govind, of abolishing these distinctions and opening a common highway to wealth and honor, naturally secured a multitude of disciples. "The peculiar disciples of the martial patriarch, Guru Govind, are all devoted to arms, though not all soldiers." "A portion of the Sikhs profess to hold exclusively the doctrines of the original founder of the sect, and are exempted from the exercise of arms."

It has not been our object to give a particular history of this sect, which has become a nation in India; but to mention such facts as afford ground to hope that the efforts to introduce Christianity among the natives in that part of the world will not be in vain. "The Sikhs are in fact Hindus," says the Reviewer, "with certain important differences, introduced by a recent and extraordinary change in their religious and civil institutions." The success of Nanac shows that the habits and prejudices of the Hindoos are not so immutably fixed as many in Great Britain have imagined. The pacific character of Nanac, and the approach of his doctrines to those of Christianity, are circumstances remarkable and important; and we need more information on the subject, than we now possess, to account for them without the aid of inspiration. As the dispersion of the Jews facilitated the spread of the gospel among the Gentiles in various parts of the world, so the existence of the Seeks may yet facilitate the spread of the gospel in India. It is devoutly to be desired, that nothing may be done on the part of Christians to introduce their religion among the nations of India, which shall tend to impress a belief that Christianity is less tolerant, mild and pacific, or in any respect less worthy of reception, than the religion of Nanac. Besides, the account we have of the principal doctrines of the Seeks, should excite our gratitude to the common Father of our race, that he has, in one way or another, diffused some correct ideas of himself, more extensively than has been generally known or supposed by Christians.

ROBERT MORRISON'S LETTER FROM CHINA (1809)

The first American missionary in China, Elijah C. Bridgman, arrived in the "Celestial Empire" in 1830. *The Missionary Herald* published his first letter from the field that September. A Congregationalist minister sent by the American Board of Commissioners for Foreign Missions, Bridgman would go on to edit a widely read missionary periodical, *The Chinese Repository*, and make important contributions as an author and translator. But Bridgman was not the first Protestant to preach to the "heathen" in China. The British Presbyterian, Robert Morrison (1782–1834), had begun work there in 1807; and it was Morrison who welcomed Bridgman and taught him Chinese. Bridgman knew about Morrison's toiling for the gospel in Asia because his letters had appeared in American and British magazines. Those reports helped form Americans' impressions of Chinese religions and, as Bridgman acknowledged in his own initial report from the mission field, inspired a generation of Americans to endure the hardships of evangelizing abroad. One of the most influential missionaries of his generation, Morrison published a dictionary of the Chinese language (1815–23) and a Chinese translation of the Bible (1823). This letter, written in Macao, China, in 1809, appeared in the American periodical, *The Panoplist, and Missionary Magazine United*. Morrison introduces the three major religions in China—Confucianism, Buddhism ("the sect of Foe"), and Taoism ("the sect of Ido-szi"). He concludes by reassuring Christian readers that the "opinions of the heathen" can be easily "overturned."

Macao: Sept. 19, 1809

Much esteemed friend,

    I have received your two favors under dates of March the 17th and April 18th, 1809. For both of these I render you my very sincere thanks. The fellow feeling of all the members of our Lord's body, the Church, has always been to me, a source of consolation. Whether one member suffer, all the other members suffer

"Mr. Morrison's Letter," *Panoplist* 3, 1 June 1811, 186–88.

with it; or if one rejoice, they rejoice with it. This truth is exemplified by the interest which you take in the Mission to China; as well as in all others.

I have to thank you for the present [letter] communicated by the ship Pacific; and in the Lord's name, tender my thanks to the Bible Society for the Bibles sent, of which I shall endeavor to make good use.

My residence here is for the present secured by my filling for the India Company the office of Chinese translator. This situation has attached to it the salary of 500 l. per an. As the duties of the situation all tend to perfect me in the language of the heathen, as the appointment whilst it continues secures my residence, and the income goes to our support, and the service of the Mission, we cannot but look upon it as a gracious interposition of the Lord in our behalf. I have made a small beginning in translating the book of God. It is, however, as yet suitable to apply closely to the Chinese classical book to be thoroughly acquainted with the language. To assist me in this, I have two persons with me in the house. One of them is a schoolmaster, who teaches me the books of Confucius, a part of which I have gone through and translated. The other writes for me, and is transcribing, with a view to printing that copy of most of the books of the New Testament in Chinese, which I brought out with me; and which I am now able to examine and correct. On the Lord's day I have been in the habit of reading this part of the Scriptures to my domestics, and explaining the truth by occasional remarks, as well as endeavoring to enforce it upon their consciences.

They occasionally remained with me at family prayer, when I expressed petitions in their own language.

You are aware of the pride and vanity of the people of this country; who form so large a proportion of the great family of man. They call *Kung-fu-tsi* [Confucius] a perfectly sinless person, a necessary assistant of Heaven, without whom the instruction of this part of mankind could not have been effected. He has not only said nothing but the truth; but he has delivered all truth necessary to be known. His doctrines are profound and inexhaustibly rich in their meaning, and boundlessly extensive in their application. The "Four books" are perfect. They hug themselves with complacency as masters of reason, and look down on us who have not the "Four books," as barbarians.

The Christian religion, as introduced by the Roman Catholics, they consider as nearly allied to the superstition of Foe [Buddhism], which also was introduced from the west.

The sect of *Ido-szi* [Taoism] is a native superstition. The rites of both these sects, as well as their opinions, are generally treated with contempt yet practiced and less or more believed, by those who profess to have any knowledge of the four books.

These four books (to the middle of the third of which I have read regularly) contain many excellent precepts for princes, and people; for fathers, and children; with turgid commendations of *Kung-fu-tsi* and his doctrines. The Four books were not written by *Kung-fu-tsi* himself but compiled by his disciples; who record his sayings, on different occasions, in a manner similar to that in which the Evangelists have recorded the sayings of our Lord.

It is not true, that *Kung-fu-tsi* never mentions the gods. He mentions them, and urges respect to them, but speaks of the subject as one which he did not understand fully and considers it a want of respect to the gods to suppose anything about them or make them a subject of discussion. He makes a doleful lamentation on account of the irregularity of a mandarin sacrificing to a *great-mountain* that should not have been approached by any inferior to a prince.

The observance, or breach, of his precepts is sanctioned by no higher penalties, than good or bad fame. Of a resurrection, future judgment, eternal life, or everlasting punishment, he has nothing. He yet speaks of Heaven inflicting present judgments and invokes its vengeance on himself if he did or taught any thing contrary to reason and truth.

A dissipated prince requested the philosopher to wait on him, which he did, and thereby gave offence to one of his pupils who thought his master should not have done so great an honor to a wicked man. *Kung-fu-tsi* said, "Heaven exterminate me, if not right; Heaven exterminate me, if not right!"

They divide men into three grades; first, the *Shing jeu*, or perfect man, who knows without learning, and who does things without exertion; who is as Heaven, and in their jargon they sometimes say, *is* Heaven. Secondly, the *Hieu jeu* or wise man, who is not absolutely perfect. He, in order to know, must learn; and to act, must exert himself. The third grade includes the bulk of mankind amongst whom there is, notwithstanding, a great variety.

Since *Kung-fu-tsi*, they have not had any perfect man. The existing Emperor is always called such by way of compliment.

Kung-fu-tsi himself says he never saw a perfect man; but speaks of the ancient Emperors *Yao, Shun*, and others, as perfect. I have lived, said he, to old age, and never saw a man without faults. Nor am I myself without faults. His commentators ascribe this to humility; he did not choose to assume the honor.

One of my people says it is to be regretted that he did not discourse more fully respecting the gods. The other insists that he, notwithstanding, understood it perfectly, and moreover knew that he himself was perfect, but he was afraid of existing doubts in the minds of men.

From this hasty sketch of some of the opinions of the heathen amongst whom I am, you perceive the ease with which they may in conversation be overturned; and moreover the utility of reading their books to become well acquainted with them, for out of the mouth of Confucius I am able often to condemn them. But though I dispute with them daily as Paul in the school of Tyrannus, all is ineffectual without the Lord's blessing on the plain simple manifestation of truth.

To say what the Chinese means by *Heaven* (*Tien*) is, I think, impossible, because they affix no definite meaning to it. That they mean by it, for one thing, the material heaven is certain, but what further they mean by it is not easy to say. In the first place they speak of the *Tai kie* (by which I cannot find what they mean); they then say that by the motion of *Tai kie* was produced the Yang, or an imaginary male energy, by the rest of the *Tai kie* was produced the *Yin*, or a female energy. After the lapse of ten thousand and odd years, *Yang* produced Heaven: and after ten thousand more years, *Yin* produced the earth. Then after ten thousand and more years, *Yin* and *Yang* unitedly produced all things. Finally after forty or fifty thousand years from the beginning to the close of the operation of *Yin* and *Yang*, the perfect men appeared. Such is the current jargon which is retained. The same work, however, from which I took this adds, "It is not worthy of credit, for from the earliest authentic records, viz. the time of *Yao* and *Shun* to the present, the time which has elapsed does not exceed three thousand odd years." "Every man of education," says the writer, "ought to examine."

My people speak of the Gods as posterior to the heavens and the earth when I ask what heaven is, I am told, it is the *Yang*. What is the *Yang*? That which was produced by the *Tai Kie*. And what is the *Tai Kie*? They cannot tell.

Sometimes I read that on the union of *Yin* and *Yang* the fine pure air ascended and became heaven; the thick gross air descended and became the earth. Men of pure and intelligent minds are allied to the pure air; men who are stupid and wicked are allied to the gross air, yet all are born good. Men become bad by neglect of education, &c. &c. How thankful should we be that we know better things. What have we that we have not received. Where then is boasting? Doubtless it is excluded. Freely we have received, let us freely give.

O blessed Jesus, who camest from the bosom of the Father to reveal Him to a benighted world, cause the light of Divine truth to shine among the millions of China; and may the whole earth be filled with thy glory. Amen! And Amen!

Dear brother pray that the day of small things in this land may not be despised.

I had a letter lately from Dr. Carey. He was well as to health, and the brethren were divided throughout Bengal to the number of eight stations. The Dr. informed me of the death of brother Cran at Vizigapatam.

By letters which I received yesterday from England I am informed of the sending out to the Birman Empire two missionaries from the London Society.

My love in the Gospel to the fathers and brethren who are interested in the welfare of the mission to China.

My dictionary and grammar of the Chinese language, from the multiplicity of my duties being unassisted and frequent slight indisposition, have not of late received that addition, which I hoped to have been able to make for them. Pray for me.

I am most affectionately, in the faith of our Lord Jesus and in the hope of eternal life through Him, Yours,

R. Morrison

ADONIRAM AND ANN JUDSON, A MISSION IN BURMA (1832)

Sixteen years before Elijah Bridgman arrived in China, the Reverend Adoniram Judson (1788–1850) became the first American missionary to evangelize in a Buddhist nation when he landed in Rangoon, Burma, on 13 July 1813. He was joined there by

Ann Hasseltine Judson (1789–1826), the first American woman to serve in the foreign mission field.

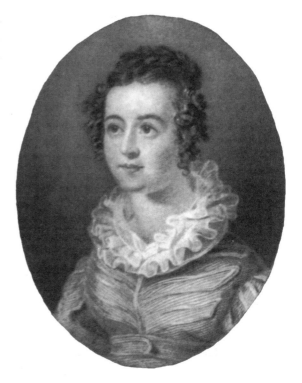

his first wife, Ann Haseltine Judson (1789–1826), the first American woman to serve in the foreign mission field. Ann, whose heart had been warmed by the fires of revivals in Massachusetts, married Adoniram in 1812, and two years later they began their work to convert the "heathen." Ann reported upon arriving in Burma that she felt certain they had made the right choice: "If we were convinced of the importance of missions before we left our native country, we now *see* and *feel* their importance. . . . We now see a whole populous empire, rational and immortal like ourselves, sunk in the grossest idolatry, given up to follow the wicked inclinations of their depraved hearts, entirely destitute of any moral principle." Adoniram shared his wife's low view of the Burmese Buddhists, and he continued to work for their salvation after Ann's early death in 1826. In the first entry below, an official letter to the sponsoring Baptists back home, the Reverend Judson (who left Congregationalism for the Baptist tradition in 1812) reported on "the perishing millions" in Burma and encouraged others to join his labors. The second entry is a summary of Adoniram's understanding of Buddhism, written by another of his missionary wives, Emily C.

Adoniram Judson to the Baptist Churches in the United States of America, 21 November 1832, in Francis Wayland, *A Memoir of the Life and Labors of the Rev. Adoniram Judson, D.D.* (Boston: Phillips, Sampson, and Company; Cincinnati: Moore, Anderson, and Company, 1853), 56–57; Emily C. Judson, "Dr. Judson's Opinion on Some of the Tenets of Buddhism," in Wayland, *A Memoir*, 407–9.

Judson. It conveys his views on the most vexing issues facing interpreters at the time: Do Buddhists believe in God? What is the origin of Buddhism? Does nirvana mean extinction?

To the Baptist Churches in the United States of America.

MAULMAIN, November 21, 1832.

DEAR BRETHREN AND SISTERS: I send this line by brother Wade, who, having had ten attacks of his disease within a year, the last of which reduced him to such a state that his life was despaired of, is obliged, at the urgent advice of his physician, to take a long voyage, as the only means of prolonging his life.

Brother Boardman has left us altogether, having obtained an honorable discharge from this warfare. Brother Jones has gone hence to Siam. In suffering him to go, we cherished the hope that in us would be fulfilled that saying, "There is that scattereth and yet increaseth." Brothers Kincaid and Mason, though indefatigable in their application to the language, are yet unable to afford much efficient aid. Brothers Bennett and Cutter are necessarily confined to the printing house. Permit us, therefore, in these straitened circumstances, with all Burmah on our hands, once more to approach your numerous and flourishing churches, sitting every man under his vine and under his fig tree, laden with the richest fruit, and to beseech you to take into compassionate consideration the perishing millions of Burmah, ignorant of the eternal God, the Lord Jesus Christ, and the blessed way of salvation; and, in consideration of the ruin impending on their immortal souls, and in remembrance of the grace of the Saviour, who shed his blood for you and for them, to send out a few of your sons and daughters to accompany brother and sister Wade, on their return to this land.

I would add, as a very powerful inducement to embrace the present opportunity, that it will not only insure the company and instructions of brother and sister Wade, but the instructions of two native converts, in consequence of which those who now volunteer their services will be able, especially if the study of the language be immediately commenced, to proclaim the glad tidings almost as soon as they land on these shores.

We have now five native churches, and above three hundred communicants; and a spirit of religious inquiry is spreading in all directions. Who will come over into Macedonia and help us?

Your brother and fellow-laborer in the kingdom and patience of Jesus Christ,

A. JUDSON.

Dr. Judson's Opinion on Some of the Tenets of Buddhism

DR. JUDSON, from a limited examination of the ancient Pali, an extensive acquaintance with the religious literature of Burmah, and a thorough knowledge of the people of that country, arrived at different conclusions with regard to some of the principal doctrines of Buddhism from those of most writers on the mythology of the East. He thought that Buddhism and Brahminism could not be "different branches of the same religion;" for though both recognize the universal oriental doctrine of metempsychosis, they are, in almost every other particular, directly antagonistic. Which of the two could justly claim the greater antiquity, he did not pretend to decide, though quite confident that Buddhism, in some form, had existed previous to the days of Gaudama.

He thought there was sufficient evidence that Gaudama flourished as a Hindoo prince, and a great heathen philosopher, some five or six hundred years before the Christian era; and he thought it probable that a devotee so wise and so sincere as this prince must have been, purified the system, and very possibly spiritualized it, to a greater extent than appears in the Buddhistic scriptures. These scriptures (the Be-ta-gat) were not written until four hundred and fifty-eight years after the death of Gaudama, and very probably do not embody the subtler teachings of the heathen sage. Be that as it may, Dr. Judson could not discover, either in the Burmese versions of these sacred books, or in conversation with professedly rigid Buddhists, any thing to redeem the system from the charge of absolute atheism. The few semi-atheists, &c., that he occasionally met, however closely they might adhere to the practices of Buddhism, readily acknowledged the latitudinous nature of their opinions. According to Dr. Judson's views of Buddhism, it acknowledges no moral governor of the universe; and though the doctrine of future rewards and punishments is one of the great pillars of the system, it recognizes no executive power, no supreme judge, no agent or minister of justice. The whole destiny of the infinitude of souls continually passing from one state of existence to another, is adjusted by the ceaseless turnings of the "unerring wheel of fate." Hence Gaudama himself endured the punishment of sins committed in previous states of existence,—"the sixteen great results of guilt,"—even during his deityship.

Dr. Judson also regarded the state of nigban as nothing less than a total extinction of soul and body. He was aware that the original Sanscrit word, nirvana, has a very different signification; but he knew also that this signification, absorption in deity, is peculiarly abhorrent to Buddhists. Buddh is their deity, and they recognize no superior. From the circumlocution incidental to the honorific language of the Burmans, it is sometimes difficult to ascertain their precise meaning. No Burman, for instance, ever says the king or the priest is dead. It would be disrespectful to say so. For the same reason, they would not say broadly, that a Buddh is extinct, that he ceases to exist. He reposes. At the same time, they readily acknowledge that he is devoid of sensation, passion, emotion, and thought; that he neither takes cognizance of the devotion of his worshippers, nor is capable of extending to them any benefit. They teach that all existence bears within itself the elements of change, suffering, disease, decay, and death; and that *therefore* nigban—exemption from these evils, these fundamental principles of existence—is the only true good. So read the books, and so the strict disciples of Buddhism in Burmah, whether learned or unlearned, believe.

It must be borne in mind, however, that there is no reliable proof of the introduction of Buddhism into Burmah earlier than A. D. 386; that it subsequently underwent some modifications, and was not fully established in its present form until about A. D. 1000. The approved translations of the Be-ta-gat are not only tediously verbal, but always give the Pali text alongside the rendering; and there is no reason to doubt their purity, or to suspect that interpolations or alterations of any kind have been admitted; though, on the other hand, there are many portions of it which have never yet been translated into the Burmese language.

On the whole, it is fair to suppose that this system is somewhat modified by the circumstances of the different nations that have adopted it; and that, in all probability, it underwent still greater modifications during the centuries that intervened between the death of Gaudama and the composition of the Be-ta-gat. —EMILY C. JUDSON

CHAPTER 2

Views from Home

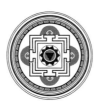

BENJAMIN FRANKLIN'S ORIENTAL TALE (1788)

For Americans who ignored travel accounts and missionary reports, the Oriental tale, the first genre of religious fiction in America, provided the most powerful impressions of the East. Oriental tales were short stories or full-length novels, set in Asia (usually the Middle East but sometimes East Asia). Although they originated centuries earlier, Oriental tales attracted widespread attention in Europe during the first half of the eighteenth century. Americans began writing them after 1780, and periodicals such as *New York Magazine* (1790–97) and *Massachusetts Magazine* (1789–96) published many. These stories were popular in America from the late eighteenth century to the middle of the nineteenth, with the greatest vogue coming about 1800. One early example, "A Letter from China," is important more for its author's stature than for its literary value. Written by statesman Benjamin Franklin (1706–90), this story appeared in a British magazine in 1788. Franklin had befriended the British Orientalist Sir William Jones, and Franklin's acquaintances reported that he liked to read about China. He was especially drawn to Confucianism, and even published excerpts of Confucius' sayings in the *Pennsylvania Gazette*. In that sense, Franklin was typical of deists in Europe and America, who applauded the naturalistic philosophy of Confucius and its emphasis on ethics. Franklin was suspicious of churches and dubious about miracles, and his own spare, rationalist creed emphasized the core beliefs that many other Enlightenment thinkers had affirmed: God, immortality, and, above all, morality.

Lisbon, May 5, 1784

Sir,

Agreeable to your desire, I have examined the sailor more particularly, and shall now give you the circumstances of his story, with all the observations he

Benjamin Franklin, "A Letter from China," *The Writings of Benjamin Franklin* (New York: Macmillan, 1905–7), vol. 9: 200, 204, 205, 207–9.

made in the country, concerning which you are so curious. He appears a more intelligent fellow than seamen in general. He says that he belonged to the *Resolution*, an English ship, one of those that made the last voyage with Captain Cook. That on their return, being at Macao, he and a comrade of his were over-persuaded by a Portuguese captain, who spoke English and Chinese, to desert, in order to go with him in a brigantine to the northwestern coast of America, to purchase sea-beaver skins from the savages, by which they hoped to make fortunes. That accordingly they took a boat belonging to the ship, got ashore in the night, turned the boat adrift, and were hid by the Portuguese captain till the *Resolution* was gone. That this was in January, 1780; and that in April following they sailed from Macao, intending to go first to a place he calls Nooky-Bay, in latitude 50. That they had twenty-five men, with eight guns and small arms for their defence, and a quantity of iron ware, cutlery, with European and Chinese toys, for trade. . . .

They have a sort of religion, with priests and churches, but do not keep Sunday, nor go to church, being very heathenish. In every house there is a little idol, to which they give thanks, make presents, and show respect in harvest time, but very little at other times; and, inquiring of his master why they did not go to church to pray, as we do in Europe, he was answered, they paid the priests to pray for them, that they might stay at home and mind their business; and that it would be a folly to pay others for praying, and then go and do the praying themselves; and that the more work they did while the priests prayed, the better able they were to pay them well for praying. . . .

There is a great deal of cheating in China, and no remedy. Stealing, robbing, and house-breaking are punished severely; but cheating is free there in everything, as cheating in horses is among our gentlemen in England. . . .

When he arrived at Canton, he did not make himself known to the English there, but got down as soon as he could to Macao, hoping to meet with his Portuguese captain; but he had never returned. He worked there in rigging of vessels, till he had an opportunity to come home to Europe; and, hearing on his arrival here, from an old comrade in the packet, that his sweetheart is married, and that the *Resolution* and *Endeavour* got home, he shall decline going to England yet a while, fearing he may be punished for carrying off the boat; therefore he has shipped himself, as I wrote you before, on a voyage to America. He was between three and four years in China. This is the substance of what I got from him, and nearly as he related it. He gave me the names of some places, but I found them hard to remember, and cannot recollect them.

JOSEPH PRIESTLEY, *A COMPARISON OF THE INSTITUTIONS OF MOSES WITH THOSE OF THE HINDOOS AND OTHER ANCIENT NATIONS* (1799)

A renowned British minister and schoolmaster who emigrated to America in 1794, Joseph Priestley (1733–1804) made contributions to religion, politics, and science. Best known for his work in chemistry, he isolated nine gases, including oxygen. In religion, he was a liberal Christian who declared himself a Unitarian in 1770. Like other Unitarians, he rejected the doctrines of original sin, election, and the trinity. Yet he celebrated the moral teachings of Jesus, worshipped a God who created and governed the world, and hoped for immortality in the afterlife. Unlike deists of his day, he believed Christianity's truth rested on revelation as well as reason. His religious convictions shaped his interpretation of Asian religions, especially Hinduism. In 1799 Priestley published a book that compared "the institutions of Moses with those of the Hindoos and other ancient nations," one of the earliest comparative studies of religion published in America. Drawing on the work of travelers and civil servants in Asia, and especially the writings of Orientalist Sir William Jones (more evidence of Jones's influence), Priestley argued for the antiquity of Judaism and presumed the superiority of Christianity. Like many other Western interpreters of his day, he was perplexed by some Hindu beliefs (especially views about caste, cows, and karma), and he delighted in recording—many Indians would say misrepresenting—the "austerities" of the Hindus (including hook swinging and, once again, suttee). Readers today might be especially interested in his comments on Hindu women. The first passage criticizes the Indian view of women; the second condemns the practice of suttee, which was neither as prevalent nor always as involuntary as Priestley suggests.

OF THE SITUATION OF WOMEN AMONG THE HINDOOS

. . . If the general character of women were such as the *Hindoo* writings exhibit, there is no supposition that can be entertained concerning them too unfavourable, nor any treatment of them too bad. In the *Heetopades*, translated by M. *Langles*, it is said, that "faithlessness, violence, falsehood, extreme avarice, a total want of good qualities, and impurity, are vices natural to the female sex." And both the *Institutes of Menu* and the *Code of Gentoo Laws*, may be quoted as better authorities in support of the same opprobrious character, but certainly not the writings of *Moses*. "It is," say the *Institutes*, "the nature of women in this world to cause the seduction of men; for which reason the wise are never unguarded in the company of females."

The same character is given more at large in the following passage: "Through their passion for men, their mutable temper, their want of settled affection, and their perverse nature, (let them be guarded in this world ever so well,) they soon become alienated from their husbands; yet should their husbands be diligently careful in guarding them, though they well know the disposition with which the Lord of the creation formed them. MENU allotted to such women a love of their bed, of their seat, and of ornament, impure appetites, wrath, weak flexibility, desire of mischief, and bad conduct. Women have no business with the texts of the *Véda*; thus is the law fully settled. Having, therefore, no evidence of *law*, and no *knowledge* of expiatory texts, sinful women must be as foul as falsehood itself; and

A Comparison of the Institutions of Moses with Those of the Hindoos and Other Ancient Nations, in *The Theological and Miscellaneous Works of Joseph Priestley*, vol. 17 (New York: Kraus Reprint Co., 1972), 227–30, 250–53.

this is a fixed rule. To this effect, many texts which may show their true disposition are chaunted in the *Védas*."

The *Gentoo Laws*, compiled by the learned *Pundits* of *Hindostan*, are in perfect unison with these *Institutes of Menu*. Of women they say something so gross, that I cannot copy it. What follows is bad enough: "Women have six qualities; the first an inordinate desire for jewels and fine furniture, handsome clothes, and nice victuals; the second, immoderate lust; the third, violent anger; the fourth, deep resentment, i.e. no person knows the sentiments concealed in their hearts; the fifth, another person's good appears evil in their eyes; the sixth, they commit bad actions." . . .

Neither can we be surprised that the birth of a female is no cause of rejoicing in a Hindoo family. If a wife bear only daughters, the husband may cease to cohabit with her. In this case, according to the *Institutes of Menu*, a man, after waiting eleven years, may marry another. The same law says, that "she who speaks unkindly" to her husband, may be superseded by another "without delay."

It is in perfect agreement with these ideas of the female character, that women must always be under the absolute controul of men. "By a girl," say the *Institutes of Menu*, "or by a young woman, or by a woman advanced in years, nothing must be done, even in her own dwelling-place, according to her mere pleasure.—A woman must never seek independence.—A woman is never fit for independence." "A man, both day and night, must keep his wife so much in subjection, that she by no means be mistress of her own actions. If the wife have her own free will, notwithstanding she be sprung from a superior caste, she yet will behave amiss."

The subjection of a wife to her husband has no bounds: "A wife must always rise before her husband, but never eat with him.—She must not dress, or take any amusement in his absence." "Though inobservant of approved usages, or enamoured of another woman, or devoid of good qualities, yet a husband must constantly be revered as a god by a virtuous wife.—A faithful wife, who wishes to attain in heaven the mansion of her husband, must do nothing unkind to him, be he living or dead.—Let her emaciate her body by living voluntarily on pure flowers, roots, and fruits; but let her not, when her lord is deceased, even pronounce the name of another man." In this case, surely she might be allowed a mansion in heaven, equal to that of her husband; but much more than this is required, if she would make sure of so great a happiness, even to be burned alive with his corpse. Whether she do this or not, she must not on any account marry again. "The marriage of a widow," say the *Institutes of Menu*, is not "even named in the laws concerning marriage. This practice, fit only for cattle, is reprehended by learned *Bráhmens*." . . .

When women are considered in this degrading light, and treated in this disrespectful manner, especially as not qualified to read their sacred books, it is no wonder that they are in general very ignorant, and perhaps undeserving of the confidence that is never reposed in them. "There are few Hindoo women to be found who can either read or write."

How much more consonant to reason is the doctrine of our Scriptures concerning the two sexes! According to them, the man has no advantage besides that superiority which must be given to one of them. In every other respect, they are considered and treated as perfectly equal. They have the same moral duties, and the same future reward in prospect, in a state in which all distinction of sex will cease, where there will be *no marrying or giving in marriage, but all will be alike, as the angels of God in heaven.* (*Matt.* xxii. 30.) As to the natural or moral disposition, there is no intimation in the Scriptures or the writings of *Moses*, of women being at all inferior to men. Both have their natural passions, but neither of them are considered as more disposed to criminal indulgence than the other. And with respect to examples, there are virtuous and excellent ones of women as well as of men. If some of the most shining characters be those of men, so are also some of the worst. And women being naturally more domestic, and coming less into public life, their characters and conduct are not in general so conspicuous, and of course not so much noticed in history as those of men. . . .

OF THE DEVOTION OF THE HINDOOS

The most affecting instances of voluntary death, if they can be said to be always voluntary, are those of the *Hindoo* women burning themselves alive with the bodies of their deceased husbands, which, though not absolutely required, is strongly recommended in the Hindoo institutions. We have seen the degraded state of women in this country, how much it is below that of men. In this way, however, and it seems to be the only one, they have an opportunity of attaining the same state of happiness with them after death. And this action is esteemed so honourable for the family in which it takes place, and to the religion itself, that nothing is omitted, especially on the part of the Bramins, to encourage, and almost compel widows to do it; and if they once give their consent, it is hardly in their power to recede. And according to the testimony of travellers, many of these widows go to the fire as much against their wills as if it was a real human sacrifice. . . .

The strict Hindoos certainly consider this action as one of the most important in all their religion, the cause of which, it is said, it would be hardly right to investigate. "It is proper," say the *Gentoo Laws*, "for a woman to burn with her husband's corpse." "Every woman who thus burns herself, shall remain in paradise with her husband three *crore*, and fifty *lacks* of years, by destiny. If she cannot burn, she must, in that case, preserve an inviolable chastity." She "then goes to paradise;" otherwise "to hell." Another powerful inducement to this practice is, "that the children of the wife who burns, become thereby illustrious, and are sought after in marriage by the most opulent and honourable of their *caste*, and sometimes received into a *caste* superior to their own."

Some of the cases of this kind, mentioned by travellers, are very affecting. The heroism and tranquillity with which some women do this, holding their husbands' heads in their laps, and lighting the fire themselves, is astonishing; while others are tied fast, or pushed into the fire, their shrieks being drowned by the Bramins. *Bernier* saw a woman burning with her husband without discovering any symptom of terror, while five of her maids, after dancing round the fire, threw themselves into it, one after another, with the greatest seeming indifference. He says, that when they discover any reluctance, the Bramins sometimes force them into the fire. In some cases, he says, that, instead of burning them, they bury them up to the neck, and then strangle them, by turning their heads round.

JOHN ADAMS TO THOMAS JEFFERSON (1813–14)

John Adams (1735–1826) was in the audience in Philadelphia when Joseph Priestley delivered his 1796 lectures on Hebrew and Hindu religions. And in the years ahead Adams, even more than his learned friend Thomas Jefferson (1743–1826), read widely in Asian religions. In the 1790s, Adams and Jefferson quarreled, but in 1812, after each had served as president, they reconciled. They then began a lively correspondence on a wide range of topics. Although Jefferson previously had been reluctant to discuss his deist religious views, Adams prodded him into frank exchanges on the subject. Adams, their letters reveal, began a serious investigation into Asian religions around this time: "I have been looking into Oriental History and Hindoo religion. I have read voyages and travels and everything I could collect." He also returned to Priestley's comparative study. In letters to Jefferson dated 25 December 1813 and 3 March 1814, Adams evaluated Priestley's book and conveyed his own religious views. Until his death on 4 July 1826, only a few hours after Jefferson's death, Adams continued to read books like Charles Dupuis's *Origine de tous les cultes* and Sir William Jones's *Works*. Adams reported that he remained a liberal and rationalist Christian, but he was more convinced than ever of the need for religious toleration, and on that point his friend Jefferson fully agreed.

Quincy Decr. 25th. 1813

Dear Sir,

Answer my Letters at Your Leisure. Give yourself no concern. I write as for a refuge and protection against Ennui.

. . .

To return to Priestley. You could make a more luminous Book, than his upon "the Doctrines of Heathen Phylosophers compared with those of Revelation."

. . . Priestley ought to have done impartial Justice to Phylosophy and Phylosophers, Phylosophy which is the result of Reason, is the first, the original Revelation of The Creator to his Creature, Man. When this Revelation is clear and certain, by Intuition or necessary Induction, no subsequent Revelation supported by Prophecies or Miracles can supercede it. Phylosophy is not only the love of Wisdom, but the Science of the Universe and its Cause. There is, there was and there will be but one Master of Phylosophy in the Universe. Portions of it, in different degrees are revealed to Creatures. Phylosophy looks with an impartial Eye on all terrestrial religions. I have examined all, as well as my narrow Sphere, my streightened means and my busy Life would allow me, and the result is, that the Bible is the best book in the World. It contains more of my little Phylosophy than all the Libraries I have seen: and such Parts of it as I cannot reconcile to my little Phylosophy I postpone for future Investigation.

Priestley ought to have given Us a Sketch of the Religion and Morals of Zoroaster of Sanchoniathon of Confucius, and all the Founders of Religions before Christ, whose superiority, would from such a comparison have appeared the more transcendant.

Priestley ought to have told us, that Pythagoras passed twenty Years, in his Travels in India, in Egypt, in Chaldea, perhaps in Sodom and Gomorrah, Tyre and Sydon. He ought to have told Us that in India he conversed with the Brahmans and read the Shast[r]a, 5000 Years old, written in the Language of the sacred Sanscrists with the elegance and Sentiments of Plato. Where is to be found Theology more orthodox or Phylosophy more profound than in the Introduction to the Shast[r]a? "God is one, creator of all, Universal Sphere, without beginning, without End. God governs all the Creation by a great Providence, resulting from his eternal designs.—Search not the Essence and the nature of the Eternal, who is one; Your research will be vain and presumptuous. It is enough that, day by day, and night by night, You adore his Power, his Wisdom and his Goodness, in his Works." ["] The Eternal willed, in the fullness of time, to communicate of his Essence and of his Splendor, to Beings capable of perceiving it. They as yet existed not. The Eternal Willed, and they were. He created Birma, Vitsnow, and Sib." These Doctrines, sublime if ever there were any sublime, Pythagoras learned in India and taught them to Zaleucus and his other disciples. He there learned also his Metempsychosis, but this never was popular, never made much progress in Greece or Italy, or any other Country besides India and Tartary, the Region of the Grand immortal Lama: And how does this differ, from the Possessions of Demons in Greece and Rome, from the Demon of Socrates from the Worship of Cows and Crocodiles in Egypt and elsewhere. After migrating [through] various Animals from Elephants to Serpents according to their behaviour, Souls that at last behaved well became Men and Women, and then if they were good, they went to Heaven. All ended in Heaven if they became virtuous. Who can wonder at the Widow of Malabar. Where is the Lady, who, if he[r] faith were without doubt, that she should go to Heaven with her Husband on the one, or migrate into a Toad or a Waspe on the other, would not lay down on The Pile and set fire to the Fuel? Modifications and disguises of the Metempsichosis had crept into Egypt and Greece and Rome and other Countries. Have you read Farmer on the Dæmons and possessions of the New Testament?

According to the Shast[r]a, Moisazor, with his Companions rebelled against the Eternal, and were precipitated, down to Ondero, the region of Darkness. Do you know any thing of the Prophecy of Enoch? Can you give me a Comment on the 6th, the 9th, the 14th verses of the Epistle of Jude?

If I am not weary of writing, I am sure you must be of reading such incoherent rattle. I will not persecute you so severely in future, if I can help it. So farewell.

JOHN ADAMS

Quincy Feb[–March 3] 1814.

DEAR SIR

. . . Your research in the Laws of England, establishing Christianity as the Law of the Land and part of the common Law, are curious and very important. Questions without number will arise in this Country. Religious Controversies, and Ecclesiastical Contests are as common and will be as Sharp as any in civil Politicks foreign, or domestick? In what sense and to what extent the Bible is Law, may give rise to as many doubts and quarrells as any of our civil political military or maritime Laws and will intermix with them all to irritate Factions of every sort. I dare not look beyond my Nose into futurity. Our Money, our Commerce, our Religion, our National and State Constitutions, even our Arts and Sciences, are so many seed Plotts of Division, Faction, Sedition and Rebellion. Every thing is transmuted into an Instrument of Electioneering. Election is the grand Brama, the immortal Lama, I had almost said, the Jaggernaught, for Wives are almost ready to burn upon the Pile and Children to be thrown under the Wheel.

You will perceive, by these figures that I have been looking into Oriental History and Hindoo religion. I have read Voyages and travels and every thing I could collect, and the last is Priestleys "Comparison of the Institutions of Moses, with those of the Hindoos and other ancient Nations," a Work of great labour, and not less haste. I thank him for the labour, and forgive, though I lament the hurry. You would be fatigued to read, and I, just recruiting a little from a longer confinement and indisposition than I have had for 30 Years, have not strength to write many Observations. But I have been disappointed in the principal Points of my Curiosity.

1. I am disappointed, by finding that no just Comparison can be made, because the original Shast[r]a, and the original Vedams are not obtained, or if obtained not yet translated into any European Language.

2. In not finding such Morsells of the Sacred Books as have been translated and published which are more honourable to the original Hindo[o] Religion than any thing he has quoted.

3. In not finding a full devellopement of the History of the Doctrine of the Metempsichosis which orig[i]nated.

4. In the History of the Rebellion of innumerable Hosts of Angells in Heaven against the Supream Being, who after some thousands of Years of War conquered them and hurled them down to the Region of total darkness, where they suffered a part of the Punishment of their Crime, and then were mercifully released from Prison permitted to ascend to Earth and migrate into all sorts of Animals, reptiles, Birds, Beasts and Men according to their Rank and Chara[c]ter, and even into Vegetables and Minerals, there to serve on probation. If they passed without reproach their Several gradations they were permitted to become Cows and Men. If as Men they behaved well, i. e. to the satisfaction of the Priests, they were restored to the Original rank and Bliss in Heaven.

5. In not finding the Trinity of Pythagoras and Plato, their contempt of Matter, flesh and blood, their almost Adoration of Fire and Water, their Metempsicosis, and even the prohibition of Beans so evidently derived from India.

6. In not finding the Prophecy of Enoch deduced from India in which the fallen Angels make such a figure.

But you are weary. Priestley has proved the superiority of the Hebrews to the Hindoos, as they Appear in the Gentoo Laws and Institutes of Menu: but the comparison remains to be made with the Shast[r]a. . . .

JOHN ADAMS

WILLIAM BENTLEY ON ASIAN TRADE IN SALEM (1794–1804)

A pioneering Unitarian minister who served East Church in Salem, Massachusetts, for thirty-six years, William Bentley (1759–1819) knew as much about Asia as any armchair Orientalist of his generation. Bentley read widely and corresponded often. One of the most accomplished linguists of his time, he knew Arabic and Persian. Thomas Jefferson was so impressed by Bentley's learning that he invited him to serve as president of the University of Virginia. Bentley declined, preferring his life of study and preaching in Salem, a port that served as a main hub of the China trade. In his four-volume diary, this liberal minister provides a glimpse of Salem's encounters with Asia. In these excerpts—from 1794, 1801, and 1804—Bentley records the arrival of a ship's captain from India and describes the expanding collection of Asian artifacts at the museum of the East India Marine Society (established 1799), an organization for men who had sailed in Asian waters. We learn about the rituals that consecrated the annual meetings of that society from the January 1804 entry: a man "dressed in Chinese habits and mask" led the procession; other members carried artifacts brought back from Asia; and African Americans, dressed in clothing from India, carried the palanquin. The final entry allows us to overhear toasts at a society dinner later that same year.

May 1. [1794] Capt. Gibaut arrived after a voyage of three years from India having been detained & embargoed in different ports 17 months. His first detention was at Pegu, where his vessel was taken into the service of the King of Ava, he then sold & took passage to the English Ports. Upon his return he found the Ship Henry at Isle of France, with the Master made a new purchase & took charge of his Ship for home. Stopped at the Cape of Good Hope long enough to have a share of British Insolence, & has safely returned.

2. Capt. Gibaut who visited the conquered province of Pegu, now subject to Ava, assured me from the Port all the circumjacent country was uncultivated. That he went above an hundred miles upon the river to the Capital which they are now restoring. That people of every condition wear only a cloth fastened at the waste reaching to the feet & open before with a short jacket with sleeves. Extremely ignorant. The religious prohibition of killing animals, tho'

William Bentley, *The Diary of William Bentley, D.D., Pastor of East Church, Salem, Massachusetts* (Gloucester, Mass.: Peter Smith, 1962), vol. 2: 88, 383; vol. 3: 68, 121. Reprinted by permission of Peter Smith Publishers, Inc.

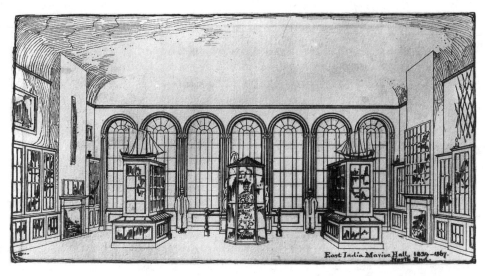

East India Marine Hall (north end), Salem, Massachusetts. Opened in 1824, this hall displayed artifacts imported from the Asia trade. Courtesy Peabody Essex Museum, Salem, Massachusetts.

not of eating them when dead, led them to many practices disagreeable to us. Some Portugese & Scotch were among them. He heard at Ragusa the tigers, & was witness of their horrid noise as he passed up the river. Executions frequent.

. . .

August 1801. Visited in Company with Capt. Hodges & Gibaut the Museum of the East India Marine Society. As they have not been long in the habit of Collecting, the Collection is entitled to notice. They are furnished with several images & paintings of Hindostan, China & Japan, with complete dresses in the Chinese fashion. They have various specimens of the Oyster shells of Sumatra. Large collections of the smaller shells & some of them beautiful. The Albatross, birds of paradise, parakets, & several birds. No fish, & but few insects. Some antiquities, & a handsome number of Coins given by E. H. Derby. A few specimens of stones, ores, &c. not arranged, petrefactions, & curiosities, in all 185 articles. They have a foundation for a Library well begun, as it contains already Cooke's Voyages, Perouse, Vancouver, &c. Their Museum is kept over the Marine office in the Brick Building, east corner of Court-Street, fronting Essex street. Communications are required on the Cape of Good Hope. Capt. Sage has lately delivered a Chart of a Voyage with the tract of his Ship, & it is a good beginning. There has been very lately opened an Indian Grave near the Iron Factory on Cowhouse or Duck river, at Waters' Bridge. Capt. Osgood who shewed me an oblong, smooth & flat stone about 7 inches long, much in the form of a Chisel but not sharpened at either end, told me that there were found graves of a grown person & of a Child. Of Mr. Goodale, who opened the grave, he got no particulars, only that he thought the Child may have been wrapped in Copper. He did not explain himself. The parts of bones remaining were left with Mr. Reid.

. . .

January 1804. This day is the Annual Meeting of the East India Marine Society. As the Clergy attend in turn, this day afforded me an opportunity to enjoy the day with them. After business & before dinner they moved in procession, but the ice limited the distance. Each of the brethren bore some Indian curiosity & the palanquin was borne by the negroes dressed nearly in the Indian manner. A person dressed in Chinese habits & mask passed in front. The crowd of spectators was great. Several gentlemen were invited to dine. The toasts were of the moment, & without any offence. The dinner was rich & elegant. The company very seasonably retired & all was quiet before four o'clock. The Instrumental Music was provided in Town, for the first time & consisted of the Bass Drum, Bassoon, Clarinet & flute, & was very acceptable. There was no singing. Application was made for subscription to an American Edition of Anderson on Commerce, with a Supplement on American Commerce. The work is to be in Eight Volumes 8vo. at 22 dollars. Many persons had subscribed before, as the patrons were Cushing & Appleton. There is most happy arrangement to deliver all the papers of this Company to Mr. Nathaniel Bowditch lately returned from a Voyage to India that they may be prepared for the public Inspection. Capt. B. Hodges, Master.

7. This day the East India Marine Society paraded & had their public dinner. The Palanquin, Holker & Dresses were exhibited in the procession, which attracted great notice. A Band of Music & the Cadet Company added to the entertainment & ceremony of the day. An elegant dinner was provided in the splendid room in which they display a large collection of natural & artificial curiosities with most happy effect.

. . .

November 1804. The Toasts of the East India Marine Society as published were—

  I Vasco da Gama, What genius performs may genius immortalize.
  II May each mariner record, so that Enterprise may discover.
  III Commerce without violence & no war upon the sea.
  IIII The riches which the arts give, may they find sacred to their support.
  V The Practical Navigator. Facts first, then theories.
  VI Natural history. May commerce never forget its obligations.
  VII A Cabinet. That every mariner may possess the history of the world.
  VIII Commerce with all the nations. But the love of our country our best happiness.
  IX Industry rich and free, always active and always content.
  X Our families never absent from our hearts.
  XI Absent members. The praise they ought to love, may they merit.
  XII The Clergy. May our reputation abroad, prove their duty at home.
  XIII The Salem East India Marine Society. Many resources from the ambition of its members continue to accomplish its designs.

HANNAH ADAMS, *A DICTIONARY OF ALL RELIGIONS* (1817)

The first American woman to earn her living by writing, Hannah Adams (1755–1831) also was a pioneer in the study of religions. The most popular and important of her nine books also was her first, *Alphabetical Compendium of the Various Sects*. It appeared in 1784 and went through three other editions by 1817. Adams, a distant relative of President John Adams, wrote her compendium in her home in Medfield, Massachusetts, because she was dissatisfied with Christian writers' portrayal of religions and denominations other than their own. Most of the religious compendia of her day identified two kinds of religions: true and false. Not surprisingly, the author's own form of Christianity typically was presented as the true one. Adams broke new ground by aiming to "avoid giving the least preference of one denomination above another." She was not always successful, but she never offered an interpretation that was more hostile than that of her sources. Her attempts to present beliefs and practices fairly advanced the study of Asian religions. In these passages from the fourth edition of her compendium, which she retitled *A Dictionary of All Religions and Religious Denominations* (1817), Adams introduces "pagan" traditions and provides sketches of religion in China and Japan. Note her classification of religions in the entry on "Pagans" and her attempts (successful and not) in the other entries to represent fairly religions that her sources had interpreted harshly.

Pagans, heathens, and particularly those who worship idols. The term came into use after the establishment of christianity; the cities and great towns affording the first converts, the heathens were called Pagans, (from *Pagus*, a Village,) because they were then found chiefly in remote country places; but we use the term commonly for all who do not receive the Jewish, Christian, or Mahometan religions. The Pagans may be divided into the following classes—

I. The Greeks and Romans, and others who admit their refined system of mythology.

II. The more ancient nations, as the Chaldeans, Phenicians, Sabians, &c.

III. The Chinese, Hindoos, Japanese, &c.

IV. The Barbarians, as the Indians of North and South America, and the Negroes of Africa.

. . .

Chinese. The religion of this great and ancient nation was certainly patriarchal, and supposed to be derived from Joktan, the brother of Peleg. (Gen. x. 29, 30.) This has degenerated to Paganism, which among their *literati* may be refined to a sort of philosophical atheism; but among the vulgar is as gross idolatry as that of other heathen nations. The grand *Lama*, or Pope of the Chinese and Tartars, who resides at Thibet in Tartary, is their visible deity, and treated with more distinction than the Pope himself, in the zenith of his power and glory, and attended by 20,000 priests or *lamas*. In addition to this general system of religion, which is

Hannah Adams, *A Dictionary of All Religions and Religious Denominations*, 4th ed. (Boston: Cummings and Hiliard, 1817), 213, 55–57, 122–24.

founded on their sacred books, said to have descended from the skies, there are three grand sects, of which we shall give a brief account; and those three are again subdivided into as many as the Christian world itself.

1. The sect of *Tao-se*, or the followers of *Laokium*, who lived, as they pretend, 500 years before Christ, and taught that God was corporeal. They pay divine honours to this philosopher, and give the same worship, not only to many emperours who have been ranked with the gods, but also to certain spirits, under the name of *zamte*, who preside over all the elements. Their morality consists in calming the passions, and disengaging themselves from every thing which tends to disquiet the soul, to live free from care, to forget the past, and not be apprehensive for the future. There are also magicians,—some of whom pretend that they derive from their founder the secret of making an elixir, which confers immortality.

2. The most predominant sect is that of *Foe*, who (according to their chronology) flourished 1000 years before our Saviour, and who became a god at the age of 30 years. This religion was transmitted from India to China 65 years after the birth of Christ. A large number of temples, or pagodas, are reared to this deity, some of which are highly magnificent, and a number of bonzes, or priests, consecrated to his service. He is represented shining in light, with his hands hid under his robes, to show that he does all things invisibly. The doctors of this sect teach a double doctrine, the one *external*, the other *internal*. According to the former they say, all the good are recompensed, and the wicked punished, in places destined for each. They enjoin all works of mercy and charity; and forbid cheating, impurity, wine, lying, and murder; and even the taking of life from any creature whatever. For they believe that the souls of their ancestors transmigrate into irrational creatures; either into such as they liked best, or resembled most, in their behaviour; for which reason they never kill any such animals.

They build temples for Foe, and monasteries for his priests, providing for their maintenance, as the most effectual means to partake of their prayers. These priests pretend to know into what bodies the dead are transmigrated; and seldom fail of representing their case to the surviving friends as miserable or uncomfortable, that they may extort money from them to procure the deceased a passage into a better state, or pray them out of purgatory, which forms a part of their system.

The *internal* doctrine of this sect, which is kept secret from the common people, teaches a philosophical atheism, which admits neither rewards nor punishments after death; and believes not in a providence, or the immortality of the soul; acknowledges no other god than the *void*, or *nothing*; and makes the supreme happiness of mankind to consist in a *total inaction*, an *entire insensibility*, and a *perfect quietude.*

3. A sect which acknowledges for its master the philosopher *Confucius*, (or *Kung-fut-si*), who lived about 500 years before our Saviour. This religion, which is professed by the literati, and persons of rank in China and Tonquin, consists in a deep inward veneration for the God, or King of Heaven, and in the practice of every moral virtue. They have neither temples nor priests, nor any settled form of external worship: every one adores the Supreme Being in the way he likes best.

Confucius, like Socrates, did not dive into abstruse notions, but confined himself to speak with the deepest regard of the great Author of all beings, whom he represents as the most pure and perfect essence and fountain of all things; to inspire men with greater fear, veneration, gratitude, and love of him; to assert his divine providence over all his creatures; and to represent him as being of such infinite knowledge, that even our most thoughts are not hidden from him; and of such boundless goodness and justice, that he can let no virtue go unrewarded, or vice unpunished.

Mr. Maurice, the author of *Indian Antiquities*, asserts, that Confucius strictly forbade all images of the Deity, and the deification of dead men; and that in his dying moments he encouraged his disciples, by predicting that *in the west the Holy One would appear!*

The Chinese honour their dead ancestors, burn perfumes before their images, bow before their pictures, and invoke them as capable of bestowing all temporal blessings.

It is remarked, that "None of the different systems of religion," above mentioned, "can be said to be the prevailing creed in China; or what is more remarkable, can be found existing pure and distinct from the rest. The greater part of the Chinese have no decided opinion whatever on the subject, and are either complete atheists, or, if they acknowledge a Supreme Being, utterly ignorant in what view he ought to be regarded; while they all combine with their peculiar sentiments the multifarious superstitions of the more popular sects. Of all these tolerated and established religious persuasions the emperour is the supreme head; without whose permission not one of them can enjoy a single privilege or point of pre-eminence; and who can diminish or increase, at his pleasure, the number of their respective temples or priests."

. . .

JAPANESE. The religion of these islanders is paganism, but under some peculiar forms which deserve attention—particularly, the *Sinto*, the ancient idol worship of the Japanese: the *Budso*, or foreign idol worship, introduced from China: and the religion of their philosophers and moralists.

I. The *Sintos* have some obscure and imperfect notions of the immortality of the soul, and a future state of bliss and misery; they acknowledge a supreme Being, who, they believe, dwells in the highest heaven: and admit of some inferiour gods, whom they place among the stars; but they worship and invoke those gods alone whom they believe to have the sovereign control over this world, its elements, productions, and animals; these, they suppose, will not only render them happy here, but, by interceding for them at the hour of death, may procure them a happy condition hereafter. Hence their *dairis*, or ecclesiastical chiefs, being thought lineally descended from the eldest and most favoured sons of these deities, are supposed to be the true and living images of their gods.

The Sintos believe that the soul, after quitting the body, is removed to the high sub-celestial fields, seated just beneath the dwelling places of their gods; that those, who have led a good life, find immediate admission, while the souls of the wicked are denied entrance, and condemned to wander till they have expiated their crimes.

Their religion enjoins abstaining from blood, from eating flesh, or being near a dead body; by which a person is for a time rendered unfit to visit their temples, or to appear in the presence of their gods. It also commands a diligent observance of the solemn festivals, in honour of their gods; pilgrimages to the holy places at Isje; that is, to the temple of Tensio-Dai-Sin, the greatest of all the gods of the Japanese; and the chastisement and mortification of their bodies. But few of them pay much regard to this precept.

II. The most essential points of the *Budso* religion are: That the souls of men and animals are immortal, and both of the same substance, differing only according to the bodies in which they are placed: and that after the souls of mankind have left their bodies, they shall be rewarded or punished according to their behaviour in this life. Their god Armida is the sovereign commander of heaven; and is considered as the patron and protector of human souls; and to obtain his approbation it is requisite to lead a virtuous life, and do nothing contrary to the five commands, viz. not to kill any thing that has life; not to steal; not to commit fornication; to avoid lies, and all falsehood; not to drink strong liquors. On the other hand, all the vicious, priests or laymen, are, after death, sent to a place of misery, to be tormented for a certain time, according to the nature and number of their crimes, the number of years they lived upon earth, and their opportunities for becoming good and virtuous. Yet they suppose the miseries of these unhappy souls may be greatly alleviated by the virtuous lives of their relations and friends, and still more by the prayers and offerings of the priests to their great god, Armida. When vicious souls have expiated their crimes, they are sent back to animate such vile animals as resembled them in their former state of existence. From the vilest of these transmigrating into other and nobler, they, at least, are suffered again to enter human bodies; and thus have it in their power, by their virtue and piety, to obtain an uninterrupted state of felicity.

III. The philosophers and moralists pay no regard to any of the forms of worship practised in the country. Their supreme good consists in the pleasure and delight which arise from the steady practice of virtue. They do not admit of the transmigration of souls; but believe that there is an universal soul diffused throughout nature, animating all things, and reassuming departed souls as the sea does the rivers. This universal spirit they confound with the supreme Being.

These philosophers consider self-murder as an heroic and commendable action, when it is the only means of avoiding a shameful death, or of escaping from the hands of a victorious enemy. They conform to the general custom of their country, in commemorating their deceased parents and relations, by placing all sorts of provisions on a table provided for the purpose; but they celebrate no other festivals, nor pay any respect to the gods of the country.

CHARLES A. GOODRICH, *RELIGIOUS CEREMONIES AND CUSTOMS* (1836)

It was not only liberal Unitarians like Adams who surveyed the religious world; more conservative Protestants did too. David Benedict, a Baptist, published *History of All*

Religions in 1824; and Charles A. Goodrich (1790–1862), a Congregationalist, followed with *Religious Ceremonies and Customs* in 1825. Goodrich's book was based on a French compendium of religions written by Bernard Picart (1663–1733). Goodrich, who attended Yale and hailed from a family of Congregationalist ministers, pastored congregations in New England for some time. His main occupation, however, was writing children's books and reference works. His *History of the United States of America* (1822) went through more than 150 editions. His survey of religions was not as popular, but it remained in print into the 1860s (though after 1840 it appeared as *Pictorial and Descriptive View of All Religions*). In this first selection, from the book's introduction, Goodrich uses images of light and darkness to compare Christian and non-Christian traditions, and he anticipates the day when all the earth "shall be full of the knowledge of God." In the second entry, Goodrich repeats a common interpretation when he highlights the parallels between Tibetan Buddhism and Roman Catholicism. At a time when anti-Catholicism was rising in America, this comparison would not have inspired admiration for the Tibetans.

The reader will have presented to him a picture of the religious world. He will perceive upon that picture many dark and distressing shades; he will see in what varied and unhallowed forms, mankind have worshipped the common Parent of all; he will be led to contemplate the delusions practiced upon millions, by the cunning and craft of imposture; the unholy devotion demanded of other millions, by an intolerant hierarchy; and the debasing superstitions and cruel abominations inculcated upon still more millions of the human family, by an earth-born system of idolatry. From the pain of dwelling upon these darker shades, he will find relief by turning his eye upon some bright spots in the picture. . . . Into the dark corners of the earth, the light of the Gospel will ultimately penetrate, and the habitations of cruelty will become the dwelling places of righteousness. Even at this present time, the Christian Church is gathering in the first fruits of this golden age. The anti-christian systems and the idolatrous superstitions of the world are rapidly approaching their fall.

. . . Yet how much remains to be done before the warfare of Zion shall be accomplished!—before that period shall arrive, when the earth shall be full of the knowledge of God! Let the reader inquire, while he hails that day as certain as its advent, what he may do to accelerate its arrival.

. . . Friar Horace says, that in the main the religion of Thibet is the counterpart of the Romish. They believe in one God, and a trinity, but full of errors; a paradise, hell, and purgatory, but full of errors also. They make suffrages, alms, prayers, and sacrifices for the dead; they have a vast number of convents filled with monks and friars, amounting to thirty thousand; who, besides the three vows of poverty, obedience, and chastity, make several others. They have their confessors, who are chosen by their superiors, and receive their licenses from the Lama, as a bishop, without which they cannot hear confessions, or impose penances.

Charles A. Goodrich, *Religious Ceremonies and Customs* (Hartford: Hutchison and Dwier, 1836) 4–6, 538–40.

They have the same form of hierarchy as in the Romish Church; for they have their inferior Lamas, chosen by the Grand Lama, who act as bishops in their respective dioceses, having under them simple Lamas, who are the religious. To these may be added, the use of holy water, crosses, beads, and other matters. . . . The Great Lama, who . . . is La or Fo [Buddha] incarnate, is, according to Grueber, called in the country, Lama Konju, or the Eternal Father. He is also styled Dalay Lama. . . . In approaching him, his votaries fall prostrate with their heads to the ground and kiss him with incredible veneration. Thus, adds the Jesuit, that the devil, through his innate malignity, transferred to the worship of this people the veneration which is due only to the Pope of Rome, Christ's vicar, in the same manner as he hath done all the other mysteries of the Christian religion.

P A R T   I I

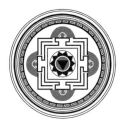

ENCOUNTERS, 1840 TO 1924

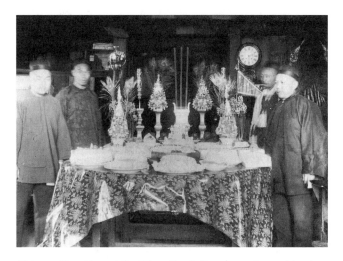

Chinese New Year at the Silver Creek "joss house" near Meadow Valley, Plumas County, California, 1890s. Courtesy Plumas County Museum.

The 1840s ushered in a new era in America's engagement with Asian religions. In the preceding period, only the most intrepid Asians made the eastward passage to the United States, and very few Americans grappled with the beliefs and practices of Asian religious traditions. But in this new era, meetings between Americans and Asians, Christians and Sikhs, Jews and Hindus became more common. Isolated contacts, in short, yielded to repeated encounters. Between 1840 and 1924, Americans encountered Asians and their religions not just abroad but at home, not just in books but face to face. As Asians came to the United States by the hundreds of thousands, they radically transformed the American religious landscape. They built temples, and worshiped their Buddhas and gods there. Thanks to the efforts of a few pioneering Hindu and Buddhist missionaries, some non-Asian Americans in this period began to embrace the East-West encounter as opportunity rather than danger. Some converted; many more sympathized. But Americans' encounters with Asians and their religions were not always friendly. Many saw Asian immigration as a threat to Christianity and the American way of life. Some responded to that perceived threat with hatred and violence. But Asian immigrants and their children persisted in their religious practices. In the process, both the United States and Asian religions were radically transformed.

Pioneering Transcendentalists such as Ralph Waldo Emerson and later Transcendentalists like James Freeman Clarke encountered Hinduism, Buddhism, and Confucianism in books, and together they formed the first American movement to press past missionary critiques of "heathen" religions toward a sympathetic engagement with Asian thought. *The Light of Asia* (1879), a poetic life of the Buddha by England's Sir Edwin Arnold, became a bestseller in America, and Bret Harte's less laudatory poem, "The Heathen Chinee" (1870), was widely quoted from San Francisco to New York City. But the encounters were not merely literary. Christian missionaries continued to meet the objects of their evangelizing in the missionary fields of Asia, while the "Boston Buddhists" encountered Buddhist images in temples in Japan, and Theosophists sat at the feet of holy men in India and Ceylon.

Asian immigration shifted the sites of these face-to-face encounters. The Chinese paved the way, followed by the Japanese and then Asian Indians. The overwhelming majority of these immigrants were men. (In 1909, a Sikh writer may have been exaggerating only slightly when he claimed there was "only one Hindoo woman on the North American continent.")[1] And laypeople predominated. But Hindu swamis, Buddhist monks, and Confucian teachers migrated too. And while many of these religious elites attended to immigrant communities, some turned the tables on the Christians by remaking America into a foreign mission field of their own. As a result of their missionizing, European Americans began in this period to convert to and sympathize with the religions of Asia. America was becoming not only a nation of immigrants but also a nation of religions.

The 1840s mark the beginning of this period of encounters. In 1841, Edward Salisbury, "the father of American Oriental studies," began teaching Sanskrit at Yale University. One year later, Salisbury and other Orientalists organized the American Oriental Society, and the Transcendentalist periodical *The Dial* began to publish "Ethnical Scriptures," a series of translations of Asian scriptures. In 1844, *The Dial* launched the American conversation about Buddhism when it published a translation by Elizabeth Palmer Peabody of portions of the *Lotus Sutra*. The annexation of California and the discovery of gold on John Sutter's sawmill in 1848 capped this key decade. Pulled by the Gold Rush and pushed by war, natural disasters, poverty, and starvation, Chinese "forty-niners" left their homes in search of happiness in *Gam Saan* or Gold Mountain. Along with hopes for peace and good fortune, these newcomers brought their faiths: Confucianism, Taoism, Buddhism, and Chinese vernacular religion. Soon they were enshrining their gods in temples up and down the West Coast.

During the first wave of Asian immigration, which extended from the opening of the Gold Rush to the shutting down of the Asian influx by the Immigration Act of 1924, roughly one million Asians came to the United States. The Chinese came first. By 1880, over 100,000 Chinese called the United States home. The Japanese came next, and in greater numbers. When the Japanese economy spiraled downward in the aftermath of the ouster of the Tokugawas and the restoration of the Meiji government in 1868, Japanese laborers began to emigrate in search of a better life. Japanese immigrants made their way in force to Hawaii in the 1880s and arrived in significant numbers on the mainland a decade later. Between 1885 and 1924, 200,000 Japanese arrived in Hawaii (which became a United States territory in 1900) and 180,000 came to the continental United States. Among the latter group were Dr. Shuye Sonoda and the Reverend Kakuryo Nishijima of Kyoto, Japan. Practitioners of Jodo Shinshu (True Pure Land) Buddhism, they became upon their arrival in San Francisco in 1899 the first full-time Buddhist missionaries to the continental United States.

Asian Indians came later and in much smaller numbers. Although there are accounts of Indian immigrants marching in a Fourth of July parade in Salem, Massachusetts, in the 1850s, immigration from India did not reach significant numbers until the late 1890s. Between 1899 and 1914, fewer than 7,000 arrived. Most were unskilled agricultural laborers from the Punjab region. Although Indian immigrants were all called "Hindoos," few actually practiced Hinduism. Approximately 10 percent were Muslims, and the overwhelming majority were Sikhs. Sikhs distinguished themselves from other Indian immigrants by wearing turbans and by refusing to shave or to cut their hair. They too built places of worship. America's first Sikh *gurdwara* or temple was built in Stockton, California, in 1912.[2] Because virtually all the Sikh migrants were men, they were forced to marry outside the faith. Many wed Mexican-American Catholics. Their families practiced a fascinating creole of Sikhism and Spanish-style Catholicism.

Neither Asian immigrants nor their religions received warm welcomes. Chinese immigration precipitated a West Coast debate about the character and destiny of America comparable only to the slavery debate on the eastern seaboard. A minority argued for what the African-American intellectual Frederick Douglass described as a "composite nation." But after the completion of the Transcontinental Railroad in 1869 (built largely with Chinese labor), most fell in behind the sentiments and slogans of nativist groups such as the Asiatic Exclusion League. Unfortunately for Americans of Chinese descent, the racists did more than chant "Keep California White" or "The Chinese Must Go!" Anti-Chinese riots left death tolls of twenty-one in Los Angeles in 1871; twenty-eight in Rock Springs, Wyoming, in 1855; and thirty-one in the Snake River Massacre in Oregon in 1877. Motivated by a combination of economics, race, and religion, anti-Chinese nativists denounced the Chinese as "cheap labor," "Chinks," and "heathen." Although Protestant missionaries as a rule embraced Asian immigrants on the theory that they would soon "bow at the same altar as our own countrymen," most Americans saw things differently.[3] Noting low rates of conversion to Christianity in America's Chinese communities, the *San Francisco Chronicle* mocked the missionaries as naifs out of step with the public, while raising the specter of Caucasian conversions to Confucianism. The answer to the "Chinese Question," its editors argued, was to cut off immigration from China.

Given the success of the anti-Chinese campaign, it is not surprising that nativists responded to Japanese and Asian-Indian immigration with similar bravado. Those who previously had warned their fellow Americans about the "Yellow Peril" now feared a tsunami of "Japs" and an invasion of "Ragheads." Once again, violence broke out. And once again legislators heeded the cries of the rioters rather than the immigrants' anguish. In 1917 the United States Congress resolved the "Hindoo Question" by creating a "barred zone" that effectively banned immigration from India and Southeast Asia. Congress finished the job by passing the Immigration Act of 1924, which added the Japanese to the list of excluded Asians.

Not all Americans treated Asians and their religions with scorn. Helena Blavatsky and Henry Steel Olcott, cofounders of the Theosophical Society (established 1875), converted to Buddhism in Ceylon (now Sri Lanka) in 1880, and three years later Episcopal rector Phillips Brooks remarked that "a large part of Boston prefers to consider itself Buddhist rather than Christian."[4] In some early versions of *Science and Health with Key to the Scriptures*, Christian Science founder (and Bostonian) Mary Baker Eddy quoted approvingly from the *Bhagavad Gita*. In 1902, Thomas Edison, an early member of the Theosophical Society, produced a documentary film called *Hindoo Fakir* (1902). Three years later, modern dance pioneer Ruth St. Denis brought Hinduism to the stage when she played the title role in *Radha: The Mystic Dance of the Five Senses.* Lafcadio Hearn, who sympathized with but never converted to Buddhism, moved to Japan, took a Japanese name (Yakumo Koizumi), and became a Japanese citizen. He was later buried in a Japanese Buddhist monastery. Finally, in 1924, in the first Buddhist ordination rite in Hawaii, Reverend Ernest "Shinkaku" Hunt, an England-born convert, was ordained a Jodo Shinshu ("True Pure Land") priest.

While a few Americans alit on Asian soil, Asians put down religious roots in the United States. Those roots were fertilized by the first generation of Asian missionaries to America. In 1893, Hindu, Zen, and Theravada Buddhist missionaries came to Chicago as delegates to the World's Parliament of Religions. Swami Vivekananda (a Hindu delegate from India), Anagarika Dharmapala (a Theravada Buddhist delegate from Ceylon), and Soyen Shaku (a Rinzai Zen master from Japan) all toured the United States following the Parliament. Dharmapala had little success transplanting his Maha Bodhi Society to America, but Vivekananda's Vedanta Society thrived in American soil. Under the leadership of Swami Abhedananda and Swami Paramananda, Vedanta spread by the 1920s to New York, San Francisco, Boston, and Los Angeles. By that time, however, Vedanta had to compete with a new form of American Hinduism, the kriya yoga of Swami Paramahansa Yogananda, who arrived in America as a delegate to the International Congress of Religious Liberals held in Boston in 1920, and stayed on as the leader of the Self-Realization Fellowship. Unlike Dharmapala, Vivekananda, and Yogananda, Soyen Shaku chose to send teachers rather than build institutions. One of his students, D. T. Suzuki, came to America in 1897 to work with Buddhist sympathizer Paul Carus at Open Court Publishing in La Salle, Illinois. The American meeting of East and West was on.

S.R.P.

NOTES

1. Saint Nihal Singh, "The Picturesque Immigrant from India's Coral Strand: Who He Is and Why He Comes to America," *Out West* 30.1 (January 1909): 42–54.

2. There is considerable confusion regarding this important date. 1906, 1909, 1912, 1915, and 1916 are all offered as the founding year by reputable historians. Research in local histories,

the Stockton City Directory, and back issues of the *Stockton Record* confirms the following story: In 1906, Stockton Sikhs bought a home, which they may have designated as their *gurdwara*. In 1912, they built a new *gurdwara* there. After acquiring an adjoining lot, they built a larger temple, which they dedicated on 21 November 1915 but may have opened as late as 1916. Finally, in 1929, they built out of brick an even larger *gurdwara*, which stands today on the site at 1930 South Grant Street. See articles in the *Stockton Record* for 17 June 1984, 6 March 1952, and 3 December 1932; Ann Wood, "East Indians in California: A Study of their Organizations, 1900–1947" (University of Wisconsin: Master's thesis, 1966); and Glenn A. Kennedy, *It Happened in Stockton: 1900–1925* (vol. 1; Stockton, Calif.: Glenn A. Kennedy, 1967), 76–77. We are grateful to Susan Benedetti, Leslie Crow, Ted Sibia, and Jane Singh for assistance with this research.

3. *Daily Alta California* (12 May 1852), quoted in Ronald Takaki, *Strangers from a Different Shore: A History of Asian Americans* (New York: Penguin, 1989), 80.

4. Alexander V. G. Allen, *Life and Letters of Phillips Brooks* (New York: E. P. Dutton, 1901), 2.

CHAPTER 3

East to America: Immigrant Landings

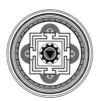

FREDERICK DOUGLASS, "OUR COMPOSITE NATIONALITY" (1869)

When Chinese immigrants began arriving in the United States in the late 1840s, the country was to them a nation of strangers. But they were not without friends. Among the earliest supporters of Chinese immigrants in the United States was Frederick Douglass (1818–95). Born a slave in Tuckahoe, Maryland, in 1818, Douglass made his way north to freedom in 1838. Three years later he joined abolitionist William Lloyd Garrison on the lecture circuit, where he would eventually champion a variety of social reforms, among them women's rights. Douglass's fiery oratory and the appearance of his classic autobiography, *Narrative of the Life of Frederick Douglass, an American Slave* (1845), made him the most recognized Black American of his century. A convert to Christianity as a teenager, Douglass chafed as an adult at the hypocrisy of Christians compromising with the sins of slavery. Slaveholding religion, he insisted, was not true Christianity. Another sin, according to Douglass, was anti-Chinese nativism. Douglass's boldest statement on "The Chinese Question" is "Our Composite Nationality," a speech he delivered in Boston in 1869. In this speech, Douglass argues for the human rights of Chinese Americans, and boldly asserts that Chinese immigration is good for America. His prophetic vision of a "composite nation" that is as harmonious as it is pluralistic has, of course, yet to be realized.

We are a country of all extremes, ends and opposites; the most conspicuous example of composite nationality in the world. Our people defy all the ethnological and logical classifications. In races we range all the way from black to white, with intermediate shades which, as in the apocalyptic vision, no man can name a number.

In regard to creeds and faiths, the condition is no better, and no worse. Differences both as to race and to religion are evidently more likely to increase than to diminish. . . .

Europe and Africa are already here, and the Indian was here before either. . . . Until recently, neither the Indian nor the negro has been treated as a part of the body politic. . . . Before the relations of these two races are satisfactorily settled, and in spite of all opposition, a new race is making its appearance within our borders, and claiming attention. It is estimated that not less than one-hundred thousand Chinamen are now within the limits of the United States. . . .

I believe that Chinese immigration on a large scale will yet be our irrepressible fact. . . . The reasons for this opinion are obvious; China is a vastly overcrowded country. . . . Men, like bees, want elbow room. When the hive is overcrowded, the bees will swarm, and will be likely to take up their abode where they find the best prospect for honey. In matters of this sort, men are very much like bees. Hunger will not be quietly endured, even in the Celestial Empire, when it is once generally known that there is bread enough and to spare in America. . . .

Not only is there a Chinese motive behind this probable immigration, but there is also an American motive which will play its part, one which will be all the more active and energetic because there is in it an element of pride, of bitterness, and revenge.

Southern gentlemen who led in the late rebellion, have not parted with their convictions at this point, any more than at others. They want to be independent of the negro. They believe in slavery and they believe in it still. . . . Hence these gentlemen have turned their attention to the Celestial Empire. They would rather have laborers who will work for nothing; but as they cannot get the negroes on these terms, they want Chinamen who, they hope, will work for next to nothing. . . .

But alas, for all the selfish inventions and dreams of men! The Chinaman will not long be willing to wear the cast off shoes of the negro, and, if he refuses, there will be trouble again. The negro worked and took his pay in religion and the lash. The Chinaman is a different article and will want the cash. He may, like the negro, accept Christianity, but, unlike the negro, he will not care to pay for it in labor under the lash. He had the Golden Rule in substance five hundred years before the coming of Christ, and has notions of justice that are not to be confused or bewildered by any of our *"Cursed by Canaan"* religion. . . .

The Chinese in themselves have first rate recommendations. They are industrious, docile, cleanly, frugal; they are dexterous of hand, patient of toil, marvelously gifted in the power of imitation, and have but few wants. . . .

The old question as to what shall be done with the negro will have to give place to the greater question, "what shall be done with the Mongolian," and perhaps we shall see raised one still greater question, namely, What will the Mongolian do with both the negro and the whites?

Already has the matter taken this shape in California and on the Pacific Coast generally. Already has California assumed a bitterly unfriendly attitude toward the Chinaman. Already has she driven them from her altars of justice. Already has she stamped them as outcasts and handed them over to popular contempts and vulgar jest. Already are they the constant victims of cruel harshness and brutal violence. Already have our Celtic brothers, never slow to execute the behests of popular prejudice against the weak and defenseless, recognized in the heads of these people, fit targets for their shillalahs. Already, too, are their associations formed in avowed hostility to the Chinese. . . .

I have said that the Chinese will come, and have given some reasons why we may expect them in very large numbers in no very distant future. Do you ask, if I would favor such immigration? I answer, *I would*. "Would you admit them as witnesses in our courts of law?" *I would*. Would you have them naturalized, and have them invested with all the rights of American citizenship? *I would*. Would you allow them to vote? *I would*. Would you allow them to hold office? *I would*. . . .

I submit that this question of Chinese immigration should be settled upon higher principles than those of a cold and selfish expediency. There are such things in the world as human rights. They rest upon no conventional foundation, but are external, universal, and indestructible.

Among these, is the right of locomotion; the right of migration; the right which belongs to no particular race, but belongs alike to all and to all alike. It is the right you assert by staying here, and your fathers asserted by coming here. It is this great right that I assert for the Chinese and the Japanese, and for all other varieties of man equally with yourselves, now and forever. . . .

It has been thoughtfully observed, that every nation, owing to its peculiar character and composition, has a definite mission in the world. . . . Ours seems plain and unmistakable. . . . and that is to make us the most perfect national illustration of the unity and dignity of the human family that the world has ever seen. . . .

The theory that each race of men has some special faculty, some peculiar gift or quality of mind or heart, needed to the perfection and happiness of the whole is a broad and beneficent theory, and, besides its beneficence, has, in its support, the voice of experience. Nobody doubts this theory when applied to animals and plants, and no one can show that it is not equally true when applied to races.

All great qualities are never found in any one man or in any one race. The whole of humanity, like the whole of everything else, is ever greater than a part. Men only know themselves by knowing others, and contact is essential to this knowledge. In one race we perceive the predominance of imagination; in another, like the Chinese, we remark its total absence. In one people, we have the reasoning faculty, in another, for music; in another exists courage; in another, great physical vigor, and so on through the whole list of human qualities. All are needed to temper, modify, round and complete the whole man and the whole nation. . . .

It is objected to the Chinaman that he is secretive and treacherous, and will not tell the truth when he thinks it for his interest to tell a lie. . . . This is the last objection which should come from those who profess the all-conquering power of the Christian religion. If that religion cannot stand contact with the Chinese, religion or no religion, so much the worse for those who have adopted it. It is the Chinaman, not the Christian, who should be alarmed for his faith. He exposes that faith to great dangers by exposing it to the freer air of America. But shall we send missionaries to the heathen and yet deny the heathen the right to come to us? I think a few honest believers in the teachings of Confucius would be well employed in expounding his doctrines among us.

The next objection to the Chinese is that he cannot be induced to swear by the Bible. This is to me one of his best recommendations. The American people will swear by anything in the heavens above or in the earth beneath. We are a nation of swearers. We swear by a book whose most authoritative command is to swear not at all. . . .

Let the Chinaman come; he will help to augment the national wealth. He will help to develop our boundless resources; he will help to pay off our national debt; he will help to lighten the burden of national taxation; he will give us the benefit of his skill as a manufacturer and tiller of the soil, in which he is unsurpassed.

Even the matter of religious liberty, which has cost the world more tears, more blood and more agony, than any other interest, will be helped by his presence. I know of no church, however tolerant; of no priesthood, however enlightened, which could be safely trusted with the tremendous power which universal conformity would confer. We should welcome all men of every shade of religious opinion, as among the best means of checking the arrogance and intolerance which are the almost inevitable concomitants of general conformity. Religious liberty always flourishes best amid the clash and competition of rival religious creeds. . . .

I close these remarks as I began. If our action shall be in accordance with the principles of justice, liberty, and perfect human equality, no eloquence can adequately portray the greatness and grandeur of the future of the Republic.

We shall spread the network of our science and civilization over all who seek their shelter whether from Asia, Africa, or the Isles of the Sea. We shall mold them all, each after his kind, into Americans; Indian and Celt, negro and Saxon, Latin and Teuton, Mongolian and Caucasian, Jew and gentile, all shall here bow to the same law, speak the same language, support the same government, enjoy the same liberty, vibrate with the same national enthusiasm, and seek the same national ends.

FUNG CHEE PANG, THE CONFUCIAN SAGE AND THE MONGOLIAN BIBLE (1876)

No group defended the rights of Chinese immigrants more ardently than Protestant missionaries. As early as 1852, William Speer, a Presbyterian minister to San Francisco's Chinatown, was trying to allay fears that Chinese immigration threatened the American way of life. But implicit in Speer's defense was the expectation that Chinese immigrants would be rapidly Americanized and Christianized. Chinese-American business leaders undercut this hope in May 1876 when they brought Fung Chee Pang to San Francisco's Chinatown to preach Confucianism. The *San Francisco Chronicle* seized upon Pang's success—he reportedly drew crowds of one thousand people at "protracted meetings" in the Luk San Fung Theater—as a chance to denounce both Chinese immigration and its missionary defenders. "Beware," the editors warned, "lest you turn over this fairest portion of the American continent to the dominion of the worst form of paganism in the attempt to convert an inconsiderable few of the benighted heathen to the gospel of Christ." Despite these warnings, the *Chronicle* allowed Fung Chee Pang to speak for himself in two long interviews. The first dealt largely with the life of Confucius. In these excerpts from the second interview, Pang and a rather sympathetic reporter discuss Confucian ritual and the teachings of the "Mongolian Bible." These interviews caught the eye of editors at the *New York Times*, which on 8 June 1876 lampooned both Confucianism (as a religion as perplexing as life insurance) and the *Chronicle* (for worrying needlessly about the prospects of Confucian priests taking over St. Patrick's Cathedral). The articles, which present a surprisingly traditional view of Confucianism, probably represent the first recorded dialogue with a Confucian in the New World.

There is no gainsaying the fact that John Chinaman is a far-seeing sort of an animal. He never gets too far away from his base of supplies. When he first came to this country he brought his rice, his chopsticks, his language, his peculiar clothing and disgusting habits, and now, to make the thing complete, he imports his religion and his literature, and whisks them fairly in the faces of our men of letters with the remark that it is more authentic and as old as the everlasting hills. If we are obliged to take it, we must know what it is like, and for this purpose a representative of the *Chronicle* has been holding a sort of literary pow-wow with the erudite Fung Chee Pang, by title Kong Lung, in order to give the public some idea of what they may expect from the advent of this new and yet old religion. It may be anticipated that the undertaking was a pleasant one. So it was. Talk no more of "feasts of reason" and a corresponding "flow of soul," but wrestle with the history, the doctrines, the sayings of the grim old Confucius as they come through the medium of an interpreter from the lips of a veritable sage who has spent twenty years of his life in a collegiate or preliminary education, and then, and only then, can one properly appreciate the length, the breadth, the thickness and the beatitude of Mongolian classics, ethics, morality and religion. The interview was held in one of the most gorgeous of the Chinese restaurants, and between the sips of delicious tea which was served, the learned pundit, with his little black silk cap on his head, told the story of Confucius. . . .

"What is the nature of the worship or homage rendered Confucius?"

"On the 1st day of every month offerings of fruit and vegetables are set forth, and on the 15th there is a solemn burning of incense. But twice a year, in the middle months of Spring and Autumn, when the first *ting* day of the month comes round, the worship of Confucius is something grand. At the Imperial College the Emperor himself is required to attend in State and is in fact the principal performer."

"Can you describe the ceremony?"

"After the Emperor has twice knelt, and six times bowed his head to the earth, the presence of Confucius' spirit is invoked in the following words: 'Great art Thou O perfect sage. Thy virtue is full, thy doctrine is complete. Among mortal

"The Chinese Sage: Fung Chee Pang Tells of the Great Confucius," *San Francisco Chronicle*, 31 May 1876, 4.

men there has not been thy equal. All kings honor thee. Thy statutes and laws have come gloriously down. Thou art the pattern in this Imperial school. Reverently have the sacrificed vessels been set out. Full of awe we sound our drums and bells.' Now the spirit is supposed to be present, and the service proceeds through various offerings; when the first has been set forth, an officer reads: 'On this month of this year the Emperor offers a sacrifice to the philosopher king, the ancient teacher, the perfect, and says: "O Teacher in virtue equal to Heaven and earth, whose doctrines embrace the past time and the present, thou didst digest and transmit the six classics, and didst hand down lessons for all generations. Now, in this second month of spring (or autumn) in reverent observance of the old statutes, with victims, silks, spirits, and fruits, I carefully offer sacrifice to thee. . . . Mayst thou enjoy the offerings.' "

"How is Confucius regarded by the masses of the people?"

"With the greatest veneration. They like to hear preaching from his texts. The whole of the magistracy of our country is versed in all that is recorded of the sage, and his sayings are in everybody's mouth. He is the God above all other gods. . . ."

"Then there are a great many scholars in the Chinese empire?"

"A great many. We have a large number of schools, as many as you have; each student, when he passes his examination, is ready to begin work, some to teach and some to preach."

"Do they all believe in Confucius and his religion?"

"They all believe Confucius. His thoughts are familiar to every one and his character more or less reproduced in every scholar. Everybody in China who has any education at all must get it from the works of the great sage. We learn of him and do him homage at the same time. In every school-room there is a tablet or inscription on the wall, sacred to the sage, and every pupil is required, on coming to school, to bow before it the first thing as an act of worship."

On being asked to explain particularly the nature of the religious teachings, the pundit took one of the volumes . . . of the four books called the "Great Learning." The translation was as follows: "My master the philosopher Ching says the Great Learning is a book left by Confucius, and forms the gate by which first learners enter into virtue." That we can now perceive the order in which the ancients pursued their learning is solely owing to the preservation of this work, the Analects and Mencius coming after it. Learners must commence their course with this, and then it may be hoped they will be kept from error.

THE TEXT OF CONFUCIUS

First—What "The Great Learning" teaches is—to illustrate illustrious virtue; to renovate the people; and to rest in the highest excellence.

Second—The point where to rest being known the object of pursuit is then determined, and that being determined a calm imperturbedness may be attained. To that calmness there will succeed a tranquil repose. In that repose there may be careful deliberation, and that deliberation will be followed by the desired end.

Third—Things have their root and their completion. Affairs have their end and their beginning. To know what is first and what is last will lead near to what is taught in "The Great Learning."

Fourth—The ancients who wished to illustrate illustrious virtue throughout the Empire first ordered well their own States. Wishing to order well their own States they first regulated their families. Wishing to regulate their families they first cultivated their persons. Wishing to cultivate their persons they first rectified their hearts. Wishing to rectify their hearts they first sought to be sincere in their thoughts. Wishing to be sincere in their thoughts they first extended to the utmost their knowledge. Such extension of knowledge lay in the investigation of things.

Fifth—Things being investigated, knowledge became complete; knowledge being complete, thoughts were sincere; thoughts sincere, hearts were rectified; hearts rectified, persons were cultivated; persons cultivated, families became well regulated; families well regulated, States became well governed; States well governed, and the whole empire is made tranquil and happy. Here the learned Fung Chee Pang—Kong Sung—stopped for breath, and the reporter, fearful that if once started the pundit might ring in the whole 1000 volumes belonging to the Confucian library, waved his hand in signification that he had got information enough. He then gracefully retired from the scholastic presence, after accepting an invitation to call again for another installment of Confucian history and to attend one of the Doctor's lectures. The latter event is looked forward to with a great deal of interest and anticipation. The extract from the book above is a fair sample of what may be expected in the way of a text.

CHINESE EXCLUSION ACT (1882)

Chinese immigrants alit on American shores as early as the 1780s, but immigration from China was miniscule until after gold was discovered in California in 1848. By 1880, there were over 100,000 people of Chinese descent in America, most of them on the West Coast. Though only 0.002 percent of the U.S. population was Chinese, white laborers in the West feared competition from the "cheap labor" of "the heathen Chinee." Anti-Chinese riots broke out beginning in the 1860s. In 1877, the Working-men's Party of California organized under the slogan, "The Chinese Must Go!" Local and state legislators responded to the rage by passing exclusionary laws. In 1882, the U.S. Congress passed the Chinese Exclusion Act, which banned the entry of Chinese laborers into the United States and forbade people of Chinese descent already living in the United States from becoming American citizens. Although the act originally prohibited immigration and naturalization for only ten years, a series of later laws first broadened the immigration ban to include "all persons of the Chinese race" and later extended its provisions indefinitely. As a result, California's Chinese population plummeted from 9 percent of the state's inhabitants in 1880 to roughly 0.5 percent in 1940. As the numbers dwindled, Chinese temples in the United States descended into disrepair. Many folded. In 1943, in an effort to effect a rapprochement with China, which was then fighting along with the United States against its newest Asian enemy, the Japanese, the Chinese Exclusion Act was repealed. But setting aside what President Roosevelt called "a historic mistake" did not put Chinese immigrants on equal footing with Europeans. An average of only fifty-nine Chinese a year came to America during the decade following the 1943 repeal.

Be it enacted, &c., That from and after the expiration of ninety days next after passage of this act, and until the expiration of ten years next after the passage of this act, the coming of Chinese laborers to the United States be, and the same is hereby, suspended; and during such suspension it shall not be lawful for any Chinese laborer to come, or having so come after the expiration of said ninety days, to remain within the United States.

Sec. 2. That any master of any vessel, of whatever nationality, who shall knowingly on such vessel bring within the jurisdiction of the United States, and permit to be landed, any Chinese laborer from any foreign port or place shall be

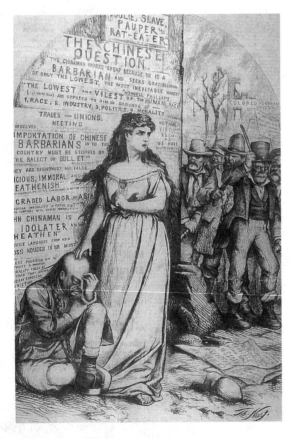

Lady Liberty comes to the defense of "John Chinaman" the "Idolater and Heathen" in this woodcut on the Chinese question by political cartoonist Thomas Nast. *Harper's Weekly*, 18 February 1871.

H.R. 3540, *Congressional Record*, 14 March 1882, vol. 13, 47th Congress, 1st Session, 1899–1900 [passed 6 May 1882, as 22 Stat. 58].

deemed guilty of a misdemeanor, and on conviction thereof shall be punished by a fine of not more than $500 for each and every such Chinese laborer so brought, and may be also imprisoned for a term not exceeding one year. . . .

Sec. 4. That in order to the faithful execution articles 1 and 2 of the treaty of the United States and the Empire of China ratified July 19, 1881, in case any Chinese residing in the United States on the 17th day of November 1880, or shall have come into the same before the expiration of ninety days next after the passage of this act, shall depart therefrom, they shall, before such departure, cause themselves to be duly registered at a custom-house in the United States, and produce to the collector of the district at which they shall seek to re-enter the United States the certificate of such registration properly vised by the indorsement of the proper diplomatic representatives or consul of the United States as required in cases of passports by the fifth section of this act. . . .

Sec 16. That hereafter no State court or court of the United States shall admit Chinese to citizenship; and all laws in conflict with this act are hereby repealed.

Sec 17. That the words "Chinese laborers," wherever used in this act, shall be construed to mean both skilled and unskilled laborers and Chinese employed in mining.

FREDERICK J. MASTERS, "PAGAN TEMPLES IN SAN FRANCISCO" (1892)

The Chinese laborers who flocked to the West Coast between the discovery of gold in California in 1848 and the Chinese Exclusion Act of 1882 brought their gods with them. The first Chinese temple in the United States emerged in San Francisco in 1853, and by the end of the century there were 400 more in the western states. These sites, which made space for Confucianism, Taoism, Buddhism, and Chinese popular piety, captured the imagination of American writers. In 1868, California's *Overland Monthly* published "Our Heathen Temples," an article on places of worship in San Francisco's Chinatown as thick with contempt as with description. Frederick J. Masters's "Pagan Temples in San Francisco" appeared in *The Californian* nearly a quarter century later. Though as ill titled as the *Overland Monthly* article, Masters's piece is far more sympathetic. In keeping with the Sinophobia of his surroundings, Masters sneers at Chinese Buddhism, but he compares favorably the "heathens" of China (fallen, from his primitivist perspective, from a glorious past) with the "pagans" of India. Masters's account of America's earliest "Joss-house"—"joss" is a corruption of *deos*, the Portuguese word for god—provides a rare early glimpse into the material culture and ritual practices of pious Chinese Americans in the nineteenth century.

Long ages ago, when our forefathers were ignorant idolaters whose altars flowed with the blood of human sacrifices, there is every reason to believe that the Chinese were a monotheistic people, who, according to their light and knowledge, wor-

Frederick J. Masters, "Pagan Temples in San Francisco," *The Californian* 2.6 (November 1892): 727–41.

shipped the Supreme Ruler, speculated upon his being and attributes, and framed a system of theology which, notwithstanding its crudeness and admixture of error, astonishes anyone who believes that in the dark ages of the world the Creator revealed himself to no people but the Hebrews. The history of their religious degradation has yet to be written. . . . Their Confucian teachers . . . taught that the most High was too exalted for ordinary mortals to approach and that the service of heaven could only acceptably offered by their Melchisedek Sovereign, "the Son of Heaven," who is responsible to Heaven for his people's welfare and offers prayer and sacrifice on their behalf. It can hardly be wondered at that when Buddhism was introduced into China at the beginning of the Christian era, this religious people should turn to images of foreign Bodhisatvas or heroes of national fame, that they were taught to believe were potent for good or ill, according as they were propitiated or neglected. The monks from the banks of the Ganges changed the whole character of Chinese religion. The so-called "Light of Asia" has made them a nation of idolaters. Amidst much that is grotesque, degrading and sinful about Chinese idolatrous rites, two negative features place their temples on a higher level than those of any other heathen land. There has been no instance of human sacrifice and no deification of vice. No human victim was ever immolated on a Chinese altar. The cruel rites practiced by the ancient Britons, Aztecs and Egyptians would horrify the humane monks of Sakyamuni with Sutras in their hands that teach the preservation of all animal life. No Chinese religious sect has ever countenanced in their temple rites the least taint of such licentious orgies as were found in the hieroduli dance to Aphrodite Pandemos or the obscene rites of the Durga-puja. . . .

While the Chinese believe in fiends and evil spirits and propitiate them just to keep them from mischief, their deepest homage is called forth in the worship of the heroes of their nation and the patriarchs of their tribes. Of the fifteen heathen temples in San Francisco, ten are erected in honor of ancient kings, statesmen or warriors famous in their history, who have become apotheosized as protectors of the people and benefactors of the nation worthy of their reverent homage. The remainder are dedicated to patriarchs of the village clans, patrons of guilds or the sages or genii of religious sects. The local Joss houses are not very imposing edifices. . . . there is nothing in this city that approaches the artistic beauty of the carvings and images of a first-rate temple in Canton. . . .

The oldest Joss-house in San Francisco is the Temple of the Queen of Heaven, on Waverly street. It was erected over forty years ago, and is the property of the Sam Yap Company. The goddess worshipped at this temple was a Chinese young lady who lived hundreds of years ago [and] was long ago canonized as the Queen of Heaven, the guardian saint of fishermen and sailors, and the protector of all good people who go down to the sea in ships. Her temples are found throughout China, where she is worshipped by landsmen and sailors alike. . . .

The most popular goddess of the Chinese pantheon is Kwan Yum, the Chinese Notre Dame. Her full title of canonization is: "Great in pity, great in love, the savior from misery and woe, the hearer of earthly cries." Her shrine is found up a dingy staircase on the southwest corner of Spofford alley and Washington streets. . . . Many are the legends told of this Buddhist Madonna. . . .

In the Spofford-alley temple are found the shrines of some twenty other gods and goddesses, the principal being the Grand Duke of Peace, the God of Medicine, and Pan Kung, a celebrated Prime Minister of the Sung dynasty. The funniest discovery in this temple was that of Tsai Tin Tai Shing. He is a beatified monkey in the image of a man. Hatched from a bowlder, this man is said to have proclaimed himself king of monkeys. At last he learned the language of men, and finding himself possessed of supernatural powers, he obtained a place among the gods. Such is the legend. Chinese idolatry thus reaches the acme of absurdity and sinfulness in the canonization of a monkey. Thoughts of Darwin's descent of man at once flashed across our mind as we looked at this image. It was disappointing to one's curiosity to find that the old temple keeper who cared more for a pipe of opium than for speculations in theology and anthropology could not tell us what part natural selection played in the evolution of Chinese deities, or whether monkey worship was the newest phase of Chinese ancestral worship. . . .

A Chinese temple has no fixed time for religious service; no congregation meets together for united praise and prayer, or sits to listen to some exposition of doctrine and duty. The worshipper comes when he has something to pray about. Family sickness, adverse fortune or some risky business undertaking drives him to the oracle. As he enters the temple he makes his bow to the gods with clasped hands, he lights his candles and incense, kneels upon a mat and calls upon the god by name three times. He then takes up two semi-oval blocks of wood called Yum Yeung Puey, bows toward the idol, prays for good luck and then tosses them up. The success of his supplication depends upon the position in which these blocks fall. If they both fall in the same position the omen is unfavorable; the god has left his office or does not wish to be disturbed. If the blocks fall one with the flat side turned up and the other with the flat surface turned down, the god is supposed to be taking some interest in his business. The worshipper now knocks his head three times three upon the floor, and he offers up his petition. This done, he takes a cylindrical bamboo pot containing bamboo slips about fifteen inches in length, each marked with a number. These are called sticks of fate, and are shaken together with the ends turned to the idol, till one is jostled out. The priest or temple keeper looks at the number, consults his book and hunts up the answer given to the man's prayer. The drum beats and the bell tolls. Offerings of paper money, consisting of beaten tinfoil, a whole armful of which can be bought for half a dollar, are burnt in the furnace and are changed by fire into the currency of the gods. It has taken only ten minutes to burn candles, incense and gilt paper, say his prayers, cast his lot, and get his answer and be on his way home.

Some happy morning he may be seen repairing to the same temple to return thanks for some profitable venture in trade, for a relative restored to health, or for some good fortune believed to have come in answer to his prayers. An express wagon drives up to the temple door, containing roast pigs and the choicest vegetables and fruits laid out in trays, which he offers to the god with libations of wine and tea. The god is supposed to feed upon the fumes of the meat and food, after which utilitarian John carts them back home to the family pantry. . . .

It is easy to condemn the impiety of this apotheosis of human beings as objects of divine worship or to ridicule the extravagance of the legends that cluster around these shrines. From seven to twenty thick centuries lie between us and the heroes and heroines whose memories are there embalmed. Much of their true history is blotted out in the twilight of the past. A rude statue, a gaudy bedizened thing of clay and wood, around which has gathered a mass of myth and fable is all that remains. But amidst the smoke of sandalwood and wax candles, the kow-towing and tomtoming and jargon of Sanscrit litanies one can discover something good—a reverence for the brave, the wise and the good, and the expression of that universal truth, however grossly symbolized, that the grave is not the goal of human greatness; that wise words and noble deeds can never die. There were heroes, patriarchs and sages in China's hoary past, who lifted up their hand against oppression and wrong—men who tried to guess out the problems of life and death, and who held out their bits of torches trying to lead men to higher and brighter paths. Such men can never be forgotten. The nation will one day return to the worship of the Highest and the faith in the True. In the dawn of a clearer light shall vanish all that is extravagant, foolish and false; but through all time and change these heroes of her national history will live and their work abide.

SHUYE SONODA, BUDDHISM IN THE KINGDOM OF LIBERTY (1899)

Although they had emigrated to Hawaii earlier, Japanese began arriving in significant numbers on the West Coast during the 1890s. Most claimed a Buddhist background. By 1906, 3,165 Japanese Buddhists lived in the continental United States, and nine Pure Land Buddhist groups had been established in California, Oregon, and Washington. The Hompa Hongwanji, one of the forms of Jodo Shinshu or the True Pure Land sect, sent two representatives in 1898 to assess the situation among immigrants. On 2 September of the following year, the Japanese organization officially recognized the Buddhist mission in America by sending to San Francisco two missionaries: Shuye Sonoda and Kakuryo Nishijima. Those Pure Land priests, and the others who followed, nurtured Japanese devotees of Amida Buddha and tutored European-American sympathizers. In the first decade of the twentieth century, Japanese-American Buddhists published two impressive magazines, one in Japanese and the other in English: *Beikoku Bukkyo* (*Buddhism in America*) and *The Light of Dharma*. They also formed the Dharma Sangha of Buddha, a Buddhist study group for Caucasians. It was one of the first Buddhist organizations for European Americans. This letter, written by one of those pioneering Buddhist priests, was addressed to Buddhist sympathizer Paul Carus, whose books had reached Sonoda in Japan. It recounts Sonoda's first public lecture in America. In this "first attempt at the propagation of the new light of the truth in the New World,"

Shuye Sonoda to Paul Carus, 14 September? 1899, Open Court Publishing Company Papers, Morris Library, Southern Illinois University Library, Carbondale. Used by permission.

Dr. Shuye Sonoda and the Reverend Kahuryo Nishijima, the first Buddhist missionaries to the United States, as depicted in the *San Francisco Chronicle*, 13 September 1899. These priests, according to the *Chronicle*, came to America to teach that God is "not a real existence, but a figment of the human imagination."

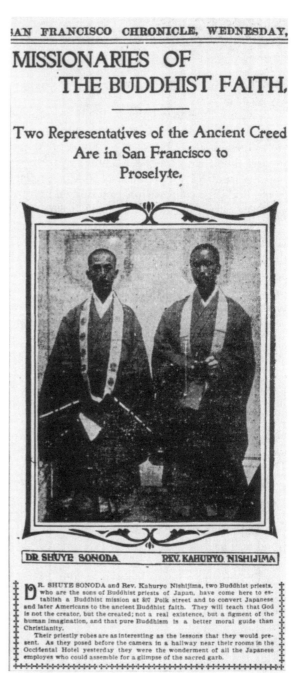

SAN FRANCISCO CHRONICLE, WEDNESDAY,

MISSIONARIES OF THE BUDDHIST FAITH.

Two Representatives of the Ancient Creed Are in San Francisco to Proselyte.

DR. SHUYE SONODA   REV. KAHURYO NISHIJIMA

DR. SHUYE SONODA and Rev. Kahuryo Nishijima, two Buddhist priests, who are the sons of Buddhist priests of Japan, have come here to establish a Buddhist mission at 807 Polk street and to convert Japanese and later Americans to the ancient Buddhist faith. They will teach that God is not the creator, but the created; not a real existence, but a figment of the human imagination, and that pure Buddhism is a better moral guide than Christianity.

Their priestly robes are as interesting as the lessons that they would present. As they posed before the camera in a hallway near their rooms in the Occidental Hotel yesterday they were the wonderment of all the Japanese employes who could assemble for a glimpse of the sacred garb.

Sonoda proclaims that Buddhism is "destined to be the universal religion" and argues that it is especially well suited to America, "the kingdom of liberty."

San Francisco
September [?] 14, 1899

My Dear Sir,

I desire to send a letter to thank you for your kindness shown to my assistant Mr. Nishijima and to inform you of our public lectures on Buddhism which were opened at last Sunday. I knew your name at home through your excellent writing tinted with candidness and I was especially interested in your "Gospel of Buddha" which I adopted as my college English text when I became the principal of the Buddhist college Honganji Bungakuryo, Kioto. On landing here I met with your late essay "Buddhism and its Christian critics" and was astonished. . . .

Though weak handed, we are now carrying on our work trusting to the protection of the merciful Buddha. My opening remarks at the first meeting read thus: My dear sisters and brethren I am very happy to see here all who wish to search earnestly after truth, but I am afraid you can not understand me well for my English is very poor and the oriental framework of thought widely differs from the occidental one. So I beg [you] to listen to me patiently a little while. I came here with my assistant Mr. K. Nishijima to instruct our countrymen who are staying here and to propagate gradually our doctrine among Americans. Buddhism is richly suited to expansion and propagation. It is destined to be the universal religion. We must propagate it throughout the world. Why have we preferred the New World? As you know, the United States was established by liberty and is governed by liberty. Liberty is the soul of the States. The United States is the kingdom of liberty. The people are very liberal. They are very tolerant. They are free from the prejudice which always accompanies the people of an old country. They are fond of seeking truth. They welcome the truth in any form. Their want is not form but essence. So every religion may find its way in the States. In the universe there is one and only one truth, and it is the common stock which ought to be equally enjoyed by mankind as a whole, free from the distinctions of race, nationality, age, sex, etc. . . , and can not be monopolized by any one. All religions have this truth for their ultimate end, but it must be borne in mind that each represents it in a different way. So from one point of view the religious differences are considered as the different methods of arriving at the truth.

Of course, some of them are merely provisional, while some are real, yet the masters of all religions made equal efforts for the benefit of humanity, and their merit must be recognized to a certain extent. Mankind is destined to seek the truth but how he should seek it is left to himself. So he is not restricted to any particular religion. If he thinks one religion inadequate to reach the goal, then he may hold other religions, for the truth is only our object and the method of finding the truth is mere means. The object must be constant but the means may be variable. If you have the privilege of believing Christianity, you also have the privilege of believing Buddhism. You are not bound to be Christians but bound to search for truth. Christianity may be the perfect way, but no Christian has any right to call Buddhism heretical, unless he thoroughly understands Buddhism and finds faults in it, for without tasting the meat we can not judge whether it is good or bad. There are some Christians who are accustomed to say that Christianity only is orthodoxical, that it alone reveals the truth, and to call Buddhism heretical, but such Christians only expose their ignorance of Buddhism.

To search for truth one must get rid of prejudice. If one will carefully and honestly look on Buddhism, he will surely find it very praiseworthy. This is not merely my supposition but many authorities support me. For instance, the learned Fausböll declares [?] as follows: "The more I learn to know Buddha the more I admire him and the sooner all mankind shall have been made acquainted with his doctrines the better it will be, for he is certainly one of the heroes of human-ity" (The Jatakas, iv of Romantic Legend of Sakya Buddha). Professor Müller says: The moral code of Buddhism is one of the most perfect the world has ever known." Dr. Paul Carus also remarks: "Whatever Buddha's doctrines may have been, this much is sure, that the principle of Buddhism is the same as the principle of the religion of Science; for Buddhism is the religion of enlightenment, and enlight-enment means a perfect comprehension of the significance of life in matters of re-ligion. How it is strange that in those two points which constitute the main dif-ference between Buddhism and Christianity, viz., creation and the nature of the soul, modern science, represented exclusively by scientists educated in Christian schools and with a Christian tradition of two millenniums, will certainly side with Buddhism."

It is very remarkable that we find the Christian missionary Bishop Bigandet speaking thus: "The Christian system and the Buddhist one, though differing from each other in their respective object and ends as much as truth from error, have it must be confessed, many striking features of an astonishing resemblance. There are many moral precepts equally commanded and enforced in common by both creeds. It will not be considered rash to assert that most of the moral tenets pre-scribed by the gospel are to be met with in the Buddhistic scriptures. In reading the particulars of the life of the last Buddha Gautama, it is impossible not to be reminded by many circumstances relating to our Savior's life as it has been sketched by the Evangelists" (p. 424, Life and Legend of Gautama). Thus one who has studied Buddhism admires it; and one who has studied Buddhism much, ad-mires it much.

So it is very evident that Buddhism is excellent. I do not come here to com-pel you to believe Buddhism blindly, but I come to ask you to investigate Buddhism honestly and earnestly. Buddha's mercy brings comfort to the weary ones of the world. It is his wish to deliver all creatures in all directions.

To realize this idea is my duty. How is it possible for me to remain idle? So I came here to explain his doctrine under his command. As Buddha taught, the truth had existed before he was born into this world, but at his birth it took its abode in his body. It was revealed by him. He is the bodily incarnation of the truth. Truth alone is the savior from mercy. Let us take refuge in Buddha.

After these few remarks I described the essential points of our doctrine as our introduction. After my lecture some questions were raised by the audience which Mr. Nishijima and I explained away. The first meeting was pretty satis-factory. This is the first attempt at the propagation of the new light of the truth in the New World, though our doctrine has been brought here in books by the endeavours of such learned scholars as you. I find much difficulty in conveying the oriental faith to occidental people. So we require your valuable aid.

I can not close my letter without expressing our indebtedness to you for your noble effort to cause the Christian people to understand Buddhism.

Yours very sincerely,
S. Sonoda

SAINT NIHAL SINGH, "THE PICTURESQUE IMMIGRANT FROM INDIA'S CORAL STRAND" (1909)

Asian Indians began coming to the United States long after the Chinese and Japanese and arrived in much smaller numbers. By 1920, only about 6,400 had made the passage. Although all Indian immigrants were called "Hindoos," the overwhelming majority were Sikhs, adherents of a distinct religious tradition that creatively combines elements of Hinduism and Islam. On 6 April 1899, the *San Francisco Chronicle* described some of the earliest Sikh immigrants to the United States as "the most picturesque

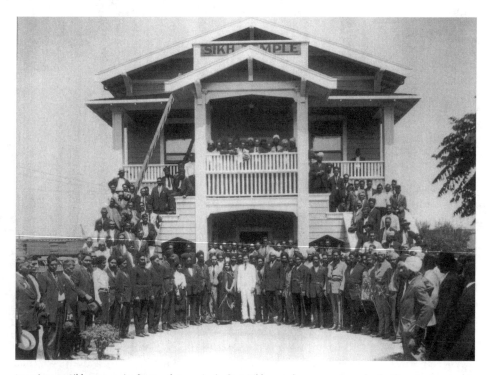

Immigrant Sikhs pose in front of America's first Sikh *gurdwara,* or temple, built out of wood in the bungalow style in Stockton, California. Dedication day, 21 November 1915. Courtesy of the San Joaquin County Historical Museum, Lodi, California.

group that has been seen on the Pacific Mall dock for many a day." All four were "fine-looking" soldiers, and each hoped to make his fortune in the New World before returning home. These "picturesque" immigrants, most of them from the Punjab region of northern India where Sikhism originated in the sixteenth century, soon became the objects of racist hatred. Defenders of racial purity who had previously decried the "Yellow Peril" now fulminated against a "tide of turbans." In 1907, the first year Asian-Indian immigration exceeded one thousand in the United States, an anti-Indian riot broke out in Bellingham, Washington. "Ragheads," as the Indians were called because of the Sikh tradition of wearing a turban, had become the Asian enemy du jour, and decrying the newest Asian invasion did not cease to be popular sport in American periodicals until the passage of restrictive immigration legislation in 1917. But America's Sikhs persevered. They established Sikh *gurdwaras*—the first was constructed in 1912 in Stockton, California—and a handful defended themselves in print. One published defense, written by Sikh immigrant Saint Nihal Singh, had enough of the exotic Oriental in it to satisfy the editors at Los Angeles's *Out West*, where it appeared in 1909. In this excerpt from "The Picturesque Immigrant from India's Coral Strand," Singh paints a portrait of Asian-Indian life in America that accents the diversity and humanity of immigrants from India.

Of all immigrants who drift to North America, none surpasses the Hindu in picturesqueness. He usually lands at one or the other of the large Pacific ports—San Francisco, Seattle, Victoria or Vancouver—although stray members of the fraternity have been known to enter the continent by way of New York, New Orleans and Montreal. He comes clad in countless curious styles. Yards upon yards of cotton, calico or silk are swathed around the head of one, forming a turban, cone-shaped or round like a button-mushroom, with a wave or point directly in the middle of the forehead or to the right or left, as variable as the styles of American women's pompadours. . . . A scarlet Turkish fez tops the head of another, while a third wears an ordinary cap or hat, and a fourth goes about bare-headed.

A smart English military uniform, with the front plastered over with metal medals, a voluminous turban and a bristling beard, distinguish the tall, lanky Sikh soldier who has served in King Edward's native army in India and elsewhere. The man with the fez is usually a Mahometan and is apt to wear a long-flowing coat reaching almost to his ankles and leaving partly visible his pajamas, which fit tightly around his shins. . . . The man with the Western cap wears clothes of pseudo-Occidental style, which he fondly believes to be up-to-date, measured by Western standards. . . . As a rule, the clothes are dilapidated in appearance and frequently second-hand, and the whole combination is grotesque except in the eyes of the newcomer himself. These specimens of the Hindoo genus homo are almost invariably workingmen or peasant-laborers.

The bare-headed Hindoo is without a coat. A longish shirt, resembling an artist's apron, reaches nearly to his ankles. He wears long stockings like a woman's and rope-soled half-shoes. Circling his left shoulder and waist like a marshal's

Saint Nihal Singh, "The Picturesque Immigrant from India's Coral Strand: Who He Is and Why He Comes to America," *Out West* 30.1 (January 1909): 42–54.

sash, is a *daupata*, a strip of cotton cloth, a handsomely-embroidered piece of silk or a long, soft shawl. In many cases, instead of the long shirt, the man drapes around his legs and trunk a sheet of cotton or silk known as a *dhoti*. . . . This type of Hindoo is usually a religious missionary intent on spreading his cult on the Western hemisphere.

Some there are in the group straggling across the gang-plank with whose dress even the most fastidious American could find no fault. Their clothes are of the latest approved style in cut, color and material. The well-dressed East-Indians are merchants, students or men of means who are traveling merely for the sake of pleasure. . . .

In stature and physique the East-Indian immigrants differ as materially as they do in their style of dress. Representatives of the soldier clans, such as Sikhs, Rajputs and Mahrattas, possess fine, athletic bodies and are usually tall and "well set-up." The peasants from the Punjab and contiguous districts are less athletic in build, but possess hardy frames, capable of great endurance. The people from the lowlands of Bengal and Deccan are somewhat shorter and slighter than the men from the North; but starvation and sun have weathered them so that they are able patiently to undergo pinching poverty and privations of every sort.

In cast of features almost all East-Indians look alike. They have intelligent faces, keen eyes, compressed lips and determined chins. This type of countenance is distinctly Aryan, as all the Hindoos who come to the land of the Stars and Stripes are descended from the same branch of the human family as the Anglo-Saxons.

One of the chief points of difference between the emigrant from India and those hailing from Europe lies in the fact that . . . only one sex is represented among the Hindoo immigrants. Probably the greater percentage of them are married—for Hindoos marry young—but they leave their wives and children behind them and venture alone to find a fortune in the West. There is only one Hindoo woman on the North American continent. She lives with her husband, a doctor of Vedic medicine, in Vancouver, B.C. So far as can be learned, only one Hindoo— the writer of this article—has married an American woman.

The East-Indian immigrants possess many forms of religion. He may be theist, atheist, agnostic or idol-worshiper. He may believe in the unity of God, or be a Christian and profess faith in the Trinity, or be a worshiper of thirty-three millions of gods.

The dusky immigrants belong to different grades and castes of society. The newcomer may be of the Brahmin caste (the priestly caste), the Kshatrya (soldier), Vaisha (merchant) or Sudra (servant) caste. This, however, makes very little difference, as wedging outside influences have broken the back-bone of caste, and are crumbling the institution into dust. . . .

Motives diverse and complex bring the Hindoo to North America. He may come to the United States with the intention of arousing the American mind, gone mad in the dollar-chase, to a sense of his higher self. He may be in the West with a view to enlisting the people's sympathy in the uplift of the East-Indian masses. He may come to the land of the free and the home of the brave to equip himself at a University to be of service to his country. Haunted by the howls of the hunger-wolf, he may emigrate to these shores hoping to be able to live in America, by hard work, in comparative comfort.

America first became aware of the presence of the Hindoos in the United States during the World's Columbian Exposition in 1893. Swami Vivekananda, a dusky man with a masterful mouth, prominent nose, large eyes and a massive forehead, lectured to the Parliament of Religions in Chicago and conquered a critical (albeit provincial) audience in a single speech. . . . The silver-tongued Swami served for Hindustan in the capacity of a John the Baptist, and his proved to be the voice of one crying in the wilderness.

The first batch of Indian workingmen landed on the North American continent somewhere between 1895 and 1900. . . . They came singly, or in very small groups, the main current directing itself to the Canadian rather than the American West. . . . The largest proportion of the immigrants came from the rural districts of the Punjab, and represented the Sikh, Mahometan and Hindu communities. By the middle of the year 1903, probably 2,500 Indian immigrants had settled in Vancouver, Victoria and neighboring territory.

The British Columbians looked upon the swarthy men from India with contemptuous indifference so long as they came to the country in straggling groups; but when they commenced to arrive by every steamer in knots of twenty or more, the white residents became alarmed and conceived the notion that Hindoo hordes were about to invade British Columbia by way of the Pacific Ocean and thrust them out of the way. . . .

Disgusted by the treatment accorded them, the Hindoos left Canada and came to the United States, drifting to Everett, Bellingham, Spokane, Seattle, Portland, San Francisco, Berkeley, Los Angeles, and other Western cities. Almost immediately they realized that instead of coming to a haven of rest, they had literally jumped from the frying-pan into the fire. The Canadian agitators contented themselves with the mere putting of obstructions in the way of the Indian immigrants to prevent them from securing lodgings and work. The American hooligans treated the peaceful Hindoo with absolute violence. A riot took place at Bellingham, Washington, and the immigrants were forced by the mob to cross the line and once more enter Canada. . . .

The East-Indian religious teachers and students have received better treatment than the Hindoo laborers. Of all the men from India who have visited the United States, the late Swami Vivekananda stands pre-eminent. He seems to have won an instant way into the hearts of American men and women, and his personality today is very much alive in the hearts of thousands of Americans of the highest intellect and culture. . . .

The Hindoo fortune teller in America is a bird of passage, flitting here, there and everywhere, evading those States where it is a criminal offence for him to follow his profession. . . . He plies his trade wherever he can, and usually makes a success of it, for there is a mystical charm attached to him in the eyes of credulous people seeking to peer into the future. It is sufficient for them that he comes from the "East." It must follow that he is a "Wise man" . . . .

No matter to what station of life he may belong, or what culture he may possess, the East-Indian immigrant, when he leaves America, takes home with him a dynamic love of liberty and sentiments of democracy. America sandpapers his caste-exclusiveness and instills within his heart a sense of brotherhood and co-operation. The Hindoo is led by his American associations to cast off his slavishness of disposition. His ideas of political and social government undergo a radical change. The American-returned East-Indian is a reformer to the core, and proves an invaluable asset for the renaissance of India.

SWAMI PARAMANANDA, *CHRIST AND ORIENTAL IDEALS* (1923)

Suresh Chandra Guha Thakurta (1884–1940) left his home in modern-day Bangladesh in 1901 to join the Ramakrishna Order (established 1886). The next year, at the age of seventeen, he renounced the world and took the name Paramananda ("he whose bliss is in the ultimate"). Inspired by the example of Swami Vivekananda, the Ramakrishna missionary who made a name for himself at the World's Parliament of Religions in Chicago in 1893, Paramananda came to New York in 1907 as an assistant to Swami Abhedananda of the New York Vedanta Society. But Paramananda's de-

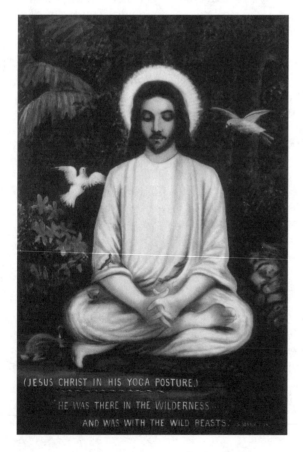

Christ the Yogi. Courtesy Vedanta Press.

votional style clashed with Abhedananda's philosophical approach, and after a couple years the two parted. Paramananda then established flourishing Vedanta societies in the Boston and Los Angeles areas. In 1912 he started a journal, *The Message of the East*, and in 1923 he founded Ananda Ashrama, a mountain retreat in Southern California. Many of Paramananda's most ardent and accomplished disciples were women. Because he wore fashionable suits, drove American cars, and delivered radio talks, some dubbed him the "Hollywood star swami." But his lifestyle was rather modest, and his practical piety did not depart radically from his teacher's. In *The Path of Devotion* (1907), a spiritual classic in the style of Thomas à Kempis's *Imitation of Christ*, Paramananda demonstrated his loving faith in the Divine Mother. In this passage from *Christ and Oriental Ideals* he urges all people of faith—Christians included—to practice what he calls the "Christ-Ideal." His claim that "Christ Himself was an Oriental" was not uncommon in his day. But Paramananda's interpretation of that claim was as controversial as it was idiosyncratic.

How often it is supposed that Christian ideals and Oriental ideals are alien to each other and can never converge; that the adoption of one means the abandonment of the other, like roads growing in opposite directions. But this idea can only exist so long as we remain on the outskirts of the religious domain, in the realm of creed and form. When we judge East and West from external appearances only, then we find great differences; but they are chiefly in manners and customs and not in the fundamental principles which lie beneath. There is vast difference between the outer expression of religion and the actual assimilation of its essence; and most of our misunderstandings and dissensions arise from variance in forms. Even to-day there can be found men and women in India who illustrate the Christ-Ideal wonderfully in their lives, although they may never have heard about Jesus of Nazareth or read the Bible, and might refuse to accept the Christian creed. What is a creed? The Supreme Ideal can never be labelled or represented by any one creed. Living the life is its only true interpretation; and the East is peculiarly adapted for this. . . .

Religion in the East is not a matter of belief in doctrine, dogma, or creed; it is being and becoming; it is actual realization. Faithful practice alone can bring true knowledge of God. No theory or creed can be accepted until it has been verified by practice. . . . It was this which Christ meant when he gave the parable of the two houses: one built on the rock, the other on the sand, typifying the two lines of the religious life, the one of theory or mere belief, the other of practice. In the Hindu teaching we find a similar parable of two servants, who worked in the garden of a rich man. One of them was lazy and idled away his time, accomplishing nothing; but when the master came he met him with flattering devotion and praised the beauty of his person; while the other labored tirelessly and at the coming of his master said little, but bringing the fruit and flowers he had raised, he laid them humbly at his feet. Is it difficult to say with which one the master was more pleased? . . .

Swami Paramananda, *Christ and Oriental Ideals,* 3d ed. (Boston: Vedanta Centre, 1923), 33–53. Reprinted courtesy of Vedanta Centre Publishers.

The East holds that to become spiritual we must make our thoughts, words and actions harmonious—that is, our whole being must work without friction or contradiction. . . . Christ taught, "Love thy neighbor as thyself"; and the Hindu sages, going one step further, tell us why we should thus love our neighbor. They say, "Thou art That"; that is, in essence you and your neighbor are one and the same; therefore to hurt your neighbor is to hurt yourself. . . . Until we have this realization of oneness with the Supreme, it is not possible to rise above all our differences and feel true love for our fellow-man. . . .

We too often forget that Christ Himself was an Oriental. The Essenes, we know, had a great influence on the life of Jesus. . . . and it is now admitted by many scholars that the foundation of the Order of the Essenes was directly due to the influence of the Buddhist monks, who were sent out as missionaries by the great Indian Emperor, Asoka, about 250 B.C. They came to Palestine, but following their habitual constructive method, they did not seek to proselytize. They merely lived a life of holiness and loving service to others without creating any antagonism; and they won followers through the force and beauty of their character, inspiring them to take up a similar life of simplicity and renunciation, such as we see embodied in the rule of the Essenes and set forth in the life and teaching of Jesus.

This has been from the beginning the method of the Aryans of India. They have always believed that there is no reason to condemn any faith or ideal, no matter how crude it might appear. Universal tolerance is the dominant note of their teaching. "He is One without a second," manifesting in the form of a Christ, a Krishna, a Buddha, a Zoroaster; and those who follow sincerely any one of these manifestations will surely reach the final goal of Truth. "In whatever way men worship Me, in the same way I fulfill their desires. O Partha in every way men follow my Path," the Lord declares in the Bhagavad-Gita. . . .

For this reason, Vedanta forbids us to dwell on the thought of sin; because sin can never beget righteousness. No one can ever gain strength by brooding over his weakness. Hence, Vedanta tells us: "Call no man a sinner. All are children of Immortal Bliss. Let each one awaken his divine nature by constantly holding his thought on the Ideal." Christ makes the same appeal when He says: "Be ye therefore perfect, even as your Father which is in Heaven is perfect." Some believe that this is possible only for a Christ; but, according to Vedanta, the Saviours and prophets come especially to show by their example how all men can attain perfection. Man possesses within himself the germs of perfection, he has only to manifest it. He is already inherently perfect. Why then talk of sin?

UNITED STATES V. BHAGAT SINGH THIND (1923)

In 1790, the U.S. Congress limited naturalization to "free white persons." That standard was broadened in 1870 to open citizenship to "persons of African descent." Who would count as "white" under the 1790 statute was not made plain, however, until the Supreme Court decided two important cases in the early 1920s. In *Ozawa* v. *U.S.*

(1922), the Court ruled unanimously that white meant "Caucasian"; because Japanese Americans were not Caucasian, they were not eligible for naturalization. Ironically, this ruling provided hope to Asian Indians in America, since even the racist Asiatic Exclusion League had admitted they were Caucasians. In *U.S. v. Thind* (1923), the Supreme Court took up the case of Bhagat Singh Thind. An Asian-Indian immigrant from the Punjab, Thind had been naturalized by a federal court in Oregon before the 1917 immigration act had disqualified virtually all Asians except the Chinese from naturalization. The suit was brought by the United States, which argued that Thind was not a "white person" and therefore did not qualify for naturalization. In an opinion written by Justice George Sutherland, the Court ruled against Thind. One year later, Congress passed the 1924 Immigration Act, which cut off virtually all immigration from Asia.

If the applicant is a white person, within the meaning of this section, he is entitled to naturalization; otherwise not. In Ozawa v. United States . . . we had occasion to consider the application of these words to the case of a cultivated Japanese and were constrained to hold that he was not within their meaning. As there pointed out, the provision is not that any particular class of persons shall be excluded, but it is, in effect, that only white persons shall be included within the privilege of the statute. . . . Following a long line of decisions of the lower Federal courts, we held that the words imported a racial and not an individual test and were meant to indicate only persons of what is *popularly* known as the Caucasian race. But, as there pointed out, the conclusion that the phrase "white persons" and the word "Caucasian" are synonymous does not end the matter. It enabled us to dispose of the problem as it was there presented, since the applicant for citizenship clearly fell outside the zone of debatable ground on the negative side; but the decision still left the question to be dealt with, in doubtful and different cases, by the "process of judicial inclusion and exclusion." Mere ability on the part of an applicant for naturalization to establish a line of descent from a Caucasian ancestor will not ipso facto and necessarily conclude the inquiry. "Caucasian" is a conventional word of much flexibility, as a study of the literature dealing with racial questions will disclose, and while it and the words "white persons" are treated as synonymous for the purposes of that case, they are not of identical meaning—idem per idem.

In the endeavor to ascertain the meaning of the statute we must not fail to keep in mind that it does not employ the word "Caucasian," but the words "white persons," and these are words of common speech and not of scientific origin. The word "Caucasian," not only was not employed in the law, but was probably wholly unfamiliar to the original framers of the statute in 1790. . . . It is in the popular sense of the word, therefore, that we employ it as an aid to the construction of the statute, for it would be obviously illogical to convert words of common speech used in a statute into words of scientific terminology when neither the latter nor the science for whose purposes they were coined was within the contemplation of the framers of the statute or of the people for whom it was framed. The words of the statute are to be interpreted in accor-

U.S. v. Bhagat Singh Thind, 261 U.S. 204 (1923).

dance with the understanding of the common man from whose vocabulary they were taken. . . .

They imply, as we have said, a racial test; but the term "race" is one which, for the practical purposes of the statute, must be applied to a group of living persons *now* possessing in common the requisite characteristics, not to groups of persons who are supposed to be or really are descended from some remote, common ancestor, but who, whether they both resemble him to a greater or less extent, have, at any rate, ceased altogether to resemble one another. It may be true that the blond Scandinavian and the brown Hindu have a common ancestor in the dim reaches of antiquity, but the average man knows perfectly well that there are unmistakable and profound differences between them to-day. . . .

The eligibility of this applicant for citizenship is based on the sole fact that he is of high-caste Hindu stock, born in Punjab, one of the extreme northwestern districts of India, and classified by certain scientific authorities as of the Caucasian or Aryan race. . . .

The term "Aryan" has to do with linguistic, and not at all with physical, characteristics, and it would seem reasonably clear that mere resemblance in language, indicating a common linguistic root buried in remotely ancient soil, is altogether inadequate to prove common racial origin. There is, and can be, no assurance that the so-called Aryan language was not spoken by a variety of races living in proximity to one another. Our own history has witnessed the adoption of the English tongue by millions of negroes, whose descendants can never be classified racially with the descendants of white persons, notwithstanding both may speak a common root language.

The word "Caucasian" is in scarcely better repute. "It is at best a conventional term, with an altogether fortuitous origin, which under scientific manipulation, has come to include far more than the unscientific mind suspects. According to [one authority], for example . . . it includes not only the Hindu, but some of the Polynesians (that is, the Maori, Tahitians, Samoans, Hawaiians, and others), the Hamites of Africa, upon the ground of the Caucasic cast of their features, though in color they range from brown to black. We venture to think that the average well-informed white American would learn with some degree of astonishment that the race to which he belongs is made up of such heterogeneous elements. . . .

It does not seem necessary to pursue the matter of scientific classification further. We are unable to agree with the District Court, or with other lower federal courts, in the conclusion that a native Hindu is eligible for naturalization. . . . The words of familiar speech, which were used by the original framers of the law, were intended to include only the type of man whom they knew as white. The immigration of that day was almost exclusively from the British Isles and Northwestern Europe, whence they and their forbears had come. When they extended the privilege of American citizenship to "any alien being a free white person" it was these immigrants—bone of their bone and flesh of their flesh—and their kind whom they must have had affirmatively in mind. . . .

What we now hold is that the words "free white persons" are words of common speech, to be interpreted in accordance with the understanding of the common man, synonymous with the word "Caucasian" only as that word is popularly understood. And so understood and used, whatever may be the speculations of the ethnologist, it does not include the body of people to whom the appellee belongs. It is a matter of familiar observation and knowledge that the physical group characteristics of the Hindus render them readily distinguishable from the various groups of persons in this country commonly recognized as white. The children of English, French, German, Italian, Scandinavian, and other European parentage, quickly merge into the mass of our population and lose the distinctive hallmarks of their European origin. On the other hand, it cannot be doubted that the children born in this country of Hindu parents would retain indefinitely the clear evidence of their ancestry. It is very far from our thought to suggest the slightest question of racial superiority or inferiority. What we suggest is merely racial difference, and it is of such character and extent that the great body of our people instinctively recognize it and reject the thought of assimilation.

It is not without significance in this connection that Congress, by the [Immigration Act of 1917] has now excluded from admission into this country all natives of Asia within designated limits of latitude and longitude, including the whole of India. This not only constitutes conclusive evidence of the congressional attitude of opposition to Asiatic immigration generally, but is persuasive of a similar attitude toward Asiatic naturalization as well, since it is not likely that Congress would be willing to accept as citizens a class of persons whom it rejects as immigrants.

CHAPTER 4

Romancing the Orient:
Literary Encounters

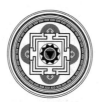

RALPH WALDO EMERSON, "BRAHMA" AND "PLATO" (1857, 1850)

New England's Transcendentalists were the first group of American intellectuals to imagine the meeting of East and West, and Ralph Waldo Emerson (1803–82) was their most imaginative thinker. Following the example of his father, who pastored Boston's First Unitarian Church, Emerson became a Unitarian minister as a young man. But he left both the ministry (for writing and lecturing) and Unitarianism (for Transcendentalism). In an 1838 address at the Divinity School at Harvard, his alma mater, Emerson declared his spiritual independence from "corpse-cold" Unitarianism and pledged his allegiance to Transcendentalism: a Romantic effort to grasp through unmediated intuition the divinity in nature and in all human beings. Emerson encountered Asian religions through books rather than teachers or artifacts. He read widely in the new translations of Hindu and Confucian scriptures but was most impressed by the *Bhagavad Gita*, the Hindu classic that he initially identified wrongly as a Buddhist text. Emerson's sympathetic encounter with Asian ideas such as maya, karma, and reincarnation can be seen in essays such as "Illusion," "Compensation," and "Fate." His finest Hindu-influenced poem, "Brahma" (the term refers to the Hindu creator God), wrestles with the claim made in the *Gita* that the distinction between the killer and the killed is ultimately as ephemeral as the distinction between Self and God. Emerson's strongest essay-length application of his beloved law of correspondences to the meeting of East and West is "Plato; Or, The Philosopher." Here Emerson imagines Plato as part Greek philosopher, part Hindu sage. Critics dispute how deeply Asian religions influenced Emerson's work—Puritan scholar Perry Miller called it "New England Puritanism decked

Ralph Waldo Emerson, "Brahma," *Atlantic Monthly* 1.1 (November 1857): 48; Ralph Waldo Emerson, "Plato, or the Philosopher," in his *The Collected Works of Ralph Waldo Emerson: Volume IV; Representative Men: Seven Lectures* (Cambridge, Mass.: Harvard University Press, 1987), 23–31. Copyright © 1987 by the President and Fellows of Harvard College. Reprinted by permission of Harvard University Press.

out in Oriental imagery"—but Transcendentalism was without question the first American movement to grapple seriously with Asian religious traditions. And in that encounter Emerson led the way.

BRAHMA

If the red slayer think he slays,
    Or if the slain think he is slain,
They know not well the subtle ways
    I keep, and pass, and turn again.

Far or forgot to me is near;
    Shadow and sunlight are the same;
The vanished gods to me appear;
    And one to me are shame and fame.

They reckon ill who leave me out;
    When me they fly, I am the wings;
I am the doubter and the doubt.
    And I am the hymn the Brahmin sings.

The strong gods pine for my abode,
    And pine in vain the sacred Seven;
But thou, meek lover of the good!
    Find me, and turn thy back on heaven.

PLATO, OR THE PHILOSOPHER

Among secular books, Plato only is entitled to Omar's fanatical compliment to the Koran, when he said, "Burn the libraries; for their value is in this book." These sentences contain the culture of nations; these are the cornerstone of schools; these are the fountainhead of literatures. A discipline it is in logic; arithmetic; taste; symmetry; poetry; language; rhetoric; ontology; morals, or practical wisdom. There was never such range of speculation. Out of Plato come all things that are still written and debated among men of thought. . . .

Philosophy is the account which the human mind gives to itself of the constitution of the world. Two cardinal facts are forever at the base; the One; and the two. 1. Unity, or Identity; and, 2. Variety. We unite all things by perceiving the law which pervades them, by perceiving the superficial differences, and the profound resemblances. But every mental act,—this very perception of identity or oneness, recognizes the difference of things. Oneness and otherness. It is impossible to speak or to think without embracing both.

The mind is urged to ask for one cause of many effects; then for the cause of that; and again the cause, diving still into the profound; self-assured that it shall arrive at an absolute and sufficient One, a One that shall be All. "In the midst of the sun is the light, and in the midst of the light is truth, and in the midst of truth is the imperishable being," say the Vedas.

All philosophy of east and west has the same centripetence. Urged by an opposite necessity, the mind returns from the one, to that which is not one, but other or many; from cause to effect; and affirms the necessary existence of variety, the self-existence of both, as each is involved in the other. These strictly-blended elements it is the problem of thought to separate and to reconcile. Their existence is mutually contradictory and exclusive; and each so fast slides into the other that we can never say what is one, and what it is not. The Proteus is as nimble in the highest as in the lowest grounds,—when we contemplate the one, the true, the good, as in the surfaces and extremities of matter.

In all nations there are minds which incline to dwell in the conception of the fundamental Unity. The raptures of prayer and ecstasy of devotion lose all being in one Being. This tendency finds its highest expression in the religious writings of the East, and chiefly in the Indian Scriptures, in the Vedas, the Bhagavat Geeta, and the Vishnu Purana. Those writings contain little else than this idea, and they rise to pure and sublime strains in celebrating it.

The Same, the Same: friend and foe are of one stuff; the ploughman, the plough and the furrow are of one stuff; and the stuff is such and so much that the variations of form are unimportant. "You are fit" (says the supreme Krishna to a sage) "to apprehend that you are not distinct from me. That which I am, thou art, and that also is this world, with its gods, and heroes, and mankind. Men contemplate distinctions, because they are stupefied with ignorance." "The words *I* and *mine* constitute ignorance. What is the great end of all, you shall now learn from me. It is soul, one in all bodies, pervading, uniform, perfect, preeminent over nature, exempt from birth, growth, and decay, omnipresent, made up of true knowledge, independent, unconnected with unrealities, with name, species, and the rest, in time past, present and to come. The knowledge that this spirit, which is essentially one, is in one's own, and in all other bodies, is the wisdom of one who knows the unity of things. As one diffusive air, passing through the perforations of a flute, is distinguished as the notes of a scale, so the nature of the Great Spirit is single, though its forms be manifold, arising from the consequences of acts. When the difference of the investing form, as that of god, or the rest, is destroyed, there is no distinction." "The whole world is but a manifestation of Vishnu, who is identical with all things, and is to be regarded by the wise as not differing from, but as the same as, themselves. I neither am going nor coming, nor is my dwelling in any one place, nor art thou, thou, nor are others, others; nor am I, I." As if he had said, "All is for the soul, and the soul is Vishnu, and animals and stars are transient paintings, and light is whitewash; and durations are deceptive; and form is imprisonment, and heaven itself a decoy." That which the soul seeks is resolution into being above form, out of Tartarus, and out of heaven, liberation from nature.

If speculation tends thus to a terrific unity, in which all things are absorbed,—action tends directly backwards to diversity. The first is the course or gravitation of mind; the second is the power of nature. Nature is the manifold. The unity absorbs, and melts or reduces. Nature opens and creates. These two principles reappear and interpenetrate all things, all thought: the one, the many. One is being; the other, intellect: one is necessity; the other, freedom: one, rest; the other, motion: one, power; the other, distribution: one, strength; the other, pleasure: one, consciousness; the other, definition: one, genius; the other, talent: one, earnestness; the other, knowledge: one, possession; the other, trade: one, caste; the other, culture: one, king; the other, democracy: and, if we dare carry these generalizations a step higher, and name the last tendency of both, we might say, that the end of the one is escape from organization, pure science; and the end of the other is the highest instrumentality, or use of means, or, executive deity.

Each student adheres, by temperament and by habit, to the first or to the second of these gods of the mind. By religion, he tends to unity; by intellect, or by the senses, to the many. A too rapid unification, and an excessive appliance to parts and particulars, are the twin dangers of speculation.

To this partiality the history of nations corresponded. The country of unity, of immovable institutions, the seat of a philosophy delighting in abstractions, of men faithful in doctrine and in practice to the idea of a deaf, unimplorable, immense fate, is Asia; and it realizes this faith on the social institution of caste. On the other side, the genius of Europe is active and creative: it resists caste by culture; its philosophy was a discipline; it is a land of arts, inventions, trade, freedom. If the East loved infinity, the West delighted in boundaries. . . .

Meantime, Plato, in Egypt and in Eastern pilgrimages, imbibed the idea of one Deity, in which all things are absorbed. The unity of Asia and the detail of Europe, the infinitude of the Asiatic soul and the defining, result-loving, machine-making, surface-seeking, operagoing Europe, Plato came to join, and, by contact, to enhance the energy of each. The excellence of Europe and Asia are in his brain.

HENRY DAVID THOREAU, *A WEEK ON THE CONCORD AND MERRIMACK RIVERS* (1849)

Like his fellow Transcendentalist Ralph Waldo Emerson, Henry David Thoreau (1817–62) was an avid reader of translations of Indian and Chinese scriptures. Thoreau pressed past Emerson, however, in attempting to practice what those texts preached—to become, in his words, "a yogin." Thoreau was born in Concord, Massachusetts, and it was there, in the woods around Walden Pond, that he lived the life of simplicity that became the subject of his most famous book, *Walden; Or, Life in the Woods* (1854). Thoreau's interests in Asian religions—particularly, Hinduism, Buddhism, and Confucianism—date to the early 1840s when, as the editor of the Transcendentalist periodical *The Dial*, he saw translations of various Eastern classics into print. His *A Week on the Concord and Merrimack Rivers* (1849) lavished such praise on the *Bhagavad Gita* and "my Buddha" that it scandalized many Christian readers. While Thoreau clearly borrowed from Asia, he also gave something back. His best-known essay, "Resistance to Civil Government," profoundly shaped the theory of nonviolent civil disobedience of Indian reformer Mohandas Gandhi, who in turn influenced the U.S. civil rights movement.

I know that some will have hard thoughts of me, when they hear their Christ named beside my Buddha, yet I am sure that I am willing they should love their Christ more than my Buddha, for the love is the main thing, and I like him too. . . .

The New Testament is an invaluable book, though I confess to having been slightly prejudiced against it in my very early days by the church and the Sabbath school, so that it seemed, before I read it, to be the yellowest book in the catalogue. . . . The reading which I love best is the scriptures of the several nations, though it happens that I am better acquainted with those of the Hindoos, the Chinese, and the Persians, than of the Hebrews, which I have come to last. Give me one of these Bibles, and you have silenced me for a while. . . .

The New Testament is remarkable for its pure morality; the best of the Hindoo Scripture, for its pure intellectuality. The reader is nowhere raised into and sustained in a higher, purer, or *rarer* region of thought than in the Bhagvat-Geeta. . . . It is unquestionably one of the noblest and most sacred scriptures that have come down to us. . . .

This teaching is not practical in the sense in which the New Testament is. It is not always sound sense in practice. The Brahman never proposes courageously to assault evil, but patiently to starve it out. His active faculties are paralyzed by the idea of cast, of impassable limits, of destiny and the tyranny of time. Kreeshna's argument, it must be allowed, is defective. No sufficient reason is given why Arjoon should fight. . . .

Behold the difference between the oriental and the occidental. The former has nothing to do in this world; the latter is full of activity. The one looks in the sun till his eyes are put out; the other follows him prone in his westward course. There is such a thing as cast, even in the West; but it is comparatively faint. It is conservatism here. It says forsake not your calling, outrage no institution, use no violence, rend no bonds, the State is thy parent. Its virtue or manhood is wholly filial. There is a struggle between the oriental and occidental in every nation; some who would be forever contemplating the sun, and some who are hastening toward the sunset. The former class says to the latter, When you have reached the sunset, you will be no nearer to the sun. . . .

I would say to the readers of Scriptures, if they wish for a good book to read, read the Bhagvat-Geeta, an episode to the Mahabharat. . . . It deserves to be read with reverence even by Yankees, as a part of the sacred writings of a devout people; and the intelligent Hebrew will rejoice to find in it a moral grandeur and sublimity akin to those of his own Scriptures.

To an American reader, who, by the advantage of his position, can see over that strip of Atlantic coast to Asia and the Pacific, who, as it were, sees the shore slope upward over the Alps to the Himmaleh mountains, the comparatively recent literature of Europe often appears partial and clannish, and, notwithstanding the limited range of his own sympathies and studies, the European writer who presumes that he is speaking for the world, is perceived by him to speak only for that corner of it which he inhabits. . . . In comparison with the philosophers of the East, we may say that modern Europe has yet given birth to none. Beside the vast and cosmogonal philosophy of the Bhagvat-Geeta, even our Shakespeare seems sometimes youthfully green and practical merely. . . . *Ex ori-*

ente lux may still be the motto of scholars, for the Western world has not yet derived from the East all the light which it is destined to receive thence.

It would be worthy of the age to print together the collected Scriptures or Sacred Writings of the several nations, the Chinese, the Hindoos, the Persians, the Hebrews, and others, as the Scripture of mankind. The New Testament is still, perhaps, too much on the lips and in the hearts of men to be called a Scripture in this sense. Such a juxtaposition and comparison might help to liberalize the faith of men. This is a work which Time will surely edit, reserved to crown the labors of the printing press. This would be the Bible, or Book of Books, which let the missionaries carry to the uttermost parts of the earth. . . .

One of the most attractive of those ancient books that I have met with is the Laws of Menu. . . . I know of no book which has come down to us with grander pretensions than this, and it is so impersonal and sincere that it is never offensive nor ridiculous. . . . It seems to have been uttered from some eastern summit, with a sober morning prescience in the dawn of time, and you cannot read a sentence without being elevated as upon the tableland of the Ghauts. It has such a rhythm as the winds of the desert, such a tide as the Ganges, and is as superior to criticism as the Himmaleh mountains. Its tone is of such unrelaxed fibre, that even at this late day, unworn by time, it wears the English and the Sanscrit dress differently, and its fixed sentences keep up their distant fires still like the stars, by whose dissipated rays this lower world is illumined. The whole book by noble gestures and inclinations renders many words unnecessary. English sense has toiled, but Hindoo wisdom never perspired. Though the sentences open, as we read them, unexpensively, and, at first, almost unmeaningly, as the petals of a flower, they sometimes startle us with that rare kind of wisdom which could only have been learned from the most trivial experience; but it comes to us as refined as the porcelain earth which subsides to the bottom of the ocean. They are clean and dry as fossil truths, which have been exposed to the elements for thousands of years, so impersonally and scientifically true that they are the ornament of the parlor and the cabinet. Any *moral* philosophy is exceedingly rare. This of Menu addresses our privacy more than most. It is a more private and familiar, and, at the same time, a more public and universal word than is spoken in parlor or pulpit now-a-days. As our domestic fowls are said to have their original in the wild pheasant of India, so our domestic thoughts have their prototypes in the thoughts of her philosophers. We are dabbling in the very elements of our present conventional and actual life; as if it were the primeval conventicle where how to eat and to drink and to sleep, and maintain life with adequate dignity and sincerity, were the questions to be decided. It is later and more intimate with us even than the advice of our nearest friends. And yet it is true from the widest horizon, and read out of doors has relation to the dim mountain line, and is native and aboriginal there. Most books belong to the house and street only, and in the fields their leaves feel very thin. They are bare and obvious, and have no halo nor haze about them. Nature lies far and fair behind them all. But this, as it proceeds from, so it addresses, what is deepest and most abiding in man. It belongs to the noontide of the day, the midsummer of the year, and after the snows have melted, and the waters evaporated in the spring, still its truth speaks freshly to our experience. It helps the sun to shine, and his rays fall on its page to illustrate it. It spends the mornings and the evenings, and makes such an impression on us over night as to awaken us before dawn, and its influence lingers around us like a fragrance late into the day. It conveys a new gloss to the meadows and the depths of the wood, and its spirit, like a more subtle ether, sweeps along with the prevailing winds of a country. The very locusts and crickets of a summer day are but later or earlier glosses on the Dherma Sastra of the Hindoos, a continuation of the sacred code. As we have said, there is an orientalism in the most restless pioneer, and the farthest west is but the farthest east.

BRET HARTE, "THE HEATHEN CHINEE" (1870)

Respected by eighteenth-century Americans as a nation of sages, China was reviled by nineteenth-century Americans as a den of iniquity. The Transcendentalists, who watched as an "age of respect" of the Chinese was giving way to an "age of contempt," were of two minds about China. Emerson praised Confucius as "the Washington of philosophy" but blasted Confucian ritualists for attending to "crockery Gods which in Europe & America our babies are wise enough to put in baby houses." Bret Harte (1836–1902) was not sure what to make of the Chinese either. Although a native of Albany, New York, Harte made his name as a chronicler of life in the hardscrabble mining towns of the Wild West. His widowed mother took him in 1854 to California, where he found his calling writing for the *Golden Era*, a San Francisco newspaper. He later wrote for the *Californian* (established 1864) and the *Overland Monthly* (established 1868), where he also worked as an editor. Although he returned with great fanfare to the East Coast in 1871, and eventually went on to a diplomatic career, Harte is remembered as a writer of frontier fiction. His best-known work is "Plain Language from Truthful James." Also known as "The Heathen Chinee," this narrative poem appeared in *Overland Monthly* in 1870, just a year after the completion of the transcontinental railroad sent many Chinese laborers scrambling for work. Whether Harte was endorsing or satirizing the racism expressed in this poem is unclear. (In other works dealing with Chinese Americans, Harte seems far more sympathetic.) But his verse clearly fueled the anti-Chinese passions of the day.

> Which I wish to remark,
>   And my language is plain,
> That for ways that are dark
>   And for tricks that are vain,
> The heathen Chinee is peculiar,
>   Which the same I would rise to explain.
>
> Ah Sin was his name;
>   And I shall not deny,

Bret Harte, "Plain Language from Truthful James (Table Mountain, 1870)," in Bret Harte, *Complete Poetical Works* (New York: P.F. Collier & Son, 1902), 129–31.

Bret Harte, "The Heathen Chinee" (1870)

In regard to the same,
    What that name might imply;
But his smile it was pensive and childlike,
    As I frequent remarked to Bill Nye.

It was August the third,
    And quite soft was the skies;
Which it might be inferred
    That Ah Sin was likewise;
Yet he played it that day upon William
    And me in a way I despise.

Which we had a small game,
    And Ah Sin took a hand:
It was Euchre. The same
    He did not understand;
But he smiled as he sat by the table,
    With the smile that was childlike and bland.

Yet the cards they were stocked
    In a way that I grieve,
And my feelings were shocked
    At the state of Nye's sleeve,
Which was stuffed full of aces and bowers,
    And the same with intent to deceive.

But the hands that were played
    By that heathen Chinee,
And the points that he made,
    Were quite frightful to see,—
Till at last he put down a right bower,
    Which the same Nye had dealt unto me.

Then I looked up at Nye,
    And he gazed upon me;
And he rose with a sigh,
    And said, "Can this be?
We are ruined by Chinese cheap labor,"—
    And he went for that heathen Chinee.

In the scene that ensued
    I did not take a hand,
But the floor it was strewed
    Like the leaves on the strand
With the cards that Ah Sin had been hiding,
    In the game "he did not understand."

In his sleeves, which were long,
    He had twenty-four jacks,—
Which was coming it strong,
    Yet I state but the facts;
And we found on his nails, which were taper,
    What is frequent in tapers,—that's wax.

Which is why I remark,
    And my language is plain,

> That for ways that are dark
> And for tricks that are vain,
> The heathen Chines is peculiar,—
> Which the same I am free to maintain.

WALT WHITMAN, *PASSAGE TO INDIA* (1870)

Walt Whitman (1819–92) wrote in the preface to his magnum opus, *Leaves of Grass* (1855), that "The United States themselves are essentially the greatest poem." Perhaps. But Whitman was undoubtedly one of the United States' greatest poets. Born on Long Island into a family of religious dissenters (Quakers and deists) who taught him to think for himself, Whitman had little formal schooling. As an adult he lived in Brooklyn, where he worked as a journalist and carpenter. The Transcendentalists clearly influenced him, but much in Whitman anticipated the Beat poets of the 1950s: his championing of the everyday experience of ordinary Americans, his Bohemian bearing, his celebration of male comradeship, his colloquial poetics, and his interests in mysticism and Asian religions. Emerson, who deemed Whitman "an American Buddh," praised *Leaves of Grass* as a daring combination of the *New York Herald* and the *Bhagavad Gita*, and more recent critics have called Whitman's poetry thoroughly Asian. But Whitman was less influenced by Asian thought than either Emerson or the major Beats. In *Passage to India* (1870), Whitman marks with his usual breathless anticipation the technological wonders—the transatlantic cable, the Suez Canal, and the transcontinental railroad—that promised to bring together New Yorkers and Californians, Americans and Asians. Significantly, Whitman never quite passes over to Asia here. The poem is finally more about America than India, more about Columbus than Krishna, more about Whitman himself than Indian swamis or Buddhist disciples.

1

[1] SINGING my days,
Singing the great achievements of the present,
Singing the strong, light works of engineers,
Our modern wonders, (the antique ponderous Seven outvied,)
In the Old World, the east, the Suez canal,
The New by its mighty railroad spann'd,
The seas inlaid with eloquent, gentle wires,
I sound, to commence, the cry, with thee, O soul,
The Past! the Past! the Past!

[2] The Past! the dark, unfathom'd retrospect!
The teeming gulf! the sleepers and the shadows!
The past! the infinite greatness of the past!
For what is the present, after all, but a growth out of the past?
(As a projectile, form'd, impell'd, passing a certain line, still keeps on,
So the present, utterly form'd, impell'd by the past.)

Walt Whitman, *Passage to India* (New York: n.p., 1870), 5–15.

2

[3] Passage, O soul, to India!
Eclaircise the myths Asiatic—the primitive fables.

[4] Not you alone, proud truths of the world!
Nor you alone, ye facts of modern science!
But myths and fables of eld—Asia's, Africa's fables!
The far-darting beams of the spirit!—the unloos'd dreams!
The deep diving bibles and legends;
The daring plots of the poets—the elder religions;
—O you temples fairer than lilies, pour'd over by the rising sun!
O you fables, spurning the known, eluding the hold of the known, mounting to heaven!
You lofty and dazzling towers, pinnacled, red as roses, burnish'd with gold!
Towers of fables immortal, fashion'd from mortal dreams!
You too I welcome, and fully, the same as the rest;
You too with joy I sing.

3

[5] Passage to India!
Lo, soul! seest thou not God's purpose from the first?
The earth to be spann'd, connected by net-work,
The people to become brothers and sisters,
The races, neighbors, to marry and be given in marriage,
The oceans to be cross'd, the distant brought near,
The lands to be welded together.

[4] (A worship new, I sing;
You captains, voyagers, explorers, yours!
You engineers! you architects, machinists, yours!
You, not for trade or transportation only,
But in God's name, and for thy sake, O soul.)

4

[7] Passage to India!
Lo, soul, for thee, of tableaus twain,
I see, in one, the Suez canal initiated, open'd,
I see the procession of steamships, the Empress Eugenie's leading the van;
I mark, from on deck, the strange landscape, the pure sky, the level sand in the distance;
I pass swiftly the picturesque groups, the workmen gather'd,
The gigantic dredging machines.

[6] In one, again different, (yet thine, all thine, O soul, the same.)
I see over my own continent the Pacific Railroad, surmounting every barrier;
I see continual trains of cars winding along the Platte, carrying freight and passengers;
I hear the locomotives rushing and roaring, and the shrill steam-whistle,
I hear the echoes reverberate through the grandest scenery in the world;
I cross the Laramie plains—I note the rocks in grotesque shapes—the buttes;
I see the plentiful larkspur and wild onions—the barren, colorless, sage-deserts;
I see in glimpses afar, or towering immediately above me, the great mountains—I see
    the Wind River and the Wahsatch mountains;
I see the Monument mountain and the Eagle's Nest—I pass the Promontory—I ascend
    the Nevadas;
I scan the noble Elk mountain, and wind around its base;

I see the Humboldt range—I thread the valley and cross the river,
I see the clear waters of Lake Tahoe—I see forests of majestic pines,
Or, crossing the great desert, the alkaline plains, I behold enchanting mirages of waters
       and meadows;
Marking through these, and after all, in duplicate slender lines,
Bridging the three or four thousand miles of land travel.
Tying the Eastern to the Western sea,
The road between Europe and Asia.

[9] (Ah Genoese, thy dream! thy dream!
Centuries after thou art laid in thy grave,
The shore thou foundest verifies thy dream!)

5

[10] Passage to India!
Struggles of many a captain—tales of many a sailor dead!
Over my mood, stealing and spreading they come.
Like clouds and cloudlets in the unreach'd sky.

[11] Along all history, down the slopes,
As a rivulet running, sinking now, and now again to the surface rising,
A ceaseless thought, a varied train—Lo, soul! to thee, thy sight, they rise,
The plans, the voyages again, the expeditions:
Again Vasco de Gama sails forth;
Again the knowledge gain'd, the mariner's compass,
Lands formed, and nations born—thou born, America, (a hemisphere unborn,)
For purpose vast, man's long probation fill'd,
Thou, rondure of the world, at least accomplish'd.

6

[12] O, vast Rondure, swimming in space;
Cover'd all over with visible power and beauty!
Alternate light and day, and the teeming, spiritual darkness;
Unspeakable, high processions of sun and moon, and countless stars, above;
Below, the manifold grass and waters, animals, mountains, trees;
With inscrutable purpose—some hidden, prophetic intention;
Now, first, it seems, my thought begins to span thee.

[13] Down from the gardens of Asia, descending, radiating,
Adam and Eve appear, then their myriad progeny after them,
Wandering, yearning, curious—with restless explorations,
With questionings, baffled, formless, feverish—with never-happy hearts,
With that sad, incessant refrain, *Wherefore, unsatisfied Soul?* and, *Whither, O mocking life?*

[14] Ah, who shall soothe these feverish children?
Who justify these restless explorations?
Who speak the secret of impassive Earth?
Who bind it to us? What is this separate Nature, so unnatural?
What is this Earth, to our affections? (unloving earth, without a throb to answer ours;
Cold earth, the place of graves.)

[15] Yet, soul, be sure the first intent remains—and shall be carried out;
(Perhaps even now the time has arrived.)

[16] After the seas are all cross'd, (as they seem already cross'd,)
After the great captains and engineers have accomplish'd their work,

After the noble inventors—after the scientists, the chemist, the geologist, ethnologist,
Finally shall come the Poet, worthy that name;
The true Son of God shall come, singing his songs.

[17] Then, not your deeds only, O voyagers, O scientists and inventors, shall be justified,
All these hearts, as of fretted children, shall be sooth'd.
All affection shall be fully responded to—the secret shall be told;
All these separations and gaps shall be taken up, and hook'd and link'd together;
The whole Earth—this cold, impassive, voiceless Earth, shall be completely justified;
Trinitas divine shall be gloriously accomplish'd and compacted by the true Son of God,
     the poet,
(He shall indeed pass the straits and conquer the mountains,
He shall double the Cape of Good Hope to some purpose;)
Nature and Man shall be disjoin'd and diffused no more,
The true Son of God shall absolutely fuse them.

7

[18] Year at whose open'd, wide-flung door I sing!
Year of the purpose accomplish'd!
Year of the marriage of continents, climates and oceans!
(No mere Doge of Venice now, wedding the Adriatic;)
I see, O year, in you, the vast terraqueous globe, given, and giving all,
Europe to Asia, Africa join'd, and they to the New World;
The lands, geographies, dancing before you, holding a festival garland,
As brides and bridegrooms hand in hand.

8

[19] Passage to India!
Cooling airs from Caucasus far, soothing cradle of man,
The river Euphrates flowing, the past lit up again.

[20] Lo, soul, the retrospect, brought forward;
The old, most populous, wealthiest of Earth's lands,
The streams of the Indus and the Ganges, and their many affluents;
(I, my shores of America walking to-day, behold, resuming all,)
The tale of Alexander, on his warlike marches, suddenly dying,
On one side China, and on the other side Persia and Arabia,
To the south the great seas, and the Bay of Bengal;
The flowing literatures, tremendous epics, religions, castes.
Old occult Brahma, interminably far back—the tender and junior Buddha,
Central and southern empires, and all their belongings, possessors,
The wars of Tamerlane, the reign of Aurungzebe,
The traders, rules, explorers, Moslems, Venetians, Byzantium, the Arabs, Portuguese,
The first travelers, famous yet, Marco Polo, Batouta the Moor,
Doubts to be solv'd, the map incognita, blanks to be fill'd,
The foot of man unstay'd, the hands never at rest,
Thyself, O soul, that will not brook a challenge.

9

[21] The medieval navigators rise before me,
The world of 1492, with its awaken'd enterprise;
Something swelling in humanity now like the sap of the earth in spring,
The sunset splendor of chivalry declining.

²² And who art thou, sad shade?
Gigantic, visionary, thyself a visionary,
With majestic limbs, and pious, beaming eyes,
Spreading around, with every look of thine, a golden world,
Enhuing it with gorgeous hues.

²³ As the chief histrion,
Down to the footlights walks, in some great scena,
Dominating the rest, I see the Admiral himself,
(History's type of courage, action, faith;)
Behold him sail from Palos, leading his little fleet;
His voyage behold—his return—his great fame,
His misfortunes, calumniators—behold him a prisoner, chain'd,
Behold his dejection, poverty, death.

²⁴ (Curious, in time, I stand, noting the efforts of heroes;
Is the deferment long? bitter the slander, poverty, death?
Lies the seed unreck'd for centuries in the ground? Lo! to God's due occasion,
Uprising in the night, it sprouts, blooms,
And fills the earth with use and beauty.)

10

²⁵ Passage indeed, O soul, to primal thought!
Not lands and seas alone—thy own clear freshness,
The young maturity of brood and bloom;
To realms of budding bibles.

²⁶ O soul, repressless, I with thee, and thou with me,
Thy circumnavigation of the world begin;
Of man, the voyage of his mind's return,
To reason's early paradise,
Back, back to wisdom's birth, to innocent intuitions,
Again with fear Creation.

11

²⁷ O we can wait no longer!
We too take ship, O soul!
Joyous, we too launch out on trackless seas!
Fearless, for unknown shores, on waves of extasy to sail,
Amid the wafting winds, (thou pressing me to thee, I thee to me, O soul.)
Caroling free—singing our song of God,
Chanting our chant of pleasant exploration.

²⁸ With laugh, and many a kiss,
(Let others deprecate—let others weep for sin, remorse, humiliation;)
O soul, thou pleasest me—I thee.

²⁹ Ah, more than any priest, O soul, we too believe in God;
But with the mystery of God we dare not dally.

³⁰ O soul, thou pleasest me—I thee;
Sailing these seas, or on the hills, or waking in the night,
Thoughts, silent thoughts, of Time, and Space, and Death, like waters flowing,
Bear me, indeed, as through the regions infinite,
Whose air I breathe, whose ripples hear—lave me all over:

Bathe me, O God, in thee—mounting to thee,
I and my soul to range in range of thee.

31 O Thou transcendant!
Nameless—the fibre and the breath!
Light of the light—shedding forth universes—thou centre of them!
Thou mightier centre of the true, the good, the loving!
Thou moral, spiritual fountain! affection's source! thou reservoir!
(O pensive soul of me! O thirst unsatisfied! waitest not there?
Waitest not haply for us, somewhere there, the Comrade perfect?)
Thou pulse! thou motive of the stars, suns, systems,
That, circling, move in order, safe, harmonious,
Athwart the shapeless, vastnesses of space!
How should I think—how breathe a single breath—how speak—if, out of myself,
I could not launch, to those, superior universes?

32 Swiftly I shrivel at the thought of God,
At Nature and its wonders, Time and Space and Death,
But that I, turning, call to thee, O soul, thou actual Me,
And lo! though gently masterest the orbs,
Thou matest Time, smilest content at Death,
And fillest, swellest full, the vastnesses of Space.

33 Greater than stars or suns,
Bounding, O soul, thou journeyed forth;
—What love, than thine and ours could wider amplify?
What aspirations, wishes, outvie thine and ours, O soul?
What dreams of the ideal? what plans of purity, perfection, strength?
What cheerful willingness, for others' sake, to give up all?
For others' sake to suffer all?

34 Reckoning ahead, O soul, when thou, the time achiev'd,
(The seas all cross'd, weather'd the capes, the voyage done,)
Surrounded, copest, frontest God, yieldest, the aim attain'd,
As, fill'd with friendship, love complete, the Elder Brother found,
The Younger melts in fondness in his arms.

12

35 Passages to more than India!
Are thy wings plumed indeed for such far flights?
O Soul, voyagest thou indeed on voyages like these?
Disportest thou on waters such as these?
Soundest below the Sanscrit and the Vedas?
Then have thy bent unleash'd.

36 Passage to you, your shores, ye aged fierce enigmas!
Passage to you, to mastership of you, ye strangling problems!
You, strew'd with the wrecks of skeletons, that, living, never reach'd you.

13

37 Passage to more than India!
O secret of the earth and sky!
Of you, O waters of the sea! O winding creeks and rivers!
Of you, O woods and fields! Of you, strong mountains of my land!
Of you, O prairies! Of you, gray rocks!

O morning red! O clouds! O rain and snows!
O day and night, passage to you!

[38] O sun and moon, and all you stars! Sirius and Jupiter!
Passage to you!

[39] Passage—immediate passage! the blood burns in my veins!
Away, O soul! hoist instantly the anchor!
Cut the hawsers—haul out—shake out every sail!
Have we not stood here like trees in the ground long enough?
Have we not grovell'd here long enough, eating and drinking like mere brutes?
Have we not darken'd and dazed ourselves with books long enough?

[40] Sail forth! steer for the deep waters only!
Reckless, O soul, exploring, I with thee, and thou with me;
For we are bound where mariner has not yet dared to go,
And we will risk the ship, ourselves and all.

[41] O my brave soul!
O farther, farther sail!
O daring joy, but safe! Are they not all the seas of God?
O farther, farther, farther sail!

T. S. ELIOT, *THE WASTE LAND* (1922)

Since the early nineteenth century, American writers had been pondering translations of Asian scriptures. But T. S. Eliot (1888–1965) was the first major American writer to study seriously Asian-Indian languages and literature. Born in St. Louis and educated at Harvard, Oxford, and the Sorbonne, this poet, literary critic, and playwright was a famous Anglophile—he became a British citizen in 1927—and a lover of India. For two years at Harvard beginning in 1911, he read Sanskrit and Pali with Professor Charles Lanman and Indian philosophy with Professor James Woods. While critics disagree about how extensively Emerson's writing was influenced by Asian thought, Eliot's encounter with Indian ideas such as karma and reincarnation clearly colored his works, most notably *The Waste Land* (1922) and *Four Quartets* (1943). Eliot considered becoming a Buddhist while he was writing *The Waste Land*, but he remained a Christian, and died an Anglo-Catholic. "The Fire Sermon," the third of *The Waste Land*'s five parts, conjures up both the Christian theologian St. Augustine and the Buddha; and "What the Thunder Said," the poem's fifth and last section (reprinted here), reflects on a passage from the *Brihad-aranyaka Upanishad* of Hinduism in light of the Christian doctrine of the resurrection. Eliot appended to *The Waste Land* (which many Western literary critics consider the most important poem of the twentieth century) a number of notes (only the final one appears here). In one he translated "*Datta, dayadhvam, damyata*" as "Give, sympathise, control."

T. S. Eliot, *The Waste Land* (1922)

WHAT THE THUNDER SAID

After the torchlight red on sweaty faces
After the frosty silence in the gardens
After the agony in stony places
The shouting and the crying
Prison and palace and reverberation
Of thunder of spring over distant mountains
He who was living is now dead
We who were living are now dying
With a little patience

   Here is no water but only rock
Rock and no water and the sandy road
The road winding above among the mountains
Which are mountains of rock without water
If there were water we should stop and drink
Amongst the rock one cannot stop or think
Sweat is dry and feet are in the sand
If there were only water amongst the rock
Dead mountain mouth of carious teeth that cannot spit
Here one can neither stand nor lie nor sit
There is not even silence in the mountains
But dry sterile thunder without rain
There is not even solitude in the mountains
But red sullen faces sneer and snarl
From doors of mudcracked houses
                        If there were water

    And no rock
    If there were rock
    And also water
    And water
    A spring
    A pool among the rock
    If there were the sound of water only
    Not the cicada
    And dry grass singing
    But sound of water over a rock
    Where the hermit-thrush sings in the pine trees
    Drip drop drip drop drop drop drop
    But there is no water

   Who is the third who walks always beside you?
When I count, there are only you and I together
But when I look ahead up the white road
There is always another one walking beside you
Gliding wrapt in a brown mantle, hooded
I do not know whether a man or a woman
—But who is that on the other side of you?

   What is that sound high in the air
Murmur of maternal lamentation

Who are those hooded hordes swarming
Over endless plains, stumbling in cracked earth
Ringed by the flat horizon only
What is the city over the mountains
Cracks and reforms and bursts in the violet air
Falling towers
Jerusalem Athens Alexandria
Vienna London
Unreal

   A woman drew her long black hair out tight
And fiddled whisper music on those strings
And bats with baby faces in the violet light
Whistled, and beat their wings
And crawled head downward down a blackened wall
And upside down in air were towers
Tolling reminiscent bells, that kept the hours
And voices singing out of empty cisterns and exhausted wells.

   In this decayed hole among the mountains
In the faint moonlight, the grass is singing
Over the tumbled graves, about the chapel
There is the empty chapel, only the wind's home.
It has no windows, and the door swings,
Dry bones can harm no one.
Only a cock stood on the rooftree
Co co rico co co rico
In a flash of lightning. Then a damp gust
Bringing rain

   Ganga was sunken, and the limp leaves
Waited for rain, while the black clouds
Gathered far distant, over Himavant.
The jungle crouched, humped in silence.
Then spoke the thunder
DA
Datta: what have we given?
My friend, blood shaking my heart
The awful daring of a moment's surrender
Which an age of prudence can never retract
By this, and this only, we have existed
Which is not to be found in our obituaries
Or in memories draped by the beneficent spider
Or under seals broken by the lean solicitor
In our empty rooms
DA
Dayadhvam: I have heard the key
Turn in the door once and turn once only
We think of the key, each in his prison
Thinking of the key, each confirms a prison
Only at nightfall, aethereal rumours
Revive for a moment a broken Coriolanus

T. S. Eliot, *The Waste Land* (1922)

DA
Damyata: The boat responded
Gaily, to the hand expert with sail and oar
The sea was calm, your heart would have responded
Gaily, when invited, beating obedient
To controlling hands

                       I sat upon the shore
Fishing, with the arid plain behind me
Shall I at least set my lands in order?
London Bridge is falling down falling down falling down
Poi s'ascose nel foco che gli affina
Quando fiam uti chelidon—O swallow swallow
Le Prince d'Aquitaine à la tour abolie
These fragments I have shored against my ruins
Why then Ile fit you. Hieronmyo's mad againe.
Datta. Dayadhvam. Damyata.
    Shantih shantih shantih[1]

---

[1]Shantih. Repeated as here, a formal ending to an Upanishad. "The Peace which passeth understanding" is our equivalent to this word.

CHAPTER 5

Journeys in the Study

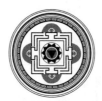

WEBSTER'S DICTIONARY ON HINDUISM AND BUDDHISM (1828, 1849, 1864)

As Americans gradually educated themselves about Asian religions, American dictionaries became more sophisticated. When Noah Webster (1758–1843) first published *An American Dictionary of the English Language* in 1828, the Buddhist and Hindu traditions received scant attention. In Webster's 1849 edition, Hinduism was slighted again, but the Buddhism entry (written with the help of Yale professor Edward Salisbury) swelled from one to eighteen lines. By 1864, thanks to William Dwight Whitney, Salisbury's heir at Yale, there were substantial definitions for both Buddhism and the Buddha (who now also merited an illustration), but the definition of Hinduism remained static. This disparity is intriguing, since Western scholars had interrogated Hindu texts long before they investigated Buddhist scriptures; while Charles Wilkins had produced the first English translation of the *Bhagavad Gita* in 1785, the first book on Buddhism by a Western scholar—Eugène Burnouf's *L'Introduction à l'histoire du buddhisme indien*—did not appear until 1844. Webster may have slighted the Hindus in part because Hinduism was (and is) extraordinarily difficult to define. He probably lavished attention on Buddhism because by 1864 European scholarly interest in Buddhism was booming.

1828

BUD'DHISM, *n.* The doctrines of the Buddhists in Asia.

HIN'DOO, *n.* An aboriginal of Hindoostan, or Hindostan.

Noah Webster, *An American Dictionary of the English Language* (New York: S. Converse, 1828); Noah Webster, *An American Dictionary of the English Language* (Springfield, Mass.: G. & C. Merriam, 1849), 136; Noah Webster, *An American Dictionary of the English Language* (Springfield, Mass.: G. & C. Merriam, 1864), 171, 628.

1849

BOODH, *n*. In *Eastern Asia*, a general name for the divinity.

BOODH'ISM., *n*. A system of religion in Eastern Asia, embraced by more than one third of the human race. It teaches that, at distant intervals, a *Boodh*, or deity, appears to restore the world from a state of ignorance and decay, and then sinks into a state of entire non-existence, or rather, perhaps, of bare existence without attributes, action, or consciousness. This state, called *Nirvana*, or *Nicban*, is regarded as the ultimate supreme good, and the highest reward of virtue among men. Four Boodhs have thus appeared in the world, and passed into *Nirvana*, the last of whom, Gaudama, became incarnate about 600 years before Christ. From his death, in 543 B.C., many thousand years will elapse before the appearance of another; so that the system, in the mean time, is practically one of pure atheism. The objects of worship, until another boodh appears, are the relics and images of Gaudama.

HIN'DOO-ISM, HIN'DU-ISM, *n*. The doctrines and rites of the Hindoos; the system of religious principles among the Hindoos.

1864

Bud'dhå (bood'då), *n*. [Skr. *buddha*, wise, sage, from *buddh*, to know.] One of the beings worshiped by the Buddhists; either the historical founder of Buddhism, or one of his fabulous prototypes or successors, of whom there are many, of different classes.

Bud'dhĭsm (bood'izm), *n*. The doctrine originally taught by the Hindu sage Gautama, surnamed Buddha, "the awakened or enlightened," in the 6th century B.C., and adopted as a religion by the greater part of Central and Eastern Asia and the Indian Islands: at first atheistic, and aiming at release from existence (*nirvâna*) as its greatest good, while yet characterized by admirable humanity and morality; later, mixed with idolatrous worship of its founder and of other supposed kindred beings.

Hĭn'doo-ĭsm, Hĭn'du-ĭsm, *n*. The doctrines and rites of the Hindoos; the system of religious principles among the Hindoos.

LYDIA MARIA FRANCIS CHILD, *THE PROGRESS OF RELIGIOUS IDEAS* (1855)

In the preface to *The Progress of Religious Ideas, Through Successive Ages* (1855), Lydia Maria Child (1802–80) says neither "bigoted Christians" nor "bigoted infidels" should buy her book. "Its tone," she writes, "will be likely to displease them." Many would-be readers apparently took Child's advice; the three-volume primer sold poorly. But disappointing sales cannot diminish the book's importance. Child, the youngest sibling in a prosperous family from Medford, Massachusetts, wrote everything from novels and antislavery pamphlets to children's books and how-to tracts for housewives. Though acquainted with many Transcendentalists, Child was a Unitarian. Unitarians had been interested in Asian religions since the late eighteenth century, but their interest quickened in 1818, when they first discerned intriguing correspondences between their own antitrinitarian faith and the monotheism of the Hindu reformer Ram Mohan Roy. Like Hannah Adams, whose work she must have known, Child contributed to these investigations, and *The Progress of Religious Ideas* was her greatest contribution. Child attempts in this book to present the world's religions impartially, but her interpretations are colored by her own convictions, among them her view that all religions were progressing from "a Golden Age of innocence long past" to "a Golden Age of holiness to come." Selections from the preface and from a chapter covering the Jains and Buddhists of "Hindostan, or India" demonstrate the tension between the ecumenical plan of the book and its partisan execution.

PREFACE

While my mind was yet in its youth, I was offended by the manner in which Christian writers usually describe other religions; for I observed that they habitually covered apparent contradictions and absurdities, in Jewish or Christian writings, with a veil of allegories and mystical interpretation, while the records of all other religions were unscrupulously analyzed, or contemptuously described as "childish fables," or "filthy superstitions." I was well aware that this was done unconsciously, under the influence of habitual reverence for early teaching; and I was still more displeased with the scoffing tone of sceptical writers, who regarded all religions as founded on imposture. Either way, the one-sidedness of the representation troubled my strong sense of justice. I recollect wishing, long ago, that I could become acquainted with some good, intelligent Bramin, or Mohammedan, that I might learn, in some degree, how their religions appeared to *them*. This feeling expanded within me, until it took form in this book. The facts it contains are very old; the novelty it claims is the point of view from which those facts are seen and presented. I have treated all religions with reverence, and shown no more favour to one than to another. I have exhibited each one in the light of its own Sacred Books; and in giving quotations, I have aimed in every case to present impartially the beauties and the blemishes. I have honestly tried never to exaggerate merits, or conceal defects. I have not declared that any system was true, or that any one was false. I have even avoided the use of the word heathen; for though harmless in its original signification, it is used in a way that implies condescension, or contempt; and such a tone is inconsistent with the perfect impartiality I have wished to observe. I have tried to place each form of worship in its own light; that is, as it appeared to those who sincerely believed it to be of divine origin. But even this candid method must necessarily produce a very imperfect picture, drawn as it is by a modern mind, so foreign to ancient habits of thought, and separated from them by the lapse of ages. The process has been exceedingly interesting; for the history of religious sentiment, struggling through theological mazes, furnishes the most curious chapter in the strange history of mankind. . . .

Lydia Maria Child, *The Progress of Religious Ideas, Through Successive Ages*, vol. 1 (New York: C.S. Francis, 1855), vii–viii, x–xi, 82–91. The "Golden Age" quotes are from vol. 2, p. 154.

I am not aware that any one, who truly reverenced the spirit of Christianity, has ever before tried the experiment of placing it precisely on a level with other religions, so far as the manner of representation is concerned. . . . The perfect openness with which I have revealed many particulars generally kept in the back ground, will trouble some devotional people, whose feelings I would not willingly wound. But I place great reliance on sincerity, and have strong faith in the power of genuine Christianity to stand on its own internal merits, unaided by concealment. . . .

HINDOSTAN, OR INDIA

The Hindoo mind early became familiar with the idea that holy men could arrive at a state of elevation transcending the gods. This led to the theory of divine incarnations in the human form; the next step was to worship saints as gods. This is done by the Djinists, or Jains. . . . One [Jain saint] named Vrischaba, whom they peculiarly revere, has many sacred titles; such as "Lord of All the Saints," "Supreme over Gods and Spirits." According to their traditions, he was a prince, who abdicated in favour of his son, retired into the forest, and became entirely absorbed in the Divine Being. They attribute to him four Sacred Books of their sect, called Yoga. They likewise regard with especial reverence the anchorite Sramana, who is said to have been absorbed in the Divine Essence, about six hundred years before the Christian era.

They opened the religious life to all castes, except Soodras; and the saints of their own sect were their priests. In old times, their hermits bound themselves by very rigorous vows, and oftentimes showed their indifference to the world by going naked. The statues of these saints in their temples are always without clothing. It is asserted that some of them never died, but gradually dissolved away into phantoms and thus imperceptibly mixed with the Universal Soul. In later times, the religious among them are less strict. They merely promise to be poor, honest, chaste, truthful, and benevolent toward all creatures. For this last trait the Jains are very remarkable. They offer no sacrifices except fruit, flowers, and incense. A prince of this sect allowed himself to be defeated, rather than march his army in the rainy season, when the fires of the camp would destroy insects then swarming. Another prince forbade printers, potters, and pressers of oil, to exercise their trades during four months of that season, when they must inevitably crush many insects. . . .

The Buddhists are by far the most important sect that have appeared in India. They have points of similarity with the Jains, and some writers have confounded the two together. But the Jains have always persecuted the Buddhists with great bitterness. They had too much tenderness to press oil, for fear of crushing insects in the process, but they slaughtered fellow-beings without mercy, under the influence of theological hatred. The Buddhists worship Spiritual Intelligences descended on earth in the form of saints; and the greatest of these is Bouddha Sakia Mouni, from whom they derive their name. The words *Bouddha* and *Mouni* both mean a Saint, or a holy Sage; thus his name is Sakia, and his titles are, the sage and the saint, the wise and the holy. European scholars suppose him to have been a great saint and reformer, who tried to restore the spiritual doctrines of the Vedas, and abolish distinctions of caste, including the priesthood. The popular belief is that he was an incarnation of a portion of Vishnu, and that he had previously appeared on earth, at various epochs, for the instruction and salvation of mankind. . . . His statues . . . represent him as a man buried in a profound meditation, with hair knotted all over his head, after the manner of hermits in ancient times, before the custom of shaving the head was introduced. From this peculiarity, some travellers have mistaken him for an African. . . .

His worshippers believe that the severe austerities he practised had a higher and more benevolent object than the attainment of perfect holiness and complete absorption for himself. He was a Heavenly Spirit, dwelling in regions of light and beauty, who, of his own free grace and mercy, left Paradise, and came down to earth, because he was filled with compassion for the sins and miseries of mankind. He sought to lead them into better paths, and he took sufferings upon himself, that he might expiate their crimes, and mitigate the punishment they must inevitably undergo. Hindoos of all sects believe that every cause has a certain effect, which must follow it by inherent necessity; thus every sin must have its exact amount of suffering; what is endured in this world will be deducted from punishment in the next; and what one voluntarily endures for another will be placed to the account of him he wishes to benefit. For these reasons, Bouddha inflicted terrible penances upon himself. So great was his tenderness, that he even descended into the hells, to teach souls in bondage there, and was willing to suffer himself, to abridge their period of torment. . . .

The Buddhists believe in One Absolute Existence, including both God and Nature. When they speak of Providence, they mean an intelligence inherent in Nature, by which her movements are regulated. Philosophers call this doctrine Naturalism. To avoid attaching any idea of form, or limit, to the original Source of Being, the Buddhists called him by a name signifying The Void, or Space.

JAMES FREEMAN CLARKE, *TEN GREAT RELIGIONS* (1871)

James Freeman Clarke's *Ten Great Religions: An Essay in Comparative Theology* (1871) was the most widely read book on Asian religions in nineteenth-century America, and its comparative method gave a tremendous boost to the aborning study of religion. Though Clarke (1818–88) is typically numbered among the later Transcendentalists, he was a lifelong Unitarian who served for nearly half a century as the minister of the Church of the Disciples in Boston. In fact, it was Clarke who gave Unitarianism its classic credo: "The fatherhood of God, the brotherhood of man, the leadership of Jesus, salvation by character, and the progress of mankind onward and upward forever." Clarke also taught at Harvard Divinity School (his alma mater), where upon his appointment in 1867 he became the first American to lecture regularly on non-Christian religions. Like Samuel Johnson's three-volume *Oriental Religions and Their Relation to Universal Religion* (1872, 1877, and 1884), with which it is often compared, Clarke's *Ten Great Religions* found both beauty and truth in Hinduism, Buddhism, and Confucianism. But Johnson did a far better job presenting the religious traditions of Asia on their own terms. As this excerpt demonstrates, *Ten Great Religions* is a deeply Christian work that, like Lydia Maria Child's *Progress of Religious Ideas* (1855), fails to live up to its author's promises of objectivity.

1. Object of the Present Work

The present work is what the Germans call a *Versuch*, and the English an Essay, or attempt. It is an attempt to compare the great religions of the world with each other. When completed, this comparison ought to show what each is, what it contains, wherein it resembles the others, wherein it differs from the others; its origin and development, its place in universal history; its positive and negative qualities, its truths and errors, and its influence, past, present, or future, on the welfare of mankind. For everything becomes more clear by comparison. . . .

2. Comparative Theology; Its Nature, Value, and Present Position

The work of Comparative Theology is to do equal justice to all the religious tendencies of mankind. Its position is that of a judge, not that of an advocate. Assuming, with the Apostle Paul, that each religion has come providentially, as a method by which different races "should seek the Lord, if haply they might feel after him and find him," it attempts to show how each may be a step in the religious progress of the races, and "a schoolmaster to bring men to Christ." It is bound, however, to abstain from such inferences until it has accurately ascertained all the facts. . . . [Comparative Theology] may be called a science, since it consists in the study of the facts of human history, and their relation to each other. It does not dogmatize: it observes. It deals only with phenomena,—single phenomena, or facts; grouped phenomena, or laws. . . .

3. Ethnic Religions. Injustice Often Done to Them by Christian Apologists

Comparative Theology, pursuing its impartial course as a positive science, will avoid the error into which most of the Christian apologists of the last century fell, in speaking of ethnic or heathen religions. In order to show the need of Christianity, they thought it necessary to disparage all other religions. Accordingly they have insisted that, while all Jewish and Christian religions were revealed, all other religions were invented; that, while these were from God, those were the work of man; that, while in the true religions there was nothing false, in the false religions there was nothing true. . . .

This view of heathen religions is probably much exaggerated. They must contain more truth than error, and must have been, on the whole, useful to mankind. We do not believe that they originated in human fraud, that their essence is superstition, that there is more falsehood than truth in their doctrines, that their

James Freeman Clarke, *Ten Great Religions: An Essay in Comparative Theology* (Boston: Houghton, Osgood and Company, 1878), 1, 3–4, 6, 15, 21–22, 24–25, 29–31.

moral tendency is mainly injurious, or that they continually degenerate into greater evil. No doubt it may be justly predicated of all these systems that they contain much which is false and injurious to human virtue. But the following considerations may tend to show that all the religions of the earth are providential, and that all tend to benefit mankind. . . .

6. It Will Show that, While Most of the Religions of the World Are Ethnic, or the Religions of Races, Christianity Is Catholic, or Adapted to Become the Religion of All Races

By ethnic religions we mean those religions, each of which has always been confined within the boundaries of a particular race or family of mankind, and has never made proselytes or converts, except accidentally, outside of it. By catholic religions we mean those which have shown the desire and power of passing over these limits, and becoming the religion of a considerable number of persons belonging to different races. . . .

7. Comparative Theology Will Probably Show that the Ethnic Religions Are One-sided, Each Containing a Truth of Its Own, but Being Defective, Wanting Some Corresponding Truth. Christianity, or the Catholic Religion, Is Complete on Every Side

Brahmanism, for example, is complete on the side of spirit, defective on the side of matter; full as regards the infinite, empty of the finite; recognizing eternity but not time, God but not nature. It is a vast system of spiritual pantheism, in which there is no reality but God, all else being Maya, or illusion. The Hindoo mind is singularly pious, but also singularly immoral. It has no history, for history belongs to time. No one knows when its sacred books were written, when its civilization began, what caused its progress, what its decline. Gentle, devout, abstract, it is capable at once of the loftiest thoughts and the basest actions. It combines the most ascetic self-denials and abstraction from life with the most voluptuous self-indulgence. The key to the whole system of Hindoo thought and life is in this original tendency to see God, not man; eternity, not time; the infinite, not the finite.

Buddhism, which was a revolt from Brahmanism, has exactly the opposite truths and the opposite defects. Where Brahmanism is strong, it is weak; where Brahmanism is weak, it is strong. It recognizes man, not God; the soul, not the all; the finite, not the infinite; morality, not piety. Its only God, Buddha, is a man who has passed on through innumerable transmigrations, till, by means of exemplary virtues, he has reached the lordship of the universe. Its heaven, Nirvana, is indeed the world of infinite bliss; but, incapable of cognizing the infinite, it calls it nothing. Heaven, being the inconceivable infinite, is equivalent to pure negation. Nature, to the Buddhist, instead of being the delusive shadow of God, as the Brahman views it, is envisaged as a nexus of laws, which reward and punish impartially both obedience and disobedience. . . .

The positive side of Brahmanism we saw to be its sense of spiritual realities. That is also fully present in Christianity. . . . It has appeared in the worship of the

Church, the hymns of the Church, the tendencies to asceticism, the depreciation of earth and man. Christianity, therefore, fully meets Brahmanism on its positive side, while it fulfils its negations. . . .

The positive side of Buddhism is its cognition of the human soul and the natural laws of the universe. Now if we look into the New Testament and into the history of the Church, we find this element also fully expressed. It appears in all the parables and teachings of Jesus, in which man is represented as a responsible agent, rewarded or punished according to the exact measure of his works. . . .

8. Comparative Theology Will Probably Show that Ethnic Religions Are Arrested, or Degenerate, and Will Come to an End, While the Catholic Religion Is Capable of a Progressive Development

The religions of Persia, Egypt, Greece, Rome, have come to an end; having shared the fate of the national civilization of which each was a part. The religions of China, Islam, Buddha, and Judaea have all been arrested, and remain unchanged and seemingly unchangeable. Like great vessels anchored in a stream, the current of time flows past them, and each year they are further behind the spirit of the age, and less in harmony with its demands. Christianity alone, of all human religions, seems to possess the power of keeping abreast with the advancing civilization of the world. As the child's soul grows with his body, so that when he becomes a man it is a man's soul and not a child's, so the Gospel of Jesus continues the soul of all human culture. It continually drops its old forms and takes new ones. It passed out of its Jewish body under the guidance of Paul. In a speculative age it unfolded into creeds and systems. In a worshipping age it developed ceremonies and a ritual. When the fall of Rome left Europe without unity or centre, it gave it an organization and order through the Papacy. When the Papacy became a tyranny, and the Renaissance called for free thought, it suddenly put forth Protestantism, as the tree by the water-side sends forth its shoots in due season. Protestantism, free as air, opens out into the various sects, each taking hold of some human need; Lutheranism, Calvinism, Methodism, Swedenborgianism, or Rationalism. Christianity blossoms out into modern science, literature, art,—children who indeed often forget their mother, and are ignorant of their source, but which are still fed from her breasts and partake of her life. Christianity, the spirit of faith, hope, and love, is the deep fountain of modern civilization. Its inventions are for the many, not for the few. Its science is not hoarded, but diffused. It elevates the masses, who everywhere else have been trampled down. The friend of the people, it tends to free schools, a free press, a free government, the abolition of slavery, war, vice, and the melioration of society. . . .

. . . This introductory chapter has been designed as a sketch of the course which the work will take. When we have completed our survey, the results to which we hope to arrive will be these, if we succeed in what we have undertaken:—

1. All the great religions of the world, except Christianity and Mohammedanism, are ethnic religions, or religions limited to a single nation or race. Christianity alone (including Mohammedanism and Judaism, which are its temporary and local forms) is the religion of all races.
2. Every ethnic religion has its positive and negative side. Its positive side is that which holds some vital truth; its negative side is the absence of some other essential truth. Every such religion is true and providential, but each limited and imperfect.
3. Christianity alone is a πλήρωμα, or a fulness of truth, not coming to destroy but to fulfil the previous religions; but being capable of replacing them by teaching all the truth they have taught, and supplying that which they have omitted.
4. Christianity, being not a system but a life, not a creed or a form, but a spirit; is able to meet all the changing wants of an advancing civilization by new developments and adaptations, constantly feeding the life of man at its roots by fresh supplies of faith in God and faith in man.

CHAPTER **6**

Postcards for the Pews:
Missionaries and Their Critics

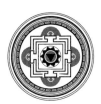

M. L. GORDON, *AN AMERICAN MISSIONARY IN JAPAN* (1892)

The foreign mission field was one of the key sites for the East-West encounter through-out the nineteenth century. For some of America's Christian missionaries, meetings with Confucians or Sikhs led to the conclusion that Asian religions were comparable to, if not fully compatible with, the Christian faith. For others, like Marquis Lafayette Gordon (1843–1900), field work only steeled certainty in Christianity's superiority. Gordon was among the best educated missionaries of his time. After graduating from both Andover Theological Seminary in Andover, Massachusetts, and from the College of Physicians and Surgeons in New York City, he sailed to Japan in 1872 as a minis-ter and physician with the American Board of Commissioners for Foreign Missions (es-tablished 1810). He soon abandoned medicine, however, on the theory that his du-ties as a doctor would undermine his effectiveness as an evangelist. Gordon's first book, *An American Missionary in Japan* (1892), published as the Americans were passing the British as the dominant force in world missions, presents the burgeoning study of comparative religion as a challenge to Christianity on par with evolution and Biblical criticism. The chapter on "Comparative Religion as a Matter of Experience" is based on interviews Gordon conducted with Shinto, Buddhist, and Confucian converts to Christianity. It begins by christening comparative religion a "Christian science" and ends with this triumphalist list of the comparative advantages of the Christian tradition.

Christianity brings a sense of sin which the other religions named above do not produce. There often has been an intellectual recognition of the fact of sin and its conse-quences, but a powerful impression of it as a personal burden is not common. . . .

M. L. Gordon, *An American Missionary in Japan* (Boston: Houghton Mifflin, 1892), 209–20.

Christianity alone brings true repentance. If the old religions bring no adequate sense of sin, how can they produce a genuine repentance? The fear of punishment is general, and often clearly defined, but a deep personal loathing of sin is practically unknown. Often repentance is the strangest and strongest element of the believer's experience.

Christianity alone awakens a true spirit of prayer. If no sense of sin and no deep repentance, true prayer by sinful man is impossible. "Before I became a Christian I prayed for temporal blessings only, for health, for children, for business prosperity. I never prayed for spiritual blessings. I did not pray for others."

Christianity alone brings the knowledge that God is our Father. Some sects of Buddhists teach that all prayer is useless; practically, the followers of both Buddhism and Shintoism worship many beings. Among scholars the idea of a Supreme Ruler, though not his worship, is common. Christianity alone teaches that this "Supreme Ruler" is our Father, and that we are his children. "Why is God called our Father?" "Because his love is greater than a human parent's love."

In his person and work Christ is unique. The doctrine of the incarnation once for all, of "the only begotten Son" of the One God, is infinitely removed from the countless transmigrations and manifestations of the innumerable buddhas. In its freedom from sin, and in its perfection as a model, Christ's life is superior to all others. "Neither Buddha nor Confucius taught of an atonement, and some object to Christianity because of the Cross; but I regard the doctrine of the Cross as the chief excellence of Christianity." "To my mind the peculiar doctrine of Christianity, the one that shows most clearly that it is divine, is the resurrection of Christ." . . .

Christianity alone teaches a certain and present forgiveness of sin. Buddhism promises deliverance from the miseries of this world and from the chain of transmigration at death rather than present forgiveness of sin. . . .

Christianity makes loving service to mankind more prominent than other religions. "Thou shalt love thy neighbor as thyself." "Love your enemies."

Christianity's doctrine of this world is superior. Buddhism makes this a world of misery to be escaped from. Strictly speaking only those are Buddhists who have "abandoned the world" and become monks or nuns. Christianity makes this world the sphere of duty to both clergy and laity, and so impels to progress and reform as Buddhism does not.

Christianity's doctrine of a future life is more rational and consistent than that of other religions. Neither Shintoism nor Confucianism has any clear doctrine of a future life. The oldest Buddhist books deny it altogether; the later books tell of an inconceivably sensuous heaven.

Christianity alone has a Sunday; a fixed day for physical rest and worship. "Sunday is a day for spiritual culture, for cleansing our hearts by meditation, Bible reading, and prayer."

Christianity places woman in a higher position and gives a higher ideal of marriage. In the civilization produced by these other religions, marriage is arranged by the parents, mutual affection before marriage is not thought of, and the parties often have no choice but to obey the parents' wishes. Gross immorality, concubinage, or repeated previous marriages on the part of the husband, make no difference. Christianity alone limits divorce to one cause, and grants it to the wife, as well as the husband, for that cause. Christianity alone makes the wife her husband's equal. This thought has already given a new impetus to female education in Japan.

Finally, Christianity alone is a living religion. Grant freely all the good that is in other religions. It is practically powerless. They are *shibutsu*, "dead things," is the often repeated assertion of our Japanese preachers; Christianity by its fruits shows that it has its Master's life within it.

MARK TWAIN, "THE UNITED STATES OF LYNCHERDOM" (1901)

A Missouri-born humorist who skewered America's Gilded Age pieties with an irreverent wit and a pointed pen, Samuel Langhorne Clemens (1835–1910) published his novels and essays as Mark Twain. Classics such as *The Adventures of Tom Sawyer* (1876) and *The Adventures of Huckleberry Finn* (1884) earned Twain recognition as one of America's greatest writers. Though no fan of Christian missions, Twain's attitudes toward Asians and their religions ranged from empathetic understanding to crude chauvinism. While on a world lecture tour in 1895–96 he judged the sacred city of Varanasi (also known as Banaras) a "vast museum of idols—and all of them crude, misshapen, and ugly." But he was an early and outspoken critic of anti-Chinese nativism, and toward the end of his life he became an ardent anti-imperialist. In "The United States of Lyncherdom," an essay from 1901, Twain brings together three themes: hatred of racism, disgust over anti-Chinese bigotry, and a keen sense of the hypocrisy of missionary do-gooders. And he does it all with his usual biting wit. The essay begins with a lament on the spread of lynching into Twain's home state of Missouri. It ends with the following plan.

Let us import American missionaries from China, and send them into the lynching field. With 1,511 of them out there converting two Chinamen apiece per annum against an uphill birth rate of 33,000 pagans per day, it will take upward of a million years to make the conversions balance the output and bring the Christianizing of the country in sight to the naked eye; therefore, if we can offer our missionaries as rich a field at home at lighter expense and quite satisfactory in the matter of danger, why shouldn't they find it fair and right to come back and give us a trial? The Chinese are universally conceded to be excellent people, honest, honorable, industrious, trustworthy, kind-hearted, and all that—leave them alone, they are plenty good enough just as they are; and besides, almost every convert runs a risk of catching our civilization. We ought to be careful. We ought to think twice before we encourage a risk like that; for, *once civilized, China can never be uncivilized again.* We have not been thinking of that. Very well, we ought to think of it now. Our missionaries will find that

Mark Twain, "The United States of Lyncherdom," in Charles Neider, ed., *The Complete Essays of Mark Twain* (Garden City, N.J.: Doubleday, 1963), 673–79.

we have a field for them—and not only for the 1,511, but for 15,011. Let them look at the following telegram and see if they have anything in China that is more appetizing. It is from Texas:

> The negro was taken to a tree and swung in the air. Wood and fodder were piled beneath his body and a hot fire was made. *Then it was suggested that the man ought not to die too quickly, and he was let down to the ground while a party went to Dexter, about two miles distant, to procure coal oil.* This was thrown on the flames and the work completed.

We implore them to come back and help us in our need. Patriotism imposes this duty on them. Our country is worse off than China; they are our country-men, their motherland supplicates their aid in this her hour of deep distress. They are competent; our people are not. They are used to scoffs, sneers, revilings, dan-ger; our people are not. They have the martyr spirit; nothing but the martyr spirit can brave a lynching mob, and cow it and scatter it. They can save their country, we beseech them to come home and do it. We ask them to read that telegram again, and yet again, and picture the scene in their minds, and soberly ponder it; then multiply it by 115, add 88; place the 203 in a row, allowing 600 feet of space for each human torch, so that there may be viewing room around it for 5000 Christian American men, women, and children, youths and maidens; make it right, for grim effect; have the show in a gradually rising plain, and let the course of the stakes be uphill; the eye can then take in the while line of twenty-four miles of blood-and-flesh bonfires unbroken, whereas if it occupied level ground the ends of the line would bend down and be hidden from view by the curvature of the earth. All being ready, now, and the darkness opaque, the stillness impres-sive—for there should be no sound but the soft moaning of the night wind and the muffled sobbing of the sacrifices—let all the far stretch of kerosened pyres be touched off simultaneously and the glare and the shrieks and the agonies burst heavenward to the Throne.

There are more than a million persons present; the light from the fires flushes into vague outline against the night the spires of five thousand churches. O kind missionary, O compassionate missionary, leave China! come home and convert these Christians!

I believe that if anything can stop this epidemic of bloody insanities it is mar-tial personalities that can face mobs without flinching; and as such personalities are developed only by familiarity with danger and by the training and seasoning which come of resisting it, the likeliest place to find them must be among the mis-sionaries who have been under tuition in China during the past year or two. We have abundance of work for them, and for hundreds and thousands more, and the field is daily growing and spreading. Shall we find them? We can try. In 75,000,000 there must be other Merrills and Beloats [sheriffs who faced lynching mobs and securely held the field against them]; and it is the law of our make that each example shall wake up drowsing chevaliers of the same great knighthood and bring them to the front.

MYRA E. WITHEE, "IS BUDDHISM TO BLAME?" (1902)

Between 1880 and 1910, some American advocates of Asian religions responded to Christian missionaries' critiques and sparked impassioned public debates. Consider the conversation between a former Protestant missionary to Japan, the Reverend Clarence Edgar Rice of Reading, Pennsylvania, and the Buddhist sympathizer, Myra Withee of St. Paul, Minnesota. Rice, who spent six years evangelizing the Japanese, published "Buddhism as I Have Seen It" in the May 1902 issue of *The Arena*. He claimed that Buddhism's central idea was that "life is essentially evil," and that in Japan, as elsewhere, it led to "an apathy as regards life, a crushing fatalism." This apathy, in turn, generated moral defects and social injustices. Like other Christian critics, Rice used pragmatic criteria to assess non-Christian religions: what fruit do they bear? Withee and her husband subscribed to *The Light of Dharma* and donated money to the Maha Bodhi Society, and she was so annoyed by the missionaries' hostile portrait of Buddhism that she immediately fired off a reply, an essay entitled "Is Buddhism to Blame?." Four months later the New Thought journal, *Mind*, printed her essay, which responds to Rice's charges. We should not assess a religion by its social effects, this Buddhist sympathizer suggests, and even if we did, tolerant Buddhism would be judged superior to aggressive Christianity. The belief in karma, according to Withee, "is a greater force in making people moral than the doctrine of the forgiveness of sins."

> "To abandon all wrong-doing, to lead a virtuous life, and to cleanse one's heart: this is the religion of all Buddhas."

The above is an extract from the Buddhists' sacred books, and to these books, or to one well acquainted with their precepts, one should look who wishes to acquaint himself with the religion taught by Prince Gautama of India.

If one wishes to become familiar with a religion, it will not do to depend upon what can be gleaned from books and articles written by devotees of some other religion; for these are certain to regard everything that seems antagonistic to their own belief as evil. Nor can one gain exact knowledge of a religion by noting the habits and moral status of its adherents; for while they may profess it, they may not *live* it. Furthermore, one invariably finds that the natural characteristics of a people form a prominent part of their religious worship. The Japanese, for instance, are universally known for their love of art; and it need not be wondered at that they aim to have their religious ceremonies attractive, and that great care is taken in locating and building their temples—that they may look picturesque.

Were a pagan desirous of studying Christianity, the intelligent Christian would not direct him to a city in Christendom and tell him to note carefully the social and moral conditions of its people. Neither would he give him the works

Myra E. Withee, "Is Buddhism to Blame?," *Mind* 10 (September 1902): 456–62.

of agnostics, nor the sacred books of the Orient; but he would be given a Bible, or directed to one well able to expound the gospel of Jesus Christ.

The writer lives in an American city of 163,000 inhabitants [St. Paul]. There are here three hundred licensed saloons and twenty-eight public houses of ill repute, besides the many dens where vice reigns unknown to the public. It is found necessary to maintain many policemen and courts of justice. Yet in this city there are one hundred and thirty Christian churches, and it is considered a model of purity compared with other cities of its size, or larger. Were she to write an article and dwell upon the many crimes that occur daily in such a city—mentioning the offenses committed by the clergy—and entitle such an article "Christianity as I Have Seen It," Christians might well object and declare that the article had not a proper title (for what had been described was not Christianity, but a lack of it), and that evil existed in spite of the churches wherein the pure gospel of Christ is preached.

An essay entitled "Buddhism as I Have Seen It" appeared in the May number of *The Arena*. The writer dwells on the immorality of the Japanese and their external forms of worship, and seems to hold Buddhism responsible. One who has studied the Buddhists' sacred books may truthfully say that the evils mentioned in the article referred to cannot properly be charged to Buddhism; for, were the teachings of Buddha obeyed, evil could not possible exist in thought, word, act.

How much of the immorality of the Japanese is chargeable to Western civilization? It will be conceded that intoxicating drinks are the cause of much immorality. These were introduced into Japan by Western enterprise. The slaughter of animals and flesh-eating came from the same source. . . .

Buddha taught kindness to animals, not because he thought they "may contain the souls of our ancestors," but because of his great kindness of heart. All sentient beings were objects of his love and mercy; and there is no other gospel in the world to which Christians could turn where they would find so much consideration shown for the so-called lower animals as is shown in the gospel of Buddha, who says: "He who wilfully and malignantly taketh the life of any harmless being, be it earth-worm or ant, is no longer a disciple of the Shakyamuni." Such were the injunctions of the Buddha to his disciples; and they are to be found on page after page of the Buddhists' sacred books. He seems to have taken special pains to impress his followers with the idea that all sentient beings should find mercy at their hands.

Considering Buddha's sentiments upon this question, it seems quite incongruous for the Christian missionary to mention any unkindness on the part of Buddhists to animals, and charge the same to Buddhism. It would be as consistent to charge all the crimes committed in Christendom to Christianity. Nor can another religion be found so free from external forms of worship. Chanting was forbidden by Buddha. One reason he gave for not allowing it was that the disciples became captivated with respect to the sound thereof. He aimed constantly to appeal to their reason, not to their senses.

Miracles were also forbidden. It appears from the sacred books that some of the disciples had power to perform what are termed supernatural acts. After making use of such power, one of them was severely criticized, and Buddha said: "I forbid you, O disciple, to employ any spells or supplications; for they are useless, since the law of *karma* governs all things. He who attempts to perform miracles has not understood the doctrine of Tathagata."

Sacrifices too were scorned. "What love can a man possess," said the Buddha, "who believes that the destruction of life will atone for evil deeds? Can a new wrong expiate old wrongs? And can slaughter of an innocent victim take away the sins of mankind? This is practising religion by the neglect of moral conduct. Purify your hearts, and cease to kill; that is true religion. Rituals have no efficacy; prayers are vain repetitions, and incantations have no saving power. But to abandon covetousness and lust, to become free from evil passions, and to give up hatred and ill-will—that is the right sacrifice, and the true worship. We reach the immortal path only by continuous acts of kindliness; and we perfect our souls by compassion and charity." A religion abounding with such sentiments cannot consistently be held responsible for the licentiousness of a people, nor for its external forms of worship.

Buddhism does *not* degrade womanhood. Women were admitted to the *sangha* (brotherhood of Buddhists) by Buddha, and they were not told to "learn in silence with all subjection" nor to adorn themselves with "shamefacedness," as they are commanded by the Christian Apostle. A religion that shows so much consideration for all sentient life as does Buddhism cannot possibly degrade womanhood.

Buddha left his wife and child for a time, and that act is often harshly criticized by Christians. But it is because the critic fails to comprehend the great unselfish love of Buddha for all beings. Had he been as selfish as the ordinary mortal he would have been content to remain about his palace—to have indulged in luxuries and enjoyed the companionship of a loving wife. But his great soul could not do thus because he felt for the many—for *all*. He had witnessed the sufferings of the poor, of the sick and of the dying, and nevermore could he be content to dwell amid plenty while a single soul knew misery. He resolved to find an escape from the ills of life. He left his wife and child amid wealth, friends, and loving relatives. The anguish such parting caused he alone knew. It must have been great, for he was an affectionate husband and father; but he felt that this sacrifice must be made for the good of the many. He went to the greatest Brahman teachers of his time, and spent years in strict discipline, contemplating their philosophy, but not until he left them and turned alone to Nature did he fine satisfaction.

When Jesus was preaching, and was told that his mother and brothers were outside and would speak with him, he replied: "Who is my mother? and who are my brethren?" and he stretched forth his hand towards his disciples and said, "Behold my mother and my brethren!" Jesus made such answer, not because he loved his mother and brothers less than others do, but because he too, like Buddha, realized that larger love which extends beyond kith and kin—a love that is an outpouring, a love not bound by propinquity, but extends to all. . . .

But though he was a model of purity, though his ethical code stands unexcelled, though he taught a religion that is above reproach, yet the system as presented today by a large percentage of its devotees appears greatly corrupted. . . .

Where the moral status of a people is low, and it is evident from their sacred books that the founder of their religion was a model of purity and taught the highest ethics, it cannot be truly said that their religion is at fault. If a professed saint is in fact a sinner, it does not prove that the path that leads to saintship is responsible for his wrongdoing; for if he follows the path he cannot err.

Judging a religion by those who profess it, how did Christianity appear at the time of the Inquisition? How does it appear today, as exemplified by the conduct of a larger percentage of its devotees? What would be the verdict of a Buddhist who should visit Christendom and judge of Christianity by what he found in her cities, especially those that are, as many Christians declare, "blots upon the earth"? Certainly, belief in the law of *karma*, which compels each one to reap exactly what he sows,—if not in his life, in some future one,—is a far greater force in making people moral than the doctrine of the forgiveness of sins. And if the Japanese Buddhists, believing in the law of *karma*,—believing that some time, somewhere, they must suffer for every evil thought, word, and act,—are as immoral as the Christian missionary asserts, what will be the result if the missionaries succeed in converting them to Christianity, and they thereby believe that they may commit all the crimes known to man, yet in a moment of mental repentance be forgiven, and their sins, "though as scarlet, be as wool"?

CHAPTER 7

The World's Parliament of Religions

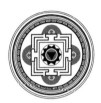

JOHN HENRY BARROWS, "WORDS OF WELCOME" (1893)

The World's Parliament of Religions, overpraised by comparative religionist F. Max Müller as "one of the most memorable events in the history of the world," took place in Chicago in 1893 under the auspices of a great fair called the World's Columbian Exposition. Christians of all stripes attended, as did Jews, Muslims, Zoroastrians, Buddhists, Hindus, Confucians, Jains, Shintos, and Taoists. John Henry Barrows (1847–1902) was one of Chicago's most prominent Presbyterian ministers when he was tapped to organize the event that would bring him international renown. Although Barrows publicly promoted the Parliament as a pluralistic gathering of all the world's faiths, he harbored a not-so-secret hope that the event would demonstrate the superiority of his beloved liberal Protestantism. Leaving the ministry after the Parliament for the lecture circuit, Barrows traveled widely in the United States and Asia before settling into the presidency at Oberlin College (his mother's alma mater) in 1898. In this opening address from the Parliament, Barrows welcomes the "wise men of the East" in the spirit of "divine Fatherhood and human brotherhood." But he does so on liberal Protestant terms.

MR. PRESIDENT AND FRIENDS,—If my heart did not overflow with cordial welcome at this hour, which promises to be a great moment in history, it would be because I had lost the spirit of mankind and had been forsaken by the Spirit of God. The whitest snow on the sacred mount of Japan, the clearest water springing from the sacred fountains of India are not more pure and bright than the joy of my heart and of many hearts here that this day has dawned in the annals of

John Henry Barrows, "Words of Welcome," in Richard Hughes Seager, ed., *The Dawn of Religious Pluralism: Voices from the World's Parliament of Religions, 1893* (La Salle, Ill.: Open Court, 1993), 23–30. Reprinted by permission of Open Court Publishing Company, a division of Carus Publishing Company, Peru, Ill. Copyright © 1993 by Open Court Publishing Company.

time, and that, from the farthest isles of Asia; from India, mother of religions; from Europe, the great teacher of civilization; from the shores on which breaks the "long wash of Australasian seas"; that from the neighboring lands and from all part of this republic, which we love to contemplate as the land of earth's brightest future, you have come here at our invitation in the expectation that the world's first Parliament of Religions must prove an event of race-wide and perpetual significance. . . .

Welcome, most welcome, O wise men of the East and of the West! May the star which has led you hither be like that luminary which guided the sages of old, and may this meeting by the inland sea of a new continent be blessed of heaven to the redemption of men from error and from sin and despair. I wish you to understand that this great undertaking, which has aimed to house under one friendly roof in brotherly council the representatives of God's aspiring and believing children everywhere, has been conceived and carried on through strenuous and patient toil, with an unfaltering heart, with a devout faith in God, and with most signal and special evidences of his divine guidance and favor.

Long ago I should have surrendered the task intrusted to me before the colossal difficulties looming ever in the way, had I not committed my work to the gracious care of that God who loves all his children, whose thoughts are long, long thoughts, who is patient and merciful as well as just, and who cares infinitely more for the souls of his erring children than for any creed or philosophy of human devising. If anything great and worthy is to be the outcome of this Parliament, the glory is wholly due to Him who inspired it, and who, in the Scriptures which most of us cherish as the Word of God, has taught the blessed truths of divine Fatherhood and human brotherhood. . . .

Christendom may proudly hold up this Congress of the Faiths as a torch of truth and of love which may prove the morning star of the twentieth century. There is a true and noble sense in which America is a Christian nation, since Christianity is recognized by the supreme court, by the courts of the several states, by executive officers, and by general national acceptance and observance as the prevailing religion of our people. This does not mean, of course, that the church and state are united. In America they are separated, and in this land the widest spiritual and intellectual freedom is realized. . . . [T]he world calls us, and we call ourselves, a Christian people. We believe in the gospels and in Him whom they set forth as "the light of the world," and Christian America, which owes so much to Columbus and Luther, to the Pilgrim Fathers and to John Wesley, which owes so much to the Christian church and the Christian college and the Christian school, welcomes to-day the earnest disciples of other faiths and men of all faiths who, from many lands, have flocked to this jubilee of civilization.

Cherishing the light which God has given us and eager to send this light everywhither, we do not believe that God, the eternal Spirit, has left himself without witness in non-Christian nations. There is a divine light enlightening every man. . . .

John Henry Barrows, "Words of Welcome" (1893)

It is perfectly evident to illuminated minds that we should cherish loving thoughts of all peoples and humane views of all the great and lasting religions, and that whoever would advance the cause of his own faith must first discover and gratefully acknowledge the truths contained in other faiths.

This Parliament is likely to prove a blessing to many Christians by marking the time when they shall cease thinking that the verities and virtues of other religions discredit the claims of Christianity or bar its progress. It is our desire and hope to broaden and purify the mental and spiritual vision of men. Believing that nations and faiths are separated in part by ignorance and prejudice, why shall not this Parliament help to remove the one and soften the other? Why should not Christians be glad to learn what God has wrought through Buddha and Zoroaster—through the sage of China, and the prophets of India and the prophet of Islam?

We are met together today as men, children of one God, sharers with all men in weakness and guilt and need, sharers with devout souls everywhere in aspiration and hope and longing. We are met as religious men, believing even here in this capital of material wonders, in the presence of an Exposition which displays the unparalleled marvels of steam and electricity, that there is a spiritual root to all human progress. We are met in a school of comparative theology, which I hope will prove more spiritual and ethical than theological. We are met, I believe, in the temper of love, determined to bury, at least for a time, our sharp hostilities, anxious to find out wherein we agree, eager to learn what constitutes the strength of other faiths and the weakness of our own. And we are met as conscientious and truth-seeking men, in a council where no one is asked to surrender or abate his individual convictions, and where, I will add, no one would be worthy of a place if he did. . . . We are not here as Baptists and Buddhists, Catholics and Confucians, Parsees and Presbyterians, Methodists and Moslems; we are here as members of a Parliament of Religions, over which flies no sectarian flag. . . .

It seems to me that the spirits of just and good men hover over this assembly. I believe that the spirit of Paul is here, the zealous missionary of Christ whose courtesy, wisdom, and unbounded tact were manifest when he preached Jesus and the resurrection beneath the shadows of the Parthenon. I believe the spirit of the wise and humane Buddha is here, and of Socrates the searcher after truth, and of Jeremy Taylor and John Milton and Roger Williams and Lessing, the great apostles of toleration. I believe that the spirit of Abraham Lincoln, who sought for a church founded on love for God and man, is not far from us, and the spirit of Tennyson and Whittier and Phillips Brooks, who all looked forward to this Parliament as the realization of a noble idea.

When, a few days ago, I met for the first time the delegates who have come to us from Japan, and shortly after the delegates who have come to us from India, I felt that the arms of human brotherhood had reached almost around the globe. But there is something stronger than human love and fellowship, and what gives us the most hope and happiness to-day is our confidence that

the whole round world is every way
Bound by gold chains about the feet of God.

SWAMI VIVEKANANDA, "HINDUISM" (1893)

While the Reverend Barrows hoped Chicago's World's Parliament of Religions of 1893 would vindicate Christianity, it actually provided a platform for Asian religious leaders like Swami Vivekananda (1863–1902) to demonstrate to Americans the reasonableness of their religions. The first Hindu missionary to America, Swami Vivekananda was born Nerendran Nath Datta in Calcutta in 1863. Though groomed by his family for secular success, he found himself drawn to Sri Ramakrishna, a Hindu mystic who initiated him into Advaita Vedanta, a monistic form of Hinduism that affirms the equivalence of *Brahman* (God) and *Atman* (Self). In 1886, the year of Ramakrishna's death, he took the vows of a *sannyasin* or world renunciant and established the Ramakrishna Order. Now called Swami Vivekananda ("he whose bliss is in spiritual discrimination"), he burst onto the world stage as a crowd favorite at the World's Parliament. One year later in New York, he established the Vedanta Society, the first Hindu organization designed to attract American adherents. Though he emphasized *jnana yoga* (the discipline of wisdom) in American lectures he delivered after the Parliament, he was, like

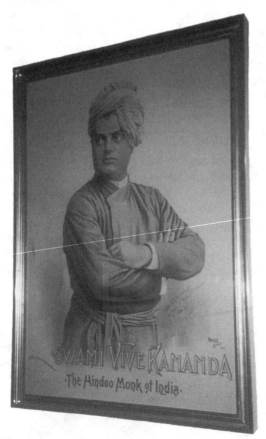

The first Hindu missionary to the United States, Swami Vivekananda represented Hinduism at the World's Parliament of Religions in Chicago in 1893. This autographed poster hangs in the Vedanta Society in Berkeley, California. Courtesy of the Pluralism Project, Harvard University.

Ramakrishna, a zealous devotee of the goddess Kali and thus a practitioner of *bhakti yoga* (the discipline of devotion). His Parliament speech epitomizes Hindu modernism. In keeping with his slashing style (British Theosophist Annie Besant once called him a "warrior-monk"), Vivekananda chastises Christian missionaries for misrepresenting Hinduism. But he also affirms the essential unity of religions—a claim that would become the rallying cry of generations of American Vedantists to come.

Three religions stand now in the world which have come down to us from time pre-historic—Hinduism, Zoroastrianism, and Judaism.

They all have received tremendous shocks and all of them prove by their survival their internal strength; but while Judaism failed to absorb Christianity, and was driven out of its place of birth by its all-conquering daughter, and a handful of Parsees, are all that remains to tell the tale of his grand religion, sect after sect have arisen in India and seemed to shake the religion of the Vedas to its very foundation, but like the waters of the seashore in a tremendous earthquake, it receded only for a while, only to return in an all-absorbing flood, a thousand times more vigorous, and when the tumult of the rush was over, they have been all sucked in, absorbed and assimilated in the immense body of another faith.

From the high spiritual flights of Vedantic philosophy, of which the latest discoveries of science seem like the echoes, the agnosticism of the Buddhas, the atheism of the Jains, and the low ideas of idolatry with the multifarious mythology, each and all have a place in the Hindu's religion.

Where then, the question arises, where is the common center to which all these widely diverging radii converge; where is the common basis upon which all these seemingly hopeless contradictions rest? And this is the question I shall attempt to answer.

The Hindus have received their religion through their revelation, the Vedas. They hold that the Vedas are without beginning and without end. It may sound ludicrous to this audience, how a book can be without beginning or end. But by the Vedas no book are meant. They mean the accumulated treasury of spiritual law discovered by different persons in different times. . . .

. . . The Hindu religion does not consist in struggles and attempts to believe a certain doctrine or dogma, but in realizing; not in believing, but in being and becoming.

So the whole struggle in their system is a constant struggle to become perfect, to become divine, to reach God and see God, and this reaching God, seeing God, becoming perfect, even as the Father in Heaven is perfect, constitutes the religion of the Hindus.

And what becomes of man when he becomes perfect? He lives a life of bliss, infinite. He enjoys infinite and perfect bliss, having obtained the only thing in which man ought to have pleasure, God, and enjoys the bliss with God. So far all

Swami Vivekananda, "Hinduism," in Richard H. Seager, ed., *The Dawn of Religious Pluralism: Voices from the World's Parliament of Religions, 1893* (La Salle, Ill.: Open Court, 1993), 421–32. Reprinted by permission of Open Court Publishing Company, a division of Carus Publishing Company, Peru, Ill. Copyright © 1993 by Open Court Publishing Company.

the Hindus are agreed. This is the common religion of all sects of India; but then the question comes, perfection is absolute, and the absolute cannot be two or three. It cannot have any qualities. It cannot be an individual. And so when a soul becomes perfect and absolute, it must become one with Brahma, and he would only realize the Lord as the perfection, the reality, of his own nature and existence, the existence absolute, knowledge absolute, and life absolute. . . .

Descend we now from the aspirations of philosophy to the religion of the ignorant? On the very outset, I may tell you that there is no polytheism in India. In every temple, if one stands by and listens, he will find the worshipers applying all the attributes of God, including omnipresence, to these images. It is not polytheism, neither would the name henotheism answer our question. "The rose called by any other name would smell as sweet." Names are not explanations.

I remember, when a boy, a Christian man was preaching to a crowd in India. Among other things he was telling the people that if he gave a blow to their idols with his stick, what could it do? One of the hearers sharply answered, "If I abuse your God what can he do?" "You would be punished," said the preacher, "when you die." "So my idol will punish you when you die," said the villager.

The tree is known by its fruits; and when I have seen amongst them that are called idolatrous men, the like of whom in morality and spirituality and love, I have never seen anywhere, I stop and ask myself, Can sin beget holiness?

Superstition is the enemy of man, bigotry worse. Why does a Christian go to church, why is the cross holy, why is the face turned toward the sky in prayer? Why are there so many images in the Catholic Church, why are there so many images in the minds of Protestants, when they pray? My brethren, we can no more think about anything without a material image than it is profitable for us to live without breathing. . . .

. . . To the Hindu man is not traveling from error to truth, but from truth to truth, from lower to higher truth. To him all the religions from the lowest fetichism to the highest absolutism mean so many attempts of the human soul to grasp and realize the Infinite, determined by the conditions of its birth and association, and each of these mark a stage of progress, and every soul is a child eagle soaring higher and higher; gathering more and more strength till it reaches the glorious sun. . . .

One thing I must tell you. Idolatry in India does not mean a horror. It is not the mother of harlots. On the other hand, it is the attempt of undeveloped minds to grasp high spiritual truths. The Hindus have their own faults, they sometimes have their exceptions; but mark this, it is always toward punishing their own bodies, and never to cut the throats of their neighbors. If the Hindu fanatic burns himself on the pyre, he never lights the fire of inquisition; and even this cannot be laid at the door of religion any more than the burning of witches can be laid at the door of Christianity.

To the Hindu, then, the whole world of religions is only a traveling, a coming up, of different men and women, through various conditions and circumstances, to the same goal. Every religion is only an evolving of God out of the material man; and the same God is the inspirer of all of them. Why, then, are there so many contradictions? They are only apparent, says the Hindu. The contradictions come from the same truth adapting itself to the different circumstances of different natures.

It is the same light coming through different colors. And these little variations are necessary for that adaptation. But in the heart of everything the same truth reigns; the Lord has declared to the Hindu in his incarnation as Krishna, "I am in every religion as the thread through a string of pearls. And wherever thou seest extraordinary holiness and extraordinary power raising and purifying humanity, know ye that I am there". . . .

. . . This, brethren, is a short sketch of the ideas of the Hindus. The Hindu might have failed to carry out all his plans, but if there is to be ever a universal religion, it must be one which would hold no location in place or time, which would be infinite like the God it would preach, whose sun shines upon the followers of Krishna or Christ; saints or sinners alike; which would not be the Brahman or Buddhist, Christian or Mohammedan, but the sum total of all these, and still have infinite space for development; which in its catholicity would embrace in its infinite arms and formulate a place for every human being, from the lowest groveling man who is scarcely removed in intellectuality from the brute, to the highest mind, towering almost above humanity, and who makes society stand in awe and doubt his human nature.

It would be a religion which would have no place for persecution or intolerance in its polity, and would recognize a divinity in every man or woman, and whose whole scope, whose whole force would be centered in aiding humanity to realize its Divine nature. Offer religions in your hand, and all the nations must follow thee. Asoka's council was a council of the Buddhist faith. Akbar's, though more to the purpose, was only a parlor-meeting. It was reserved for America to call, to proclaim to all quarters of the globe that the Lord is in every religion.

May he who is the Brahma of the Hindus, the Ahura Mazda of the Zoroastrians, the Buddha of the Buddhists, the Jehovah of the Jews, the Father in Heaven of the Christians, give strength to you to carry out your noble idea. The star arose in the East; it traveled steadily toward the West, sometimes dimmed and sometimes effulgent, till it made a circuit of the world, and now it is again rising on the very horizon of the East, the borders of the Tasifu, a thousand-fold more effulgent than it ever was before. Hail Columbia, mother-land of liberty! It has been given to thee, who never dipped her hand in her neighbor's blood, who never found out that shortest way of becoming rich by robbing one's neighbors, it has been given thee to march on at the vanguard of civilization with the flag of harmony.

ANAGARIKA DHARMAPALA, "THE WORLD'S DEBT TO BUDDHA" (1893)

Anagarika Dharmapala (1864–1933) arrived at the World's Parliament of Religions in Chicago in 1893 as the first Theravada Buddhist missionary to the United States. Born in 1864 in Colombo, Ceylon (now Sri Lanka), he embraced Theosophy in his youth after meeting Helena Blavatsky and Colonel Olcott during their triumphant tour of his island homeland in 1880. He worked alongside Olcott to revitalize Buddhism in Ceylon, and in 1889 traveled with him to Japan in an effort to construct an ecumenical "International Buddhist League." Two years later, Dharmapala founded the Maha Bodhi Society, which in its infancy aimed to restore the site of Gautama Buddha's enlightenment in Bodhgaya, India, as a sacred space for all the world's Buddhists. He achieved international acclaim at the Parliament, in part because just days after its conclusion he officiated at a ceremony in which C.T. Strauss, a New York Jew, became the first American to convert to Buddhism on American soil. In the Parliament's afterglow, Dharmapala returned to his homeland, but he made his way back to the United States for an occasional lecture tour. "The World's Debt to Buddha," which Dharmapala delivered at the Parliament in a captivating Irish brogue, demonstrates Dharmapala's debts to Theosophy, academic Orientalism, and what some scholars have called "Protestant Buddhism."

Ancient India, twenty-five centuries ago, was the scene of a religious revolution, the greatest the world has ever seen. Indian society at this time had two

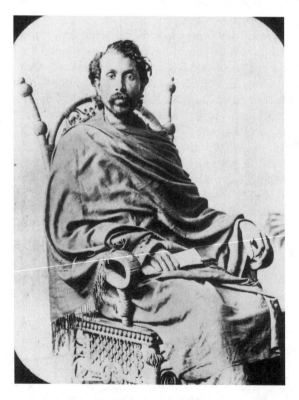

Anagarika Dharmapala of Ceylon (now Sri Lanka) came to Chicago in 1893 as a delegate to the World's Parliament of Religions. Courtesy of the Theosophical Society in America.

Anagarika Dharmapala, "The World's Debt to Buddha," in Richard H. Seager, ed., *The Dawn of Religious Pluralism: Voices from the World's Parliament of Religions, 1893* (LaSalle, Ill.: Open Court, 1993), 410–20. Reprinted by permission of Open Court Publishing Company, a division of Carus Publishing Company, Peru, Ill. Copyright © 1993 by Open Court Publishing Company.

large and distinguished religious foundations—the Sramanas and the Brahmanas. Famous teachers arose and with their disciples went among the people preaching and converting them to their respective views. The air was full of a coming spiritual struggle, hundreds of the most scholarly young men of noble families (Kulaputta) leaving their homes in quest of truth, ascetics undergoing the severest mortifications to discover a panacea for the evils of suffering, young dialecticians wandering from place to place engaged in disputations, some advocating scepticism as the best weapon to fight against the realistic doctrines of the day, some a life of pessimism as the nearest way to get rid of existence, some denying a future life. It was a time of deep and many-sided intellectual movements, which extended from the circles of Brahmanical thinkers far into the people at large. The sacrificial priest was powerful then as he is now. He was the mediator between God and man. Monotheism of the most crude type, from fetichism and animism and anthropomorphic deism to transcendental dualism, was rampant. So was materialism, from sexual Epicureanism to transcendental Nihilism. In the words of Dr. Oldenberg, "When dialectical scepticism began to attack moral ideas, when a painful longing for deliverance from the burden of being was met by the first signs of moral decay, Buddha appeared."

> . . . The Saviour of the World,
> Prince Siddhartha styled on Earth,
> In Earth and Heavens and Hells incomparable,
> All-honored, Wisest, Best, most Pitiful
> The Teacher of Nirvana and the Law.
> —SIR EDWIN ARNOLD'S "LIGHT OF ASIA"

The Dawn of a New Era. . . . History is repeating itself. Twenty-five centuries ago India witnessed an intellectual and religious revolution which culminated in the overthrow of monotheism, priestly selfishness, and the establishment of a synthetic religion, a system of life and thought which was appropriately called *Dhamma*—Philosophical Religion. All that was good was collected from every source and embodied therein, and all that was bad discarded. The grand personality who promulgated the Synthetic Religion is known as BUDDHA. . . .

His First Message. . . . A systematic study of Buddha's doctrine has not yet been made by the Western scholars, hence the conflicting opinions expressed by them at various times. The notion once held by the scholars that it is a system of materialism has been exploded. The Positivists of France found it a positivism; Buchner and his school of materialists thought it was a materialistic system; agnostics found in Buddha an agnostic, and Dr. Rhys Davids, the eminent Pali scholar, used to call him the "agnostic philosopher of India"; some scholars have found an expressed monotheism therein; Arthur Lillie, another student of Buddhism, thinks it a theistic system; pessimists identify it with Schopenhauer's pessimism, the late Mr. Buckle identified it with pantheism of Fichte; some have found in it a monism; and the latest dictum of Prof. Huxley is that it is an idealism supplying "the wanting half of Bishop Berkeley's well-known idealistic argument."

In the religion of Buddha is found a comprehensive system of ethics, and a transcendental metaphysic embracing a sublime psychology. To the simple-minded it offers a code of morality, to the earnest student a system of pure thought. But the basic doctrine is the self-purification of man. . . .

Human Brotherhood. This forms the fundamental teaching of Buddha; universal love and sympathy with all mankind and with animal life. Everyone is enjoined to love all beings as a mother loves her only child and takes care of it, even at the risk of her life. The realization of the idea of brotherhood is obtained when the first stage of holiness is reached; the idea of separateness is destroyed, and the oneness of life is recognized. There is no pessimism in the teachings of Buddha, for he strictly enjoins on his holy disciples not even to suggest to others that life is not worth living. On the contrary, the usefulness of life is emphasized for the sake of doing good to self and humanity.

Religion Characteristic of Humanity. From the first worshiping savage to the highest type of humanity, man naturally yearns after something higher; and it is for this reason that Buddha inculcated the necessity of self-reliance and independent thought. To guide humanity in the right path a Tathagata (Messiah) appears from time to time.

The Theism of Buddhism. Speaking of deity in the sense of a Supreme Creator, Buddha says that there is no such being. Accepting the doctrine of evolution as the only true one, with its corollary, the law of cause and effect, he condemns the idea of a creator and strictly forbids inquiry into it as being useless. But a supreme god of the Brahmans and minor gods are accepted; but they are subject to the law of cause and effect. This supreme god is all love, all merciful, all gentle, and looks upon all beings with equanimity, and Buddha teaches men to practice these four supreme virtues. But there is no difference between the perfect man and this supreme god of the present world-period.

Evolution as Taught by Buddha. The teachings of the Buddha on this great subject are clear and expansive. We are asked to look upon the cosmos "as a continuous process unfolding itself in regular order in obedience to natural laws. . . .

The Attributes of Buddha.
1. He is absolutely free from all passions, commits no evil, even in secrecy, and is the embodiment of perfection; he is above doing anything wrong.
2. Without a teacher by self-introspection he has reached the state of supreme enlightenment.
3. By means of his divine eye he looks back to the remotest past and future, knows the way of emancipation, is accomplished in the three great branches of divine knowledge, and has gained perfect wisdom. He is in possession of all psychic powers, is always willing to listen, full of energy, wisdom, and Dhyana.
4. He has realized eternal peace of Nirvana and walks in the perfect path of virtue.
5. He knows the three states of existence.
6. He is incomparable in purity and holiness.
7. He is teacher of gods and men.

8. He exhorts gods and men at the proper time according to their individual temperaments.
9. He is the supremely enlightened teacher and the perfect embodiment of all the virtues he preaches.

The two characteristics of the Buddha are wisdom and compassion. . . .

The Compassionateness Shown by Buddhist Missionaries. Actuated by the spirit of compassion, the disciples of Buddha have ever been in the forefront of missionary propaganda. The whole of Asia was brought under the influence of Buddha's law. Never was the religion propagated by force, not a drop of blood has ever been spilt in the name of Buddha. . . .

The Ultimate Goal of Man. The ultimate goal of the perfected man is eternal peace. To show humanity the path on which to realize this state of eternal peace, Buddha promulgated the noble eight-fold path. The Nirvana of Buddha is beyond the conception of the ordinary mind. Only the perfected man realizes it. It transcends all human thought. Caught in the vortex of evolution man undergoes change and is constantly subject to birth and death. The happiness in the highest heaven comes some day to an end. This change, Buddha declared, is sorrowful. And until you realize Nirvana you are subject to birth and death. Eternal changefulness in evolution becomes eternal rest. The constantly dissipating energy is concentrated in Nirvanic life. There is no more birth, no more death. It is eternal peace. On earth the purified, perfected man enjoys Nirvana, and after the dissolution of the physical body there is no birth in an objective world. The gods see him not, nor does man.

The Attainment of Salvation. It is by the perfection of self through charity, purity, self-sacrifice, self-knowledge, dauntless energy, patience, truth, resolution, love, and equanimity that the goal is realized. The final consummation is Nirvana.

The Glorious Freedom of Self—the last words of Buddha. "Be lamps unto yourselves. Be ye a refuge to yourselves. Betake yourself to no external refuge. Hold fast to the truth as a lamp. Hold fast as a refuge to the truth. Look not for refuge to any one besides yourselves. Learn ye then, O Bhikshus, that knowledge have I attained and have declared unto you, and walk ye in it, practice and increase, in order that this path of holiness may last and long endure, for the blessing of many people to the relief of the world, to the welfare, the blessing, the joy of gods and man. O Bhikshus, everything that cometh into being changeth. Strive on unceasingly for the consummation of the highest ideal."

SOYEN SHAKU, REPLY TO A CHRISTIAN CRITIC (1896)

A reform-minded abbot at the Engaku Monastery in Kamakura, Japan, and the first Zen missionary to America, Soyen Shaku (1859–1919) came to the United States in 1893 as a Rinzai Zen delegate to the World's Parliament of Religions. Because he did not speak English (his speeches were translated by D.T. Suzuki and read by Parliament organizer John Henry Barrows), Soyen did not make the same splash in Chicago as did

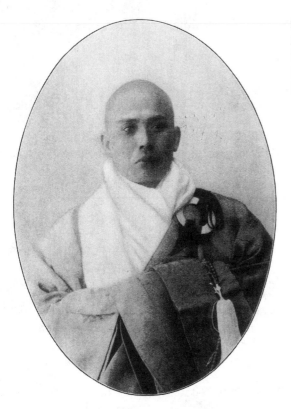

Soyen Shaku, from *Sermons of a Buddhist Abbot* (1906), the first book on Zen printed in the English language. Courtesy of Open Court Publishing Company.

Vivekananda and Dharmapala. Still he influenced the course of American Buddhism, largely through the work of disciples such as Nyogen Senzaki and D. T. Suzuki, both of whom came to the United States at his urging. Prompted by Buddhist sympathizer Paul Carus (who might have drafted portions of the letter himself), Soyen addressed this piece in 1896 to Barrows. Soyen takes his correspondent to task for misrepresenting Buddhism in a lecture Barrows delivered in January 1896 at the University of Chicago. He also holds Jesus up to the light of the Buddha and finds him wanting. Soyen's letter, written later in 1896, first appeared in *Open Court* in January 1897. It was later published in *Sermons of a Buddhist Abbot* (1906). A collection comprising largely the talks he delivered during an American lecture tour in 1905 and 1906, this was the first book on Zen published in the English language.

Dear Sir:

Friends in America have sent me a number of the *Chicago Tribune*, dated Monday, January 13, 1896, which contains the report of your second Haskell lecture, delivered at the Kent Theater in the Chicago University. The subject is

Soyen Shaku, *Sermons of a Buddhist Abbot* (Chicago: Open Court, 1906), 121–25. This book was later reprinted as *Zen for Americans* (La Salle, Ill.: Open Court, 1974). Reprinted by permission of Open Court Publishing Company, a division of Carus Publishing Company, Peru, Ill. Copyright © 1906 by Open Court Publishing Company.

"Christianity and Buddhism," and I anticipated a friendly and sympathetic treatment of Buddhism at your hands, for I do not doubt that you desire to be just in your judgment. Your utterances are of importance because they will be received as an impartial representation of our religion, since you, having been Chairman of the Religious Parliament, are commonly considered to have the best of information about those religions that were represented at this famous assemblage. I was greatly disappointed, however, seeing that you only repeat those errors which are common in the various Western books on Buddhism. You say, "The goal which made Buddha's teachings a dubious gospel, is Nirvana, which involves the extinction of love and life, as the going out of a flame which has nothing else to feed upon." Now the word *Nirvana* means "extinction" and it means the eradication of all evil desires, of all passions, of all egotism, so that the flame of envy, hatred, and lust will have nothing to feed upon. This is the negative side of Nirvana. The positive side of Nirvana consists in the recognition of truth. The destruction of evil desires, of envy, hatred, extinction of selfishness implies charity, compassion with all suffering, and a love that is unbounded and infinite. Nirvana means extinction of lust, not of love; extinction of evil, not of existence; of egotistic craving, not of life. The eradication of all that is evil in man's heart will set all his energies free for good deeds, and he is no genuine Buddhist who would not devote his life to active work, and a usefulness which would refuse neither his friends nor strangers, nor even his very enemies.

You say that "human life does not breathe, in Buddhism, the atmosphere of divine fatherhood, but groans under the dominion of inexorable and implacable laws." Now, I grant that Buddha taught the irrefragability of law, but this is a point in which, as in so many others, Buddha's teachings are in exact agreement with the doctrines of modern science. However, you ought to consider that while the law is irrefragable, no one but those who infringe upon it groan under it. He who understands the laws of existence, and especially the moral law that underlies the development of human society, will accommodate himself to it, and thus he will not groan under it, but in the measure that he is like Buddha he will be enlightened, he will be a master of the law and not a slave. In the same way that the ignorant savage is killed by the electric shock of lightning, while an electric engineer uses it for lighting the halls and streets of our cities, the immoral man suffers from the moral law, he groans under its inexorable and implacable decree, while the moral man enjoys it, and turning it to advantage glories in its boundless blessings.

This same moral law is the source of enlightenment and its recognition constitutes Buddhahood. This same moral law we call Dharmakaya, which is eternal, omnipresent, and all-glorious. We represent it under a picture of a father, and it was incarnated not only in Gautama-Buddha, but also in all great men in a higher or lesser degree, foremost among them in Jesus Christ, and, allow me to add, in George Washington, Abraham Lincoln, and other great men of your country. Allow me to add, too, that Buddha's doctrine, far from being skepticism, proclaims the doctrine that man *can* attain enlightenment and that he attains it not only through study and learning, which, as a matter of course, are indispensable, but also and mainly through *the earnest exertions of a life of purity and holiness.*

There are many more points in your lecture which I feel tempted to discuss with you, but they refer more to Christianity than to Buddhism, and may imply a misunderstanding of Christian doctrines on my part. I am anxious to know all that is good in Christianity and the significance of your dogmas, so that I may grow in a comprehension of truth, but I have not as yet been able to see that mankind can be benefited by believing that Jesus Christ performed miracles. I do not deny the miracles nor do I believe them; I only claim that they are irrelevant. The beauty and the truth of many of Christ's sayings fascinate me, but truth does not become clearer by being pronounced by a man who works miracles. You say that, "We explain Buddha without the miracles which later legends ascribe to him, but we cannot explain Christ—either his person or his influence—without granting the truth of his own claim that he did the supernatural works of his father." We may grant that Jesus Christ is the great master and teacher that appeared in the West after Buddha, but the picture of Jesus Christ as we find it in the Gospel is marred by the accounts of such miracles as the great draft of fishes, which involves a great and useless destruction of life (for we read that the fishermen followed Jesus, leaving the fish behind), and by the transformation of water into wine at the marriage-feast at Cana. Nor has Jesus Christ attained to the calmness and dignity of Buddha, for the passion of anger overtook him in the temple, when he drove out with rope in hand those that bargained in the holy place.

How different would Buddha have behaved under similar conditions in the same place! Instead of whipping the evil-doers he would have converted them, for kind words strike deeper than the whip.

I do not dare to discuss the statements you make about Christianity, for fear that I may be mistaken, but I am open to conviction and willing to learn.

I hope you will not take offense at my frank remarks, but I feel that you, if any one in Christendom, ought to know the real teachings of Buddha, and we look to you as a leader who will make possible the way for a better understanding between all the religions of the world, for I do not doubt that as you unknowingly misrepresent the doctrines of the Tathagata, so we may misunderstand the significance of Christianity. We shall be much obliged to you if in justice to the religion of Buddha you will make public this humble protest of mine, so that at least the most important misconceptions and prejudices that obtain among Christians may be removed.

I remain, with profound respect,

Your obedient servant,
Soyen Shaku

Kamakura, Japan

CHAPTER **8**

Turning East: Sympathizers and Converts

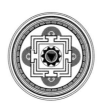

HENRY STEEL OLCOTT, *OLD DIARY LEAVES*
AND *THE BUDDHIST CATECHISM* (1900, 1881)

The first American formally to convert to Buddhism, Henry Steel Olcott (1832–1907), was born into a Presbyterian household in Orange, New Jersey, in 1832. But he embraced spiritualism as a young man, and soon he was championing myriad social reforms, including temperance, antislavery, women's rights, cremation, and agricultural, educational, and civil service reform. In 1874, while reporting on spiritualism for the New York *Daily Graphic*, Olcott met Helena Petrovna Blavatsky, a Russian occultist who gradually introduced him to the esoteric truths of "ancient wisdom." One year later in New York City, Olcott and "H. P. B." cofounded the Theosophical Society, which would serve as one of the most important conveners of America's Gilded Age meeting with Asian religions. The "theosophical twins," as Olcott and Blavatsky were called, moved themselves and their society to India in the winter of 1878–79. In 1880, on a trip to Ceylon (now Sri Lanka), they publicly embraced Buddhism in a ceremony described in Olcott's six-volume memoir, *Old Diary Leaves* (1895–1935). Soon Olcott was leading a revival of Buddhism in Ceylon and trying to knit Mahayana and Theravada Buddhists together into a "United Buddhist World." Olcott's *Buddhist Catechism* (1881), which helped to popularize in Ceylon a religious creole called "Protestant Buddhism," is divided into five parts. The first three—"The Life of the Buddha," "The Dharma or Doctrine," and "The Sangha"—reflect a traditional Theravada Buddhist emphasis on Buddha, Dharma, and Sangha. The last two—"The Rise and Spread of Buddhism" and

Henry Steele Olcott, *Old Diary Leaves: The History of the Theosophical Society* (Wheaton, Ill.: Theosophical Publishing House, 1974), 165–69; Henry S. Olcott, *The Buddhist Catechism*, 45th ed. Wheaton, Ill.: Theosophical Publishing House, 1970), 1–4, 109–12, 114. Both reprinted by permission of Theosophical Publishing House.

"Buddhism and Science"—reflect Olcott's interests in religious history and "occult science." These catechism selections come from the first and last chapters. They are preceded by a short *Old Diary Leaves* account of Olcott's pioneering conversion rite.

OLD DIARY LEAVES

. . . In a land of flowers and ideal tropical vegetation, under smiling skies, along roads shaded by clustering palm trees and made gay with miles upon miles of small arches and ribbon-like fringes of tender leaves, and surrounded by a glad nation, whose joy would have led them into the extravagance of actually worshipping us, if permitted, we passed from triumph to triumph, daily stimulated by the magnetism of popular love. The people could not do enough for us, nothing seemed to them good enough for us: we were the first white champions of their religion, speaking of its excellence and its blessed comfort from the platform, in the face of the Missionaries, its enemies and slanderers. It was that which thrilled their nerves and filled their affectionate hearts to bursting. I may seem to use strong language, but in reality it falls far short of the facts. If anybody seeks

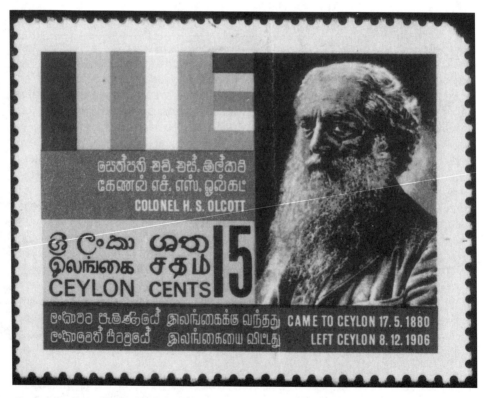

The "White Buddhist" Henry Steel Olcott as he appears on a commemorative stamp issued in Ceylon (now Sri Lanka) in 1967.

for proof, let him go through the lovely Island now, after fifteen years, and ask what they have to say about this tour of the two Founders and their party. . . .

As this visit of ours was the beginning of the second and permanent stage of the Buddhist revival begun by Megittuwatte, a movement destined to gather the whole juvenile Sinhalese population into Buddhist schools under our general supervision, even its details acquire a certain importance. . . .

On 25th May [1880], H. P. B. and I "took *pānsil*" from the venerable Bulatgama, at the temple of the Ramanya Nikāya, whose name at the moment escapes me, and were formally acknowledged as Buddhists. A great arch of greenery, bearing the words: "Welcome to the members of the Theosophical Society," had been erected within the compound of the Vihāra. We had previously declared ourselves Buddhists long before, in America, both privately and publicly, so that this was but a formal confirmation of our previous professions. H. P. B. knelt before the huge statue of the Buddha, and I kept her company. We had a good deal of trouble in catching the Pāli words that we were to repeat after the old monk, and I don't know how we should have got on if a friend had not taken his place just behind us and whispered them *seriatim*. A great crowd was present and made the responses just after us, a dead silence being preserved while we were struggling through the unfamiliar sentences. When we had finished the last of the *Sīlas*, and offered flowers in the customary way, there came a mighty shout to make one's nerves tingle, and the people could not settle themselves down to silence for some minutes, to hear the brief discourse which, at the Chief Priest's request, I delivered. I believe that attempts have been made by some of my leading colleagues of Europe and America to suppress this incident as much as possible, and cover up the fact that H. P. B. was as completely accepted a Buddhist as any Sinhalese in the Island. This mystification is both dishonest and useless, for, not only did several thousand persons, including many *bhikkus*, see and hear her taking the *pānsil*, but she herself boldly proclaimed it in all quarters. But to be a regular Buddhist is one thing, and to be a debased modern Buddhist sectarian quite another. Speaking for her as well as for myself, I can say that if Buddhism contained a single dogma that we were compelled to accept, we would not have taken the *pānsil* nor remained Buddhists ten minutes. Our Buddhism was that of the Master-Adept Gautama Buddha, which was identically the Wisdom Religion of the Aryan Upanishads, and the soul of all the ancient world-faiths. Our Buddhism was, in a word, a philosophy, not a creed.

THE BUDDHIST CATECHISM

Part I. The Life of the Buddha

1. *Question.* *Of what religion[1] are you?*
   Answer. The Buddhist.

---

[1]The word *religion* is most inappropriate to apply to Buddhism which is not a religion, but a moral philosophy, as I have shown later on. But by common usage the word has been

2.   Q.   *What is Buddhism?*

         A.   It is a body of teachings given out by the great personage known as the Buddha. . . .

9.   Q.   *Was the Buddha God?*

         A.   No. Buddha Dharma teaches no "divine" incarnation.

10.   Q.   *Was he a man?*

         A.   Yes; but the wisest, noblest and most holy being, who had developed himself in the course of countless births far beyond all other beings, the previous Buddhas alone excepted. . . .

Part V. Buddhism and Science

323.   Q.   *Has Buddhism any right to be considered a scientific religion, or may it be classified as a "revealed" one?*

         A.   Most emphatically it is not a revealed religion. The Buddha did not so preach, nor is it so understood. On the contrary, he gave it out as the statement of eternal truths, which his predecessors had taught like himself. . . .

325.   *Do Buddhists accept the theory that everything has been formed out of nothing by a Creator?*

         A.   The Buddha taught that two things are causeless, namely Akāsha and Nirvāna. Everything has come out of Akāsha, in obedience to a law of motion inherent in it, and, after a certain existence, passes away. Nothing ever came out of nothing. We do not believe in miracles; hence we deny creation, and cannot conceive of a creation of something out of nothing. Nothing organic is eternal. Everything is in a state of constant flux, and undergoing change and reformation, keeping up the continuity according to the law of evolution. . . .

329.   Q.   *Should Buddhism be called a chart of science or a code of morals?*

         A.   Properly speaking, a pure moral philosophy, a system of ethics and transcendental metaphysics. It is so eminently practical that the Buddha kept silent when Malunka asked about the origin of things. . . .

332.   Q.   *Is anything said about the body of the Buddha giving out a bright light?*

---

applied to all groups of people who profess a special moral doctrine, and is so employed by statisticians. The Sinhalese Buddhists have never yet had any conception of what Europeans imply in the etymological construction of the Latin root of this term. In their creed there is no such thing as a "binding" in the Christian sense—a submission to or merging of self in a Divine Being. . . . With this explanation, I continue to employ under protest the familiar word when speaking of Buddhistic philosophy, for the convenience of the ordinary reader. [Footnote in original.]

       A.   Yes, there was a divine radiance sent forth from within by the power of his holiness. . . .

340.   *How is it described?*

       A.   As a halo of a fathom's depth.

341.   *Q.*   *What do the Hindus call it?*

       A.   *Tejas:* its extended radiance they call *Prakāsha.*

342.   *Q.*   *What do Europeans call it now?*

       A.   The human aura.

SISTER CHRISTINE, "MEMORIES OF SWAMI VIVEKANANDA" (1945)

Christine Greenstidel was in many respects a typical American convert to Vedanta. Most early American Vedantists were women, many were foreign born, and a good number came to Hinduism out of alternative religious traditions such as Theosophy, New Thought, and Christian Science. But Greenstidel was atypical in one respect: she did not come from money. An early disciple of Swami Vivekananda, Greenstidel was born in Germany but came to the United States in 1869 at the age of three. Raised in poverty, she worked while a young adult as a schoolteacher. She also practiced Christian Science. In 1894, however, she encountered her guru in Detroit, and eight years later she moved to India to work with the Ramakrishna Mission. In Baghbazar, India, she and Margaret Noble (an important British Vedantist also known as Sister Nivedita) cofounded the Sister Nivedita Girl's School. "Sister Christine," as Greenstidel was now known, went back to the United States in 1914 but returned to her adopted Indian homeland in 1923. She died in New York in 1930. This memoir of her life with her guru provides an unusually intimate picture of Swami Vivekananda's charismatic (and controversial) appeal to American women, and of the allure of the *Advaita Vedanta* Hindu teaching of "the divinity of man."

Little did I think when I reluctantly set out one cold February night in 1894 to attend a lecture at the Unitarian church in Detroit that I was doing something which would change the whole course of my life. . . . The forceful, virile figure which stepped upon the platform was unlike the emaciated, ascetic type which is generally associated with spirituality in the West. A sickly saint everyone understands, but who ever heard of a powerful saint? The power that emanated from this mysterious being was so great that one all but shrank from it. It was overwhelming. It threatened to sweep everything before it. This one sensed even in those first unforgettable moments.

Later we were able to see this power at work. It was the mind that made the first great appeal, that amazing mind! What can one say that will give even a faint idea of its majesty, its glory, its splendor? It was a mind so far transcending other

Sister Christine, "Memories of Swami Vivekananda," in Christopher Isherwood, ed., *Vedanta for Modern Man* (New York: Harper, 1945), 134–52. Reprinted by permission of Vedanta Press.

minds, even of those who rank as geniuses, that it seemed different in its very nature. Its ideas were so clear, so powerful, so transcendental that it seemed incredible that they could have emanated from the intellect of a limited human being. Yet marvelous as the ideas were and wonderful as was that intangible something that flowed out from the mind, it was strangely familiar. I found myself saying, *"I have known that mind before."* Vivekananda burst upon us in a blaze of reddish gold, which seemed to have caught and concentrated the sun's rays. He was barely thirty, this preacher from faraway India. Young with an ageless youth and yet withal old with the wisdom of ancient times. For the first time we heard the age-old message of India, teaching of the Atman, the true Self.

The audience listened spellbound while he wove a fabric as glowing and full of color as a beautiful Kashmir shawl. Now a thread of humor, now one of tragedy, many of serious thought, many of aspiration, of lofty idealism, of wisdom. Through it all ran the woof of India's most sacred teaching: the divinity of man, his innate and eternal perfection; that this perfection is not a growth nor a gradual attainment, but a present reality. *That thou art.* You are that now. There is nothing to do but realize it. The realization may come now in the twinkling of an eye, or in a million years, but "all will reach the sunlit heights." This message has well been called "the wondrous evangel of the Self." We are not the helpless limited beings which we think ourselves to be, but birthless, deathless, glorious children of immortal bliss.

Like the teachers of old, Vivekananda too spoke in parables. The theme was always the same—man's real nature. Not what we seem to be, but what we *are.* We are like men walking over a gold mine, thinking we are poor. We are like the lion who was born in a sheepfold and thought he was a sheep. When the wolf came he bleated with fear, quite unaware of his true nature. Then one day a lion came, and seeing him bleating among the sheep called out to him, "You are not a sheep. You are a lion. You have no fear." The lion at once became conscious of his nature and let out a mighty roar. . . .

Which of us who heard Vivekananda then can ever forget what soul memories were stirred within us when we heard the ancient message of India: "Hear ye, children of immortal bliss, even ye who dwell in higher spheres, I have found the Ancient One, knowing whom alone ye shall be saved from death ever again." Was it possible to hear and feel this and ever be the same again? All one's values were changed. The seed of spirituality was planted to grow and grow throughout the years until it inevitably reached fruition. . . . We knew we had found our teacher. The word *guru* we did not know then. Nor did we meet him personally, but what matter? It would take years to assimilate what we had already learned. And then the master would somehow, somewhere, teach us again!

It happened sooner than we expected; for in a little more than a year, we found ourselves at Thousand Island Park in the very house with him. It must have been the 6th of July, 1895, that we had the temerity to seek him out. . . .

Of all the wonderful weeks that followed, it is difficult to write. Only if one's mind were lifted to that high state of consciousness in which we lived for the time, could one hope to recapture the experience. We were filled with joy. We did not know at that time that we were living in the man's radiance. On the wings of inspiration, he carried us to the height which was his natural abode. He himself, speaking of it later, said that he was at his best at Thousand Islands. Then he felt that he had found the channel through which his message might be spread, the way to fulfill his mission, for the guru had found his own disciples. Swamiji's first overwhelming desire was to show us the path to *mukti*, to set us free. "Ah," he said with touching pathos, "if I could only set you free with a touch!" His second object, not so apparent perhaps, but always in the undercurrent, was to train this group to carry on the work in America. "This message must be preached by Indians in India, and by Americans in America," he said. . . .

The training Swamiji gave was individualistic and unique. Unless the desire for discipleship was definitely expressed, and unless he was convinced that the aspirant was ready for the step, he left the personal life of those around him untouched. . . . But once one accepted him as a guru, all that was changed. He felt responsible. He deliberately attacked foibles, prejudices, valuations—in fact everything that went to make up the personal self. Did you in your immature enthusiasm see the world as beautiful and believe in the reality of good and the unreality of evil? He was not long in destroying all your fine illusions. If good is real, so is evil. Both are different aspects of the same thing. Both good and evil are in maya. Do not hide your head in the sand and say, "All is good, there is no evil." Worship the terrible even as now you worship the good. Then get beyond both. Say, "God is the only reality". . . .

Swami refused to solve our problems for us. Principles he laid down, but we ourselves must find the application. He encouraged no spineless dependence upon him in any form, no bid for sympathy. "Stand upon your own feet. You have the power within you!," he thundered. His whole purpose was not to make things easy for us but to teach us how to develop our innate strength. "Strength! Strength!," he cried. "I preach nothing but strength. That is why I preach the *Upanishads*." From men he demanded manliness and from women the corresponding quality for which there is no word. Whatever it is, it is the opposite of self-pity, the enemy of weakness and indulgence. The attitude had the effect of a tonic. Something long dormant was aroused and with it came strength and freedom. . . .

Then we found that this man whom we had set up in our minds as an exalted being did not observe the conventions of our code. All fine men reverence womanhood; the higher the type, the greater the reverence. But here was one who gave no heed to the little attentions which ordinary men paid us. We were allowed to climb up and slide down the rocks without an extended arm to help us. When he sensed our feeling he answered, as he so often did, our unspoken thought. "If you were old or weak or helpless, I should help you. But you are quite able to jump across this brook or climb this path without help. You are as able as I am. Why should I help you? Because you are a woman? That is chivalry, and don't you see that chivalry is only sex? Don't you see what is behind all these attentions from men to women?" Strange as it may seem, with these words came a new idea of what true reverence for womanhood means. And yet, he it was, who, wishing to get the blessing of the one who is called the Holy Mother, the wife and disciple of Sri Ramakrishna, sprinkled Ganges water all the way so that he might be purified when he appeared in her presence. She was the only one to whom he revealed his intention. Without her blessing, he did not wish to go to the West. Never did he approach her without falling prostrate at her feet. Did he not worship God as Mother? Was not every woman to him a manifestation in one form or another of the Divine Mother? . . . Knowing the criticism that awaited him in India, he still dared in America to initiate into *sannyas* a woman, for he saw in her only the sexless Self.

PAUL CARUS, *THE DHARMA* (1898)

Paul Carus (1852–1919) once described himself as "a religious parliament incarnate." Because of his conviction that he was as Christian and Taoist as he was Buddhist, he never formally converted to Buddhism, but he was the most influential Buddhist sympathizer in Gilded Age America. The son of a Reformed minister in Germany, he earned a doctorate in Tübingen in 1876 before coming to the United States in 1884. In 1887, he took the helm at Open Court Publishing Company. Soon he was editing *The Monist* and *Open Court*, and tilting both toward what he called the "Religion of Science." At

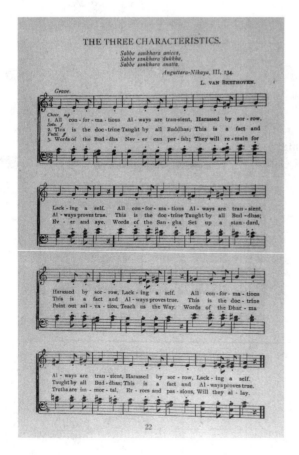

Sheet music for "The Three Characteristics" (*anicca*, or transiency; *dukkha,* or suffering; and *anatta,* or no-self) from Paul Carus's *Buddhist Hymns* (1911). Lyrics by Carus, music by German composer Ludwig van Beethoven. Courtesy of Open Court Publishing Company.

the World's Parliament of Religions in 1893, he befriended two important Buddhists: Soyen Shaku of Japan and Anagarika Dharmapala of Ceylon. Within a few years, Soyen's disciple, D. T. Suzuki, was working for Open Court, and Dharmapala was on a cross-country lecture tour facilitated by Carus. Convinced that Buddhism would thrive in the modern West only if it adapted to Western circumstances, Carus presented Buddhism as a philosophical and ethical system fully in accord with reason and science. The Buddha, he wrote, was "the first radical freethinker." Though Carus agreed with the Theosophists on the essential unity of religions, he had little sympathy for "esoteric Buddhism." He wrote more than sixty books, most notably *The Gospel of Buddha* (1894). In *The Dharma* (1898), Carus the committed rationalist provides a concise statement of his interpretation of Buddhism as rooted in reason rather than revelation. Nonetheless, he draws parallels between Buddhist philosophy and Christian theology. Carus's interpretations significantly influenced Suzuki's later views of Zen, and, through Suzuki, the views of millions of others in both America and Japan.

The following explanations will serve to remove some of the most important misconceptions:

1. Buddhism has no dogmas and is not based upon a revelation in the sense in which the words "dogma" and "revelation" are commonly used. Every Buddhist is free to investigate for himself the facts from which the Buddhist doctrines have been derived. Buddha had no other revelation than the experience which every human being is confronted with; however, he had a deeper insight into the nature of things than any other man, and could, therefore, trace the cause of evil and propose a remedy.
2. A conflict between religion and science is impossible in Buddhism. According to Buddha's injunctions we must accept all propositions which have been proved to be true by careful scientific investigation. Buddha taught only those truths which are necessary for salvation; yet it is noteworthy that modern psychology, as worked out by the most advanced western scientists who have heard little of Buddha, confirm Buddha's doctrines of the soul.
3. Buddhism is commonly said to deny the existence of the soul. This statement is correct or incorrect according to the sense in which the word soul is used. Buddhism denies the reality of the selfhood of the soul. It denies the existence of a soul-substratum, of a metaphysical soul-entity behind the soul; but not of the feeling, thinking, aspiring soul, such as from experience we know ourselves to be. To deny the existence of the soul in the latter sense would be a denial of the surest facts of the existence of which we have the most direct and most reliable knowledge.

Paul Carus, *The Dharma or the Religion of Enlightenment: An Exposition of Buddhism*, 4th ed. (Chicago: Open Court, 1898), 45–50. Reprinted by permission of Open Court Publishing Company, a division of Carus Publishing Company, Peru, Ill.

4. Buddhism does not propose the doctrine of the annihilation of the soul in death, but teaches the continuance of the soul in reincarnations according to the deeds done during life, which is called the law of Karma.

Enlightenment is the cessation of ignorance, not of thinking; the suppression of lust, not of love; the quiescence of passion, not of life.

Nirvana is not self-annihilation, but the extinction of sin; it is not non-existence, but the destruction of selfishness; it is not dissolution into nothing, but the attainment of truth; it is not resignation, but bliss.

5. Buddhism is commonly said to deny the existence of God. This, too, is true or not true, according to the definition of God. While Buddhists do not believe that God is an individual being like ourselves they recognize that the Christian God-idea contains an important truth, which, however, is differently expressed in Buddhism. Buddhism teaches that Bodhi, or Sambodhi, or Amitabha,[2] i.e., that which gives enlightenment, or, in other words those verities the recognition of which is Nirvana (constituting Buddhahood), is omnipresent and eternal. Bodhi is that which conditions the economic order of the world and the uniformities of reality. Bodhi is the everlasting prototype of truth, partial aspects of which are formulated by scientists in the various laws of nature. Above all, Bodhi is the basis of the Dharma; it is the foundation of religion; it is the objective reality in the constitution of being from which the good law of righteousness is derived; it is the ultimate authority for moral conduct.

6. Buddhism is not pessimism. Buddhism, it is true, boldly and squarely faces the problem of evil, and recognizes the existence of evil; but it does so in order to show to mankind the way of escape. Buddhism does not preach annihilation, but salvation; it does not teach death, but life. Buddhism would abolish lust, not love; it does not enjoin asceticism or self-mortification, but preaches the right way of living; its aim is Nirvana, the abandonment of selfhood and the leading of a life of truth, which is attainable here upon earth in this life of ours.

7. Buddhists do not believe that they alone are in possession of truth, and hail truth and purity wherever they find it, be it in the prophets of Israel, in the New Testament, or in the Dharmapada. We read in the twelfth edict of Ashoka: "There ought to be reverence for one's own faith and no reviling of that of others."

8. While Buddhists would not accept dogmas which stand in contradiction to science, they gladly recognize many remarkable resemblances of their own faith with other religions; especially the ethics of Christ are truly elevating and remind Buddhists of the noble injunctions of Buddha.

9. Buddhists are all those who, like Buddha, seek salvation in enlightenment. There are Buddhists who officially join the Buddhist brotherhood

---

[2]*Bodhi* (wisdom), *Sambodhi* (perfect wisdom), *Amitabha* (infinite light), remind one of the Christian term *Logos*, word, and the Chinese *Tao*, word, path, reason. [Footnote in original.]

by voluntarily taking the vows with the purpose of leading a life of perfect holiness. There are others who by a solemn pronunciation of the refuge-formula join the Buddhist Church as lay-members, and lay members may, equally with those who have taken the vows, attain the bliss of salvation. In addition there are unconscious followers of Buddha who without any external connection with Buddhist communities accept the truths of Buddhism, and walk in the noble eightfold path.

MARIE DE SOUZA CANAVARRO, *INSIGHT INTO THE FAR EAST* (1925)

Marie Canavarro (1849–1933), or "Sister Sanghamitta" as she was known in the press, was the second American and first woman of European descent to ritually declare her Buddhist allegiance on U.S. soil. She did that in a public ceremony in New York City in 1897, with the Sinhalese Buddhist Anagarika Dharmapala officiating. Although obscure today, Canavarro was a minor celebrity in 1900 and 1901; she lectured as an authoritative representative of Buddhism in San Francisco, Chicago, and New York. In later years she went on to speak for other religions too. A restless former Roman Catholic, Canavarro moved from one tradition to the next seeking a broader and more inclusive faith, one that elevated women and reconciled religions. Her spiritual journey took her from Catholicism to Theosophy to Buddhism to Baha'i to Hinduism. By the time her autobiography appeared in 1925, she had embraced the Vedanta Hinduism taught at Swami Paramananda's Ananda Ashrama in California. In this autobiographical narrative, she retraces every twist and turn in her spiritual journey. Near the start of the book she explains her 1890s conversion to Buddhism. Later she recalls her sea journey to Asia in 1897, describing her plan to work at a Buddhist school for girls in Ceylon, a part of the "noble and useful and sacrificing work" that she yearned for when she was a bored diplomat's wife in Honolulu. Canavarro labored at that school for several years. She then returned to the United States to lecture about Buddhism, and to continue her spiritual journey.

HOW I CAME TO EMBRACE BUDDHISM

I was reared in the Roman Catholic faith, but never thoroughly espoused it, though I loved going to mass, especially to the Cathedral: the quiet solemnity of the services, the soft coloring, the sublime music, all appealing to my mystic temperament.

An unsatisfying craving for something, I knew not what, pursued me. I sought a solution in many ways. First, I took up philanthropic work, then the study of the different sciences.

Marie de Souza Canavarro, *Insight into the Far East* (Los Angeles: Wetzel Publishing Company, 1925), 13–15, 35–36.

I observed greed, selfishness, and deceit everywhere and in every sphere of life; it seemed to me one could not succeed in the feverish life of the world without pulling another down. Everything was unreal, artificial, my own life no less so than others. Sometimes the emptiness of my life appalled me; at such times I turned to religion, but found no comfort. Those who profess to live the most pious lives were, upon the whole, the most egotistical and selfish people; they were incessantly wrangling over creeds. The prevalent idea of God given by the early Protestant teachers, and still held as a cornerstone of orthodox theology, confused rather than gave peace. I studied and searched deeply, but everywhere the same old platitudes met me; then my soul cried out, "Can I ever find answers to my longings?" Thus my mind rocked back and forth.

Many and many a time in the midst of some gaiety I was overcome by thoughts, too weighty for the moment, and I longed to be out of the stifling atmosphere of the pleasure, to be far away from it all, doing some noble, useful and sacrificing work.

About this time I read a little book entitled *Ben-Hur*, by Lew Wallace; doubtless my readers know it. This little book braced up my sinking courage for a short time. In its pages Jesus Christ, the man, came nearer; and as the man came nearer, so did God. In itself, the Christ legend is a simple little narrative, but so full of human passion, human sorrow and suffering, that it appealed to my soul.

At this time, I was living in Honolulu. There were many poor immigrants constantly coming to the island, and among whom there was so much suffering. I thought it was a good opportunity to embark in charitable work, so I began visiting these homes of squalor, filth and misery, taking with me food and other necessaries.

I used to go from the homes of the wealthy to those of squalor. There I found children, tiny babes whose eyelids were eaten away by mosquitoes; little ones crying with hunger, cheerless and forlorn. Seeing this I began to question God's mercy.

After weighing the question spiritually on the one hand, technically and physically on the other, I finally concluded that the task of solving the mystery of God's love and of the hereafter was beyond my power of understanding. I gave up seeking phenomena and turned inward to the numen. The study of numina led me back to phenomena and then I began to study nature. To do this I retired from society for three years till I had learned to listen to nature's voice—the music of spheres. The contemplation of nature led me to take up a systematic study of the sciences—especially chemistry and astronomy. These studies opened to my mind a vista heretofore unfathomed.

One thing still troubled me: Look wherever I might, into the bowels of the earth or into the vast ocean, into space, everywhere, there was one unwavering law, namely, that one life was sustained by the sacrifice of another. In the waters greater life fed upon the lesser; on land and in space the same law prevailed—it was ever the survival of the fittest. Even man, whom God is said to have made after his own likeness, supported life by killing and consuming other lives.

At last I left the silence which had meant so much to me during the last three years and came from my retreat. I sought kindred spirits, whom I found in the Theosophical Society.

Through connection with this fraternity, I came to know a Buddhist from Ceylon. I told him of my long search for truth, and explained that I had not yet found what I had been seeking. He then told me of the Buddha and his long search for truth. He spoke no ill of anyone, and had sympathy for everything that lived. I became interested, and commenced the study of Buddha's scriptures. In these I came to know the meaning of Christ and that many Christs had lived before Jesus, even before time was, and would live when time had ceased to be. That Truth (as Buddha called God) was above reality; that there was a divine law of cause and effect which balanced good and evil and that this law can be reasoned out, also pointing the way to reach this understanding, and that moreover there was nothing preventing any mortal from attaining the same goal, but that the Self, which through ignorance had caused the world often to err, had brought suffering even to the innocent.

I now knew that I never understood the true teachings of Christ Jesus and that but few have done so. How can the Occident understand the subtle mind of the Orient, without knowing the Orient? And Jesus of Nazarene was an Oriental. The error of the present teachings of Christianity lies with those who teach the doctrine. They are too unyielding and ununited.

The study of Buddhist scriptures satisfied my craving for Truth and led me to embrace that religion and venerate that concept of my relation to things about me.

ON THE STEAMER FOR CEYLON

Oct.—

Weather pleasant, sea smooth. This morning while I was sitting in the salon a Ceylonese lady came and sat beside me and began a conversation. In reply to her questions I told her who I was, and where I was going and some of my immediate plans. She is a native of Ceylon she said and a Christian, though her husband is a Hindoo. There were, she said, many philosophies and creeds even in Ceylon; the people were divided and there was much inharmony among them. She also told me of the degraded condition of the so-called Buddhist devotees; they were ignorant, dirty and shiftless, despised by the people as common beggars; and that they became devotees only when too old or too lazy to work.

All this was rather discouraging; first the degraded condition of the Upasakas; then the caste system is in itself a great evil, raising a wall, which prevents the true understanding of brotherly love. With so many creeds the followers of each believing firmly in their own, and with the immobility of the Hindoos' nature there is not a very bright prospect ahead of me for my work among these people.

It is slowly presenting itself to my mind that I ought to do something for this poor despised class calling themselves Buddhist devotees. One cannot ignore such a class; something should make their lives more useful and decent. I have thought out many plans of work of which one seems the most feasible. These women might be made useful by inducing them to help in the care of little children left homeless by their parents.

An institution where little girls of the people could be brought together and taught useful arts, such as housekeeping, needlework, and be trained in the habits of cleanliness. Besides receiving a rudimentary education, in their own language, would be a great benefit to these people.

WILLIAM STURGIS BIGELOW TO KWANRYO NAOBAYASHI (1895)

American intellectuals traveled to Japan starting in the 1870s, and among them were William Sturgis Bigelow (1850–1926) and Ernest Francisco Fenollosa (1851–1903). Some of the first Americans to practice Buddhism in Asia, these two aesthetically-inclined Bostonians lived in Japan for years (Bigelow stayed seven years and Fenollosa fifteen) and then returned to shape literature and the arts in America. Together they received the precepts of Tendai Buddhism on 21 September 1885 at Homoyoin Temple, a subtemple of the Tendai monastery where they had studied. Bigelow delivered the Ingersoll Lecture at Harvard on Buddhism and immortality in 1908, but he wrote less about the tradition than his friends had hoped he would. He is remembered as one of the elite "Boston Buddhists," but his greatest significance might be as a patron and collector of East Asian art. It was in that capacity that he received from the Japanese government the decoration of the Third Order of the Rising Sun, the highest honor bestowed on a foreigner. Fenollosa, a poet and student of Asian art, made an even greater mark on the arts in America. Like Bigelow, Fenollosa donated objects to the Boston Museum of Fine Arts, where he served as curator of the Oriental collection. These American Buddhists, who were inspired by the Romantic movement and animated by a love of Japanese culture, continued to have connections with Asia after they returned to the United States. In this letter written six years after he left Japan, Bigelow writes to the new chief priest of Homoyoin Temple in Japan. With his beloved teacher Keitoku Sakurai now dead, Bigelow seems unsure about how to continue his Tendai and Shingon Buddhist practice without temples or teachers nearby. In this letter and later ones, Bigelow poses a range of religious questions. He also offers information about Fenollosa and seeks help in guiding George Cabot Lodge (1873–1909), a young poet whom Bigelow had been tutoring in Buddhist doctrine and practice. Lodge, son of the senator from Massachusetts, continued to meditate and went on to write a poetic tribute to nirvana.

Boston, Mass, U.S.A.
April, 1895

Rt. Rev. Kwanryo Naobayashi
My dear Sir

It is with the greatest pleasure that I have received your kind letter, which contained many pleasant words for Prof. Fenollosa and myself.

William Sturgis Bigelow to Rt. Rev. Kwanryo Naobayashi, April 1895, in Akiko Murakata, *Selected Letters of Dr. William Sturgis Bigelow*, Ph.D. diss., The George Washington University, 1971 (Ann Arbor, Michigan: University Microfilms, 1971), 117–20. Reprinted by permission of Akiko Murakata.

William Sturgis Bigelow, Edward Morse, and Ernest Fenollosa donated vast collections of East Asian art to American museums. This portable Buddhist shrine, which the Boston Museum of Fine Arts gave to Salem's Peabody Essex Museum in 1914, is made of black lacquered wood with engraved brass fixtures. Inside is a polychrome image of the Bodhisattva Jizo. This lightweight shrine from Japan's Edo Period (1615–1867) was designed so a monk could carry it on his back. Courtesy of the Peabody Essex Museum, Salem, Massachusetts.

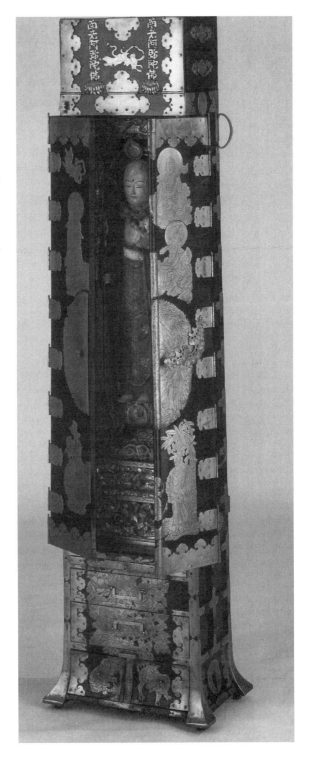

It is very long since I met you, and I am very glad to know that you still think of me sometimes.

I am always earnestly hoping to see you again, but have not been able to come to Japan. But I hope to come some day before this life is over.

In the year of the Chicago Fair, Mr. Machida kindly paid me a visit. It was a great honor to be visited by the first Buddhist priest who had ever come to Boston. Mr. Machida told me that you had become Jushoku [chief priest] of Homioin, which I was very glad to hear. Also, he told me more important news about you, in regard to which I respectfully congratulate you.—

Here, it is not so easy to practice as in Japan, because when something happens in practice there is no one to ask what it means. In Japan it was always easy to ask the Ajari.

But now I know you have a good translator, and I may perhaps trouble you with some questions, because I have had some difficulties that I cannot quite understand, and which seem to have come through trying to help other people.

But now that I am sure that the Rt. Rev. Chiman [head priest of Zuishin-in] and you are sometimes thinking of me, I shall begin practice again, with hope of improving.—

It is a matter of no importance, but I have also had some trouble in the world and in daily life since I came home, such as being ill for a long time, and of late I have been annoyed by a lawsuit, which is very soon to begin again.

But such things are not worth mentioning.

You will be glad to know that Prof. Fenollosa is well, and is still working at the Museum of Fine Art in Boston, and now is giving many public lectures on Japanese Art, which are of great value to people here.

Lately, I received a very well-written letter from Mr. Kakichi Ohara of Otsu. Do you know this gentleman? He speaks of taking the Kai with Prof. Fenollosa and myself. His letter is extremely good, and I should like to know more of him.—

It would be very pleasant if I could come to the Dempo-Kwancho-Kai [transmission ceremony] this spring but many things keep me here—especially this lawsuit. But perhaps next year I may be able to come to visit you, and shall be very glad to talk with you, and to pay my respects to the Rt. Rev. Chiman. I shall try to bring with me a young man who seems to have some talent for the study of Buppo [Buddhism], and who is very desirous to receive the Kai and Kwanjo [moral precepts]. I shall perhaps write more fully about him either to you or to the Rt. Rev. Chiman, before long.— He seems to be able to practice meditation very well, and finds no difficulty in leaving his body, and seems to enter the mushiki-kai [the formless world] quite easily, but cannot enter the world of Buddha because he has not been shown the path, and of course I am not far enough advanced to show it to him by giving him the Kai or by teaching him the Shingons. But, is not it possible for you or the Rt. Rev. Chiman to help him? Is there no ceremony to give the Kwai or the Kwanjo at a distance, so that you, in Japan, can give him some help while he is here in America? I should be very happy if this were possible.

With many thanks for your letter, and with kindest regards to the Rt. Rev. Chiman and yourself, I am very sincerely yours

W. Sturgis Bigelow

The death of our great teacher, Sakurai Ajari, was a great misfortune to us, to Buddhism, and to the whole world.

I always think of him with gratitude, reverence, and affection.

It sometimes seems to me that his kindness to me did not cease when he died.

I am very unworthy to say such a thing, but you will understand what I mean.

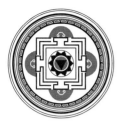

PART III

EXCLUSION, 1924 TO 1965

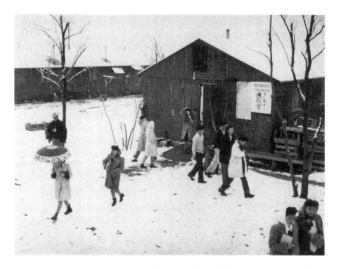

Japanese Americans interned during World War II exit a Buddhist Church at the Manzanar War Relocation Center in Manzanar, California. Photograph by Ansel Adams.

When the Indian poet Rabindranath Tagore arrived in Los Angeles for a lecture tour in 1929, immigration officials insulted him. Angelinos, full of the libel of Katherine Mayo's *Mother India* (1927) and the silver-screen images of the sinister Dr. Fu Manchu, treated him with suspicion. Rather than suffer these indignities, Tagore canceled his tour and left the country abruptly. But not before getting in a parting shot. "Jesus could not get into America," Tagore remarked, "because . . . he would be an Asiatic."[1]

Tagore was not the only "Asiatic" to endure the slings of public policy and the arrows of public opinion in the 1920s. In lawsuits in 1922 and 1923, the Supreme Court ruled that neither the Japanese nor Asian Indians were by law "white" persons eligible for citizenship. In 1924, the Asian Exclusion Act effectively cut off immigration from Asia. As Tagore discovered, it was difficult for Hindu and Buddhist teachers even to visit the United States, let alone settle there. And it was nearly impossible for lay people to make the passage through San Francisco's Angel Island.

Though the Asian Exclusion Act became law during the Roaring Twenties, it ushered in a period of quiescence in the history of Asian religions in the United States. In this period of exclusion, which lasted until 1965, the Chinese population fell, the Japanese population stagnated, and Asian-Indian immigration shrank to almost nothing. Buddhism, Hinduism, and other Asian religious traditions were set adrift. Although the Chinese Exclusion Act was repealed in 1943 and the Luce-Celler Bill of 1946 lifted India out of the Asiatic Barred Zone, immigration quotas for the Chinese and Asian Indians were so miniscule (roughly 100 per year for each nationality) that this legislation did little to reverse the demographic slide started in 1924.

As the Chinese who remained in the United States moved from rural to urban areas, and from small cities to big ones, many previously thriving Chinatowns declined, and many Chinese temples shut down. Inside the Japanese-American community, the Nisei generation rose to prominence. In its rush to the mainstream, this American-born and English-speaking cohort was more likely than the Japanese-born Issei generation to neglect the faiths of their fathers and mothers.

Holding fast to the religion of your Asian ancestors became far more than a threat to your American identity during World War II. It became a threat to your freedom. After the Japanese bombed Pearl Harbor on 7 December 1941, one of the first groups to be rounded up were Buddhist priests of Japanese descent. Before, during, and after the era of incarceration in wartime internment camps brought on by President Roosevelt's Executive Order 9066 of 1942, many Buddhists stopped practicing their faith for fear of being labeled anti-American. Others converted to Christianity in a show of patriotism. In 1944, leaders of the Buddhist Mission of North America—with forty-four temples in the early 1940s it was the largest Buddhist group in the United States during this period—met in the Topaz camp in Arizona and voted to rename their organization the Buddhist Churches of America. Their point was as plain as it was poignant: Japanese-American Buddhism was American Buddhism, and it deserved a place alongside Christianity at the table of American faiths.

The actions of Congress and the orders of President Roosevelt had a chilling effect on immigrant Buddhism and Hinduism between 1924 and 1965. But those same actions and orders provided an opportunity for non-Asian Americans to assume leading roles in the unfolding saga of Asian religions in America. In fact, Buddhism and Hinduism refused to fade away in this era because of the efforts of a handful of Asian-born teachers, on the one hand, and a small but influential group of their non-Asian converts and sympathizers on the other.

Consider the course of Buddhism in this period of exclusion. While Chinese temples shut down and the Buddhist Churches of America fought a war of attrition, Buddhism survived. And at least in its Zen form, it prospered among a new crop of "White Buddhists." Introduced in America by Rinzai Zen master Soyen Shaku at the World's Parliament of Religions in Chicago in 1893, Zen carved out a place for itself in many American cities in the twentieth century. After Rinzai Zen reformer Soyen Shaku contributed the first American book on Zen, *Sermons of a Buddhist Abbot* (1906), Nukariya Kaiten, a Soto Zen priest and a Harvard lecturer, contributed the second, *Religion of the Samurai*, in 1913. After these books came a series of Zen centers, attended almost entirely by the non-Asian converts and sympathizers who were buying Zen books. The peripatetic Nyogen Senzaki established Zen centers in San Francisco in 1925 and Los Angeles in 1931. Shigetsu Sakaki, also known as Sokei-an, incorporated the Buddhist Society of America (later renamed the First Zen Institute in America) in New York City in 1931. Meanwhile, D. T. Suzuki kept Zen on the minds of fashionable elites on the two coasts through a combination of lectures, books, and interpersonal contacts. His two series of *Essays in Zen Buddhism*, published in London in 1927 and 1933, were the most influential Zen texts in America in this period.

Largely because of Suzuki's efforts, Zen emerged after World War II as the Asian religion of choice among non-Asian Americans. W. Y. Evans-Wentz introduced a generation of Americans to the Vajrayana ("Diamond Vehicle") Buddhism of Tibet upon the publication of his *Tibetan Book of the Dead* (1927), but there were few Tibetan teachers around to transform whatever interest that book generated into serious practice inside Tibetan Buddhist communities. Dwight Goddard, author of the *Buddhist Bible* (1932) and founder of the Followers of Buddha (established 1934), tried to bring the rigors of Buddhist monasticism to the heartland of America, but his experiment failed. At least in this period, Americans were not prepared to do their Dharma before dawn. What they were eager for was a heavy dose of Zen humor and paradox: the free spirit of Eisai and the wandering of Dogen. Suzuki delivered that in lectures at Columbia and Harvard, in television interviews, and in profiles in *Vogue* and the *New Yorker*. The Beat Generation of the postwar decade embraced Zen (and other forms of Buddhism, including the "mind only" teachings of the Yogacara school of Mahayana) as an alternative to what it saw as the stultifying, and hypocritical, Judeo-Christian orthodoxy of Eisenhower's America. Thanks to the efforts of the Beats, Zen principles of freedom, naturalness, silence, and spontaneity made their way into American music, dance, painting, and literature. John Cage's "4'33," an avant-garde celebration of the chance sounds ever erupting out of silence (first performed in 1952), was informed by Zen, as was Jack Kerouac's *Dharma Bums*, which became upon its publication in 1958 as sure a symbol of hipster status as the white T-shirt or the James Dean scowl. Although Rinzai Zen dominated in this period, Soto Zen (which emphasized seated meditation over against the koan) also had a presence, most notably in the form of the San Francisco Zen Center, established by Shunryu Suzuki-roshi in 1961. No longer widely denounced as a heathen religion, Buddhism had become (once again, and not for the last time) trendy. "Zen Buddhism," *Time* magazine announced in 1958 (a sentiment it would echo in a cover article in 1997), "is growing more chic by the minute."[2]

While Zen thrived at least toward the end of this relatively placid period, Sikhism and Hinduism barely survived. Sikhs, who did not win non-Asian converts until the late 1960s, could not justify establishing a second American temple until the late 1940s, when they bought a Japanese Buddhist temple in El Centro, California (emptied, ironically, by wartime circumstances), and converted it into a *gurdwara*, or temple. Swami Vivekananda and his followers had established Vedanta societies in key American cities early in the century, but in this period many folded and others barely hung on. Meanwhile, a spate of European-American gurus like "Oom the Omnipotent" (a.k.a. Pierre Bernard) gave Hinduism a bad name. Not long after Swami Paramahansa Yogananda imported to America the kriya yoga teachings of the Yogoda Satsanga

Society of India (established 1917), his Self-Realization Fellowship (S.R.F.) passed the Vedanta Society as the most influential Hindu movement in the country. In 1937, *Self-Realization* magazine reported over 150,000 had been initiated into Yogananda's quick and easy path to God-consciousness—the "airplane route" in Swami-speak—but Yogananda's 1952 death devastated the S.R.F., which has not yet bounced back to its peak strength of an estimated 150 American centers.

American impressions of Asians and Asian religions improved somewhat over this period. The Chinese enjoyed a brief era of respect between the Japanese bombing of Pearl Harbor in 1941 and the Communist victory in China in 1949, but for much of the period they were viewed with suspicion or contempt. Mohandas Gandhi, by contrast, emerged as an international and American hero—a "Mahatma" or Great Soul—in the years leading up to Indian independence in 1947. The Fourteenth Dalai Lama (who would achieve his greatest fame in the 1990s) earned the respect of Americans and the cover of *Time* for his Gandhian perseverance before and after the Chinese takeover of Tibet in 1959. Finally, Maharishi Mahesh Yogi ascended to the status of "Guru to the Stars" after bringing his Hindu-based (but ostensibly nonreligious) technique of Transcendental Meditation to the United States in 1959. By reinforcing long-standing American stereotypes about the inscrutable spirituality of Asian holy men, Gandhi, the Dalai Lama, and the Maharishi helped set the stage for the eastward turn of the late sixties and early seventies. Things would be far easier in Los Angeles for martial artist Bruce Lee than they had been for Rabindranath Tagore.
S.R.P.

NOTES

1. Ronald Takaki, *Strangers from a Different Shore: A History of Asian Americans* (New York: Penguin Books, 1989), 298.

2. Quoted in Karin Higa, "From Enemy Alien to Zen Master: Japanese American Identity in California During the Postwar Period," in Jeffrey Wechsler, ed., *Asian Traditions/Modern Expressions: Asian American Artists and Abstraction, 1945–1970* (New York: Harry N. Abrams, 1997), 192.

CHAPTER 9

Closed Ports and
Open Camps

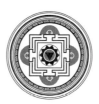

ASIAN EXCLUSION ACT (1924)

The Immigration Act of 1924 capped a series of legal restrictions of immigration begun with the Chinese Exclusion Act of 1882. In 1917, the United States Congress passed, over the veto of President Wilson, an immigration bill creating an Asiatic Barred Zone. This legislation effectively ended immigration from all of Asia except the Philippines (which was under American influence) and Japan (which continued to be subject to the Gentleman's Agreement of 1907–8). Commonly known as the Asian Exclusion Act, the Immigration Act of 1924 established a "national origins quota system" that included the Japanese among the supposedly unassimilable and, therefore, undesirable nonwesterners. This system, which would not be overturned until 1965, produced the intended effect. After 1924, Asian immigration declined precipitously. Not until the sixties would it match, and then wildly exceed, pre-1924 levels. But the act did more than curtail immigration. By cutting off the flow of both Asian teachers and lay practitioners, it severely restricted the development of Asian religions in the United States among immigrants and converts alike. More than any other event, the passage of this bill set Asian religions in America adrift, and ushered in the exclusionary era.

EXCLUSION FROM UNITED STATES

SECTION 13.

(a) No immigrant shall be admitted to the United States unless he (1) has an unexpired immigration visa or was born subsequent to the issuance of the im-

Eliot Grinnell Mears, *Resident Orientals on the American Pacific Coast: Their Legal and Economic Status* (Chicago: University of Chicago Press [1928]), 515.

migration visa of the accompanying parent, (2) is of the nationality specified in the visa in the immigration visa, (3) is a non-quota immigrant if specified in the visa in the immigration visa as such, and (4) is otherwise admissible under the immigration laws.

(b) In such classes of cases, and under such conditions as may be by regulations prescribed, immigrants who have been legally admitted to the United States and who depart therefrom temporarily may be admitted to the United States without being required to obtain an immigration visa.

(c) No alien ineligible to citizenship shall be admitted to the United States unless such alien (1) is admissible as a non-quota immigrant under the provisions of subdivision (b), (d), or (e) of Section 4, or (2) is the wife, or the unmarried child under 18 years of age, of an immigrant admissible under such subdivision (d) and is accompanying or following to join him, or (3) is not an immigrant as defined in Section 3.

(d) The Secretary of Labor may admit to the United States any otherwise admissible immigrant not admissible under clause (2) or (3) of subdivision (a) of this section, if satisfied that such inadmissibility was not known to, and could not have been ascertained by the exercise of reasonable diligence by, such immigrant prior to the departure of the vessel from the last port outside the United States and outside foreign contiguous territory, or, in the case of an immigrant coming from foreign contiguous territory, prior to the application of the immigrant for admission.

PRESIDENT FRANKLIN D. ROOSEVELT, EXECUTIVE ORDER 9066 (1942)

When President Franklin D. Roosevelt signed Executive Order 9066 on 19 February 1942 he authorized the Secretary of War to exclude people of Japanese ancestry from so-called "danger zones" on the West Coast. Over the next three years, the newly established War Relocation Authority (WRA) incarcerated more than 120,000 Japanese Americans in assembly centers, relocation camps, and internment camps as far east as Arkansas. Two-thirds of the detainees were American-born citizens. When the war ended in August 1945, 44,000 people were still interned, and not until 20 March 1946 was the last WRA camp shut down. Executive Order 9066 profoundly affected the Japanese-American Buddhist community. Virtually all ministers of the Buddhist Mission of North America (renamed the Buddhist Churches of America in 1944) were interned. In the 1970s and 1980s, the United States government revisited this painful issue. President Gerald Ford publicly apologized in 1976 for the government's actions. In 1981, the Commission on the Wartime Relocation and Internment of Civilians (CWRIC) concluded after exhaustive hearings that "a grave injustice" had been done to Japanese Americans because of "race prejudice, war hysteria and a failure of political leadership." In 1989, President George Bush signed a law allocating $20,000 to each living Japanese-American internee.

Whereas, The successful prosecution of the war requires every possible protection against espionage and against sabotage to national-defense material, national-defense premises and national-defense utilities. . . .

Now, therefore, By virtue of the authority vested in me as President of the United States, and Commander in Chief of the Army and Navy, I hereby authorize and direct the Secretary of War, and the Military Commanders whom he may from time to time designate, whenever he or any designated Commander deems such action necessary or desirable, to prescribe military areas in such places and of such extent as he or the appropriate Military Commander may determine, from which any or all persons may be excluded, and with respect to which, the right of any person to enter, remain in, or leave shall be subject to whatever restriction the Secretary of War or the appropriate Military Commander may impose in his discretion. The Secretary of War is hereby authorized to provide for residents of any such areas who are excluded therefrom, such transportation, food, shelter, and other accommodations as may be necessary, in the judgment of the Secretary of War or the said Military Commander, and until other arrangements are made, to accomplish the purpose of this order. The designation of military areas in any region or locality shall supersede designations of prohibited and restricted areas by the Attorney General under the Proclamations of December 7 and 8, 1941, and shall supersede the responsibility and authority of the Attorney General under the said Proclamations in respect of such prohibited and restricted areas.

I hereby further authorize and direct the Secretary of War and the said Military Commanders to take such steps as he or the appropriate Military Commander may deem advisable to enforce compliance with the restrictions applicable to each Military area hereinabove authorized to be designated, including the use of Federal troops and other Federal Agencies, with authority to accept assistance of state and local agencies.

I hereby further authorize and direct all Executive Departments, independent establishments and other Federal Agencies, to assist the Secretary of War or the said Military Commanders in carrying out this Executive Order, including the furnishing of medical aid, hospitalizations, food, clothing, transportation, use of land, shelter, and other supplies, equipment, utilities, facilities, and services.

This order shall not be construed as modifying or limiting in any way the authority heretofore granted under Executive Order 8972, dated December 12, 1941, nor shall it be construed as limiting or modifying the duty and responsibility of the Federal Bureau of Investigation, with respect to the investigations of alleged acts of sabotage or the duty and responsibility of the Attorney General and the Department of Justice under the Proclamations of December 7 and 8, 1941, prescribing regulations for the conduct and control of alien enemies, except as

President Franklin D. Roosevelt, "Executive Order No. 9066, Authorizing the Secretary of War to Prescribe Military Areas, February 19, 1942," in United States Army, *Final Report: Japanese Evacuation from the West Coast, 1942* (Washington: U.S. Government Printing Office, 1943), 26–27.

such duty and responsibility is superseded by the designation of military areas hereunder.

NYOGEN SENZAKI, *LIKE A DREAM, LIKE A FANTASY* (1978)

The life of Nyogen Senzaki (1876–1958) can be read as an extended meditation on the Buddhist teaching of impermanence. Senzaki was born in Siberia to a Japanese mother who died when he was a boy. After being raised by a series of mentors who educated him in the scripture and poetry of Japan and China, he became a pupil of Rinzai Zen master Soyen Shaku in 1896. For the next five years he studied at Soyen's Engaku Monastery. He followed Soyen to San Francisco in 1905, but, following his teacher's admonition to not "utter the B of Buddhism" for seventeen years, did not set himself up as an instructor until 1922. In that year, he began teaching in rented halls, leading what students called a floating zendo. More stable Zen centers under Senzaki's direction emerged in San Francisco in 1925 and Los Angeles in 1931. During World War II, Senzaki was incarcerated in a camp in Heart Mountain, Wyoming. There he established yet another floating zendo. He also wrote poetry. Some of Senzaki's Heart Mountain poems appear in a posthumous collection of his Zen writings called *Like a Dream, Like a Fantasy* (1978). They provide a haunting glimpse into the emotional and spiritual complexities of daily life in the camps, and into the paradoxical power of Zen's "empty fist."

Thus have I heard:
The army ordered
All Japanese faces to be evacuated
From the city of Los Angeles.
This homeless monk has nothing but a Japanese face.
He stayed here thirteen springs
Meditating with all faces
From all parts of the world.
And studied the teaching of Buddha with them.
Wherever he goes, he may form other groups
Inviting friends of all faces,
Beckoning them with the empty hands of Zen.
May 7, 1942

A swarm of demons infests the whole of humanity
It resembles the scenery of Gaya where Buddha fought his last battle to attain
      Realization.
We, Zen students in this internment, meditate today
To commemorate the Enlightened One.
We sit firmly in this Zendo while the cold wind of the plateau
Pierces to our bones.

Nyogen Senzaki, *Like a Dream, Like a Fantasy: The Zen Writings and Translations of Nyogen Senzaki* (Eido Shimano, ed.; Tokyo and New York: Japan Publications, 1978), 22–47. Copyright © 1978 The Zen Studies Society, Inc. Reprinted courtesy of Eido Tai Shimano-roshi.

All demons within us freeze to death.
No more demons exist in the snowstorm
Under the Mountain of Compassion.
December 6, 1942

Morning haze gives an illusion of California.
The east wind promises the coming of spring.
Within the snow-covered plateau of internment,
Evacuees can go no place else.
They can admire only the gorgeous sunrise
Beyond the barbed wire fence,
Above the hills and mountains.
January 1, 1943

Sons and daughters of the Sun are interned
In a desert plateau, an outskirt of Heart Mountain,
Which they rendered the Mountain of Compassion or Loving-kindness.
They made paper flowers to celebrate Vesak, the birthday of the Buddha.
"Above the heavens, beneath the earth, I alone am the World Honored One," said the
      baby Buddha,
Declaring the spirit of independence and self-respect of each sentient being of the world.
Hey! You! Stupid sagebrush and timid cactus!
Why don't you stretch out your green buds to answer the call of spring?
April 13, 1943

"In the spring garden of discipline,
Perseverance blooms its first flower."
So the Buddha said in his last teaching.
Hundred thousand brothers and sisters!
You have pined long enough.
The emancipation is not far from you.
February 13, 1944

An evacuee artist carved the statue of baby Buddha.
Each of us pours the perfumed warm water
Over the head of the newly born Buddha.
The cold spell may come to an end after this.
A few grasses try to raise their heads in the tardy spring,
While the mountain peaks put on and off
Their veils of white cloud.
April 9, 1944

Man makes enclosures by himself
When he thinks himself
Separated from other beings.
Bars as such should be taken off.
The sooner the better.
One hesitates and loses time in vain.
Nothing disturbs unselfish man
Who harmonizes with heaven and earth.
He goes freely like a floating cloud
Or running rivulet—
Without fighting.
January 7, 1945

On his deathbed
Buddha taught his disciples
To practice forbearance.
Man should act like the willow branches,
Which bend gently against the wind.
Three times we have commemorated
Buddha's Nirvana Day in this plateau.
We did not learn much during the past three years.
We are ready, however,
To face the world with equanimity,
Taking smilingly the snowstorm of abuse
As well as the sunshine of honeyed words.
Praise be to the Buddha, the Enlightened One.
February 18, 1945

Land of Liberty!
People of Independence!
The Constitution is beautiful.
It blooms like the spring flower.
It is the scripture by itself.
No foreign book can surpass it.
Like the baby Buddha,
Each of the people
Should point to heaven and earth, and say,
"America is the country of righteousness."
April 8, 1945

Fellow students:
Under Heart Mountain
We formed a Sangha for three years
And learned to practice
The wisdom of Avalokitesvara.
The gate of the barbed wire fence opens.
You are now free
To contact other students,
Who join you to save all sentient beings
From ignorance and suffering.
August 15, 1945

For forty years I have not seen
My teacher, Soyen Shaku, in person.
I have carried his Zen in my empty fist,
Wandering ever since in this strange land.
Being a mere returnee from the evacuation
I could establish no Zendo
Where his followers should commemorate
The twenty-sixth anniversary of his death.
The cold rain purifies everything on the earth
In the great city of Los Angeles, today.
I open my fist and spread the fingers
At the street corner in the evening rush hour.
October 29, 1945

SHIGEO KIKUCHI, *MEMOIRS OF A BUDDHIST WOMAN MISSIONARY IN HAWAII* (1991)

The U.S. government's wartime internment policy extended beyond the mainland to Hawaii, and it affected not only the individuals who were arrested, evacuated, and incarcerated, but also family members left behind. In her moving *Memoirs of a Buddhist Woman Missionary in Hawaii*, Shigeo Kikuchi describes how her life was changed and her Buddhist faith deepened during World War II. Kikuchi emigrated in 1914 from her homeland of Japan to Hawaii, where her husband, the Reverend Chikyoku Kikuchi, was serving as a minister in the Hompa Hongwanji mission of Jodo Shinshu ("True Pure Land") Buddhism. Long before the promulgation of Executive Order 9066, police came to round him up under existing "alien enemies" regulations. Kikuchi's memoirs describe how faith in Amida Buddha and the chanting of the *nembutsu* ("Namu Amida Butsu," or "I take refuge in Amida Buddha") sustained her Pure Land community during this agonizing ordeal.

The night before December 7, 1941, we honored the elders of the temple at a Bodhi Day celebration sponsored by the YBA [Young Buddhist Association] mem-

Shigeo Kikuchi. Courtesy of the Buddhist Studies Center, Honolulu, Hawaii.

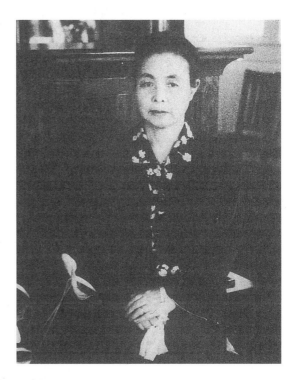

Shigeo Kikuchi, *Memoirs of a Buddhist Woman Missionary in Hawaii* (Honolulu: Buddhist Study Center Press, 1991). Copyright © 1991 Florence Okada. Reprinted courtesy of Buddhist Study Center Press.

bers. Early the next morning I sent my husband off to Hilo to attend the opening meeting of the education committee at Hilo Betsuin. While I was preparing for my Sunday school service, Mr. Hamada, the YBA president, dashed in and said, "Okusan, an awful thing has happened. There is a rumor that Japan has bombed Pearl Harbor." I was shocked and disbelievingly turned on the radio. Unmistakably an announcer was confirming that this terrible thing had occurred. The announcer went on to give details of the great confusion in Honolulu. As the innocent children came for Sunday school, I told them, "We will not have Sunday school service today; and you must go home." Shocked and fearful at hearing of the Pearl Harbor attack, many people came to the temple seeking advice.

My husband came home from Hilo in the afternoon. He said that they, too, were not aware of the incident at the morning meeting but just as they were about to have lunch, a message was received stating that war had broken out between Japan and America and that everyone should return home immediately. This was shocking information. Panic-stricken, the ministers left Hilo with empty stomachs.

We were warned that lights were to be made invisible from our houses but every household was not prepared to handle this situation. Even when a tiny streak of light was seen, the soldiers from a guardpost came and issued warnings.

At midnight, someone knocked at the door. My husband got up to answer the knock and found a Hawaiian police officer friend standing at the door. "Rev. Kikuchi, I want you to come to the office for a minute." My husband left with him but soon returned home. The policeman told him, "I want you to go to Volcano and because it is cold there you should take some warm clothing. You may have to stay there two or three days." I borrowed the policeman's flashlight and in the darkness, gathered some warm clothing and put them into a bag. After changing his clothes, he picked up the "Shinshu Seiten" from the bookcase and put it into his pocket. As he left he said, "There is nothing to worry about, I will return in two or three days. But I want you to inform the resident Japanese that we are now in an unexpected situation. Because we are governed by the United States everyone must respect and obey the law of the government and continue to work earnestly. Whatever happens, be patient, control yourself, and never argue or fight with people of other ethnic groups. As for me, nothing to worry about because I have done nothing wrong. After this investigation is over, I will come home." Then he disappeared into the darkness with the officer.

Early the next morning, Mr. Beatty, the plantation boss, came and comforted me, saying, "Mrs. Kikuchi, the situation between the United States and Japan has become bad, but I think that Reverend Kikuchi will be coming home soon." After saying this, however, he requested that all of the Japanese-American men, regardless of whether they were first or second generation, report to the Japanese language school at 2 o'clock that afternoon. I immediately telephoned those persons in charge of Waiohinu, Honuapo, and Hiilea, using the plantation boss's home phone.

The war had changed our friendly climate overnight. We were now consid-ered enemies. It caused me great pain to face members from other ethnic groups. So with a heavy heart, I went again to the home of the plantation boss. His wife said, "Mrs. Kikuchi, war is between the United States and Japan; not you and me." Her compassionate words struck me and tears began to flow from my eyes. . . .

As soon as the investigation was over, I had hoped that my husband would be returned home, but I waited a week, then two weeks, and yet he did not re-turn. Perhaps by Christmas, I thought. Maybe by New Year's. My hopes and ex-pectations were in vain. I received no word from him.

As an enemy alien, my bank savings account and my checking accounts were frozen, and I suffered a great deal. . . .

During the war, I completely lost interest in reading books, except religious ones. I put my heart, day and night, into reading Buddhist books. I realized that despite the circumstances, I must not forget "I am a Buddhist, and a Japanese woman, and not to take any action to dishonor this heritage."

. . . One day in February [1942], an unexpected news was released saying, the internees will be allowed to see their families. The members of the families were very excited and happy and began preparing favorite foods day and night, for their fathers, husbands or brothers. . . . As I approached closer to the wire-fence, I could see the internees' faces fastened to the fence as they eagerly awaited the arrival of their family members. "Mrs. Kikuchi, sensei is here," I heard a voice. After three months of insecurity and a feeling of uneasiness due to our separa-tion, we were finally allowed to see each other. Holding each other's hands there was no word necessary to express the joy of reunion. . . .

Finally the time of departure arrived. Volcano towards the evening is rather chilly. We do not know when we will be able to meet again. Perhaps this might be the last time! Those remaining, those leaving, both said reluctant farewells to each other. There was a scene where a little child waved his hand crying, "Daddy bye-bye." There were other scenes of mothers or wives, with tears in their eyes, waving their hands, loathing to part. I can still see these scenes vividly before my mind's eye. This moment of farewell was very, very sad indeed.

It was not long after this visit that the families were informed the internees were being transferred to the mainland. . . .

Soon after, a notice was sent to the families stating, "If the families desire to transfer to the mainland and wish to live together with husbands, parents, or with brothers, you will be granted the privilege to do so." It was a notification from the Army. At the time practically all the island ministers' wives and their fami-lies moved to the mainland, but . . . I made a firm decision to stay on and vowed to work and help as much as I could. . . .

[At a sendoff for Japanese-American inductees] I told each young man, "The Buddha is always with you," and gave them a Buddhist rosary, but whatever "nenju" I had at hand soon were all gone. I could only grasp the hands of the re-maining boys and say, "The Buddha is always with you no matter when or where. When you are lonely or when you're in trouble, repeat 'Namu Amida Butsu.'

Even if you cannot repeat His name, He will always be with you, so don't worry." Because they were all regular Sunday School pupils, they readily understood what I was saying. . . .

During the war, my husband was sent to the mainland internee camp. He was gone for four years, but returned safely back home to Hawaii on November 13, 1945. The ship entered the Honolulu harbor at 2:30 pm. The following day I went to Hilo harbor with persons in charge of Naalehu Hongwanji to meet my husband. Seeing my husband at first glimpse, I was surprised at seeing him so thin, but he had a happy smile on his face and he exchanged greetings in high spirits. I was relieved. I took a deep breath. How grateful I felt to see him once again. We paid homage together at Hilo Betsuin then, at Hilo Inn, twenty to thirty people welcomed us. . . . As we approached Pahala, members of the temple turned out to welcome my husband who had returned after four years of absence. As soon as we arrived there my husband kneeled down in front of the temporary altar of Amida Buddha, reciting nembutsu as he shed his tears.

JULIUS GOLDWATER, WARTIME BUDDHIST LITURGY (1940s)

The incarceration of Japanese Americans in World War II internment camps had a devastating impact on Japanese-American Buddhist institutions such as the Buddhist Mission of North America (later the Buddhist Churches of America). The internment of virtually all Japanese-American Buddhists elevated Julius Goldwater, a minister at the BMNA temple in Los Angeles, to a position of nationwide significance in the BMNA. Born to German-American Jewish parents in Los Angeles in 1908, Goldwater became one of America's first Jewish Buddhists when he formally converted in Honolulu, Hawaii, in July 1928. During a trip to Asia in the 1930s, he was ordained in Kyoto, Japan, and again in Hangchow, China. Now known as Subhadra, he devoted himself after World War II broke out to ministering to incarcerated Buddhists. He traveled to every internment camp, distributing devotional and liturgical materials. To facilitate the production and distribution of these texts, he founded the Buddhist Brotherhood of America. Among the texts he and the BBA distributed in the camps was *A Book Containing an Order of Ceremonies for Use by Buddhists*. An adaptation of *The Vade Medum* (1924), a liturgical manual produced in Hawaii by Goldwater's mentor, the Reverend Ernest Hunt, this book contains two catechisms, numerous *gathas* or hymns, a liturgy for Wesak (the Buddha's birthday), orders for marriages and funerals, excerpts from Buddhist scripture, and a history of Buddhism in which Jodo Shinshu founder Shinran is likened to Martin Luther. Reproduced here is an order for an initiation ceremony. In form and content, this "Dedication Ceremony" bears witness to Goldwater's Americanization and Protestantization of the BCA.

Anonymous, *A Book Containing an Order of Ceremonies for Use by Buddhists* (Los Angeles, Buddhist Brotherhood of America, n.d.), 12–15. Reprinted courtesy of the Reverend Julius Goldwater.

GATHA

(Here Shall Be Chanted the Three Refuges)

Officiant: Buddham Saranam Gacchami. *(Gong)*

Answer: Buddham Saranam Gacchami.

Officiant: Dhammam Saranam Gacchami. *(Gong)*

Answer: Dhammam Saranam Gacchami.

Officiant: Sangham Saranam Gacchami. *(Gong)*

Answer: Sangham Saranam Gacchami.

SALUTATION

(Which Shall Be Sung by All)

> To all the Buddhas of the ancient days,
> To all the Buddhas of all future time,
> We offer adoration evermore.
> To all the Buddhas of the ancient days,
> To all the Buddhas of the present age,
> We offer adoration evermore.
> For me there is no other refuge,
> The Buddha is my refuge
> He is the best, He is the best.
> By the power of the Truth
> May I attain the glorious victory.

RESPONSIVE READING, CONGREGATION SEATED

Officiant: Buddha our Lord hath found the Way of Salvation.

Answer: And hath redeemed us from the terror of death.

Officiant: He giveth courage to them that are weak.

Answer: And comfort to the weary and sorrow-laden.

Officiant: In His Law there is balm for the wounded.

Answer: And bread for them that are hungry.

Officiant: There is hope for the despairing.

Answer: And light for them that sit in darkness.

Officiant: Trust in the Truth, ye that love the Truth.

Answer: For the Kingdom of Righteousness is founded upon earth.

Officiant: Take refuge in the Buddha, our Lord.

Answer: For He hath found the Truth and blessed be His Name for ever and ever.

(All Stand and Say this Affirmation)

Reverently we come before the shrine of the Holy One, the Buddha of Eternal Light and Boundless Love.

We offer Him our gratitude and devotion for showing to us the Way of Salvation.

We resolve earnestly to strive, not only to learn and to understand His Holy Teaching, but also to walk every day in His Holy Path, so that like Him, we may attain Perfection and enter into the Eternal Bliss of Nirvana. Namu Amida Butsu.

GATHA   Before the Sermon

As they of old in faith drew near
Thy holy doctrine to attend
We come with joy Thy Word to hear,
Lord Buddha, Teacher, Guide and Friend.

Clearly to man hast Thou revealed
Within Thy Law the Way assured
Whereby all mortal woes are healed
And peace eternal is procured.

O may we all Thy Truth receive
With earnest purpose, pure intent,
Thy Path to tread and thus achieve
The bliss of full enlightenment.

DISCOURSE

GATHA   Before the Sermon

Sing with one accord
Praise to him, the Lord
Who to us the Truth hath given
Whereby error's bonds are riven
And our hearts set free
From captivity.

Buddha's Doctrine true
Shall our minds endue
With the strength to fight temptation
And in time of tribulation
Still to persevere
Though the skies be drear.

Lead us, Lord of Light,
Through this vale of night;

By Thy Word Thine aidance lending
Till, Nirvana's height ascending,
We have found release
In Thy perfect peace.

EXHORTATION

Officiant: (Turning to people): Dear Children (or people), you have come together in this holy place, to dedicate yourselves to the service of Him, Who, through self-effort and renunciation, attained Enlightenment, and found for us the way of Salvation.

Before taking upon yourselves these obligations, listen well to the words of the Blessed One, who exhorts you to avoid the ten evils.

1 Kill not, but have regard for life.
2 Steal not, but help each man to be master of the fruit of his labor
3 Keep from impurity, lead a Life of chastity.
4 Lie not, but be truthful
5 Invent not evil reports, neither repeat them.
6 Swear not; but speak decently and with dignity.
7 Waste not time in idle gossip.
8 Covet not, nor envy, but rejoice at another's good.
9 Cherish no hatred, but embrace all beings with love.
10 Free your minds from ignorance, be anxious to learn the truth.

(Here the Candidates Shall Stand Up)

Officiant: Do you realize the seriousness of the words you are about to speak?

Answer: We do.

Officiant: Have you chosen the Blessed One, the Lord Buddha to be your guide?

Answer: We have chosen Him to be our guide forever.

Officiant: As the Sun shineth upon the earth, awakening into growth and fruitfulness the seed that lieth therein, so doth the Light of Truth, Love and Wisdom, manifested in our Lord Buddha shed its glorious Radiance into the hearts and minds of mankind, calling forth into activity the Buddha-seed within. Come ye therefore with confidence, and with sincerity give your hearts into His keeping, that they may be received into His great Buddha-Heart of Compassion.

If you accept the Lord Buddha as your guide, if you acknowledge His Law as your rule of life, and if you firmly purpose to remain faithful to His Holy Brotherhood, then repeat after me this dedication.

(All Repeat, With or After the Officiant)

Candidates:	Here today in this Holy Temple, in the presence of the congregation here assembled, we solemnly pledge our allegiance to the Lord Buddha. We promise to follow Him faithfully all our days. His religion shall be first in our hearts, and His teaching the guiding star of our lives.
Officiant:	In the name of the Lord Buddha, I receive you as His disciples. In witness of your dedication to His service do I offer this incense (here the officiant offers incense) and as a symbol of the Light of His Holy Doctrine which shall guide you to Nirvana, do I light for you this candle. (Here officiant lights a candle.)
Officiant:	I take my refuge in the Buddha.
Candidates:	I take my refuge in the Buddha.
Officiant:	I take my refuge in His Law.
Candidates:	I take my refuge in His Law.
Officiant:	I take my refuge in His Brotherhood.
Candidates:	I take my refuge in His Brotherhood.

GATHA

Lord of divine compassion,
Unfailing Friend and Guide,
Who with us in Thy Doctrine
Forever dost abide.

To Thee, as to a father,
Our little ones we bring
That they on life's long journey
To thy dear hand may cling.

O may Thy love enfold them,
Thy peace their way attend;
Nirvana's bliss await them
When earthly life shall end.

METTABHAVANA

(Ancient Buddhist Thought-Wave)

We surround all men and all forms of life with Infinite Love and Compassion. Particularly do we send out compassionate thoughts to those in suffering and sorrow; to all those in doubt and ignorance, to all who are striving to attain Truth and to those whose feet are standing close to the great change men call death, we send forth oceans of wisdom, mercy and love.

Peace be unto you!

CHAPTER **10**

Hindu Crossings:
Gurus and Disciples

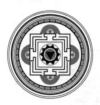

KRISHNALAL SHRIDHARANI, "MY BRIEF
CAREER AS A YOGI" (1941)

A journalist, playwright, poet, and political activist who wrote in both English and his native Gujarati, Krishnalal Shridharani (1911–60) embodied from birth the religious diversity of India. His mother was a Jain and his father a devotee of Vishnu. A controversial figure in his homeland, Shridharani was jailed for participating in Gandhi's 240-mile March to the Sea in 1930, and a novel based on his imprisonment, *I Shall Kill the Human in You!* (1932), was banned by the British as subversive. Shridharani came to America as a student sojourner in 1934. When he returned to India twelve years later he had earned three degrees, including a Ph.D. at Columbia University (for a dissertation on Gandhian nonviolence later published as *War Without Violence*). An early and outspoken advocate of African-American civil rights, Shridharani helped to organize the Congress of Racial Equality (CORE, established 1942). He was also a staunch Indian nationalist who devoted a substantial portion of his autobiography, *My India, My America* (1941), to excoriating (as "vividly dramatized claptrap") Katherine Mayo's best-selling exposé of the treatment of women in India, *Mother India* (1927). "My Brief Career as a Yogi," this selection from *My India, My America*, comes from a clever chapter called "Hindus Are Human Beings." With Twain-like wit and irreverence, Shridharani takes Indophilic Americans to task for stereotyping Asians as navel-gazing contemplatives—and for embracing Indian spiritual humbuggery. It was not a lesson Americans would learn quickly.

Krishnalal Shridharani, *My India, My America* (New York: Duell, Sloan and Pearce, 1941), 95–99.

A middle-aged lady in Rhode Island, exquisite and luminous, one of those favored creatures of the gods who are at their best between forty and forty-five, took an interest in me in the early years of my stay in the United States. When I had shared enough of her time to know her friends also, I learned that she had the proper and glamorous connections with the *Mayflower,* and that mixed with her blue blood was the blood of the Indians, the "originals" in this land of foreigners, and apparently her favorite forebears. Red or blue, she was the veritable warden of a self-imposed concentration camp of Society.

My first introduction to her came through an American writer whom I had met at Abu in western India during one of those summer months when an entire stratum of India moves to "hill stations" to escape the heat. The first day I entered milady's home, I was more pleased than surprised when she introduced me to the only other Indian at her party, a sort of an Indian-ola engulfed in a large pink turban. When she introduced him as Swami Sulaiman, I very nearly broke down, what with the incongruity of a turban on a Swami, and a Mohammedan name tacked onto a Hindu religious title. In spite of his profession of "detachment alike in bliss and sorrow," Swami Sulaiman looked definitely disconcerted under the eye of an unexpected compatriot. However, that was our first and last encounter, as he soon sailed for India with the financial blessings of my hostess, to conduct research on "Proper Breathing as a Means to World Peace."

For reasons unknown to me, the departure of the so-called Swami coincided with the increased frequency of my visits to Rhode Island. Fortnight after fortnight I went there, enjoying thoroughly all the little attentions which are the lot of a combination guest and exhibit. To my lasting sorrow, however, I soon discovered that a chance remark of mine had been taken with unnecessary seriousness by my hostess. In an off moment I had told her that according to my experience meditation came naturally in an early morning under an open sky. Every time I visited her sea-side sanctuary after that unfortunate remark, I was expected to get up at five in the morning, parade across the lawn in her company to the water front, and sit on the pebbles for half an hour meditating. It was during these performances that I really came to appreciate the foresight of my ancestors who had prescribed "closing of the eyes" while meditating.

Greater trials were in store for me. One morning while on my way to the meditation ground, I discerned a group of women fluttering in the early morning shadows. My hostess was already there, awaiting my arrival along with the others. It soon transpired that I was to give an illustrated talk on meditation, proper breathing—and "Yoga in general."

There and then we agreed, as amicably as possible under the circumstances, that we had arrived at the parting of the ways.

That was perhaps the first time in history when Yoga stood between two souls.

Not all Indians enjoy a religious station. They are not all Swamis, or Yogis, or Sadhus, or Rishis.

In the United States one may hear about one Yogi Tincanwalla, advertising himself as "The Einstein of Spiritual Relativity," and giving "soul-instilling free lectures"—always with a subtle suggestion for a "silver offering" at the end. But however strong his influence may be in the discovery of "The Boundless Being," a Tincanwalla's name can only belong to a Parsi, and thus he can hardly call himself a Yogi, any more than a Baptist preacher could call himself an Archbishop of Canterbury. Often Americans are invited to attend classes ("$2.00 for each attendance; $25.00 for the series of fifteen") in "Yogic breathing" given by some Swami Sulaiman; but to a Hindu "Swami Sulaiman" sounds as incongruous as "Pope Bernstein" would sound to a Catholic. Once in a while, a Christian is heard calling himself a Rishi just because he hails from India and is unemployed otherwise. More frequently, however, Americans with Yogic proclivities repair to some "Yogashram" conducted by one of their compatriots, Yogi Edwin Russell or Sadhu Smith. What with their native understanding of business and advertising, Americans invariably make showier and more successful Swamis and Yogis than Indians; their annual incomes mount into the thousands. But not all of them can be Swamis or Yogis, for not even all Indians can be Swamis or Yogis. One has to be a Hindu, and fortunately or unfortunately, one has to be born a Hindu.

What limits the field still further, and casts doubt on many professional Indian spiritualists in the United States, is the fact that not even all Hindus can be Rishis. King Rama, the Ideal King and an Incarnation of God, hunted down a Shudra, that is, a man belonging to the fourth caste of menial laborers, and killed him simply because the Shudra was disciplining himself in order to be a Rishi. It is fortunate for the phoney Swamis of today that Rama no longer haunts the earth with his bow and arrow.

Now, it should be made clear that a Yogi is to be found in a remote cave of the Himalayas, or in the thick forests of central India, or sometimes on the banks of the Ganges. He has no earthly possessions, and he shuns social contacts; even his daily bread is provided by admiring devotees. He does not go out even to teach, or spread knowledge of what, through living in harmony with nature and away from the lustful crowds, he may have discovered in realms of the spirit; he is to be sought after by votaries of truth. Nor does he proudly style himself a Yogi or a Rishi; he is given such a title only by the faithful when they become aware of his selfless wisdom. The designation comes unsought and falls in his lap like a ripe mango. There are fakers galore in India, to whom God's name is a salable commodity to be bartered to the superstitious masses; but they are called Bahvas and always are distinguished from Yogis and Rishis. With an understanding of all this, it is perhaps easier to grasp why the sensitivity of one brought up in the Hindu tradition is shocked when he finds some of his own countrymen in the United States dragging spiritual qualities down to the market place.

There are probably half a dozen genuine Hindu Swamis in America who do fulfill all the requirements of caste and religion, of birth and training, and who have created a lasting place for themselves in various communities. Of the ten or twenty Indians who have some claim to upper-bracket earnings in the United States, curiously enough, these Swamis are at the top of the list. One or two of these priests have real-estate interests in some of the most fashionable purlieus of New York, Boston, and Los Angeles, and some are millionaires. Such facts, together with the realization that India is already over-advertised with respect to her religiosity, render many a young Indian visiting America unappreciative if not seriously critical of the activities of even these genuine Swamis. Yet there is a case, as there is a place for this transplanted clergy. They have gone a long way toward establishing a real community of religions. They have also brought the wisdom of the Hindus to a distant shore, and, unlike the Christian missionaries in the Orient, without any intention of proselytizing "the heathens." And very likely their greatest contribution lies in answering a dire American need. The uncertainties of an industrial economy, the speed and noise of the modern city, the dreadful stresses and strains of modern times have had their effects on countless Americans. To a few of these victims of modern "civilization" the Swamis do bring a serenity of mind by teaching the wisdom of a people who for centuries have lived peacefully and valiantly in face of want.

SWAMI PARAMAHANSA YOGANANDA, *AUTOBIOGRAPHY OF A YOGI* (1946)

Swami Paramahansa Yogananda's Self-Realization Fellowship (SRF) was the largest and most influential Hindu religious movement in America before World War II. Yogananda (1893–1952) first came to the United States as a delegate to the International

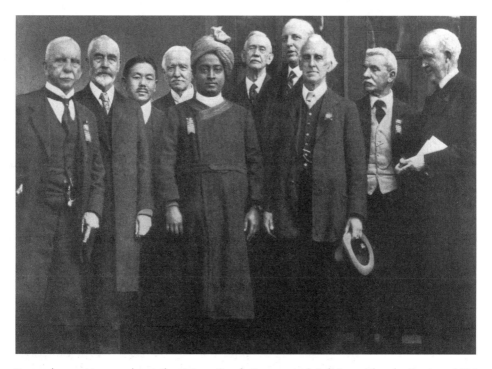

Paramahansa Yogananda at the International Congress of Religious Liberals, Boston, 1920. Copyright © 1970 Self-Realization Fellowship. Used by permission.

Congress of Religious Liberals held in Boston in October 1920. Unlike Swami Vivekananda, who returned to India a few years after the World's Parliament of Religions of 1893, Yogananda settled in the United States. Born in Gorakhpur in northeastern India in the shadow of the Himalayas, Yogananda left his homeland at the behest of his teacher, Sri Yukteswar Giri (1855–1936), who encouraged him to adapt the beliefs and practices he had learned for use in the West. In the United States, Yogananda lectured widely, spreading the message of kriya yoga: "the scientific technique of God-realization." At its height, the SRF—an American outgrowth of the Yogoda Satsanga of India—claimed 150,000 devotees at 150 centers, but its influence and numbers declined sharply after its founder's death in 1952. Yogananda wrote a number of books, most notably *Autobiography of a Yogi* (1946), which became a countercultural hit in the 1960s. Two selections from that book are reproduced here. In "The Science of Kriya Yoga," a portion of a chapter from the first edition, Yogananda argues that his method is as quick as it is easy. "Aims and Ideals of Self-Realization Fellowship," a later text promulgated by Sri Daya Mata (who ascended to the presidency of both the Yogoda Satsanga Society of India and the SRF in 1955), lists key SRF principles.

AUTOBIOGRAPHY OF A YOGI

The science of *Kriya Yoga*, mentioned so often in these pages, became widely known in modern India through the instrumentality of Lahiri Mahasaya, my guru's guru. The Sanskrit root of *kriya* is *kri*, to do, to act and react; the same root is found in the word *karma*, the natural principle of cause and effect. *Kriya Yoga* is thus "union (*yoga*) with the Infinite through a certain action or rite (*kriya*)." A yogi who faithfully follows its technique is gradually freed from karma or the universal chain of causation.

Because of certain ancient yogic injunctions, I cannot give a full explanation of *Kriya Yoga* in the pages of a book intended for the general public. The actual technique must be learned from a *Kriyaban* or *Kriya Yogi*; here a broad reference must suffice.

Kriya Yoga is a simple, psychophysiological method by which the human blood is decarbonated and recharged with oxygen. The atoms of this extra oxygen are transmuted into life current to rejuvenate the brain and spinal centers. By stopping the accumulation of venous blood, the yogi is able to lessen or prevent the decay of tissues. The advanced yogi transmutes his cells into pure energy. Elijah, Jesus, Kabir, and other prophets were past masters in the use of *Kriya* or a similar technique, by which they caused their bodies to dematerialize at will.

Kriya is an ancient science. Lahiri Mahasaya received it from his guru, Babaji, who rediscovered and clarified the technique after it had been lost in the Dark Ages.

Paramhansa Yogananda, *Autobiography of a Yogi* (New York: Philosophical Library, 1946), 243–52; Paramahansa Yogananda, *Autobiography of a Yogi* (Los Angeles: Self-Realization Fellowship, 1983), 573. Both reprinted courtesy of the Self-Realization Fellowship. Yogananda initially spelled his first name "Paramhansa"; it was later changed to "Paramahansa."

"The *Kriya Yoga* which I am giving to the world through you in this nineteenth century," Babaji told Lahiri Mahasaya, "is a revival of the same science which Krishna gave, millenniums ago, to Arjuna, and which was later known to Patanjali, and to Christ, St. John, St. Paul, and other disciples." . . .

St. Paul knew *Kriya Yoga*, or a technique very similar to it, by which he could switch life currents to and from the senses. He was therefore able to say: "Verily, I protest by our rejoicing which I have in Christ, *I die daily*." By daily withdrawing his bodily life force, he united it by yoga union with the rejoicing (eternal bliss) of the Christ consciousness. In that felicitous state, he was consciously aware of being dead to the delusive sensory world of *maya*.

In the initial states of God-contact (*sabikalpa samadhi*) the devotee's consciousness merges with the Cosmic Spirit; his life force is withdrawn from the body, which appears "dead," or motionless and rigid. The yogi is fully aware of his bodily condition of suspended animation. As he progresses to higher spiritual states (*nirbikalpa samadhi*), however, he communes with God without bodily fixation, and in his ordinary waking consciousness, even in the midst of exacting worldly duties.

"*Kriya Yoga* is an instrument through which human evolution can be quickened," Sri Yukteswar explained to his students. "The ancient yogis discovered that the secret of cosmic consciousness is intimately linked with breath mastery. This is India's unique and deathless contribution to the world's treasury of knowledge. The life force, which is ordinarily absorbed in maintaining the heart-pump, must be freed for higher activities by a method of calming and stilling the ceaseless demands of the breath."

The *Kriya Yogi* mentally directs his life energy to revolve, upward and downward, around the six spinal centers (medullary, cervical, dorsal, lumbar, sacral, and coccygeal plexuses) which correspond to the twelve astral signs of the zodiac, the symbolic Cosmic Man. One-half minute of revolution of energy around the sensitive spinal cord of man effects subtle progress in his evolution; that half-minute of *Kriya* equals one year of natural spiritual unfoldment.

The astral system of a human being, with six (twelve by polarity) inner constellations revolving around the sun of the omniscient spiritual eye, is interrelated with the physical sun and the twelve zodiacal signs. All men are thus affected by an inner and an outer universe. The ancient rishis discovered that man's earthly and heavenly environment, in twelve-year cycles, push him forward on his natural path. The scriptures aver that man requires a million years of normal, diseaseless evolution to perfect his human brain sufficiently to express cosmic consciousness.

One thousand *Kriyas* practiced in eight hours gives the yogi, in one day, the equivalent of ten thousand years of natural evolution: 365,000 years of evolution in one year. In three years, a *Kriya Yogi* can thus accomplish by intelligent self-effort the same result which nature brings to pass in a million years. The *Kriya* short cut, of course, can be taken only by deeply developed yogis. With the guidance of a guru, such yogis have carefully prepared their bodies and brains to receive the power created by intensive practice.

The *Kriya* beginner employs his yogic exercise only fourteen to twenty-eight times, twice daily. A number of yogis achieve emancipation in six or twelve or twenty-four or forty-eight years. A yogi who dies before achieving full realization carries with him the good karma of his past *Kriya* effort; in his new life he is harmoniously propelled toward his Infinite Goal.

The body of the average man is like a fifty-watt lamp, which cannot accommodate the billion watts of power roused by an excessive practice of *Kriya*. Through gradual and regular increase of the simple and "foolproof" methods of *Kriya*, man's body becomes astrally transformed day by day, and is finally fitted to express the infinite potentials of cosmic energy—the first materially active expression of Spirit.

Kriya Yoga has nothing in common with the unscientific breathing exercises taught by a number of misguided zealots. Their attempts to forcibly hold breath in the lungs is not only unnatural but decidedly unpleasant. *Kriya*, on the other hand, is accompanied from the very beginning by an accession of peace, and by soothing sensations of regenerative effect in the spine. . . .

Introspection, or "sitting in the silence," is an unscientific way of trying to force apart the mind and senses, tied together by the life force. The contemplative mind, attempting its return to divinity, is constantly dragged back toward the senses by the life currents. *Kriya*, controlling the mind *directly* through the life force, is the easiest, most effective, and most scientific avenue of approach to the Infinite. In contrast to the slow, uncertain "bullock cart" theological path to God, *Kriya Yoga* may justly be called the "airplane" route.

AIMS AND IDEALS OF SELF-REALIZATION FELLOWSHIP AS SET FORTH BY PARAMAHANSA YOGANANDA, FOUNDER, SRI DAYA MATA, PRESIDENT

To disseminate among the nations a knowledge of definite scientific techniques for attaining direct personal experience of God.

To teach that the purpose of life is the evolution, through self-effort, of man's limited mortal consciousness into God Consciousness; and to this end to establish Self-Realization Fellowship temples for God-communion throughout the world, and to encourage the establishment of individual temples of God in the homes and in the hearts of men.

To reveal the complete harmony and basic oneness of original Christianity as taught by Jesus Christ and original Yoga as taught by Bhagavan Krishna; and to show that these principles of truth are the common scientific foundation of all true religions.

To point out the one divine highway to which all paths of true religious beliefs eventually lead: the highway of daily, scientific, devotional meditation on God.

To liberate man from his threefold suffering: physical disease, mental inharmonies, and spiritual ignorance.

To encourage "plain living and high thinking"; and to spread a spirit of brotherhood among all peoples by teaching the eternal basis of their unity: kinship with God.

To demonstrate the superiority of mind over body, of soul over mind.

To overcome evil by good, sorrow by joy, cruelty by kindness, ignorance by wisdom.

To unite science and religion through realization of the unity of their underlying principles.

To advocate cultural and spiritual understanding between East and West, and the exchange of their finest distinctive features.

To serve mankind as one's larger Self.

KRISHNAMURTI, THE TURNING POINT (1975)

Jiddu Krishnamurti (1895–1986) is an example of the rare Indian-born teacher whose success as an American guru was rooted in his reluctance to play the role. An unorthodox spiritual teacher who defied conventional labels and eschewed institutional ties, Krishnamurti was born in Madanapalle, India, in 1895 to theosophically inclined parents. When Krishnamurti was only fourteen, Annie Besant, who had succeeded Colonel Olcott as the president of the Theosophical Society, prophesied the advent of a World Teacher. She then tapped Krishnamurti for the part, and founded the Order of the Star of the East (established 1911) with him as its spiritual head. In 1929, Krishnamurti rejected this messianic role and set off on his own, though he never fully outgrew the Theosophical education he had received in India and England. In lectures he delivered around the globe in a public career that spanned more than five decades, he taught a form of mysticism that rejected all authority, including his own. But his teaching that you cannot approach truth by any path only prompted followers to beat a path to his door. He died in 1986 at the age of ninety in his American home of Ojai, California, but his legacy of spiritual self-reliance lives on in the Ojai-based Krishnamurti Foundation of America (established 1969). In this passage from a biography by Mary Lutyens, Krishnamurti describes his celebrated mystical breakthrough under a pepper tree in Ojai in August 1922. The "Masters" Krishnamurti refers to are the Theosophical adepts Helena Blavatsky had popularized decades earlier.

Well, since August 3rd, I meditated regularly for about thirty minutes every morning. I could, to my astonishment, concentrate with considerable ease, and within a few days I began to see clearly where I had failed and where I was failing. Immediately I set about, consciously, to annihilate the wrong accumulations of the past years. With the same deliberation I set about to find out ways and means to achieve my aim. First I realized that I had to harmonize all my other bodies with the Buddhic plane and to bring about this happy combination I had to find out what my ego wanted on the Buddhic plane. To harmonize the various bodies I had to keep them vibrating at the same rate as the Buddhic, and to do this I had to find out what was the vital interest of the Buddhic. With ease which rather astonished me I found the main interest on that high plane was to serve

Mary Lutyens, *Krishnamurti: The Years of Awakening* (New York: Farrar, Straus & Giroux, 1975), 157–60. Reprinted courtesy of the Krishnamurti Foundation of America.

the Lord Maitreya and the Masters. With that idea clear in my physical mind I had to direct and control the other bodies to act and to think the same as on the noble and spiritual plane. During that period of less than three weeks, I concentrated to keep in mind the image of the Lord Maitreya throughout the entire day, and I found no difficulty in doing this. I found that I was getting calmer and more serene. My whole outlook on life was changed.

Then, on the 17th August, I felt acute pain at the nape of my neck and I had to cut down my meditation to fifteen minutes. The pain instead of getting better as I had hoped grew worse. The climax was reached on the 19th. I could not think, nor was I able to do anything, and I was forced by friends here to retire to bed. Then I became almost unconscious, though I was well aware of what was happening around me. I came to myself at about noon each day. On the first day while I was in that state and more conscious of the things around me, I had the first most extraordinary experience. There was a man mending the road; that man was myself; the pickaxe he held was myself; the very stone which he was breaking up was a part of me; the tender blade of grass was my very being, and the tree beside the man was myself. I almost could feel and think like the roadmender, and I could feel the wind passing through the tree, and the little ant on the blade of grass I could feel. The birds, the dust, and the very noise were a part of me. Just then there was a car passing by at some distance; I was the driver, the engine, and the tires; as the car went further away from me, I was going away from myself. I was in everything, or rather everything was in me, inanimate and animate, the mountain, the worm, and all breathing things. All day long I remained in this happy condition. I could not eat anything, and again at about six I began to lose my physical body, and naturally the physical elemental did what it liked; I was semi-conscious.

The morning of the next day (the 20th) was almost the same as the previous day, and I could not tolerate too many people in the room. I could feel them in rather a curious way and their vibrations got on my nerves. That evening at about the same hour of six I felt worse than ever. I wanted nobody near me nor anybody to touch me. I was feeling extremely tired and weak. I think I was weeping from mere exhaustion and lack of physical control. My head was pretty bad and the top part felt as though many needles were being driven in. While I was in this state I felt that the bed in which I was lying, the same one as on the previous day, was dirty and filthy beyond imagination and I could not lie in it. Suddenly I found myself sitting on the floor and Nitya and Rosalind asking me to get into bed. I asked them not to touch me and cried out that the bed was not clean. I went on like this for some time till eventually I wandered out on the verandah and sat a few moments exhausted and slightly calmer. I began to come to myself and finally Mr. Warrington asked me to go under the pepper tree which is near the house. There I sat crosslegged in the meditation posture. When I had sat thus for some time, I felt myself going out of my body, I saw myself sitting down with the delicate tender leaves of the tree over me. I was facing the east. In front of me was my body and over my head I saw the Star, bright and clear. Then I could feel the vibrations of the Lord Buddha; I beheld Lord Maitreya and Master K.H. I was so happy, calm and at peace. I could still see my body and I was hovering near it. There was such profound calmness both in the air and within myself, the calmness of the bottom of a deep unfathomable lake. Like the lake, I felt my physical body, with its mind and emotions, could be ruffled on the surface but nothing, nay nothing, could disturb the calmness of my soul. The Presence of the mighty Beings was with me for some time and then They were gone. I was supremely happy, for I had seen. Nothing could ever be the same. I have drunk at the clear and pure waters at the source of the fountain of life and my thirst was appeased. Never more could I be thirsty, never more could I be in utter darkness. I have seen the Light. I have touched compassion which heals all sorrow and suffering; it is not for myself, but for the world. I have stood on the mountain top and gazed at the mighty Beings. Never can I be in utter darkness; I have seen the glorious and healing Light. The fountain of Truth has been revealed to me and the darkness has been dispersed. Love in all its glory has intoxicated my heart; my heart can never be closed. I have drunk at the fountain of Joy and eternal Beauty. I am God-intoxicated.

JOHN YALE, "WHAT VEDANTA MEANS TO ME" (1960)

While American Vedantists such as Sister Christine came to Hinduism through face-to-face encounters with Indian-born swamis, John Yale was initially attracted to Hinduism by a book: the *Bhagavad Gita*. A midwestern child of the Depression who came of age long after Swami Vivekananda had made his triumphal, post-Parliament return to India, Yale struggled early in his life to make the Protestant revivalism of his youth his own. But his doubts about Christianity never resolved into faith. "What Vedanta Means to Me" describes Yale's pilgrimage from Sunday School through Episcopalianism and psychoanalysis to the Vedanta teachings of Swami Prabhavananda, the leader of the Vedanta Society of Southern California. Vedanta-style Hinduism resolved his personal crisis, and concluded his search for a spiritual home. In addition to editing the volume in which this essay originally appeared, Yale has written *A Yankee and the Swamis* (1961), a memoir of his travels through India in the early fifties. During the sixties, he worked as an editor at Vedanta Press in Hollywood, California. In the late 1990s, Yale was known as Swami Vidyatmananda and was living as a Ramakrishna monk in France.

I think of myself as a representative product of my age—a Depression child who grew up in the era of Roosevelt, Red Russia, and Freud. I was from a middle-class Midwestern, Protestant family. Like many others, as I reached my adolescence I rebelled against much in my background, went through a short period of radicalism, and then became committed to the new science of human engineering. So far, at least, I was representative. But that is as far as I went. I do not know what people of my generation believe in now; for I left them in 1950 for the life of monasticism which I follow today.

John Yale, "What Vedanta Means to Me," in John Yale, ed., *What Vedanta Means to Me: A Symposium* (Garden City, N.Y.: Doubleday, 1960), 141–42, 146–47, 150–57. Reprinted by permission of Vedanta Press.

As a child in Sunday School I was vastly attracted to Jesus Christ. I was per-fectly sure then—and I have never since believed otherwise—that Christ was God and came to earth to show man how to find truth and freedom. The intention came to me early to be a good man and to find and follow some noble ideal. I would be a genuine Christian and devote my life to helping mankind.

But I found this easier said than done. . . .

After many unsuccessful attempts to make a "decision for Christ" which would work and be permanent, toward the end of my teens I made a trembly, guilt-ridden withdrawal from church. In deep conflict, I came to the conclusion that I was an anomaly who must seek his ideal through some other means. . . .

After an uncertain period of school teaching and textbook writing, I finally found what seemed to be the right career, and progressed in it. . . . The business flourished better than anyone could have expected it to, so that before I was thirty I had become that most admirable of modern beings, a business success.

I played the assured leader at the office, but at home alone at night, or on gray Sunday mornings, I was something quite different—a very average human being bewildered by life and afraid of death. . . .

In a panic I reached out for help. I considered psychotherapy, but soon aban-doned hope of finding help there. . . . I became an Episcopalian hoping to find aid in the old wisdom, and balm in the ritualistic beauties, of this faith.

And I began to study anew the teachings of Christ, and for the first time the writings of Vedanta, especially the Swami Prabhavananda-Christopher Isherwood translation of the Bhagavad-Gita. In the New Testament I read: "And he said to them all, if any man will come after me, let him deny himself, and take up his cross daily, and follow me. For whosoever will save his life shall lose it; and whosoever will lose his life for my sake, the same shall save it. For what is a man advantaged, if he gain the whole world, and lose himself, or be cast away?"

And in the Bhagavad-Gita was a like teaching:

> Adore me only
> With heart undistracted;
> Strive without ceasing
> To know the Atman,
> Seek this knowledge
> And comprehend clearly
> Why you should seek it:
> Such, it is said,
> Are the roots of true wisdom:
> Ignorance, merely,
> Is all that denies them.

What I came to understand as a result of almost tearing the words from the pages was this: the cause of frustration is the wish to get—to get ego-fulfillment, possessions, pleasure. The route to peace of mind is self-abnegation—the system-atic restraining of one's identification with matter, and the re-identification with spirit. I later realized that what I was interested in was what Christianity once understood simply to be religion, but what we in the West—now that religion has become mainly instruction in ethical living—at present term mysticism. . . .

So in 1948, suffering from stage fright and the fear that perhaps I was only being melodramatic, I withdrew from the business, sold my home, and started out—in a brand-new black Mercury convertible with white-wall tires—to seek my spiritual fortune.

I don't remember now just where I expected to find help; certainly not at the Vedanta Society of Southern California. Indeed, I ended up there only after I had exhausted every other alternative. For my prejudice against Eastern religion was strong. . . .

I made a trip to one of the few American monasteries of the Episcopal Church. . . . I even went back once to my old revivalist sect, determined, should there be an altar call, to try yet again to reach salvation by the instantaneous method. . . .

Finally ready to take help—since there was no avoiding it—from a Hindu, and Indian, a swami, I found my way to the little white and gold chapel standing in a garden just above the intersection of Hollywood Boulevard and Vine Street. After all, was he not the teacher . . . of Christopher Isherwood, who had lived at this place for two years as a probationary monk, during which time he and the Swami had made the translation I so much liked, of the Gita? Others, also, had found Swami Prabhavananda quite acceptable. About him I had read in Henry Miller's *The Air-Conditioned Nightmare*: "The most masterful individual, the only person I met whom I could truly call 'a great soul,' was a quiet Hindu swami in Hollywood." . . .

When I met Swami he was then about fifty-five years of age, a golden-colored Indian about the size of and somehow rather like a twelve-year-old boy, wearing gray flannel trousers and a yellow sweater. The only thing that seemed adult about him physically was his gait—his way of walking with his arms behind his back, the body bent forward a little, slippers flapping on his feet. He was most charming, with a big smile. I forgot instantly I was talking to an Oriental; he was just a most intelligent, permissive, engaging man.

I told Swami my story; what a big man I was, and what a grandiose quest I was on.

So Swami gave my ego the first of the many jabs he has been applying ever since, by advising me against seeking God, by telling me to go back to the business and try to lead a good, clean, ethical, mundane life.

Although I didn't recognize it as such then, this was also a come-on, to get me off balance, to make me do the asking—and the challenge worked. "But Swami," I flared, "don't you think I've tried all that? There's just nothing there."

"Then how do you want to visualize God?"

What a question! I didn't even know what it meant. I had no wish for anything but to be taken seriously, given some prohibitions, assigned some renunciations, so that I might begin to grow spiritual.

"I don't understand you," I said.

"Slavery is in the mind; liberation is in the mind. Restlessness and unhappiness are in the mind; peace is there too. The only way to be happy is to think of God, to visualize him in some form attractive to you. When you don't think of God you cannot be happy; when you can see him all the time, then you are in bliss all the time—and incidentally a saint."

"What about self-abnegation?" I asked. "Isn't that important?"

"Only as a means of freeing the mind to think of God. Yes, it is fairly important, but we don't stress it; it comes about naturally in time without much effort, as one becomes more devoted."

"I see."

"If it's God you really want," Swami went on, "I can show you how to find him."

"I want meaning, closure. I guess that's God."

"Then I request you to meditate for at least a half hour three times a day."

This was a surprise. "Meditate?" I asked.

"Yes."

"What good will that do?"

"That will do everything. Try it, as I will instruct you, and see."

That was the end of my anti-Orientalism and my search. I have followed Swami Prabhavananda since that day, for on that day, as always later, he spoke as one having authority. And as I have lived with him all these years and watched his every move, I have seen that he is a demonstration of the discipline he preaches. The sought-after ideal example at last!

CHAPTER **11**

Buddhist Crossings:
Masters and Students

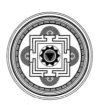

DAISETZ TEITARO SUZUKI, "WHAT IS ZEN?" (1959)

A prolific writer and translator, Daisetz Teitaro Suzuki (1870–1966) exemplified and personified Zen to twentieth-century Americans. Though trained in Rinzai Zen at the Engaku Monastery in Kamakura, Japan, he never became a monk. At the urging of his teacher, Soyen Shaku, he came to the United States in 1897 to work for philosopher Paul Carus's Open Court Publishing Company in La Salle, Illinois. He stayed until 1909. In 1911 in Japan, he married Theosophist Beatrice Erskine Lane. Ten years later, while he was teaching at Otani University in Kyoto, Suzuki and his wife founded *The Eastern Buddhist*, an English-language Buddhist journal. After returning to the United States in the 1950s, Suzuki lectured widely, including at Columbia University. In 1959 he founded the Cambridge Buddhist Association in Cambridge, Massachusetts. During the 1950s, he influenced musician John Cage, novelist Jack Kerouac, poet Allen Ginsberg, Catholic monk Thomas Merton, psychologist Erich Fromm, and fellow Zen popularizer Alan Watts. He died in 1966 in Kamakura at the age of 96, but not before his idiosyncratic understanding of Zen—as a mystical teaching known only through spiritual experience yet somehow present in all the world's religions—achieved canonical status in the West. In this short selection from *Zen and Japanese Culture* (1959), a classic distillation of Zen into English, Suzuki winnows his Zen down to eleven short propositions.

(1) Zen discipline consists in attaining enlightenment (or *satori*, in Japanese).

D. T. Suzuki, "What Is Zen?," in his *Zen and Japanese Culture* (New York: Bollingen, 1959), 16–17. This book is a revision of Suzuki's *Zen Buddhism and Its Influence on Japanese Culture* (Kyoto: Eastern Buddhist Society, 1938). Copyright © 1959 and © renewed 1987 by Princeton University Press. Reprinted courtesy of Princeton University Press.

(2) *Satori* finds a meaning hitherto hidden in our daily concrete particular experiences, such as eating, drinking, or business of all kinds.

(3) The meaning thus revealed is not something added from the outside. It is in being itself, in becoming itself, in living itself. This is called, in Japanese, a life of *kono-mama* or *sono-mama*. *Kono-* or *sono-mama* means the "isness" of a thing, Reality in its isness.

(4) Some may say, "There cannot be any meaning in mere isness." But this is not the view held by Zen, for according to it, isness is the meaning. When I see into it I see it as clearly as I see myself reflected in a mirror.

(5) This is what made Hō Koji (P'ang Chü-shih), a lay disciple of the eight century, declare:

How wondrous this, how mysterious!
I carry fuel, I draw water.

The fuel-carrying or the water-drawing itself, apart from its utilitarianism, is full of meaning; hence its "wonder," its "mystery."

(6) Zen does not, therefore, indulge in abstraction or in conceptualization. In its verbalism it may sometimes appear that Zen does this a great deal. But this is an error most commonly entertained by those who do not at all know Zen.

(7) *Satori* is emancipation, moral, spiritual, as well as intellectual. When I am in my isness, thoroughly purged of all intellectual sediments, I have my freedom in its primary sense.

(8) When the mind, now abiding in its isness—which, to use Zen verbalism, is not isness—and thus free from intellectual complexities and moralistic attachments of every description, surveys the world of the senses in all its multiplicities, it discovers in it all sorts of values hitherto hidden from sight. Here opens to the artist a world full of wonders and miracles.

(9) The artist's world is one of free creation, and this can come only from intuitions directly and immediately rising from the isness of things, unhampered by senses and intellect. He creates forms and sounds out of formlessness and soundlessness. To this extent, the artist's world coincides with that of Zen.

(10) What differentiates Zen from the arts is this: While the artists have to resort to the canvas and brush or mechanical instruments or some other mediums to express themselves, Zen has no need of things external, except "the body" in which the Zen-man is so to speak embodied. From the absolute point of view this is not quite correct; I say it only in concession to the worldly way of saying things. What Zen does is to delineate itself on the infinite canvas of time and space the way the flying wild geese cast their shadow on the water below with-

out any idea of doing so, while the water reflects the geese just as naturally and unintentionally.

(11) The Zen-man is an artist to the extent that, as the sculptor chisels out a great figure deeply buried in a mass of inert matter, the Zen-man transforms his own life into a work of creation, which exists, as Christians might say, in the mind of God.

DWIGHT GODDARD, *FOLLOWERS OF BUDDHA: AN AMERICAN BROTHERHOOD* (1934)

Few American missionaries who went to Asia during the heyday of American Protestant missions in the late-nineteenth and early-twentieth centuries returned unchanged. Many came back with a better understanding of Asians and Asian religions. Dwight Goddard (1861–1939), converted. After a lucrative career as an inventor and industrial engineer, Goddard decided to devote himself to spiritual matters. In 1894, he was graduated from Hartford Theological Seminary, not far from his boyhood home of Worcester, Massachusetts, and was dispatched as a Baptist missionary to Foochow, China. But he was gradually drawn to Buddhism, and after wandering into a Buddhist monastery in Kushan, he decided to become a Buddhist. He studied Buddhism in China and Japan before returning to the United States to practice. Goddard is best known for his *Buddhist Bible* (1932), an anthology of Buddhist scriptures toted in the rucksacks of the Beat Generation. But he was also a pioneering American advocate of Buddhist monasticism whose taste of monastic life in Asia convinced him that efforts to laicize Buddhism in America were misguided. *Followers of Buddha: An American Brotherhood* (1934) describes Goddard's unrealized dream, hatched in the summer of 1933, of a decidedly American monasticism: itinerant monks traveling back and forth in a van between retreats in Vermont and California in an effort to live out the admonition of Gautama Buddha to "have no abiding place." Because Goddard was far more attentive to ritual than other pioneering American Buddhists, *Followers of Buddha* also includes an intriguing list of practical rules for his all-male "American Buddhist Brotherhood," a monastic institution that now lives on only in his writings.

INTRODUCTION

The plan is as follows: To have inexpensive refuges in Vermont and California and then to have a motor-van by which some of the Brothers can motor back and forth between the two places taking advantage of favorable climatic conditions, teaching and explaining the Dharma to those they meet by the way, selling

Dwight Goddard, *Followers of Buddha: An American Brotherhood* (Santa Barbara, Calif.: J. F. Rowny Press, 1934), vi, 19–22.

Buddhist books, distributing literature, seeking new members and wider support for the Brotherhood.

The plan has certain advantages that earlier plans have lacked. A fixed location tends to become an "institution" with mounting expenses, routine and a tendency to lapse into easy going ways. The plan of itinerating—of having no abiding place—keeps the Brothers awake, active and earnest. It was the plan that Buddha, Jesus and St. Francis followed. It presents a life of freedom from, dependence upon, and conformity to, the conventional life of the world. It gives opportunity for meeting many people and awakening interest in Buddha and his way of life. It is comparatively inexpensive, there are no salaries to be paid, no deficits to be made up, it is friendly and peaceful, it does not antagonize anyone, and it keeps true to the example and spirit of Buddha. . . .

PRACTICAL RULES FOR THE DAILY LIFE OF THE BROTHERS

1. THE FIVE PRECEPTS. (1) Not to kill or be unkind to any living creatures. (2) Not to cherish impure thoughts. (3) Not to deceive. (4) Not to take anything that does not belong to one. (5) Not to partake of drugs or intoxicating drinks.

2. FIVE ADDITIONAL PRECEPTS. (1) To have as little to do with money and valuable things as possible. (2) To live a strictly pure and celibate life. (3) Not to sleep on soft beds. (4) Not to use ointments and condiments. (5) Not to attend entertainments or take part in games of chance.

3. THE SIX PARAMITAS. (1) Charity and sympathy. (2) Behavior to be determined by its relation to the happiness and benefit of others. (3) Humility and patience. (4) Zeal and perseverence. (5) Concentration and tranquility of mind. (6) Wisdom.

4. OBSERVANCE OF RULES. Brothers are to be cheerfully obedient to the rules they are asked to observe and to the duties they are asked to perform. All questions as to the meaning of the rules are to be referred to the Director and his interpretation is final. In grave cases an appeal may be made to the whole body of Brothers but a two-thirds vote is necessary to reverse the Director's decision.

5. HARMONY AMONG THE BROTHERS. In cases of flagrant immorality or serious dissension among the Brothers the Director shall try to settle the matter privately, but in case of failure, he shall summon a meeting of all the Brothers and together they shall try to compose the difference. If this fails, the Director shall request the recalcitrant Brother to withdraw from the Brotherhood. If asked to go away, a Brother shall do so promptly and without unpleasantness. If later on an ex-Brother should have a change of heart and desire to return to the Brotherhood his request shall be considered as in the case of a new Brother.

6. OUTSIDE INTERESTS. Brothers are not to have any outside interests, employment or worldly friends to distract their attention and interest from the main purpose of the Brotherhood. Worldly newspapers, magazines and books are not to be brought onto the premises, for the same reason. Brothers should not use their free time to relapse into worldly ways, or concern with world affairs, or idle talk, or discussions, or joking, or anything that tends to weaken one's mind-control and tranquility. Brothers are not to go away from the premises without notifying the Director, nor are they to invite worldly friends to visit them.

7. KINDNESS. Brothers are expected at all times and under all circumstances to practice kindness toward all people and all creatures. It is especially important that nothing shall be said or done to cause another Brother to feel badly, or that will cause strife within the Brotherhood, for harmony among the Brothers is of highest importance.

8. FOOD. Only two meals will be served, at six and twelve. Only vegetables, fruits, cereals, and nuts, with eggs and milk, will be served and only in limited quantities. The meal is to be partaken of in silence. Grace is to be said before and after the noon meal. No food is to be eaten between meals, except tea and a slight lunch after the evening practice of Dhyana [meditation], if there has been hard labor during the day. Indulgence in sweets, unnecessary condiments, and coffee is to be restrained and the use of tobacco is forbidden.

9. CLOTHING. Clothing is to be simple and inexpensive and is to be used until it is worn out. The possession of expensive, stylish and unnecessary clothing is forbidden. The use of silk and leather is to be avoided.

10. USE OF MONEY. Brothers are to have no private money. All private money or property is to be relinquished to relatives or friends, or given to the Brotherhood to be used for the common good. If a Brother needs money, he may ask for it from the treasurer who will supply what is necessary, as far as he is able to do so.

11. LABOR. Every Brother is expected to have some work assigned to him for each morning. The work may be frequently rotated and changed, or it may be a continuing task according to the ability of each Brother, to be determined by the Director. At the request of the Director Brothers may be asked to do outside work for which no money payment will be accepted. If food or other things are offered in exchange they may be gratefully accepted.

12. GUESTS. Any man who is sincerely interested in Buddhism and who desires instruction in it may be received as a guest for a limited time by the approval of the Director. Such a guest is expected to observe in a general way the rules of the Brotherhood, and to give evidence of his sincere purpose to profit by the instruction and practice. In their attitude toward a guest the Brothers should be very careful to reflect the spirit of Buddha, seeking above all else to recommend the Dharma by their own conduct. They should avoid general conversation and shall seek to teach and to explain the Dharma to the best of

their ability, always remembering that the best gift is the gift of the Dharma. There should be no urging upon a guest to become a Buddhist, leaving that to the guest's own decision. All callers and friends shall be considered as guests of the Brotherhood, and shall not be invited to private rooms or to meals.

13. LADIES. As the Brothers are trying to live a tranquil life, the presence of ladies at the Refuge is not desired. If they call they are to be received courteously, but they are not to be invited to call, or to be received in private, or to eat with the Brothers, or to be present at any of their exercises.

14. DHYANA. Whatever the Brothers may be doing, or wherever they may be, they should always arrange the day so as to include some time for the quiet practice of Dhyana.

15. THE DAY'S DUTIES:
    4:30—Rising bell.
    4:45-6:45—Practice of Dhyana.
    7:00—Breakfast.
    7:30-11-30—Labor.
    12:00—Dinner.
    12:30-2:00—Free time.
    2:00-4:00—Practice of Mindfulness.
    4:00-5:00—Free time.
    5:00-7:00—Practice of Dhyana.
    7:00—Light lunch and free time.
    9:00—Lights out.

JACK KEROUAC, *DHARMA BUMS* (1958)

The name of Jack Kerouac (1922–69) is forever entwined with the Beat Generation, postwar hipsters who prepared the way for the hippies by writing spontaneous prose, doing drugs, practicing free love (including homosexuality), and generally renouncing the obligations of home and work place—and all quite before the sixties. Although the media interpreted the term "beat" in negative terms (as in "beat down" or "beat up"), Kerouac insisted on a more positive reading: beat as "beatific." The Beat movement was no mere literary or social protest, he was saying, it was a spiritual quest for a "new consciousness." Kerouac, who was born in Lowell, Massachusetts, into a family of French-Canadian Catholics, came to Buddhism through Thoreau's *Walden* (1854), which inspired him in the winter of 1953–54 to hunt up Buddhist books at his local library. Soon Kerouac was devouring Dwight Goddard's *The Buddhist Bible* (1932), urging his fellow Beats to "dig" the Buddha, and doing his level best to meditate on bum knees. Kerouac found a fellow traveler in Zen poet Gary Snyder, who encouraged Kerouac's study and practice. Although Kerouac returned toward the end of his life to the comforts of the Roman Catholicism of his youth, Buddhism—especially Zen spontaneity and the affirmation of the Yogacara ("mind only") school that our world

Sketch of the Buddha (1991) by Beat poet Allen Ginsberg. Copyright © Allen Ginsberg Trust. Used by permission.

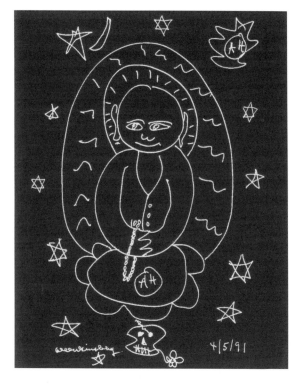

of suffering is an illusion created by ignorant minds—influenced many of his works, including *Mexico City Blues* (1959), a long poem of 242 choruses, and the novel *Dharma Bums* (1958). In these passages from that novel, Kerouac reconstructs Gary Snyder as Japhy Ryder and Beat poet Allen Ginsberg as Alvah Goldbook. He names his own alter-ego Ray Smith.

The little Saint Teresa bum was the first genuine Dharma Bum I'd met, and the second was the number one Dharma Bum of them all and in fact it was he, Japhy Ryder, who coined the phrase. Japhy Ryder was a kid from eastern Oregon brought up in a log cabin deep in the woods with his father and mother and sister, from the beginning a woods boy, an axman, farmer, interested in animals and Indian lore so that when he finally got to college by hook or crook he was already well equipped for his early studies in anthropology and later in Indian myth and in the actual texts of Indian mythology. Finally he learned Chinese and Japanese and became an Oriental scholar and discovered the greatest Dharma Bums of them all, the Zen Lunatics of China and Japan. At the same time, being a Northwest boy with idealistic tendencies, he got interested in oldfashioned I.W.W.

anarchism and learned to play the guitar and sing old worker songs to go with his Indian songs and general folksong interests. I first saw him walking down the street in San Francisco the following week (after hitchhiking the rest of the way from Santa Barbara in one long zipping ride given me, as though anybody'll believe this, by a beautiful darling young blonde in a snow-white strapless bathing suit and bare-footed with a gold bracelet on her ankle, driving a next-year's cinnamon-red Lincoln Mercury, who wanted benzedrine so she could drive all the way to the City and when I said I had some in my duffel bag yelled "Crazy!")— I saw Japhy loping along in that curious long stride of the mountain-climber, with a small knapsack on his back filled with books and toothbrushes and whatnot which was his small "goin-to-the-city" knapsack as apart from his big full rucksack complete with sleeping bag, poncho, and cookpots. He wore a little goatee, strangely Oriental-looking with his somewhat slanted green eyes, but he didn't look like a Bohemian at all, and was far from being a Bohemian (a hanger-onner around the arts). He was wiry, sun-tanned, vigorous, open, all howdies and glad talk and even yelling hello to bums on the street and when asked a question answered right off the bat from the top or bottom of his mind I don't know which and always in a sprightly sparkling way.

"Where did you meet Ray Smith?" they asked him when we walked into The Place, the favorite bar of the hepcats around the Beach.

"Oh I always meet my Bodhisattvas in the street!" he yelled, and ordered beers. . . .

He claimed at once that I was a great "Bodhisattva," meaning "great wise being" or "great wise angel," and that I was ornamenting this world with my sincerity. We had the same favorite Buddhist saint, too: Avalokitesvara, or, in Japanese, Kwannon the Eleven-Headed. He knew all the details of Tibetan, Chinese, Mahayana, Hinayana, Japanese and even Burmese Buddhism but I warned him at once I didn't give a goddamn about the mythology and all the names and national flavors of Buddhism, but was just interested in the first of Sakyamuni's four noble truths, *All life is suffering*. And to an extent interested in the third, *The suppression of suffering can be achieved*, which I didn't quite believe was possible then. (I hadn't yet digested the Lankavatara Scripture which eventually shows you that there's nothing in the world but the mind itself, and therefore all's possible including the suppression of suffering.) . . .

Japhy leaping up: "I've been reading Whitman, know what he says, *Cheer up slaves, and horrify foreign despots*, he means that's the attitude for the Bard, the Zen Lunacy bard of old desert paths, see the whole thing is a world full of rucksack wanderers, Dharma Bums refusing to subscribe to the general demand that they consume production and therefore have to work for the privilege of consuming, all that crap they didn't really want anyway such as refrigerators, TV sets, cars, at least new fancy cars, certain hair oils and deodorants and general junk you finally always see a week later in the garbage anyway, all of them imprisoned in a system of work, produce, consume, work, produce, consume, I see a vision of a great rucksack revolution thousands or even millions of young Americans wandering around with rucksacks, going up to mountains to pray, making children laugh and old men glad, making young girls happy and old girls happier, all of 'em Zen Lunatics who go about writing poems that happen to appear in their heads for no reason and also by being kind and also by strange unexpected acts keep giving visions of eternal freedom to everybody and to all living creatures, that's what I like about you Goldbook and Smith, you two guys from the East Coast which I thought was dead."

"We thought the *West* Coast was dead!"

"You've really brought a fresh wind around here. . . . Just think how truly great and wise America will be, with all this energy and exuberance and space focused into the Dharma."

"Oh"—Alvah—"balls on that old tired Dharma."

"Ho! What we need is a floating zendo, where an old Bodhisattva can wander from place to place and always be sure to find a spot to . . . lay up in and learn to drink tea like Ray did, learn to meditate like you should Alvah, and I'll be a head monk of a zendo . . . Yessir, that's what, a series of monasteries for fellows to go and monastate and meditate in, we can have groups of shacks up in the Sierras or the High Cascades or even Ray says down in Mexico and have big wild gangs of pure holy men getting together to drink and talk and pray, think of the waves of salvation can flow out of nights like that, and finally have women, too, wives, small huts with religious families, like the old days of the Puritans. Who's to say the cops of America and the Republicans and Democrats are gonna tell everybody what to do?"

[Ryder:] "We'll write poems, we'll get a printing press and print our own poems, the Dharma Press, we'll poetize the lot and make a fat book of icy bombs for the booby public."

[Smith:] "Ah the public ain't so bad, they suffer too. You always read about some tarpaper shack burning somewhere in the Middlewest with three little children perishing and you see a picture of the parents crying. Even the kitty was burned. Japhy, do you think God made the world to amuse himself because he was bored? Because if so he would have to be mean."

"Ho, who would you mean by God?"

"Just Tathagata, if you will."

"Well it says in the sutra that God, or Tathagata, doesn't himself emanate a world from his womb but it just appears due to ignorance of sentient beings."

"But he emanated the sentient beings and their ignorance too. It's all too pitiful. I ain't gonna rest till I find out *why*, Japhy, *why*."

"Ah don't trouble your mind essence. Remember that in pure Tathagata mind essence there is no asking of the question why and not even any significance attached to it."

"Well, then nothing's really happening, then."

"He threw a stick at me and hit me in the foot.

"Well, that didn't happen," I said.

"I really don't know, Ray, but I appreciate your sadness about the world. 'Tis indeed. Look at that party the other night. Everybody wanted to have a good time and tried real hard but we all woke up the next day feeling sorta sad and separate. What do you think about death, Ray?"

"I think death is our reward. When we die we go straight to nirvana Heaven and that's that."

"But supposing you're reborn in the lower hells and have hot redhot balls of iron shoved down your throat by devils."

"Life's already shoved an iron foot down *my* mouth. But I don't think that's anything but a dream cooked up by some hysterical monks who didn't understand Buddha's peace under the Bo Tree or for that matter Christ's peace looking down on the heads of his tormenters and forgiving them."

"You really like Christ, don't you?"

"Of course I do. And after all, a lot of people say he is Maitreya, the Buddha prophesied to appear after Sakyamuni, you know, Maitreya means 'Love' in Sanskrit and that's all Christ talked about was love."

"Oh, don't start preaching Christianity to me, I can just see you on your deathbed kissing the cross like some old Karamazov or like our old friend Dwight Goddard who spent his life as a Buddhist and suddenly returned to Christianity in his last days. Ah that's not for me, I want to spend hours every day in a lonely temple meditating in front of a sealed statue of Kwannon which no one is ever allowed to see because it's too powerful. Strike hard, old diamond!"

"It'll all come out in the wash."

RUTH FULLER SASAKI, "ZEN: A METHOD FOR RELIGIOUS AWAKENING" (1959)

A partisan of what her son-in-law Alan Watts derided as "square Zen," Ruth Fuller Sasaki (1893–1967) helped turn Zen into what she called "the magic password at smart cocktail parties" in 1950s Manhattan. She spent some time in the twenties at the Nyack, New York, ashram of Pierre Bernard, an early and controversial convert to Hinduism also known as "Oom the Omnipotent." In 1930 she and her husband, Charles Everett, went on a world tour. In Japan they met D. T. Suzuki, who handed her a copy of his *Essays in Zen Buddhism* and showed her how to meditate. Two years later she went back to Japan, where she practiced Rinzai Zen for three-and-a-half months at Nanzen-ji in Kyoto. Returning to her New York City home, she joined the Buddhist Society of America and became an integral part of the East Coast Buddhist scene. After her husband's death in 1940, she grew close to Sokei-an, the founder of the Buddhist Society of America (later renamed The First Zen Institute of America). After his release from wartime internment, they were married, but he died shortly thereafter. She returned to Japan in 1949, translating Zen texts and advancing her Zen training. In 1956 she established a First Zen Institute of America branch on the grounds of Daitoku-ji. Two years later she pioneered the role of the American woman Zen master when, under Sesso Oda Roshi's sponsorship, she became the first foreigner to be ordained in the Zen tradition in Japan. In this excerpt from a lecture she originally delivered at MIT in 1958, Sasaki describes her encounter with the foundational practices of traditional Rinzai Zen: the koan and the *sanzen*, or interview between roshi and student.

I am a Zen Buddhist and have been one for over twenty-five years. So I speak from within Zen, not as one who observes it from the outside. Though brought up in a strict Presbyterian family, I became a Buddhist in my twenties. The study of early Buddhism, into which I soon plunged, brought me to the conclusion that the pivot of that religion was Awakening and the Buddhist life a life lived in accordance with Awakening. Meditation was the means through which Śākyamuni, the historical Buddha, had come to his enlightenment. The forty-nine years of his life after his great experience were spent in trying to show other men how they, by following the path he had pursued, might attain this awakening for themselves. Therefore, to find a teacher who could give me instruction in how to practice Buddhist meditation became my aim. Also, I wanted to see if meditation methods that eastern people had for centuries found successful would work equally well for a westerner. At forty I first had the privilege of practicing under a famous Rinzai Zen master or *rōshi*, Nanshinken of the Nanzen-ji monastery in Kyoto, Japan. Later, as the obligations of a normal family life permitted, I continued my practice and study in Japan under Nanshinken, and in America under the late Sōkei-an Rōshi. For the past ten years, free of household responsibilities, I have lived almost continuously in Kyoto, devoting myself to Japanese and Chinese language studies as they relate to Zen, and to Rinzai Zen practice under my third Zen teacher, Gotō Zuigan Rōshi. Though I have not yet completed my Zen study, perhaps I can share with you a little of what I have learned. . . .

Zen does not hold that there is a god apart from the universe who first created this universe and then created man to enjoy, or even master it—and these days it seems not to be enough to master the planet Earth; we must now master the universe as well. Rather, Zen holds that there is no god outside the universe who has created it and created man. God—if I may borrow that word for a moment—the universe, and man are one indissoluble existence, one total whole. Only THIS—capital THIS—is. Anything and everything that appears to us as an individual entity or phenomenon, whether it be a planet or an atom, a mouse or a man, is but a temporary manifestation of THIS in form; every activity that takes place, whether it be birth or death, loving or eating breakfast, is but a temporary manifestation of THIS in activity. When we look at things this way, naturally we cannot believe that each individual person has been endowed with a special and individual soul or self. Each one of us is but a cell, as it were, in the body of the Great Self, a cell that comes into being, performs its functions, and passes away, transformed into another manifestation. Though we have temporary individuality, that temporary, limited individuality is not either a true self or our true self. Our true self is the Great Self; our true body is the Body of Reality, or the Dharmakāya, to give it its technical Buddhist name.

Ruth Fuller Sasaki, "Zen: A Method for Religious Awakening," in Nancy Wilson Ross, ed., *The World of Zen: An East-West Anthology* (New York: Random House, 1960), 16–19, 24–25, 28–29. Reprinted by permission of First Zen Institute of America, Inc.

Buddhism, and Zen, grant that this view is not one that can be reasoned about intellectually. Nor, on the other hand, do they ask us to take this doctrine on faith. They tell us it must be experienced, it must be realized. Such realization can be brought about through the awakening of that intuitive wisdom which is intrinsic to all men. The method for awakening this intuitive wisdom is meditation. . . .

It is the generally accepted view today that, as far as doctrines are concerned—and, as you see, Zen does have them, contrary to what you may have heard—Zen is developed Mahayana Buddhism as the Chinese mind, steeped in the Chinese world view and classical Taoism, realized it. In fewer words, we might say that Zen is Indian Buddhism dyed with the dye of Chinese Taoism. Japanese Zennists, however, while conceding this, consider Zen to be rather a return to the Buddha's Buddhism . . . a return to Śākyamuni's basic teaching that every man can and should attain this transforming religious experience of awakening for himself. . . .

Now how does one go about studying and practicing Zen today? A would-be student goes to a Zen roshi, one for whom he has deep respect, in whom he has faith, and with whom he has a distinct feeling of relationship. In a polite and humble manner the student requests to be accepted as a disciple. If the roshi consents, he will turn the student over to his head monk or senior disciple to be instructed in zazen, or meditation practice. The student will be told how to sit and how to breathe; he will be given certain concentration exercises to practice. For a considerable period the student pursues these elementary practices at home several hours a day, or sits with a group of other students who meet for zazen practice at certain specified times. When the head monk or senior disciple decides that the student has acquired a "good seat," that is, can sit in the correct posture for a considerable length of time and is proficient in concentration, he will inform the roshi that the student is now prepared to begin his koan study.

The student then goes to the roshi and, during the private interview known as *sanzen*, an interview conducted in a formal and specifically prescribed manner, the master gives the student a koan which he is now to meditate upon. At definite times from then on the student is expected to go to the roshi for a like interview, and during each interview to express to the master his view at the moment of the inner meaning or content of the koan on which he has been continuously meditating. . . .

Since each koan deals with some aspect of Truth as it is held in Zen Buddhism, little by little the student is brought to realize the total of Zen doctrine which is wholly concerned with the THIS, of which I have spoken earlier, and its relative, or manifested, aspects. The doctrines of Zen are not stated specifically either in written or spoken words, but, through long-continued meditation upon the succession of koans, deeper and deeper levels of the student's intuitive mind are opened, levels where these unspoken doctrines are realized as truths. For the Zen master teaches his student nothing. . . . The treasure of Truth lies deep within the mind of each one of us; it is to be awakened or revealed or attained only through our own efforts. . . .

I don't profess to know clearly what is causing so many Americans and Europeans to interest themselves in Zen today. In fact I should like to have someone tell me. I know they are said to be unable to have faith in traditional religious doctrines, to find in scientific materialism poor nourishment for their spirits, to feel that modern life, with its multitude of machines, is an exhausting and unrewarding way of life for them as human beings. And, of course, there are always the few who don't like to conform and who seem to think that perhaps in Zen they will find justification for their own personal interpretations of freedom. . . .

In Zen, when we must speak, everyday words are preferred to quotations from the scriptures. So, in conclusion, let me put more simply what I have just said. The aim of Zen is first of all awakening, awakening to our true self. With this awakening to our true self comes emancipation from our small self or personal ego. When this emancipation from the personal ego is finally complete, then we know the freedom spoken of in Zen and so widely misconstrued by those who take the name for the experience. Of course, as long as this human frame hangs together and we exist as one manifested form in the world of forms, we carry on what appears to be an individual existence as an individual ego. But no longer is that ego in control with its likes and dislikes, its characteristics and its foibles. The True Self, which from the beginning we have always been, has at last become the master. Freely the True Self uses this individual form and this individual ego as it will. With no resistance and no hindrance it uses them in all the activities of everyday life, whatever they are and wherever they may be.

ELSON B. SNOW, ENTRY INTO THE DHARMA GATE (1994)

Not all the interest in Buddhism during the 1950s focused on Zen, and not all the interested were New York painters or San Francisco poets. This previously unpublished memoir offers a glimpse of other religious crossings during this period of exclusion. Elson Snow, a printer with a high school education, reflects on his conversion to Jodo Shinshu in 1954. Born in Modesto, California, in 1925, Snow visited Japan while serving in the Navy during World War II. Nine years later he turned to Buddhism. In San Francisco, where he worked as a printer for a local newspaper, Snow stumbled into a Japanese Buddhist temple. That experience changed his life. He was not the first European American, or *hakujin*, to join the Buddhist Churches of America (BCA); some, like Julius Goldwater, had even served as priests. But not many of Snow's generation followed him into the predominantly Japanese Pure Land community, with its family-oriented piety and its haunting memories of internment. Fewer still rose to positions of authority. A devoted member of the BCA since 1954, in recent years Snow has served as editor of its monthly paper, *Wheel of Dharma*. Snow's story is important not because it is typical but because it challenges stereotypes about sympathizers and converts: not all were artists or intellectuals; not all turned to the Zen of Watts or Suzuki. Some, like this working-class Pure Land devotee, chanted to Amida Buddha in Japanese temples on Sundays, seeking solace "in a chaotic world of unease and unrest."

Elson B. Snow to Thomas A. Tweed, personal correspondence, 10 November 1994. The abridged (and previously unpublished) letter is used with the permission of Elson B. Snow.

A rainy day and with a handful of picture cards of some Shingon related images with Sino-Japanese captions, I went to *nihon machi* (Japanese Town) to see if I could find someone to translate them for me as I thought the statuary, particularly, was interesting. The photo reproductions are well known, and as far as I know, the Asian Arts at the Boston Museum are still intact, but I doubt they come close to the Brundage Collection in value and quantity. The first person I met was Tokuhiro Miura, working in a broken down second hand store at the edge of the Nikkei (Japanese ancestry) community. He was a student at the University of California, and although he was hesitant in translating the Sanskrit transliteration in Sino-Japanese, Kambun said there was a Buddhist temple up the street and I should inquire there, which I did.

My first "known" Buddhist acquaintance was Noburo Hannyu, still an active member of the BCA and long associated with the administrative side of the organization; he was one of the charter signers of corporate papers with the State of California filed during the war years in the early 1940's. When I first saw him he was perched on a ladder fiddling with some arrangements in the temple gymnasium preparing for the annual Bazaar. He told me to come back during the day and talk with Reverend Seiji Kobara, residential minister, and he would be able to translate the captions for me. This was in 1954, the year in which I became a Buddhist. A convert.

I always like to think that I became a Buddhist at the same age that Sakyamuni, the historical Buddha, left home to become the Great Ascetic, and eventually assume the role of the Great Guide for Humanity. I was 29 years old. It is difficult to remember just how much Buddhism was familiar to me, it was certainly known to me as a "general reader," but my knowledge of the dharma was deficient. It embarrasses me today to recall that only a few weeks after my first contact I was asked to give a talk on Buddhism. In giving "dharma talks" later I was still embarrassed by stumbling efforts. It is, in my opinion, that in the days before the war and those years following, it was assumed in BCA temples that the *hakujin* had a kind of understanding which could interpret the religion to an audience limited to the English language. This kind of hakujin-embracement has always nourished a hope that an assimilation of religion and American culture is happening—it is my conviction that there is more to this bussei (buddhist) attitude than the explanation I am able to construct; that it has to do with the way an ethnic minority was able to survive over a long period of time which spanned the *Yellow Peril Era* and finally a defense mechanism as "enemy aliens." What counts is that in some way prevailing attitudes in the BCA jurisdiction allowed me an autodidactic education I received by way of the back door.

My formal education goes no further than a High School shop curriculum, and I successfully graduated as a result of credit for serving in the military, a draftee in the Navy during my senior year not completed in 1943. . . .

I can recall only three times of hearing about Buddhism before 1954:

1) In Japan (1945 occupation) I was told by a shipmate (USS Oklahoma City) that he visited a Buddhist temple; I remember how surprised I

was to hear of such a thing. I had learned nothing about Buddhism from this experience.

2) Helped my mother (in the late 1940's) to prepare a talk on Buddhism for her Christian Sunday School Class—all information extracted from an encyclopedia.

3) About the same time a friend asked me, "What is Zen Buddhism?" as a result of one of his fellow printers attending Zen temple in San Francisco.

I had received journeyman pointer status in the late forties at a very early date due to the demise of the *Marin Journal,* a small daily newspaper in San Rafael, California. This was possible as I had served apprentice time one year before going into the Navy, working for the four Weeklies in San Anselmo, California, while still in High School. The next few years I traveled across the western part of the United States as a printer before settling down to working steady for *The San Francisco Chronicle,* and was married in 1961. I was active in the Young Democrat organization in San Francisco before marriage. I was especially active in the Adlai Stevenson Campaign and this campaign marks the real beginning of my life-long labor union and liberal views, but it was preceded by my union activity, the hassle of unions resulting from the Taft-Hartley law, and the presence of Richard Milhaus Nixon whose dirty congressional and senate campaigns earned him the reputation as our most despicable national politician before Watergate. . . .

I was born in Modesto, California, 1925. I am the oldest and have two brothers and two sisters. My mother considers herself a Californian, although she was born in Washington. My father was an Iowan, and in my eyes a typical Midwesterner whose importance to me is that my grandfather loved books and left Christianity, exactly how and why I do not know except that he loved debating the representatives in the Bible belt on the question of Darwin evolutionism. This position caused my father to declare himself an "agnostic" in consistency with his father's beliefs, and he delighted in swearing in favor of a simplistic evolutionary belief. How deep my grandfather's belief, I do not know but I think it was the popular materialistic view of the time which rubbed fundamentalist Christian's fur the wrong way.

My father told me that he had "to stay home and take care of his invalid mother" during the crucial years when he could have served in France during World War I. He only went as far as the eighth grade, but I believe the Midwestern background of his time was on par with our present day High School. In his early twenties he came to California in a Model T Ford with "a friend" earning their way cross country by repairing cars breaking down along American roads. In 1930 we moved to Iowa. Because this was my formative years until I was ten, it always seemed that I was a Midwesterner, too—and it seems that these years were long and full with one continuous adventure from the unsettled country along a river, to a farm just outside town on the Iowa-Missouri State-Line, and to *the big city* of Davenport Iowa. "The worst years," my father said. But they were the greatest for me living near the Mississippi River, going to western movies for a nickel on Saturday afternoons, and the excitement of city neighborhoods before returning to California at the height of the great economic depression. I don't remember the cinch bugs, dust storms, crop failures, and poverty. My grandfather had gone through the depression of 1898 and he swore, "never again" so he invested in property. The 1930 depression, however, ate up all money for seeding and other things undreamed of by my grandfather. Whether my father was a poor manager of agriculture could be partly possible, for he hated farming and was much more successful as a carpenter after moving back to California.

One of his first jobs on his return to California was a carpenter on the Waldo Tunnel, an entry onto the Golden Gate Bridge. . . . I really grew up in Marin County, a conservative and sheltered community, but I always advertised myself as coming from the working class, at my father's expense and embarrassment. "The County" to this day remains a haven for the yuppies (unrecognized as such in that era). My political consciousness did not ripen until after leaving Marin County following the War, although I do remember bad-mouthing *Southern Pacific* for ripping up the tracks in '40–41, sending the rails to Japan for scrap iron and installing Greyhound busses. The slogan, at the time was "Guns for Japan, Bandages for China." I do remember having a deep prejudice against corporate America (and the British!), but they were mostly "feelings" and had little to do with real politics and/or real people.

I sincerely believe that I have a conservative bent in the acceptance of Buddhism, and this is traced to my family background of a mother who sent us to Sunday School spasmodically to a Methodist Church, to Salvation Army, to Presbyterian, etc., but our attendance was irregular and reinforced, I think, by my father's strange evolutionary doctrine inherited from his father. . . .

One favorite philosopher for adolescents and post-adolescents, I believe, is Arthur Schopenhauer, and I'm sure that it was his essays that made it easy for me to enter the gate of Buddhism. I have always thought it strange that the label "pessimism" was often placed on his ideas—the teaching that sorrow is rampant in the world is the experience I thought about in my own struggle to become an adult and the loosening of restraints. I had the romantic idea, also, to be *uprooted*, which I enacted as a transient printer. Contrary to the belief of many Japanese American friends, I have never consciously turned to Buddhism as a reaction to the *Dogmas of Christianity*. Buddhism came to me at the right time convincing me that there is no soul problem, and as for things like *Resurrection* and other marvelous events there seemed to me no approach to them in Christianity other than that they are "mysteries." Naive, or not, doctrinal beliefs in Buddhism for me were no barrier. . . .

Why Jodo Shinshu? Right from the very first I was attracted by: (1) anatman theory; (2) bhakti-type religion; I later learned that this designation is considered doctrinally incorrect; (3) The Absolute Other, which I have always felt to be unique in world religions, and that the *tariki* (other-power) aspect is comparable only to the Taoist; and, (4) the radical ethics of Shinran Shonin. Of course, I admit of having primitive views at this stage of religious development, and would not argue with anyone who says I had arrived for wrong reasons! In any case, I was lucky that the residential minister Reverend Kobara was very doctrinal in approach, and the fact of the lack of Buddhist material in English made it imperative to read everything about Buddhism outside Jodo Shinshu and the Pure Land tradition. I was also cautious from the very beginning to refrain from pushing my political views in this new religious context which I enthusiastically found by *a series of accidents* [or, was it ripened karma similar to Calvinism?]. My liberal views were easily submerged in this environment, but it did not prevent me from voicing disapproval from time to time of the hesitancy to take a stand on social issues. This posture is a very difficult problem to unravel in the BCA. First of all, it is hardly likely in the foreseeable future that the BCA will come to terms with the conflict of "church and state" and its related matters as long as its members see themselves as not yet an assimilated group in mainstream america (is this buzz word correct?). It is my criticism that some of our Reverends in spite of a vigorous denial see ourselves as a small sect and not as representatives of a great tradition like Mahayana.

Although I volunteered a week or two of "hard labor" at the construction of the Buddhist temple in China Town, and attended lectures of other Buddhist sects, I have never veered far from the temple organization of the BCA, and never gave much thought to crossing over to a tradition other than the Hongwanji transmission of Jodo Shinshu. . . .

I could have been comfortable in a Shingon, a Nichiren (not *sogagakkai*), or a Zen setting (in the Japanese community only) as it would have satisfied my need for ritual-imagery and for activism—but the doctrine of the "total-other with its radical ethical posture" is an ingredient that makes religious experience a possibility for me. I also could not see playing the role of a vegetarian and a quiet sitter on the week-end. The tension between the secular and the sacred is too strong for half-involvement, and the householder status seemed to me to be the only option in the ultimate sense of spiritual participation. And then, of course, there is the conviction that comes from faith, "feeling we could do nothing else" known in Shin Buddhism as the *shinjin experience,* or, "the awakening of faith."

There are two topics that have never appealed to me but I always had to admit them as valuable avenues of inquiry, and perhaps should never be left out in the real business of discussing personal religion and commitment: (1) Why are you a Buddhist, or have become one? (2) How can we adapt Buddhism to America? Both these questions are asked with frequency. Perhaps after there has been a legitimate development of maturation and assimilation, the question will be asked with less frequency. I think that the questions should be stated differently somehow including references to descriptions of individual and institutional conditions already present. Something like, "what is your commitment and present role in the Buddhist community, and what spiritual goals would you like to set for yourself—and what obstacles are there which prevent you from realizing them?"

It is certain that there have been many influences on me within the community of Jodo Shin Buddhists, and I would not want to try to sort them out for fear of unintentionally devaluating the most important of them. The Academic influence must be given to Professor Ryosetsu Fujiwara whose lectures on Shin doctrine I paid close attention and appreciated them. The Sanskrit courses from Reverend M. Fujitani at least gave me a taste for the broad interest in Mahayana Buddhism, and much later I was able to attend classes in reading Chinese texts at the IBS on Haste Street that have proven very valuable. My earlier study "on the hill of San Francisco" (College of the Pacific) was confined to conversational Japanese which did not take me very far, but it had a cultural impact. I reflect on this past with some sadness as there were not widely available good sources for the study of Buddhism, unless one had plenty of time, money, and ambition to study. In my opinion popular Buddhism at the time was disastrous because we could only acquire pop psychology and watered down Zen. There were the hippie movement, and flower children later on that added color and a possible spur for religious imagination, but the drug and sex coloration of the vagabond mentality, I felt, was artificially drawn. . . .

My family history does not lend itself to an established religion, and I see little in it that would promote a stability in religious belief, except a healthy attitude of *acceptance*, whenever the opportunity psychologically presents itself which would fit a life-time mood and perspective for individual liberation by spiritual means. My mother was tolerant of my beliefs, but my agnostic father thought it odd to accept a Japanese religion, "giving up one's heritage!"

I do not think my account here is of any use, nor do I feel that such an attempt could possibly be truthful; it seems apparent that we are always pasting our present attitudes to events and anticipations occurring years ago. Today, I am an enthusiastic admirer of Rennyo Shonin, whose career ended 500 years ago. The usual reason for admiring him is an interest in the historical institution, but my fondness for him lies in his personality as a charismatic leader whose orientation is one for the ideal layman in a chaotic world of unease and unrest.

My own status as a "convert" I share with most hakujin Buddhists who feel that we have not been converted at all, but that the Buddha and his followers has verified the truths we already know. . . .

. . . *In gratitude to the light and life of tathagata amitabha*
gassho, Elson
November 10, 1994

CHAPTER 12

Artists, Preachers, and Missionaries

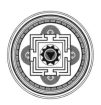

E. STANLEY JONES, *THE CHRIST OF THE INDIAN ROAD* (1925)

In the period between World War I and World War II, American Protestants vigorously debated the means and ends of foreign missions. Should missionaries stress evangelism or social service? Was Christianity the only way to salvation, or were there nuggets of truth in Asian religions? In 1930, philanthropist John D. Rockefeller Jr. funded an interdenominational mainline Protestant commission charged with answering such questions. *Re-Thinking Missions* (1932), the report of this "Layman's Inquiry," articulated a forward-looking view that would resonate among mainline Protestants for the rest of the century. It recast the aim of missions as collaboration rather than conversion, and redefined the ideal missionary as an ambassador, not a salesman. One man who came close to meeting this new modernist ideal was E. Stanley Jones (1884–1973). A Maryland-born Methodist minister who went to India in 1907 to teach Christianity, Jones discovered after his arrival that he had much to learn from the Indian people. His first book, *The Christ of the Indian Road* (1925), sold over half a million copies and brought Jones international renown as a liberal spokesperson for the new missions. Deeply influenced by Mohandas Gandhi, whom he considered a friend, Jones later established a number of Christian ashrams or spiritual retreat centers, first in India and later in the United States. During World War II, he was a frequent visitor to Japanese-American internment camps. In this passage from *The Christ of the Indian Road*, Jones demonstrates his determination to foster both an India that is more Christian and a Christianity that is more Indian.

As Christ meets India and her past what is his demand?

When Mohammedanism confronted Hinduism the demand was of absolute surrender—a complete wiping of the slate of the past and the dictates of the prophet written in its stead. It is no wonder that Hinduism withstood it, and does withstand it, for its very life and past are involved.

Does Jesus take that same attitude? Are his demands upon India the same as Mohammed? Is the slate to be wiped clean and the past absolutely blotted out?

It must be confessed that this has often been the attitude and demand of the Christian missionary. If Christianity is more or less identified with Western civilization and presented as such, or if it is a system of church government and a more or less fixed theological system, blocked off and rigid and presented as such, then I do not see how we can escape the attitude of the Mohammedan. The past must be wiped out and a clean slate presented for our theological systems, our ecclesiastical organizations, and our civilization to be written in its stead.

But if our message be Christ, and Christ alone, then this does not necessarily follow. He may turn to India as he turned to Judaism and say, "I came not to destroy but to fulfill." . . .

There is no doubt that devout Hindus who see worth-while and beautiful things in their faith are deeply concerned as they see the decay of that faith and wonder what the future will bring. Hindus themselves frankly tell of that decay, but always with a pang. . . .

A keen Hindu put the matter to me in rather vulgar but vivid language: "Christianity is increasing and Hinduism is dying—damn it!"

When he says that Hinduism is dying it must be qualified a bit. Some of the outward practices of Hinduism are dying, but there are behind these practices some ideas that constitute the living spirit of Hinduism and have made it survive through the centuries. Caste and idolatry and Brahmanism will drop away, but there will be left what will constitute the core of the Indian heritage. It will be worth preserving. A lady in Baltimore found some seeds in the hands of an Egyptian mummy and planted them. Morning glories came up. In the hand of the mummified forms and customs of Hinduism I think there are five living seeds: (1) That the ultimate reality is spirit. (2) The sense of unity running through things. (3) That there is justice at the heart of the universe. (4) A passion for freedom. (5) The tremendous cost of the religious life. I do not believe that the world can afford to lose those five things so deeply imbedded in India's thought and life. . . .

Would these ideas that form the finest things in India's past find new life should they die into Christianity? Would they be expressed in a new living way? Would Christ be the new mold and motive? . . .

The role of the iconoclast is easy, but the role of the one who carefully gathers up in himself all the spiritual and moral values in the past worth preserving is infinitely more difficult and infinitely more valuable. Hence we can go to the East and thank God for the fine things we may find there, believing that they are the very footprints of God. He has been there before us. . . .

To see how Jesus remarkably fulfills the finest striving of both East and West note the ends of life discovered by the Greeks and those discovered by the Hindus and the announcement that Jesus made about himself. The Greeks were the brain of Europe and did its philosophic thinking, just as the Hindus are the brain of Asia and have done the philosophic thinking for Asia. The Greeks said the ends of life were three: the Good, the True, and the Beautiful. The Hindus also say the ends of life are three: Gyana, Bhakti, and Karma. With this difference that the Hindus were the more religious people and made these ends means—the end was Brahma, the means to attain that were the three ways: the Gyana Marga, the way of knowledge; the Bhakti Marga, the way of devotion or emotion; the Karma Marga, the way of works or deeds.

Jesus stood between the Greeks and the Hindus, midway between East and West, and made this announcement, "I am the Way, the Truth, and the Life." Turning toward the Greeks he says, "I am the Way"—a method of acting—the Greek's Good; "I am the Truth"—the Greek's True; "I am the Life"—the Greek's Beautiful, for Life is beauty—plus. Turning toward the Hindus he says, "I am the Way"—the Karma Marga, a method of acting; "I am the Truth"—the Gyana Marga—the method of knowing; "I am the Life"—the Bhakti Marga—the method of emotion, for Life is emotion—plus. . . .

As I have sat writing the experiences of these seventeen years two simple incidents have kept recurring again and again. They were so simple that they should have faded with the moment, but while the introductory statements of chairmen of our meetings have been forgotten, these two things persist, and in their persisting bless. A little Indian girl of about seven years was playing around the bungalow with our little girl. I was seated on the veranda at my writing. As they darted past me the little Indian girl paused, and in her shy way came up to me, passed her little brown hand across my cheek and said, "Apke munh mujhe bahut piyara lagta"—"Your face is very dear to me." As she ran on I brushed away a tear and went on with my writing. But my heart was very warm. As I have sat writing this book here in America I have felt again the soft touch of India's hand upon my cheek, and my heart has been warm, for India has become very dear to me. But I find that my love for India has a quality in it now that it did not have in the early days. I went to India through pity, I stay through respect. I love India because she is lovable, I respect her because she is respectable; she has become dear to me because she is endearing.

The other occurred when I was in Shantineketan at the Ashram of Tagore. I sat on the edge of the steps and watched the temple service one day. At the close a student went forward, took a lotus flower—the national flower of India—from a bowl upon the table in front, came back and presented it to me. As I arose to receive it he bent and touched my feet, as is the custom with their gurus, or teachers. It was done very simply and very beautifully. I had come there a stranger and a foreigner, I had come openly with another faith, and I wondered how I would be received, but when this student gave me this lotus flower before all, then I knew I was accepted as friend and brother—and teacher. To be accepted as teacher was the goal of my hopes. But I felt myself as much a learner as a teacher. I had come to India with everything to teach and nothing to learn. I stay to learn as well, and I believe I am a better man for having come into contact with the gentle heart of the East. . . .

There is a beautiful Indian marriage custom that dimly illustrates our task in India, and where it ends. At the wedding ceremony the women friends of the bride accompany her with music to the home of the bridegroom. They usher her into the presence of the bridegroom—that is as far as they can go, then they retire and leave her with her husband. That is our joyous task in India: to know Him, to introduce Him, to retire—not necessarily geographically, but to trust India with the Christ and trust Christ with India. We can only go so far—he and India must go the rest of the way.

India is beginning to walk with the Christ of the Indian Road. What a walk it will be!

MERSENE SLOAN, *THE INDIAN MENACE* (1929)

The modest success of Hindu teachers in America in the early twentieth century did not go unpunished in the missionary press. In "The Heathen Invasion of America," a 1912 article in *The Missionary Review of the World*, Mabel Potter Daggett claimed that Hinduism was antiwoman and that Indian swamis were stripping well-heeled American women of their money, their sanity, and, in some cases, their virginity. Though she offered little evidence for the accusation, Daggett's diatribe spawned a series of article- and book-length imitations. The best known was Katherine Mayo's *Mother India* (1927), a relentless attack against India's supposed sins against womanhood. The most florid example of this genre, however, is Mersene Sloan's *The Indian Menace* (1929). Like Daggett and her ilk, Sloan blasts Hindu teachers for conning American women, but he saves his most incendiary rhetoric for missionaries like E. Stanley Jones ("emissaries of the Devil") and mainline Protestant institutions such as the Federal Council of Churches ("a synagogue of Satan"). In denouncing what he calls the "oriental craze" of the twenties, Sloan also anticipates an argument that would become fashionable in the seventies: that Asian religious imports succeed only by "brainwashing" unwitting American followers.

It is amazing how people who profess to follow Jesus Christ as the only and sufficient world-saviour look to and welcome, even run after, the "Light of Asia" as the world's hope. . . . Infatuation for the oriental flavor has reached the stage where "The Christ of the Indian Road"—"The Oriental Christ"—is more appealing to some than is the Christ of history, the Christ of Palestine, the Christ of God, the Christ of the Universe. . . . There is nothing of oriental mysticism in the Christ of the New Testament. To attempt to dress him in such garb is to disguise him beyond recognition as the Light of the world. . . .

Certain theorists who shut their eyes to realities think they see in Indian religion some lovely things. . . . The alleged spirituality of oriental idolatry is a stupid myth utterly contrary to the rationality claimed by the high-brow apologists for Paganism. . . . Intelligent Hindus confess that idols are not regarded as symbols but are real objects of worship. Living idols (plants or animals) are regarded

Mersene Elon Sloan, *The Indian Menace: An Essay of Exposure and Warning Showing the Strange Work of Hindu Propaganda in America and Its Special Danger to Our Women* (Washington: Way Press, 1929), 5, 7–8, 11–12, 17–20, 29–31, 33–35, 63.

as actual incarnations, not mere symbols. Degradation and debauchery always accompany idolatry. . . . Hindu piety never bothers with morals. It is merely a superstitious bondage to forms of idol-worship. Even if a Hindu knew what purity is, how could he pray for it or think of it before an idol in a temple ornamented [!] with obscene sculptures and attended by a crowd of prostitute priestesses? . . .

"India has something to teach us" in religion implies a failure of the New Testament to completely meet human needs. It repudiates all warnings against adding to or modifying the gospel of the grace of God. . . . Nobody who understands the really spiritual sees spirituality in oriental religions. India can give only what she has. What she has is idolatry. . . . No pagan system has any right to offer its interpretation of religion as a substitute for, or improvement on, original Christianity. It is up to India to accept the Gospel of Christ as set forth in the New Testament, without the effrontery of suggesting modifications out of its own twisted fancies. Christ makes no bargain or compromise with the Devil, and Paganism is surely of him.

. . . A big show of broadness is being made in the cry for tolerance—off-color people demanding concessions from the faithful. Some of them would even dictate to God!! Destroy all distinctions between religions. . . . Only high-brows from modern colleges are able to grasp such stupendous wisdom! Only believe, no matter what. . . . One of the latest developments, alongside the religious Round-Table, is the FELLOWSHIP-OF-FAITH movement. Meetings are held from time to time where representative speakers from all sorts of religions are on a common platform. Renegade Christian preachers make mockery of God by trying to make him acknowledge that even Satan's religious delusions are as good as Christianity. It is a shameless humbug, an affront to reason and a burlesque on idiocy—in the name of higher education! As there can be no fellowship between light and darkness, this movement is only a fellowship of different shades of darkness. No light of real Christianity is in it. Evil associations corrupt virtuous habits. Even affected Christianity loses to the Devil when it tries to sop at the same platter.

Such a Fellowship-of-Faith pats the Devil on the back and says his clever imitations are as good as the original light of god. But God is no mollycoddle jellyfish Modernist to consent to any such monstrosity of infatuation. Truth is not double-faced nor multi-colored. All roads do not lead to Heaven. Christ is *the* door, not just one of a number. He is *the* way, *the* truth, *the* life. *No one* CAN *come to the Father but by him.* All who try some other access are thieves and robbers. Other foundation *can not* be laid. Jesus Christ is the ONLY basis for salvation and godliness. Religions not so based and directed may not be grouped with Christianity. Some of the false systems are so vile that the Lord says he hates them—he does not belong to the Fellowship-of-Faith gang! . . .

. . . The verdict of every sensible reader will be that HINDU SWAMIS MUST GO. Indeed, they should be denied entrance to our ports. It is quite true that, as some say, India has something for us, but that something is quite different from what is intended by such advisers. I was about to say that India does not need invitation, being quite willing to push this propaganda. But, in part, India did receive an invitation some time ago. When the Parliament of Religions was held at the Chicago World's Fair most cordial invitations were extended to representatives of oriental religions. Much honor was accorded prominent Hindu teachers. Along with that strange visitation by oriental teachers came, logically, certain conspicuous exhibitions of sex incitements which were welcomed and became established features of entertainment programs. The prevalence of present-day sex debauchery is but the logical result of the welcome given by leaders of nominal Christianity to representatives of eastern cults. There is now a considerable craze for eastern things, even to the point of cherishing oriental fabrics, colors, music and entertainments. With strange inconsistency this country excludes poor, ignorant laborers from the Far East, but admits a thousand-fold worse element—teachers of Hinduism who push corrupting propaganda too vile for full description. . . .

Contrary to suppositions in this country and to false pretenses by the strangers, yogis and swamis are not from the alleged higher classes of India. They come from the lower castes in matters of morals and decency. . . . They are from devil-worshipping castes, and pride themselves for being in a long line of descent from "black" magicians. A special school prepares them for expert practice of magic and hypnotism in America—the land where humbugs are thrice welcome. . . . Americans, true to Barnum's estimate,[1] fall for the humbugs, throwing away reason and Christian faith to become dupes of devils, the worst of all bondage. The foxy foreigners direct their occult influence especially towards women, as being more susceptible to psychic control. . . .

When American women by such delusion come under continued influence of a swami, they are easy victims to whatever suggestions may be proposed. It is said that a certain Hindu fakir of this breed successfully fooled a class of several hundred "high-brow" New York women into the belief that he was Christ reincarnated and had occupied the new body for towards a thousand years. When he died of TB, they refused to credit it. Another swami influenced a prominent and wealthy woman in New York to marry him. Several rich women of that city have bought fine homes for such Hindu teachers who had claimed to be Christs, and even God. I know a woman of superior natural ability who came under such influence until she now claims to be the first person to attain full super-human life and power. She claims power to confer eternal life upon whom she will, and makes other insane claims. Such are the effects of oriental so-called philosophy that India has for us and is selling us!

The peculiar intonations and chanting by Hindu swamis are a phase of a psychic process to secure special passivity to occult influences—a very dangerous hypnotism. . . . Monotonous chanting of the "Aum, Aum," and certain breathing exercises, with posturing, are among the simpler yogas. . . . So-called Negro spirituals (not spirituals, but psychicals) are sometimes of this order, notably the song "Shout It All About Heaven," in which the nasal final is much prolonged until nervous collapse is nearly effected. That may be religious, but is far from Christian. It is plain paganism.

---

[1]Presumably, "There's a sucker born every minute." [Footnote not in original.]

Women pupils practicing yoga often reach a point of perplexity, even a condition of felt danger, when they seek advice from the swamis. . . . The deluded women will do whatever the swamis suggest. At this stage the women have been alienated from their husbands and families . . . and become victims of abnormal erotic urge. What is called "Hatha Yoga" frequently results in insanity. . . .

Religious freedom? The men who established our institutions knew nothing of the diabolical things parading under guise of religion now so active. Provision for free exercise of religion did not anticipate such hideous perversions as are now so active. Laws against fragrant evils should not tremble before hypocritical pretenders to religious sanctity to propagate monstrous vileness. Integrity to genuine American intentions demands positive exclusion of all oriental propaganda. Repudiation of Christianity endangers our civilization, and our worst foes are propagators of orientalism in whatever form. Put the yogis and swamis out, and keep them out.

HOWARD AND SUE BAILEY THURMAN MEET MAHATMA GANDHI (1936)

The ties that bind the struggle for Indian independence and America's civil rights movement are as old as they are complex. Mohandas Gandhi's strategy of *satyagraha* or nonviolent direct action was informed by the Jain principle of *ahimsa* ("noninjury"), Jesus's Sermon on the Mount, and Thoreau's essay "Civil Disobedience." During the civil rights era of the 1950s and 1960s, Black leaders like the Reverend Martin Luther King, Jr., pointed to Gandhi's success (India achieved independence in 1947) in support of their own strategy of nonviolent civil disobedience. But King, who traveled to India himself in 1959, was not the first African American inspired by Gandhi. In fact, African-American newspapers began covering Gandhi and his strategic imprisonments extensively in the early 1920s. In 1929 W. E. B. DuBois solicited and the African-American newspaper *Crisis* published an open letter from Gandhi, "To the America Negro." Black interest in Gandhi was so great that in 1939, Krishnalal Shridharani, an Indian sojourner in the United States featured in an earlier entry in this book, prophesied that *satyagraha* might have "more fertile fields in which to grow and flourish in the West than in the Orient." One Black leader who took an early interest in Gandhi was theologian Howard Thurman (1900–81). Born into a Baptist household in Daytona, Florida, in 1900, Thurman attended Morehouse College in Atlanta and Colgate-Rochester Divinity School in Rochester, New York. An ordained Baptist minister, he later worked as a professor at Howard University and Boston University, and served for nearly a decade as the founding co-minister of the Church for the Fellowship of All Peoples in San Francisco. In 1935–36, Thurman and his wife, Sue Bailey Thurman, went on a "pilgrimage of friendship" to India, Burma (now Myanmar), and Ceylon (now Sri Lanka). In February of 1936 they met Gandhi in Bardoli, India. In this historic East-West exchange, the Thurmans discussed with Gandhi voting rights, lynching, Islam, and Christianity. But as this excerpt from *Mahatma* (1952), an Indian biography of Gandhi, indicates, their conversation centered on the Jain principle of *ahimsa*. Roughly two

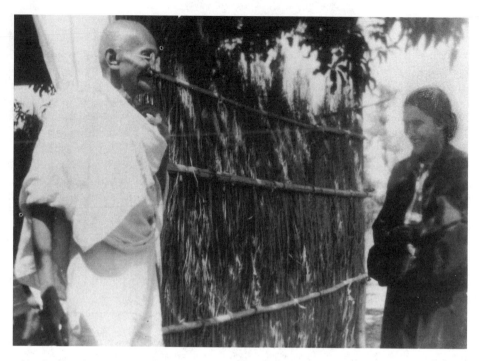

Mohandas Gandhi greets Sue Bailey Thurman in Bardoli, India, in 1936. Thurman and her husband, Howard Thurman, spoke with Gandhi about parallels between his nonviolent struggle for Indian independence and their campaign for civil rights for African Americans. Courtesy of the Department of Special Collections, Boston University.

decades after this exchange, the Reverend King would lead the Montgomery bus boycott of 1955. He was well on his way to becoming "the Black Gandhi."

Now the talk centred on a discussion which had mainly drawn the distinguished members to Gandhi. "Is non-violence from your point of view, a form of direct action?" inquired Dr. Thurman. "It is not one form, it is the only form," replied Gandhi. "I do not, of course, confine the words 'direct action' to their technical meaning. But without any direct active expression of it, non-violence, to my mind, is meaningless. It is the greatest and the activest force in the world. One cannot be passively non-violent. In fact, 'non-violence' is a term I had to coin, in order to bring out the root meaning of ahimsa. In spite of the negative particle 'non,' it is no negative force. Superficially we are surrounded in life by strife and bloodshed, life living upon life. But some great seer, who ages ago penetrated the centre of truth, said: it is not through strife and violence, but through non-violence that man can fulfil his destiny and his duty to his fellow creatures. It is a force which is more positive than electricity and more powerful than even ether. At the

D. G. Tendulkar, *Mahatma: Life of Mohandas Karamchand Gandhi, Volume Four, 1934–1938* (Bombay: Vithalbhai K. Jhaveri & D. G. Tendulkar, 1952), 59–62.

centre of non-violence is a force which is self-acting. Ahimsa means 'love' in the Pauline sense, and yet something more than the 'love' defined by St. Paul, although I know St. Paul's beautiful definition is good enough for all practical purposes. Ahimsa includes the whole creation, and not only human. Besides, love in the English language has other connotations too, and so I was compelled to use the negative word. But it does not, as I have told you, express a negative force, but a force superior to all the forces put together. One person who can express ahimsa in life exercises a force superior to all the forces of brutality."

Question:	"And is it possible for any individual to achieve this?"
Gandhi:	"Certainly. If there was any exclusiveness about it, I should reject it at once."
Question:	"Any idea of possession is foreign to it?"
Gandhi:	"Yes. It possesses nothing, therefore, it possesses everything."
Question:	"Is it possible for a single human being to resist the persistent invasion of the quality successfully?"
Gandhi:	"It is possible. Perhaps your question is more universal than you mean. Is it not possible, you mean to ask, for one single Indian, for instance, to resist the exploitation of 300 million Indians? Or, do you mean the onslaught of the whole world against a single individual personally?"
Dr. Thurman:	"Yes, that is one half of the question. I wanted to know, if one man can hold the whole violence at bay?"
Gandhi:	"If he cannot, you must take it that he is not a true representative of ahimsa. Supposing I cannot produce a single instance in life of a man who truly converted his adversary, I would then say that is because no one had yet been found to express ahimsa in its fulness.
Question:	"Then it overrides all other forces?"
Gandhi:	'Yes, it is the only true force in life."

"Forgive now the weakness of this question," said Dr. Thurman, "but may I ask how are we to train individuals or communities in this difficult art?"

Gandhi:	"There is no royal road, except through living the creed in your life which must be a living sermon. Of course, the expression in one's own life presupposes great study, tremendous perseverance, and a thorough cleansing of one's self of all the impurities. If for mastering of the physical sciences you have to devote a whole lifetime, how many lifetimes may be needed for mastering the greatest spiritual force that mankind has known? But why worry even if it means several lifetimes? For, if this is the

only permanent thing in life, if this is the only thing that counts, then whatever effort you bestow on mastering it, is well spent. Seek ye first the Kingdom of Heaven and everything else shall be added unto you. The Kingdom of Heaven is ahimsa.

Mrs. Thurman had restrained herself until now. But she could not go away without asking the question with which she would be confronted any day. "How am I to act, supposing my own brother was lynched before my very eyes?"

"There is such a thing as self-immolation," he said. "Supposing I was a Negro, and my sister was ravished by a white or lynched by a whole community, what would be my duty?—I ask myself. And the answer comes to me: I must not wish ill to these, but neither must I co-operate with them. It may be that ordinarily I depend on the lynching community for my livelihood. I refuse to co-operate with them, refuse even to touch the food that comes from them, and I refuse to co-operate with even my brother Negroes who tolerate the wrong. That is the self-immolation I mean. I have often in my life resorted to the plan. Of course, a mechanical act of starvation will mean nothing. One's faith must remain undimmed whilst life ebbs out, minute by minute. But I am a very poor specimen of the practice of non-violence, and my answer may not convince you. But I am striving very hard, and even if I do not succeed fully in this life, my faith will not diminish."

"We want you to come to America," said the guests. Mrs. Thurman reinforced the request, "We want you not for White America, but for the Negroes; we have many a problem that cries for solution, and we need you badly. "How I wish I could," said Gandhi, "but I would have nothing to give you, unless I had given an ocular demonstration here of all that I have been saying. I must make good the message here, before I bring it to you. I do not say that I am defeated, but I have still to perfect myself. You may be sure that the moment I feel that call within me, I shall not hesitate."

Dr. Thurman explained that the Negroes were ready to receive the message. "Much of the peculiar background of our own life in America is our interpretation of the Christian religion. When one goes through the pages of the hundreds of Negro spirituals, striking things are brought to mind which remind me of all that you have told us today."

"Well," exclaimed Gandhi, "if it comes true, it may be through the Negroes that the unadulterated message of non-violence will be delivered to the world."

JOHN CAGE, "LECTURE ON NOTHING" (1949)

Although the Beat poets and novelists are the best known Zennists of the postwar period, Zen also commended itself to painters like Robert Rauschenberg, choreographers like Merce Cunningham, and composers like John Cage. One of America's most influential avant-garde composers, John Cage (1912–92) believed that music, like meditation, was intended to still the mind and open it to "divine influences." Although informed by the I Ching, *Advaita Vedanta*, and Dadaism, Cage was most profoundly

John Cage, "Lecture on Nothing" (1949)

influenced by Zen, which he first encountered in the late thirties at a Seattle lecture on "Zen Buddhism and Dada" by Nancy Wilson Ross. In the late forties, Cage heard D. T. Suzuki lecture at Columbia University, and he later visited Suzuki in Japan. He did not call himself a Buddhist, but Cage was an avid reader of Buddhist texts who acknowledged Buddhism's impact on his work. In his most famous score, "4' 33"" (1952), musicians sit silently for four minutes and thirty-three seconds; the performance consists of the random bits of sound audible in the concert hall. Silence, randomness, chance, and humor are also important themes in Cage's first and best known book, *Silence* (1961). Cage first delivered "Lecture on Nothing," which appears in that book, at a 1949 meeting of abstract painter Robert Motherwell's Artists' Club in New York City. Despite the title, the piece is more poem than lecture. It too is intended to quiet the mind, to open it up to the influence of emptiness.

```
I am here              ,           and there is nothing to say              .
                                                            If among you are
those who wish to get   somewhere           ,            let them leave at
any moment          .                          What we re-quire             is
silence            ;           but what silence requires
         is         that I go on talking          .
                                                    Give any one thought
            a push              :         it falls down easily
;         but the pusher      and the   pushed          pro-duce         that enter-
tainment            called            a  dis-cussion               .
                  Shall we have one later     ?


Or               ,       we could simply de-  cide                      not to have a dis-
cussion          .                          What ever you like.              But
now                           there are   silences                      and the
words              make              help make                          the
silences           .
                                          I have nothing to say
         and I am saying it                                   and that is
poetry                             as I   need it          .


            This space of time                                   is organized
.                      We need not fear these       silences,—


we may love them          .
                                              This is a composed
talk              ,         for I am making it           It is like a glass
      just as I make      a piece of music.            glass
         of milk              We need the            it is like an
and we need the       milk               .          Or again              at any
empty glass                           into which
moment              anything                          may be poured
.                      As we go along      ,          (who knows?)
            an i-dea may occur in this    talk              .
                                       I have no idea      whether one will
         or not.              If one does,             let it.              Re-
```

Exclusion, 1924 to 1965

gard it as something   seen   momentarily   ,   as
though   from a window   while traveling   .
If across Kansas   ,   then, of course,   Kansas
.   Arizona   is more interesting,
almost too interesting   ,   especially   for a New-Yorker   who is
being interested   in spite of himself   in everything.   Now he knows he
needs   the Kansas in him   .   Kansas is like
nothing on earth   ,   and for a New Yorker   very refreshing.
It is like an empty glass   ,   nothing but wheat   ,   or
is it corn   ?   Does it matter which   ?
Kansas   has this about it: at any instant,   one may leave it,
and whenever one wishes one may return to it   .

Or you may leave it   forever   and never return to it   ,
            for we pos-sess nothing   .   Our poetry now
            is the reali-zation   that we possess   nothing
.   Anything   therefore   is a delight
(since we do not   pos-sess it)   and thus   need not fear its loss
.   We need not destroy the   past: it is gone;
at any moment,   it might reappear and   seem to be   and be the present
.   Would it be a   repetition?   Only if we thought we
owned it,   but since we don't,   it is free   and so are we
            and how un-certain it is   Most anybody knows a-bout the future
            and how un-certain it is   .

What I am calling   poetry   is often called   content.
I myself   have called   it form   .   It is the continuity   of a piece of music.   Continuity   today,
when it is necessary   ,   is a demonstration   of dis-
interestedness.   That is,   it is a proof   that our delight
lies in not   pos-sessing anything   .   Each moment
presents what happens   .   How different
this form sense is   from that   which is bound up with
memory: themes   and secondary themes;   their struggle;
their development;   the climax;   the recapitulation   (which is the belief
that one may   own one's own home)   .   But actually,
unlike the snail   ,   we carry   homes   within us,

which enables us   to fly   or to stay
, —   to enjoy   each.   But beware of
that which is   breathtakingly   beautiful,   for at any moment
        the telephone   may ring   or the airplane
come down in a   vacant lot   .   A piece of string
or a sunset   ,   possessing neither   ,
each acts   and the continuity   happens
.   Nothing more than   nothing   can be said.
Hearing   or making this   in music   is not different
—   only simpler—   than living this way   .
        Simpler, that is   ,   for me,—because it happens
        that I write music   .

That music is   simple to make   comes from   one's willingness to accept   the limitations   of structure.   Structure is
simple   be-cause   it can be thought out,   figured out,
measured   .   It is a discipline   which,

John Cage, "Lecture on Nothing" (1949)

```
accepted,              in return         accepts whatever        ,           even those
rare moments           of ecstasy,       which,         as sugar  loaves train horses,
train us               to make what we make  .                    How could I
better tell            what structure    is                 than simply to
tell           about this,               this talk                which is
contained              within            a space of time          approximately
forty minutes          long              ?

That forty minutes     has been divided into   five           large parts,          and
each unit              is divided        likewise.                 Subdivision      in-
volving        a square root        is the only       possible subdivision which
permits                this micro-macrocosmic   rhythmic structure        ,
which I find so        acceptable        and accepting            .
As you see,            I can say anything    .
It makes very little   difference        what I say     or even how I say it.
At             this par-ticular moment,   we are passing through    the fourth
part                   of a unit which is the        second unit in the second large
part of this talk      .             It is a little bit        like passing through Kansas
.                      This, now, is the     end           of that second unit
.


Now begins the         third unit        of the second part       .
                                                                   Now the

second part of that    third unit        .
                       Now its third part     .


                                                                   Now its fourth
part                                     (which, by the way,       is just the same
length         as the third part)        .
                       Now the fifth      and last part            .

You have just          ex-perienced      the structure     of this talk         from a
microcosmic            point of view     .               From a macrocosmic
point of view          we are just passing the halfway point       in the second
large part.            The first part         was a rather rambling   discussion of
nothing                ,                  of form,                 and continuity
```

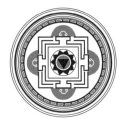

PASSAGES, 1965 TO THE PRESENT

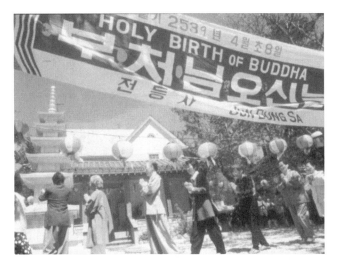

Korean-American Buddhists celebrate the Buddha's birthday at the Jun Dung Sa Temple on a residential street in Flushing, New York. © Audrey Gottlieb. Used by permission.

In 1989 some residents of a southwestern Miami neighborhood protested when Thai Buddhist immigrants decided to build a temple, one large enough that all 350 members could gather to celebrate the Buddha's birthday. County zoning laws prohibited the construction, and the neighbors had their own reasons for challenging the building plans. At a public meeting to resolve the dispute, one European-American resident explained his objections: "They've gotten their foot in the door, and now they want to build this huge edifice. I have nothing against Buddhism and nothing against Buddhists, but it's not a community church. You're taking a church that's not even in the mainstream of American life and putting it in a place where the congregation doesn't come from. It's just out of place here." Other residents shared his views, but the Thai Buddhist community won this dispute when a Catholic priest, a rabbi, and other local religious leaders defended the Buddhists at the county commissioners meeting later that year. Since the 1970s similar disputes have erupted in towns and cities across the country, and local Buddhists, Sikhs, Jains, and Hindus have not always fared so well.[1]

At first glance these controversies seem quite familiar. After all, hostility against Asians and their religions had broken out in town after town since the onset of Asian immigration in the middle of the nineteenth century, especially in communities along the West Coast that had attracted large numbers of Asian immigrants. Americans had been meeting each other and mapping the religious world long before the 1960s, and their encounters would continue into the last decades of the twentieth century.

But the 1965 immigration law opened a new period in America's encounter with Asian religions, and migration emerged as its predominant theme. Almost 40 percent of the new immigrants arrived from Asia, and millions of them practiced an Asian religious tradition. In turn, that Miami resident's complaint—that Asian religions were not in the "mainstream of American life"—sounded less persuasive. Christians remained the majority, but the cultural landscape of many cities had changed, with more temples and gurdwaras around the corner and more Asians, and American converts, next door. Faced with this new terrain, Americans began to remap the landscape during this period of passages, when revisions of the immigration laws combined with advances in communications and travel technology as well as Asian economic instability and political upheaval to generate crisscrossing transnational movements. In the post-1965 period, peoples, artifacts, beliefs, and practices moved back and forth between Asia and America more quickly and more often than ever before. Those passages, and the concomitant cultural exchanges, transformed both Asia and America.

The passages were driven not only by social forces; people in the East and the West had their personal reasons for crossing. For the American generation that came of age during the countercultural movements of the sixties—which might best be dated from the assassination of President Kennedy in 1963 to the energy crisis of 1973—that meant turning east to find alternatives to the Western traditions that had produced, in their judgment, a materialistic and destructive society. Disillusioned with the West, the cultural descendants of the Beats turned to Asian spirituality. For some—like Timothy Leary, "the pied piper of the psychedelic sixties"—that journey began with drug experimentation. Many who influenced the counterculture—from Alan Watts to the Beatles—traveled to Asia, where they practiced with Hindu, Sikh, or Buddhist teachers. And some of the eastward travelers returned to lecture and write about Asian religions. For example, Ram Dass (formerly Richard Alpert) wrote a volume, *Be Here Now*, that lay on many coffee tables and nightstands in the early 1970s.

Passages also went the other way: Asian teachers toured and lived in the United States. Vivekananda and Dharmapala had come earlier, so had D. T. Suzuki and Paramahansa Yogananda, but the sixties and seventies saw an explosion of Asian masters coming to the West. Some of them founded new religious movements that drew on Indian or Japanese traditions. Yogi Bhajan, who arrived in 1968 from India, spread Sikhism among European-American converts in the Healthy, Happy, Holy Organization. Maharishi Mahesh Yogi taught Transcendental Meditation to millions of Americans, and Masayasu Sadanaga promoted Soka Gakkai, the Buddhist-inspired Japanese new religion. Some of these teachers and organizations, including the International Society for Krishna Consciousness (Hare Krishnas) and the Rajneesh International Foundation, attracted controversy as well as converts. National news shows labeled Bhagawan Shree Rajneesh "the sex guru," while other gurus became icons of pop culture. Swami Satchidananda, for example, preached tolerance and peace to the crowds at Woodstock, and went on to establish a large Hindu community in Virginia. Most Asian leaders of new religious movements labored more anonymously, however, struggling to adapt their messages to Western audiences.

Other Asian teachers also transplanted Asian traditions in America. Tibetan Vajrayana Buddhist teachers attracted American converts. Geshe Wangyal arrived in 1955 in New Jersey, where he later established the first Tibetan monastery open to Americans. It was there that Robert Thurman, the first American to be ordained as a Tibetan monk, studied. Other Tibetan teachers, including Tarthang Tulku in Berkeley and Chogyam Trungpa Rinpoche in Boulder, arrived to nurture American converts in the late sixties and seventies, and exiled Tibetan teachers—such as Lama Thubten Yeshe and Lama Thubten Zopa Rinpoche—toured and lectured throughout the United States. Asians, and Americans who had studied Vipassana meditation in Asia, established Theravadin Buddhist centers, such as the Insight Meditation Society in Massachusetts and the Desert Vipassana Center in California. Japanese and Korean masters, including Soen-sa-nim in Providence and Hakuun Yasutani-roshi in Los Angeles, founded Zen centers.[2]

In one of the most interesting developments of the period, American-born teachers, some of whom were women and most of whom had studied in Asia, ascended to leadership roles in American centers. Consider the case of Zen Buddhism. Philip Kapleau, after thirteen years in Japan, returned to head a Zen center in Rochester, and Robert Aitken-roshi, the "unofficial American dean of Zen," studied with Nyogen Senzaki in Japan and later established a Zen center in the hills above Honolulu. Maurine Stuart-roshi led the Cambridge Buddhist Association, and Jiyu Kennett-roshi taught at Shasta Abbey, the community in northern California she founded. Similar stories could be recounted for other groups—Buddhist, Taoist, and Sikh.[3]

Some Asian and American teachers, among them the Vietnamese monk Thich Nhat Han, wrote best-selling books on Asian traditions, and there were many more signs that Asian religions had influenced American culture. In martial arts and tai chi centers, instructors tutored students in practices shaped by Taoism and Buddhism. Asian religions inspired American painters, sculptors, and architects. The same was true in modern dance and contemporary music, from Philip Glass's new music to the Beastie Boys' hip hop. The rock star Tina Turner credited Nichiren Buddhism with granting her peace and prosperity. Asian religions influenced the sports world too: Phil Jackson, the professional basketball coach, credited Zen with his success in the game. How-to books promised improvement in everything from sex to business, if only readers would apply the principles of yoga, Zen, or Taoism. Advertisers, script writers, and filmmakers also used Asian religious images to move an audience or sell a brand. Asian-American artists, like the novelists Bharati Mukherjee and Amy Tan, explored religious themes from the religions of India, Japan, and China.

With Asian religions more prominent in American culture, it was difficult at the end of the twentieth century for Christians and Jews to ignore them, although some managed to act as if little had changed. Although in smaller numbers than during the early-twentieth-century peak of Protestant missions, some Christian groups still sent evangelists abroad. Most Orthodox Jews and evangelical Protestants at home reaffirmed the uniqueness and centrality of their own faith. Evangelicals, for example, armed born-again believers with surveys, including Fritz Ridenour's *So What's the Difference* (1979), which listed purported weaknesses of Asian religions. During the 1970s and 1980s, liberal Jews and Christians began formal dialogues with adherents of other religions. Thomas Merton, the Trappist monk, led the way for Roman Catholics when he traveled to Asia in 1968 to meet with Buddhists. That Catholic-Buddhist encounter deepened after his untimely death. As a symbol of how far the exchanges had gone in two decades, on 24 May 1989, a Catholic priest, the Reverend Patrick Hawk-roshi, was formally recognized as an authorized Zen master (and Aitken-roshi's dharma heir) in a ceremony in Honolulu. Mainline Protestants and Reform and Conservative Jews also participated in these ongoing conversations. In the early 1990s, for instance, writer Rodger Kamenetz and other American Jews journeyed to meet with the Dalai Lama and Tibetan monks, where they exchanged views on a wide range of topics. The movement peaked in vitality during the 1980s, but interreligious dialogue, which involved participants from all Asian religions, continued to attract attention at the end of the twentieth century—even if most American Christians and Jews did not take part and many remained sure their own faith surpassed all others.

In the most important development of all, the post-1965 period witnessed a new wave of Asian immigration. Los Angeles, New York, and Chicago could boast that within their urban boundaries lived representatives of all the major religions. But Sikhs in Seattle, Jains in St. Paul, Taoists in Denver, Buddhists in Oklahoma City, and Hindus in Houston also formed new organizations and built new temples. Occasionally, these Asian immigrants encountered American converts, but usually the two groups remained separated by language, custom, and values. Where they coexisted in the same temple or center, they often formed "parallel congregations," as one scholar has called them, gathering together only for major festivals or special events. Whether or not they encountered American converts regularly—and the vast majority did not—post-1965 immigrants struggled with many challenges that previous generations of immigrants from Europe and Asia had faced: how to construct new buildings, attract religious leaders, socialize the children, and confront America's political system and cultural values.[4]

Sometimes immigrants, and converts to Asian new religious movements, confronted American values in legislatures and courtrooms, facing vexing questions about the relation of religion and the state. Do three children from a Sikh family in California have the right to wear *kirpans*, daggers that symbolize Sikh faith, to their public school? What are parents' rights, and the state's obligations, when an adolescent or young adult joins a Hindu-inspired communitarian movement? And how do zoning codes, and First Amendment religious liberties, apply when residents protest that followers of Asian religions have no right to build a new temple in the neighborhood? In these legal disputes, and in many other kinds of interpersonal contacts, Americans decided not only how to interpret the First Amendment's religious liberty clause, but how to define America, which by the end of the twentieth century had become a nation reshaped by years of encounter and exchange.

T.A.T.

NOTES

1. The speech by the local resident, Jim Roach, was recorded in Sean Rowe, "Buddhist Temple Plan Criticized in Redland," *Miami Herald,* 20 August 1989, 16.

2. An explanation of Tibetan titles: *Lama* is a term reserved for senior members of the Tibetan monastic order. *Geshe* signifies that the person has completed a rigorous course of study in Buddhism, roughly equivalent to a doctorate in theology. *Rinpoche*, meaning "precious jewel," is a title given to those who have been judged to be a *tulku*, or a reincarnation of a deceased enlightened teacher.

3. The quote about Aitken-roshi is from Helen Tworkov, *Zen in America: Profiles of Five Teachers* (San Francisco: North Point Press, 1989), 25.

4. Paul David Numrich uses the term *parallel congregations* in *Old Wisdom in the New World: Americanization in Two Immigrant Theravada Buddhist Temples* (Knoxville: University of Tennessee Press, 1996), 63–79.

CHAPTER **13**

Countercultural Appropriations

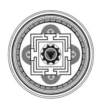

ALAN WATTS, "BEGINNING A COUNTERCULTURE" (1972)

Perhaps the most influential popularizer of Asian religions of his generation, Alan Watts (1915–73) served as a spiritual teacher for many in the counterculture of the sixties and seventies. Disillusioned with the Church of England and the Christian God, whom he called "a bombastic bore," the young Watts turned East, where he found an appealing aesthetic, a tolerant spirit, a spontaneous ethic, and a monistic view of ultimate reality. The Asian artifacts his mother had collected and the Buddhist books he read (including volumes by Lafcadio Hearn, Dwight Goddard, and D. T. Suzuki) opened new paths for the disquieted adolescent. Watts never attended a university but read widely, gradually finding his niche as a writer and lecturer. From 1934 to 1938 he edited the British Buddhist magazine, *The Middle Way*. He then moved to New York, where he encountered Sokei-an (Shigetsu Sasaki), the Japanese Zen teacher, but Watts was temperamentally disinclined to follow teachers or join groups. For most of his adult life, Watts remained outside religious institutions, even though he worked as an Episcopalian chaplain for five years (1945–50). The period of his greatest influence began after that, and in more than twenty-six books and as many as one thousand lectures, Watts interpreted Taoism and Buddhism for American audiences. He also served on the faculty of San Francisco's American Academy of Asian Studies (established 1951). In his autobiography, Watts describes his own hybrid spirituality as "between Mahayana Buddhism and Taoism, with a certain leaning towards Vedanta and Catholicism, or rather the Orthodox Church of Eastern Europe." In these passages from that book, published the year before his death, Watts records his impressions of Buddhists he encountered in San Francisco and reflects on his role in a counterculture that was just then declining.

Alan Watts, *In My Own Way: An Autobiography* (New York: Vintage, 1973), 301–7, 309–12. Reprinted by the permission of Russell & Volkening as agents for the author.

Rudyard Kipling made the famous statement that "East is East and West is West, and never the twain shall meet." He also said that "he does not know England who only England knows," and though this might be taken to mean that un-traveled Englishmen cannot realize how good it is at home, the two statements, taken together, suggest something more profound. Kipling was . . . one of those channels of British colonialism through which Himalayan culture backed up into England. . . .

My own interest in this cultural encounter was peculiar, in the sense that I was not simply a fact-seeker, like a historian or journalist, nor a missionary try-ing to convert Westerners to Buddhism—though I have been taken for that. No one, however, has ever accused me of being a scholarly Orientalist. I am more of-ten considered a popularizer of Zen, Vedanta, and Taoism, who often twists the facts to suit his own views. One reason for this impression is that my style of writ-ing does not lend itself to the torturous course of fine distinctions. But I am well aware of them when I leave them out, and can (and do) refer those who want the fine points to the proper sources, and can, furthermore, produce the necessary scholarly evidence for my conclusions if asked. Another is that I am not inter-ested in studying, say, Buddhism in terms of what most Buddhists think about it—that is, as an anthropological phenomenon. I am interested in the work of those who are, and have been, its most creative exponents, and, above all, in the actual nature of the inner experiences which they describe. Thus if I am berated for a facile equation of the Buddhist *nirvana* with the Hindu *moksha*, or of Nagarjuna's *sunyata* with Shankara's Brahman, I can give excellent reasons for so doing to anyone prepared to listen for the time required. It is believed in some circles that I have seriously misrepresented Zen by failing to bring out, and in-deed even questioning, the importance of the discipline of *za-zen*—or sitting in meditation for long hours—as the royal road to Buddhist enlightenment. It is therefore also said—perhaps with truth—that my easy and free-floating attitude to Zen was largely responsible for the notorious "Zen boom" which flourished among artists and "pseudo-intellectuals" in the late 1950s, and led on to the friv-olous "beat Zen" of Kerouac's *Dharma Bums*, of Franz Kline's black and white ab-stractions, and of John Cage's silent concerts. . . .

What I saw in Zen was an intuitive way of understanding the sense of life by getting rid of silly quests and questions. The archetypal situation was when Hui-k'e asked Bodhidharma how to attain peace of mind. Bodhidharma said, "Bring your mind out, and I will pacify it." "But when I look for it," said Hui-k'e, "I can't find it." "In that case," the master concluded, "it's pacified al-ready." It is thus that almost every morning, when I first awaken, I have a feel-ing of total clarity as to the sense of life, a feeling of myself and the universe as a matter of the utmost simplicity. "I" and "That which is" are the same. Always have been and always will be. I could say that what constitutes me is the same jazz that constitutes the cosmos, and that there is simply nothing special to be achieved, realized, or performed. . . .

I am saying all this to suggest the spirit in which I was working at the Academy of Asian Studies to start something which—based primarily on Lao-tzu and Chuang-tzu—would counterbalance, out-fox, soften, and allay the martial, mechanically marching, tick-tock, and saw-toothed jagged life-rhythm which has been rattling the world at least since the Caesars' legionnaires stamped out of Rome. Cultures, religions, and political attitudes have characteristic rhythms which must be watched and studied as carefully as a doctor feels the pulse or listens to the heartbeat. When President Eisenhower warned us to keep an eye on "the military-industrial complex" he was surely hearing the danger to life in this marching and mechanical rhythm which jolts, fractures, and interrupts everything organic, oceanic, and vegetative, and is being beaten out by people who do not realize that Earth is for all its creatures and not merely for human beings. I knew that I could not preach against this rhythm, because the style of preaching is its own bombast, but that I must rather woo it—like Orpheus—with a different music.

Zen, because of its association with the *banzai-bushido* spirit of the samurai, might have seemed an unlikely ally in this project. But I had learned from D. T. Suzuki, Sokei-an, and later, Sabro Hasegawa that Zen is basically Taoism—the water-course way of life—and that it attempted to tame samurai brigands precisely by showing them that the utmost perfection in swordsmanship and archery was to fence without a sword and shoot without an arrow. In other words, if you practice fencing, archery, or judo by Zen methods that attainment of real skill puts you in a state of consciousness where you are so free from egocentric desire that warfare ceases to have any point.

. . . Among our students at this time [at the Academy of Asian Studies] were Michael Murphy and Richard Price, who together founded the Esalen Institute at Big Sur; Richard Hittleman, who subsequently taught Yoga to the nation on television; and on occasion, Gary Synder the poet, who first appeared unaccountably and amazingly dressed in a formal black suit, British style, with a neatly rolled umbrella, but who later emerged in history as Japhy Ryder—the Buddhist beatnik hero of Kerouac's *Dharma Bums*—in a characterization which hardly begins to do him justice. I am not Gary's teacher. He studied Chinese at the University of California with Shih-hsiang Chen and Zen at Daitokuji in Kyoto with Goto and Oda; but when I am dead I would like to be able to say that he is carrying on everything I hold most dearly, though with a different style. To put it another way, my only regret is that I cannot formally claim him as my spiritual successor. He did it all on his own, but nevertheless he *is* just exactly what I have been trying to *say*. For Gary is tougher, more disciplined, and more physically competent than I, but he embodies these virtues without rubbing them in, and I can only say that a universe which has manifested Gary Synder could never be called a failure.

. . . Naturally, the Academy was in touch with the great Chinese community of San Francisco. Chingwah Lee, its antiquarian and public relations officer, used to talk with us and sometimes lend me objects of art from his considerable collection. There was, however, a large active Chinese-Buddhist group whose leaders came to study with us, who wined and dined us with the most sumptuous hospitality, whose physicians took care of our ailments, and from whom—in working over such texts as the *T'an Ching*, or *Sutra of the Sixth Patriarch*—I learned a great amount of written Chinese. These lovable and generous people were, however, bending over backward to be Rotarian Americans and, with the exception of their diet, had forgotten the taste of Chinese culture. They could have afforded Sung paintings and Han statuary but instead preferred enormous television sets, and such works of Chinese art as they displayed were deplorable cliches. I was aesthetically baffled in trying to show them the grandeur of T'ang and Sung, as also in attempting to warn them that a protestantized Buddhism would have small appeal for the West. The same was true of the Japanese-Buddhist communities, which were falling between the two stools of archaic and mechanical ritualism, on the one hand, and rationalized modernism, on the other, so that their younger Jaycee-type members had the heebijeebies when their priests chanted the sutras, and preferred instead to sing:

> Buddha loves me this I know
> For the sutra tells me so.

They were incapable of seeing that this kind of Buddhism gave no substantial alternative to what was already being offered in the Presbyterian and Methodist churches.

Finally, however, the Soto Zen Temple, then lodged in an abandoned synagogue on Bush Street, got the message—first under Hodo Tobase and later under Shunryu Suzuki. They saw that there was no future in being a circumscribed service center for the Japanese community, for the superstitious and sentimental old folks or for their over-Americanized second- and third-generation children. They saw that what was needed was an authentic and intelligent school of Zen practice designed for Westerners . . . . Under Shunryu Suzuki the Soto Temple blossomed into the thriving Zen Center to which was later added the Zen Mountain Center at Tassajara Springs, far beyond the end of Carmel Valley. But aside from its priests, there are hardly any other Japanese people involved.

TIMOTHY LEARY, "THE BUDDHA AS DROP-OUT" (1968)

Condemned by Richard Nixon as "the most dangerous man in America" and revered by others as the "Pied Piper of the psychedelic sixties," Timothy Leary (1920–96) set out on a life-long campaign to advocate the use of mind-altering drugs when he first ingested hallucinogenic mushrooms in Mexico in 1960. Then a Harvard psychologist, Leary was dismissed from the university in 1963 for giving undergraduates hallucinogens. Using the slogan he coined—"Turn on, tune in, drop out"—he told anyone who would listen that LSD expanded consciousness and overcame repression. Many listened, and Leary became one of the icons of the counterculture. In 1966, however, he was arrested for drug use. The next ten years found Leary in and out of prison. After his release in 1976, he spent the remainder of his life, as his *Newsweek* obituary put it, "being famous for being famous." In his last years, Leary became convinced of the transformative possibilities of the new computer technology. He set up an elaborate web site (www.leary.com) to allow his fans to follow his last days on line, reporting even his daily drug intake. His final words—"Why not?"—summarized much of his philosophy of life. But that philosophy did not only draw on drugs or technology; it also incorporated Asian religions. Although never a serious or systematic student of Buddhism or Hinduism, Leary did discuss those traditions from time to time. In 1967 the editors of *Horizon* magazine planned an issue on the hippies and invited Leary to submit an article. He penciled an essay on the Buddha, which the magazine (to Leary's amusement and annoyance) never published. In this satirical piece, finally published in 1968, Leary portrays the founder of Buddhism as the first hippie.

The message of the Buddha, Gautama, is the familiar, ancient always to-be-rediscovered divine instruction:

> Drop out
> Turn on
> Tune in

The avatar, the divine one, is he who discovers and lives out this rhythm during his earthly trip.

The life of the Buddha, Gautama, is simply another case illustration in the venerable library of tissue manuals on "How to Discover Your Own Buddha-hood."

Gautama Sakyamuni was born a prince. His father, the king, and his mother, the queen, were determined that he should carry on the family business and not discover his divinity. According to familiar parental tradition, they attempted to protect their son from confronting the four basic dimensions of the human time span: sickness, age, death, and the existence of eccentric, barefoot holy men—alchemists who could show him how to solve the time riddle by—

> Dropping out
> Turning on
> Tuning in

The truth of the matter is that the Buddha was born and brought up in Westchester County, educated at an Ivy League college and groomed for that pinnacle of princely success which would allow him in 1967 to subscribe to *Horizon*, a magazine particularly unlikely to confront him with the prospect of his own divinity.

First Gautama dropped out. Horrors! Did he really desert his wife and child? Run out on the palace mortgage payment? Welsh on his commitments to his 10,000 concubines? Leave the Internal Revenue Service holding the bag for the Vietnam War bill? Maybe he just moved with his wife and kids to Big Sur, not even leaving a forwarding address for fourth-class mail. Lost *Horizon*. Or maybe the dropout was internal (where it always has to be). Maybe he just detached himself invisibly from the old fears and ambitions.

Timothy Francis Leary, *The Politics of Ecstasy* (New York: Putnam, 1968), 304–9. Reprinted by permission of the Putnam Publishing Group.

After his drop-out he struggled to turn on. It's never easy, you know, to turn on. He memorized the Vedas. Read the Upanishads and the *Village Voice* and Alan Watts and Krishnamurti. Studied at the feet of gurus. Got the message. "Sorry young man. We can't teach it. Divinity is a do-it-yourself proposition, located somewhere inside your own body."

So he spent several years practicing lonely austerities. Diet and physical yoga. Gave up smoking. Ate macrobiotic rice. Got thin. Let his beard grow. Looked holy but felt wholly terrible.

One day, as he was sitting under a tree, a dairy maid offered him a bowl of milk and honey, maybe laced with mushroom juice. It was a forbidden, dangerous potion, against all the laws of yoga abstinence.

Then he started his trip. Session delights. The marijuana miracle! Vision! Touch! Smell! Sound! Beautiful! Ecstasy!!! But don't get caught, Buddha! All the manuals warn you! Center your mind! Float to the beginning!

Next came the sexual visions. Mara the devil sent his naked daughters to entrance. The devil, you say? Oh, didn't they tell you in Bronxville Sunday School and the comparative religions seminar at Princeton that the devil is part of your own mind that wants you to cop out and sell short your timeless divinity? You're a junior executive now with the narcotic security needle hooked in your liberal Republican vein, and the secretaries at the office think you're cute Mr. *Horizon-Reading* Buddha. But remember the teachings! Enjoy but don't chase the erotic fantasies. Center!

Then came the terrors. You'll go insane! You'll lose your ambition! Brain damage! Permanent psychosis! Bellevue Hospital! Chromosome destruction! Jump out a palace window! Who are you, anyway? Spoiled prince, arrogant Brooks Brothers Faust, to grab with greedy hands the delicate web of God? You're crazy now and will never get back. Help! Paranoia! Call the court physician! Call a psychiatrist!

But Gautama remembered the prayer. He centered his mind and body. He spun through the thousand past reincarnations. Tumbled down his DNA code and died, merging in the center of the solar, lunar, diamond, peacock eye of fire that men call God. Illumination.

From whence he looked back up and saw the fibrous unfolding of life to come, all past, all future, hooked up, the riddle of time and mortality solved by the unitive, turn-on perspective.

And at that moment of highest Samhadi, Gautama opened his eyes in delight and wonder at the paradise rediscovered by his trip, and looked around and said that great line—"Wonder of all wonders, all men are the Buddha." . . .

Tradition has it that Gautama Buddha after his illumination sat for days under the bo tree, wondering whether he should come back. Why bother? Gautama's question is exactly that anguishing dilemma faced by several million young Americans who have taken the psychedelic trip in the last 5 years. Because, when seen *sub specie aeternitatis*, American society really does appear quite destructive and insane. What can LBJ or Billy Graham offer a dropped-out, turned-on, ill-prepared, confused teen-ager visionary? Why not stay dropped out? . . .

But the message of the Buddha is to tune in. Glorify! Tune back in, not to the old game. You have to stay dropped out of that. You drop back in to life. You come back down and express your revelation in acts of glory and beauty and humor. Help someone else drop out and turn on.

The Buddha dropped back in with his four noble truths:

> All life is suffering.
> The suffering is caused by striving.
> You can end the suffering by dropping out of the chase.
> The dropping out involves an eightfold discipline, hard work, continual attention, constant centering of consciousness. . . .

Gautama, the Nepalese drop-out, is the greatest spiritual master of recorded history. His message is bleak and direct. Each man is Buddha. The aim of human life is to discover your Buddha-hood. You must do this yourself. You can't rely on any of the divine avatars of the past. Jesus is dead. Krishna is dead. Lao-tse is gone. You must retrace the ancient path yourself. Discover your own Christ-hood. Stagger down from the mountain, flipped-out Moses, with your own moral code fashioned in the ecstatic despair of your own revelation. The only help you have is the teaching. Fashion a prayer and keep your sense of humor. Use the guidebooks and manuals left by the inspired drop-outs of the past. The Buddha himself spent forty years teaching the most accurate and detailed psychological system the world has ever known. This was his tuning-back-in exercise. Use it and go beyond it.

But the old texts mainly tell you what not to do. The timing, the direction, the style, the rhythm, the ritual of your search is for you to evolve. But this much is known. It's all right. It's all worked out. It's all on autopilot. Remember the Buddha message. Turn on, tune in, drop out.

RAM DASS, *THE ONLY DANCE THERE IS* (1974)

Ram Dass burst onto the American scene in 1971 with *Be Here Now*, a best-seller that exhorted readers to "be fully in the moment." He continued to write and lecture on psychology and spirituality into the 1990s, when he had come to be associated with the New Age Movement. Born Richard Alpert in 1931 in Boston, he earned a Ph.D. in psychology from Stanford in 1957 and taught at Stanford, Berkeley, and Harvard. As a Harvard faculty member, Alpert first ingested psilocybin in 1961, and he later joined Timothy Leary to research the effects of psychedelics such as LSD. Alpert himself ingested hallucinogenic drugs more than three hundred times, but his quest to expand his consciousness also led him to search out holy men in India in 1967. He suspected, as did others in the counterculture, that Asian traditions had stores of wisdom unknown to the materialistic and shallow West. In the East, Alpert studied at a tiny temple in the Himalayas under the direction of Neem Karoli Baba. The following year he returned to America as Ram Dass, a name given him by his guru, to pass on what he had learned. Two years later he wrote *Be Here Now*, a book that became one of the most popular spiritual texts for the countercultural generation. In 1974, Ram

Dass's public lectures at the Menniger Foundation and Spring Grove Hospital appeared as *The Only Dance There Is*. These selections from that book discuss his views about LSD and explain his strategies for gaining higher consciousness.

THE PATH OF CONSCIOUSNESS

Last evening, here in Topeka, as one of the journeyers on a path, a very, very old path, the path of consciousness, I, in a sense, met with the Explorers Club to tell about the geography I had been mapping. The people who gather to hear somebody called Ram Dass, formerly Richard Alpert, have somewhere, at some level, in some remote corner, some involvement in this journey. All that I can see that we can do with one another is share notes of our exploration. I can say, "Watch out, because around that bend the road falls off sharply to the left . . . stay far over on the right when you do that."

The motivation for doing this is most interesting—it's only to work on myself. It's very easy to break attachments to worldly games when you're sitting in a cave in the Himalayas. It's quite a different take you do of sex, power, money, fame, and sensual gratification in the middle of New York City in the United States with television and loving people around and great cooks and advertising and total support for all of the attachments. But there is the story of a monk who got very holy up on the mountain until he had some thousands of followers. After many years he went down into a city and he was in the town and somebody jostled him. He turned around angrily and that anger was a mark of how little work he had really done on himself. For all the work he had done he still hadn't clipped the seed of anger; he still got uptight when somebody pushed him around.

So that what I see as my own *sadhana* (my work on my own consciousness—it could also be called my spiritual journey) is that it is very much cyclic. There are periods of going out and there are periods of turning back in, periods of going out and periods of going back in. Just as living here in the market place is forcing things into the forefront, so sitting in a room by myself for 30 or 40 days in a mountain is forcing other things to be confronted. Each hides from the other, each environment hides from the other sets of stimulus conditions. . . .

. . . So, what I'm saying is that this evening is part of my work on myself because I realize that *the only thing you have to offer to another human being, ever, is your own state of being.* You can cop out only just so long, saying I've got all this fine coat—Joseph's coat of many colors—I know all this and I can do all this. But everything you do, whether you're cooking food or doing therapy or being a student or being a lover, *you are only doing your own being, you're only manifesting how evolved a consciousness you are.* That's what you're doing with another human being. That's the only dance there is! When you're protesting against somebody, the degree of consciousness with which you're protesting determines how well they can hear what it is you're really saying.

CONSCIOUSNESS AS FREEDOM FROM ATTACHMENT

Consciousness does not mean attachment to polarity, at any level. It means freedom from attachment. And once you see that the highest mother is the mother who is the most *conscious* mother, the highest student, the highest therapist, the highest lover, the highest anything is the most conscious one, you begin to see that the way you serve another human being is by freeing him from the particular attachments he's stuck in that turn him off to life. You realize that the only thing you have to do for other human beings is to keep yourself really straight, and then do whatever it is you do.

I stop at a Shell station, and the man starts to wash my windshield and put in gas. I've got an old Buick usually, a 1938 limousine, and I live in it, and I'm driving around, and I'm sitting there with one leg under me, driving along at 45 miles an hour, full speed, and I'm doing my *mantra* . . . I'm doing my cognitive centering device. When I stop I'm in a very high state of consciousness just from doing that. I haven't been going anywhere, the car's doing it. It's like a movie of driving down the road in an old Buick. It's like cinerama, a four-day movie of cinerama. I'm just sitting. I've got a really good seat, and I see it all. I stop at the Shell station and I look at the man and of course he is somebody Central Casting sent over—right?—to give me gas and wash my windshield. He is playing like he's a Shell service man. He and I are both from Central Casting. I've been billed this round, in his consciousness, as a kind of strange far-out-looking guy in a weird old car and he is billed as a Shell salesman in my karmic unfolding. We meet, right there. At the moment he's washing my windshield and I look at him and . . . it's saying, "How's the show going, man?" He says, "Groovy." But you don't say it quite that way, you just . . . be there. Nothing to do, you don't come on to anybody, you don't have to change anybody. Just look at them. And so, he finishes and he starts talking about old cars, and then about how during this meat strike he carried turkeys in a car just like this back in 1929, or '39, rather, into New York City and sold them down the market. After we've been going at this for a while and I'm just signing my credit card slip he says, "Would you like to see my car?" "O.K." I get out and go see his car. It's a Mercedes and we look at that and talk about Mercedes. He says, "Say, I'd really like to have you meet my wife." "O.K." So we go upstairs—his wife lives upstairs—and we sit down with his wife. She says, "Would you like to stay for lunch?" "Sure."

So I stay for lunch and pretty soon his son comes home from college and we're all settling in, and we've all got our feet up and we're all home. I realize, this is my home. Where am I? Am I going to say, "Well, I gotta go home?" How did I define what that concept is all about? Here I am and here we are. We're here again, we're all here. Behind the Shell man and behind the weirdo, here we are! I begin to see that every moment of my life is that same place. So, tomorrow when I get in a car and go from Topeka to Albuquerque, the question is how much of my consciousness is spent going to Albuquerque, how much consciousness is spent leaving Topeka, and how much consciousness is right here and now, wherever here and now happens to be on the highway. To the extent that I keep the mantra going all the time, I will stay right here all the time. I can never get more than a little flicker away and I'm pulled right back to the here and now. So from the Shell man I begin to see that *the environment is as high as I am.* If I come to the station thinking I'm just a guy getting gas, that's all I am—a guy getting gas. The Shell man goes through his platitudes and I go through mine and I drive away. And that's what my whole life becomes. My whole life becomes this exquisite dance of being in one role after another where we do our on-stage routine, we do our *Lady Macbeth* scene again or *Twelfth Night* or *Blithe Spirit* or whatever it is we're doing.

. . .

MANTRA

A mantra is a phrase, or it could be a sound or a phrase. It is a phrase that you repeat over and over and over again. Take for example the phrase, the Tibetan one (you can use English ones, but . . . I'll show you why you use Sanskrit or Tibetan ones) *Om Mani Padme Hum.* This phrase is perhaps one of the most widely used mantras in the world today. In fact in Nepal you'll see rocks twenty feet long and ten feet high with *Om Mani Padme Hum* written in tiny letters over the whole rock, so you can just read it like a letter. And there are prayer wheels at the temples where written in them ten million times is the phrase *Om Mani Padme Hum* . . . and you see lamas going around stupas saying *Om Mani Padme Hum.* Now, when you first start to say a mantra, the first involvement is in hearing it outside, through your ears, saying it aloud and hearing it and thinking about its meaning. That's the first game you play with mantra. So, if I give you that mantra, *Om Mani Padma Hum,* you think about it and you think, "Well, what does it mean?" Now, there are many meanings—there's a whole book written about its meaning by Lama Govinda. One of the ways of understanding its meaning is that *Om* means, like Brahma, that which is behind it all, the unmanifest. *Mani* means jewel or crystal. *Padme* means lotus, and *Hum* means heart. So, on one level what it means is the entire universe is just like a pure jewel or crystal right in the heart or center of the lotus flower, which is me, and it is manifest, it comes forth in light, in manifest light, in my own heart. That's one way of interpreting it. You start to say *Om Mani Padme Hum* and you're thinking, "God in unmanifest form is like a jewel in the middle of a lotus, manifest in my heart." You go through that and feel it in your heart—that's one trip. O.K., that's the first. That's the lowest level of operation of mantra. It's putting one set of thoughts into your head in place of another set of thoughts. Instead of thinking, "Gee, it's hot out. Shall I have a milk shake at the next stop? Gee, the engine sounds a little strange. Those new Chevy's don't look very good at all. Boy, I've been on this trip!" Instead of all of that stuff, which is terribly profound and important, but isn't really that relevant, you go into the mantra.

Once the mantra has been going on that way for a while, it starts to change in its nature. You stop thinking about what it means; you just get sort of addicted or hooked on the Tibetan sound of it. And then it starts to move into your head, and then from your head sort of down into your chest, until pretty soon it's going around like a little wheel, going around inside your chest, just *Om Mani Padme Hum.* Right? Now, at that point it has stopped meaning anything to you. Any time you want to bring it back into consciousness, you can rerun its meaning, which will do that thing for you again. But you can keep it down in the place where it's just running off. Now, it's got another quality to it. That is, when a mantra is done sufficiently it gets into a certain kind of vibration or harmony with the universe in a certain way which is its own thing. The conscious beings who evolve certain languages such as Sanskrit specifically evolve the sounds of these languages to be connected with various states of consciousness—unlike the English language—so that a Sanskrit mantra, if you do it over and over again, will take you to a certain state of consciousness.

. . .

LSD

When I said that God came to the United States in the form of LSD, I was quoting my teacher, with whom I lived for six months, who was, as far as I could see, one of the purest and highest beings I have met. When I asked him what LSD was he went away and several weeks later he came back and he wrote, and the quote is almost exact, "LSD is like a Christ coming to America in the *Kali-Yuga.* America is a most materialistic country and they wanted their Avatar in the form of a material. The young people wanted their Avatar in the form of a material. And so they got LSD. If they had not tasted of such things, how will they know— how they will know?" was his actual wording. Now, this plus the fact that my guru took 900 micrograms of LSD and nothing happened to him, and I watched this process happen, were the two bits of new information I had collected about LSD which I reported back to the intellectual community. I am not at this moment using LSD nor am I not using LSD. Right, I'm doing a type of yoga which does not require at this moment the use of LSD.

I honor LSD; LSD has, for me, anyway, made a major change in my perceptual field, and I feel that under suitable conditions it is a major breakthrough of technology, allowing man to change his levels of consciousness. I share Tim's vision in almost every way. I think I'm not as attached to certain kinds of polarities in terms of establishment and good and evil and dropping out and so on as Timothy is, but I think he is a great visionary and my feelings about LSD are: I honor it. I also think that it is very quickly becoming an anachronism. I think it is totally falling out of date because the types of consciousness that it opened allowed the Maharishi to do the work he did in the United States and allowed the Beatles to do the work they've done and allowed all of that process to happen. I think that only took about five years and it seems to me that the values in the culture shifted dramatically enough, as a result of the psychedelic movement, to bring in another set of cognitive consciousness possibilities into the *Zeitgeist*, enough so that they would become researchable, they would become studyable, and explorable; and yoga, which was a dirty word seven years ago, can now become a highly respected and thoughtful science, as it should be, as it is.

CHAPTER **14**

Asian Indian Gurus,
Converts, and Movements

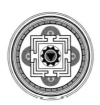

A TM CATECHISM (1975)

Of all the spiritual imports that benefited from the lifting of immigration restrictions in 1965, Transcendental Meditation was initially the most popular. TM came to the United States with Maharishi Mahesh Yogi, an Indian-born guru who earned a physics degree from Allahabad University before turning to the study of meditation under his teacher, Jagadguru Bhagavan Shankaracharya. In an effort to share what he had learned, Maharishi founded the Spiritual Regeneration Movement in 1958. His first book, *Science of Being and Art of Living*, appeared in 1963. TM took off in the 1970s after it was endorsed by the Beatles and New York Jets quarterback Joe Namath. At first Maharishi applied TM to individual spiritual advancement, but in 1972 he promulgated a World Plan aimed at remaking society. Today TM's social goals are promoted by the Maharishi International University (established 1975) and by the Natural Law Party, a political party devoted to healing America's social ills through TM practice. Like the Hare Krishna movement, TM has been more successful in the West than in India. It has been promoted among Americans not as a religion—in fact, members insist it is not—but as a simple and easy-to-learn technique of chanting a mantra (a sacred sound repeated as a meditation tool). In *The TM Book* (1975), a popular catechism-style guide sprinkled liberally with cartoons, TM practitioners Denise Denniston and Peter McWilliams repeatedly emphasize TM's practical results. Chanting a TM mantra, they say, will reduce stress, drug abuse, and crime, and increase intelligence, self-esteem, and world peace. This excerpt focuses on the theory and practice of TM rather than its purported effects.

Denise Denniston and Peter McWilliams, *The TM Book: How to Enjoy the Rest of Your Life* (Allen Park, Mich.: Three Rivers Press, 1975). Reprinted courtesy of Prelude Press.

The TM program is not a religion? I've heard it was just some Westernized form of Hinduism.
No, no—it's absurd to assume that just because the TM technique comes from India it must be some Hindu practice. . . . The TM technique is a scientific discovery which happens to come from India. . . . The TM program does not involve any religious belief or practice—Hindu or otherwise. . . .

Does TM conflict with any form of religion?
NO. People of any religion practice the TM technique. In fact, they find the increased clarity of mind brought about through the TM program greatly broadens the comprehension and enhances the appreciation of their individual religious practices. Priests practice it, rabbis practice it, ministers practice it, and they recommend the TM program to their congregations. . . .

Aren't most who practice the TM program vegetarians?
Some are. Many aren't. But then, a lot of nonTMer's are vegetarians, too. The point is, there are no dietary restrictions or recommendations involved with the TM program. . . .

I can still eat Big Macs?
You can eat anything you want. . . .

No funny clothes?
No. . . .

No change of life style?
There is no need to change in any way to start the TM program. There are no pleasures you must abandon, nor any new traditions you must uphold. . . .

Now that I know what the TM program is not, tell me what the TM technique is.
. . . The Transcendental Meditation technique is a simple, natural, effortless process that allows the mind to experience subtler and subtler levels of the thinking process until thinking is transcended and the mind comes into direct contact with the source of thought.

. . . Just how many years does it take to learn this technique?
Years? Days. Hours, actually. Four two-hour sessions with a qualified teacher of the TM program, and that's it.

And then I do the TM technique whenever I want?
No. The TM technique is practiced twice a day, morning and evening, for 15–20 minutes each time. It's preparation for activity. We sit comfortably anywhere we happen to be: propped up in bed, on a train, in the office, in your living room, any where.

This twice-daily practice of the TM technique forms the basis of the TM program. . . .

If I decide to do it, how do I go about learning the TM technique?
You can learn the Transcendental Meditation technique in seven steps. They are:

- A. Introductory steps:
  1. *Introductory lecture.* If you've read our book thus far you are already acquainted with the introductory material. (What can the TM program do for me?)
  2. *Preparatory lecture.* This lecture is about the practice of the TM technique—specific explanations of how the technique works, how it differs from other techniques, where it comes from, how it is taught, and why it is taught in that way.
  3. *Personal interview.* Just after the preparatory lecture, you meet with a teacher of the TM program, get to know each other, and clear up any questions you may have.

- B. Four consecutive days of instruction (two hours each day):
  4. *Personal instruction.* This is the private session where you learn the TM technique from your teacher, who was personally trained and qualified by Maharishi Mahesh Yogi.
  5. *First day checking.* In this group session you receive further instruction and answers to your questions about your experiences while discussing practical details about the TM program.
  6. *Second day checking.* The group discusses the mechanics of the process of the TM technique and the release of stress in the light of their experience with the practice.
  7. *Third day checking.* This group session explores the goal of the TM program—life free from stress, with the full use of mental and physical potential. . . .

Course fee?
As of 1975, the course fee in the USA is $125 per person. Couples, and their children under 15, may all start together for $200. The fee for college students is $65, for high school students $55, and for junior high school students $35. Children between four and ten are asked to bring two weeks' allowance. . . .

How does the TM technique work?
. . . During the TM technique, we take a specific thought, our "mantra." Because of the nature of the mantra, and the way we are taught to experience it, the mind automatically goes within, following the thought of the mantra back to the source of all thought. Each "step" toward pure consciousness is more and more fulfilling, and the final step—the experience of pure creative intelligence—is the most fulfilling of all.

Mantra?
"Mantra" means a specific sound, the effects of which are known for the individual in every way—mentally, physically, and environmentally. The ones used

in the TM program come from an ancient tradition which assures their beneficial effectiveness. They are taught in a very specific way. Everyone learns individually and privately, from a teacher personally trained and qualified by Maharishi Mahesh Yogi. The teaching procedure is a very simple exchange of information and instructions between the teacher and the student. . . .

If it is so easy, why don't you just print a list of mantras and a few directions and I can learn from a book?
There are several reasons. First, there's that interchange between teacher and student which ensures that you have correct experiences. Second, it's necessary that the mantra be personally selected by a trained teacher, and that it be imparted properly and usefully.

THE BEATLES AND A. C. BHAKTIVEDANTA SWAMI PRABHUPADA, *SEARCH FOR LIBERATION* (1981)

The International Society for Krishna Consciousness (ISKCON) was the most conspicuous and successful Hindu-based new religious movement in 1970s America. Its moving force was A. C. Bhaktivedanta Swami Prabhupada (1896–1977), a businessman and devotee of the Hindu god Krishna who renounced the world in 1956 and came to New York City nine years later. ISKCON, which he started in 1966, teaches a devotional form of Hinduism that worships Krishna as "the Supreme Lord." "Hare Krishnas," as members are often called, read the *Bhagavad Gita* as a core scripture and chant a mantra: "Hare Krishna, Hare Krishna, Krishna Krishna, Hare, Hare Rama, Hare Rama, Rama, Hare." Although ISKCON is often classified as a new religious movement, it has roots in the Krishna-based devotionalism of Caitanya (1486–1533), a Bengali holy man from the sixteenth century. The Beatles rock group is typically associated more with Maharishi Mahesh Yogi and TM than with Prabhupada and ISKCON, but its members were attracted enough to the Hare Krishna movement to engage Prabhupada in this dialogue. Later published as *Search for Liberation*, the conversation is dominated by Prabhupada's voice. But John Lennon and George Harrison also weigh in, as does Yoko Ono, Lennon's Japanese-American wife. It is now something of a cliché to note that the ideals of movements like ISKCON and TM shared much with countercultural values. This dialogue demonstrates there were also some significant fault lines—both between the Hare Krishnas and the counterculture, and between ISKCON and TM.

Śrīla Prabhupāda [to John Lennon]: You are anxious to bring about peace in the world. I've read some of your statements, and they show me that you're anxious to do something. Actually, every saintly person should be anxious to bring peace

A. C. Bhaktivedanta Swami Prabhupada and John Lennon, *Search for Liberation* (Los Angeles: Bhaktivedanta Book Trust, 1981), 1–21. Copyright © 1981 Bhaktivedanta Book Trust. Reprinted courtesy of Bhaktivedanta Book Trust International.

to the world. But we must know the process. In *Bhagavad-gītā* [5.29], Lord Kṛṣṇa explains how to achieve peace: "The sages, knowing Me as the ultimate purpose of all sacrifices and austerities, the Supreme Lord of all planets and demigods, and the benefactor and well-wisher of all living entities, attain peace from the pangs of material miseries."

People can become peaceful by knowing three things. . . . First of all, Lord Kṛṣṇa says that he is the real enjoyer of all the sacrifices, austerities, and penances that people undertake to perfect their lives. For instance, your own musical activities are also a form of austerity. . . . That is called *yajña*, or sacrifice. It is also called *tapasya*, or penance. So Kṛṣṇa says that He is the enjoyer of the results of your *tapasya*. He claims, "The result of your *tapasya* should come to Me. Then you'll be satisfied."

The second thing people should remember is that Kṛṣṇa is the supreme proprietor. People are claiming, "This is my England," "This is my India," "This is my Germany," "This is my China." No! Everything belongs to God, Kṛṣṇa. Not only this planet belongs to Kṛṣṇa, but all other planets in the universe. . . .

Thirdly, we should always remember that Kṛṣṇa is the real friend of every living entity and that He is sitting as a friend within everyone's heart. . . . He is the best friend of all living beings. He's not just the friend of a select few, but is dwelling even within the heart of the most insignificant creature, as Paramātma, or Supersoul.

THE PEACE FORMULA

So if these three things are understood clearly, then one becomes peaceful. This is the real peace formula. Everything is there in *Bhagavad-gītā*. One simply has to study it. Just like arithmetic—there are so many types of mathematical calculations, such as addition, subtraction, multiplication, division, and fractions. One has to learn them by careful study. So *Bhagavad-gītā* is the best book to study for learning the spiritual science. . . .

Bhagavad-gītā is accepted by scholars and philosophers of all nationalities. Therefore, I think people should have one scripture, one God, one *mantra*, and one activity: one God, Kṛṣṇa; one scripture, *Bhagavad-gītā*; one *mantra*, Hare Kṛṣṇa; and one activity, to serve Kṛṣṇa. Then there will actually be peace all over the world. I request you to at least try to understand this philosophy to your best ability. And if you think that it is valuable, then please take it up. You want to give something to the world. So why not give them Kṛṣṇa consciousness? . . .

MUSIC AND MANTRAS

Śrīla Prabhupāda: . . . What kind of philosophy are you following? May I ask?

John Lennon: Following?

Yoko Ono: We don't follow anything. We are just living.

George Harrison:	We've done meditation. Or I do my meditation—*mantra* meditation.
Śrīla Prabhupāda:	Hare Kṛṣṇa is also *mantra.*
John Lennon:	Ours is not a song, though.
George Harrison:	No, no. It's chanting.
John Lennon:	We heard it from Maharishi. A *mantra* each.
Śrīla Prabhupāda:	His *mantras* are not public.
George Harrison:	Not out loud . . . no.
John Lennon:	No—it's a secret.
Śrīla Prabhupāda:	There's a story about Rāmanujācārya, a great Kṛṣṇa conscious spiritual master. His spiritual master gave him a *mantra* and said, "My dear boy, you chant this *mantra* silently. Nobody else can hear it. It is very secret." Rāmanujācārya asked his *guru,* "What is the effect of this *mantra*?" The *guru* said, "By chanting this *mantra* in meditation, you'll get liberation." So Rāmanujācārya immediately went out to a big public meeting and said, "Everyone chant this *mantra.* You'll all be liberated." [*Laughter.*] Then he came back to his spiritual master, who was very angry, and said, "I told you that you should chant silently!" Rāmanujācārya said, "Yes, I have committed an offense. So whatever punishment you like you can give me. But because you told me that this *mantra* will give liberation, I have given it to the public. Let everyone be liberated, and let me go to hell—I am prepared. But if by chanting this *mantra* everyone can be liberated, let it be publicly distributed." His spiritual master than embraced him, saying, "You are greater than me." You see? If a *mantra* has so much power, why should it be secret? It should be distributed. People are suffering. So Caitanya Mahāprabhu said to chant this Hare Kṛṣṇa *mantra* loudly. Anyone who hears it, even the birds and beasts, will become liberated.

WHICH MANTRA TO CHANT?

Yoko Ono:	If Hare Kṛṣṇa is such a strong, powerful *mantra,* is there any reason to chant anything else? For instance, you talked about songs and different *mantras.* Is there any point in the chanting of another song or *mantra*?
Śrīla Prabhupāda:	There are other *mantras,* but the Hare Kṛṣṇa *mantra* is especially recommended for this age. . . .

John Lennon: If all *mantras* are just the name of God, then whether it's a secret *mantra* or an open *mantra* it's all the name of God. So it doesn't really make much difference, does it, which one you sing?

Śrīla Prabhupāda: It *does* make a difference. For instance, in a drug shop they sell all types of medicines for curing different diseases. But still you have to get a doctor's prescription in order to get a particular type of medicine. Otherwise, the druggist won't supply you. You might go to the drug shop and say, "I'm diseased. Please give me the medicine you have." But the druggist will ask you, "Where is your prescription?" . . . Similarly, in this age of Kali the Hare Kṛṣṇa *mantra* is prescribed in the *śāstras*, or scriptures. . . .

YOU CAN'T MANUFACTURE A MANTRA

Śrīla Prabhupāda: . . . if you don't receive the *mantra* through the proper channel, it may not really be spiritual.

John Lennon: How would you know, anyway? How are you able to tell? I mean, for any of your disciples or us or anybody else who goes to any spiritual master—how are we to tell if he's for real or not?

Śrīla Prabhupāda: You shouldn't go to just *any* spiritual master.

WHO'S A GENUINE GURU?

John Lennon: Yes, we should go to a true master. But how are we to tell one from the other?

Śrīla Prabhupāda: It is not that you can go to just any spiritual master. He must be a member of a recognized *sampradāya*, a particular line of disciplic succession.

John Lennon: But what if one of these masters who's not in the line says exactly the same thing as one who is? What if he says his *mantra* is coming from the *Vedas* and he seems to speak with as much authority as you? He could probably be right. It's confusing—like having too many fruits on a plate.

Śrīla Prabhupāda: If the *mantra* is actually coming through a bona fide disciplic succession, then it will have potency.

John Lennon: But the Hare Kṛṣṇa *mantra* is the best one?

Śrīla Prabhupāda: Yes.

Yoko Ono: Well, if Hare Kṛṣṇa is the best one, why should we bother to say anything else other than Hare Kṛṣṇa?

Śrīla Prabhupāda: It's true, you don't have to bother with anything else. We say that the Hare Kṛṣṇa *mantra* is sufficient for one's perfection, for liberation.

George Harrison: Isn't it like flowers? Somebody may prefer roses, and somebody may like carnations better. Isn't it really a matter for the individual devotee to decide? One person may find that Hare Kṛṣṇa is more beneficial to his spiritual progress, and yet another person may find that some other *mantra* may be more beneficial for himself. Isn't it just a matter of taste, like choosing a flower? They're all flowers, but some people may like one better than another.

Śrīla Prabhupāda: But still there is a distinction. A fragrant rose is considered better than a flower without any scent.

Yoko Ono: In that case, I can't—

Śrīla Prabhupāda: Let's try to understand this flower example.

Yoko Ono: O.K.

Śrīla Prabhupāda: You may be attracted by one flower, and I may be attracted by another flower. But among flowers a distinction can be made. There are many flowers that have no fragrance and many that have fragrance.

Yoko Ono: Is that flower that has fragrance better?

Śrīla Prabhupāda: Yes.

YOGI BHAJAN, "AWAKENING THE MIND TO PRAYER" (1984)

Not all the Asian teachers who converged on the United States in the sixties and seventies were Hindus or Buddhists. Harbhajan Singh, popularly known as Yogi Bhajan, was a Sikh. Born in India, he earned a degree in economics and worked for the government before moving from Delhi to Toronto in 1968. He settled later that year in Los Angeles, where he taught the techniques of kundalini yoga (physical exercises aimed at awakening the spiritual energy latent at the base of the spine). In 1969, he founded the Healthy, Happy, Holy Organization (3HO) and began to attract Gora ("white") Sikhs to a religious tradition that had previously been reserved in the United States for Asian Indians. Two years later Yogi Bhajan was named the chief authority for Sikh Dharma in the West. 3HO is now the educational arm of the broader organization known as Sikh Dharma, which runs over one hundred American ashrams (teaching centers) and maintains headquarters in Los Angeles and Espanola, New Mexico, where Yogi Bhajan lives. Sikh Dharma's roughly five to ten thousand members do not cut their hair, and women as well as men wear white clothes and turbans. One scholar has called the largely European-American Sikh Dharma and the much bigger Punjabi Sikh community in the United States "estranged." Indian-American Sikhs have condemned Yogi Bhajan for departing from his Sikh orthodoxy by emphasizing kundalini

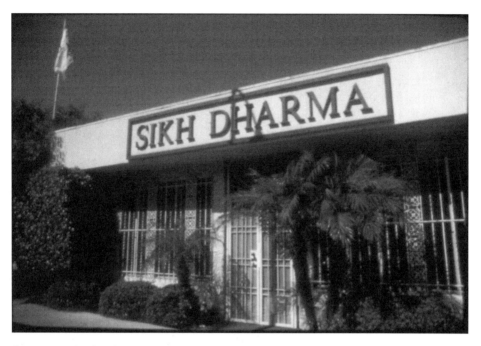

The Los Angeles headquarters of Yogi Bhajan's Sikh Dharma. Courtesy of The Pluralism Project, Harvard University.

yoga and, more recently, "white tantric yoga," while Sikh Dharma members have criticized Punjabi Sikhs for giving up the traditional turban. In the late 1990s, Yogi Bhajan, known to his followers as Siri Singh Sahib Bhai Sahib Harbhajan Khalsa Yogiji, was spreading his message through talks, books, videotapes, and the internet. His extensive web site (www.yogibhajan.com) boldly proclaimed, "You have a right to be healthy, happy and holy." This internet excerpt, which originally appeared in a book called *Identical Identity* (1984), marks Yogi Bhajan as a creative contributor to both Sikhism in the diaspora and the longstanding American tradition of the power of positive thinking.

Every person is born into the world with the concept and capability to realize and access the Infinite Energy within them. Some people call that experience "God," while others quake in fear at the sound of that well-used word. No matter what you call it, the fact remains that the experience of that Infinite Energy is a critical facet of human existence, and to tap that Energy gives us strength, knowledge, and contentment.

Every human has three aspects. You have the lower self, which is the gross or physical self; you have the central self, which is known as the existing self; and you have the higher self, which is a powerful sophisticated and delicate self. The higher self is the aspect of our existence which separates us from other forms of animal life. The higher self is the experience of the subtle and meditative reality for which we are all born. When you give the mind the regular experience of an Infinite horizon, you are maintaining the higher self and experiencing the level and caliber of a basic human being. When you further develop the facets of the higher self and become a God-conscious individual, it means you have the power of mental infinity. It is a great help and a special treat if you find some teacher who can stand by you and let you go through the experience of the higher self.

You can get knowledge from anybody, and it will always yield a beautiful bounty, but a teacher cannot give you mental infinity. That is your job alone. You have to train yourself to be wise and effective through your own experience of awakening the heart and mind to prayer. A normal, fully-aware human being has a mind that is stable, accurate, and neutral. However, today you will find most people are erratic, commotional, and upset by the smallest thing. Actually, nothing should upset you. You are beautiful. What upsets you is your own mind. It is the ugly mind that makes you think you are ugly. In fact, there is no such thing as an ugly human nature. It doesn't exist.

When the mind supports the thought pattern that you are ugly, then it can put you under a deep spell of self-delusion and depression. Under that spell, you can do undesirable and destructive actions. Your mind can drag you to the lowest level of your consciousness. We pass our years with such speed and anxiety that we do not know what maintains us, except the blessing of God's compassion. When there is constant pressure and no relaxation, when there is no outlet, when there is constant boredom or when there is a constant deficit in mental capacity, it results in a shattered mind and the loss of happiness. Then you must get to a psychiatrist, to a counselor, or to some yogi. You have to depend on someone to redirect your energy and help you. I do not believe you should be dependent and be led around by some wise man like a donkey with a string in your nose. What you need is the inner experience of God. But you have been brainwashed to misunderstand this idea.

You think God is a guy who stands on a seventh sky at the head of Time, watching you. I believe that every single person represents God. And if you cannot see God in all, you cannot see God at all. Factually speaking, this universe is an electromagnetic field. It has the longitude and latitude of magnetic wavelengths. This cosmic universe is very communicative and interactive. It talks. It is in this talking that all personalities are built and marred. Therefore always speak very carefully and consciously. Remember the Word is God and God is the Word. You are what your words are and you live by the definition of your prayers. You are an individual magnetic psyche working in this huge magnetic field. This pranic energy by which we live is nothing more than an electromagnetic field. This whole universe is the coexistence of a working electromagnetic field.

Each individual magnetic field has its own frequency, its own rhythm, its own axis and its own orbit. You are in perfect harmony with another person whenever you cross the range of another field and the psyches intertwine. For any progressive contribution you make, you must have the absolute connection with the entire psyche of the electromagnetic computerized system, which we call God. You project at a certain frequency through your little tiny electromagnetic field to the universal psyche. For your prayers to be effective, your frequency must intertwine with the infinite electromagnetic field. If your signals are correct the results shall be perfect. Your signals are called prayers. This is the mechanics of how the creatures send prayers to the Creator.

Guru Gobind Singh says: Savaa laakh se ayk laraanoo tabai Gobind Singh naam kahaaoo. When it is one hundred twenty-five thousand against one, Only then can my name be Gobind Singh! Guru Gobind Singh. That only means that one electromagnetic psyche was so perfect and computerized that it can send a signal to the master electromagnetic psyche to rearrange the strength and coordinate the fulfillment by that psyche which shall give the victory. Don't misunderstand that prayer is only that which you say or utter. Prayer is also that, but real prayer means attention. Where you, your soul, your mind pays attention, that is called prayer.

MARGARET SIMPSON, AN EXPERIENCE OF SIDDHA YOGA MEDITATION (1991)

On a 550-acre ashram in the Catskill mountains of New York, Swami Chidvilasananda, known to her devotees as Gurumayi, teaches Siddha Yoga meditation. The SYDA (or Siddha Yoga Dham Associates) Foundation comprises more than three hundred meditation centers and several ashrams around the world. It was founded by Swami Muktananda (1908-82), who first visited the United States in 1970 and returned in the next decade for extended stays during several world tours. Baba Muktananda, following the teachings of his own guru (Bhagawan Nityananda)—and drawing on Kashmir Shaivism, Vedanta, and the Bhakti sants—emphasized that students need the guidance of a spiritually realized being. It is the guru's grace (*guru-kripa yoga*) that awakens the seeker's spiritual energy (*kundalini-shakti*) and leads to further spiritual progress—and (eventually) full realization of the inner Self. As with many guru-centered traditions, and new and transplanted religious movements generally, a decisive moment arrived when the founder died. For several years after Muktananda's death in 1982 Gurumayi and her brother Swami Nityananda led the movement as co-heirs. However, in 1985, under circumstances that are described differently by the parties involved, Gurumayi's brother stepped down as co-leader of the community. He has since formed his own ashram just a few miles east of the Siddha Yoga Meditation International headquarters in South Fallsburgh, New York. The forty-two-year-old Gurumayi, whom *Hinduism Today* named one of the ten most influential international Hindu leaders, continues to be revered by many followers in the United States and around the world. In this excerpt from SYDA's monthly magazine, one devotee describes the life-transforming effects of Siddha Yoga meditation.

Margaret Simpson, "From the Inside Out," *DARSHAN*, 52 (1991): 21–25. Reprinted by permission of Margaret Simpson and *DARSHAN*.

Recently I had to fill in a form about myself. I listed all the usual things: educational establishments, degree, jobs, publications, TV credits, marital status, children. Then I came to hobbies and leisure activities. I paused. Was meditation a hobby? True, it's not something I'm paid to do and sitting still for an hour a day *sounds* more like leisure than work. Yet to put meditation under that heading would trivialize it. Because, quite simply, sitting for meditation is one of the most important and satisfying activities in my life. It fills me with feelings of well-being and calm. It gives me a sunnier perspective on life. It has made me much less dependent on outside events and circumstances for gratification, because I have discovered a wellspring of contentment within myself to which I can turn at any time. It refreshes me. It has put me in touch with and given me trust in the intuitive part of myself. I am less angry, less fearful, more accepting, more creative than I used to be. This is not just my opinion. Other people, including my grown-up children, have remarked on it. . . .

When I discovered Siddha Meditation—seemingly by chance—I was first impressed by its simplicity. I was invited to sit quietly, with a straight back; to breathe naturally; and to repeat silently to myself the Siddha mantra, *Om Namah Shivaya*—I honor my own inner Self—on each incoming and outgoing breath. This process would calm the mind, I was told, and take me to the still center at the very heart of myself that is, in the words of Baba Muktananda, "the abode of deep peace, where love gushes, steadfastness is entrenched, and the image of God shines forth."

Baba addressed directly the two issues that had been fueling my search, and explained, in very simple terms, the connection between them: human beings are always searching in the outside world for a happiness that lies right within them all the time. This happiness is our birthright, and to experience it is to know our own inner Self, the pure "I am" that lies beneath our roles and our talents and even our personality and deepest relationships. This "I am" is pure Consciousness. It is God, manifest within us. And the one great obstacle that keeps us from seeing this truth is the mind—"our worst enemy, our greatest friend."

"The mind veils the inner Self and hides it from us," wrote Baba. "It makes us feel that God is far away and that happiness must be found outside. Yet the same mind that separates us from the Self also helps us reunite with it. . . . When we practice meditation, the mind goes deeper and deeper within, and becomes more and more quiet. When it is truly still, we begin to drink the nectar of the Self."

These words moved me. If they were true, then I wasn't a lone radio operator after all, beaming messages randomly across the cosmos in the hope of picking up God in His heaven. If they were true, all I had to do was turn within and I could reach God on my very next breath!

And of course, Baba's words were true, they *are* true, because Siddha Yoga had already given me more than theory. It had already given me the *experience* of their truth. From the very first day I meditated using the Siddha mantra, there had been perceptible effects—unexpectedly physical, given the spiritual and mental nature of my longings. My back spontaneously straightened up, for example, and there was a pleasurable tingling in the back of my head. When I emerged from these sessions of meditation, I noticed, rather to my surprise, that my senses were particularly acute. Food looked, smelled, and tasted quite delicious. As I went about my daily life, I found myself delighting in sights I saw—the blossoms in the gardens as I walked down the road with my dog, the moss on the trees, bright green on wet mornings, a spider's web in the kitchen window, streetlights reflected in wet tarmac.

At first my busy mind used to try and find rational explanations for all this. Perhaps the secret lay in the meaning of the mantra. "After all, if you keep repeating, 'I honor my own inner Self,' it's bound to increase your self-esteem," I told myself. Since then I have come to understand that there is a lot more to it than that. The Siddha mantra is a *chaitanya*, or living, mantra. It has been passed on from Guru to disciple down through the ages. As such, it carries not only the power of the living Guru, Gurumayi, but all the accumulated power, wisdom, and understanding of the whole Siddha lineage. What was awakened in me that very first day I used it was the dormant spiritual energy known as Kundalini. It was this energy I experienced as a tingling in my head; later I was to feel it at other points in my back, or in my lips, or at my throat, or between my eyebrows. It was a surprise to discover that there were energy pathways for the spirit, every bit as specific and full of sensation as those that transmitted physical pleasure, but the experience was undeniable. I came to trust it, even to think of these sensations as a sort of Geiger counter, because they intensified when I was in the presence of the Guru, or in places made sacred by spiritual practice—the meditation cave in Ganeshpuri, at the English ashram, and sometimes in town, if I visited a cathedral or a church, or listened to a particularly beautiful piece of music. Then, at other times, Kundalini would manifest in other sensations—excessive salivation, for example, which as I tried to control it, made my throat ache as it had when I tried to control sobs as a child; and a series of nightmares that abated only when I offered them to the Guru in meditation. For the Siddha path is just that—a path—and the Kundalini, once awakened, clears out every unresolved conflict in the way of our spiritual growth. Rather like removing splinters, it's not always pleasant, but—in my experience—it always passes, and it's always healing.

The goal to which this path leads is not a place, but a state. It is to live in the awareness of our own inner Self—our own divinity—not just when we are seated in meditation, but in every moment of our lives. This is the state of the Guru.

SWAMI SATCHIDANANDA, "INTEGRAL YOGA" (1996)

Swami Satchidananda has been one of the most visible Hindu teachers in America since he arrived in 1966, at the invitation of two American devotees, filmmaker Conrad Rooks and pop artist Peter Max. Sri Gurudev, as his students call him, was born C. K. Ramaswamy Gounder in Chettipalayam, South India, on 22 December 1914. He entered the Ramakrishna Mission in 1946 and later found the guru who would set the course of his life: Swami Sivananda (1887–1963), the leader of Divine Life Society,

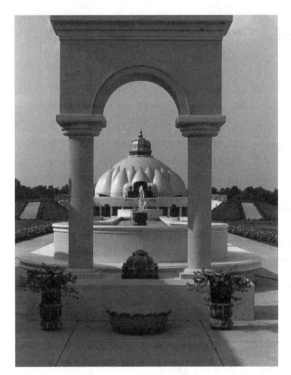

Light of Truth Universal Shrine, Satchidananda Ashram, Yogaville, Buckingham, Virginia. This shrine is dedicated to "the Light of all faiths and to world peace." Courtesy Satchidananda Ashram, Yogaville.

a nonsectarian Hindu organization. At his guru's request, Satchidananda traveled to Sri Lanka to set up Divine Life Society branches, and many Westerners (including Rooks) sought him out for spiritual direction there. Shortly after his arrival in New York City on 31 July 1966, Gurudev began teaching students in Peter Max's apartment, and in October of that year he founded the Integral Yoga Institute. He subsequently lectured widely, wrote several books, and appeared on talk shows. For many, he is best remembered as the bearded Indian guru who gave the opening words at the Woodstock Festival in 1969. At the festival, and in the years ahead, he taught a form of Hinduism that combined multiple Hindu practices and emphasized religious tolerance. By the 1990s, Gurudev had become a well-known advocate of interreligious dialogue and world peace. The Light of Truth Universal Shrine, which was dedicated in 1986, might be the clearest expression of his ecumenical views. That lotus-shaped temple to tolerance is located on the mountainous grounds of the Satchidananda Ashram in Virginia, known as Yogaville. The building includes twelve altars, each representing a major faith. Like these two pamphlets published by his ashram, the shrine expresses clearly the guru's desire to honor multiple traditions and celebrate religious cooperation.

Integral Yoga International, "Integral Yoga," pamphlet (Buckingham, Va.: Satchidananda Ashram—Yogaville, n.d.); Swami Satchidananda, "Truth Is One, Paths Are Many," pamphlet (Buckingham, Va.: Satchidananda Ashram—Yogaville, n.d.). Copyrighted material of Satchidananda Ashram-Yogaville. Reprinted by permission of Satchidananda Ashram Yogaville.

INTEGRAL YOGA

Facets of Yoga

> "A mind free from all disturbances is Yoga."
>
> THE YOGA SUTRAS OF PATANJALI

The teachings of Yoga are the same essential principles that lie at the foundation of all faiths. The true Yogi respects all traditions, recognizing that although the paths are many, the Truth is One.

The practice of Yoga is based on such moral and ethical precepts as: non-violence, truthfulness, non-stealing, moderation, non-greed, purity, contentment, self-discipline, study of spiritual books, and dedication to God.

When the word Yoga is mentioned, most people think of some physical postures for relaxing and limbering the body. This is only one facet of Yoga. The practice of Yoga addresses itself to every aspect of the individual; physical, psychological, emotional, spiritual and social, and leads to the understanding and mastery of one's own mind. When the mind becomes clear and balanced, we are able to look within ourselves to experience the peace and happiness that is in us as our true nature.

The goal of Integral Yoga, and the birthright of every individual, is to realize the spiritual unity behind all the diversities in the entire creation and to live harmoniously as members of one universal family. This goal is achieved by maintaining our natural condition of: a body of optimum health and strength, senses under total control, a mind well-disciplined, clear and calm, an intellect as sharp as a razor, a will as strong and pliable as steel, a heart full of unconditional love and compassion, an ego as pure as crystal, and a life filled with Supreme Peace and Joy.

Integral Yoga, as taught by Sri Swami Satchidananda, combines the methods of Yoga to develop all the capabilities bestowed upon us by nature. These methods are: Hatha Yoga (physical postures, breathing practices, and relaxation techniques), Karma Yoga (selfless service), Raja Yoga (concentration and meditation, based on ethical perfection), Japa Yoga (repetition of a sound vibration), Bhakti Yoga (love and devotion to God) and Jnana Yoga (self-inquiry). All of these practices help one to find the peace and happiness within.

Yogaville

Satchindananda Ashram-Yogaville, in Buckingham, Virginia, is the headquarters for Integral Yoga International. Here, people of all faiths and backgrounds have come together to study and practice the principles of Integral Yoga under the guidance of Sri Swami Satchidananda.

This fast-growing spiritual center is designed to serve as a model of how we can all live and work together in harmony, while still enjoying our individual differences.

Situated near the Blue Ridge Mountains, on the banks of the James River, the center encompasses almost 1000 acres of serene, natural landscape. Yogaville has a programs and dining hall, two dormitories, a meditation hall, a library, a guest inn and general store, a school, an organic garden and orchard, a garage, a woodworking shop, an office building, a fine arts society, an audio/video production department (Shakticom), an archives, a photo lab, a publications/distribution center, an art department, an affiliated credit union, and a law office.

At Yogaville, guests are always welcome for a short visit, overnight, a week, or longer.

TRUTH IS ONE, PATHS ARE MANY

The purpose of any religion is to educate us about our spiritual unity. However, more people have been killed in the name of God and religion than in all of the natural calamities and world wars combined. That means religion has gotten caught in the hands of egoistic groups who are fighting with each other, who are claiming only their path is right. If you follow the teaching of one individual, that does not mean that everyone should follow your teacher. The one and the same Spirit expresses itself in many forms and names to suit the age, time, and place. In one place the Spirit is called Jesus; in another place, Buddha; in another, Mohammed. There is no need to claim that only one should be worshipped.

It is not the religions or the founders of the religions, the sages and the prophets, who gave us these beautiful paths, who are dividing us. They want us all to be together. It is the people who make use of religion for their own benefit who are literally dividing humanity in the name of that which is supposed to unite us. We have to do everything within our capacity to follow the principle that we should not and cannot divide ourselves in the name of God and religion, and to so educate others also.

We are one in Spirit. That does not mean that you should renounce your own path or approach. That is not unity; that is conversion. Real unity means accepting all the various approaches, and that is what ecumenism means. Sometimes people ask if the ecumenical approach is an effort to have all faiths merge into one. No, that is not the purpose of ecumenism. When things become uniform they become boring. Variety is the spice of life. God created all these differences for a reason. Our aim is to understand the unity and enjoy the variety. Ultimately we aim for the same truth while walking on different paths.

So, let us not fight in the name of religion. The moment the understanding comes that essentially we are one appearing as many, all the other problems, physical and material, will be solved. Until then, they will never be solved, because the basic cause for all the world problems is the lack of understanding of this spiritual unity. Wherever you go say, "We look different, but we are all one in Spirit. Hello, brother, hello, sister." Care and share, love and give. Apply it in your very own life.

OM Shanthi, Shanthi, Shanthi

Swami Satchidananda

ELSIE COWAN, "SAI BABA AND THE RESURRECTION OF WALTER COWAN" (1976)

In this age of fast travel and instant communication, even Asian teachers who never have visited the United States can attract a following. Sathya Sai Baba, the red-robed, bushy-haired Hindu guru, might be modern India's most famous deity-saint, although in his homeland mention of his name elicits a range of responses, from ridicule to reverence. Those in India who revere him, especially but not exclusively the English-speaking, high-caste middle and upper-middle classes, tell the story of his holy life and miraculous deeds. Satyanarayana, the future Sai Baba, was born in 1926 in a village in what is now Andhra Pradesh, and the biography Indian devotees recount centers around his gradual recognition of his divine status as an *avatar*, or earthly descendant, of the Hindu deity Shiva. It also highlights his miracles: according to his followers, Sai Baba materializes objects, cures illness, foresees the future, and even raises the dead. In the United States, Sai Baba is less well known, but his followers have established

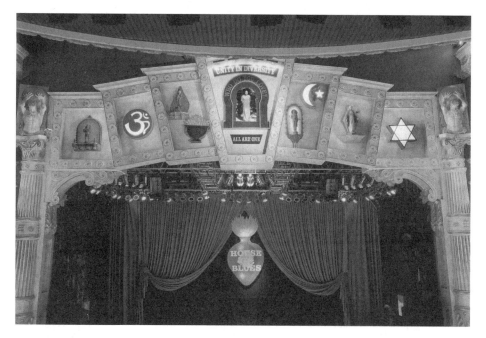

House of Blues "God Wall." House of Blues was founded by Isaac Tigrett, a devotee of Sai Baba. The God Wall, which appears above the stage at each House of Blues nightclub, features Sai Baba surrounded by phrases such as "Unity in Diversity" and symbols from Hinduism, Buddhism, Judaism, Christianity, and Islam. Copyright © House of Blues. Used by permission.

Elsie Cowan, "Sai Baba and the Resurrection of Walter Cowan," in Satya Pal Ruhela and Duane Robinson, eds., *Sai Baba and His Message: A Challenge to Behavioral Sciences* (Delhi: Vikas Publishing House, 1976), 236–45.

dozens of centers and study groups since 1967. Potential devotees can encounter him elsewhere too: enshrined above the stage of New York's Hard Rock Cafe and New Orleans' House of Blues, and on the Internet at www.sathyasai.org. That web page provides a useful summary of Sai Baba's rather conventional Hindu injunctions: believe in the one god, though he may be called by many names; live "in consonance with the teachings of good behavior and morality"; respect all other religions; and perform "selfless service" to the less fortunate. More representative of the movement's focus, however, is this account, in which American followers describe a 1971 miracle attributed to Sai Baba.

SAI BABA AND THE RESURRECTION OF WALTER COWAN

We have come back from India, my husband and I, brimfull of the most astonishing news that could happen to anyone. It is so fantastic that many may doubt it, because hardly any of us realize the great importance and the tremendous power of this Great High God, who not only walks the earth, but cares for all the planes from earth into eternity. He gives us strength and power. He is compassionate. But most of all, He gives us the protection, which is His Grace. In time of need, He wraps His Grace around us like a very warm blanket, soft and lovely, to soothe us into a state of bliss. Without Him there would be no one to turn to; no father to ask; and even greater than that, at the very deepest feelings, He makes us strong. There are no tears, for the body goes back to the earth.

This is a story of how our Great Lord Sai Baba resurrected Walter, who died in Madras. Little did we know what was going to happen at the time, and when it did happen, what could I say but, "Where would I rather die, than at the feet of this Great, Great Lord?" It is a blessing to know that the Great Lord takes care of us, places us where we should be placed, or else as in this case, after several hours, He brings one back to life as he did Walter, my husband.

There were many people present, but Jack Hislop was there throughout almost the entire experience. Since he is a wonderful devotee, and is very, very close to our Lord, Sai Baba, I have asked Jack to tell the story as a third party.

Jack Hislop's Account of This Event

"*Dear Elsie Cowan*, this is a letter in response to your request that I say what I know about your husband's experience in India, while you were there in December of 1971 and January of 1972. My name is Jack Hislop. I live in Mexico. My wife and I had visited Sathya Sai Baba a number of times in the past, and we will be there again in 1972. We returned from India on February 27th of this year, after some four months with Sathya Sai Baba.

As I recall, Walter and you arrived in Madras on 23 December 1971, and came to the building where Baba was holding a conference with some 3,000 presidents of his Seva Samitis. Baba at once came to you and gave Walter and yourself a warm and affectionate greeting. Walter was obviously not feeling well, and ushers had provided chairs as soon as you arrived. Thus, you were quite visible amidst the great crowd of people, all of whom were sitting on the floor, as is the custom in India.

On the morning of the 25th of December, news quickly spread that an elderly American had had a fatal attack of what was thought to be heart trouble, and had passed away. Upon hearing the rumor, my wife and I at once went to your hotel. You confirmed the news, and told us how the attack had felled Walter in the hotel room. You had prayed to Sathya Baba for help at this most trying moment of your life, but with great self-control and recollection of human mortality, had ended your prayer with—"Let God's will be done." You at once remember that Mr and Mrs Ratan Lal were staying in a room almost next door to your room, and you called her. Mrs Ratan Lal came immediately. With her help, you summoned a room boy, and Walter was lifted from the floor to the bed. Mrs Ratan Lal joined you in prayer for it was soon evident to you that Walter had indeed passed away from the body.

Someone called an ambulance to take Walter to the hospital, but it was your experience that Walter had died in your arms, soon after having been lifted from the floor to the bed, and you were so exhausted that you could not accompany the then lifeless body into the ambulance. These events had taken place in the early morning hours of 25 December. But at 7 a.m. you had recovered sufficient strength to go with Mrs Ratan Lal to Baba's place of residence to tell him the news and ask for his advice and help. Baba said he would visit the hospital about 10 a.m.

At 10 a.m., Mrs Ratan Lal accompanied you to the hospital, but you were told that Baba had already been there, and had left just before you arrived. Upon entering the hospital, you found Walter alive. That Walter was alive at 10 a.m. on 25 December is certain. But how about his death? Was there medical verification that he had died? After all, two ladies—very much upset at a tragic event—could not, perhaps, make the same tests for life as would a medical doctor not personally involved in the emotional impact of the situation.

To clarify this point, at my request, Judge Damodar Rao of Madras interviewed the doctor who had attended Walter when he arrived at the hospital. This attending physician is well-known to Judge Damodar Rao personally, and the doctor told Judge Rao that Walter was indeed dead when he had examined Walter shortly after the ambulance had delivered him to the hospital. The doctor said there was no sign of life; that he pronounced Walter as dead; that Walter's ears and nose were stuffed with cotton; that Walter was covered with a sheet and moved into an empty room.

The doctor then left the hospital on some professional duty, and had missed seeing Baba when He was at the hospital. The doctor arrived back at the hospital after Baba had left. When the doctor returned to the hospital, Walter was alive. The doctor found himself unable to explain this situation. It seemed worthwhile to me to make an investigation for medical verification of Walter's death, because such verification might be a factor of interest to people who had never seen Sathya Sai Baba, and who might have a very limited knowledge of him. But, medical testimony is not a factor of any importance to devotees of Baba. To his devotees, what He said about Mr Cowan was the truth of the matter.

I saw Baba at His place of residence after He had returned from the hospital. He told me and others within hearing that Walter Cowan had died; that the hospital had stuffed his ears and nose with cotton, and covered him with a sheet, and put the body in a closed room. Baba said that He had brought Walter back to life. I did not inquire of Baba as to how he had brought Walter back to life, or his reasons for doing so, nor to the best of my knowledge, did anyone else. That is a mystery that Baba has not as yet chosen to explain.

. . .

Thus Walter had a most extraordinary experience in December 1971 and January 1972. Both of you know directly the Divine Grace of Shri Sathya Sai Baba. *Jack Hislop*".

Walter Cowan's Account of His Resurrection

"While in the Connemara Hotel in Madras, two days after I arrived, I was taken very sick with pneumonia and was in bed. As I gasped for breath, suddenly the body's struggle was over, and I died. I found myself very calm, in a state of wonderful bliss, and the Lord, Sai Baba, was by my side. Even though my body lay on the bed, dead, my mind kept working throughout until Baba brought me back. There was no anxiety or fear, but a tremendous sense of well-being, for I had lost all fear of death.

Baba took me to a very large hall where there were hundreds of people milling around. It was the hall where all of the records of all my lives were kept. Baba and I stood before the Court of Justice. The one in charge knew Baba very well, and He asked for the records of all my lives. He was very nice and kind, and I had the feeling that whatever was decided would be the best for my soul.

The records were brought into the hall—armloads of scrolls—and all of them seemed to be in different languages. As they were read, Baba interpreted them. In the beginning, they told me of countries that have not existed for thousands of years, and I could not recall them. When they reached King David, the reading of my lives became more exciting. I could hardly believe how great I apparently was in each life that followed. As they continued reading my lives, it seemed that what really counted was my motives and character, as I stood for outstanding peace and spirituality. I do not remember all the names, but I am included in almost all of the history books of the world from the beginning of time. As I incarnated in the different countries, I carried out my mission—which was peace and spirituality.

After about two hours, they finished reading the scrolls, and the Lord, Sai Baba, said that I had not completed the work that I was born to do, and He asked the Judge that I be turned over to Him to complete my mission of spreading the Truth; and he requested that my soul be returned to my body, under Baba's Grace. The Judge said, "So be it." The case was dismissed and I left with Baba to return to my body. I hesitated to leave this wonderful bliss, but I knew it was best to complete my mission so that I could merge with the Lord, Sai Baba.

I related the story to Elsie at once, and she recorded it. I also talked it over with Baba, and He said it was not my imagination—it was a true experience. My life goes on now under the Grace of Sai Baba, whom I adore and to whom I owe my life. *Walter R. Cowan*."

CHAPTER **15**

Buddhist Teachers, Converts, and Movements

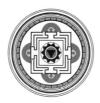

SHUNRYU SUZUKI, "POSTURE" (1970)

One of the most important of the second-generation Zen teachers, Shunryu Suzuki (1905–71) led San Francisco Zen Center during its early period and established the first Zen monastery on American soil. This son of a Japanese Zen priest left for the United States in 1959 to serve the elderly Japanese-American congregation at Sokoji, the Soto Zen temple in San Francisco that Hosen Isobe had founded in 1934. But Suzuki-roshi is best known for his role in instructing American converts. Some European-Americans in the San Francisco area were practicing Soto Zen earlier, but their numbers increased dramatically after Suzuki-roshi arrived. Slowly a vibrant community of American students emerged, and San Francisco Zen Center was born. A few years later, in 1966, the community located 160 acres in the Los Padres National Forest, where they built the first Zen monastery in America, Tassajara Zen Mountain Center. At that monastery, and at the urban Zen Center, American Buddhism took root in practice. Suzuki-roshi repeatedly said that the practice of *zazen* (or seated meditation) was the heart of Zen. Following a long line of Soto Zen teachers, Suzuki taught that we all have Buddha nature, so there is nothing to do, nothing to accomplish. Seated meditation, in this view, is the *expression* of one's original enlightened nature, not a means to attain another state. The problem, of course, is that most of us do not seem to think or act like Buddhas. The solution, according to Suzuki: just sit. Suzuki made this point regularly as he instructed students privately, and he reiterated it in his many Zen talks. In this talk, which was recorded by a student and published in his only book, *Zen Mind, Beginner's Mind*, Suzuki describes the proper meditation posture. Posture

Shunryu Suzuki, *Zen Mind, Beginner's Mind: Informal Talks on Zen Meditation and Practice* (New York and Tokyo: Weatherhill, 1970), 25–28. Reprinted by permission of Weatherhill, Inc.

is central, he suggests, because "the state of mind that exits when you sit in the right posture is, itself, enlightenment."

Now I would like to talk about our zazen posture. When you sit in the full lotus position, your left foot is on your right thigh, and your right foot is on your left thigh. When we cross our legs like this, even though we have a right leg and a left leg, they have become one. The position expresses the oneness of duality: not two, and not one. This is the most important teaching: not two, and not one. Our body and mind are not two and not one. If you think your body and mind are two, that is wrong; if you think that they are one, that is also wrong. Our body and mind are both two *and* one. We usually think that if something is not one, it is more than one; if it is not singular, it is plural. But in actual experience, our life is not only plural, but also singular. Each one of us is both dependent and independent.

After some years we will die. If we just think that it is the end of our life, this will be the wrong understanding. But, on the other hand, if we think that we do not die, this is also wrong. We die, and we do not die. This is the right understanding. Some people may say that our mind or soul exists forever, and it is only our physical body which dies. But this is not exactly right, because both mind and body have their end. But at the same time it is also true that they exist eternally. And even though we say mind and body, they are actually two sides of one coin. This is the right understanding. So when we take this posture it symbolizes this truth. When I have the left foot on the right side of my body, and the right foot on the left side of my body, I do not know which is which. So either may be the left or the right side.

The most important thing in taking the zazen posture is to keep your spine straight. Your ears and your shoulders should be on one line. Relax your shoulders, and push up towards the ceiling with the back of your head. And you should pull your chin in. When your chin is tilted up, you have no strength in your posture; you are probably dreaming. Also to gain strength in your posture, press your diaphragm down towards your *hara*, or lower abdomen. This will help you maintain your physical and mental balance. When you try to keep this posture, at first you may find some difficulty breathing naturally, but when you get accustomed to it you will be able to breathe naturally and deeply.

Your hands should form the "cosmic mudra." If you put your left hand on top of your right, middle joints of your middle fingers together, and touch your thumbs lightly together (as if you held a piece of paper between them), your hands will make a beautiful oval. You should keep this universal mudra with great care, as if you were holding something very precious in your hand. Your hands should be held against your body, with your thumbs at about the height of your navel. Hold your arms freely and easily, and slightly away from your body, as if you held an egg under each arm without breaking it.

You should not be tilted sideways, backwards, or forwards. You should be sitting straight up as if you were supporting the sky with your head. This is not just form or breathing. It expresses the key point of Buddhism. It is a perfect expression of your Buddha nature. If you want true understanding of Buddhism, you should practice this way. These forms are not a means of obtaining the right state of mind. To take this posture itself is the purpose of our practice. When you have this posture, you have the right state of mind, so there is no need to try to attain some special state. When you try to attain something, your mind starts to wander about somewhere else. When you do not try to attain anything, you have your own body and mind right here. A Zen master would say, "Kill the Buddha!" Kill the Buddha if the Buddha exists somewhere else. Kill the Buddha, because you should resume your own Buddha nature.

Doing something is expressing our own nature. We do not exist for the sake of something else. We exist for the sake of ourselves. This is the fundamental teaching expressed in the forms we observe. Just as for sitting, when we stand in the zendo we have some rules. But the purpose of these rules is not to make every-one the same, but to allow each to express his own self most freely. For instance, each one of us has his own way of standing, so our standing posture is based on the proportions of our own bodies. When you stand, your heels should be as far apart as the width of your own fist, your big toes in line with the centers of your breasts. As in zazen, put some strength in your abdomen. Here also your hands should express your self. Hold your left hand against your chest with fingers en-circling your thumb, and put your right hand over it. Holding your thumb point-ing downward, and your forearms parallel to the floor, you feel as if you have some round pillar in your grasp—a big round temple pillar—so you cannot be slumped or tilted to the side.

The most important point is to own your own physical body. If you slump, you will lose your self. Your mind will be wandering about somewhere else; you will not be in your body. This is not the way. We must exist right here, right now! This is the key point. You must have your own body and mind. Everything should exist in the right place, in the right way. Then there is no problem. If the micro-phone I use when I speak exists somewhere else, it will not serve its purpose. When we have our body and mind in order, everything else will exist in the right place, in the right way.

But usually, without being aware of it, we try to change something other than ourselves, we try to order things outside us. But it is impossible to organize things if you yourself are not in order. When you do things in the right way, at the right time, everything else will be organized. You are the "boss." When the boss is sleeping, everyone is sleeping. When the boss does something right, everyone will do everything right, and at the right time. That is the secret of Buddhism.

So try always to keep the right posture, not only when you practice zazen, but in all your activities. Take the right posture when you are driving your car, and when you are reading. If you read in a slumped position, you cannot stay awake long. Try. You will discover how important it is to keep the right posture. This is the true teaching. The teaching which is written on paper is not the true teaching. Written teaching is a kind of food for your brain. Of course it is neces-sary to take some food for your brain, but it is more important to be yourself by practicing the right way of life.

That is why Buddha could not accept the religions existing at his time. He studied many religions, but he was not satisfied with their practices. He could not find the answer in asceticism or in philosophies. He was not interested in some metaphysical evidence, but in his own body and mind, here and now. And when he found himself, he found that everything that exists has Buddha nature. That was his enlightenment. Enlightenment is not some good feeling or some particular state of mind. The state of mind that exists when you sit in the right posture is, itself, enlightenment. If you cannot be satisfied with the state of mind you have in zazen, it means your mind is still wandering about. Our body and mind should not be wobbling or wandering about. In this posture there is no need to talk about the right state of mind. You already have it. This is the conclusion of Buddhism.

CHOGYAM TRUNGPA, *MEDITATION IN ACTION* (1969)

If Shunryu Suzuki-roshi transplanted a form of Mahayana Buddhism (Zen), a Tibetan-born teacher, the Venerable Chogyam Trungpa Rinpoche (1939–87), helped introduce Americans to Vajrayana Buddhism. Trungpa Rinpoche (*rinpoche*, meaning "precious jewel," is an honorific title given to those who have been judged to be a *tulku*, or reincarnation of a deceased enlightened teacher) would become the most influential Tibetan teacher on American soil. He met and admired the older and more established Suzuki-roshi, whom he described in his autobiography as "a man of genuine Buddhism, delightful and profound, full of flashes of Zen wit." Their teachings converged in some ways: for example, both emphasized that Buddhist practice had no goal or aim. But Trungpa Rinpoche came from a very different Buddhist tradition. He was a teacher in the Kagyu-pa order of Tibetan Buddhism, which the Tantric master Marpa (1012–92) had founded. (There are four main orders or schools in Tibetan Buddhism: the other three are the Kadam-pa, the Sakya-pa, the Nyingma-pa.) He received full monastic ordination in 1958. The following year he narrowly escaped capture by the Chinese and crossed the Himalayas to India, where the Fourteenth Dalai Lama (who also fled Tibet in 1959) appointed him spiritual adviser at the Young Lamas Home School. After four years in that position, Trungpa Rinpoche traveled to England. He studied art, philosophy, and religion at Oxford University, and began to instruct Western students in Buddhism. In 1967 he cofounded the Samye-Ling Meditation Centre in Scotland, and in 1970 he arrived in North America. By July of that year Trungpa Rinpoche had settled in Boulder, Colorado, where he founded one of the major centers for American convert Buddhism. In 1974, he opened the Naropa Institute, an accredited Buddhist-inspired university (where Ram Dass and Allen Ginsberg, among others, would teach). Controversy erupted in the Boulder community, however, after Osel Tendzin (Thomas F. Rich) was appointed Trungpa's Vajra Regent, or dharma heir, in 1976. Osel Tendzin, who died in 1990, was one of several Buddhist and Hindu teachers across the country to be charged with sexual misconduct: he allegedly had unprotected sex after he knew he had the AIDS virus. But the community survived the controversy, in part because many still found Trungpa Rinpoche's Vajrayana teachings edifying. The exiled Tibetan spread those teachings in lectures, seminars, and books. *Meditation in Action*, a collection of Trungpa's talks at Samye-Ling, was published in

1969, only months before he arrived in America. The last chapter of that book describes wisdom (*prajna* in Sanskrit or *sherab* in Tibetan) and the three methods to cultivate it: study (*topa*), contemplation (*sampa*), and meditation (*gompa*).

Prajna. Wisdom. Perhaps the English word has a slightly different sense. But the word used in Tibetan, *sherab*, has a precise meaning: *she* means knowledge, knowing, and *rab* means ultimate—so primary or first knowledge, the higher knowledge. So sherab is not specific knowledge in any technical or educational sense of knowing the theology of Buddhism, or knowing how to do certain things, or knowing the metaphysical aspect of the teaching. Here knowledge means knowing the situation, *knowingness* rather than actual knowledge. It is knowledge without a self, without the self-centered consciousness that one is knowing—which is connected with ego. So this knowledge—prajna or sherab—is broad and far-seeing, though at the same time it is tremendously penetrating and exact, and it comes into every aspect of our life. It therefore plays a very important part in our development, as does upaya, method, which is the skillful means for dealing with situations in the right way. These two qualities, in fact, are sometimes compared to the two wings of a bird. Upaya is also described in the scriptures as being like a hand, which is skillful, and prajna as being axlike, because it is sharp and penetrating. Without the ax it would be impossible to cut wood: one would simply hurt one's hand. So one may have the skillful means without being able to put it into effect. But if there is also prajna, which is like an eye, or like light, then one is able to act properly and skillfully. Otherwise the skillful means might become foolish, for only knowledge makes one wise. In fact upaya by itself could make the greatest of fools, because everything would still be based on ego. One might see the situation up to a point and be partially able to deal with it, but one would not see it with clarity and without being affected by past and future, and one would miss the immediate nowness of the situation.

But perhaps we should examine how to develop this knowingness, or sherab, before we go into any further details. Now, there are three methods which are necessary for the cultivation of sherab, and these are known in Tibetan as töpa, sampa, and gompa. Töpa means to study the subject, sampa means to contemplate it, and gompa means to meditate and develop samadhi through it. So first töpa—study—which is generally associated with technical knowledge and the understanding of the scriptures and so on. But true knowledge goes much further than that, as we have already seen. And the first requirement for töpa is to develop a kind of bravery, to become a great warrior. We have mentioned this concept before, but perhaps it would be as well to go into it in more detail. Now, when the true warrior goes into battle he does not concern himself with his past and with recollections of his former greatness and strength, nor is he concerned with the consequences for the future and with thoughts of victory or defeat, or pain and death. The greatest warrior knows himself and has great confidence in

Chogyam Trungpa, *Meditation in Action* (Boston and London: Shambhala, 1996), 79–84, 87–90. © 1991 by Diana Mukpo. Reprinted by arrangement with Shambhala Publications, Inc.

himself. He is simply conscious of his opponent. He is quite open and fully aware of the situation, without thinking in terms of good and bad. What makes him a great warrior is that he has no opinions; he is simply aware. Whereas his opponents, being emotionally involved in the situation, would not be able to face him, because he is acting truly and sailing through their fear and is able to attack the enemy with effect. Therefore töpa, study and understanding, demands the quality of a great warrior. One should try to develop theoretical knowledge without being concerned with the past or the future. At first one's theories may be inspired by reading books, so we do not altogether dismiss learning and studying, which are very important and can provide a source of inspiration. But books can also become merely a means to escape from reality; they can provide an excuse for not really making an effort to examine things in detail for oneself. Reading can be rather like eating food. Up to a point one eats from physical necessity, but beyond that one is doing it for pleasure, because one likes the taste of food, or possibly just to fill up time: it is either breakfast time or lunch time or tea time or time for dinner. In the development of sherab it is clear that we do not read merely to accumulate information. We should read with great openness without making judgments, and just try to receive. . . .

This is the first stage of töpa, where one develops theory. And it often happens at a certain point that this theory appears almost in the guise of experience, so that one may feel one has reached a state of spiritual ecstasy or enlightenment. There is a great excitement and one almost feels one has seen Reality itself.

Of course this theoretical knowledge is very interesting. One can talk so much about it—there are a great many words involved—and there is great pleasure in telling other people all about it. . . .

But that is still theory. And from there we come to sampa, which is reflective meditation, or contemplating and pondering on the subject. Sampa is not meditating in the sense of developing mindfulness and so on, but meditating on the subject and digesting it properly. In other words what one has learned is not yet sufficiently developed to enable one to deal with the practical things of life. For example, one might be talking about one's great discovery when some catastrophe occurs; say, the milk boils over or something like that. It might be something quite ordinary, but it seems to be rather exciting and terrible in a way. And the transition, from discussing this subject to controlling the milk, is just too much. The one is so elevated and the other is so ordinary and mundane that somehow one finds it very difficult to put one's knowledge into effect on that level. The contrast is too great and, as a result, one becomes upset, suddenly switches off and returns to the ordinary level of ego. So in this kind of situation there is a big gap between the two things, and we have to learn to deal with this and somehow make the connection with everyday life, and to identify our activities with what we have learned in the way of wisdom and theoretical knowledge. Of course our theory is something far beyond just ordinary theory, which one might have worked out mathematically to produce a feasible proposition. One is involved and there is great feeling in it. Nevertheless this is only theory, and for that very reason one finds it difficult to put it into effect. It seems true, it seems to convey something, when you only think on that subject, but it tends to remain static. So sampa, reflective meditation, is necessary because one needs to calm down after the initial excitement of discovery and one has to find a way of relating one's newfound knowledge to oneself on a practical level.

. . .

Finally we come to gompa, meditation. First we had theory, then contemplation, and now meditation in the sense of samadhi. The first stage of gompa is to ask oneself, "Who am I?" Though this is not really a question. In fact it is a statement, because "Who am I?" contains the answer. The thing is not to start from "I" and then want to achieve something, but to start directly with the subject. In other words one starts the real meditation without aiming for anything, without the thought, "I want to achieve." Since one does not know "Who am I?" one would not start from "I" at all, and one even begins to learn from beyond that point. What remains is simply to start on the subject, to start on what *is*, which is not really "I am." So one goes directly to that, directly to the "is." This may sound a bit vague and mysterious, because these terms have been used so much and by so many people; we must try then to clarify this by relating it to ourselves. The first point is not to think in terms of "I," "I want to achieve." Since there is no one to do the achieving, and we haven't even grasped that yet, we should not try to prepare anything at all for the future.

There is a story in Tibet about a thief who was a great fool. He stole a large sack of barley one day and was very pleased with himself. He hung it up over his bed, suspended from the ceiling, because he thought it would be safest there from the rats and other animals. But one rat was very cunning and found a way to get to it. Meanwhile the thief was thinking, "Now, I'll sell this barley to somebody, perhaps my next-door neighbor, and get some silver coins for it. Then I could buy something else and then sell that at a profit. If I go on like this I'll soon be very rich, then I can get married and have a proper home. After that I could have a son. Yes, I shall have a son! Now what name shall I give him?" At that moment the moon had just risen and he saw the moonlight shining in through the window onto his bed. So he thought, "Ah, I shall call him Dawa" (which is the Tibetan word for moon). And at that very moment the rat had finished eating right through the rope from which the bag was hanging, and the bag dropped on the thief and killed him.

Similarly, since we haven't got a son and we don't even know "Who am I?," we should not explore the details of such fantasies. We should not start off by expecting any kind of reward. There should be no striving and no trying to achieve anything. One might then feel, "Since there is no fixed purpose and there is nothing to attain, wouldn't it be rather boring? Isn't it rather like just being nowhere?" Well, that is the whole point. Generally we do things because we want to achieve something; we never do anything without first thinking, "Because . . ." "I'm going for a holiday *because* I want to relax, I want a rest." "I am going to do such-and-such *because* I think it would be interesting." So every action, every step we take, is conditioned by ego. It is conditioned by the illusory concept of "I," which has not even been questioned. Everything is built around that and everything begins with "because." So that is the whole point. Meditating without any purpose may sound boring, but the fact is we haven't sufficient courage to go into it and just give it a try. Somehow we have to be courageous. Since one is interested and one wants to go further, the best thing would be to do it perfectly and not start with too many subjects, but start with one subject and really go into it thoroughly. It may not sound interesting, it may not be exciting all the time, but excitement is not the only thing to be gained, and one must develop patience. One must be willing to take a chance and in that sense make use of will power.

One has to go forward without fear of the unknown, and if one does go a little bit further, one finds it is possible to start without thinking "because," without thinking "I will achieve something," without just living in the future. One must not build fantasies around the future and just use that as one's impetus and source of encouragement, but one should try to get the real feeling of the present moment. That is to say that meditation can only be put into effect if it is not conditioned by any of our normal ways of dealing with situations. One must practice meditation directly without expectation or judgment and without thinking in terms of the future at all. Just leap into it. Jump into it without looking back.

THICH NHAT HANH, *THE MIRACLE OF MINDFULNESS* (1975)

Nominated for the Noble Peace Prize by Dr. Martin Luther King, Jr., Thich Nhat Han has been an international figure since his public criticism of the Vietnam War brought him widespread attention during the 1960s. ("Thich" is an abbreviation of "Thich-ca," Vietnamese for "Sakya," which is the name of the Buddha's clan; it is a title taken by Vietnamese monks to denote kinship in the spiritual family of the Buddha.) Thich Nhat Hanh was born in central Vietnam in 1926 and ordained a Zen monk at the age of sixteen. The Vietnam War changed his life irrevocably. He returned from his studies and teaching at Columbia and Princeton to lead a peace movement in his native land. Barred from Vietnam since 1966, Nhat Hanh now lives in France at Plum Village, a community he established in 1982, but he travels widely, including in the United States, giving talks and guiding practice. On 14 November 1997 he officially opened the Maple Forest Monastery (*Tu Vien Rung Phong*) in Hartland, Vermont, where the community also plans to start a retreat center (Green Mountain Dharma Center) and a Mindfulness Training Institute. Nhat Hanh also has written many best-selling books; the Beacon Press edition of *The Miracle of Mindfulness* alone had sold approximately 125,000 copies. After the Dalai Lama, Nhat Hanh might be the most influential contemporary Buddhist teacher. Although celebrated as an "engaged Buddhist" for his emphasis on social action, he is probably best known in the United States for his teachings on mindfulness. In this selection from *The Miracle of Mindfulness* Nhat Han instructs readers to attend fully to each moment of daily life.

Thich Nhat Hanh, *The Miracle of Mindfulness: A Manual on Meditation*, revised ed. (1975; Boston: Beacon Press, 1987), 6–8, 23–24. © 1975, 1976 by Thich Nhat Hanh. English Translation © 1975, 1976, 1987 by Mobi Ho. Used by permission of Beacon Press, Boston.

THE ESSENTIAL DISCIPLINE

More than thirty years ago, when I first entered the monastery, the monks gave me a small book called "The Essential Discipline for Daily Use," written by the Buddhist monk Doc The from Bao Son pagoda, and they told me to memorize it. It was a thin book. It couldn't have been more than 40 pages, but it contained all the thoughts Doc The used to awaken his mind while doing any task. When he woke up in the morning, his first thought was, "Just awakened, I hope that every person will attain great awareness and see in complete clarity." When he washed his hands, he used this thought to place himself in mindfulness: "Washing my hands, I hope that every person will have pure hands to receive reality." The book is comprised entirely of such sentences. Their goal was to help the beginning practitioner take hold of his own consciousness. The Zen Master Doc The helped all of us young novices to practice, in a relatively easy way, those things which are taught in the Sutra of Mindfulness. Each time you put on your robe, washed the dishes, went to the bathroom, folded your mat, carried buckets of water, or brushed your teeth, you could use one of the thoughts from the book in order to take hold of your own consciousness.

The Sutra of Mindfulness says, "When walking, the practitioner must be conscious that he is walking. When sitting, the practitioner must be conscious that he is sitting. When lying down, the practitioner must be conscious that he is lying down. . . . No matter what position one's body is in, the practitioner must be conscious of that position. Practicing thus, the practitioner lives in direct and constant mindfulness of the body . . ." The mindfulness of the positions of one's body is not enough, however. We must be conscious of each breath, each movement, every thought and feeling, everything which has any relation to ourselves.

. . .

EVERY ACT IS A RITE

In my small class in meditation for non-Vietnamese, there are many young people. I've told them that if each one can meditate an hour each day that's good, but it's nowhere near enough. You've got to practice meditation when you walk, stand, lie down, sit, and work, while washing your hands, washing the dishes, sweeping the floor, drinking tea, talking to friends, or whatever you are doing: "While washing the dishes, you might be thinking about the tea afterwards, and so try to get them out of the way as quickly as possible in order to sit and drink tea. But that means that you are incapable of living during the time you are washing the dishes. When you are washing the dishes, washing the dishes must be the most important thing in your life. Just as when you're drinking tea, drinking tea must be the most important thing in your life. When you're using the toilet, let that be the most important thing in your life." And so on. Chopping wood is meditation. Carrying water is meditation. Be mindful 24 hours a day, not just during the one hour you may allot for formal meditation or reading scripture and reciting prayers. Each act must be carried out in mindfulness. Each act is a rite, a ceremony. Raising your cup of tea to your mouth is a rite. Does the word "rite" seem too solemn? I use that word in order to jolt you into the realization of the life-and-death matter of awareness.

AN INTERVIEW WITH ROSHI JIYU KENNETT (1986)

The most distinctive feature of American convert Buddhism is that women participate and lead, much more than they traditionally have in Asian lands. Many women, including Maurine Stuart in Cambridge and Karuna Dharma in Los Angeles, have led American Buddhist centers. One of the first female Buddhist teachers in the United States was Roshi Jiyu Kennett, who died in 1996. Born to Buddhist parents in England, Kennett studied in Japan with the Venerable Chisan Koho Zenji, a Soto Zen teacher, from whom she received the dharma transmission in 1963. In 1970 she founded Shasta Abbey at the foot of Mt. Shasta in northern California as a place to train male and female monks, although lay followers also participate in the community. At Shasta Abbey she introduced a number of somewhat controversial innovations, including clerical collars and Gregorian-style chanting, in her attempt to acculturate Buddhism. In this interview conducted in 1986 and published a few years later, Kennett outlines her approach to adapting Buddhism to American culture, focusing especially on the role of women.

I speak with Reverend Roshi Jiyu Kennett in the backyard of the Berkeley Buddhist Priory, a modest house on a busy street, one of a number of priories staffed by priests from Shasta Abbey. She often comes to the Bay Area to lecture at the University of California, and this summer she has stayed longer because of health problems. I am greeted by a jocular-seeming woman in a brown robe who sports a short crewcut dappled with gray. She is as large and commanding as I remembered, flanked this morning by two male monks who stay with us throughout the interview and now and then interject a comment. We seat ourselves below a sun umbrella at a round metal table, and Jiyu Kennett begins to talk with the authority of one who is used to holding forth, in a strong voice that I can only describe as juicy, her stories underlined now and then by hearty laughter.

One story concerns her graduation ceremony in Japan.

"When I was in Japan, as a woman you could officially become a priest, but you didn't do it in public," she begins, "because that would mean that the emperor would have to recognize that a woman existed. So you paid him four times the price that a man did, to get the certificate, and you did it in private.

"My master said, 'We're going to do it in public, because this is totally wrong.' And he forced the issue. I have never done a ceremony with more terror inside me, than that one with twelve men down each side, each one with the curtains drawn over his eyes as if to say 'I'm not here.' Those were the witnesses. Try that

Sandy Boucher, "Shasta Abbey," in Sandy Boucher, *Turning the Wheel: American Women Creating the New Buddhism*, updated and expanded edition (1988; Boston: Beacon Press, 1993), 137–38, 141–44. Used by permission of Beacon Press, Boston.

Roshi Jiyu Kennett, the Zen teacher who founded Shasta Abbey in 1970. Courtesy of Shasta Abbey.

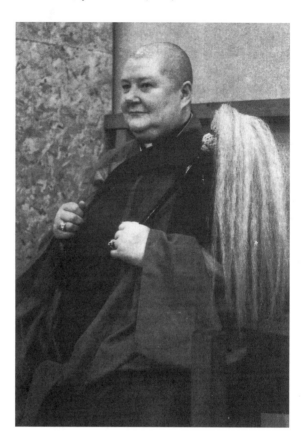

sometime! That can be pretty scary—in a foreign county, in a language you're not one hundred percent sure of, with a lot of people who are hating your guts. And the reason Koho Zenji did it—and I've got it on tape—was for the benefit of women in his country.

"The weirdest thing was sitting on the floor in the guest department with the chief guest master chanting words in front of you as he offered you the big red teacup, and a look of total disbelief on his face. He could not believe this was happening. It would make a wonderful film."

She leans back to chuckle in appreciation of the scene and comments on the significance of it.

"As I see it, if women want to do this, they've got to make their minds up just what it is they're going into it for. Are they going into it because they want to become one with the Buddha and find their own Buddhahood, or are they going into it because men say they can't?

"I've never had a fight with men. I've always loved 'em. I don't trust 'em and I don't admire 'em, but I love every one of 'em. Fair enough? That's experience."

She has a way of taking an idea, spinning it out then reeling it back in, closing it down, and snapping the lid shut on it. She has already told me how she made it through her difficult training in Japan, where she was discriminated against as a woman and a foreigner. The Buddha had said woman could make it, she said, and as far as she was concerned, all the rest was simply trappings from the Indian culture of the Buddha's time. She tells the story of the monk Ananda's having asked the Buddha whether women who had gone forth into the nun's life could reach the highest level of attainment. The Buddha replied, "Women, Ananda, having gone forth . . . are able to realize . . . perfection."

"Obviously a lot of women feel frustration and jealousy and hurt and pain because of what's happened to them. And I understand that. But in religion that's gotta fly out the window. What are we in religion for? Yes, in religion you have a lot of people who you're insulting because you're a female, and a lot of people who won't come to you for funerals or weddings or the like, but that's their problem, it's not mine. Somehow or other women have to get to that stage, if they want true spiritual equality. They've gotta stop letting the men put them down.

"In my case, at Shasta Abbey, I have created, if you like, an oasis. Or I've tried to make an oasis—where people really are equal. That's bringing the essence of Buddhism rather than women shall walk three paces behind, we shall use chopsticks, we must all sit on the floor, chairs are illegal, going round with a loincloth instead of an ordinary pair of undershorts. I mean, my god, all of these things are not us! The norm for religious dress in this country is a collar turned backwards and a shirt. Why have we got to go around pretending we're Japanese or Chinese or Thai?

. . . "Has women's participation changed over the fifteen years the abbey has been in existence?" I ask her, and she answers by telling of a difficulty some women encounter in pursuing a spiritual path.

"It's been subtle. Most of them when they first came didn't believe they could do it. And I had to keep holding out my certainty, because I knew they could. And it became very obvious that they could, but they weren't totally sure of it. And therefore a lot of them have been slower than the men, simply because they had to believe. Now we have at least three senior females totally capable of doing any job that the men do in the temple. But it's taken a good five, six, maybe ten years, in some cases longer—simply because of the brainwashing that was done prior to their getting there.

"When I was in the Far East, they said, 'Women are much slower than men.' And Koho Zenji said, 'Yeah, they are, guess who made them so!' And the old boy was right. There were monks around who said he was mad. I mean, he wasn't like any other Japanese. No, nobody else was archbishop either! How did they think he got the job?!"

From a discussion of the position of women in the Christian Church she moves to the declaration that some of the problems of women within Buddhism in the West derive from Christian concepts.

"The Japanese word for monk-priest has both male and female forms; when you translate it as nun, what you have is a Christian thing that automatically puts the woman down. If you translate it as female monk or female priest, you immediately have a thing which is a distinction but not a put-down. The words monk and nun are Christian."

. . . As a conspicuous and outspoken religious leader, and the only female head of a Buddhist monastery, Kennett Roshi is sometimes criticized by people who either disagree with her or misunderstand her methods or intentions. Among these criticisms is the assertion that she discourages sexual expression for her students. Indeed, she tells me, she does favor celibacy for her monks, and she gives her position on this persistently challenging issue in monastic life.

"Over here, when I first started teaching, I believed utterly that married priests were possible. That was because in Japan that was all I saw. As I watched, I realized that you could have much better priests, male and female, of a much higher caliber from the point of view of the congregation, if they were not married. And if you wanted to go beyond a certain distance in spirituality, it didn't matter whether you wanted to be married or not, you couldn't be. That explains to me why a lot of the Chinese priests, who were celibate, seemed to be going a lot further in their spirituality than did the Japanese. I did not come to this conclusion easily. It took me something like fourteen, fifteen years to be certain of it."

"In your view," I ask, "is it because relationships take too much time and effort? Are they a distraction?"

She fixes me with an intent look.

"The scriptures say, 'If you want spirituality, give up everything.' That means all attachments. Give up everything. The scriptures tell it as it is. Everything means everything. You have to get to the state where it doesn't matter if you're dead— if you would go the whole way. You cannot even have the comfort of fondling another person, if you go the whole way.

"Now anyone and everyone, including the laity, can have what the Japanese call a first kensho, or enlightenment experience, and from which most of the priests teach. The first kensho is the first certainty of spirituality. You know in the Bible it says that many are called and few chosen. Buddhism has it that all are called and few answer. Sometime or other, in everyone's life, that call will come. If it is answered, it becomes a first kensho, and one has the absolute certainty of the unborn, undying, unchanging, and uncreated. You know in a way that you can never forget or lose, that this is so. It is from that certainty that a lot of priests teach.

"But in actual fact if you want to go on further than that in your spiritual training, you've got to understand this is like taking down the plaque from the door and sticking it up outside and saying 'I'm ready now.' You've got to go into the house and go through everything in the house. . . . Do you see what I'm saying? If you're married, the singleness of mind, the devotion, the oneness with that eternal can't take place, because you're dividing it off for a member of the opposite sex or member of the same sex, or whatever. If you're going to follow the eternal, he's the one you're gonna be fond of. He-she-it. That's the difference."

"Is there a loss," I ask her, "for people who are going to minister to others, in life experience, for instance, the experience of raising children?"

"I've not found it so," she answers. "But I personally think that it's probably wiser to go into the priesthood later in life rather than earlier. You come in at seventeen or eighteen when all your juices are flowing eagerly, and you can have an awfully rough time. A lot of Buddhist countries won't take people until they've been married and had children. So there is that side of it, but they do say you've got to be separated off afterward."

WOMEN, BUDDHISM, AND VIPASSANA MEDITATION (1991)

Theravada Buddhism has found its place in the American religious landscape too. At Insight Meditation Center in Barre, Massachusetts, male teachers such as Jack Kornfield and Joseph Goldstein have tutored Buddhist converts and sympathizers, and exerted influence nationally. But female teachers have had a place in this movement too. This essay by the feminist lay Buddhist Sandy Boucher (who conducted the preceding Kennett interview) explores gender and sexuality as it documents an encounter with an important Theravada Buddhist teacher, Ruth Denison. Denison guides students in "insight meditation" at the Desert Vipassana Center in California. The German-born Denison, who also has taught regularly at the Insight Meditation Society, was trained in Burma by the Theravadin teacher U Ba Khin. She later studied in a Soto Zen monastery in Japan with Soen Roshi and Yasutani Roshi, with whom she continued to practice later in Los Angeles. Denison and other Vipassana teachers distinguish insight meditation from concentration meditation, which focuses attention on a single object. As Jack Kornfield explained it in *Living Buddhist Masters* (1977), Vipassana (or insight) meditation "develops the quality of concentration on changing objects as a tool for probing the nature of the mind-body process. Insight meditation is practiced by developing a bare attention, a seeing-without-reacting to the whole process of our world of experience. . . ." But Boucher's textured essay does more than introduce Vipassana meditation. By focusing on Denison, a female teacher who was the first to lead an all-woman meditation retreat, it also raises questions about the status of women in Buddhism. According to Boucher, the tradition has not lived up to the egalitarian teachings of its founder. At the same time, this essay also hints at another issue that troubled some converts in American Buddhist centers in the 1970s and 1980s: sexual misconduct by male Buddhist teachers. Osel Tendzin, the Vajrayana teacher in Boulder, was not the only one accused. For example, Richard Baker-roshi, Suzuki-roshi's dharma heir at San Francisco Zen Center, reportedly slept with some of his female students. As with some Protestant ministers and Catholic priests, Buddhist leaders have not always lived up to their tradition's moral ideals. This essay by Boucher confronts the sexual controversy, and considers women's status, as it reveals some European-American women's ambivalence about the Buddhist tradition.

Sandy Boucher, "In Love with the Dharma," Ms. (May/June 1991): 80–81. Reprinted by permission of Ms. Magazine, © 1991.

IN LOVE WITH THE DHARMA

When I began to hear about Buddhism in the late 1970s, I felt great relief that you didn't have to believe anything, that there was no god involved, and that one could do the practices without having to come up against the "furniture" of a religion. (Of course, my view of Buddhism is quite different from that of Asian or Asian American women, for whom Buddhism is often a family religion carrying a weight of cultural baggage.

Then a friend took me down to the Mojave Desert in California to attend a week-long meditation retreat. Even the concept of "retreat" was new to me—and suspect, from my political point of view: why should one separate oneself from ordinary life? But I went. Arriving at the Desert Vipassana Center perched among the Joshua trees, we met Ruth Denison, a German-born teacher in her sixties. She welcomed us to the small concrete-block meditation hall where we would practice Vipassana (Vee-PAH-sah-na), or "insight meditation."

There followed a week of interminable days of sitting meditation, walking and movement meditation, and "Dharma talks" by Ruth Denison. My body declared war upon me almost from the start—nerves twitching, muscles cramping as I tried to sit still on my meditation pillow. My mind took off in an extravaganza of memory, fantasy, and self-denigrating nattering. But finally my resistance exhausted itself, and I was able to settle in and follow Ruth Denison's precise guidance to help me attend to the sensations of my body, and to observe my mind. Sometimes, playfully, she led us in a conga line out across the desert, or had us dance with slow, sweeping, carefully observed movements in a circle. I began to experience flashes of joy. By the final days of the retreat a tenderness awakened in me for all of those people who sat with me in the meditation hall. I understood that I was not separate from people and animals, earth and sky, and surprising myself, I cried tears of gratitude.

This Buddhist practice, I realized, was an *investigation:* a deep probing into our own natures and the nature of what it is to be a human being. It illuminated the Buddhist teachings of the persistent unsatisfactoriness of existence, the impermanence of all phenomena, the insubstantiality of the self. As Ruth presented them, these concepts did not loom with the bulk of a *religion*, but seemed the logical explanation for the experiences I had been having. At home in Oakland, I began to meditate almost daily by myself. This practice did not cause me to drop my political activism. On the contrary, it set up a healthy continuum: out into the world of action, back into meditation to ponder that action, out into the world bringing the fruits of "sitting," and so forth. The practice influenced me toward a more nonviolent and thoughtful approach to political actions. Over the years I returned regularly to the Desert Vipassana Center. There we practiced silence and consideration of others, careful attention to the simple actions of life—folding up one's blanket, sweeping the concrete porch—and this steadied me. At moments, after an hour of concentration on my body, I pierced to the truth of the impermanence of my own flesh and of matter in general, and experienced grief for all that dies, love for all that lives.

But I was curious about the theory behind Buddhist practice, so I enrolled at a meditation and teaching institute in Berkeley where I took courses in the "Abhidharma," the distillation of the teachings of the Buddha.

Soon it dawned on me that I had walked in off the bare porch of Buddhist practice into the house itself, which was stuffed, after all, with furniture—some of it archaic, exotic, arbitrary. To make matters worse, I saw the male bias of much of the information and ceremony: the teaching had been passed down almost exclusively through male lineage; woman had been viewed as temptress and/or lesser being. (In the institute itself woman were not allowed to ring the dinner bell.)

Troubled, I began to read the very few works that existed in the early 1980s that addressed the question of women's relationship to Buddhism. The Buddha had broken the male-supremacist code of his sixth-century B.C.E. culture to acknowledge women as spiritual equals, but after his death his male followers sank back into their privilege and began to exclude women from religious agency and influence.

The relationship of this Asian past to present-day North American Buddhist practice became a matter of vital concern to me. I joined other women at the first women and Buddhism conferences, held in 1981 and 1982 in Boulder, Colorado; in 1983 through 1985 in Providence, Rhode Island. I heard other women talk about their difficulties with male teachers, problems in accommodating Buddhist practice to their lives as mothers and workers, struggles to have a say in the running of their Buddhist institutions.

Communications with Buddhist women revealed that in the larger picture of Buddhism in the U.S. (estimates range from two to ten million meditators), most women learned to mediate in heavily male-supremacist environments, often headed by Asian teachers who had previously engaged only with male students. These women told of strict hierarchies, the relegation of women to second-rate or supportive status. And the practice itself, in many Zen centers, for instance, smacked of military boot camp, with physical fortitude put at a premium, endurance of extreme discomfort held out as a prerequisite for spiritual progress.

By early 1983, a pattern of corruption began to emerge. A disturbing number of the major, most respected male Buddhist teachers had transgressed their role and taken advantage of women students' vulnerability to initiate sexual intercourse. A few had also misused their power financially.

Shock waves ran through the Buddhist community as one after another of the best-known teachers were exposed. The pain, the sense of betrayal, cut deep. Some of the women turned away from any form of spiritual practice, afraid to join a group, trust a teacher. Others stayed to reform the structure of their communities, giving rise to an intricate net of women's commentary and culture. . . .

After a period of residence as a nun in a Buddhist nunnery in Sri Lanka, and travel in Thailand and Burma (where I learned firsthand about the Asian origins of this spiritual practice I had adopted), I now augment my Buddhism with women's spirituality and shamanic practices. But the teachings of the Buddha ring so deeply in me that I know I belong here, as a member—admittedly a sometimes disgruntled one—of the Buddhist community. Recently, after a lecture, Ruth

Denison spread her hands and, with a disarming smile, admitted, "I can't help it: I'm in love with the Dharma." The 'Dharma' is the "truth," the teachings, what *is*. For me, both the Dharma and feminism are arrows pointing toward liberation, both are tools for investigation of our lives, and they *can* be brought into harmonious relationship.

But I must ask, in each instance, "What in this practice comes from the Buddha's universal teachings, and what is an expression of Asian culture?" This question comes not from an anti-Asian position, but merely recognizes the inappropriateness of a wholesale carryover of Asian practices or attitudes to contemporary Western institutions. In my relationship with other North American Buddhists I need to discover how to point out injustice without rancor, how to help women meditators break free of their idealization of male teachers so that they can protect themselves and other women and children from abuse. How to do this while remaining grounded in the compassion, sympathetic joy, and equanimity that are the heart of this spiritual path! And I remind myself that the vast majority of women Buddhists live in or come from Asian countries, and have a different relationship to this practice than I: we need to communicate more across cultural lines, in the context of shared practice, about differences.

This path is not easy, comfortable, or safe. Sincere spiritual practice never is. But I have hope that we in North America, together with all women in Buddhist communities worldwide, will fully acknowledge our capacity and achievement in Buddhism, profoundly affecting its future.

BELL HOOKS, "WAKING UP TO RACISM" (1994)

Race is as important a dividing line in American Buddhism as gender. One of the greatest challenges facing American Buddhism today, Buddhist scholar Charles Prebish has argued, is to find "a means of reconciling the vastly different emphases of ethnic Buddhist and export Buddhist groups." Prebish and other observers have acknowledged the fissures between Buddhists of Asian and European heritage. Members of these two groups do not typically have sustained contact with one another, and they practice their faith differently. For example, American converts focus more on meditation, and women play more prominent roles in their religious communities. Another Buddhist scholar, Jan Nattier, has distinguished Asian-American Buddhism ("ethnic Buddhism") from two kinds of convert Buddhism: "elite" Buddhism, in which the potential convert seeks out the tradition, for example, Zen; and "evangelical" Buddhism, which is spread by missionary activity, for example, the Soka Gakkai International. But there are still other divisions among American Buddhists, as bell hooks notes in this 1994 essay. An African-American feminist theorist and cultural critic who practices Zen Buddhism, hooks points to the racial divide between black and white Buddhists. As many observers have noticed, the Soka Gakkai attracts more ethnically diverse followers, including African Americans and Latinos/as, but people of color are absent in many Buddhist centers, even if many African Americans privately practice and study the tradition. When they do join Buddhist communities, hooks suggests, African

Americans often feel marginalized. In this essay hooks challenges white Buddhists to be more sensitive to the subtle (and not so subtle) impositions of power in Buddhist centers, and to consider more fully the politics of speaking for this Asian tradition. At the same time, she invites people of color who meditate or chant privately "to move out of the shadows of silence and speak about the nature of their spiritual practice."

For some time now I have been writing fragments of a book, *Buddha Belly*, about the meaning of Buddhism in my life, about the buddha I have been carrying in my belly for more than twenty years now. These writings are often funny, witty takes on my experience as a black female with Buddhism. I have been lucky because Buddhism has come to me from so many different directions that even when I was not seeking, I was always found. That thought, too, makes me laugh, because many of my religious white comrades are obsessed with seeking. When I was young, talking Buddhism all the time with them, I was always amazed and sometimes envious that to them longing to seek meant taking a trip, backpacking to Tibet, joining this community somewhere on the other side of the planet, finding that special teacher. Inwardly, I was a bit ashamed that I could never gather the courage to share that I had no intention of going anywhere—that to go places was about time and money and a will to travel that simply was not in me. The time I needed to study and write, and the journey to blessedness, to enlightenment, well, that could take place anywhere, or so the confinement and limitations of my circumstances made it essential for me to believe.

We cannot separate the will of so many white comrades to journey in search of spiritual nourishment to the "third world" from the history of cultural imperialism and colonialism that has created a context where such journeying is seen as appropriate, acceptable, an expression of freedom and right. Nor does it surprise me that black people, and other people of color who have grown up in the midst of racial apartheid and racist domination, often feel the need to stay home, to stay in our place. Often we feel we have no right to move into a world that belongs to someone else seeking to discover treasures—not even if they are spiritual gems. It is important to recognize and interrogate these two positions without the judgment of good and bad. We can hold the reality that imperialism paved the way for white folks seeking to go anywhere in the world and claim ownership to walk on many paths, simultaneously with the understanding that much of what has been found there—in that initial violent colonialism, continuing neocolonialism, and journeying rooted in compassion and good will—gives life as much as it takes and has taken life away. We can hold the understanding that enlightenment as an expression of spiritual devotion and practice is not bound by time and space even as we recognize the necessity of cultural borrowing and the mixing of traditions, lifestyles, and practices. We can understand racism within the circles of Buddhism in the United States if we surrender our attachment to binary, either/or thinking, if we let go the need to "own" any position as better, right, more correct.

bell hooks, "Waking Up to Racism," *Tricycle* (Fall 1994): 42–45. Reprinted by permission of bell hooks and the Watkins/Loomis Agency.

To many of my white comrades who accepted their interest in Buddhism as "natural," my engagement always made me suspect, the object of spectacle, someone to be interrogated. "And why are you interested in Zen? And where did you first become interested? And who do you follow?" These questions are usually asked of anyone new to Buddhism, but what a person of color hears, whether it's intended or not, is that we are being singled out. These interrogations presuppose that I—and not they—am the other, that there is no ancestral connection between me or other people of color and the cultures in which they search to find Buddhist truth. This is the cultural arrogance that white supremacy allows. No wonder, then, that many black people, people of color, have felt that they cannot maintain a connection with their race and culture of origin and walk a Buddhist path. To some of them, choosing such a path in this country has been synonymous with choosing whiteness, with remaining silent about racism for fear of being dismissed, for fear of bringing in issues that are not really important. Often the disillusionment people of color feel is a response to idealized assumptions that spiritual communities will be places where the racism encountered in everyday life will have disappeared. Why do we think working at the Bodhi Tree Bookstore (which I did) will be any freer of racial tension and hostilities than working at Macys? While some of us hear the dilemmas of the rare individual black person who has lived in a Buddhist community, who has studied with teachers, who has served, most folks refuse to write about these experiences. Many people of color have retreated from communities into a monastic culture within. When the openness is there, they will speak their experiences. Often white people share the assumption that simply following a spiritual path means that they have let go of racism: coming out of radical movements—civil rights, war resistance—in the sixties and seventies and going on to form Buddhist communities, they often see themselves as liberal and marginalized, proudly identifying with the oppressed. They are so attached to the image of themselves as nonracists that they refuse to see their own racism or the ways in which Buddhist communities may reflect racial hierarchies. This is made more problematic where the emphasis in the predominantly white communities is on letting go of the self.

I am often asked when talking about racism in Buddhist circles to be specific, give examples. In part, this longing emerges from the reluctance of white people in power to accept, and see clearly by opening their eyes, that white supremacy informs the shaping of Buddhist communities, individual interactions, publications, etc. That reluctance can only be transformed in spiritual practice, not by proof. There is never enough proof. We see the absence of people of color in predominantly white Buddhist circles. We hear the silence of those voices. What will it take for the individuals in those circles to seek an understanding of that absence, which comes from within?

To understand that absence there has to be a concrete understanding of how racism works, of how white supremacy shapes personal interactions. Progressive whites who have no difficulty challenging institutionalized racism may have no clue about challenging the day-to-day xenophobia and racism inside everyone. When people of color are reluctant to enter predominantly white Buddhist settings it is not out of fear of some overt racist exclusion, it is usually in response to more subtle manifestations of white supremacy. Even to speak or write for a Buddhist publication where white people are in power evokes the concern, and sometimes the fear, that one's words, thoughts, and being may be distorted, presented in a way that speaks only to the need of white readers. It is no simple matter to find a space within Buddhist circles where compassion has surfaced with an intensity that overshadows racial injustice and racial hierarchy.

In the United States there are many black people and people of color engaged with Buddhism who do not have visibility or voice. Contrary to a certain cultural arrogance that enjoys calling attention to—in a trivializing way—the quantifiable presence of black people in Nichiren Shoshu, there are many black people who identify with diverse traditions, walk on various paths, who practice in silence, who rely on the monastic culture within. It is a challenge to the white supremacist capitalist patriarchy to accept that not seeing something does not mean it does not exist. Clearly, the time has come for more people of color in the United States to move out of the shadows of silence and speak about the nature of their spiritual practice. That silence is often imposed, a response to fears that we might not know enough, that we will be looked down upon, especially by whites. I have always been reluctant to speak about Buddhism, for fear I will mispronounce words, not have all the details and information that will prove me a card-carrying Buddhist and not just a dharma voyeur. Surely it is often racism that allows white comrades to feel so comfortable with their "control" and "ownership" of Buddhist thought and practice in the United States. They have much to learn, then, from those people of color who embrace humility in practice and relinquish the ego's need to be recognized. Rarely have I heard or read any really prominent white person engaged with Buddhism discuss any fear of being arrogant when speaking about the subject, grappling with issues of ownership or authenticity, posing the question, "Will the real Buddhist please stand up?" I am quick to say, "I am not a 'real' Buddhist." It has been useful to meditate on the subject of being a real Buddhist. In those moments of contemplation and quiet, the awareness surfaces that so many people of color fear not being worthy in ways that escape the attention of our white comrades. This fear of not being worthy is not always a response to the reality of subjugation. It also has to do with the practice of humility, not being presumptuous, not assuming rights, and/or the experience of being in awe, I am always reminded of that spirit of awe when I contemplate the passage in the biblical Book of Psalms where the seeker marvels at the wisdom of the teacher, completely open to the possibility that "such knowledge is high, I cannot attain to it."

Lately, I often playfully want to ask the "real Buddhists to please stand up." Studying different traditions, I learned early on that "real" Buddhists have teachers they know and name, have studied specific paths, done translations, can speak with authority. Certainly there is always a need for experience and knowledge rooted in traditions, but it is not a spiritual given that these are the places where peace, union, and spiritual awareness are found. What am I to make of the fact that every journey I start that is to lead me to a face-to-face encounter with a teacher is interrupted, short-circuited? Each time I have set out in the direction of Thich Nhat Hanh, who teaches and guides my heart, something happens. Often my teachers have no faces, no bodies I can touch with my eyes or hands, no skin color I can see, no race. This absence may keep me on the path, for it is an absence that does not preclude contact, connection, transmission—even though there are times when I wonder, Am I never to be a "real" Buddhist? And what of all those white men, those writers—Jack Kerouac, Gary Snyder, and many others— who may never have and will never feel the need to ask that question, including some who can find their way to "legitimate" Buddhism even in death? Then there are all the nonwhite people, many Asians from various ethnic groups with long traditions of Buddhist practice, who are angry, who want to counter the hegemony of whiteness with their own insistence on received right, authority, realness. How to separate the need to dismantle racism and white supremacy in Buddhist circles from the desire to construct more diverse hierarchies of domination? That is a challenge only profound spiritual practice can help us meet.

JACCI THOMPSON-DODD, SOKA GAKKAI AND THE POWER OF CHANTING (1996)

The Soka Gakkai International (literally "Society for the Creation of Value"), a religious movement that originated in Japan, has attracted a wider range of members in terms of ethnicity and class than any other convert-centered American Buddhist group. Commonly known as SGI, the movement traces its lineage to the Japanese religious leader Nichiren (1222–82), who established a distinctive Buddhist sect anchored in the authority of the Lotus Sutra, a Buddhist sacred text. Practice has traditionally centered on the "three great hidden truths": the *gohonzon*, the embodiment of the Lotus Sutra's teachings and Nichiren's life in the form of a scroll, which members enshrine in their homes; the *daimoku* (literally "title"), the invocation or chanting of Nam-myoho-renge-kyo, the title of the Lotus Sutra, which is inscribed on the *gohonzon*; and the *kaidan*, or the ordination platform that Nichiren wanted to establish on the slopes of Mt. Fuji. SGI, which until recently was a lay organization within Nichiren Shoshu, was founded in 1937 by a Japanese schoolteacher named Makiguchi Tsuneasburo. In 1960 the group's third president, Daisaku Ikeda, established organizations in the United States. According to religion scholar Jane Hurst, by the mid-1990s SGI probably counted between 5 and 8.5 million member families in 115 countries. A major split occurred in 1991, primarily over the issue of religious authority, and the priests of Nichiren Shoshu in Japan excommunicated Soka Gakkai lay members because they allegedly had defied and slandered the High Priest. A bitter battle ensued. In a sixty-four page pamphlet published in 1996 by the Myohoji Temple in West Hollywood (*Refuting the Soka Gakkai's Counterfeit Object of Worship*), Nichiren Shoshu's Doctrinal Research Committee reiterated its claim to hold the true object of worship (or *gohonzon*). The two groups now compete for the allegiance of Nichiren admirers in the United States, although SGI counts many more adherents and centers: Nichiren Shoshu has six U.S. temples and claims 5,000 active members; the SGI-USA has more than sixty centers and about 50,000 American followers. Because SGI is much larger, the excerpts below focus on that movement. The first entry is the latest official summary of SGI's "purposes and principles," published four years after the 1991 split. The second entry is a testimony by Jacci Thompson-Dodd, an African-American SGI member from Seattle. This testimony, published in the SGI's official newspaper, shows that however bitter the institutional split has been, the movement's diverse devotees continue to practice the faith. They continue to chant in front of the *gohonzon*, or sacred scroll, and they continue to claim that practice transforms their lives.

CHARTER OF THE SOKA GAKKAI INTERNATIONAL

Preamble

We, the constituent organizations and members of the Soka Gakkai International (hereinafter called "SGI"), embrace the fundamental aim and mission of contributing to peace, culture and education based on the philosophy and ideals of the Buddhism of Nichiren Daishonin.

We recognize that at no other time in history has humankind experienced such an intense juxtaposition of war and peace, discrimination and equality, poverty and abundance as in the 20th century; that the development of increasingly sophisticated military technology, exemplified by nuclear weapons, has created a situation where the very survival of the human species hangs in the balance; that the reality of violent ethnic and religious discrimination presents an unending cycle of conflict; that humanity's egoism and intemperance have engendered global problems, including degradation of the natural environment and widening economic chasms between developed and developing nations, with serious repercussions for humankind's collective future.

We believe that Nichiren Daishonin's Buddhism, a humanistic philosophy of infinite respect for the sanctity of life and all-encompassing compassion, enables individuals to cultivate and bring forth their inherent wisdom and, nurturing the creativity of the human spirit, to surmount the difficulties and crises facing humankind and realize a society of peaceful and prosperous coexistence.

We, the constituent organizations and members of SGI, therefore, being determined to raise high the banner of world citizenship, the spirit of tolerance, and respect for human rights based on the humanistic spirit of Buddhism, and to challenge the global issues that face humankind through dialogue and practical efforts based on a steadfast commitment to nonviolence, hereby adopt this charter, affirming the following purposes and principles:

"Charter of the Soka Gakkai International," *World Tribune*, 8 December 1995, 5; Jacci Thompson-Dodd, "Finding Faith Again," *World Tribune*, 15 November 1996, 3. Reprinted by permission of *World Tribune*.

Purposes and Principles

1. SGI shall contribute to peace, culture and education for the happiness and welfare of all humanity based on Buddhist respect for the sanctity of life.
2. SGI, based on the ideal of world citizenship, shall safeguard fundamental human rights and not discriminate against any individual on any grounds.
3. SGI shall respect and protect the freedom of religion and religious expression.
4. SGI shall promote an understanding of Nichiren Daishonin's Buddhism through grass-roots exchange, thereby contributing to individual happiness.
5. SGI shall, through its constituent organizations, encourage its members to contribute toward the prosperity of their respective societies as good citizens.
6. SGI shall respect the independence and autonomy of its constitutent organizations in accordance with the conditions prevailing in each country.
7. SGI shall, based on the Buddhist spirit of tolerance, respect other religions, engage in dialogue and work together with them toward the resolution of fundamental issues concerning humanity.
8. SGI shall respect cultural diversity and promote cultural exchange, thereby creating an international society of mutual understanding and harmony.
9. SGI shall promote, based on the Buddhist ideal of symbiosis, the protection of nature and the environment.
10. SGI shall contribute to the promotion of education, in the pursuit of truth as well as development of scholarship, to enable all people to cultivate their characters and enjoy fulfilling and happy lives.

THE POWER OF CHANTING

I have been practicing consistently for more than 21 years. In that long history, I have never doubted the Gohonzon—not until recently.

In January 1995, I embarked on an ambitious million daimoku campaign to live my true identity. Now, 20 months later, I am midway through my second million daimoku chart toward the goal.

I could never have imagined the muck that would surface through this campaign. As it cleared away, I discovered a deep passion for writing—especially about the arts and culture. I dreamed that someday I could turn this creative energy into a vigorous life for kosen-rufu. So when a job opportunity appeared unsought in a new arts institution, I thought my prayer had been answered.

Anxious to show actual proof, I chanted three hours before my final set of interviews, and was confident in my presentations. The director of this organization even hosted a dinner in my honor with trustees and senior staff.

Since this was in another city, I began chanting for the perfect house for kosen-rufu activities. As mystically as the job appeared, the perfect house also emerged—light, airy, beautiful and well within my price range. It was even four doors away from one of the best elementary schools in the city, ideal for my young daughter to attend. The future seemed assured.

A week later, a tersely worded letter arrived, informing me that I did not get the job. I was devastated. For the first time in 21 years, my faith was deeply shaken—so much so that I stopped doing gongyo and decided not to practice anymore. I spent a night crying in the depth of despair, castigating myself for trusting the Gohonzon. I felt foolish, betrayed, and hopeless.

At work the next day, I felt numb and worthless. Despite the fact that I had renounced my practice the night before, out of instinct I called my leader for guidance. She reminded me of *The Opening of the Eyes*, and shared her 35 years of faith experiences, determined to reach into my life.

"Although I and my disciples may encounter various difficulties, if we do not harbor doubt in our hearts, we will as a matter of course attain Buddhahood. Do not have doubts simply because heaven does not lend you protection. Do not be discouraged because you do not enjoy an easy and secure existence in this life. This is what I have taught my disciples morning and evening, and yet they begin to harbor doubts and abandon their faith. Foolish men are likely to forget the promises they have made when the crucial moment comes" (*Major Writings of Nichiren Daishonin*, vol. 2, p. 205).

Crying together with me, she begged me to take my tears to the Gohonzon one more time and chant. Hesitantly, I agreed to try again.

When I arrived home in front of the altar, the wall went up again between me and the Gohonzon, and I couldn't chant. I called another long-time member and explained my torment. The wisdom of her 27 years of practice came pouring through the phone. We chanted three times together through the phone—my first daimoku in several days. Many daimoku and tears followed, washing away my suffering and showing me how turned around my values had been.

Slowly, the illusion that this job would have taken me closer to my dream lifted. I realized that it would actually have sent me careening away from my heart's desire of writing. That revelation was followed by others, including the tremendous fortune I have in my family, friends and faith. Unbeknownst to me, my husband, Mel (who does not practice), called a Buddhist friend for guidance about how to encourage me to chant again. Even my 4-year old daughter, Nailah, encouraged me, saying: "Mommy, you should be happy! You have me and Daddy and the Gohonzon to be happy about. Please don't be sad anymore!" Members showered me with inspiring phone calls, visits, and letters. This incredible outpouring of support confirmed the precious benefit of living as the Buddha we all truly are.

This experience helped anchor my practice into a much deeper foundation.

Seeking my true identity has brought me bountiful rewards. I am convinced that this faith-challenging ordeal was a blessing in disguise. What I was seeking outside was inside me all along.

As a result, writing opportunities are springing up everywhere! My first article is being published in a prestigious international art journal this winter, and a New York publishing house is very encouraging about my book manuscript. What sweet victories!

I know now to renew my appreciation for my practice and our beautiful organization and, most of all, trust my dreams and never presuppose what their fulfillment will look like. Through this practice, I know that every dream will always come true.

BERNARD GLASSMAN AND RICK FIELDS, "RECIPES FOR SOCIAL CHANGE" (1996)

When European Americans first started turning to Buddhism in the late nineteenth century, many of those converts and sympathizers thought of the Buddha as a social reformer and presented Buddhism as morally superior to Christianity. Many emphasized personal and social moral action—being good and doing good—as an integral part of their faith. Since the 1960s, a more organized Buddhist social activism, or "engaged Buddhism" as some have called it, has emerged in the United States with the creation of groups like the Buddhist Peace Fellowship (established 1978). The activities of the Zen Center of New York (ZCNY) provide an illuminating example of this socially responsible Buddhism. ZCNY was founded by Bernard Tetsugen Glassman Sensei, an ordained Soto Zen priest. Born into a Jewish family in Brooklyn in 1939, this former aerospace engineer studied with Maezumi-roshi (1931–95) at the Zen Center of Los Angeles, another major Buddhist institution in America. Maezumi-roshi named Glassman his first dharma-heir. After serving as chief administrator of the Los Angeles Center, Glassman founded ZCNY in 1979 on the banks of the Hudson River. Drawing on the example of San Francisco Zen Center's successful bakery, ZCNY opened Greyston Bakery, which has been the community's primary revenue source. Once ZCNY was financially secure, Glassman decided to reach out to the surrounding community by confronting social problems such as poverty, homelessness, and AIDS. In *Instructions to the Cook*, Glassman returns to a familiar Soto Zen theme. (In 1237, the Japanese teacher Dogen wrote a classic text with the same title, *Tenzo Kyokun*.) But Glassman adds a twist. He uses the analogy of food preparation to explain Buddhist values and describe his community's humanitarian programs, including the Greyston Family Inn, which opened in 1987 to address the problem of homelessness in New York.

WHO ARE YOU COOKING FOR?

It's very important to remember that we have to take care of our own life. We have to cook for ourselves before we can really invite guests to join us for dinner. We have to nourish ourselves first.

A sick cook won't make a good meal, and a hungry cook won't wait for the meal to be served. If we don't begin by befriending ourselves, our meal will not taste right, no matter how hard we work, or how many ingredients we have, or how fancy our equipment is.

When we learn how to cook for ourselves, though, we find that our vision or understanding of the self grows and expands. The smell of food cooking and the warmth of the kitchen always invites people in. Even though it may seem as if we're cooking for ourselves, we're always cooking for everybody at the same time. This is because we are all interconnected. We are actually one body.

I sometimes use the analogy of one person with two hands. One hand is Sam, the left. The other is Bill, the right. Each has its own identity. When money arrives in the mail and Sam reaches for it, Bill gets a little jealous. When Bill burns himself on a hot stove, Sam thinks, "I should help him, but if I put the wrong kind of medicine on his hand maybe I'll get sued."

Eventually, they find that they have to work together to get anything done. Sam needs Bill to lift a heavy package, or drive a car, or even to open a can of soup. In this way, they discover that they are a part of one body. They are one interdependent world. There is no more separation. When money comes, a hand reaches out, and it doesn't matter whether it's left or right. If a hand gets burned, there's no thinking about what to do, the other just automatically helps.

Of course, I don't say, "I have two hands." It's so obvious that I don't even say, "These are my hands." They're just a part of me. I see you and me as separate until I realize that we are both part of one interconnected world as well. Eventually, all there is is one whole universe unfolding, and everything is taking care of everything else.

SELF AND OTHER

So the Zen cook cooks for others because he or she sees that the separation between self and other is illusory. This is actually very different from feeding others to help "them" or to do good.

My own interest in feeding others—in what people call social action—has a lot do with what I can learn from people I seem to be helping. By becoming one with them, by seeing the world as much as I can through their eyes, I learn what their needs are. At the same time, I broaden and expand my own view of life.

. . . When we decided to build housing for the homeless, we wanted to help folks get off welfare. But when we went out to the welfare motels and talked to people, we found that most people wanted jobs but needed child care first. Working together, we came up with a comprehensive model for the Greyston Family Inn, which included housing, child care, counseling, and job training.

THE COMPLETE MEAL

Most people could see that only a holistic, totally integrated approach could break the cycle of homelessness and poverty. We had to include all the elements and ingredients of a good meal. The biggest and most immediate problem, of course, was to provide some kind of stability, which for the homeless meant permanent housing. In order to do this we formed an entirely independent corporation with its own board of directors called Greyston Family Inn. Calling on some of the wealthy and influential people we met in Westchester, we began to work our way through the maze of red tape and bureaucracies until we finally obtained a grant from the New York State Housing Assistance Program to buy and renovate a deserted building a few blocks from the bakery, at 68 Warburton Avenue.

. . . So we formed a construction company, headed by minority managers and supervisors, that offered on-the-job training to unemployed and homeless people. Then we went to work, completely gutting and reconstructing the building. In this way, the money stayed in the community, and the homeless were involved from the very beginning in building their own homes as well as learning a trade. Finally, in October, two years after we had begun the process, the first eighteen families moved into their own building.

Once the building was complete, we began to add the other ingredients according to plan. Because the homeless were mainly single-parent families, we added a child care center. Because none of the parents had jobs, we added job training as well. We started a tenant's organization, encouraging people to take more and more control of running the building.

. . . So far the results of the program have far exceeded our expectations. One tenant had a job when people began to move into the building—he lost it almost immediately, partly due to the pressures of being reunited with his wife and kids. But within five months, eleven out of twenty-five adults in the building were working. Four were employed as child-care aides in the building, and some were planning to get further training to become assistant teachers and then teachers. One person was working in the bakery, another as the superintendent of the building. And the rest had jobs outside. Six were completing high school equivalency courses. One was studying radiology in college, and three completed a beginning word processing course taught by Greyston Family Inn and were enrolled in a more advanced course in a local education center.

But the greatest change is the change from despair to hopefulness. As one tenant says, "Besides everything else—besides the apartment, child care, and job help—the one thing Greyston offers is encouragement. After you're homeless for a while, once you feel you're alone, it takes its toll on your self-esteem. You look at yourself the same way the public looks at someone who's homeless: as someone who can offer the community nothing."

Another tenant, who came to Greyston along with her newborn child and husband after two years of homelessness and unemployment, sums it up this way: "At this time last year," she says, "if someone came and told me I would have a beautiful apartment, and I would have day care, and I would be able to go to school and, hopefully, within six months get a job, I wouldn't have believed them—because I've never seen anyone who was homeless and ever came out of it. But I'm doing it. I'm not successful yet, but I will be—I know I will."

Such progress is wonderfully heartening. But every up has a down; every success creates more "problems." The meal served at the Greyston Family Inn is a very rich one. Even though we've been successful, we have to be careful that people don't get sick from eating too much too fast. There has to be enough time to chew and digest all the new information and experience. Recovering from homelessness, we've learned, doesn't happen overnight. It's an ongoing process.

CHAPTER 16

Asian Indian Immigrants:
Hindu, Jain, and Sikh

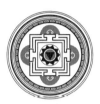

ANAND MOHAN, "THE PILGRIMAGE" (1994)

Pilgrimage, or religious journey to a sacred site, is important in many religions, but it plays an especially prominent role among Hindus in India. With the dedication of two major Indian-style Hindu temples in the United States during the summer of 1977, American Hindus had local pilgrimage destinations too. America's first two Indian-style temples were the Sri Ganesha Temple (now called the Maha Vallabha Ganapati Devasthanam) in Flushing, New York, and the Sri Venkateswara Temple in Pittsburgh, Pennsylvania. The Flushing Hindu community began planning their building earlier, and they broke ground first. But there is some polite disagreement about which building was dedicated first: Hindus in Pittsburgh date their temple dedication as 8 June 1977, almost a month earlier than the Flushing temple's Fourth of July ceremony, while devotees at the Flushing temple claim the Pittsburgh building was consecrated a few days after their own. In any case, devotees at the two temples agree that 1977 was a decisive year for American Hinduism. Both temples have become popular pilgrimage sites, and since they opened Hindus have built almost fifty major Asian-style temples across the United States, often with financial support and technical assistance from temples in India. Many urban areas, including New York, Chicago, Los Angeles, Philadelphia, Flint, Atlanta, Washington, D.C., San Francisco, and Houston, now boast impressive buildings. These temples—in an effort to accommodate a wide variety of Indian-American devotees—often lump together Hindu deities in ways that would be unimaginable in India. Home shrines, which range in

Anand Mohan, "The Pilgrimage," in Marella L. Hanumadass, ed., *A Pilgrimage to Hindu Temples in North America* (Flushing: The Council of Hindu Temples of North America, 1994), np. Reprinted by permission of the Council of Hindu Temples of North America, Flushing, New York.

size from a cabinet shelf to an entire room, continue to be important to Hindu devotion too, but the new temples have become crucial religious and cultural centers for Hindu immigrants. In 1994 the Flushing-based Council of Hindu Temples of North America published a guide to American Hindu pilgrimage sites. Its introductory essay, which is excerpted here, explores the meaning of Hindu pilgrimage in India and America.

When some of our Indian immigrants first entered the United States as students some forty years ago or more, there was not a single Hindu temple anywhere in North America. Today, almost every major city in the United States and Canada boasts of a temple, large or small. So much so, that one can go temple-hopping from the shores of the Atlantic to those of the Pacific. And it would make not merely for a grand tour but also an imposing pilgrimage.

Strange indeed are the twists and turns of time. Half a millennium ago, when Christopher Columbus was fired with the zeal of discovering a sea route to India, among the things which attracted him to undertake that arduous adventure were not only the famed treasures of Hindoostan but also reports of the celebrated devotional exercises practiced in such temple-towns as Srirangam. The wheel of history has turned full circle, and the people of the Old World of *Sanatana Dharma* can now join the citizens of the New World of change and challenge.

But change and challenge are not attributes peculiar to modern American culture alone. The *Tirtha-Yatra* or pilgrimage of ancient Hindu India was actually a response to the desire for a change of scene as much as an urge to accept the challenge of the spirit. So persistent and ubiquitous a habit of the Hindus was the *Tirtha-Yatra* that no foreign observer failed to notice it. Hsuan-tsang, who travelled in India between 629 and 645 A.D., Alberuni in his famous *Kitab-ul-Hind*, written around 1030 A.D., and Abut Fazl, in his *Ain-i-Akbari* dedicated to Emperor Akbar in 1593 A.D., all conceded the importance of the institution of pilgrimage in the Hindu tradition.

Another Arab geographer of the tenth century, Ibn Haukal, commenting on the sanctity attached to Multan, which is now in Pakistan, reports:

"There is an idol there held in great veneration by the Hindus, and every year people from the most distant parts undertake pilgrimages to it, and bring vast sums of money, which they expend upon the temple."

So firmly entrenched in the consciousness of the Hindu was this notion of pilgrimage that Hsuan-tsang could follow very closely the route described in the *Mahabharata*. A special section, entitled *Tirtha-Yatra,* of the *Anusana Parva* of that great epic, which is devoted exclusively to pilgrimage, mentions 270 sacred spots—evidence that Hindu places of pilgrimage were spread over the entire length and breadth of the country.

Starting from Pushkara, one proceeded to Mahakala (Ujjain), then to the river Narmada, onwards to Mount Abu (the asylum of the *rishi*, Vasishta), thence to Prabhasa (Somnath), down to the mouth of the mythical river Saraswati, to the Dwaravati (Dwaraka), and then to the mouth of river Sindhu (Indus). Then one travelled upstream to the Yoni *Tirtha* (northeast of Peshawar, now in Pakistan) and then eastward to the vale of Kashmir for a dip in the holy ponds surround-

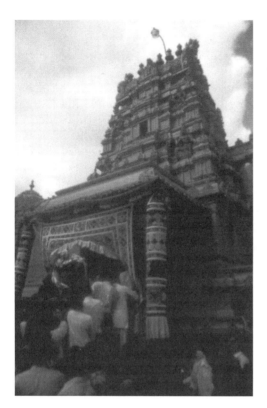

Maha Vallabha Ganapati Dev-asthanam, popularly known as the Ganesha Temple, Flushing, New York. Courtesy of The Pluralism Project, Harvard University.

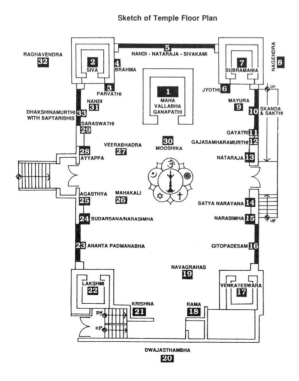

Sketch of Temple Floor Plan

RAGHAVENDRA **32**

NANDI · NATARAJA · SIVAKAMI **5**

SIVA **2** BRAHMA **4**

3 PARVATHI

SUBRAMANIA **7**

NAGENDRA **8**

NANDI **31**

DHAKSHINAMURTHI WITH SAPTARISHIS **33**

SARASWATHI **29**

1 MAHA VALLABHA GANAPATHI

JYOTHI **6**

MAYURA **9** **10** SKANDA & SAKTHI

GAYATRI **11** **12**

GAJASAMHARAMURTHI

NATARAJA **13**

VEERABHADRA **27** **30** MOOSHIKA

AGASTHYA **25** MAHAKALI **26**

AYYAPPA **28**

SATYA NARAYANA **14**

24 SUDARSANA/NARASIMHA

NARASIMHA **15**

23 ANANTA PADMANABHA

GITOPADESAM **16**

NAVAGRAHAS **19**

LAKSHMI **22**

VENKATESWARA **17**

KRISHNA **21** RAMA **18**

DN UP

DWAJASTHAMBHA **20**

Ganesha Temple floor plan. In an effort to accommodate as many area Hindus as possible, the floor plan makes space for a wide variety of Hindu deities. The logo at the center of the image demonstrates the belief of temple members in the unity of all religions. Courtesy Maha Vallabha Ganapati Devasthanam.

ing Mount Meru in the trans-Himalayana region which is also a source of the three rivers, Yamuna, Ganga and Sindhu.

The journey then turned southward to Kurukshetra (the battle field of the celebrated *Bhagavad Gita*) and then passing through Naimisharanya (the retreat of the *rishis* and sages mentioned in the *Satyanarayana Katha*), one proceeded to Varanasi or Kashi, for a break at Markandeya, the confluence of the rivers Ganga and Gomati. The next stop was Gaya, so much eulogized because the performance of *sraddha* (rites for the deceased) here was considered most desirable. Setting out from there to the confluence of the Ganga with the Gandaki, one wound one's way to Visala (Vaisali) to the river Bhagirathi (the easternmost limit of Aryan expansion) to the Gangasagara-Sangama where the river Ganges emptied itself into the Bay of Bengal.

The southward journey now began down the river Vaitarani in Orissa to Mahendra Giri (in the eastern ghats of present Andhra Pradesh) to Srisailam, close to the Krishna river, to Kaveri and Rishabha to the southernmost tip of the sub-continent, Kanya Kumari, where the three watery expanses met. One then veered westward and northward to Gokarna, then to the confluence of the Godavari and Varada (Wardha), and passing through the Dandakaranya (of Ramayana fame) reached Kalanjara and Chitrakoota, and concluded the pilgrimage in Prayaga (Allahabad).

During the medieval period, when South India enjoyed political stability and economic prosperity, the flow of royal grants transformed several temples into powerful religious, cultural and social institutions. A great spiritual revival, which peaked in the seventh century, witnessed the rise of a number of new pilgrim centers—Kanchipuram, Rameswaram, Setubandha (Adam's Bridge) and Tirumala-Tirupati.

Needless to say, that if the grand pilgrim route of the *Mahabharata* saw the traveller scale magnificent peaks, navigate majestic rivers, venture across thicket and jungle, and roam through the plains, resting in rustic village and trumpeting through temple-town, the pilgrimage itself was seen as an arduous journey that made enormous demands on the strength, stamina and staying power of the traveller. And add to it the rigor or religious ritual and the austerities of personal purification—fasting, sleeping on the floor, or at best, on a hard bed, sexual abstinence, avoidance of the use of vehicles, and walking barefoot!

Why did they go through it all, and how did they endure it? The *Mahabharata* offers a variety of reasons why select places are sacred: "Just as certain limbs of the body are purer than the others, so are certain places on earth more sacred—some on account of their situation, others because of their sparkling waters, and still others because of the association of saintly people with them, or the habitation of sages in them." Such places are called *tirthas*, and the *Puranas—Garuda*, *Matsya*, and *Agni*—inform us that *tirthas* may be sacred rivers, mountains or forests, places where the gods dwell and reveal themselves to us, hollowed nodes in a circumambient realm of consecrated space.

The *Brahmapurana* provides us with a ranking of the various *tirthas*, classifying them into four basic categories.

First come the *Daiva Tirthas* or sacred places resulting directly from the benevolent and divine acts of the major *devatas* or deities. Examples of such sites are Varanasi, Pushkara, Prabhasa (Somnath), Badrinath, Kedarnath and Dwaraka.

The second type are the *Asura Tirthas* or sacred places where *asuras* or demons were destroyed by the gods, and *dharma* or the moral order restored. A supreme example of this is Gaya, where Lord Vishnu subdued the demon Gayasura.

The third type are *Arsha Tirthas* or those consecrated by the actions of *rishis,* saints and sages through their penances, and sacrifices. One of the most important of these is Naimisharanya in Uttar Pradesh. Other examples are the *guha* or cave of Vyasa near Badrinath, the *ashramas* of Kanwa and Narada near Rudra Prayag on the bank of the river Alaknanda, and the *ashramas* of Atri and Bharadwaja in Central India.

Lastly, there are the *Manusha Tirthas,* built and sanctified by the rulers of the Surya and Chandra *vamshas* or solar and lunar dynasties.

Here in North America, all the temple sites are *Manusha Tirthas,* examples of religious societies and temple authorities creating sacred space. How sacred are they? Although they are considered to belong to a lower order of sanctity than the others they do embody the idea of the sacred. Why these temples have come up in certain cities or locations and not others, what accounts for the selection of their sites, which deities have come to be installed there, what odds have been encountered and what obstacles surmounted are all questions which, even if they can be persuasively answered and given a rational account, are still not totally devoid of mystery. And it is this great mystery of Being which arouses awe and inspires reverence, which staggers the imagination and stirs the spirit, and which also beckons the pilgrim to seek *darsan,* which is at once the fleeting sight of the form divine and ultimate insight into the nature of formless reality.

What kind of pilgrimage is apposite for experiencing the sacred in Hindu America? Smear oneself with ash, wear sackcloth, meander on foot, with staff in one hand and a bowl in the other, and soulful song on tongue? No, not quite. The temper of the times, the spirit of the age, and the *mores* of society dictate the conduct even of the pilgrim, be he or she a Freemason or Rotarian, Lion or Kiwani.

One can fly or undertake a Tirtha-Yatra in the United States in one's own car.

Suffering is not necessarily or exclusively the badge of true spirituality. Let us do away with the mortification of the flesh and the flagellation of the spirit! Fasting in the land of feasting is downright sinning. When you stop for gas and cannot bear to do justice to a quarter-pound cheeseburger and a cone with a double scoop of Baskin-Robbins ice cream, look in the trunk of your car for some lighter and fluffier edibles—*poori bhaji* or *idli* and *vada* wrapped in aluminum foil, and down it with a mug of Mysore coffee.

The faith of our fathers and mothers is transparently honest and commonsensically crystal clear. As a *grihastha* or house-holder, you are enjoined to pursue *artha* or wealth of all kinds, and *kama* or the aesthetic enjoyment of worldly pleasures—all in conformity with, and not in contravention of, *dharma,* the cosmic principle of the moral and divine order that sustains the earth. The stomach satiated and the senses satisfied, you are now ready for *moksha,* liberation from *maya* or illusion, and freedom from the bondage of *samsara,* the recurrent cycle of birth, death and rebirth.

Leaf through the pages of this helpful guide to track down the sacred spots presided over by your *ishtha devatas,* whose grace is the essential precondition for your *moksha.* Be it Durga or Lakshmi or Meenakshi, Balaji, Shivji or Ganeshji, or a host of others conjured up by the fertile polytheistic imagination of the Hindu, you will not fail to find them at some temple or the other.

But as you traverse the length and breadth of this vast land, and stand in awe of the stolidity of its mountains, its rolling meadows, its raging rivers, its towering trees, and the stillness of its forests, do recognize that this splendid, stupefying spectacle of nature, too, is suffused with the Spirit. Our predecessors and the first inhabitants of this land, the American Indians, contemplated nature, as did the Hindu Indians, with the poetic vision of a Wordsworth who saw in the sunrise or sunset not merely a pageant of beauty but a moment of spiritual consecration. The American Indians venerated, as do we Hindus, the mountain and the river, the Earth and the Sky, not merely as the natural expression of God's bounty but as *Prakriti,* the very embodiment of God's life-sustaining energy and power.

The Council of Hindu Temples of North America is pleased to present this guide to aid the progress of our pilgrims in this new land of their adoption. This guide, however, can hardly vie with the *Mahabharata* in its monumental success. But even great enterprises have small beginnings, and the Council trusts that this modest effort is the harbinger of future hopes of an ever-expanding pilgrimage in the New World.

RITUALS AT SRI VENKATESWARA TEMPLE (1995)

At Hindu temples priests and lay devotees engage in ritual action. Pittsburgh's Sri Venkateswara Temple was built in the South Indian style and named for the presiding deity (a form of Vishnu) of one of the most sacred pilgrimage sites in South India (the hilltop shrine of Tirupati). It was dedicated in an elaborate *Maha Kumbhabhishekam* ceremony in 1977, as priests poured water over the top of the fifty-foot *gopuram* or towered gateway. Since then the temple's four resident priests have conducted the usual daily ceremonies—at sunrise, noon, sunset, and midnight. They also offer a wide range of traditional religious services. Rituals mark the transitions in life (*samskaras*), and the priests conduct initiation ceremonies for boys (*upanayana*). They also preside at weddings, and the first entry is the instruction sheet temple officials distribute to couples who plan a traditional Vedic wedding ceremony. Other rituals are important too. Festivals attract large numbers of pilgrims, and many devotees attend for a special *puja*, or veneration of a deity who dwells in a temple image. The Pittsburgh temple's official periodical, *Saptagiri Vani*, prints its weekly ritual schedule and describes the materials (usually fruit or flowers) that devotees should bring or purchase. The temple's ritual schedule is reprinted in the second entry. These two selections, then, offer a glimpse of the ritual life at a typical American Hindu temple. Note that *Archana* means "worship" and implies veneration of a deity's image, accompanied by an offering of fruit, especially bananas and coconut. *Abhisheka* is the ritual bathing of deities, and *Satyanarayana puja* is an elaborate rite of veneration dedicated to Vishnu in the form of Satyanarayana. *Kalyana Utsavam* is the wedding festival of the deities, in this case the celebration of the marriage of Venkateswara (Vishnu) to Padmavati (Lakshmi).

THE WEDDING CEREMONY

Weddings at the S. V. Temple take place in the Kalyana Mandapam (wedding pavilion), symbolizing the Universe. According to Hindu tradition, the Universe rests on the back of the Great Tortoise, which is balanced by a thousand heads of the Great Serpent, navigated by the sharp sight of eight elephants, surrounded by twenty-seven constellations, protected by nine planets, and guided by the lords of the eight corners of the world. The ceremony is conducted in Sanskrit, the language of the Hindu scriptures.

1. Snataka

The bridegroom celebrates his graduation with his parents and offers presents to his guru. The parents and guru advise him to marry a suitable girl to enter Grahastasrama (family life). He stubbornly refuses to marry and instead sets off to the holy city of Benares in pursuit of knowledge. Then the bride's brother appeals with some gifts and persuades him to marry his illustrious sister.

2. Preparation for the Ceremony

The priest begins the ceremony with an offering of prayers to God Almighty and all his representations, the pantheon of gods. The bride's parents, after self-purification, introduce themselves.

3. Worship of Ganesha

Lord Ganesha is invited, installed and offered hospitality by the bride's parents. He is worshipped with a request to oversee the ceremony, remove any obstacles to its progress and help in its successful completion.

4. Punyahavachanam (Purification)

The bride's parents prepare three special kalashas (vessels) and invite all the sacred rivers to contribute and fill the vessels with their waters. These waters are purified and are used during the entire ceremony. The time of the ceremony and the place of the ceremony are established as sacred and pure. The minds of the participants and witnesses are purified with the blessings of the gods.

Saptagiri Vani, a publication of Sri Venkateswara Temple, vol. 26 (November 1995), 40, 43; "Information on Performance of Weddings at S.V. Temple, Pittsburgh, PA," unpublished document, Sri Venkateswara Temple, Pittsburgh, 1990. Reprinted by permission of Sri Venkateswara Temple, Pittsburgh.

5. Arrival of Bride and Groom

The bridegroom, escorted by his friends, arrives at the pavilion and takes his seat. The priest helps to remove all evils. He gives him a bracelet of protection. The bride, accompanied by her friends and relatives, is escorted to the pavilion by her uncle. The bride's parents receive the bride, thanking her uncle for safe escort. The bride is given a bracelet of protection by the priest. The bride's father then washes the feet of the bridegroom as a symbol of purification in preparation for the ceremony. The priest recalls the history of the Universe since creation and identifies the space and time coordinates of the present event in relation to the sacred places and times. The bride's father requests the bridegroom to accept his daughter as his wife, recalling the names of the three past generations on both sides. He asks him to promise to treat his daughter as an equal partner in all walks of his life. The bridegroom promises that he shall treat the bride as his equal and agrees to marry her.

6. Churnika (Proclamation)

The priest proclaims the sacredness and importance of the Muhurtam (moment) of the wedding and assures that the gods, the heavens, the earth and the seats of knowledge and prosperity are all in consonance and are ready to bless the couple.

7. Muhurtam (Moment of Wedding)

At the moment of wedding, the bride and bridegroom place their right hands on each other's heads, with a symbolic gesture of sweet and bitter tastes in their palms, while the priest invokes the powers of gods to provide stability and continuity to their married life.

8. Wedding Symbols

The curtain is removed. The bride and the bridegroom face each other. Together they do homage to the symbols of their marriage. The bridegroom ties the necklace of wedding medallions around the bride's neck. He ties a sacred rope around her waist. They smear each other's palms with milk. They exchange rings. They pour rice on each other's heads. They garland each other. The priest symbolically ties the ends of their upper garments in a sacred knot.

9. Pradhana Homam (Worship of Agni)

Agni, who is the messenger from heaven and is symbolized as light and fire, is invited, installed and worshipped by the bride and bridegroom.

10. Sapta Padi (The Seven Steps)

The bride and bridegroom take seven steps together around Agni. After the seventh step they take the following vows:

By walking seven steps with me you have become my friend. With these seven steps we have become friends. I am blessed with your friendship. I shall always be with you. You shall always be with me. We shall live together. We shall combine our minds in our thoughts. We shall combine our hands in our actions.

11. Invocation of Stability and Strength

The bride and bridegroom stand on a stone slab to symbolize stability of their marriage and strength to overcome all distracting influences.

12. Worship of the Stars

The bride and bridegroom pay homage to the seven sacred sages of the Universe, who are now represented by the seven stars in the constellation Ursa Major and in particular the companion star named Arundhati. The bride is given a necklace of blue-black beads representing the stars.

   The bride and bridegroom, to signify the goals of their married life, search for a treasure at the bottom of a vessel filled with waters of happiness. The couple pay their respect to the priest, the parents and the assembly.

13. Asirvadam (Blessings)

The priest recites selected hymns from Hindu scriptures invoking the blessings of all the gods and wishing prosperity to the newlyweds as well as to all those who have assembled to witness the ceremony. He will place the sacred rice on the couple to signify these blessings, the rice previously touched by everyone present.

14. Mangala Harathi (Presentation to the Light of God)

The ceremony ends when the friends of the family bring the sacred lights to the newlyweds and wish them happiness and prosperity.

TEMPLE SCHEDULE

Monday Through Friday		Saturday & Sunday	
9:00 AM	Suprabhatham	7:30 AM	Sathyanarayana Pooja
9:45 AM	Sahasranama Archana (for Venkateswara)	9:00 AM	Suprabhatham
		9:45 AM	Sahasranama Archana
10:30 AM	Sathyanarayana Pooja*	10:30 AM	Hair Offering
12:00 noon	Kalyana Utsavam*	11:00 AM	Abhishekam**
4:00 PM	Kalyana Utsavam*	12:30 PM	Kalyana Utsavam*
5:30 PM	Lakshmi Sahasranama Archana	3:00 PM	Sathyanarayana Puja*
6:00 PM	Unjal Seva* and Sahasranama Archana	4:00 PM	Kalyana Utsavam*
8:00 PM	Sayanotsavam	5:30 PM	Lakshmi Sahasranama Archana
		6:00 PM	Unjal Seva* and Sahasranama Archana
		8:00 PM	Sayanotsavam

Fridays

7:00 PM   Bhajans every third Friday of the month (Please check with Temple office)
9:00 PM   Sayanotsavam
*   These are performed on sponsorship only.
**   To Venkateswara on Sundays. 1st Saturday to Ganesha, 2nd Saturday to Padmavathi and 3rd
      Saturday to Andal. 4th Saturday to Anjaneya.
***   Fall & Winter Timings: Sayanotsavam will be advanced by one hour (7:00 PM) on all days except
      Fridays when it will be at 8:00 PM
Swarna Pushpa Archana on Special days & long weekends. Puja timings are likely to be changed during
festivals.

INFORMATION ON PERSONAL SERVICES

After deciding a suitable/auspicious date for the service, in consultation with the priest, if necessary, please call the Manager (9:00 AM–5:00 PM) at least two weeks in advance for approval of the use of the temple facilities. The services will be made available subject to the availability of priests and space. The facilities are available for 1 to 4 hours. For weddings please remit a deposit of $100 as soon as the date is finalized. The deposit will be adjusted towards the total donation. Please inform the Manager if the service is cancelled. ($50 will be recovered from the deposit in case of cancellation.)

Materials to be brought by devotees for all personal services: Turmeric, kumkum, flowers, a new bath towel, camphor, agarbathi, three varieties of fruits, six coconuts and twelve bananas. Other needed items are noted in the respective columns below. Please consult the priest for further information.

Services to be performed	Wedding	Akshara Abhyasam/ Anna Prasanam	Seemantham Ayush/ Navagraha/ Sudarsana Homams	Upanayanam	Sashtyabdi Poorthi/ Sathabhishekam
Materials to be brought other than those mentioned above. Bananas and coconuts are available at the temple for a nominal price.	Betal leaves and nuts, 4 garlands,* 2 lb. rice, 1/2 lb. ghee, sari for the bride and dhoti for the groom, wedding chain (*Thiruman-galyam*)	2 lb. rice, Cooked sweet rice (Payasam) for Anna-prasanam	2 lb. rice, 1/2 lb. ghee, *Seemantham:* sari for the would-be mother. *Homams:* New clothes for the child; nava dhanyam and cashew nuts.	4 lb. rice 1/2 lb. ghee 2 metal spoons 2 silk dhotis 1 garland*	2 lb rice 1/2 lb. ghee Mangalyam 2 garlands* Navadhanyam
Donation	**$300.00**	**$11.00**	**$51.00**	**$120.00**	**$120.00**

*The temple can arrange for four garlands for $51.00. For use of multipurpose room for lunch or dinner, please add $250.00.

SRI GANESHA TEMPLE, NASHVILLE, RECOUNTING HISTORY AND NURTURING YOUTH (1985–95)

Over the last two decades Hindu temples have been dedicated not only in New York and Pittsburgh but also in unexpected places like Nashville, Tennessee. In the capital of country music the Pittsburgh temple's chief priest presided at a ground-breaking ceremony for Sri Ganesha Temple in 1982. Three years later the new Nashville temple opened. In Nashville, as in many other cities since the 1970s, Asian Indian immigrants formed a building committee, and then struggled to raise funds and organize people. In the first of three brief entries from temple publications, Buntwal N. Somayaji, the chairman of the temple's Board of Trustees, recounts the origins of the Nashville project and exhorts devotees to continue their support. In the second entry, written six years later, Somayaji takes stock, as he considers the community's future in its fully functioning temple. Somayaji and the other members of the temple's building committee were able to attract donors and volunteers in part because the Hindu immigrants around Nashville were worried about their children. Would the second generation preserve the cultural and religious traditions of India? That concern for the next generation also led followers to establish a "Sunday School," as Hindus at other American temples have done. In the final entry instructors and students at Nashville's Sri Ganesha Temple reflect on religious education.

HOW IT ALL BEGAN

Those of us who arrived here in the late 60's and early 70's were of the notion that we would "go home eventually to settle down." But soon we realized that "home is here in America," thousands of miles away from Mother India. In a sense, as pioneers, we were confronted with the reality of raising a new generation, born on this soil, without the emotional and spiritual support provided by our great religious institutions. The need for a strong religious and cultural center to foster our rich heritage was strongly felt here and in several other communities around the U.S.A.

Informal discussions were held in 1978 and 1979 and a committee was formed in 1980 to provide an organizational structure for a temple and cultural center. There was considerable discussion regarding the name of the organization as well as its long term goals. Finally in October 1980, "The Hindu Cultural Center of Tennessee" was officially incorporated in the state of Tennessee to get our project underway. The logo for the center was drawn by an eminent artist, Mr. S. V. Rama Rao, who now resides in Chicago.

Buntwal N. Somayaji, "How It All Began," reprinted from *Phase One Completion Souvenir* (April 1985), in *Sri Ganesha Temple: Inauguration Souvenir, 1991* (Nashville: Hindu Cultural Center of Tennessee, 1991), 3; Buntwal N. Somayaji, "The Long Road—Both Behind and Ahead," in *Sri Ganesha Temple: Inauguration Souvenir, 1991* (Nashville: Hindu Cultural Center of Tennessee, 1991), 1; Sujata Wasudev, "Sunday School," *Aradhana,* a publication of Sri Ganesha Temple, Tenth Anniversary issue, vol. 2 (Summer 1995): np. Reprinted by permission of Sri Ganesha Temple, Nashville.

Under the auspices of the Hindu Cultural Center, we began meeting at various homes to observe several religious functions and festivals. As the number of participants was steadily increased, we found it necessary to locate a larger meeting place for our functions. The facilities of the First Unitarian Universalist Church at 1808 Woodmont Blvd. were obtained in early 1982 and we have been meeting there regularly ever since. We are grateful to the church for their help in this regard. The center has also had the privilege of sponsoring several well known artists, such as the Kuchipudi dancers, Sangita Siromani Narasimhachari and his wife Vasantalakshmi, Garimella Sisters of Chicago, Odissi dancer Sanjukta Panigrahi, Geetashree Sandhya Mukherjee, Veena artist Balachander, Vempati Chinna Satyam and his Kuchipudi Academy Troupe and several other artists. We also had the pleasure of bringing several lecture series on Gita conducted by Swami Dayananda Saraswati over the last three years and a lecture on Hinduism by Jagadguru Mathe Mahadevi.

Almost immediately after the founding of the Hindu Cultural Center the search was on for a suitable place for a permanent home. We did not have to wait too long. The divine hands were already at work and an ideal land of 13 acres with gentle sloping hills and a magnificent view was purchased on Old Hickory Blvd. near Interstate 40 West in the Bellevue area. On Ganesha Chaturthi Day, on August 22, 1982, the ground breaking ceremony for Hindu Temple was performed on the temple site by Sri. Iyengar, chief priest at Pittsburgh Venkateshwara Temple. This grand event was witnessed by several hundred devotees from Middle Tennessee and several members in the community took the pledge to support the cause. We were fortunate to have one of the leading temple architects from India, Muthiah Stapathi, visit us in 1983. A survey of the membership revealed that the overwhelming majority of the people wanted three dieties installed in the temple—Ganesha, Shiva and Vishnu and it was decided to have Lord Ganesha as the main diety in accordance with the wishes of the community. Muthiah Stapathi has incorporated these wishes in his plans. In January 1984 it was decided to have the temple project completed in several phases, the details of which are provided elsewhere in this brochure. On Ganesha Chaturti Day in 1984 construction for the first phase of the project began.

We do not view this temple project as an effort that is to be started and completed by us alone. It is a continuously evolving thing and constant nurturing by all the devotees is essential. It has to grow along with the community, meetings its various needs as they arise. We may only take credit for starting such a monumental task but it is up to our future generations to see that it functions as an active institution. To this end, it is up to us to inform and encourage the younger generations to actively participate in the various activities of the temple and be a part of history in the making. We have had some setbacks but they have only made us more determined. We have left all our trials and tribulations in the hands of Lord Vigneshwara and we are hopeful that His blessings will be upon us in all our efforts.

THE LONG ROAD—BOTH BEHIND AND AHEAD

We have come a long way since the opening of the Sri Ganesha Temple in Nashville six years ago. Instead of a small building, we now have a fully-functioning temple and an organization which can support it. There is much that is left to be done, just as there is much to maintain; but before looking at where we are going, it is important to review the recent past.

The Hindu Cultural Center was a very different organization six years ago. With the opening of the Sri Ganesha Temple we found ourselves, a bunch of amateurs, trying to manage the complexities of running a religious institution. Though we had a very small building, the demands were anything but small. From the start there was a priest to take care of, bills to pay, a building to maintain, and grounds to keep. As the number of visiting devotees increased, additional responsibilities of numerous receipts, a growing mailing list, increased needs for supplies, and other welcome signs of a growing following made life ever more complicated at the Temple. From the confusion of these early days an order has now evolved which allows the Sri Ganesha Temple to have two priests, one of whom is always available to perform services throughout the community while the other maintains the steady schedule of services that devotees have come to depend on.

This dependability was not easy to achieve. The HCC was fortunate to have the most important asset for any non-profit organization: a core of dedicated volunteers. They have devoted many hours each week, every week, to the running of the Temple. Organized into several committees, different groups have specific responsibilities, each essential to the smooth running of the institution. Whether it is the maintenance of the books, the purchasing of supplies, the vacuuming of the hall, or the transportation of the priests, they all have helped both with their time and often their own money with the long and short term needs of the Temple, allowing most of the donated funds to be saved for the building of the new Temple complex. These people know who they are, and for them the rewards have been intangible; their lives have been changed by the Temple and most would say it was for the better.

It is thus that the Hindu Cultural Center has embarked upon this even larger project. With the experience acquired from the smaller temple we are quite confident we will be able to expand upon the religious services offered by the HCC in the past. However, in order for the investment in the new structure to be justified, the Temple needs to do more. It should not only be a religious but also a cultural center, providing a place for visiting artists and opportunities for learning about all aspects of our culture. We have started on this path, but much work remains.

As a regional Hindu center, it should provide solace and comfort to devotees for years to come. This institution should take an active role in various social causes by working closely with other religious and civic groups. Family support services, financial assistance for needy students, and the establishment of retirement homes are just a few of the things that are planned for the future.

Leadership is necessary to achieve these goals, and for the future that leadership must come from the Youth of our community—a role they are already starting to accept.

None of this is possible without financial security. The HCC currently has a $1.5 million debt which will have to be serviced for some time to come. After that is paid off, we need to establish an endowment fund which will provide for the daily running of the Temple. However, the Center cannot run without the other half of the equation: volunteers who will give their time and abilities willingly. The Hindu Cultural Center is for our entire community, and it needs all of our support to keep it strong into the next century and beyond.

May the blessings of Lord Ganesha be with us all.

SUNDAY SCHOOL

It's 10:30 A.M. on Sunday at the Sri Ganesha Temple. Services haven't started yet, but some of the Temple's most active devotees are already there, in the auditorium on the first floor, discussing Hindu philosophy and chanting prayers. They come every Sunday, as only the most devoted do, but this is a group with distinctly unique needs and demands; they seek not only to *learn* but to *understand* the rituals and philosophies of Hinduism. And they love a good story.

They are the Temple's youngest devotees—some as young as 6 years old—but they are also the most curious, the most eager of the Sunday crowd. And it's becoming increasingly obvious that their enthusiasm is spreading fast. "I get 100% participation," says Radha Babu, who along with Asha Rao teaches a group of 30 to 40 younger children, ages 6–10, each week. "They have such a thirst to learn." She says that teaching is fulfilling and energizing, and that she learns as much from her students as they learn from her. "I know that what I'm doing will live on for generations—I'm planting seeds," Mrs. Babu says. "The amount of satisfaction I get and the amount of education the kids get is priceless."

The Sunday School classes follow the 10-year Vedic Heritage Teaching Program, developed by the Arsha Vidya Gurukulum in Pennsylvania. Teachers use three volumes of workbooks, each of which match a specific age group. Last year, the Temple's junior class learned introductory prayers and the Bhagavatha Purana; this year Mrs. Babu and Mrs. Rao are guiding them through daily prayers and the Ramayana. The 10-year curriculum includes: Hindu samskaras, prayers to deities, practice of values, smrti literature, historical India, introduction to sruti and Vedic dharma, a comparative study of values and contemporary teen issues.

Mrs. Babu says she believes attendance at these classes will continue to grow. And, while many young second-generation Indians initially go to the Temple because their parents force them to, the converse is true as well. These Sunday School students require transportation to and from the Temple, and many parents who drive their children end up staying to attend services. "The kids are drawing their parents in," Mrs. Babu says.

But developing religious faith in children is a complicated process, says Vedavyas Biliyar, who teaches the older class of Sunday School students, ages 12 to 18. "Encouraging faith is an important first step and bringing that faith into the Temple is the second step," he says. "It's a complicated process because it depends on the parents' lifestyles. Children learn by how we (as parents) do things on a day-to-day basis."

However, Sunday School alone doesn't completely define the experience of second-generation Indians with Hinduism or with the Temple. Roopa Srinivas, 14, says that religion plays a major role in her life—she even recites prayers on the way to school each morning. She attends services each Sunday and volunteers much of her time to the Temple, yet she doesn't always make it to the Sunday School class.

The classes for the younger group and the older group are held simultaneously each week, but attendance among the older children is smaller—12 to 15 students usually show up. High schoolers are forced to divide their time between several activities and often don't prioritize visits to the Temple, Dr. Biliyar says.

Among college-age students, attendance can become even weaker. "Once we go to college and we're no longer with our families, there's no longer the push to go," says Niranjan Bhat, 22. "I didn't go (to a temple) much when I was at Harvard. I didn't feel a connection to the community there." Niranjan and Sudhir Channabasappa, 25, are determined to reverse that trend in Nashville, however. Starting in January, they're hoping to bring in a series of guest lecturers to speak with an advanced class of undergraduate and graduate students at the Temple on Sundays. "Parents don't always want to explain the 'why' of certain holidays and actions. Teaching to high school and elementary kids can become didactic. As adults we can learn it on a different level," Niranjan says.

Like others, Sudhir says he first went to the Temple because his parents forced him to go. Today, however, going to the Temple is so important to him that he considers it a part of his identity. "I enjoy going there, so there's no one making me go. It allows me to learn the religion and find a sense of peace. This temple will always be an important part of my life," he says. "I feel a sense of pride when my friends say this is one of the neatest buildings in Nashville."

HINDUISM IN THE PUBLIC REALM: *HINDUISM TODAY* ON CHRISTIANITY AND CLONING (1996)

The term *Hinduism* refers to diverse movements with no single institutional center, so when it comes time to speak publicly on controversial policy issues it is not always clear who, if anyone, should speak for the Hindu tradition. One periodical, *Hinduism Today*, has assumed that role for itself. Founded in 1979 by Satguru Sivaya Subramuniyaswami (Gurudeva), who is a teacher in the Nandinatha lineage in Sri Lanka and spiritual head of a Hawaiian monastic community, *Hinduism Today* "was created to strengthen all the many diverse expressions of Hindu spirituality, to give them a single, combined voice." Of course, not all Hindus feel represented by the magazine, which is published in seven editions around the world (including a North American one). Still it has offered a Hindu viewpoint on many current issues, entering into conversation with non-Hindus in the public sphere. In "A Contrast of Convictions," the editor collaborates with counterparts at *Christianity Today* to provide a one-page summary of differences between the two religions. In "Playing God?," the magazine confronts a contemporary moral problem, human cloning. In this case, it was asked to speak for Hinduism. In March 1997, shortly after the cloning of a sheep in England focused worldwide attention on the issue, President Bill Clinton's National Bioethics Advisory Committee telephoned the magazine to ask for Hindu views on the subject. The editor, "honored and stunned" by the request from the high-profile presidential committee, surveyed Hindu teachers on the topic. In a 1997 issue *Hinduism Today* published this summary reflection.

A CONTRAST OF CONVICTIONS

Hinduism Today and Christianity Today Craft a Point-Counterpoint

Back in 1993, our editors were contacted by *Christianity Today* magazine to be interviewed for a major story called *Hindus in America.* Thus began a series of dialogs that added to their article crucial and often corrective insights to dispel common myths and misinformation about the world's oldest religion. Perhaps most significantly, they agreed to publish our own nine fundamental Hindu beliefs. The editors of *Christianity Today* counter-composed nine parallel Christian convictions, written just before press time in a series of grueling sessions by the best theologians they could assemble. The resulting point-counterpoint—whose brevity is both its strength and its weakness—summarizes the cosmic perspective of two of the world's largest faiths.

HINDUS BELIEVE IN THE DIVINITY OF THE Vedas, the world's most ancient scripture, and venerate the *Agamas* as equally revealed. These primordial hymns are God's word and the bedrock of Sanátana Dharma, the eternal religion which has neither beginning nor end.	1	CHRISTIANS BELIEVE THAT THE BIBLE IS the uniquely inspired and fully trustworthy word of God. It is the final authority for Christians in matters of belief and practice, and though it was written long ago, it continues to speak to believers today.
HINDUS BELIEVE IN A ONE, ALL-PERVASIVE supreme being who is both immanent and transcendent, both Creator and Unmanifest Reality.	2	CHRISTIANS BELIEVE IN ONE GOD IN THREE persons. He is distinct from his creation, yet intimately involved with it as its sustainer and redeemer.

"A Contrast of Convictions: *Hinduism Today* and *Christianity Today* Craft a Point-Counterpoint," *Hinduism Today*, December 1996, 32; "Playing God?," *Hinduism Today*, June 1997, 22. Reprinted by permission of *Hinduism Today*.

HINDUS BELIEVE THAT THE universe undergoes endless cycles of creation, preservation and dissolution.

3 CHRISTIANS BELIEVE THAT THE WORLD WAS created once by the divine will, was corrupted by sin, yet under God's providence moves toward final perfection.

HINDUS BELIEVE IN KARMA, THE LAW of cause and effect by which each individual creates his own destiny by his thoughts, words and deeds.

4 CHRISTIANS BELIEVE THAT, THROUGH God's grace and favor, lost sinners are rescued from the guilt, power and eternal consequences of their evil thoughts, words and deeds.

HINDUS BELIEVE THAT THE SOUL reincarnates, evolving through many births until all karmas have been resolved, and *moksha*, spiritual knowledge and liberation from the cycle of rebirth, is attained. Not a single soul will be eternally deprived of this destiny.

5 CHRISTIANS BELIEVE THAT IT IS APPOINTED for human beings to die once and after that face judgment. In Adam's sin, the human race was spiritually alienated from God, and that those who are called by God and respond to his grace will have eternal life. Those who persist in rebellion will be lost eternally.

HINDUS BELIEVE THAT DIVINE BEINGS EXIST in unseen worlds and that temple worship, rituals, sacraments as well as personal devotionals create a communion with these *devas* and Gods.

6 CHRISTIANS BELIEVE THAT SPIRIT beings inhabit the universe, some good and some evil, but worship is due to God alone.

HINDUS BELIEVE THAT A SPIRITUALLY awakened master, or *satguru*, is essential to know the Transcendent Absolute, as are personal discipline, good conduct, purification, pilgrimage, self-inquiry and meditation.

7 CHRISTIANS BELIEVE THAT GOD HAS GIVEN us a clear revelation of Himself in Jesus and the sacred Scriptures. He has empowered by his Spirit prophets, apostles, evangelists, and pastors who are teachers charged to guide us into faith and holiness in accordance with his Word.

HINDUS BELIEVE THAT ALL LIFE IS sacred, to be loved and revered, and therefore practice *ahimsa*, "noninjury."

8 CHRISTIANS BELIEVE THAT LIFE IS TO BE highly esteemed but that it must be subordinated in the service of Biblical love and justice.

HINDUS BELIEVE THAT NO PARTICULAR religion teaches the only way to salvation above all others, but that all

9 CHRISTIANS BELIEVE THAT JESUS IS GOD incarnate and, therefore, the only sure path to salvation. Many religions

genuine religious paths are facets of God's Pure Love and Light, deserving tolerance and understanding.

may offer ethical and spiritual insights, but only Jesus is the Way, the Truth and the Life.

PLAYING GOD?

In July 1996 a Blackface ewe gave birth to lamb 6LL3, an outwardly normal baby sheep, at the Roslin Institute's genetic research facility in Edinburgh, Scotland. In the February 27, 1997, issue of *Nature* magazine, Roslin's chief researcher Dr. Ian Wilmut stunned the world when he announced that 6LL3 (now named Dolly, after American country singer Dolly Parton) was the first successfully cloned mammal. Wilmut was summoned to the British Parliament, and later to the U.S. Senate. He informed alarmed committees on both sides of the Atlantic that he foresaw no particular obstacle to the cloning of humans—the accomplishment coupled with advancements in genetic engineering could alter the future of the human race in a manner not seen since the discovery of atomic energy. . . .

The prospects get scary when cloning is combined with genetic engineering (the actual intent of Wilmut's research with sheep). DNA could be taken from a person, customized with genes for disease resistance, intelligence, beauty and then grown into a baby. The perfect musician or the creative genius could be ordered up by calculating parents to be—as could be the perfect unquestioning soldier or murderous sociopath by the less altruistic.

The territory is so new that world leaders are in an ethical void on what to think about it. A host of questions are suddenly being addressed by scientists, politicians, philosophers, and religious leaders. After Wilmut's announcement, U.S. President Clinton forbade any federal research on human cloning pending formal review by the U.S. National Bioethics Commission—a significant part of which is to solicit opinions of the world's religions.

Most religious leaders, including Hindu, are opposed to cloning humans. Many consider it "playing God" and therefore wrong. Others question the necessity for another way to make people at a time when we have too many people. Putting these opinions in perspective requires a certain amount of technical background as to exactly what cloning is, how it was accomplished and where genetic engineering fits in. . . .

Human Cloning

1. A single cell is taken from the donor woman (or man), for cloning.
2. The donor cell is starved into a state of quiescence in which it stops reproducing on its own.
3. An unfertilized egg is taken from a second woman and the genetic nucleus is removed.
4. The enucleated egg is kept alive in a test tube.
5. After 36 hours (for sheep; humans may differ), the donor cell is fused into the egg with an electrical spark which also starts cell division.

According to Hinduism, an incarnating soul enters at this point, drawn by its karma and by the consciousness and karma of those involved in the conception.

6. For six days (in sheep) the developing egg is kept alive in a test tube.
7. If the embryo is growing normally, it is implanted in a surrogate mother who carries it to term and gives birth normally.
8. The offspring is an exact genetic duplicate of the cell donor, and has no genetic relationship to the egg donor or to the surrogate birth mother.

Cloning from the Hindu View

Cloning in India took a wrong turn about 6,000 years ago with the creation of Raktabija ("blood drop"), a mythological demon who appears in the Markandeya Purana. Another of him sprung from every drop of his blood spilled on the battlefield. Only with great effort were he and his clones finally destroyed. More benign results were obtained by dozens of other methods of asexual procreation found in the vast scope of Hindu literature. For example, Lord Ganesha was created from the skin of His Mother and Lord Murugan by a spark from Siva's third eye. Kunti conceived her sons, the Pandavas, by means of mantras (sacred formulas) offered to the Gods.

Even so, there is really no easily found scripture directly addressing the practice of cloning, just as there was no need for a Federal Aviation Agency before airplanes were invented and started to crash. In Hinduism and the other religions, endorsements or objections to cloning are necessarily based upon induction and extrapolation.

Hindus analyze cloning in Hindu terms—karma, reincarnation, ahimsa, all-pervasive Divinity and soul's evolving nature—along with the benefit or danger to society as a whole. In a survey of seven Hindu leaders conducted by *Hinduism Today*, all called strongly for strict regulation. Acharyas and swamis were unanimous that scientists were in no way creating a soul by cloning, in contrast to the Abrahamic belief that the soul is created at conception. In the Hindu view, the God-created soul inhabits the body, but is not the body. The question arises: what kind of soul would take birth in a body created so uniquely. At a gathering of the American Association of Vedic Astrologers (AAVA) Chakrapani Ullal said religious sanctification of marriage helps insure the birth of high souls. Lacking such sanctification, he warned, "people born through cloning will be fraught with problems." Speaking from the view of ayurveda (India's traditional medicine), Dr. David Frawley (Vamadeva Shastri) pondered, "You are trying to have birth without prana [vital life energy]. What kind of creature is going to be created without direct participation of the pranic force?" Mrs. Ullal asked how a normal being could be born from a "conception" devoid of love. The 2000-year-old Tirumantiram supports their wisdom, describing how each embodied soul is influenced by the consciousness and energies of the parents before and during coitus. Without these pranas, life would certainly be different though not all think negatively. Perhaps a highly evolved soul would choose to take such a passionless birth. Dr. M. M. Sankhdher, ex-professor of political science, University of

Delhi, offered: "To a Hindu, a cloned human being, when this reality material-izes, would be another manifestation of a new species as an outcome of the Divine Will."

The research itself violates the tenets of *ahimsa*, non-injuriousness. Several of Wilmut's sheep, for example, were killed and autopsied by the researchers after their fetuses died. In ayurveda, research on animals is allowed only to benefit the animal. If human cloning is permitted, deformed fetuses will certainly be aborted as part of the larger process. Dr. Dennis Harness, of the AAVA, warned of po-tential long-term problems, "Cloning involves altering energies on a very subtle level where we don't even realize what we are doing."

Bhairava Sundaram Sivacharya, who belongs to an ancient lineage of Saivite priests, said that Hinduism has always welcomed new discoveries. He asks, "A soul is born with a parabdha karma [the karma it is destined to ex-perience in this life]. When it lives through the parabdha karma, that body will die. Now if we take a cell from that body and make another man, do the parab-dha karmas of the first man continue in some way? If so, the original soul can-not get released into the next world upon the body's death. It will bring a great confusion."

Several prominent swami leaders questioned the need for cloning in an over-populated world, where abortion of unwanted children occurs daily. Rev. Swami Satchidananda warned about unanticipated consequences, the problem of "let-ting the genie out of the bottle" and not being able to get it back in. Many warned cloning would result in the same havoc to society and the environment as have so many other scientific inventions of the last few centuries.

In a joint statement, Dr. Ajit Ram Verma, ex-director of the National Physical Laboratory of New Delhi, and Dr. I. S. Kothari, ex-professor of physics, Delhi University, said, "In an intelligent society, cloning could be used for the better-ment of the society. But today decisions may be based on considerations other than society's good. Therefore, research in the field should be carefully con-trolled." A poll of the U.S. Hindu Students Council concluded, "Hindus believe that man is neither superior nor inferior, but simply a part of nature as are the trees, animals, and so on. By manipulating nature, we may be upsetting natural and spiritual balances." . . .

Hindu leaders are divided on whether possible benefits outweigh the risks. Some urge an outright ban; others call for close supervision. Mata Amritanandamayi said, "Historically, it is impossible and unwise to interfere with the advance of sci-ence." She and others call for a forum of "spiritually aware and responsible people" to advise industry and governments on cloning. No one polled was willing to leave the regulation to science or business alone, recognizing that the consequences im-pact all of humanity.

Other Religions React

Jewish Rabbi Gershon Gewirtz said, "I think there are too many things we just don't understand. In my view, the risk is just too great." Roman Catholic Cardinal John O'Connor said, "Contrary to the right of every human person to be conceived and born within marriage and from marriage, the clone is reduced to the level of a product made rather than a person begotten." The Navajo Indians of the Southwest U.S. hold the sheep in particular sacredness, and complained that the scientist desecrated the animal. Muslim scholar Abdulaziz Aachedina, a medical ethicist at the University of Virginia, worries about the long-term implications of separating reproduction from human relationship. "Imagine a world with no need for marriage," he invites.

Governments Act

Malaysia and France reacted by banning human cloning. In February [1997] the U.S. Senate considered a permanent ban, and the research for this article will be part of future deliberation. Senator Tom Harkin protested any ban, defending the impossibility of limiting human knowledge. "What nonsense. What utter, utter nonsense to think that somehow we are going to hold up our hand and say, 'Stop,'" he told his colleagues.

Cloning will not stop. It has been done for a sheep. In a few years it will be done with humans. Cloning may become as easy as ordinary reproduction, with profound consequences for human society. For this reason, and remembering we represent one-sixth of the human family, all Hindus should take a serious interest in this issue.

JAIN SOCIETY OF METROPOLITAN CHICAGO, AN ANCIENT HERITAGE AND A PROMISING FUTURE (1993)

Jainism, an Indian religion probably founded by Vardhamana Mahavira in the sixth century BCE, is followed by tens of thousands of Indian immigrants in America. The editor of the *Jain Directory* estimates that 75,000 Jains live in North America. Jains in New England, for example, established the Jain Center of Greater Boston in 1973, and they moved into their first building, a former Protestant church, eight years later. Jains in the Midwest formed the Jain Society of Metropolitan Chicago in 1970, and when their temple opened for use in 1993 it was the largest Jain center in North America. That Indian-style complex in Bartlett, a western suburb of Chicago, serves more than 500 families, or approximately 2,000 Jains. To commemorate the center's opening, the group published a *Souvenir Booklet*. One brief article in that booklet, "A Promising Future," portrays this ancient religion, and especially its core teaching on *ahimsa* (nonviolence), as well suited to present problems and future needs. Another article reminds midwestern Jains of the center's history and functions, exhorting members to express their gratitude by supporting the recently completed construction project.

"A Promising Future" and "It Is Time We Return Our Gratitude to Jainism," in Jain Society of Metropolitan Chicago, *Souvenir Booklet*, June 1993, 8. Reprinted by permission of the Jain Society of Metropolitan Chicago.

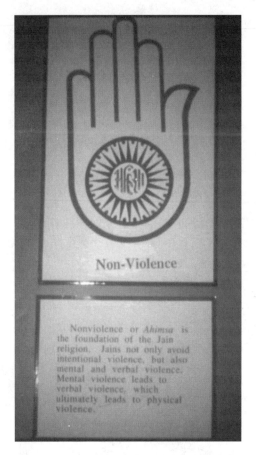

Jain display at a convention of the Federation of Jain Associations in North America (JAINA), Pittsburgh, Pennsylvania, 1993. The word *ahimsa* (noninjury or nonviolence) appears in the center of the palm. Courtesy of The Pluralism Project, Harvard University.

A PROMISING FUTURE

In a world rampant with conflicts and disenchantment the effect of the Jain doctrine is to fill the mind with a glad certainty about the future. The Jain doctrine and its concepts relate amazingly to modern science and many of its revolutionary theories. The Jain scriptures emphasize the "prevalence of knowledge over compassion" (Desa-caikalika-sutra, verse 10, chapter 4). This is consistent with one of the greatest scientists of this century, Albert Einstein, who maintained, "Religion without science is blind. Science without religion is lame." One of Einstein's most revolutionary ideas about the interchangeability of matter and energy has been a concept known to Jainism for centuries. The word "Pudgala" is used to describe matter. Explicit in this word is the fact that matter and energy are two sides of the same coin.

Similarly, Jainism inherently addresses the problems of the modern day world. Jainism puts the greatest emphasis on "Ahimsa," usually translated as "non-violence." "Himsa" means "harm," the prefix "a," is a negative. So Ahimsa is the very negation of harm, it precludes violence not only in action but also in thought intention. It is applicable to individuals as well as to nations.

The effect of the adoption of the vow of "Ahimsa" by the world in general, will bring to an end the unholy rivalries, unrighteous wars and all forms of racial and religious prejudice.

So, Jainism gives hope, it teaches the negation of harm. It teaches non-acquisitiveness too. The fifth of the five vows of the Jains is to avoid perpetual striving for material possessions beyond a reasonable sufficiency. Today's society measures success in possessions, the Jains are by no means exempt from this. We are not going to change society overnight. But the quest for possessions must not be carried on to the extent of depriving others of their necessities. Perhaps non-acquisitiveness is linked with generosity, and charity is another virtue in the eyes of Jains.

So Jainism has a lot to offer in the light of the problems of the world—a heritage to be re-explored and revived in our lives.

IT IS TIME WE RETURN OUR GRATITUDE TO JAINISM

Jain Society of Metropolitan Chicago, established in 1970, has been doing significant work to promote and perpetuate Jainism. Since its inception, it has grown to include more than 500 families actively participating in religious and social work. We celebrate all major religious festivals and have been inviting scholars and sages to address our people from time to time. Our Paryushana celebrations have been occasions for attracting people from distant places. For over a year, we have been publishing a monthly magazine called *Jain Darshan*. The magazine has been well received.

The biggest Jain Center in the North American Continent is open for its use from May 23rd, 1993. Major construction work has been already completed. The center is located on a spacious 15 acre lot in Bartlett, a western suburb of Chicago. It includes a temple and a community hall covering 30,000 square feet of constructed area. The following are the highlights of the Center:

- Jain Temple with Shwetambar and Digambar idols
- Shrimad Rajchandra Center
- Sthanak for meditation and other religious activities
- Pathshala for teaching Jainism to our children
- Library for studying Jainism in depth
- Community hall for social and religious functions
- Dining hall
- Youth activity center

With your help, we have the ambition to make this center a place for pilgrimage where rooms can be made available for visitors from outside. Such a comprehensive center, with all its facilities and activities will be one of its kind.

The cost of this project is $2.5 million.

In the Jain religion, construction of temples and contribution to such construction has been treated as the most meritorious deed. We encourage you to donate to this noble cause generously. By doing so, you will be contributing to the preservation of our heritage and culture which is all so important to us and our future generations in this country.

SIKH RELIGIOUS SOCIETY, "THINGS THAT MAKE YOU ASK 'KION'?" (1994)

If American Sikhs still seemed exotic to many of their neighbors, who still confused them with Hindus, by the 1990s they had become a more visible part of the religious landscape in several urban centers. Khalsa Diwan Society of Stockton, California, had built America's first *gurdwara* or temple in 1915. But the post-1965 Indian immigrants have been most active constructing places of worship, for example in Houston, New York, and Los Angeles. In 1981 the Sikh Religious Society of Chicago became the first Asian-Indian immigrants in the area to construct their own building when they occupied a gurdwara in the suburb of Palatine. The Society reports that 500 local Sikhs attend services weekly at the family-oriented gurdwara. As at many immigrant Hindu, Jain, and Buddhist temples, tensions between the generations sometimes emerge there. An anonymous teenager from the Chicago gurdwara speaks for many of her Asian-American contemporaries when she lists the intergenerational differences that make her ask *"kion?"* ("why?"). She is especially irritated by the religiously sanctioned gender roles and the "double standard" she finds among Sikh parents in America.

THINGS THAT MAKE YOU ASK "KION"?

When a child is growing up, he or she is taught certain standards by which he or she is expected to live by. These requirements are largely set by parents who mold their child through the impressions they, themselves, have of the world. But as the child matures, he or she develops a new way of seeing the world and he or she defines his or her relationship to this world by creating a new set of standards or moral ethics by which to live by. During the teenage years, a time of journey from adolescence to young adulthood, many decisions must be made and many dilemmas faced by teenagers. Unfortunately, this process of maturing during adolescence often involves the evolution of differences between our parents generation and ourselves. We find that they just don't understand us and visa versa and along with this lack of understanding comes the inability to communicate. Perhaps in our case, this is due to not only the generational gap but it has more to do with the differences in the cultures we were raised in.

Sikh parents who live in America, today, to a large degree still uphold the "traditional" beliefs and customs taught to them by their parents. And these be-

"Things That Make You Ask 'Kion?,'" *Kesri Pages, 1994*, a publication of the Sikh Religious Society of Chicago, 15–18.

liefs still include double standards in the upbringing of Sikh boys and girls. In our mother's time, girls were taught that they should be quiet and shy. These traits were considered jewels which embellished the young girl and were external signs of a good upbringing in a reputable family. Girls were not supposed to voice their opinions unless it was solicited by her elders. They were supposed to help their mothers with the domestic chores which would prepare them to take up similar tasks in their future husband's home.

The times have changed and although women are given more equality, they are still subjected to the old ingrained ideals of the past. I can remember as a young child being taught that boys can play and go places with their friends on trips, etc., whereas girls should not because the world is unsafe for them to romp about so carelessly. When I asked my parents "Why?," they informed me that parents have to protect their daughters whereas their sons could and should learn to take care of themselves. This role assignment, I later realized, sustained the age old roles where the female must be "protected" and the male must always be the "protector." But isn't today's world just as unsafe for young boys as young girls and if the boys must learn to take care of themselves shouldn't a girl be taught to do the same?

By giving their boys free reign to the world with little restrictions and by enforcing strict restrictions on their girls, parents are facing a dual problem today. The boys are not held accountable for their activities by the parents, who have no knowledge of them, whereas the girls end up resenting their parent's bias on gender grounds. In either case, the teenagers no longer confide in their parents who all the while want what's best for their children.

Many a times, I have heard Sikh parents complain about how distant their teenager is becoming. How that once open child no longer shares her or his little tid-bits with them. But how can they when their parents can not understand the different world their children are living in. Sikh teenagers today are confused and need answers, not lectures or condemnation. They want answers dealing with questions on hair, the opposite sex, peer pressure, and the double standard society holds for girls on behavior and expectations, etc. There has always been silence on these subjects and though many parents won't admit it, they will not speak to their children openly about these subjects, leaving their teenagers to go and find answers from a culture which is not synonymous to their home life. Because the teenagers can not go to their parents for answers they often end up hiding things from them, which eventually leads to distrust from the parents and an unhealthy relationship between parent and child. Believe me, many children just do not confide in their parents because they know their parents won't try to understand. Of course, this depiction may not be true of every household but a great many families face these problems without realizing it.

The problem of being teenagers arises mainly because this period of growing up is when young people facing puberty are trying desperately to find their identity in their own world. This identity is contingent upon the society that the child lives in and the acceptance gained by conforming to certain norms of that society. Whether that be piercing one's ear if you are a boy or piercing one's nose if you are a girl or visa versa. I can remember seeing my parent's pictures of their teenager years. They were decked out in the latest fashions, things which they now condemn. While my mother was trying out the beehive hair do, my father was wearing tight "beatle" pants, and I, in my teenage years, am trying out what the norms are in my peer group. Luckily, my friends are not into some of the crazy "in" things that many teenagers are into these days but regardless my parents went through the same things that any teenager goes through. They just did it in India, where trends still conformed with the Indian culture for the most part.

The Sikh teenagers must deal with trends that have nothing to do with their home culture but rather with the culture that they must be a part of on a daily basis. But we are not talking of trends as much as the need all humans, especially teenagers, have for conforming or fitting in somewhere. This is the issue that must be reckoned with and no matter how good a child's upbringing is every teenager faces this dilemma to some degree. Perhaps rather than scolding or chastising their children Sikh parents should remember that the process of growing up is difficult in itself and that this is America and the culture their children belong to is one of two distinct worlds. Of course, I am not condoning drugs, alcohol, and such things but I am saying that issues such as dating, should be reevaluated and dealt with on a level that was not necessary before hand. And above all I am asking that all Sikh parents should deal with their American Sikh teenagers with an understanding that certain dimensions of their familial lives have changed with the change of country and culture. Please be patient and listen to your child and try as hard as you can to understand before you disagree.

CHAPTER **17**

Buddhist Immigrants

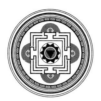

THE BUDDHA'S BIRTHDAY IN A
VIETNAMESE-AMERICAN TEMPLE (1986)

The Most Venerable Dr. Thich Thien An, who trained in the Lieu Quan tradition (the Vietnamese equivalent of the Rinzai Zen school) was the first teacher of Vietnamese Buddhism in America. He arrived in the United States in 1966 to serve as a visiting professor at the University of California at Los Angeles and decided to stay. Initially he guided American students at the International Buddhist Meditation Center, which he founded in 1970. But after the fall of Saigon on 30 April 1975, when hundreds of thousands of Vietnamese fled their homeland, he reached out to the Buddhist refugees. He formed the Vietnamese United Buddhist Churches in 1975 and established Chua Vietnam (or Vietnam Temple) in Los Angeles the following year. Between 60 and 80 percent of the 593,213 Vietnamese in the United States in 1990 were Buddhists, and Chua Vietnam, with approximately 5,000 participants, had become one of the country's largest and most important Vietnamese Buddhist centers. In the first entry below, excerpted from a 1980 speech, Thich Thien An discusses how to transplant Buddhism in American soil. After Thich Thien An's death in 1981, the Most Venerable Dr. Thich Man Giac took over as leader of Chua Vietnam. Since then he has balanced competing concerns—to "adapt to American customs," to transmit Vietnamese culture, and "to improve the current situation in Vietnam." Those concerns are evident in the second entry, which describes the 1986 commemoration of Buddha's birthday. Along with Tet, or the New Year's celebration, the Buddha's birthday is one of the temple's two most important annual rituals.

Thich Thien An, "Three Month Training Period: An Adaptation of An-Cu to American Training," in *The Presence of Vietnamese Buddhists in America* (Los Angeles: Vietnamese Buddhist Temple, 1981), 5; Rick Fields, "Los Angeles Vesak Day," *Vietnamese Buddhist Temple in Los Angeles*, undated and unpaginated pamphlet, published by Chua Vietnam, Los Angeles, California. Reprinted by permission of the Vietnamese United Buddhist Churches.

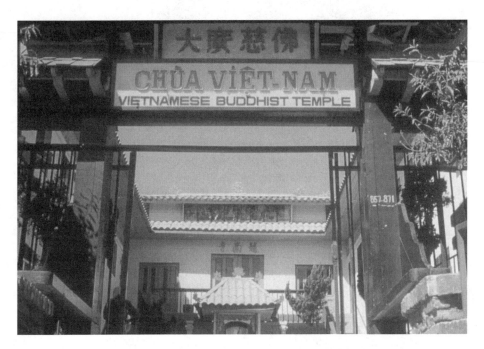

Chua Viet-nam, Los Angeles, California. Courtesy The Pluralism Project, Harvard University.

BUDDHIST ACCULTURATION

As Buddhism moves into new lands, the Buddhist teachers who teach in the new cultures must pass on the essence of Buddhism in a way appropriate to the new culture. While they need to teach the depth of Buddhism, they must strip away from it the attached cultural ideas and practices from their own land which are inappropriate for the new society and slowly, carefully and methodically try to adapt it to suit the new culture.

This adaptation does not mean that the Buddhism passed on to the new land is changed or modified itself, but that an examination to find what is truly Buddhist is required. For this essence, this heart of wisdom, is what must be transmitted. Slowly Buddhism will develop traditions and practices appropriate to the new country, as Buddhism has done for 25 centuries as it spread from India into all of Asia.

Buddhism is quite new in the United States and many different Asian forms of it are being practiced. This "Asian" Buddhism will slowly become an "American" Buddhism, and we can help the process of acculturation if we use *upaya*, skillful means, to help in spreading Buddhist practice appropriate for Twentieth Century America.

LOS ANGELES VESAK DAY

Vietnamese Buddhists celebrate two major holidays every year, Tet—which is the Chinese New Year—and the Buddha's birthday. Tet usually falls sometime in mid-February. It is a night-time celebration, and during it the temple courtyard is filled with people and fireworks. The fireworks are such an important part of the Tet celebration that each year the temple receives special dispensation from the Los Angeles fire department.

The Buddha's birthday, however, is a Spring day-time celebration, which is observed each year on the Sunday closest to the full moon day of May. It is a holiday that is observed by Buddhists throughout the world, though the exact date may differ somewhat from country to country. It is a festive holiday, a time for children and their parents, to come together with the whole Buddhist community. There are always flowers everywhere on the Buddha's birthday.

On this particular Sunday in May, 1986, the 2530th year since the birth of the Buddha, the Buddha's birthday is being celebrated in a big way. The Vietnamese Buddhist community seems to have the sense that they have come through, they have once more survived a difficult time against great odds, and though the future is uncertain and even perilous, there is much to be thankful for.

A large green parachute has been spread over the central courtyard, from roof to roof. Beneath its soft, nearly translucent shelter, the Vietnamese community and assorted guests and friends are gathered. There is a large wooden platform in front, and the Buddhist flag, with its orange and white and red and yellow and blue stripes is strung along the rooftops, and in the hands of nearly everyone there. It is a bright, happy sort of flag—the same flag that Diem had forbidden the Buddhists of Hue to fly back in 1963.

The image of the Buddha stands painted on an immense backdrop behind the platform. "All Buddhists Happily Celebrate Buddha's Birthday," it says, in English and Vietnamese. It is the traditional image used for today's celebration. The Buddha is standing, with one hand pointing up, towards the sky, and the other pointing down, towards the earth, and looking straight ahead. This posture refers back to the tradition that says that when the Buddha was born, he took seven steps in the four directions, and then proclaimed, "In heaven and earth, I am the only one."

This year's celebration coincides with the U.N. International Year of Peace, and there is a speaker from the Los Angeles chapter of the Friends of the U.N., as well as other dignitaries, representatives of the mayor's and Governor's offices and Buddhist monks and nuns from many of the other Buddhist traditions now making their homes in Los Angeles and the United States. There are also a fair number of American Buddhists representing newer Buddhist groups.

There is no question that this is a Vietnamese celebration, but there is also no question that many others are included in it. This is in no small part due to the Ven. Thich Man Giac's vision realization that in order for Buddhism to flourish in America, whether among Vietnamese or Americans or Vietnamese Americans for that matter, it must adapt to its new home. "The customs of Americans are different than

Asians," he says. "If we want Buddhism to develop and grow in the U.S., we must adapt to American customs."

Whatever the future may hold, today is a day to celebrate the continuing strength and resilience of the Vietnamese Buddhist's traditions. It is like any Sunday at the temple, only more so. The women have been cooking for days, flowers and flags and balloons with the legend, "Happy Birthday," are everywhere, particularly clutched in the small hands of toddlers bouncing around under the watchful eyes of slightly older brothers and sisters.

There are speeches, and words of greetings from the speakers on the platform, and there is chanting in praise of the Buddha in many of the languages of Buddhism, in Vietnamese, and Korean, and Japanese, and Pali, and Sanskrit, and, also, in English. The President of the Organizing Committee of the celebration, a scholarly layman, wearing a round black Confucian hat that seems all brim, sums it all up, when he says, "What happened in Vietnam—the misery and sorrow have no end—but I want to make a solemn vow for peace and freedom in Vietnam." A number of pigeons are released, as is the custom on many Buddhist holidays, and then some people file past a small figure of the Buddha, with hands pointing up and down, and pour sweet milk over the figure with a small ladle, which is the custom on this particular day.

Berendo Street has been closed, or at least slowed down by two motorcycle police, and the main concern is how to start and maneuver the float that is the centerpiece of the parade. The float has been constructed on top of a pick-up truck, and entirely covers it. The only way to see out is through a few small holes bored in the flower-covered wood panel covering the front of the truck. The whole float is covered with flowers. There is a large pink and white and red and yellow and blue paper heart on one side framed by flowers, and on the other side is the Eight-Spoked Wheel. The spokes are made of flowers, red, orange, pale green, and pink, with blue in the center. On top of the float the Buddha stands, his pointing up and down, with backdrop of India, cool and looking very blue and green and Himalayan cool in the Los Angeles heat. There are live trees on top of the float, too, with beautifully made orange and yellow paper flowers fixed in their leaves. Paper dragons with benevolent toothy smiles guard each side. Someone mentions that the monk in charge of getting the float ready hasn't slept in a month—while someone else waters the flowers, in danger of wilting in heat, with a spray bottle.

Finally, the Buddha's float moves slowly out away from the curb towards the center of the street. There four young girls wearing floral wreaths in their hair, and wearing traditional clothes, climb on top, and take positions on the float.

First are two men holding a large banner that reads: "950 Million Buddhists All Over the World Happily Celebrate the Buddha's Birthday."

Then come four men, wearing Confucian official black robes, carrying an American flag, the Buddhist flag, the flag of the United Nations, and the yellow and red striped flag of South Vietnam.

Then comes the Venerable Thich Man Giac, Supreme Patriarch of Vietnamese Buddhists in America, wearing a bright yellow robe, a red transparent over-robe, flecked with gold thread, and a high peaked hat. He is followed by four members of the Buddhist youth group, the Long Hoa, bearing a palaquin with a large incense burner. They are followed by more members of the Long Hoa bearing flags from all over the world, the green banners of the Long Hoa, and kids with lots of balloons.

Then a Vietnamese brass band, the players in dark trousers and white shirts.

Then the float with the Buddha and the four little girls moving slowly and carefully, guided by members of the Long Hoa.

Then the oil painting of Quang Duc, the first monk to burn himself, his robes in flame, held aloft on a palaquin by four scouts.

Then the banners, in Vietnamese and English:

"There Is No Religious Freedom in Vietnam."

"Long Live the Sacrificial Spirit of the Venerable Thich Quan Duc."

"Long Live World Buddhism." (in Korean and German)

"Unity Is Strength."

And, finally, "950 Million Buddhists All Over the World Unite With Other Religions to Serve World Peace."

The rear is taken up by a troupe of Dragon Dancers, twisting and swirling inside a two-man dragon costume to drums, cymbals, and gongs.

The parade goes up the street, and pauses before the nun's A-D: Da temple, the College of Oriental Studies, and the International Buddhist Meditation Center. At each place The Venerable Thich Man Giac and the other monks chant and offer incense. At the International Meditation Center they are greeted by a banner. "Government In Vietnam Has to Give Freedom Back to Monks, Nuns, Buddhists, and Prisoners of War."

After circling the block, the parade returns to the temple. There, as on every Sunday, everybody is fed, though today there were so many people that most take their paper plates out to the courtyard or the street below. There are Vietnamese popular songs being sung now, and the kids are playing and the old men and women exchanging gossip. And I don't think that I was the only one who noticed that the doves which had been set free that day had nearly all decided to stay and take refuge in the temple of Chua Vietnam.

THE DALAI LAMA MEETS THE BUDDHIST SANGHA COUNCIL OF SOUTHERN CALIFORNIA (1989)

In the 1980s, as the Buddhist population grew in some urban areas, pan-Buddhist organizations began to form. One of the most important of these, the Buddhist Sangha Council of Southern California, was founded in 1980 to establish "firm lines of communication" among Buddhists, "give aid and support" to Buddhist leaders, act on all matters concerning the Buddhist community, and "engage in ecumenical cooperation with all religious groups." The council membership has altered the usual pattern in Asia by including Buddhist monks, nuns, and ministers from all three major "vehicles" (or branches). Its members represent a wide range of ethnic groups: Burmese, Cambodians, Chinese, European Americans, Japanese, Koreans, Laotians, Sri Lankans,

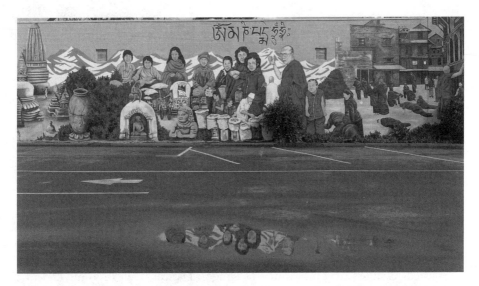

The Fourteenth Dalai Lama pleads for a free Tibet on a mural painted on a pizza restaurant wall in Eugene, Oregon. Copyright © 1998 Herman Krieger. Used by permission.

Thais, Tibetans, and Vietnamese. This entry records an exchange sponsored by the Buddhist Sangha Council on 5 July 1989 at Kwan Um Sa, a Korean Buddhist temple in Los Angeles. Moderated by the Venerable Dr. Karuna Dharma, the influential European-American female teacher who was Thich Tien An's first American student, the event included a speech by one of the founding members of the Council, the Venerable Dr. Havanpola Ratanasara. He posed several questions for their distinguished guest, Tenzin Gyatso (b. 1935), the Fourteenth Dalai Lama, who is the most visible (and probably the most influential) Buddhist leader in the world. One of those questions for the exiled religious and political leader of Tibet solicited advice about how to adapt Buddhism to American society.

CONVERSATION WITH THE DALAI LAMA

In light, then, of some of the topics broached here, I ask Your Holiness to comment upon some of these issues and to suggest methods by which we may help in the adaptation of Buddhism to this new society.

More specifically, we realize that you and many of the Tibetan people left Tibet thirty years ago and have established yourselves in India, Europe, and around the world. You, therefore, have the experience of being an immigrant in a culture radically different from your own, and you have experienced the strains

Changing Faces of Buddhism in America: The Dalai Lama Meets the Buddhist Sangha Council of Southern California, July 5, 1989 (Los Angeles: Buddhist Sangha Council of Southern California, 1989), 12–13, 16–17. Reprinted by permission of the Buddhist Sangha Council of Southern California.

of this movement into a new society. From your own personal experience, what advice can you give us? How can we become full members of a new society without compromising our own individuality? To put the question more obviously, how can we become Americanized, yet hold to the core of Buddhism? How can we keep our children from being seduced by a Western secular culture or its religious traditions?

In the United States there are present all Buddhist traditions. How can we develop an American Buddhism, which will be vital and appropriate to this society and still retain our individual, unique traditions? More specifically, how would you advise the followers of Tibetan tradition to interact with other Buddhist traditions here in the States? And most finally, do you have any suggestions on how to best effect a meaningful inter-faith dialogue? . . .

Response by the Dalai Lama

Spiritual brothers and sisters, I am very happy to have this opportunity to be with you today.

Since you have asked me to say something about some of your questions, I will respond to those important points.

A problem you mentioned are the groups of people who come from different traditions, different cultures and live in a new environment. This is quite complicated. And practically in this respect, I think, the culture, one's own culture, is very important; yet at the same time, some aspects of one's own culture may not be very useful. So as time changes, some aspects of culture ought to change. And then some aspects of a culture may be useful to preserve. If it is something useful in our daily life, that kind of culture can be preserved and is worthwhile to preserve. So now you see, it is important for a Buddhist community who comes from different traditions, different countries, different cultures, to make a distinction between the true aspect of Buddhist teaching and cultural essence. So, I think, it is easier and more worthwhile to preserve the aspects of Buddhist teachings than cultural aspects. For example, that Buddhism which flourished in India and went from there to Tibet and Mongolia and other places changed as it moved into new cultures. Buddhism also went from India to Thailand, Burma, Sri Lanka, China, Korea, Japan, Cambodia, Laos and Vietnam and even to Indonesia. As it moved, its cultural aspects changed. You see, then the same teaching: one Buddhism, but when it meets new places, new environments, new cultures, then Buddhism makes some kind of adjustment with the local culture, the local conditions. This process of assimilation eventually occurred everywhere: China, Burma, Japan, etc., so therefore, eventually, there will appear western Buddhism or American Buddhism or English Buddhism. It really will happen, the same essence yet some change, the cultural aspects will change. So, a Buddhist community coming from another Buddhist country, from Asia, and remaining in this country, with no definite idea to return to their old country, must eventually adapt to the existing environment. Sometimes this need to adapt is difficult to accept, but this is a fact. Now, as far as the Tibetan experience is concerned, you see, we have for the last 30 years kept our basic role and our identification with the determination of the Tibetan people inside of Tibet. We kept the Tibetan community with our own identity, our own culture. I think that comparatively we Tibetan people are quite fortunate, we have some success regarding preserving Tibetan culture, Tibetan identity. But of course there are many factors; our situation with our factors, we kept our essential culture. In different situations, with different factors, adaptations should occur.

DHARMA VIJAYA BUDDHIST VIHARA'S
TENTH ANNIVERSARY (1990)

Thai, Kampuchean, Laotian, Burmese, and Sinhalese immmigrants have consecrated more than 142 Theravada temples in the United States. Dharma Vijaya Buddhist Vihara, a temple (*vihara* means temple or monastery) not far from South Central Los Angeles, is one of at least eight Sinhalese temples in America. A committee of monks and laypersons came together in 1975 to build that place of worship, and in May 1979 they oversaw its official opening. The community split within a year, however. By March 1980 the two monks, Venerable Piyananda and Pannila Ananda, had left to establish a rival temple, Dharma Vijaya. That temple, which moved in 1981 to its present location, a neighborhood of mostly African-American, Korean, and Latino/a residents, was organized by Sinhalese immigrants and is staffed by Sinhalese monks. But it has attracted a wide range of Buddhist followers, Asians and converts alike. The breakaway community celebrated its tenth anniversary in 1990, and in these two entries from its official publication a monk and a layperson reflect on their temple's significance. Venerable Lenagala Sumedha, senior monk at Dharma Vijaya, emphasizes its ethnic diversity. A lay follower, Chintana Tang Lintong, describes the transformative effects of Buddhist practice there.

THE VENERABLE LENAGALA SUMEDHA
(SENIOR MONK AT DHARMA VIJAYA)

There was no Sri Lankan temple in Los Angeles before Ven. Walpola Piyananda arrived here. For the first time he came to L.A. on July 4, 1976, the 200th anniversary of American independence. Now, Los Angeles has an active, vibrant Sri Lankan Buddhist temple which serves Buddhists of all communities.

The outstanding characteristic of Dharma Vijaya Buddhist Vihara is its inclusion of so many different ethnic groups. Sri Lankans (Sinhalese, Tamils, Moslems), Americans, Thai, Laotians, Cambodians, Vietnamese, Burmese, Chinese, Koreans, Japanese, and others: all these participate in our activities without problems.

Our Thai devotees are singular in their dedication to the temple. They never fail to bring all kinds of necessities to the temple, and come often. Sri Lankans

Dharma Vijaya, Tenth Anniversary Issue, 4 (September 1990): 29–30, 31–32. Reprinted by permission of Dharma Vijaya Buddhist Vihara, Los Angeles.

come to enjoy their national traditions while participating in religious ceremonies, and always bring and share food. Many of our Sri Lankan members are professionals, and unhesitatingly offer their services to our other members and friends in time of need. Our abbot, Ven. Piyananda, has made the temple a refuge for many newcomers from Sri Lanka, of whatever ethnic group or religion, often giving them a temporary place to stay and helping them look for jobs and more permanent lodging. Our Laotian refugee members, many of whom have suffered problems in adjusting to Western society, bring all sorts of family problems to the temple rather than going to see, say, a psychiatrist. In fact, Thai, Lao, and Cambodians usually bring family matters to deal with monks, a tradition which they have brought from their country, which enhances the sense of community here.

All our traditional Asian Buddhists have something to learn from the American and other Western members of our Vihara. American Buddhists often dedicate themselves to meditation and really apply their mindfulness to religious activities. When we hold a special ceremony, it is most likely the American members who will sit up all night at a chanting ceremony, not leaning against a wall half-asleep. It is our American members who are most likely to sit in meditation for an hour. Some of our traditional Buddhists could learn from this! Personally, I have found it a pleasure to teach Americans Buddhism and meditation, and have enjoyed their directness of manner and their inquisitiveness. They have made me think even more deeply about many matters, and of course, they have made me think about them in English!

It is relatively rare even in Sri Lanka to see monks gather as they do at this temple. Here every morning at 6 AM you can see all the monks gathering to chant and meditate. And unless some duty carries them to separate destinations, they always eat breakfast and lunch together, and discuss issues that arise like brothers, in total harmony.

Certainly we monks of the Vihara are most grateful to all the devotees of whatever nationality, all of whom contribute to make this temple a lively, friendly, yet serious place where all can take refuge in the Buddha, the Dhamma, and the Sangha, as well as develop the wisdom and compassion necessary for our fulfillment as living beings.

CHINTANA TANG LINTONG (LAY MEMBER)

I have been associated with Dharma Vijaya Buddhist Vihara for ten years. I have felt fortunate to meet many monks and lay persons from around the world. It is a special privilege to associate with Sri Lankan, Thai, Burmese, Japanese, Korean, Chinese, and American monks. Through the monks' kindness, I have learned to be kind and compassionate. It is true that association is very important for our lives. The Buddha mentions to Ven. Ananda that association with good friends is for one's whole life.

Thanks to the temple's invitation, I have had many good teachers and have had a chance to practice what the Buddha taught. The four foundations of mindfulness is one of my favorite practices. I can apply it in my work, at home, at the temple, with friends and children, and wherever I am. I feel it is very practical. The practice of loving-kindness is also very important for me to get through my day, to calm down all my emotions.

I would like to share some of my experiences through the practice of loving-kindness and the four foundations of mindfulness.

1. I was able to be aware of my goal clearly. I learned more about myself. I have gotten to know who I am.
2. My expectations are lower than before.
3. I have learned to reduce greed through the practice of giving my time, energy, effort, and money to support the temple.
4. I am able to live in harmony with others and create only good kamma.
5. I have more chances to meet good people through the temple, and I am able to share my experience.
6. I learn to look within, be introspective, and find happiness within.
7. Finally, I would like to emphasize that mindfulness can clear away boredom and loneliness and bring us to live at the present moment. Happiness can be acquired through our right understanding and right effort. The Buddha has given us the eightfold path as a map to happiness and bliss. We only have to put forth some effort in the direction he pointed out for us. It is so important to learn about ourselves, as only then can we learn about others. The end result is that nobody can fool us easily. We then can acquire what everybody is looking for, which is happiness, health, wealth, fame, popularity, security, and peace of mind.

LATER GENERATIONS OF JAPANESE AMERICANS ON JODO SHINSHU (1990)

Japanese-American Buddhism did not disappear after the internment camps' barbed wire was pulled down and the immigrant generation (Issei) died. The younger members of the second generation (Nisei), most of whom were born between the 1910s and the 1940s, and their children (Sansei), who were born after the horrors of internment, continued to affiliate with the Buddhist Churches of America (BCA) in the post-1965 period. In 1997 the Japanese-dominated BCA reported 16,902 adult members in sixty temples, and thousands more had looser connections to the Jodo Shinshu tradition. Even if the cultural climate grew somewhat less hostile after 1965, later generations of Jodo Shinshu Buddhists have continued the earlier struggles—to deal with pervasive racism and nurture an authentic Buddhism—as this memoir from Kanya Okamoto shows. Okamoto, who was born in 1943 in Gila River, Arizona, one of the many wartime "relocation centers," now serves as a Pure Land priest in Denver. He continues to feel the sting of America's enduring racism, even though, as he puts it in his autobiographical account, "I was born behind barbed wire and machine gun towers on U.S. government property, so I'm more American than most Americans." In the second entry, Kenneth K. Tanaka, a Jodo Shinshu priest and Buddhist scholar, reflects on another aspect of Japanese Buddhists' relation to American culture. To help BCA members respond effectively to the questions posed by their Christian neighbors, Tanaka offers *Guidelines for Talking with Non-Buddhists*. In this pamphlet published by the organization's religious education department, Tanaka takes on some of the usual questions: Is Amida Buddha God? What kind of practice do you do? What happens when you die?

KANYA OKAMOTO

The emperor of Japan died this month, as I'm sure you know. I had many phone calls from people in the press asking me, basically, "How do you feel about the emperor's death?" And I thought about it and, you know, I'm an American. I was born here; I went to school here. A lot of my values are American. And I remember my feelings when President Kennedy died. I was in the United States Navy, a thousand miles out to sea, when I heard this. I was shocked. And my feelings were more intense than when I heard that the emperor of Japan had died.

I'm not American like apple pie. But I'm not Japanese like Japan. Back in '74, when I was studying in Japan, I remember when a Japanese soldier was found on Guam. Since the end of the war he hid out in a cave, continuing to do his reconnaissance or whatever. And, you know, he came back to Japan a hero. I asked my fellow students (they were all born and raised in Japan), I said, "What d'you think about this guy?" And they said, "Oh, that's really great . . . never giving up." And what I flashed on was, "This guy is crazy!" (Laughs.) I woulda given up a long time ago. So I knew I wasn't Japanese like my fellow students.

Here in America I'm always asked, "What are you? Are you Chinese or Japanese?" And when I meet a person who's white, I don't ask them, "Are you French or German?" I don't worry about that. If I meet a person who's black, I don't ask them, "Are you from Ethiopia or South Africa?" I don't ask them that. But I'm always asked, "Are you Japanese or Chinese?" So I am fully aware this is a racist society. And racism is the oldest tradition known to human beings. Racism is taught from father to son, mother to daughter. Wars are fought because of racism, you know. And that's why understanding the evacuation of Japanese Americans is really important, because as a Japanese American born in the camp, I don't want to see it happen again to any other minority.

I was just two years old when we left the camp. My family moved to northern California, and my mother took me to a Methodist church five miles away from where we lived. There was a Buddhist temple in Stockton, California, but it was fifty miles away. So my mom, being very practical, said you're gonna go to

"Kanya Okamoto," in Phillip L. Berman, *The Search for Meaning: Americans Talk About What They Believe and Why* (New York: Ballantine Books, 1990), 424–25, 427. Reprinted by permission of Ballantine Books, a Division of Random House, Inc.; The Reverend Kenneth K. Tanaka, *Guidelines for Talking with Non-Buddhists: Entering the Heart of Jodo-Shinshu Teaching* (San Francisco: Department of Buddhist Education, Buddhist Churches of America, 1992), 1–2, 3–4. Reprinted by permission of the Reverend Kenneth K. Tanaka.

the Methodist church because it's only five miles away. I enjoyed going there. But I had questions. And every time I asked a question, the minister said, "You have to have faith." But I said, "I have questions."

When I was nine, my family moved to Los Angeles, and at that time my mother said, "Well, there's a Buddhist temple there, the Methodists are there, the Protestants over there." And she said, "Choose." So I went to three or four different places and I ended up at the Buddhist temple. The reason was, all the cute Japanese girls were at the temple. (Laughs.) When I was at the Buddhist temple, I was very fortunate that I had an English-speaking priest. And every time that I asked a question, he would say, "Very interesting question." And he would explain his own answer to my question and then ask me a question. Which made me ask another question. So one thing that was very interesting about the Buddhist temple was questions were allowed. . . .

Depending upon what country you live in, that determines a lot of what's right, you know, the laws of your country, the norms and values. So, as Buddhism enters a country, it doesn't change a country; it accepts a country's customs into Buddhism. So Japanese Buddhism is uniquely Japanese. Vietnamese Buddhism is uniquely Vietnamese; Thai Buddhism uniquely Thai. They have their own language, their own customs.

Our school of Buddhism is uniquely Japanese. It's called Jodo Shinshu. And we talk a lot about the three poisons. The three poisons are greed, anger, and stupidity. It's called gas. (Laughs.) I'm fulla gas, man. (Laughs.) So if what I say is based on greed, anger, or stupidity, it's best for me to remain silent. If what I'm going to do is based on greed, anger, or stupidity, I better not do it. Greed, anger, and stupidity are controlled by my ego. But my ego won't let go of them. So there's a problem there, because it's impossible to use my ego to become egoless. (Laughs.) The ego will not allow that to happen, okay? Other schools of Buddhism say you can do it. Zen, for instance, says you can do it through meditation. But our school says that the only way is to not give up, but give in. So we give in to the compassionate beauty of Amitabha Buddha. Amitabha Buddha is a Buddha of immeasurable light and life, and his compassionate beauty surrounds you and me.

So my goal, and the goal of this temple, is to become aware of this compassion . . . to feel the compassion. And with the feeling of the compassion of the Buddha comes a deep sense of *arigatai*, or gratefulness; gratefulness for the many things that support and sustain my life. Realizing this, you come to fully appreciate all manifestations of life and live in harmony.

TALKING WITH NON-BUDDHISTS

What Does the Statue in the Shrine Represent?

It represents Amida Buddha, the Buddha of Boundless Life and Boundless Light, a personification (in human characteristics) of universal compassion and wisdom.

Is Amida Some Kind of God?

What do you mean by God? (*Note: We should not simply assume that the questioner is confident in his own understanding of what he means by "God"; many questioners are often not as certain or knowledgable as we expect. Discussions have proven more lively and meaningful when I began asking the questioner about what he or she means by "God." After the questioner responds, we can speak about Amida.*)

Amida Buddha is pure selfless compassion and wisdom which are qualities also attributed to God in Christianity. But Amida is not considered a supreme being who created the universe and now resides in heaven to watch over me, judging my thoughts and actions in this life according to some divine standard.

Instead, Amida is the dynamic "spiritual power" manifesting as wisdom and compassion that I am made aware of in the ordinary experience of my daily life. Wisdom helps me to see myself and life as they really are, not just as I wish them to be. Compassion enhances my appreciation for things and assures me that I am embraced by a wider community and not forsaken as an isolated individual.

So Amida Has Nothing to Do with the Creation of the Universe?

That's right. Though knowledge is important in our lives, our knowing how the world/universe began (even if it could be known for sure) does not help us to attain the main Shinshu goal of true awareness or enlightenment. To be overly concerned about creation reminds us of the famous "Poison Arrow" parable in which a dying man shot with a poison arrow would not allow the physician to pull out the arrow until he got answers to such questions as the type of arrow and the background of the man who shot him.

. . .

What Happens After You Die?

People of Shinjin-awareness no longer worry seriously about life after death because they are at peace with themselves. According to our founder, Shinran Shonin (1173–1263), we are assured of realizing Oneness (nirvana) immediately upon death in becoming one with the cosmic wisdom and compassion. Then, as part of the dynamic benefit of Oneness, we help liberate all beings. Oneness is the dynamic cycle of compassion, like the river water that flows into the ocean only to eventually return as rain water to nourish the plants and all other living beings.

How Does Your Idea of "Pure Land" Fit in with All This?

The Pure Land is the same as Oneness or nirvana. It's a more concrete and aesthetically appealing way of speaking about the same truth.

Do Shinshu Followers Believe in Reincarnation?

Some do and some don't. Some take it literally, while others see it symbolically.

The idea of reincarnation goes back to India but it is also esteemed by many Western thinkers, past and present. Belief in reincarnation is not part of the core teaching in Shinshu and thus is not a requirement for the realization of the most important goal, Shinjin-awareness.

. . .

What Kind of Practice Do You Do?

Our teaching does not prescribe any one particular form of practice as many other Buddhist schools do, such as sitting meditation, since it is not our action that directly causes our enlightenment. However, it does not mean we do nothing. In our daily affairs we strive for awareness of our self-centered imperfections and our indebtedness to the interdependent nature of our existence. In appreciation of the teachings we try to learn more about ourselves. We take part, for example, in listening to and discussing the Dharma, participating in religious services at home and temple, reflecting on the before-and-after meal recitations, and engaging in efforts to reduce suffering whenever possible. These activities serve as a mirror to increase our awareness of our imperfections and indebtedness to our family and friends, the community, and the world.

. . .

THAI YOUTH CLUB, "DJ OR NOT WE'RE STILL UPSET" (1994)

Thais arrived in the United States in significant numbers after the changes in the immigration laws in 1965, and like other first-generation immigrants they have not always agreed with their children about how to practice their religion or live as Americans. The 1990 Census counted 91,275 Thai Americans, who have gathered mostly in major cities in five states: California, New York, Texas, Illinois, and Florida. Their predominant religion is Theravada Buddhism. "To be Thai is to be Buddhist," one Thai saying proclaims, and their immigrants have built more than fifty-five Buddhist temples across the United States. One of those temples, Wat Dhammaram, is in a former elementary school in Chicago's southwest side. In 1976 Thai Buddhists in Chicago purchased property for their first temple, a three-story brick building that had served as a Christian church, and there they practiced their religion until they moved to the larger southwest Chicago site in the 1980s. At this new temple, intergenerational tensions arise. As in most immigrant communities, the second-generation Thai Buddhists struggle to live between two worlds—the old one they find in the home and temple and the new one they encounter at the mall and school. In the *Thai Youth Journal*, Wat Dhammaram's Thai Youth Club frankly addresses intergenerational tensions, expressing frustrations that might sound familiar. The teenagers complain, first, that their parents will not allow them to have a DJ at a temple dance and, second, that "Thai parents expect too much from their kids."

Thai Youth Club, "DJ or Not We're Still Upset," *Thai Youth Journal*, 9 April 1994, 5–6; Anonymous, "Thai Parents Expect Too Much from Their Kids," *Thai Youth Journal*, 9 April 1994, 10. Reprinted by permission of Wat Dhammaram, Chicago, Illinois.

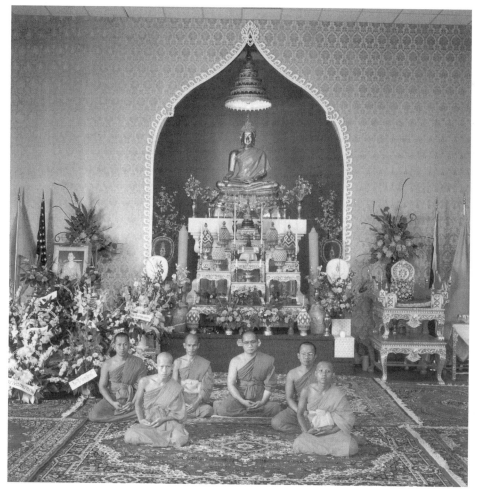

Thai Buddhist monks in Chicago photographed by James Newberry. Courtesy of the Chicago Historical Society.

DJ OR NOT WE'RE STILL UPSET

On the Sunday of March 27, 1994, the Thai Youth Club was invited to attend one of this year's Songkran meetings for the first time. We were proud to be asked to participate in the organization of that night and had recently gone over our ideas. Among our ideas was the controversial topic of having a dance for the younger generation at Wat. A few of us attended the meeting willing to discuss and compromise on the issue. However, as we sat down and read the agenda, we were surprised to find that it had already been decided that we wouldn't be allowed to have the dance.

In turn, we became upset. We do not understand the purpose of us being called to the meeting. We wanted to present our point of view, but felt that their intention was to dictate to us what had priorly been decided without our knowledge. Because of this, we began to feel that the Youth Club would not be taken as seriously as we had previously hoped. Consequently, a heated argument began among those in the meeting, mainly between the youths and some strongly opposed adults. Still, we hoped that the adults would listen to our arguments since they mentioned that they would be willing to compromise on the issue.

We understood that there would be no room if the weather was not suitable for the food to be placed outside, but what if the weather would make it capable? We stated that we would be willing to turn up the lights and turn the music down if asked to. Adults would also be welcomed to join us.

By the end of the meeting, we thought that we had possibly been able to convince the adults into letting us have a DJ, but that did not occur. They stayed with their claim that it was inappropriate for the occasion. They have also claimed that the reason was stated in the board meeting note (bylaws ?) of the temple, any type of dancing is forbidden. Our only concerns with that decision was that we have had dances prior to this meeting, and there had never been any opposition before. It seemed to us that the decision had occurred somewhat spontaneously.

In spite of the fact that the outcome had not been what we had hoped, we are still proud to have had the chance to have been represented in the meeting. Because the adults gave us the opportunity to speak our position, we feel that they have confidence in what the Thai Youth Club stands for: the chance for the youth of the Thai community to speak their opinions to the public. All that we have hoped to occur in the meeting that did not occur was a compromise of the clashing views. Respect takes time.

THAI PARENTS EXPECT TOO MUCH FROM THEIR KIDS

You are sitting in your room working diligently on your homework from school when your father knocks on the door. "Come out and play some music for me," he says, "You need to practice your (song/dance/Thai)."

You yell back through your door, "I'm doing my homework!"

He says, "Come now!" What can you do? You can't just sit there and ignore his request, that would only make him angry. Being the good kid that you are, you get up and do whatever he wants without complaint. When you are done, it's late, you still haven't finished your homework, and you have a major test tomorrow on electron configuration in chemistry class. On top of all that, your parents don't want you to stay up late, so they command you to go to sleep.

Two days later, you come home with a "D" on your chemistry test and a note from your teacher about not doing your homework. Your father starts to give you a lecture, and when you try to explain about the night that he took you away from your schoolwork, he says, "Don't talk back to me!"

What's a kid to do?

HSI LAI TEMPLE, BUDDHISM COMING TO THE WEST (1997)

On fifteen acres in Hacienda Heights, an affluent suburb of Los Angeles, stands the largest Buddhist temple in the western hemisphere—Fo Kuang Shan Hsi Lai Temple. It was completed in 1988 at the cost of $30 million. Most of its 20,000 members are Chinese immigrants from Taiwan, where Master Hsing Yun founded Fo Kuan Shan Monastery. Combining elements from several Chinese schools of Mahayana, the founder teaches a "Humanistic Buddhism" that aims to spread Buddha's teachings widely and establish an earthly Pure Land, a peaceful and just world community. The California temple's many activities reflect those aims. Hsi Lai offers opportunities not only for monastic training and lay practice, but also for continuing education, cultural exchange, and community service. It sponsors television programs, operates a Buddhist university, organizes recycling drives, hosts international conferences, translates Buddhist writings, and distributes food to the poor. And the California temple attracts visitors. In 1996, for example, more than 110,000 took the guided tour. Vice President Al Gore visited that year too, unwittingly drawing the temple into a political controversy about Democratic Party fund raising that made front page news and embarrassed temple officials. The temple's name, Hsi Lai, means "coming to the West," and its imposing buildings and public activities announce that Buddhism has arrived, taking a prominent place in the American cultural landscape. This excerpt from an official publication describes the movement's aims, teachings, and activities.

BUDDHIST TEACHING COMING TO THE WEST FOR THE BENEFITS OF ALL

Hsi Lai Temple, the largest international monastery in the West, was founded by Ven. Master Hsing Yun, the founder of Fo Kuang Shan. Taking ten years of planning and untiring efforts to complete, Hsi Lai Temple follows the architectural design of a traditional Chinese monastery to facilitate the Dharma propagation. Since its inauguration in 1988, monastics and lay devotees have worked jointly to achieve goals in community services, education, charity, and international cultural exchange, etc. The temple has not only been functional in benefiting society, it has also built the bridge between the cultures of the East and the West.

. . .

CARING FOR THE WORLD

As a guide to future developments, Ven. Master Hsing Yun offers the following four points:

International Buddhist Progress Society, Hsi Lai Temple, "Buddhist Teaching Coming to the West for the Benefits of All," "Caring for the World," "Charity," and "Education," (Hacienda Heights, Calif.: Hsi Lai Temple, 1997), 1–2, 5, 6–7. Reprinted by permission of Hsi Lai Temple.

1. There will be Dharma functions and chanting sessions conducted in English. Translation will be provided at all meetings to facilitate English speaking enthusiasts.
2. To respect groups of all ethnic backgrounds, Hsi Lai Temple will hold various international activities and strive to be the "United Nation for Buddhism."
3. Emphasis will be placed on translating sutras and Dharma lectures. In addition to an expansion in television and radio broadcasting, an audio-visual library will be planned.
4. With the joint efforts of monastics and devotees to spread the Dharma, let the seeds of Buddhism grow, blossom, and bear fruits in the West.

It is the wish of every Fo Kuang Buddhist to "let the Buddha's light shine and the Dharma water forever flow." With everyone's support, let us strive forward.

CHARITY

According to the sutra, we should "teach generosity to the poor, give medicine to the sick, protect those who are vulnerable, provide shelter to the homeless, and help those who are without help." Hsi Lai Temple follows the Buddha's com-

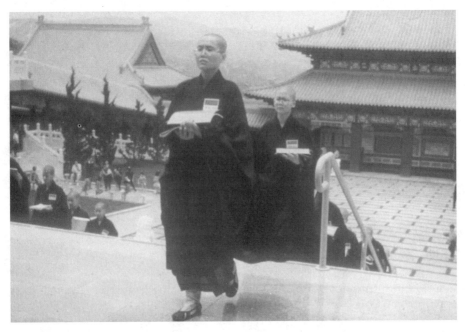

Nuns processing during a Triple Platform Ordination ceremony at Hsi Lai Temple, Hacienda Heights, California, May 1992. Courtesy of the Pluralism Project, Harvard University. Hsi Lai is the largest Buddhist temple in the United States.

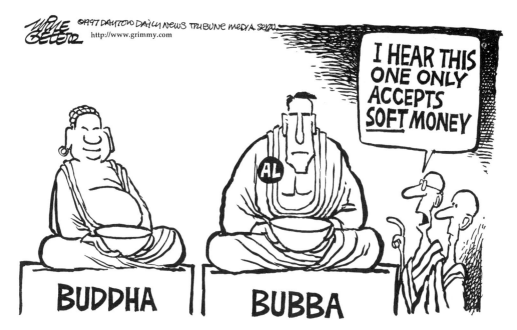

After Vice President Al Gore visited Hsi Lai Temple in 1996, members were reluctantly drawn into a national debate about political campaign fund raising. This cartoon by Mike Peters contrasts the Buddha's humble begging bowl with Gore's fund-raising techniques. Copyright © 1997 Dayton Daily News & Tribune Media Services. Courtesy of Grimmy, Inc.

passionate spirit in delivering our concerns to different corners of our society. Besides the annual winter relief programs for the needy, we actively reach out and comfort those in illness or difficulty. In 1996, we have expanded our efforts of delivering "caring kits" and food coupons to the poor and distributing food and necessities to the homeless. We have frequently visited senior citizens in convalescent homes, and provided spiritual guidance to abused children. We have organized community blood pressure screening and "Bone Marrow Drive." We have provided comfort for the dying and terminally ill. We visit the sick and donate emergency relief funds. There are over thousands of such events—all in accordance with the Buddha's spirit of "compassion and loving kindness regardless of karmic bond." Hsi Lai Temple aspires to bring warmth to all sentient beings through the material goods and spiritual encouragement.

EDUCATION

Hsi Lai University

It is through education of our youngsters that we have hope for the future. Ven. Master Hsing Yun places tremendous emphasis on education. In Taiwan, he founded 16 Buddhist colleges, Fo Kuang University, and Nan Hua University. In

1990, he also founded Hsi Lai University in Los Angeles. While undergoing approval processes, Hsi Lai University has received the rating of "excellence" in the areas of faculty, curriculum, administration, and library book collections.

In 1996, Hsi Lai University was relocated to Rosemead. With well-equipped buildings and meticulously maintained campus grounds, Hsi Lai University is poised to expand its operation and recruitment for more US and international students. In addition to the Bachelor of Arts (B.A.) and Master of Arts (M.A.) programs in Buddhist studies and comparative religious studies, Master of Business Administration (MBA) program will be offered in the near future. With Buddhist dual emphases on compassion and wisdom, we hope to benefit even more students in the future. The *San Gabriel Valley Tribune* once reported and praised Hsi Lai University as "the Buddhist Harvard."

Buddha's Light Hsi Lai School

Since its establishment in 1989, Buddha's Light Hsi Lai School has promoted education in Chinese language and culture. The balanced curriculum, placing equal emphasis on honor, wisdom, physical conditioning, and interpersonal relationship, has the following special features:

1. Leaning on Buddhism: this is the most unique feature of this school and is popular among students and parents.
2. After school guidance: in addition to helping with homework and teaching Chinese courses, this school guides students on everyday issues and helps with transportation to the school. For the newly immigrated or busy parents, this service can alleviate their parental concerns.
3. Youth symphony orchestra: since its formation in 1993, the orchestra has given many well received concerts and has set the precedent for overseas Chinese schools.
4. Halloween costume and pumpkin carving contests: by celebrating Halloween festivity, students express their creativity.
5. Winter and Summer camps: these camps provide students opportunity to enrich their lives during the major school breaks.

Currently there are over 300 students. In its seven years of operation, this school has received numerous recognitions and awards.

Community Activities

There is a saying, "Actions bring out life; actions bring out strength." To bring out the vitality of Buddhist teachings, the best way is to plan a variety of activities to put everyone in action. During the year of 1996, Hsi Lai Temple has held a series of family activities, children's summer camp, "Fo Kuang Ceremony of Adulthood," youth camps, classes for volunteers, and workshops for BLIA staff. With the rich curriculum and solemn ceremonies, these activities have attracted Buddhists over and over again. Together they cultivate right understanding in dealing with people and events of their lives.

CHAPTER 18

Asian Religions in Popular and Elite Culture

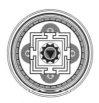

"Diaspora" by Michael Yue Tong. Tong, who came to the United States from China in 1982, lived inside this sheet metal Buddha head during an art exhibition held in New York City in 1994. Courtesy of Exit Art/The First World.

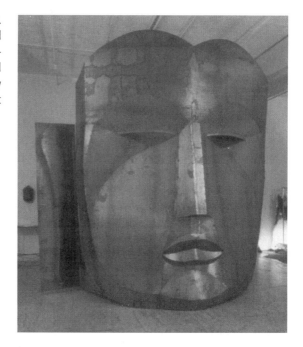

BRUCE LEE, *TAO OF JEET KUNE DO* (1975)

Americans have encountered Asian religions, especially Zen and Taoism, through the martial arts. Some have attended martial arts academies; many more have viewed representations of the martial arts on television and in film. The most important popularizer of the martial arts was Bruce Lee (1940–73). Born Lee Jun Fan in San Francisco's

Chinese Hospital to a well-known comic actor from Hong Kong and a Shanghai-born mother, Lee and his family traveled abroad from their Hong Kong home. Claiming to be "bullied" at school, Lee took up in 1954 the Wing Chun style of Kung Fu as taught by master martial artist, Yip Man. Expelled from school in Hong Kong five years later, he went to America to make something of himself. Lee ended up in Seattle, where he majored in philosophy at the University of Washington and met his wife, Linda Emery. In 1964 he began to instruct students in Kung Fu in Oakland, but it was not until he made his TV debut in 1966 as Kato, the Green Hornet's valet and chauffeur, that he attracted a large following. The show flopped after one season, but his career as a television and film star had just begun. Lee became an international figure in a series of martial arts movies. He even developed the concept for the successful TV series, "Kung Fu," but David Carradine got the role because Lee was judged "too Chinese looking." After appearing in several movies, including *Fists of Fury* and *The Chinese Connection,* that drew large audiences Lee died mysteriously from an allergic reaction shortly after finishing the film that would make him a pop icon, *Enter the Dragon* (1973). Although acting brought Lee fame, it was not his first love. As his widow reminded fans after his death, "My husband Bruce always considered himself a martial artist first and an actor second." Lee's understanding of the martial arts, which he called *Jeet Kune Do* or Way of the Intercepting Fist, stressed economy of motion and freedom of expression. As these excerpts from a posthumously published book demonstrate, that philosophy was shaped by his interpretation of Zen.

ON ZEN

To obtain enlightenment in martial art means the extinction of everything which obscures the "true knowledge," the "real life." At the same time, it implies *boundless expansion* and, indeed, emphasis should fall not on the cultivation of the particular department which merges into the totality, but rather on the totality that enters and unites that particular department.

The way to transcend *karma* lies in the proper use of the mind and the will. The oneness of all life is a truth that can be fully realized only when false notions of a separate self, whose destiny can be considered apart from the whole, are forever annihilated.

Voidness is that which stands right in the middle between this and that. The void is all-inclusive, having no opposite—there is nothing which it excludes or opposes. It is living void, because all forms come out of it and whoever realizes the void is filled with life and power and the love of all beings.

Turn into a doll made of wood: it has no ego, it thinks nothing, it is not grasping or sticky. Let the body and limbs work themselves out in accordance with the discipline they have undergone.

If nothing within you stays rigid, outward things will disclose themselves. Moving, be like water. Still, be like a mirror. Respond like an echo.

Nothingness cannot be defined; the softest thing cannot be snapped.

I'm moving and not moving at all. I'm like the moon underneath the waves that ever go on rolling and rocking. It is not,"I am doing this," but rather, an inner realization that "this is happening through me," or "it is doing this for me." The consciousness of self is the greatest hindrance to the proper execution of all physical action.

The localization of the mind means its freezing. When it ceases to flow freely as it is needed, it is no more the mind in its suchness.

. . .

An assertion is Zen only when it is itself an act and does not refer to anything that is asserted in it.

In Buddhism, there is no place for using effort. Just be ordinary and nothing special. Eat your food, move your bowels, pass water and when you're tired go and lie down. The ignorant will laugh at me, but the wise will understand.

Establish nothing in regard to oneself. Pass quickly like the non-existent and be quiet as purity. Those who gain lose. Do not precede others, always follow them.

Do not run away; let go. Do not seek, for it will come when least expected.

Give up thinking as though not giving it up. Observe techniques as though not observing.

There is no fixed teaching. All I can provide is an appropriate medicine for a particular ailment.

Buddhism's Eight-Fold Path

The eight requirements to eliminate suffering by correcting false values and giving true knowledge of life's meaning have been summed up as follows:

1. *Right views (understanding):* You must see clearly what is wrong.
2. *Right purpose (aspiration):* Decide to be cured.
3. *Right speech:* Speak so as to aim at being cured.
4. *Right conduct:* You must act.
5. *Right vocation:* Your livelihood must not conflict with your therapy.
6. *Right effort:* The therapy must go forward at the "staying speed," the critical velocity that can be sustained.

7. *Right awareness (mind control):* You must feel it and think about it incessantly.
8. *Right concentration (meditation):* Learn how to contemplate with the deep mind.

. . .

JEET KUNE DO

For security, the unlimited living is turned into something dead, a chosen pattern that limits. To understand Jeet Kune Do, one ought to throw away all ideals, patterns, styles; in fact, he should throw away even the concepts of what is or isn't ideal in Jeet Kune Do. Can you look at a situation without naming it? Naming it, making it a word, causes fear.

It is indeed difficult to see the situation simply—our minds are very complex—and it is easy to teach one to be skillful, but it is difficult to teach him his own attitude.

Jeet Kune Do favors formlessness so that it can assume all forms and since Jeet Kune Do has no style, it can fit in with all styles. As a result, Jeet Kune Do utilizes all ways and is bound by none and, likewise, uses any techniques or means which serve its end.

Approach Jeet Kune Do with the idea of mastering the will. Forget about winning and losing; forget about pride and pain. Let your opponent graze your skin and you smash into his flesh; let him smash into your flesh and you fracture his bones; let him fracture your bones and you take his life! Do not be concerned with your escaping safely—lay your life before him!

The great mistake is to anticipate the outcome of the engagement; you ought not to be thinking of whether it ends in victory or in defeat. Let nature take its course, and your tools will strike at the right moment.

Jeet Kune Do teaches us not to look backward once the course is decided upon. It treats life and death indifferently.

Jeet Kune Do avoids the superficial, penetrates the complex, goes to the heart of the problem and pinpoints the key factors.

Jeet Kune Do does not beat around the bush. It does not take winding detours. It follows a straight line to the objective. *Simplicity is the shortest distance between two points.*

The art of Jeet Kune Do is simply to simplify. It is being oneself; it is reality in its "isness." Thus, isness is the meaning—having freedom in its primary sense, not limited by attachments, confinements, partialization, complexities.

Jeet Kune Do is the enlightenment. It is a way of life, a movement toward will power and control, though it ought to be enlightened by intuition.

. . .

BENJAMIN HOFF, *THE TAO OF POOH* (1982)

Whether they admit it or not, many Americans first encounter Asian religions in popular books and how-to manuals. In 1997, *Books in Print* listed 197 titles that began with the word *Zen*. Among them were seventy-seven prescriptive books that applied Zen to one or another aspect of life. They include *Zen and Creative Management, Zen in the Art of Golf*, and even *Zen and the Art of Changing Diapers*. The same pattern appears in popular books about Taoism: *Tao of Management, Tao of Baseball*, and *Tao of Motherhood*. Scholars and adherents of these East Asian traditions typically dismiss these popular books, but they are the primary source of information on Buddhism and Taoism for many American readers. One of the most widely read of these popular texts is Benjamin Hoff's *The Tao of Pooh*. In that inventive book, the Oregon writer offers an interpretation of A. A. Milne's *Winnie-the-Pooh* (1926) that conveys the principles of Taoism. In the opening chapter, Hoff presents a lighthearted summary of China's three primary religions—Confucianism, Buddhism, and Taoism— and introduces their founders: K'ung Fu-tzu or Confucius (551–479 BCE), the originator of the philosophical and religious tradition that bears his name; Lao-tzu, allegedly the author of the Taoist philosophical classic, *Tao te ching* (mid-fourth century BCE); and Siddhartha Gautama (566–486 BCE), the founder of Buddhism.

THE *HOW* OF POOH?

"You see, Pooh," I said, "a lot of people don't seem to know what Taoism is . . ."

"Yes?" said Pooh, blinking his eyes.

"So that's what this chapter is for—to explain things a bit."

"Oh, I see," said Pooh.

"And the easiest way to do that would be for us to go to China for a moment."

"*What?*" said Pooh, his eyes wide open in amazement. "Right now?"

"Of course. All we need to do is lean back, relax, and there we are."

"Oh, I see," said Pooh.

Let's imagine that we have walked down a narrow street in a large Chinese city and have found a small shop that sells scrolls painted in the classic manner.

We go inside and ask to be shown something allegorical—something humorous, perhaps, but with some sort of Timeless meaning. The shopkeeper smiles. "I have just the thing," he tells us. "A copy of *The Vinegar Tasters!*" He leads us to a large table and unrolls the scroll, placing it down for us to examine. "Excuse me—I must attend to something for a moment," he says, and goes into the back of the shop, leaving us alone with the painting.

Although we can see that this is a fairly recent version, we know that the original was painted long ago; just when is uncertain. But by now, the theme of the painting is well known.

We see three men standing around a vat of vinegar. Each has dipped his finger into the vinegar and has tasted it. The expression on each man's face shows his individual reaction. Since the painting is allegorical, we are to understand that these are no ordinary vinegar tasters, but are instead representatives of the "Three Teachings" of China, and that the vinegar they are sampling represents the Essence of Life. The three masters are K'ung Fu-tse (Confucius), Buddha, and Lao-tse, author of the oldest existing book of Taoism. The first has a sour look on his face, the second wears a bitter expression, but the third man is smiling.

To K'ung Fu-tse (kung FOOdsuh), life seemed rather sour. He believed that the present was out of step with the past, and that the government of man on earth was out of harmony with the Way of Heaven, the government of the universe. Therefore, he emphasized reverence for the Ancestors, as well as for the ancient rituals and ceremonies in which the emperor, as the Son of Heaven, acted as intermediary between limitless heaven and limited earth. Under Confucianism, the use of precisely measured court music, prescribed steps, actions, and phrases all added up to an extremely complex system of rituals, each used for a particular purpose at a particular time. A saying was recorded about K'ung Fu-tse: "If the mat was not straight, the Master would not sit." This ought to give an indication of the extent to which things were carried out under Confucianism.

To Buddha, the second figure in the painting, life on earth was bitter, filled with attachments and desires that led to suffering. This world was seen as a setter of traps, a generator of illusions, a revolving wheel of pain for all creatures. In order to find peace, the Buddhist considered it necessary to transcend "the world of dust" and reach Nirvana, literally a state of "no wind." Although the essentially optimistic attitude of the Chinese altered Buddhism considerably after it was brought in from its native India, the devout Buddhist often saw the way to Nirvana interrupted all the same by the bitter wind of everyday existence.

To Lao-tse (LAOdsuh), the harmony that naturally existed between heaven and earth from the very beginning could be found by anyone at any time, but not by following the rules of the Confucianists. As he stated in his *Tao Te Ching* (DAO DEH JEENG), the "Tao Virtue Book," earth was in essence a reflection of heaven, run by the same laws—*not* by the laws of men. These laws affected not only the spinning of distant planets, but the activities of the birds in the forest and the fish in the sea. According to Lao-tse, the more man interfered with the natural balance produced and governed by the universal laws, the further away the harmony retreated into the distance. The more forcing, the more trouble. Whether heavy or light, wet or dry, fast or slow, everything had its own nature already within it, which could not be violated without causing difficulties. When abstract and arbitrary rules were imposed from the outside, struggle was inevitable. Only then did life become sour.

To Lao-tse, the world was not a setter of traps but a teacher of valuable lessons. Its lessons needed to be learned, just as its laws needed to be followed; then all would go well. Rather than turn away from "the world of dust," Lao-tse advised others to "join the dust of the world." What he saw operating behind everything in heaven and earth he called *Tao* (DAO), "the Way." A basic principle of Lao-tse's teaching was that this Way of the Universe could not be adequately described in words, and that it would be insulting both to its unlimited power and to the intelligent human mind to attempt to do so. Still, its nature could be understood, and those who cared the most about it, and the life from which it was inseparable, understood it best.

Over the centuries Lao-tse's classic teachings were developed and divided into philosophical, monastic, and folk religious forms. All of these could be included under the general heading of Taoism. But the basic Taoism that we are concerned with here is simply a particular way of appreciating, learning from, and working with whatever happens in everyday life. From the Taoist point of view, the natural result of this harmonious way of living is happiness. You might say that happy serenity is the most noticeable characteristic of the Taoist personality, and a subtle sense of humor is apparent even in the most profound Taoist writings, such as the twenty-five-hundred-year-old *Tao Te Ching*. In the writings of Taoism's second major writer, Chuang-tse (JUANGdsuh), quiet laughter seems to bubble up like water from a fountain.

"But what does that have to do with vinegar?" asked Pooh.
"I thought I had explained that," I said.
"I don't think so," said Pooh.
"Well, then, I'll explain it now."
"That's good," said Pooh.

In the painting, why is Lao-tse smiling? After all, that vinegar that represents life must certainly have an unpleasant taste, as the expressions on the faces of the other two men indicate. But, through working in harmony with life's circumstances, Taoist understanding changes what others may perceive as negative into something positive. From the Taoist point of view, sourness and bitterness come from the interfering and unappreciative mind. Life itself, when understood and utilized for what it is, is sweet. That is the message of *The Vinegar Tasters*.

"Sweet? You mean like honey?" asked Pooh.
"Well, maybe not *that* sweet," I said. "That would be overdoing it a bit."
"Are we still supposed to be in China?" Pooh asked cautiously.
"No, we're through explaining and now we're back at the writing table."
"Oh."

"Well, we're just in time for something to eat," he added, wandering over to the kitchen cupboard.

GARY SNYDER, "SMOKEY THE BEAR SUTRA" (1969)

As Americans have converted to Buddhism, they have also made it their own, in part by translating its beliefs and practices into familiar idioms. One such idiom is contemporary American poetry. There are now at least two anthologies devoted to Buddhist-inspired poetry in the United States: *Big Sky Mind: Buddhism and the Beat Generation* (1995) and *Beneath a Single Moon: Buddhism in Contemporary American Poetry* (1991). The work of Gary Snyder (born 1930) appears in both. Immortalized as "Japhy Ryder" in Jack Kerouac's *Dharma Bums* (1958), Snyder was born in San Francisco and raised in the Pacific Northwest, where he cultivated a love of the wild and a commitment to environmental activism. He earned a B.A. in anthropology and literature at Reed College, and was studying Asian languages as a graduate student at the University of California at Berkeley in the mid-fifties when he met Kerouac. Although often pigeonholed as a Beat writer, Snyder was a more serious practitioner of Buddhism than most East Coast Beats. He went to Japan in 1956 to study under Rinzai Zen master Oda Sesso-roshi at Kyoto's Daitoku-ji monastery, and did not return permanently to the United States until 1969. Five years later he won the Pulitzer Prize for *Turtle Island*. He lives today in the Yuba River watershed of the Sierra Nevadas and teaches writing at the University of California, Davis. Snyder resembles no one in American letters as much as Thoreau, who like Snyder was an accomplished essayist who tried to live his life in tune with nature's rhythms and Asian teachings. In "Smokey the Bear Sutra" (a sutra is a form of Buddhist scripture), Snyder transforms the mascot of the Forest Service into a cosmic Buddha with an ecological conscience. Here, and elsewhere, Snyder takes a Buddhist seed, plants it in American soil, and fertilizes it with his poetic imagination. The result is a poetics that is as thoroughly Buddhist as it is American.

> Once in the Jurassic about 150 million years ago,
> the Great Sun Buddha in this corner of the Infinite
> Void gave a Discourse to all the assembled elements
> and energies: to the standing beings, the walking beings,
> the flying beings, and the sitting beings—even grasses,
> to the number of thirteen billion, each one born from a
> seed, assembled there: a Discourse concerning
> Enlightenment on the planet Earth.
>
> "In some future time, there will be a continent called
> America. It will have great centers of power called
> such as Pyramid Lake, Walden Pond, Mt. Rainier, Big Sur,
> Everglades, and so forth; and powerful nerves and channels
> such as Columbia River, Mississippi River, and Grand Canyon.
> The human race in that era will get into troubles all over
> its head, and practically wreck everything in spite of
> its own strong intelligent Buddha-nature."

Snyder wrote "Smokey the Bear Sutra" in 1969 and had it published as a broadside. The poem can be found at http://web.mit.edu/afs/athena.mit.edu/user/d/r/dryfoo/www/Spritz-yule/snyder.html.

Gary Snyder, "Smokey the Bear Sutra" (1969)

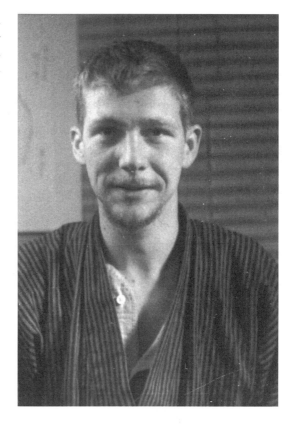

Poet Gary Snyder in Zen robes, Berkeley, California, 1955. Copyright © Allen Ginsberg Trust. Courtesy of the Fahey/Klein Gallery, Los Angeles.

"The twisting strata of the great mountains and the pulsings
of volcanoes are my love burning deep in the earth.
My obstinate compassion is schist and basalt and
granite, to be mountains, to bring down the rain. In that
future American Era I shall enter a new form; to cure
the world of loveless knowledge that seeks with blind hunger:
and mindless rage eating food that will not fill it."

And he showed himself in his true form of

SMOKEY THE BEAR

A handsome smokey-colored brown bear standing on his hind legs,
showing that he is aroused and watchful.
Bearing in his right paw the Shovel that digs to the
truth beneath appearances; cuts the roots of useless attachments,
and flings damp sand on the fires of greed and war;
His left paw in the Mudra of Comradely Display—indicating
that all creatures have the full right to live to their limits
and that deer, rabbits, chipmunks, snakes, dandelions,
and lizards all grow in the realm of the Dharma;
Wearing the blue work overalls symbolic of slaves and

laborers, the countless men oppressed by a civilization
that claims to save but often destroys;
Wearing the broad-brimmed hat of the West, symbolic of
the forces that guard the Wilderness, which is the Natural
State of the Dharma and the True Path of man on earth:
all true paths lead through mountains—
With a halo of smoke and flame behind, the forest fires
of the kali-yuga, fires caused by the stupidity of those
who think things can be gained and lost whereas in truth all
is contained vast and free in the Blue Sky and Green Earth
of One Mind;
Round-bellied to show his kind nature and that the great
earth has food enough for everyone who loves her and trusts
her;
Trampling underfoot wasteful freeways and needless
suburbs; smashing the worms of capitalism and totalitarianism;
Indicating the Task: his followers, becoming free of cars,
houses, canned foods, universities, and shoes; master the
Three Mysteries of their own Body, Speech, and Mind; and
fearlessly chop down the rotten trees and prune out the
sick limbs of this country America and then burn the leftover
trash.

Wrathful but Calm. Austere but Comic. Smokey the Bear will
Illuminate those who would help him; but for those who would hinder or
slander him,

       HE WILL PUT THEM OUT.

Thus his great Mantra:
       Namah samanta vajranam chanda maharoshana
       Sphataya hum traks ham nam

       "I DEDICATE MYSELF TO THE UNIVERSAL DIAMOND
       BE THIS RAGING FURY DESTROYED"

And he will protect those who love woods and rivers,
Gods and animals, hobos and madmen, prisoners and sick
people, musicians, playful women, and hopeful children:

And if anyone is threatened by advertising, air pollution, television,
or the police, they should chant SMOKEY THE BEAR'S WAR SPELL:

       DROWN THEIR BUTTS
       CRUSH THEIR BUTTS
       DROWN THEIR BUTTS
       CRUSH THEIR BUTTS

And SMOKEY THE BEAR will surely appear to put the enemy out
with his vajra-shovel.

Now those who recite this Sutra and then try to put it in
practice will accumulate merit as countless as the sands
of Arizona and Nevada.
Will help save the planet Earth from total oil slick.
Will enter the age of harmony of man and nature.

Will win the tender love and caresses of men, women, and
beasts.
Will always have ripe blackberries to eat and a sunny spot
under a pine tree to sit at.
AND IN THE END WILL WIN HIGHEST PERFECT
ENLIGHTENMENT.

thus have we heard.

(may be reproduced free forever)

AN INTERVIEW WITH COMPOSER PHILIP GLASS (1991)

Asian religions have inspired American artists—painters, choreographers, playwrights,
and musicians. For example, India's rich religious and cultural heritage has shaped the
"new music" of composer Philip Glass. Born in Baltimore in 1937, Glass studied vio-
lin and flute as a child, and after graduating from college at age 19 he attended New
York's Julliard School to study musical composition. He then moved to Paris to work
with Nadia Boulanger. Soon after, Glass's composing career took a decisive turn when
he agreed to transcribe the Indian music of Ravi Shankar, whom George Harrison had
introduced to the West. Glass had journeyed to India previously, in 1966, and he returned many times later. Those encounters with Indian culture transformed his compositions, which include a large collection of new music composed for dance, theater,
and film. He wrote the score for Martin Scorsese's *Kundun*, the cinematic biography
of the Fourteenth Dalai Lama. Glass also has composed a series of operas about social change and nonviolence—*Einstein on the Beach*, *Satyagraha*, and *Akhnaten*—that
explore, among other things, the philosophy and legacy of Mahatma Gandhi. As he
reveals in this 1991 interview, Glass first encountered Hindu yoga in 1962, but it was
John Cage's *Silence* that introduced him to Buddhism. Glass's Buddhist interests deepened in later years, as he traveled to Asia regularly. Glass acknowledges Buddhism's
profound influence on his personal life but denies that it has directly inspired his musical compositions. Even so, it seems indisputable that Glass's new music owes much
to his encounter with India's cultures and religions.

> *Tricycle:*   As your Buddhist studies followed an interest in yoga, let's start
> there. That puts us back in 1962, when even a yoga teacher was
> hard to come by.
>
> *Philip Glass:*   I found one in the Yellow Pages, under the Y's. For the next
> three years I studied with Indian yoga teachers, including one
> who started me being a vegetarian.
>
> *Tricycle:*   And did yoga put you under some kind of Eastern umbrella
> that extended to Buddhism?

"First Lesson, Best Lesson: An Interview with Philip Glass," *Tricycle* (Winter 1991): 8–9, 13–14, 16, 18.
Reprinted by permission of *Tricycle: The Buddhist Review*.

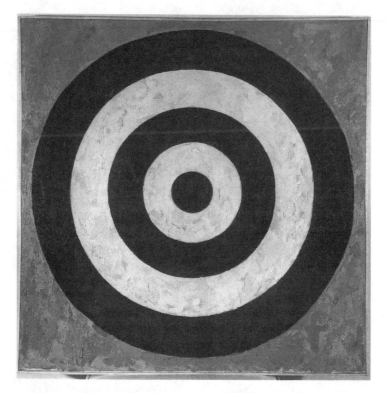

Target (1958), oil and collage on canvas by Jasper Johns. Johns painted his first in a series of *Target* paintings in 1955, just two years after Eugen Herrigel's *Zen in the Art of Archery* appeared. Asian religious influences continued to shape some of Johns' later paintings (for example, his 1981 work *Tantric Detail III*), just as other American artists—including Ad Reinhardt, Robert Rauschenberg, and William Wiley—looked East for inspiration. Copyright © Jasper Johns/Licenses by VAGA, New York, New York. Used by permission.

Philip Glass:	I never heard anything about Buddhism through my yoga teachers. It was through John Cage that I knew anything at all, through his book *Silence*. And just a year or two before that, the first really good edition of the *I Ching* came out, which I knew about through an English painter who had joined the Native American Church and was a peyote eater. Throughout the late Fifties and early Sixties the painters were the most adventurous people in the arts, the ones most committed to searching out new ideas. So it's not surprising that I would know of the *I Ching* through a painter. And then John Cage. I certainly did not learn about him at music school. He was not considered a serious musical influence at that time. Certainly not by the people at

Julliard. Then in *Silence* there were all these references to Zen koans. But the big explosion in the culture happened in 1968 when the Beatles went to India to study with the Maharishi. They brought back Indian culture. Only after that did people like Ravi Shankar begin performing in large concert halls—and filling them. George Harrison made Ravi Shankar a household name. But when I started out, any kind of Eastern interest was still pretty marginal.

. . .

Tricycle: There are perhaps other ways of talking about your music and your own Buddhist meditation practice, but it's tricky, because the newness of Buddhism in the United States fosters an irksome imperialistic tendency to co-opt ideas, people, or music, for that matter, as "Buddhist" when they are not really so. Yet in spite of this, there seem to be recognizable interconnections between your music and your studies in Buddhism.

Philip Glass: Certainly. But not in the music itself. The real impact of Buddhist practice affects how you live your life on a daily basis, not how you do your art. How you live day by day, moment by moment. The impact of Buddhism is not theoretical, as in how you paint or how you write a novel. That's hardly as interesting as how you live on a daily basis, don't you think? Aspects of Buddhist studies, such as the development of compassion and equanimity and mindfulness, are the practical aspects of daily life.

Tricycle: This is a big departure from the exoticism you pursued in India thirty years ago.

Philip Glass: You start out pursuing the exotic, and it brings you around to the most basic daily activities. Also, the music world encourages such an exhausting and compulsive way of living that it is important to balance your life against the demands of that kind of career.

Tricycle: It took a generation to discover that it's about how you put your shoes on in the morning.

Philip Glass: But that's what turns out to be the most interesting thing. That's why I de-emphasize the impact on the actual music itself.

. . .

Tricycle: Have there ever been conflicts between Tibetan practice and making music?

Philip Glass: My Tibetan friends have always encouraged my music practice. I've been encouraged to devote myself entirely to music. There is some kind of recognition on their part, I think, that music is a kind of "practice," too—that this is practice in their terms. This is a practice of a kind that need not be profane or self-cherishing.

Tricycle: And then, too, you did a series of operas with overt social themes.

Philip Glass: I did three operas about social change through nonviolence. It started with *Einstein on the Beach*, which I did with Bob Wilson, though at the time, I didn't know what I was doing and would not have seen it that way. But with the next one, *Satyagraha* (in which Mahatma Gandhi was the main character), I was consciously thinking about a religious revolutionary. Again with Ahknaten and with his impact on the social order—in terms of the society as a whole or the individual in society. In my own work, those polarities went from *The Making of Another from Planet Eight* by Doris Lessing, which is about the transcendence of a whole society, to a personal hallucination such as Poe's *The Fall of the House of Usher*. That's the range, and the concern reflects Buddhist practice.

Tricycle: How deliberately did that enter your music?

Philip Glass: At a certain point, I wanted the music to reflect my feelings of social responsibility. Take the image of the artist as someone cut off from society. We learn from dharma teachers that this separateness is an illusion, and things begin to shift—we begin to see ourselves as connected.

. . .

Tricycle: So addressing the illusion of a separate self, for example, or taking on a social issue for the benefit of society, justifies liberal artistic interpretation?

Philip Glass: The artist who does that, in being a purveyor of the idea, becomes partly the teacher. I was not that ambitious. I never felt that I knew that much. All I knew was that there was something mysterious and interesting and wonderful about Gandhi. And I really didn't try to explicate it anymore than that.

Tricycle: In the Glass opera *Satyagraha*, there is an Indian subject and an Indian story line about a great secular saint of our times. The sets are very distilled and stylized, and everything, from linguistic content, to sound—voices, pitch, rhythm—to the sets, communicates great holiness.

Philip Glass: The music does not sound Indian.

Tricycle: No. But there is an overt transcendence to the music that we had been hearing for several years before *Satyagraha*.

Philip Glass: But it's also true that *Satyagraha* makes a very big statement. I think that the occasion of an opera about Gandhi inspired that "transcendent" quality to go to another level.

Tricycle:	And are we still getting it all wrong to make associations between this music and a personal spiritual evolution?
Philip Glass:	In 1979, when I wrote *Satyagraha*, I was forty-two, just entering my middle age, so to speak. And that's what we have come to expect from artists, with or without a spiritual practice. The late works of Beethoven are transcendent, and so are the late works of Shostakovich. You can see that with some visual artists, too. There are changes, I think, that you can find in the work of any artist who has seriously plied his trade for a solid twenty years and where the intention of the work has been honorable. So this is not personal to me. But you know, the most beautiful part of *Satyagraha*, to me, is in the very last scene, when Lord Krishna says to Arjuna, "I have known many a birth and you have not; and I have come to be reborn to move and act with men and to set virtue on her seat again." That's what he's saying. That is the Bodhisattva Vow: "I've come back on earth to move with men and to place virtue on her seat again." I'm not certain, but I wouldn't want to deny that the music is inspired by the text. Because of my interests, I do use texts and materials that inspire transcendence in some pieces. But not in others. But still, I would have to say, Buddhism has affected my life more directly than my work.
Tricycle:	How you put on your shoes?
Philip Glass:	There is a kind of ordinariness, a kind of ordinary thinking—is there such as thing as high ordinary?—I mean, there is a way of thinking about ordinary life in a distinctly Buddhist way; and I think that's the real practice. Funny, isn't it? It turns out that the pie in the sky is the same pie that's in your refrigerator.

THE BEASTIE BOYS, "BODHISATTVA VOW" (1994)

The connection between pop music and Asian religions is at least as old as the sixties. The Beatles traveled to India in 1968, and experimented with mantra chanting. Other bands also have looked East for spiritual edification. Among those groups is the Beastie Boys, whose music combines hip hop, punk, and funk. By the mid-1990s, they had sold more than seven million records, with four platinum albums. They have played songs with Buddhist themes and toured with the Namgyal monks of Tibet, who performed purification rituals and sacred dances to open each day of the 1993 Lollapalooza, a musical tour with political aims. The band's Buddhist interests have been sparked by bassist Adam Yauch. Yauch, who visited Nepal and Kathmandu in the early 1990s, explained what attracted him to Buddhism: "The feeling I get from the rinpoches and His Holiness [the Dalai Lama] and even many of the Tibetan people in general. The people I've met are really centered in the heart; they are coming from a real clear, compassionate place." After studying Buddhism for four years, Yauch became a Buddhist in mid-1996. He also has worked diligently to educate Americans about the plight of the Tibetan people and to raise money to help Tibet regain its independence. Yauch wrote "Bodhisattva Vow," a song from the Beastie Boys' 1994 release *Ill Communication*, after an informal encounter with the Dalai Lama in Arizona in 1993: "He grabbed both of my hands and looked at me for a second, and I felt all this energy. . . . I thought, I need to write a song about the Bodhisattva vow." The song's lyrics follow closely a traditional version of the vow, which Yauch himself has taken. In the Buddhist tradition a *bodhisattva* is a living being who has committed to reach the full enlightenment of a Buddha, and anyone who takes the bodhisattva vow promises to compassionately help all sentient beings.

> As I develop the awakening mind
> I praise the Buddhas as they shine
> I bow before you as I travel my path
> To join your ranks, I make my full the task
> For the sake of all beings I seek
> The enlightened mind that I know I'll reap
> Respect to Shantideva and all the others
> Who brought down the dharma for sisters and brothers
>
> I give thanks for the world as a place to learn
> And for the human body that I'm glad to have earned
> And my deepest thanks to all sentient beings
> For without them there would be no place to learn what I'm seeing
> There's nothing here that's not been said before
> But I put it down now so that I'll be sure
> To solidify my own views
> And I'll be glad if it helps anyone else out too
>
> If others disrespect me or give me flack
> I'll stop and think before I react
> Knowing that they're going through insecure stages
> I'll take the opportunity to exercise patience
> I'll see it as a chance to help the other person
> Nip it in the bud before it can worsen
> A chance for me to be strong and sure
> As I think of the Buddhas who have come before
> As I praise and respect the good they've done
> Knowing only love can conquer hate in every situation
> We need other people in order to create
> The circumstances for the learning that we're here to generate
> Situations that bring up our deepest fears
> So we can work to release them until they're cleared

Beastie Boys, *Ill Communication*, musical recording, Hollywood, Calif.: Grand Royal/Capitol Records, 1994. "Bodhisattva Vow" reprinted by permisson of Adam Yauch. The quotations from Adam Yauch included in the headnote are taken from "Beastie Boys: The Big Show: An Interview with Adam Yauch," *Tricycle* (Winter 1994): 85–90.

Therefore it only makes sense
To thank our enemies despite their intent

The bodhisattva path is one of power and strength
A strength from within to go the length
Seeing others are as important as myself
I strive for a happiness of mental wealth
With the interconnectedness that we share as one
Every action that we take affects everyone
So in deciding for what a situation calls
There is a path for the good for all
I try to make my every action for that highest good
With the altruistic wish to achieve buddhahood
So I pledge here before everyone who's listening
To try to make my every action for the good of all beings
For the rest of my lifetime and even beyond
I vow to do my best to do no harm
And in times of doubt I can think on the dharma
And the enlightened ones who've graduated samsara.

CHILDREN RESPONDING TO *LITTLE BUDDHA* (1994)

Episodes of television shows like *Kung Fu* and *Bonanza* interpreted Asians and Asian religions for American audiences since the 1960s, and many other television and film writers sprinkled Asian religious references into their scripts. In one 1990 episode of *The Simpsons*, Bart turned to a strange blend of Zen and Taoism to improve his miniature golf game. A number of films have explored American military involvement with Japan, Korea, and Vietnam—or violence and oppression in Cambodia or Burma— and sometimes Buddhists and their temples formed part of the setting for these stories. The first film by an American director to explore Asian religions seriously was Oliver Stone's *Heaven and Earth* (1994), which followed closely the autobiographical books by Le Ly Hayslip, a Vietnamese Buddhist. A year earlier, however, another film that highlighted Buddhism appeared in U.S. theaters, Bernardo Bertolucci's *Little Buddha*. Like two films that followed a few years later (*Kundun* and *Seven Years in Tibet*), *Little Buddha* focuses on Tibetan Buddhism. The film tells the story of a Seattle boy whom a Tibetan lama has identified as the reincarnation of his own deceased master. Along the way the movie also narrates the life of the Buddha. *Little Buddha* did not meet with financial or critical success: one reviewer for an American Buddhist periodical dismissed it as so disappointing "that it could make *The Ten Commandments* seem understated by comparison." But understatement rarely appeals to children, and Bertolucci reported that he wanted to make a film his kids could watch. Of course, many more young moviegoers saw Leonardo (the adolescent crime-fighting turtle) meditate in the lotus position in *Teenage Mutant Ninja Turtles: The Movie* (1990), but as this survey of Buddhist childrens' reactions indicates, some Buddhist elementary school students across the country found something they liked in *Little Buddha*. The lasting value of this entry, however, is not its interpretations of the film. By recording *children's* interpretations, it provides a window into the religious worlds of these young Buddhists.

Josh Ikeda-Nash, age 5
Oakland, California
"What I want to know is, why were there two buddhas at the end? And I liked the part where Mara threw fireballs at Buddha. I think Buddha is the best person. Buddha and Martin Luther King Jr."

Courtney Flynn, age 8
Boston, Massachusetts
"I would be honored for being picked to be a great teacher."

Kate M. Linthicum, age 8
Albuquerque, New Mexico
"I liked the part where the monks sat down on the floor in the little boy's living room, because that doesn't usually happen—you usually sit on the chair. The monks think one of the three kids is the lama. At the end of the movie, though, the head monk bows to each of the three kids and calls them 'teacher.' "

Ten Ley Palsang, age 14
Boston, Massachusetts
"I liked when he pulled his own reflection out of the water. That was really cool. Last summer I went to Tibet and had the privilege to go to the Tsurpu monastery and witness the installment of His Holiness Karmapa's reincarnation, who was about seven years old. The movie did a very good job representing it. I never thought that three children could all be the reincarnations, but my mother told me after the movie that they each represented the lama's mind, body, and spirit."

Shane Jaynes, age 5
Los Angeles, California
"I didn't like the burning body. And I just don't understand the movie. I need to get a book on Siddhartha."

Nicholas Gaylord-Scott, age 6
Durham, North Carolina
"It was great! I liked the part when Siddhartha was having all those thoughts sitting by the tree. They tried to scare him, but he wasn't scared because it was just his imagination."

"Children Responding to Bernardo Bertolucci's *Little Buddha*," *Tricycle* (Fall 1994): 30–31. Reprinted by permission of *Tricycle: A Buddhist Review*.

Stuart Gaylord-Scott, age 8
Durham, North Carolina
"Awesome! My favorite part was when the children were visualizing Siddhartha getting enlightened. I especially liked when the army was trying to scare him."

Sonam Liberman, age 11
Somerville, Massachusetts
"The background and places were really pretty—I saw some places I remember from Nepal. I liked when they were doing the Buddha story and I liked the actor who played Buddha, Keanu Reeves."

Liza Walsh, age 6
Butte, Montana
"I never knew Buddha wore makeup!"

Rebecca Levin, age 11
Los Angeles, California
"The part I liked was when these people told the three kids the story of Prince Siddhartha and the most amazing part was when he got to *go out* and see how people lived their own life. If I were in that movie and I got picked to be one of the three kids that got chosen to be the head Buddhist, then I would meditate and meditate and meditate like Prince Siddhartha and then tell the story about him to my children and my grandchildren and it would be passed on in the family."

Tseten Zalichin, age 8
Takoma Park, Maryland
"There were a few scary parts. It explained to me that luxury isn't the best in life. In the beginning the Buddha had lots of fear. In the end he is fearless."

Francis Simon Gayek, age 8
Yellow Springs, Ohio
"I liked how the boy was reading the book and imagining the story, and also I really liked when they were doing the sand painting. If I were chosen as a tulku I would kind of feel sad about being taken away from my family, but I would kind of feel happy about being special."

PHIL JACKSON, "IF YOU MEET THE BUDDHA IN THE LANE, FEED HIM THE BALL" (1995)

Two passions—religion and basketball—have dominated Phil Jackson's life. He grew up in a strict and pious Protestant home. His father was a Pentecostal preacher who served small churches in Montana and North Dakota. His mother traveled throughout Montana before she married, spreading the Pentecostal message and forming new congregations. She continued to serve Christian churches alongside her husband during Jackson's youth. Jackson began to pull away from his inherited tradition as early as age twelve, when he was unable to experience the presence of the Holy Spirit by "speaking in tongues." His religious journey deepened during the 1960s at the University of North Dakota. There he studied religion, psychology, and philosophy and starred on the basketball court. After college, he played in the National Basketball Association for the New York Knicks. Jackson was appointed head coach of the NBA's Chicago Bulls in 1989. *Sacred Hoops* recounts his spiritual journey and explains his philosophy of sport, which is influenced in large measure by Zen Buddhism's emphasis on meditation and compassion.

What I was missing was spiritual direction. The unfulfilled legacy of my devout childhood had left an emptiness, a yearning to reconnect with the deeper mysteries of life.

. . . I started exploring a variety of paths. Inspired by *Sunseed*, a film about the search for enlightenment, I began taking yoga classes, reading books about Eastern religion, and attending lectures by Krishnamurti, Pir Vilayat Khan, and other spiritual teachers. By then my brother Joe had left academia and moved to the Lama Foundation in New Mexico to experience the Sufi way. I visited him there and participated in many of the rituals.

. . . My next step was to explore meditation. First I tried the simple breath-counting technique outlined in Lawrence LeShan's book, *How to Meditate*. That kept me busy for a while, but it was devoid of spiritual content and began to feel like mental calisthenics. I turned to Joel Goldsmith's *Practicing the Presence*, a book that attempts to bridge the gap between East and West by using Christian maxims as guidelines for meditation. Goldsmith demythologized meditation and helped me understand it within a Christian context. But the technique he recommended, which involved visualization and repeating inspirational phrases, was far too cerebral for me. The last thing I needed was to increase my level of mental activity.

Then I turned to Zen. Though my brother Joe had already introduced me to the basics, it wasn't until the mid-seventies that I started practicing seriously, using *Zen Mind, Beginner's Mind*, by the late Japanese roshi, Shunryu Suzuki, as my guide. One summer I began sitting with a small group of Zen students in Montana who were connected with the Mt. Shasta Abbey in northern California. By then I had remarried, to my present wife, June, and had another daughter, Chelsea. When I met June a few years earlier at a pinochle game in New York, she had just graduated from the University of Connecticut and was working at a job she hated at Bellevue Hospital. I invited her to spend the summer travelling around the northwest on my motorcycle. After that magical trip, June moved into my loft, and marriage soon followed.

The summer I discovered the Mt. Shasta group, Joe and I were consumed with building a vacation home for my family on Flathead Lake. Every morning at 5:30 he and I would start the day with a half hour of meditation, then in the afternoon we'd take a break to do Sufi grounding exercises. After we finished putting up the rough-cut pole-and-beam frame, we recruited one of the members

Chicago Bulls superstar Michael Jordan on the cover of a "Special Spirituality Issue" of *Swing* magazine, March 1996. Jordan's coach, Phil Jackson, wrote the Zen-inspired autobiography *Sacred Hoops* (1995). Copyright © 1996 Swing magazine. Used by permission.

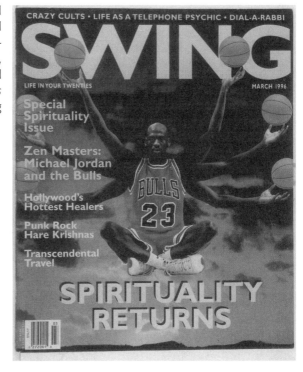

of the Zen group to help us build the deck. I was impressed by his demeanor as he worked. He was fast and efficient, and radiated a peaceful self-assurance, developed through years of daily Zen practice, that put everyone at ease.

What appealed to me about Zen was its emphasis on clearing the mind. As the Buddha put it in the Dhammapada, "Everything is based on mind, is led by mind, is fashioned by mind. If you speak and act with a polluted mind, suffering will follow you, as the wheels of an oxcart follow the footsteps of the ox. . . . If you speak and act with a pure mind, happiness will follow you, as a shadow clings to a form." But the Zen idea of a polluted mind is quite different from the traditional Christian perspective, which dictates that "impure" thoughts be rooted out and eliminated. What pollutes the mind in the Buddhist view is our desire to get life to conform to our peculiar notion of how things *should* be, we spend the majority of our time immersed in self-centered thoughts. *Why did this happen to me? What would make me feel better? If only I could make more money, win her heart, make my boss appreciate me*. The thoughts themselves are not the problem; it's our desperate clinging to them and our resistance to what's actually happening that causes us so much anguish.

. . . I found the Zen perspective on concentration particularly intriguing. According to Suzuki, concentration comes not from trying hard to focus on something, but from keeping your mind open and directing it at nothing. "Concentration means freedom," he writes in *Zen Mind, Beginner's Mind*. "In zazen practice we say your mind should be concentrated on your breathing, but the way to keep your mind on your breathing is to forget all about yourself and just to sit and feel your breathing. If you are concentrating on your breathing, you will forget yourself, and if you forget yourself you will be concentrated on your breathing."

As a basketball player this made a lot of sense to me. I knew from experience that I was far more effective when my mind was clear and I wasn't playing with an agenda of some kind, like scoring a certain number of points or showing up one of my opponents. The more skilled I became at watching my thoughts in zazen practice, the more focused I became as a player. I also developed an intimate knowledge of my mental processes on the basketball court.

. . . Basketball happens at such a fast pace that your mind has a tendency to race at the same speed as your pounding heart. As the pressure builds, it's easy to start thinking too much. But if you're always trying to figure the game out, you won't be able to respond creatively to what's going on. Yogi Berra once said about baseball: "How can you think and hit at the same time?" The same is true with basketball, except everything's happening much faster. The key is seeing and doing. If you're focusing on anything other than reading the court and doing what needs to be done, the moment will pass you by.

Sitting zazen, I learned to *trust the moment*—to immerse myself in action as mindfully as possible, so that I could react spontaneously to whatever was taking place. When I played without "putting a head on top of a head," as one Zen teacher puts it, I found that my true nature as an athlete emerged. It's not uncommon for basketball players, especially young ones, to expend a great deal of mental energy trying to be somebody they're not. But once you get caught up in that game, it's a losing battle. I discovered that I was far more effective when I became completely immersed in the action, rather than trying to control it and fill my mind with unrealistic expectations.

Another aspect of Zen that intrigued me was its emphasis on compassion. The goal of Zen is not just to clear the mind, but to open the heart as well. The two, of course, are interrelated. Awareness is the seed of compassion. As we begin to notice ourselves and others, just as we are, without judgment, compassion flows naturally.

. . . What does all this have to do with professional basketball? Compassion is not exactly the first quality one looks for in a player. But as my practice matured, I began to appreciate the importance of playing with an open heart. Love is the force that ignites the spirit and binds teams together.

. . . The most dramatic example of this occurred in 1990 when Scottie Pippen's father died while we were in the middle of a tough playoff series against the Philadelphia 76ers. Pippen skipped Game 4 to attend the funeral and was still in a solemn mood before the start of the next game. I thought that it was important for the team to acknowledge what was going on with Scottie and give him support. I asked the players to form a circle around him in the locker room and recite the Lord's Prayer, as we often do on Sundays. "We may not be Scottie's family," I said, "but we're as close to him as anyone in his life. This is a critical time for him. We should tell him how much we love him and show compassion for his loss." Demonstrations of heartfelt affection are rare in the NBA, and Scottie was visibly moved. That night, buoyed by his teammates, he went on a 29-point romp, as we finished off the 76ers to take the series.

AMY TAN, *THE KITCHEN GOD'S WIFE* (1991)

Some Asian-American writers explore religious themes in their poetry and fiction. Bharati Mukherjee, the Indian-born novelist, weaves Hindu symbols and themes into her writings. Amy Tan, working in a literary tradition that began in 1945 with the publication of *Fifth Chinese Daughter* by Jade Snow Wong, explores intergenerational tensions among Chinese Americans. For her characters that means confronting the cultural and religious inheritances of their ancestors. Best known for *The Joy Luck Club*, which was made into a film, Tan, who was born in Oakland in 1952, considers religion most directly in her 1991 novel *The Kitchen God's Wife*. Set in San Francisco's Chinatown, the story focuses on narrator Winnie Louie's relationship with her mother and her mother's generation. In chapter two, Winnie brings her non-Chinese husband, Phil, and their two young daughters to the Buddhist funeral of her Grand Auntie Du. Her aunt and her mother had attended the First Chinese Baptist Church, but both left when Winnie's father, a minister, had died. "I don't think Grand Auntie ever gave up her other beliefs, which weren't exactly Buddhist," Winnie says, "just all the superstitious rituals concerning attracting good luck and avoiding bad." In this scene the funeral presided over by two Buddhist monks has just ended, and Louie's husband has returned with the children, who went for a walk with their father to avoid the open-casket viewing. Then the family begins to talk about Auntie Du's will. Winnie is told that her aunt left her a small red lacquer altar of the Kitchen God, which she had played with as a child and (because Winnie was raised Christian) had viewed as "a Chinese version of a Christmas crèche." Disturbed by the story of the Kitchen God, a Chinese deity who decides which families deserve good luck in the coming year, Winnie ponders what to do with the gift from her deceased aunt—just as other Asian Americans have struggled to make sense of the religious symbols their ancestors' have bequeathed them.

GRAND AUNTIE DU'S FUNERAL

. . .

 Phil returns with Cleo, Tessa is right behind. And now I am actually sorry we have to leave.

 "We better hit the road," says Phil. I put the teacup down.

 "Don't forget," my mother says to Phil. "Grand Auntie's present in the laundry room."

 "A present?" Cleo says. "Do I have a present too?"

Phil throws me a look of surprise.

"Remember?" I lie. "I told you—what Grand Auntie left us in her will."

He shrugs, and we all follow my mother to the back.

"Of course it's just old things," says my mother. She turns on the light, and then I see it, sitting on the clothes dryer. It is the altar for Grand Auntie's good-luck god, the Chinese crèche.

"Wow!" Tessa exclaims. "A Chinese dollhouse."

"I can't see! I can't see!" Cleo says, and Phil lifts the altar off the dryer and carries it into the kitchen.

The altar is about the size of a small upturned drawer, painted in red lacquer. In a way, it resembles a miniature stage for a Chinese play. There are two ornate columns in front, as well as two ceremonial electric candles made out of gold and red plastic and topped by red Christmas tree bulbs for flames. Running down the sides are wooden panels decorated with gold Chinese characters.

"What does that say?" I ask my mother.

She traces her finger down one, then the other. "*Jye shiang ru yi*. This first word is 'luck,' this other is another kind of luck, and these two mean 'all that you wish.' All kinds of luck, all that you wish."

"And who is this on the inside, this man in the picture frame?" The picture is almost cartoonlike. The man is rather large and is seated in regal splendor, holding a quill in one hand, a tablet in the other. He has two long whiskers, shaped like smooth, tapered black whips.

"Oh, this we call Kitchen God. To my way of thinking, he was not too important. Not like Buddha, not like Kwan Yin, goddess of mercy—not that high level, not even the same level as the Money God. Maybe he was like a store manager, important, but still many, many bosses above him."

Phil chuckles at my mother's Americanized explanation of the hierarchy of Chinese deities. I wonder if that's how she really thinks of them, or if she's used this metaphor for our benefit.

"What's a kitchen god?" says Tessa. "Can I have one?"

"He is only a story," answers my mother.

"A story!" exclaims Cleo. "I want one."

My mother's face brightens. She pats Cleo's head. "You want another story from Ha-bu? Last night, you did not get enough stories?"

"When we get home," Phil says to Cleo. "Ha-bu is too tired to tell you a story now."

But my mother acts as if she has not heard Phil's excuses. "It is a very simple story," she says to Cleo in a soothing voice, "how he became Kitchen God. It is this way."

And as my mother begins, I am struck by a familiar feeling, as if I am Cleo, again three years old, still eager to believe everything my mother has to say.

"In China long time ago," I hear my mother say, "there was a rich farmer named Zhang, such a lucky man. Fish jumped in his river, pigs grazed his land, ducks flew around his yard as thick as clouds. And that was because he was blessed with a hardworking wife named Guo. She caught his fish and herded his pigs. She fattened his ducks, doubled all his riches, year after year. Zhang had everything he could ask for—from the water, the earth, and the heavens above.

"But Zhang was not satisfied. He wanted to play with a pretty, carefree woman named Lady Li. One day he brought this pretty woman home to his house, made his good wife cook for her. When Lady Li later chased his wife out of the house, Zhang did not run out and call to her, 'Come back, my good wife, come back.'

"Now he and Lady Li were free to swim in each other's arms. They threw money away like dirty water. They slaughtered ducks just to eat a plate of their tongues. And in two years' time, all of Zhang's land was empty, and so was his heart. His money was gone, and so was pretty Lady Li, run off with another man.

"Zhang became a beggar, so poor he wore more patches than whole cloth on his pants. He crawled from the gate of one household to another, crying, 'Give me your moldy grain!'

"One day, he fell over and faced the sky, ready to die. He fainted, dreaming of eating the winter clouds blowing above him. When he opened his eyes again, he found the clouds had turned to smoke. At first he was afraid he had fallen down into a place far below the earth. But when he sat up, he saw he was in a kitchen, near a warm fireplace. The girl tending the fire explained that the lady of the house had taken pity on him—she always did this, with all kinds of people, poor or old, sick or in trouble.

" 'What a good lady!' cried Zhang. 'Where is she, so I can thank her?' The girl pointed to the window, and the man saw a woman walking up the path. Aiya! That lady was none other than his good wife Guo!

"Zhang began leaping about the kitchen looking for some place to hide, then jumped into the kitchen fireplace just as his wife walked in the room.

"Good wife Guo poured out many tears to try to put the fire out. No use! Zhang was burning with shame and, of course, because of the hot roaring fire below. She watched her husband's ashes fly up to heaven in three puffs of smoke. Wah!

"In heaven, the Jade Emperor heard the whole story from his new arrival. 'For having the courage to admit you were wrong,' the Emperor declared, 'I make you Kitchen God, watching over everyone's behavior. Every year, you let me know who deserves good luck, who deserves bad.'

"From then on, people in China knew Kitchen God was watching them. From his corner in every house and every shop, he saw all kinds of good and bad habits spill out: generosity or greediness, a harmonious nature or a complaining one. And once a year, seven days before the new year, Kitchen God flew back up the fireplace to report whose fate deserved to be changed, better for worse, or worse for better."

"The end!" shouts Cleo, completely satisfied.

"Sounds like Santa Claus," says Phil cheerfully.

"Hnh!" my mother huffs in a tone that implies Phil is stupid beyond words. "He is not Santa Claus. More like a spy—FBI agent, CIA, Mafia, worse than IRS, that kind of person! And he does not give *you* gifts, you give *him* things. All year long you have to show him respect—give him tea and oranges. When Chinese

New Year's time comes, you must give him even better things—maybe whiskey to drink, cigarettes to smoke, candy to eat, that kind of thing. You are hoping all the time his tongue will be sweet, his head a little drunk, so when he has his meeting with the big boss, maybe he reports good things about you. This family has been good, you hope he says. Please give them good luck next year."

"Well, that's a pretty inexpensive way to get some luck," I say. "Cheaper than the lottery."

"No!" my mother exclaims, and startles us all. "You never know. Sometimes he is in a bad mood. Sometimes he says, I don't like this family, give them bad luck. Then you're in trouble, nothing you can do about it. Why should I want that kind of person to judge me, a man who cheated his wife? His wife was the good one, not him."

"Then why did Grand Auntie keep him?" I ask.

My mother frowns, considering this. "It is this way, I think. Once you get started, you are afraid to stop. Grand Auntie worshipped him since she was a little girl. Her family started it many generations before, in China."

"Great!" says Phil. "So now she passes along this curse to us. Thanks, Grand Auntie, but no thanks." He looks at his watch and I can tell he's impatient to go.

"It was Grand Auntie's gift to you," my mother says to me in a mournful voice. "How could she know this was not so good? She only wanted to leave you something good, her best things."

"Maybe the girls can use the altar as a dollhouse," I suggest. Tessa nods, Cleo follows suit. My mother stares at the altar, not saying anything.

"I'm thinking about it this way," she finally announces, her mouth set in an expression of thoughtfulness. "You take this altar. I can find you another kind of lucky god to put inside, not this one." She removes the picture of the Kitchen God. "This one, I take it. Grand Auntie will understand. This kind of luck, you don't want. Then you don't have to worry."

"Deal!" Phil says right away. "Let's pack 'er up."

. . .

CHAPTER 19

Interreligious Dialogue

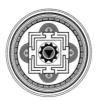

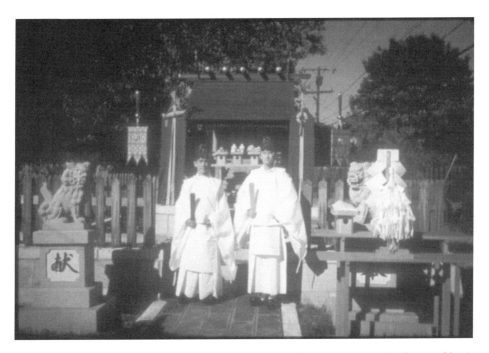

Rev. Ochiai (left) and Rev. Iwasaki (right) at Tsubaki Grand Shrine of America, Stockton, California. Members of both the Tsubaki Grand Shrine in Japan and this American outgrowth (dedicated 1987) have been active in Shinto-Unitarian interfaith dialogue. Courtesy of The Pluralism Project, Harvard University.

THOMAS MERTON, LETTER FROM ASIA (1968)

Thomas Merton (1915–68) was the most influential Roman Catholic monk of the twentieth century and a leader in the Christian encounter with Asian religions. Born in France and raised an Anglican, he converted to Catholicism in 1938. He then joined a religious order. Catholics have a number of religious orders. Some are "contemplative," while others focus on teaching, nursing, missions, or other more "active" pursuits. Merton joined a contemplative monastic order, the Trappists or Reformed Cistercians of the Strict Observance, which required not only the usual vows of poverty, chastity, and obedience, but also a vow of silence. In Our Lady of Gethsemani Abbey near Bardstown, Kentucky, Merton continued his search for the experience of God, while never forgetting the world outside. From the silence of that monastery, Merton wrote over three hundred articles and sixty books, including his best-selling spiritual autobiography, *The Seven Story Mountain* (1948). Merton also spoke out often on social issues like war, poverty, and racism. But at heart he was a contemplative, and during the last year of his life he traveled to Asia to attend two meetings, one with Catholic abbots and one with representatives of Asian religions. While in Asia, he conversed about monasticism and inquired about meditation. In this letter from New Delhi, India, just one month before his accidental death by electrocution in Thailand, Merton describes his encounters with the Dalai Lama, the exiled head of the Tibetan Buddhists, and Chogyam Trungpa Rinpoche, the young Tibetan abbot who later would establish an important Buddhist center in Colorado.

NOVEMBER CIRCULAR LETTER TO FRIENDS

November 9, 1968
New Delhi, India

Dear Friends:

This newsletter is not a reply to mail because I have not been getting mail on this Asian trip and have not had time to write letters either. As you probably know, I have received permission to be absent from my monastery for several months, chiefly because I was invited to attend a meeting of Asian Catholic abbots in Bangkok and give a talk there. Since this gave me an opportunity to be in Asia, I have been permitted to extend the trip a little in order to learn something about Asian monasticism, particularly Buddhist. I will also be visiting our Cistercian monasteries in Indonesia, Hong Kong, and Japan, and giving some talks there. Apart from that, the trip is not concerned with talking but with learning and with making contact with important people in the Buddhist monastic field. I am especially interested in Tibetan Buddhism and in Japanese (possibly Chinese) Zen.

Thomas Merton, "November Circular Letter to Friends," 9 November 1968, in Thomas P. McDonnell, ed., *A Thomas Merton Reader*, revised edition (Garden City, New York: Image Books, 1974), 447–52. Reprinted by permission of the Merton Legacy Trust.

(Maybe there are still some Chinese Ch'an [Zen] centers in Taiwan.) I hope to see John Wu in Taiwan.

. . .

I don't want to waste time and paper in gossip. The main point of this letter is to tell you something about my contacts with Tibetan mysticism and my meeting with the Dalai Lama in his new headquarters, high on a mountain at Dharamsala, which is an overnight train trip from Delhi, up in the Himalayas. (The Himalayas are the most beautiful mountains I have ever seen. There is something peculiar about the light there, a blue and a clarity you see nowhere else.) I spent eight days at Dharamsala making a kind of retreat, reading and meditating and meeting Tibetan masters. I had three long interviews with the Dalai Lama and spoke also with many others.

The Dalai Lama is the religious head of the Tibetan Buddhists and also in some ways their temporal leader. As you know, he had to escape from Tibet in 1959 when the Chinese Communists took over his country. There are many Tibetan refugees living in tents in the mountains, and many also forming colonies on tea plantations. I have seen some monastic communities on these plantations. The Dalai Lama is much loved by his people, and they are the most prayerful people I have seen. Some of them seem to be praying constantly, and I don't mean monks, lay people. Some always have rosaries in their hands (counting out Buddhist mantras), and I have seen some with prayer wheels. It is customary in the West to laugh at prayer wheels, but the people I have seen using them looked pretty recollected to me. They were obviously deep in prayer and very devout.

The Dalai Lama is thirty-three years old, a very alert and energetic person. He is simple and outgoing and spoke with great openness and frankness. He is in no sense what you would expect of a political emigré, and the things he said about Communism seemed to me fair and objective. His real interests are monastic and mystical. He is a religious leader and scholar, and also a man who has obviously received a remarkable monastic formation. We spoke almost entirely about the life of meditation, about samadhi (concentration), which is the first stage of meditative discipline and where one systematically clarifies and recollects his mind. The Tibetans have a very acute, subtle, and scientific knowledge of "the mind" and are still experimenting with meditation. We also talked of higher forms of prayer, of Tibetan mysticism (most of which is esoteric and kept strictly secret), especially comparing Tibetan mysticism with Zen. In either case the highest mysticism is in some ways quite "simple"—but always and everywhere the Dalai Lama kept insisting on the fact that one could not attain anything in the spiritual life without total dedication, continued effort, experienced guidance, real discipline, and the combination of wisdom and method (which is stressed by Tibetan mysticism). He was very interested in our Western monasticism and the questions he asked about the Cistercian life were interesting. He wanted to know about the vows, and whether the vows meant that one became committed to a "high attainment" in the mystical life. He wanted to know if one's vows constituted an initiation into a mystical tradition and experience under a qualified master, or were they just "equivalent to an oath"—a kind of agreement to stick around. When

I explained the vows, then he still wanted to know what kind of attainment the monks might achieve and if there were possibilities of a deep mystical life in our monasteries. I said well, that is what they are supposed to be for, but many monks seem to be interested in something else. . . . I would note, however, that some of the monks around the Dalai Lama complain of the same things our monks do: lack of time, too much work, inability to devote enough time to meditation, etc. I don't suppose the Dalai Lama has much time on his hands, but in the long talks we had on meditation I could see that he has certainly gone very thoroughly and deeply into it and is a man of high "attainment." I have also met many other Tibetans who are impressive in this way, including Tibetan lay people who are very far advanced in a special type of Tibetan contemplation which is like Zen and is called dzogchen.

At this point in the letter I was interrupted, and went out to meet a Cambodian Buddhist monk who has been running a small monastery in India for years. He is of the Theravada (Southern or Hinayana) tradition, different from the Tibetan. Here too the emphasis is on disciplining the mind and knowing it inside out. But the methods are simpler than the Tibetan ones and go less far. He told me that the best monks in the Theravada tradition are in Burma and Thailand. In fact I did see a monastery in Bangkok and met a very interesting English Buddhist monk [Phra Khantipalo] who has a great reputation for scholarship and fervor among the Thais. He was just about to withdraw to one of the "forest wats" or small eremitical meditation monasteries in the northern jungles of Thailand where the best masters are found. These are almost completely unknown to Westerners.

One of the most interesting people I have met is a young Tibetan abbot who, since escaping from Tibet, has been trained at Oxford and has started a small monastery in Scotland. He is very successful there, apparently, and is a talented man. He has written a book called *Born in Tibet* about his experiences in escaping. I recommend it. (His name is Chogyam Trungpa Rimpoche.)

I have also had some contact with the Sufi tradition (Moslem), which has penetrated India in the Delhi area (which used to be capital of the Mogul empire and is still quite Moslem.) I met an expert on Sufism who told me of the meetings at which the Sufis of this area use singing to induce contemplation, but I have not been to any of them. I do hope to hear some singing of this type in Urdu at a local restaurant where it is featured on week ends. The food here by the way is wild, it is a positive menace. For the most part I try to stick to Chinese food rather than Indian, which is (for me at least) lethal.

In summary: I can say that so far my contacts with Asian monks have been very fruitful and rewarding. We seem to understand one another very well indeed. I have been dealing with Buddhists mostly, and I find that the Tibetans above all are very alive and also generally well trained. They are wonderful people. Many of the monasteries, both Thai and Tibetan, seem to have a life of the same kind as was lived, for instance, at Cluny in the Middle Ages: scholarly, well trained, with much liturgy and ritual. But they are also specialists in meditation and contemplation. This is what appeals to be most. It is invaluable to have direct contact with people who have really put in a lifetime of hard work in training their minds and liberating themselves from passion and illusion. I do not say they are all saints, but certainly they are men of unusual quality and depth, very warm and wonderful people. Talking with them is a real pleasure. For instance, the other day one of the lamas, at the end of our meeting, composed a poem for me in Tibetan, so I composed one for him (in English), and we parted on this note of traditional Asian monastic courtesy. There is much more I could write about: the rich art, music, etc. But it would get too involved.

I hope you will understand why I cannot answer my mail these days. I am entirely occupied with these monastic encounters and with the study and prayer that are required to make them fruitful. I hope you will pray for me and for all those I will be meeting. I am sure the blessing of God will be upon these meetings, and I hope much mutual benefit will come from them. I also hope I can bring back to my monastery something of the Asian wisdom with which I am fortunate to be in contact—but it is something very hard to put into words.

I wish you all the peace and joy in the Lord and an increase of faith: for in my contacts with these new friends I also feel consolation in my own faith in Christ and His indwelling presence. I hope and believe He may be present in the hearts of all of us.

With my very best regards always, cordially yours in the Lord Jesus, and in His Spirit.

THOMAS MERTON

MASAO ABE AND JOHN COBB, "BUDDHIST-CHRISTIAN DIALOGUE" (1981)

An international movement that encouraged interreligious dialogue grew from the exchanges that Merton and many others had been having in Asia and America. Some Americans—mostly liberal Catholics, Protestants, and Jews—sought in-depth conversations with members of other religions. They held meetings, formed organizations, and started journals. Participants brought to the table different aims, but most agreed that they had come together to explore similarities and differences, while remaining open to the possibility that they might be changed by the encounters. These dialogues occurred among members of many faiths, including Hindus, Sikhs, Jains, Confucians, Muslims, and Jews—especially during the 1980s, when the movement had enormous vitality. One of the liveliest dialogues crossed Buddhist and Christian boundaries, and those conversations continued into the 1990s. Two leading participants in this interreligious encounter were the Japanese Zen Buddhist philosopher Masao Abe and the American Methodist theologian John Cobb. In 1981, an American journal published an interview with Abe and Cobb, who candidly, if politely, discussed the strengths and weaknesses of the Christian and Buddhist traditions.

Masao Abe and John Cobb, interviewed by Bruce Long, "Buddhist-Christian Dialogue: Past, Present, and Future," *Buddhist-Christian Studies* (1981): 15–16, 18–19, 24–25. Reprinted by permission of *Buddhist-Christian Studies*.

MASAO ABE AND JOHN COBB: A DIALOGUE

Abe: Besides organized forms of Buddhist-Christian dialogue, I published an article "Buddhism and Christianity as a Problem Today" in *Japanese Religions* in 1963 (Vol. 3) . . . . To my surprise, I received many responses from abroad: Christians, scholars, and philosophers. . . .

Long: Would you describe, briefly, what you stated in that article to be the central problem of Christianity and Buddhism in Japan?

Abe: I think Buddhism and Christianity have differing problems. Buddhism may be compatible with the scientific view of the world, whereas Christianity may have more difficulty in being compatible because of its emphasis on the personal God as the creator of the world and its generally personalistic character.

On the other hand, Buddhism is rather weak in its personalistic and historical aspects. Therefore, the weakness of Buddhism may be viewed as the strength of Christianity and vice-versa. Hence Buddhist-Christian dialogue might be focused on these divergences and each side learn from each other.

Long: Could you summarize the main thrust of the responses that you got, particularly from the Christian side? Was there some disagreement with your evaluation of Christianity and Buddhism?

Abe: Father Hans Waldenfels, for instance, disagreed with my interpretation of the Christian notion of God and *creato ex nihilo* [creation out of nothing] because I stated that the *nihil* implied by *creato ex nihilo* was a principle of privation in Christianity, whereas Absolute Nothingness is positive in Buddhism. He insisted that we should compare "Being" in Christianity and "Nothingness" in Buddhism because they are the last words for the two religions, respectively.

Long: Did anyone address the practice of veneration of various Buddhas in personalistic terms (such as Avalokitesvara and Maitreya) as being comparable to the Christian veneration of a personal god, though recognizing that the Buddhas aren't revered as creators? Nonetheless, they were personal foci of religious reverence. Were you challenged at any point on this matter?

Abe: Not in connection with that article.

Cobb: But you have, yourself, developed that idea very clearly in recent times.

Abe: Yes, the personal manifestation of the impersonal dharma is very important, and that point must be defined in Buddhism. In that connection, we have many things to learn from Christianity. . . .

Long: Now I would like to know from you, a Christian theologian, why *Buddhism*? What is the symbiotic relation or what are the ingredients in Christianity and Buddhism, historically and theologically, that would lead you and others like yourself to think that it is with Buddhism that our most fruitful dialogue can occur, and not with any number of the other great world religions?

Cobb: My view is that the reason Buddhism so fascinates us is that it is the most different from Christianity of the great religious traditions. It is interesting for Christians to have dialogue with a parent religion (Judaism), or with a sibling religion (Islam)—and that's very important and very fruitful. But that dialogue does not raise questions that probe so deeply to the heart of what the faith is all about. Hinduism is another option. But even there, perhaps because of common linguistic roots, there seems to be an easier basis to find equivalence.

Long: You're thinking, now, not of Pali or Sanskrit Buddhism, but of Japanese Buddhism?

Cobb: It is Mahayana Buddhism that is, in some way, dealing with the same level of the spiritual quest, and yet saying things that are so strikingly opposed to what we have taken for granted as the way one would speak if one were religious.

    Also, the Christian observing what happens to Buddhists, quickly recognizes that there are Buddhist saints. So although Buddhism doesn't talk about the self and doesn't talk about God (two central categories which we would ordinarily relate to sainthood), the result is one which we also recognize: sanctity.

    So how is it possible, on such a profoundly different basis, to arrive at results which, though not the same, are immediately impressive and attractive to Christian eyes? To deal with that is a theological problem. And, of course, one which involves practical problems.

    I think there is one other argument for saying Buddhism is the most important conversation partner, and that might be that it is, in another respect, most *like* Christianity. Of all the traditions in the world, Buddhism and Christianity seem to have been most successful in separating themselves from dependence upon the cultural matrix out of which they arose, and adapting to other cultural matrices in forming them and being transformed by them.

    Islam, of course, is very impressive in this respect too, but it seems to me generally, that you can speak of Islamic culture more than you can speak of Christian culture or Buddhist culture. So, in a certain sense, these two traditions seem to be the ones that have the greatest potentiality for a pluralistic universality. That, I think, is fascinating to Christians, also. . . .

Abe: Most Buddhist thinkers have rather strong convictions that
        Buddhism is deeper than Christianity as a religion, both spiri-
        tually and intellectually.

Cobb: And this has been, if anything, reinforced by the dialogue?

Abe: Maybe. Reinforced or evidenced.

Cobb: So for the Buddhist there is no sense of a need to move to some
        other position regarding this conviction?

Abe: Basically, no. Nevertheless, Buddhist thinkers are trying to cope
        with contemporary issues such as "science and religion," "his-
        tory and religion," "nihilism and religion" on the basis of the
        Buddhist realization of "emptiness."

Cobb: Whereas Christians have been forced to realize that the way they
        have thought about God is not nearly so penetratingly and sat-
        isfactorily established and thus, they are set in motion in some
        way.

        You have said some of this already. But to me, you seem
        also to be suggesting that there is a certain advantage which the
        Christians might have as a result of this: they are "on the way"
        to something else, whereas Buddhists have no such sense of be-
        ing "on the way." That is also my view: that there is an excit-
        ing promise in this Christian instability which may or may not
        be realized through the dialogue. I think Christians involved in
        the dialogue are learning new things. And up until now, I don't
        see that Buddhists have been learning new things in any really
        fundamental way.

Abe: But some Buddhist thinkers, including myself, are aware that
        Buddhism must develop itself through confrontation with
        Christianity. It may not be related to the most fundamental
        point. But, with such problems, as that of justice and the un-
        derstanding of history in regard to justice, I think Buddhists
        must learn from Christianity, because the idea of justice is very
        weak and unclear in Buddhism.

Cobb: The difference would still be that if you learn about history and
        justice from Christianity, for Buddhists this is *not* at the deepest
        level; whereas for many Christians one cannot go to a deeper
        level than history and justice. To suggest that there *is* a deeper
        level would have already been—for many Christians, though
        not for all—a misunderstanding of what God is doing in the
        world, and thus of what it means to be faithful.

        This point—as to whether the interest in history and justice
        is a secondary level or primary level interest—which seems to
        me to be a very fundamental issue for the dialogue has not as
        yet been very effectively engaged in the dialogue. This is partly
        because of the tendency for the Christians who have given lead-

ership to the dialogue to be themselves the more mystically inclined Christians.

RODGER KAMENETZ, *THE JEW IN THE LOTUS* (1994)

Since the day in Chicago in 1893 that C. T. Strauss, a Jew from New York, became
the first U.S. citizen formally to convert to Buddhism in the United States, Jews have
been drawn disproportionately to American Buddhism. Although only about 2.5 percent of the U.S. population is Jewish, between 6 and 30 percent of American Buddhists
are Jewish-born. Perhaps because of their "twoness"—as one put it, "I have Jewish
roots and Buddhist wings"—America's Jewish Buddhists ("Jubus") have been active
participants in interreligious dialogue. In 1989, a group of Jewish scholars and rabbis
met with the Dalai Lama in New Jersey, and in 1997 the Dalai Lama participated in
a Tibetan Freedom Passover Seder in Washington, D.C., with Supreme Court Justice
Stephen Breyer. In 1990, Rodger Kamenetz, a poet and English professor from
Louisiana State University, traveled with a Jewish delegation to Dharamsala, India, to
meet with the Dalai Lama in his homeland in exile. A self-described "secular Jew" who
does not identify himself as a Buddhist, Kamenetz reflects on his Indian encounters
with both Tibetan Buddhists and Jubus in *The Jew in the Lotus* (1994). In "Jewish
Buddhists, Buddhist Jews," a chapter from his book, Kamenetz describes an informal
exchange between Jews and Jubus at a Sabbath service in Dharamsala—an exchange
that caused Kamenetz to quicken his own commitment to "Jewish renewal."

A stroll through the Tibetan market at McLeod Ganj on Friday morning had already convinced me that a good number of Jews were seeking spiritual wisdom
in Dharamsala. . . . Since the sixties Dharamsala has been a way station for spiritual travelers, including Thomas Merton, Gary Snyder, and Allen Ginsberg. Now
a new generation, the long-haired and the monastically shorn, mingled freely with
Hindu beggars by the steps of the Llasa Guest House. . . .

I overheard some voices speaking Hebrew, then saw Moshe Waldoks in front
of a T-shirt shop in an animated conversation with three Israelis in khaki shorts.
Moshe was buying Tibetan yarmulkes for himself and his kids: beautiful pillbox
caps with fancy, thickly threaded embroidery and bits of blue glass glued in. They
were very princely. He introduced us and told the Israelis about our meeting with
the Dalai Lama, but they'd already heard about it from the buzz in the streets.
Moshe told them that all of Yiddishe Dharamsala was invited to the Saturday
morning service, and they promised to come. . . .

Still, when I hiked the quarter mile up from my quarters to Kashmir Cottage
Saturday morning, I was surprised by the size and variety of the crowd we'd
gathered. More than a *minyan* [a prayer quorum, typically of ten men]. . . .

Rabbi Schachter and Rabbi Greenberg officiated at Congregation Beth Kangra in delightful sunshine. Our old traveling companion, the Sephardi Torah, stood upright in its case, once more showing its power to bring Jewish sparks together. Rabbi Greenberg announced the portion we'd been mulling over all week, *Lekh Lekha* [Genesis 12:1–17:27]. The Hebrew means: Take yourself out. Go travel. Seek foreign lands. So Reb Zalman announced an aliyah for "those, like Abram, who travel, those who seek truth in other places." Most of our guests identified with that one and crowded around the Torah, including an academic couple from Massachusetts traveling through India with their kids, and four Jewish Buddhist nuns in robes, among them Henrietta Szold's great-granddaughter. From Hadassah to Dharamsala in three generations! . . .

With the mass aliyah of Jews and JUBUs assembled, Yitz and Zalman chanted the Torah. They spot translated the Hebrew into English. At the same time, they maintained the Hebrew cantillation. It was a gracious and nimble performance that showed a remarkable command of the text. I realized that whatever their differences in outlook, they shared a deep reverence for the Torah.

Sitting around on lawn chairs, and in the cool grass, we later discussed a passage from the Torah portion. One nun asked if Abram's wars against the kings of Sodom could be interpreted as spiritual struggles against delusion.

But to Rabbi Greenberg at least, the wars were real. They illustrated an actual struggle to establish religion against violent opposition. They were like the wars Israel has to fight today. For Yitz, "Humans live in history. We have to make choices, sometimes painful choices."

A Western Buddhist challenged him. "What are we faced with in our present culture? Many of us see that Buddhism provides the balance we need in this world today."

Yitz Greenberg admitted being impressed by the Buddhist commitment to nonviolence. But he felt pacifism was only possible in the context of a balance of terror between larger nations. Neither Buddhists nor Jews could afford to be pacifists if their survival was at stake. For instance, on analogy to Israel's battles, Yitz very much supported the Tibetans fighting for their freedom and was skeptical of their winning in any other way. Likewise, to Dr. Isaac Bentwich, the young Israeli I'd met the night before, spiritual growth was always colored by historical circumstances. He compared the Dalai Lama to Abram, and the kings of Sodom to the rulers of China.

The discussants tried to resolve the conflict between survival and spiritual values. Could Buddhists fight to preserve a tradition of non-violence? Many Buddhists thought not. . . .

We moved on. The Jewish Buddhists had some of the same questions I had. They wanted to know if Judaism was flexible enough to adapt to our times. Could it respond to feminism, the ecological crisis, and the need for individual spiritual growth? Zalman Schachter, in the Hasidic style, offered a story as an answer. "A man opens a bank account in Switzerland. He's dying and he believes in reincarnation. Thirty years from now, he tells the bank officials, someone will come with a syllable. I want you to give him control of the account.

"Thirty years later a man comes and asks to withdraw all the money. When they question his judgment, saying that, after all, the original depositor told them to hold on to it, he says, 'I gave you the order last time around, but now I want to do what I want to do.'

"We're invested in a tradition so we have a continuity. The best people to invest in tradition are conservative. But the best people to spend it are those willing to take a risk.

"Our treasures—what a fantastic bank account we have grown. The past and the tradition have a vote but can't have a veto, because we are in unprecedented conditions. Now there's an understanding emerging that we are an organic part of all species, that religions are the organs of humanity."

The Jewish delegates and Jewish Buddhists replayed an old family quarrel. Jewish Buddhists felt that the bank account of Judaism had been empty for them when they came to make a withdrawal, whereas they had found real spiritual wealth in Buddhism.

I knew the immediate defensive reaction to that, it was the mountain or barrier I had put up in my own thinking: the Jewish community tends to dismiss such people as flakes or apostates. I had come to Dharamsala with a few of these attitudes myself.

But in the Shabbat sun, those mountains were melting. I'd been deeply impressed with the Dalai Lama and other Buddhist masters, and having felt firsthand the attraction of another religion, I could no longer be judgmental about Jewish Buddhists. I'd been moved when the Dalai Lama addressed our group as his Jewish brothers and sisters. Well, the JUBUs were certainly my brothers and sisters! So I was eager to talk to them, to learn in depth about their Jewish backgrounds, how they came to Buddhism, how they feel about Judaism.

Extremely open about their lives and beliefs, what they had to say that morning seemed revealing not just about them, but about the problems of gaining access to Jewish spirituality—and the need for a new way of teaching it, for a Jewish renewal.

THE PARLIAMENT OF THE WORLD'S RELIGIONS CENTENNIAL (1993)

To celebrate the centennial of the 1893 World's Parliament of Religions, a diverse group of religious leaders planned and attended a similar event in the same city, Chicago, in 1993. The nineteenth-century Parliament continued to occupy a place in the American imagination a hundred years later because, its champions claimed, it had bridged religious chasms and symbolized America's diversity. Although differences over doctrine and practice divided the 1993 participants, many found agreement on ethical issues. A group of religious leaders met during the Parliament to discuss a joint statement on ethics, and 143 prominent participants signed the resulting declaration, "Towards a Global Ethic." Among the signers were Hindus, Buddhists, Baha'is, Zoroastrians, Muslims, Neo-Pagans, Native Americans, Taoists, Christians, Sikhs, Jains, and Jews. The Dalai Lama, Louis Farrakhan, and Joseph Cardinal Bernardin endorsed the document. However, another signator, the Venerable Samu Sunim from the Buddhist Society of Compassionate Wisdom in Chicago, joined five other Buddhists from Korea, Sri Lanka, Thailand, and Kampuchea in sending a protest letter to the organizing council. In an unpublished document dated 7 August 1997, Samu Sunim explained that his discomfort began on 5 August 1993 when the Trustee reception, which was organized to publicize the upcoming Parliament, opened and closed with prayers to "Almighty God." His displeasure with the theistic language grew when the Parliament opened. "At the end of the evening [28 August]," Samu Sunim recalled, "I had a strong feeling that the Parliament was being held under the sponsorship of God for theistic religions." To express his feelings, the Korean Buddhist drafted a letter to the conference's organizing body and distributed copies to the other participants. It did not seem to have much effect, however. In his welcome speech on 2 September the chairperson of the Assembly of Religious and Spiritual Leaders urged participants to appeal to God for guidance. To respond to Buddhist concerns, organizers did allow Samu Sunim to read this statement to the assembled religious leaders that day— although only after the media had left the hall. History was repeating itself. Just as some Buddhists at the 1893 Parliament had been offended because the speakers privileged Christianity and presupposed theism, these Buddhists at the 1993 event felt compelled to remind the Parliament's Council that Buddhists do not regard Buddha as a god and do not worship a creator.

TOWARDS A GLOBAL ETHIC (AN INITIAL DECLARATION) 1993 PARLIAMENT OF THE WORLD'S RELIGIONS CHICAGO, ILLINOIS, USA

This interfaith declaration is the result of a two-year consultation among scholars and theologians representing the world's communities of faith.

On September 2–4, 1993, the document was discussed by an assembly of religious and spiritual leaders meeting as part of the 1993 Parliament of the World's Religions in Chicago. Respected leaders from all the world's major faiths signed the declaration as individuals, agreeing that it represents an initial effort: a point of beginning for a world sorely in need of ethical consensus.

The Council for a Parliament of the World's Religions and the persons who have endorsed this text offer it to the world as an initial statement of those rules for living on which the world's religions agree.

    . . .

"Towards a Global Ethic (An Initial Declaration), 1993 Parliament of the World's Religions, Chicago, Illinois, USA," reprinted in *The United Nations and the World's Religions: Prospects for a Global Ethic* (Cambridge, Mass.: Boston Research Center for the 21st Century, 1995), 123–25. Reprinted by permission of the Boston Research Center for the 21st Century; The Venerable Samu Sunim, et al., "To the Council for a Parliament of the World's Religions," unpublished document, 31 August 1993. Used by permission of the Venerable Samu Sunim and the Buddhist Society for Compassionate Wisdom.

The Declaration of a Global Ethic

The world is in agony. The agony is so pervasive and urgent that we are compelled to name its manifestations so that the depth of this pain may be made clear.

Peace eludes us . . . the planet is being destroyed . . . neighbors live in fear . . . women and men are estranged from each other . . . children die.

This is abhorrent!

We condemn the abuses of Earth's ecosystems.

We condemn the poverty that stifles life's potential: the hunger that weakens the human body; the economic disparities that threaten so many families with ruin.

We condemn the social disarray of the nations; the disregard for justice which pushes citizens to the margin; the anarchy overtaking our communities; and the insane death of children from violence. In particular we condemn aggression and hatred in the name of religion.

But this agony need not be.

It need not be because the basis for an ethic already exists. This ethic offers the possibility of a better individual and global order, and leads individuals away from despair and societies away from chaos.

We are women and men who have embraced the precepts and practices of the world's religions.

We affirm that a common set of core values is found in the teachings of the religions, and that these form the basis of a global ethic.

We affirm that this truth is already known, but yet to be lived in heart and action.

We affirm that there is an irrevocable, unconditional norm for all areas of life, for families and communities, for races, nations, and religions. There already exist ancient guidelines for human behavior which are found in the teachings of the religions of the world and which are the condition for a sustainable world order.

We Declare:

We are interdependent. Each of us depends on the well-being of the whole, and so we have respect for the community of living beings, for people, animals, and plants, and for the preservation of Earth, the air, water and soil.

We take individual responsibility for all we do. All our decisions, actions, and failures to act have consequences.

We must treat others as we wish others to treat us. We make a commitment to respect life and dignity, individuality and diversity, so that every person is treated humanely, without exception. We must have patience and acceptance. We must be able to forgive, learning from the past but never allowing ourselves to be enslaved by memories of hate. Opening our hearts to one another, we must sink our narrow differences for the cause of the world community, practicing a culture of solidarity and relatedness.

We consider humankind our family. We must strive to be kind and generous. We must not live for ourselves alone, but should also serve others, never forgetting the children, the aged, the poor, the suffering, the disabled, the refugees, and the lonely. No person should ever be considered or treated as a second-class citizen, or be exploited in any way whatsoever. There should be equal partnership between men and women. We must not commit any kind of sexual immorality. We must put behind us all forms of domination or abuse.

We commit ourselves to a culture of nonviolence, respect, justice, and peace. We shall not oppress, injure, torture, or kill other human beings, forsaking violence as a means of settling differences.

We must strive for a just social and economic order, in which everyone has an equal chance to reach full potential as a human being. We must speak and act truthfully and with compassion, dealing fairly with all, and avoiding prejudice and hatred. We must not steal. We must move beyond the dominance of greed for power, prestige, money, and consumption to make a just and peaceful world.

Earth cannot be changed for the better unless the consciousness of individuals is changed first. We pledge to increase our awareness by disciplining our minds, by meditation, by prayer, or by positive thinking. Without risk and a readiness to sacrifice there can be no fundamental change in our situation. Therefore we commit ourselves to this global ethic, to understanding one another, and to socially beneficial, peace-fostering, and nature-friendly ways of life.

We invite all people, whether religious or not, to do the same.

TO THE COUNCIL FOR A PARLIAMENT OF THE WORLD'S RELIGIONS

August 31, 1993

We the undersigned Buddhists and friends are deeply concerned with the following and urge the Parliament to take proper measures in order to rectify the situation.

Having listened to invocations, prayers and benedictions offered by religious leaders of different host committees during the Opening Plenary and having attended the evening Plenary on Interfaith Understanding, we could not help but feel that the 1993 Parliament of the World's Religions is being held for the worshippers of Almighty and Creator God and efforts are being made towards "achieving oneness under God."

Further, with great astonishment we watched leaders of different religious traditions define all religions as religions of God and unwittingly rank Buddha with God. We found this lack of knowledge and insensitivity all the more surprising because we, the religious leaders of the world, are invited to this Parliament in order to promote mutual understanding and respect, and we are supposed to be celebrating one hundred years of interfaith dialog and understanding!

We would like to make it known to all that Shakyamuni Buddha, the founder of Buddhism, was not God or a god. He was a human being who attained full Enlightenment through meditation and showed us the path of spiritual awakening and freedom. Therefore, Buddhism is not a religion of God. Buddhism is a religion of wisdom, enlightenment and compassion. Like the worshippers of God who believe that salvation is available to all through confession of sin and a life of prayer, we Buddhists believe that salvation and enlightenment is available to all through removal of defilements and delusion and a life of meditation. However, unlike those who believe in God who is separate from us, Buddhists believe that Buddha which means "one who is awake and enlightened" is inherent in us all as Buddhanature or Buddhamind.

Our concern is threefold:

1. We feel that mutual understanding and appreciation of different approaches to spirituality and salvation should be a prerequisite for an interreligious gathering like A Parliament of the World's Religions.
2. We feel that we the religious leaders of the world gathered here at this historic Parliament of the World's Religions must establish strong guidelines for religious tolerance and cooperation and serve as inspirations for the different religious communities in the world.
3. Language and communication skills are important elements in bringing about agreement and cooperation. We must train ourselves to be sensitive to each other and learn to use language that is inclusive and all embracing. We suggest we use "Great Being" or "power of the transcendent" or "Higher Spiritual Authority" instead of God in reference to the ultimate spiritual reality. We are open to other suggestions and discussions on this matter.

Today we religious leaders and teachers of the world are facing unprecedented new opportunities for our future together in the global village as well as severe challenges from the secular world. In order to seize upon these opportunities for our common future we must change. We would have to depart from our traditional religious attitudes and open our hearts in order to introduce to the world community a new religious consciousness and vision for peace, happiness and ecological justice. And we believe that Buddhism can contribute to this new vision with the message that we can practice religion with or without God. In other words, we must broaden our religious base in order to meet the challenges of our secular world, so that the civilizing influence of the liberal religious traditions would prevail over secular forces.

We the undersigned respectfully request that Mr. Daniel Gomez-Ibanez, Executive Director, and members of the Executive Board of the Council for a Parliament of the World's Religions bring this matter to the attention of the Parliament and respond to us.

Respectfully,

Venerable Samu Sunim,   Buddhist Society of Compassionate
                                          Wisdom Zen Buddhist Temple,
                                          Chicago

Venerable Maha Ghosananda,	Supreme Patriarch of Cambodian Buddhism, Inter-Religious Mission for Peace in Cambodia
Zen Master Seung Sahn,	Founder and Head, Kwan Um Zen School, International
Venerable Walpola Piyananda,	Abbot, Dhamma Vijaya Buddhist Temple Chief Sangha Nayaka, Sri Lankan Buddhism U.S.A.
Rev. Chung Ok Lee,	Head, Won Buddhists (Korea) in the U.S.A. Vice-chair, Committee on Religious NGOs at the U.N.
Dr. Chatsumarn Kabilsingh,	Professor, Thammasat University, Bankok, Thailand

WALTER MARTIN, *THE KINGDOM OF THE CULTS* (1985)

Not all American Christians and Jews engaged in interreligious dialogue or celebrated ecumenical "Parliaments"; some were deeply suspicious of all activities that seemed to grant too much to other religions or to diminish the uniqueness of their own faiths. Many evangelical Protestants, convinced that Jesus offered the only way to salvation, denounced the new relativism that threatened to chip away at the Christian faith. Some published books and pamphlets comparing the truths of Christianity with the falsehoods of other religions. Fritz Ridenour's *So What's the Difference?*, which has sold more than 800,000 copies since it appeared in 1967, summarized and assessed major religious traditions. Its evangelical readers learned that "the Hindu's god is too small" and that Buddhism's goals "are beyond man's ability to reach." A similar book, Walter Martin's *The Kingdom of the Cults*, catalogs the errors of various new religious movements in America. Chapter nine takes on Zen Buddhism. After acknowledging that Zen has "grown by leaps and bounds" in America, Martin dismisses it as a "cult," with all the negative connotations that term had acquired since the 1978 mass suicide of more than nine hundred of Jim Jones's followers in Guyana. Zen, this conservative Protestant suggests, "is not only Biblically and theologically untenable, but also psychologically and socially detrimental."

ZEN BUDDHISM

The second oldest of all the cult systems considered in this book is a form of Buddhism, one of the major world religions with a following of many millions.

Walter Martin, *The Kingdom of the Cults* (Minneapolis: Bethany House Publishers, 1985), 261, 268–69. Reprinted by permission of Bethany House Publishers.

"Zen," as it is known in America, is derived from the Japanese branch of the "meditation" school of Buddhist philosophy introduced into Japan from China in the seventh century A.D. . . .

In the United States Zen has grown by leaps and bounds in the last few years. This is largely because of American's disillusionment with a valueless system of society and their turning to the counterfeit values of Eastern religion and philosophy.

Zen cannot be taken lightly, especially when it receives favorable attention from magazines of the standing of *Time, Newsweek, Life, U.S. News and World Report,* and *Reader's Digest,* to name a few. Zen itself is far more complex than the garbled jargon of pseudo-intellectuals who desperately want "a place in the sun," not by virtue of their capacity to earn it, but on the singularly selfish principle that they are entitled to it because of their own imagined intellectual and philosophical superiority to their fellow man. This is no exaggeration, and anyone acquainted with pseudo adherents to Zen will readily testify to it. They literally believe that the world owes them a living. So, ceaselessly mouthing fragmented sentences, liberally sprinkled with symbolic language, Zen terminology and fractured logic, they urge the general populace to embrace what they claim has emancipated them. . . .

Zen attracts people by its specious arguments, but offers not truth. It is the delusion of "blind guides," but is not the true way. It casts some dim light, but does not give the true light, nor the life, "the life (that) was the light of man." The whole creation groans and travails in pain, searches and probes in darkness. Yet man comprehended not the light which is come into the world and shines in darkness; they loved the darkness rather than the light and thus became easy preys of false prophets.

Zen is objectionable not only because it is inadequate in its teachings but also futile in its effects. Zen is inadequate, because (1) it denies the infinity and transcendence of a living and personal God by identifying Him with nature. It is in fact a very subtle form of atheism, disguised by the language of theism, and embellished with seductive eloquence. (2) It engenders a spirit of mysticism by taking refuge in its doctrine of radical intuition by looking into one's own nature. But to look "within" for an authoritative guide without divine revelation will surely fall into the delusion of Satan. . . . (3) It denies the need of external rules of morality. This will inevitably plunge mankind into pure anarchic relativism. (4) It rejects the grace of God and the need of a Savior by exalting and deifying man. This will surely lead the world to eternal perdition because "the whole godless world lies in the power of the evil one." Indeed, it is "a way which seems right unto a man, but the end thereof are the ways of death!" . . .

In a word, Zen is not only Biblically and theologically untenable, but also psychologically and socially detrimental. . . . Zen is a technique by which to achieve "a mental breakdown." . . . Now many Westerners, weary of their conventional religion and philosophy, find some charm in Zen and have become prey to its plausible teachings. If unchecked, the consequences will be surely disastrous to our culture.

CHAPTER 20

Mapping Legal Boundaries:
Religion and State

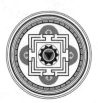

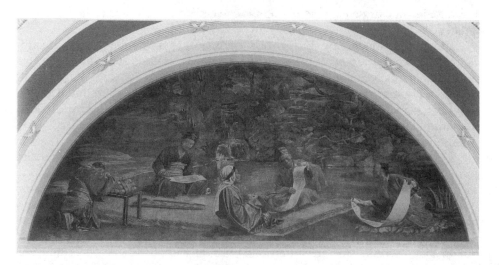

"The Recording of Precedents" (1905) by American painter John La Farge, a lunette of Confucius and his pupils transcribing documents, Supreme Court Room of the State Capitol, St. Paul, Minnesota.

JUSTICE WILLIAM DOUGLAS, ASIAN RELIGIONS ACCORDING TO THE SUPREME COURT (1965)

The First Amendment to the United States Constitution states that "Congress shall make no law respecting an establishment of religion, or prohibiting the free exercise thereof." But what is religion? Does Buddhism, for example, count? Hinduism? In 1965, the U.S. Supreme Court took up these questions. Three citizens had claimed draft exemptions as conscientious objectors, and their cases were consolidated into *U.S.* v. *Seeger*. In 1940, the Selective Training and Service Act had exempted from combat and the draft individuals who by "religious training and belief" were conscientiously opposed to war. That same year, Chief Justice Charles Hughes had written, "The essence of religion is belief in a relation to God involving duties superior to those arising from any human relation." In 1948, Congress defined "religious training and belief" as "an individual's belief in a relation to a Supreme Being involving duties superior to those arising from any human relation, but [not including] essentially political, sociological, or philosophical views or a merely personal moral code." None of the litigants in *U.S.* v. *Seeger* were avowed atheists, but none professed belief in either "God" or a "Supreme Being." So the justices had to decide whether what they did believe constituted "religious training and belief." The Court determined it did: all three, in its judgment, deserved draft exemptions. In the Court's published opinion, Justice Tom Clark tried to craft workable definitions of terms such as *religion* and *God.* Mindful of the fact that "over 250 sects inhabit our land," Clark proffered elastic definitions that drew on Protestant theologian Paul Tillich's understanding of God as "the power of being" and religion as "ultimate concern." Justice William Douglas agreed with the Court's decision, but wrote a concurring opinion that considered the implications of the case for the freedom of religion of America's Hindus and Buddhists. Rebuking those who would characterize the United States as a Christian nation, he called the country "a nation of Buddhists, Confucianists, and Taoists, as well as Christians." Excerpted here are portions of Justice Douglas's concurring opinion, the U.S. Supreme Court's first extended reflection on Buddhist and Hindu thought.

The legislative history of this Act leaves much in the dark. But it is, in my opinion, not a tour de force if we construe the words "Supreme Being" to include the cosmos, as well as an anthropomorphic entity. If it is a tour de force so to hold, it is no more so than other instances where we have gone to extremes to construe an Act of Congress to save it from demise on constitutional grounds. . . .

The words "a Supreme Being" have no narrow technical meaning in the field of religion. Long before the birth of our Judeo-Christian civilization the idea of God had taken hold in many forms. Mention of only two—Hinduism and Buddhism—illustrates the fluidity and evanescent scope of the concept. In the Hindu religion the Supreme Being is conceived in the forms of several cult Deities. The chief of these, which stand for the Hindu Triad, are Brahma, Vishnu and Siva. Another Deity, and the one most widely worshipped, is Sakti, the Mother Goddess, conceived as power, both destructive and creative. Though Hindu religion encompasses the worship of many Deities, it believes in only one single God, the eternally existent One Being with his manifold attributes and manifestations. This idea is expressed in Rigveda, the earliest sacred text of the Hindus, in verse 46 of a hymn attributed to the mythical seer Dirghatamas (Rigveda, I, 164):

United States v. *Seeger*, 380 U.S. 163 (1965). Supreme Court opinions typically contain myriad footnotes as well as internal references. This decision, like the opinions that follow, has been edited to make the text more accessible to readers unfamiliar with this legal format.

They call it Indra, Mitra, Varuna and Agni. And also heavenly beautiful Garutman: The Real is One, though sages name it variously—They call it Agni, Yama, Matarisvan.

Indian philosophy, which comprises several schools of thought, has advanced different theories of the nature of the Supreme Being. According to the Upanisads, Hindu sacred texts, the Supreme Being is described as the power which creates and sustains everything, and to which the created things return upon dissolution. The word which is commonly used in the Upanisads to indicate the Supreme Being is Brahman. Philosophically, the . . . Supreme Being is the transcendental Reality which is Truth, Knowledge, and Bliss. It is the source of the entire universe. In this aspect Brahman is Isvara, a personal Lord and Creator of the universe, an object of worship. But, in the view of one school of thought, that of Sankara, even this is an imperfect and limited conception of Brahman which must be transcended: to think of Brahman as the Creator of the material world is necessarily to form a concept infected with illusion, or maya—which is what the world really is, in highest truth. Ultimately, mystically, Brahman must be understood as without attributes, as neti neti (not this, not that).

Buddhism—whose advent marked the reform of Hinduism—continued somewhat the same concept. As stated by Nancy Wilson Ross, "God—if I may borrow that word for a moment—the universe, and man are one indissoluble existence, one total whole. Only THIS—capital THIS—is. Anything and everything that appears to us as an individual entity or phenomenon, whether it be a planet or an atom, a mouse or a man, is but a temporary manifestation of THIS in form; every activity that takes place, whether it be birth or death, loving or eating breakfast, is but a temporary manifestation of THIS in activity. When we look at things this way, naturally we cannot believe that each individual person has been endowed with a special and individual soul or self. Each one of us is but a cell, as it were, in the body of the Great Self, a cell that comes into being, performs its functions, and passes away, transformed into another manifestation. Though we have temporary individuality, that temporary, limited individuality is not either a true self or our true self. Our true self is the Great Self; our true body is the Body of Reality, or the Dharmakaya, to give it its technical Buddhist name."

Does a Buddhist believe in "God" or a "Supreme Being"? That, of course, depends on how one defines "God," as one eminent student of Buddhism [Edward Conze] has explained: "It has often been suggested that Buddhism is an atheistic system of thought, and this assumption has given rise to quite a number of discussions. Some have claimed that since Buddhism knew no God, it could not be a religion; others that since Buddhism obviously was a religion which knew no God, the belief in God was not essential to religion. These discussions assume that God is an unambiguous term, which is by no means the case."

Dr. Conze then says that if "God" is taken to mean a personal Creator of the universe, then the Buddhist has no interest in the concept. But if "God" means something like the state of oneness with God as described by some Christian mystics, then the Buddhist surely believes in "God," since this state is almost indistinguishable from the Buddhist concept of Nirvana, "the supreme Reality; . . . the eternal, hidden and incomprehensible Peace." And finally, if "God" means one of the many Deities in an at least superficially polytheistic religion like Hinduism, then Buddhism tolerates a belief in many Gods: "the Buddhists believe that a Faith can be kept alive only if it can be adapted to the mental habits of the average person. In consequence, we find that, in the earlier Scriptures, the deities of Brahmanism are taken for granted and that, later on, the Buddhists adopted the local Gods of any district to which they came."

When the present Act was adopted in 1948 we were a nation of Buddhists, Confucianists, and Taoists, as well as Christians. Hawaii, then a Territory, was indeed filled with Buddhists, Buddhism being "probably the major faith, if Protestantism and Roman Catholicism are deemed different faiths." Organized Buddhism first came to Hawaii in 1887 when Japanese laborers were brought to work on the plantations. There are now numerous Buddhist sects in Hawaii, and the temple of the Shin sect in Honolulu is said to have the largest congregation of any religious organization in the city.

In the continental United States Buddhism is found "in real strength" in Utah, Arizona, Washington, Oregon, and California. "Most of the Buddhists in the United States are Japanese or Japanese-Americans; however, there are 'English' departments in San Francisco, Los Angeles, and Tacoma." The Buddhist Churches of North America, organized in 1914 as the Buddhist Mission of North America and incorporated under the present name in 1942, represent the Jodo Shinshu Sect of Buddhism in this country. This sect is the only Buddhist group reporting information to the annual Yearbook of American Churches. In 1961, the latest year for which figures are available, this group alone had 55 churches and an inclusive membership of 60,000; it maintained 89 church schools with a total enrollment of 11,150. According to one source, the total number of Buddhists of all sects in North America is 171,000.

When the Congress spoke in the vague general terms of a Supreme Being I cannot, therefore, assume that it was so parochial as to use the words in the narrow sense urged on us. I would attribute tolerance and sophistication to the Congress, commensurate with the religious complexion of our communities. In sum, I agree with the Court that any person opposed to war on the basis of a sincere belief, which in his life fills the same place as a belief in God fills in the life of an orthodox religionist, is entitled to exemption under the statute. None comes to us an avowedly irreligious person or as an atheist; one, as a sincere believer in "goodness and virtue for their own sakes." His questions and doubts on theological issues, and his wonder, are no more alien to the statutory standard than are the awe-inspired questions of a devout Buddhist.

U.S. SUPREME COURT, EVEN BUDDHIST PRISONERS HAVE RIGHTS (1972)

In *Ho Ah Kow* v. *Nunan*, a California case from 1879, Justice Stephen Field overturned a San Francisco ordinance that would have required a Chinese citizen with a traditional long braid to conform to a rule requiring all prisoners to cut their hair to a length of one inch. The prisoner's queue, wrote Field, was a religious symbol; to force him to cut it off would be tantamount to forcing an Orthodox Jew to eat pork. For much of the next century, Field was a justice crying in the wilderness. Across the United States, prisoners' rights were severely circumscribed. In 1972, however, a case called *Cruz v. Beto* turned things around. Cruz, a member of the Jodo Shinshu-based Buddhist Churches of America and a practitioner of "the gospel of Buddhism," claimed his First Amendment rights were being violated in the Texas prison where he was incarcerated. According to the complaint, Cruz was prevented in prison from holding Buddhist services, borrowing Buddhist books, and preaching Buddhist truths. Justice William Rehnquist voted against Cruz, and another justice found some of Cruz's claims "frivolous," but the Court decided in his favor. Because the Court ruled *per curiam* ("by the court"), the opinion is brief and not attributed to any particular jurist. Nonetheless, the decision, excerpted here, helped (at least for a time) to turn the tide of constitutional law back in a direction Justice Field might have applauded.

Federal courts sit not to supervise prisons but to enforce the constitutional rights of all "persons," including prisoners. We are not unmindful that prison officials must be accorded latitude in the administration of prison affairs, and that prisoners necessarily are subject to appropriate rules and regulations. But persons in prison, like other individuals, have the right to petition the government for redress of grievances which, of course, includes "access of prisoners to the courts for the purpose of presenting their complaints." Moreover, racial segregation, which is unconstitutional outside prisons, is unconstitutional within prisons, save for "the necessities of prison security and discipline". . . .

If Cruz was a Buddhist and if he was denied a reasonable opportunity of pursuing his faith comparable to the opportunity afforded fellow prisoners who adhere to conventional religious precepts, then there was palpable discrimination by the state against the Buddhist religion, established 600 B.C., long before the Christian era.* The First Amendment, applicable to the states by reason of the Fourteenth Amendment, prohibits government from making a law "prohibiting the free exercise" of religion. If the allegations of this complaint are assumed to be true, as they must be on the motion to dismiss, Texas has violated the First and Fourteenth Amendments.

The motion for leave to proceed *in forma pauperis* is granted. The petition for certiorari is granted, the judgment is vacated, and the cause remanded for a hearing and appropriate findings.

So ordered.

Cruz v. Beto (1972), 405 U.S. 319.

---

*We do not suggest, of course, that every religious sect or group within a prison—however few in number—must have identical facilities or personnel. A special chapel or place of worship need not be provided for every faith regardless of size; nor must a chaplain, priest, or minister be provided without regard to the extent of the demand. But reasonable opportunities must be afforded to all prisoners to exercise the religious freedom guaranteed by the First and Fourteenth Amendments without fear of penalty.

CHIEF JUSTICE WILLIAM REHNQUIST, THE KRISHNA RELIGION (1992)

In the seventies, members of the International Society for Krishna Consciousness, or Hare Krishnas, became fixtures on street corners and in airport terminals across the nation. As complaints about their fund-raising tactics mounted, new ordinances restricting proselytizing were passed and old ones enforced. Meanwhile, friends and relatives of Hare Krishnas, convinced their loved ones had been "brainwashed" by a dangerous "cult," began kidnapping and trying to "deprogram" ISKCON members. In a case called *Shapiro* v. *Shapiro* (1976), a father sued and obtained guardianship of his son. He then placed him in a mental hospital. Hare Krishnas responded to these and other threats by taking to the courts themselves to defend their First Amendment rights. In *Heffron* v. *International Society for Krishna Consciousness* (1981), for example, ISKCON contested a Minnesota Agricultural Society rule that required a license to sell or distribute printed matter at the state fair. The rule, it argued, violated members' religious obligation to practice *sankirtan*, or proselytizing for the faith. But the Supreme Court ruled against this "organization espousing the views of the Krishna religion." In *International Society for Krishna Consciousness* v. *Lee* (1992), the Hare Krishnas challenged, again on First Amendment grounds, a regulation forbidding the solicitation of money inside airport terminals of the Port Authority of New York and New Jersey. Again the case made its way to the Supreme Court, and again ISKCON lost. The decision

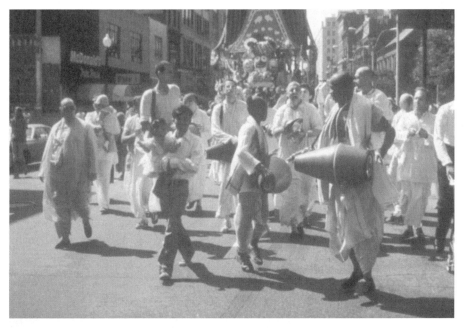

Hare Krishnas marching in a parade in Boston, Massachusetts. Courtesy of The Pluralism Project, Harvard University.

excerpted here was written by Chief Justice William Rehnquist, whose Court earned a reputation in the 1990s for chipping away at the religious freedoms of U.S. citizens.

It is uncontested that the solicitation at issue in this case is a form of speech protected under the First Amendment. But it is also well settled that the government need not permit all forms of speech on property that it owns and controls. . . .

Airports are commercial establishments funded by users fees and designed to make a regulated profit . . . and where nearly all who visit do so for some travel related purpose. As commercial enterprises, airports must provide services attractive to the marketplace. In light of this, it cannot fairly be said that an airport terminal has as a principal purpose "promoting the free exchange of ideas." To the contrary, the record demonstrates that Port Authority management considers the purpose of the terminals to be the facilitation of passenger air travel, not the promotion of expression. Even if we look beyond the intent of the Port Authority to the manner in which the terminals have been operated, the terminals have never been dedicated (except under the threat of court order) to expression in the form sought to be exercised here: i.e., the solicitation of contributions and the distribution of literature. . . . Thus, we think that neither by tradition nor purpose can the terminals be described as satisfying the standards we have previously set out for identifying a public forum.

The restrictions here challenged, therefore, need only satisfy a requirement of reasonableness. We reiterate [that] the restriction " 'need only be reasonable; it need not be the most reasonable or the only reasonable limitation.' " We have no doubt that under this standard the prohibition on solicitation passes muster.

We have on many prior occasions noted the disruptive effect that solicitation may have on business. "Solicitation requires action by those who would respond: The individual solicited must decide whether or not to contribute (which itself might involve reading the solicitor's literature or hearing his pitch), and then, having decided to do so, reach for a wallet, search it for money, write a check, or produce a credit card." Passengers who wish to avoid the solicitor may have to alter their path, slowing both themselves and those around them. The result is that the normal flow of traffic is impeded. This is especially so in an airport, where "air travelers, who are often weighted down by cumbersome baggage . . . may be hurrying to catch a plane or to arrange ground transportation." Delays may be particularly costly in this setting, as a flight missed by only a few minutes can result in hours worth of subsequent inconvenience.

In addition, face to face solicitation presents risks of duress that are an appropriate target of regulation. The skillful, and unprincipled, solicitor can target the most vulnerable, including those accompanying children or those suffering physical impairment and who cannot easily avoid the solicitation. The unsavory solicitor can also commit fraud through concealment of his affiliation or through deliberate efforts to shortchange those who agree to purchase. Compounding this problem is the fact that, in an airport, the targets of such activity frequently are

International Society for Krishna Consciousness v. *Lee*, 505 U.S. 672 (1992) 505 U.S. 672.

• *384* •

on tight schedules. This in turn makes such visitors unlikely to stop and formally complain to airport authorities. As a result, the airport faces considerable difficulty in achieving its legitimate interest in monitoring solicitation activity to assure that travelers are not interfered with unduly.

The Port Authority has concluded that its interest in monitoring the activities can best be accomplished by limiting solicitation and distribution to the sidewalk areas outside the terminals. . . . This sidewalk area is frequented by an overwhelming percentage of airport users . . . Thus the resulting access of those who would solicit the general public is quite complete. In turn we think it would be odd to conclude that the Port Authority's terminal regulation is unreasonable despite the Port Authority having otherwise assured access to an area universally traveled.

The inconveniences to passengers and the burdens on Port Authority officials flowing from solicitation activity may seem small, but viewed against the fact that "pedestrian congestion is one of the greatest problems facing the three terminals," the Port Authority could reasonably worry that even such incremental effects would prove quite disruptive. Moreover, "the justification for the Rule should not be measured by the disorder that would result from granting an exemption solely to ISKCON." For if petitioner is given access, so too must other groups. "Obviously, there would be a much larger threat to the State's interest in crowd control if all other religious, nonreligious, and noncommercial organizations could likewise move freely." As a result, we conclude that the solicitation ban is reasonable. For the foregoing reasons, the judgment of the Court of Appeals sustaining the ban on solicitation in Port Authority terminals is

Affirmed.

SIKH KIRPANS IN PUBLIC SCHOOLS (1994)

When is a sacred object a dangerous weapon? California schoolchildren, legislators, lawyers, and jurists took up that question in 1994. So did the American Civil Liberties Union and California Governor Pete Wilson. The trouble started in January 1994 when children playing with eleven-year-old Rajinder Cheema (also known as Rajinder Singh) caught a glimpse of a "kirpan" he was wearing under his shirt and reported their findings to the principal. Sikhs initiated into the Khalsa sect observe the "Five K's": *kes* (uncut hair), *kangha* (comb), *kara* (steel bangle), *kacch* (short pants), and the symbol at issue here: the *kirpan*, or short curved sword. Like other religious symbols, the kirpan, which has been worn by Sikhs for hundreds of years, has multiple meanings. It is a sign of self-respect, a reminder of one's duty to come to the aid of the oppressed, and a symbol of peace. To this elementary school principal, however, the kirpan was a knife. He suspended Rajinder and his siblings, Jaspreet (age 7) and Sukhjinder (age 8), for violating a state law outlawing weapons on school grounds. The ACLU filed suit on behalf of the Cheema family, but the U.S. District Court ruled in favor of the Livingstone School District. Democratic Senator Bill Lockyer then filed a bill in the state

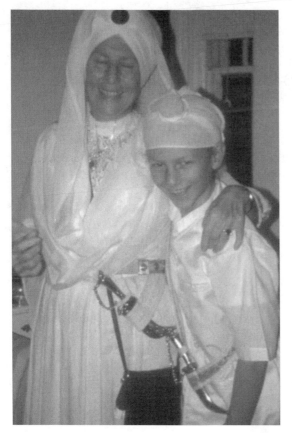

A mother and son display the Sikh kirpan (ceremonial dagger). The mother, Sat Kirn Kaur Khalsa, converted to Sikhism in 1973 after encountering the teachings of Yogi Bhajan of 3HO. Courtesy of The Pluralism Project, Harvard University.

legislature that would have permitted California's Sikhs to wear kirpans on school grounds. The bill was initially voted down, but it passed in August, only to be vetoed by Governor Pete Wilson in September. The U.S. Court of Appeals, meanwhile, overturned the lower court ruling, finding in favor of the children, who promptly returned to school with their kirpans. Not all the state's Sikhs were happy with this outcome. One said handing a kirpan to a Sikh child was "like giving a baby a razor blade." Another reasoned: "If they don't carry the sword when they go to school, God is not going to be angry with them. I still love my religion. But we have to obey the rules and regulations of the country we are living in." Exactly what those rules and regulations were to be for practitioners of minority religious traditions such as Sikhism remained, at the end of the twentieth century, very much in doubt. Arrayed on the one hand were Governor Wilson and the logic that "a knife is a knife." But arrayed on the other were most, if not all, of the nation's Sikhs. Coming to their aid were the editors at the *Oakland Tribune*, who introduced their editorial on the subject with familiar words.

"Assembly Tramples Religious Freedom," *Oakland Tribune,* 24 August 1994, A12. Reprinted courtesy of the *Oakland Tribune.*

> Congress shall make no law respecting an establishment of religion, or prohibiting the free exercise thereof; or abridging the freedom of speech, or of the press, or the right of the people peaceably to assemble, and to petition the Government for a redress of grievances.
>
> FIRST AMENDMENT TO THE CONSTITUTION OF THE UNITED STATES, RATIFIED DEC. 15, 1791

Religious freedom in California took a solid kick in the teeth last week when confused state legislators, mistaking a religious symbol for a dangerous weapon, banned the kirpan from the state's schools.

The kirpan is a ceremonial sword used by practitioners of the Sikh religion, of whom there are many in California, especially in the Central Valley and the San Francisco Bay Area. It signifies the power that binds members of the Sikh spiritual brotherhood known as the Khalsa to righteousness and obligates them to defend the poor, the weak and the innocent, to preserve freedom of religious worship, and to end tyranny.

Sword is too strong a word to describe the kirpan, however. Although it is made of steel, it is sewed into a sheath and kept beneath the clothing. Its edges are blunted and its size is much smaller than the image the word "sword" brings to mind. The kirpan is only a few inches long, a little longer than three inches on average.

Fifth-grader Rajinder Singh of Livingstone, south of Modesto, wears a kirpan. He was wearing one last year on the playground when his shirt slid up. Other youngsters saw the kirpan and reported him to school officials. Worried about crime in the schools, and ignorant of different cultures and religions, the principal banned the kirpan under the school's no-weapons policy.

Rajinder, a brother and a sister were excluded from school if they wore the kirpan. They have been getting their education at home.

Banning the kirpan was unnecessary; there has never been a case of violence reported in a United States school involving a kirpan.

Beyond that, the kirpan is clearly a religious symbol, akin to the Christians' crucifix. The Sikhs took the school district to court, on the grounds that their religious freedom was being violated.

The U.S. District Court ruled last spring that the kirpan could be banned. Sikhs appealed in early August to the 9th U.S. Circuit Court of Appeals in San Francisco. No decision has been announced.

Meanwhile, State Sen. Bill Lockyer, D-Hayward, troubled by the religious implications, sought to have the kirpan exempted from state weapons laws. It is a crime to bring a dagger, switchblade, ice pick, razor or any knife with a blade longer than two and a half inches to school. It's also against the law to conceal one.

Lockyer sought to have an exception made for "any knife or dagger which is an integral part of (the) recognized religious practice of the carrier." The student's parents would have to notify the school that their child had the kirpan, and the youngster would have to keep it in a sheath beneath his or her clothing. The right to wear the knife would be revoked if the student brandished it.

The bill would have made wearing a kirpan legal. It protected religious freedom while minimizing the prospects of violence. It was a well-crafted solution to the conundrum. It sailed through the state Senate with a unanimous vote. But the Assembly failed to adopt it.

Lockyer's bill needed 41 votes in the Assembly. It received 34. The usual small parade of know-nothings, with troglodyte right-wing Republican Ross Johnson of Fullerton out front, led the charge against the bill.

Ignoring all the evidence, Johnson raised the specter of knife fights on school grounds. Republican Assemblywoman Paula Boland of Granada Hills said anyone could wear a kirpan and claim religious freedom, an eventuality that is specifically forbidden by the wording of Lockyer's bill.

The most upsetting thing about the discussion is some lawmakers' ignorance of the principles of religious freedom. Some of these folks—Johnson, for example—are the first to complain that the Christian religion is not getting a fair shake in the schools and in the culture in general. Yet freedom of religion applies to all religions, including those that originated in Asia.

Lockyer plans to bring the bill back up, perhaps today, for another vote in the Assembly. It will be carried there by Republican Assemblyman Bernie Richter, whose Chico-area district has a large Sikh population.

We urge those Assembly members who voted against the Lockyer legislation to examine the evidence more closely this time, and cast a vote for religious tolerance. They would be celebrating our many cultures and the principle of religious freedom that binds them together.

A VIETNAMESE HOME TEMPLE ZONING DISPUTE (1996)

In city councils and zoning boards across the nation, the religious rights of Asian immigrants came under fire in the 1980s and 1990s. In the immigrant-rich Los Angeles area, lawsuits over Asian-American temples became commonplace. In 1993, city officials turned down a proposal by Sikhs to transform two houses in North Hills into a religious center. "We feel we're being inundated by outsiders and the traffic they bring," one North Hills resident said. "We're having to put up with all the new churches: a Buddhist temple, a Korean church, a Chinese church and then another Korean church." In 1994, after a long legal battle, Hindus won approval to construct a temple in Norwalk, but only after agreeing to adapt their architecture to conform to the Catholic mission style. Three years later, Burmese Buddhists petitioned to build a monastery in Yorba Linda. At a city council meeting, a Mormon resident supported the plan but a Christian argued against it on the theory that God had "commanded his people to rid the land of those who worship pagan gods." The permit was denied. This article from the *Los Angeles Times* describes a dispute that simmered for much of the 1990s between a Vietnamese Buddhist monk at the Lien Hoa Temple (established 1987) and his Garden

Lily Dixon, "Tranquil Temples Nettle O.C. Neighbors," *Los Angeles Times* (Orange County Edition), 7 October 1996, A1. Copyright © 1996 by the *Los Angeles Times*. Reprinted with permission.

Grove neighbors. In Vietnam, monks have traditionally lived in home temples that double as sacred spaces and living quarters. But this traditional arrangement has not met with favor in suburban Los Angeles, where roughly one-half of America's Vietnam refugees reside.

Everything about the Lien Hoa Temple evokes sublime tranquillity.

There are huge, shady jacaranda and fig trees whose knotty trunks are stakes for two low-slung hammocks. Leafy trees heavy with unripe persimmons, grapefruits, tangerines, guavas and cherimoyas fill the garden. A sloping concrete bridge graces the man-made lotus pond. A statue of the Buddha Goddess sits at the center of the verdant courtyard. . . .

Yet it hasn't always been so serene in the neighborhood around the temple, a salmon-hued structure the size of a double-car garage in a most unlikely place: the backyard of a four-bedroom house on Bixby Avenue.

Cities in Orange County increasingly are cracking down on "home temples" that are located in residential areas or that operate without proper permits. Lien Hoa is but one of many such temples, maintained primarily by Vietnamese monks, that in the last several years have faced complaints from neighbors and city inspectors about noise, litter, traffic and zoning violations.

To some of the monks, it never occurred to check out zoning laws when they bought their property.

"It's not that complicated to explain," said Thu Van Nguyen, the head monk at Lien Hoa Temple, which was cited recently because ceremonies drew more than the 64 people allowed on his property under city codes. "In Vietnam, we can build a temple, big or small, anywhere. So, many of us just automatically assumed in the beginning that we can have our houses also be temples.

"Zoning ordinance? We only learn about them later."

Generally, private homes are not allowed to operate as places of worship without conditional-use permits, which are issued only if the property meets safety requirements such as adequate parking, building space and emergency exits. But enforcing the law can be problematic because officials must weigh individuals' constitutional rights to assembly.

"It's a gray area," said Don Anderson, community development director of Westminster, which has several Vietnamese temples in the city but has seen few complaints at City Hall. "If somebody says, 'It's my home and I will have an occasional religious gathering,' do you define that as . . . a place of worship? And then, of course, there's a question of how occasional is occasional?"

There are 44 Vietnamese Buddhist temples from San Diego to Sacramento—most of them in Garden Grove and Santa Anna—listed in the 1996 Nguoi Viet Yearbook, a directory of Vietnamese businesses and organizations in California. No statistics are available for the number of private homes that also function as places of worship, but according to local monks there are at least a dozen in Orange County.

A Vietnamese Communist government crackdown on religion in the early 1980s caused many Buddhist monks to join the wave of refugees who fled to the West by boat. The majority came to Orange County, now home to at least 100,000

Vietnamese expatriates, the largest such population outside Southeast Asia.

Many of the monks recalled arriving literally with just the robes and sandals they had on. They rebuilt their already ascetic lives with the help and kindness of compatriots who welcomed them into their homes.

Vietnamese Buddhists in the community pooled their resources to buy houses for the monks, who then converted them into religious temples. They had no choice, the monks said. They had no money to buy or build structures that were up to code.

In the beginning, the home temples were more a curiosity than anything else. City officials were vaguely aware of their existence, but in respect to cultural differences generally left the monks and their worshipers alone. But as the crowds grew, so did the residents' complaints.

Usually it is during Tet, the celebration of the new year on the lunar calendar, when neighborhood complaints rise. Thousands of Buddhists flock to their temples at this time to pray and pay respect to their ancestors.

But even during normal times, some residents object to the temples because of the steady flow of traffic during services, which primarily take place on Saturdays and Sundays but also sometimes during the week.

"I don't want to stop anyone from worshiping, but there just are so many people and they block my driveway, make a lot of noise and just come and go at all hours," said Betty Parker, who lives three houses from Thanh Tung Duong, a monk who was sued in April by Garden Grove city officials on grounds of holding religious services at his home on Magnolia Street without a permit. . . .

Parker said that she still sees a lot of activity around the temple, but that things have quieted down since the city of Garden Grove settled the case against Duong, who agreed to limit the number of worshipers at his home.

The city also settled a case against Lien Hoa Temple last spring after it too promised to keep down the number of people there.

The monks say they are the victims of unfortunate circumstances. They can't afford to build temples outside of residential areas, but at the same time they must find a place to minister to their flocks. . . .

"Monks are poor. We don't have money," said Dao Van Bach, the head monk at the Vietnam Temple, whose Garden Grove house in 1989 became the first home temple to be sued in Orange County for a zoning violation. Bach is known in the Vietnamese community by his honorific Buddhist title, Thich Phap Chau. (All Vietnamese Buddhist monks have honorific titles beginning with "Thich.") Bach has since razed his house and in its place has built what he and other monks maintain is among the largest Vietnamese Buddhist temples in size in the U.S. . . .

Some monks say they do not use their homes as temples but acknowledge they have religious artifacts often found in temples and occasionally invite over many guests for prayer.

"This is where I work and live, where monks come to pray or live," said Dong (Thich Quang Thanh), one of the two monks sued by Garden Grove officials earlier this year. "Yes, it has an altar, but I am a monk, so my home will have one."

When Dong applied for a permit last year to renovate his home to build a patio and raise his ceiling to accommodate a 30-foot altar for the Buddha, city officials asked if his home would be used as a place of worship. "I said no," the monk recalled. "I meant it then, and I mean it now: This is the home of a monk and not a temple."

There was never a debate as to whether Lien Hoa is a temple or not. Its sign in front—"Lien Hoa Temple"—is as plain as day.

But Nguyen, the head monk, says he has inadvertently violated his permit allowing up to 64 worshipers many times since 1987, when the temple opened. The last violation occurred on the eve of Tet when hundreds of Vietnamese Buddhists flitted in and out of the temple from morning till night. Their prayers and chants filled the air, already thickened with incense smoke. Their parked cars virtually plugged the streets.

"I test and test to see to what degree I can push . . . and what I can get away with," said Nguyen (Thich Chon Than). "When they took me to court this year after Tet, I knew I couldn't push any more."

Like Nguyen, other monks whose temples have been cited said they also have tested their city officials over time—and found them generally patient and accommodating.

"I think the city just looks the other way most of the times," said Bach, the Vietnam Temple monk. "They just have to respond to complaints, we know that. But they have given us much leeway."

Bach said Garden Grove officials, who could not be reached for comment, have yet to carry out threats to jail him for repeated code violations. By allowing him to continue to hold services, he reasons, they indirectly gave him time to appeal to his 2,000-family membership for the $2.6 million necessary to build his temple into what it is today: the Vietnam Temple, an imposing pagoda whose size rivals many of the bigger churches.

Vietnam Temple still has more upgrading to do—the latest inspection required that Bach fix the parking drainage system, improve lighting and build a fence. But the monk is certain that by its opening early next year, the temple, which can hold up to 1,000 people, will meet city codes.

Meantime, even though the temple hasn't met all zoning requirements, Bach said he continues to hold regular weekly ceremonies on the property—as he has since 1983.

"We just need to do everything we can to meet their standards if we want to continue our services," Bach said. "Or else, we can just hide—hide and continue them illegally. Most of the monks here do that anyway."

CHRONOLOGY

1784
- *Empress of China* sails into the port of Canton and the *United States* anchors off Pondicherry. U.S. trade with China and India begins.

- Hannah Adams's *An Alphabetical Compendium of the Various Sects* discusses Asian religions in an appendix.

- British Orientalists establish the Asiatik Society of Bengal, whose journal will later publish many early translations and interpretations of Asian religions.

1785
- Sir Charles Wilkins, a British colonial administrator in India, offers the first English translation of a Hindu scripture: *The Bhagavat-geeta, or, Dialogues of Kreeshna and Arjoon*.

- Three Chinese arrive in Baltimore.

1788
- Benjamin Franklin's Oriental Tale, "A Letter from China."

1790
- Naturalization Act restricts citizenship to "free white persons."

- A man from Madras, India, visits Massachusetts.

1799
- Joseph Priestley's *A Comparison of the Institutions of Moses with Those of the Hindoos and Other Nations*.

- The East India Marine Society is founded in Salem, Massachusetts. Its collection of artifacts from the Asia trade is the first major American collection of Asian art.

1800
- Henry Sherburne writes *The Oriental Philanthropist*, one of the first pieces of American fiction set in Asia.

1810
- The foundation of the American Board of Commissioners for Foreign Missions (ABCFM) inaugurates the "Great Century" in American missions. India, Burma, and Ceylon are among the mission fields of this Congregationalist-dominated voluntary association.

1812
- The ABCFM sends the first American missionaries to India.

1813
- Adoniram Judson becomes the first American missionary to a Buddhist nation when he arrives in Rangoon, Burma. His first wife, Ann Judson, becomes America's first woman to evangelize abroad.

1818 • News of the alleged conversion to Unitarianism of Ram Mohun Roy, a Hindu reformer who will found the Brahmo Samaj in 1828, reaches the United States, galvanizing the interest of Unitarians in Asian religions.

1830 • Elijah Coleman Bridgman docks in Canton. This Congregationalist minister is the first American missionary in China.

1836 • The Transcendental Club is established in Boston, Massachusetts.

1841 • Edward Salisbury, "the father of American Oriental studies," begins teaching at Yale University. His post is the first U.S. professorship in Sanskrit.

1842 • Emerson and Thoreau inaugurate "Ethnical Scriptures," a series of translations of the world's scriptures, in the Transcendentalist periodical, *The Dial*.

• The American Oriental Society becomes the first organization devoted to the scholarly study of the languages and literatures of the "Orient."

1844 • A translation by Elizabeth Palmer Peabody of portions of the *Lotus Sutra* published in *The Dial* launches the American conversation with Buddhism.

1848 • The discovery of gold in California inaugurates the Gold Rush, which sparks Chinese emigration to the United States.

1853 • The first Chinese temple in America opens in San Francisco's Chinatown.

• The Reverend William Speer establishes a Presbyterian mission to the Chinese in San Francisco.

1853–54 • Commodore Matthew Perry sails a fleet of U.S. Navy ships into Tokyo Bay, forcibly opening Japan to Western "friendship" and ending an era of commercial and cultural isolation initiated in 1639.

1868 • The Meiji Restoration replaces Japan's closed-door policy with a mandate for "westernization." The first Japanese immigrant group arrives in Hawaii.

• The Burlingame Treaty allows for the "free migration" of the Chinese to the United States and reciprocal privileges for Americans in China.

1869 • The Transcontinental Railroad is completed, sending Chinese laborers hunting for work.

1871 • James Freeman Clarke's *Ten Great Religions* demonstrates the continued interest of Unitarians and Transcendentalists in Asian religious traditions.

1875 • The Theosophical Society is established in New York City.

1877 • White laborers organize the Workingmen's Party of California under the slogan, "The Chinese Must Go!"

1879 • *The Light of Asia* by English poet Edwin Arnold renders the life of the Buddha in free verse. It will sell over one million copies in the United States and Great Britain and help stimulate the first American Buddhist vogue.

1880 • Theosophists Helena Blavatsky and Henry Steel Olcott formally convert to Buddhism in Ceylon.

1882 • The Chinese Exclusion Act effectively bans Chinese immigration and naturalization.

1885 • Ernest Fenollosa and William Sturgis Bigelow officially embrace the precepts of Tendai Buddhism in Japan.

• Anti-Chinese nativism erupts into a massacre at Rock Springs, Wyoming, killing twenty-eight Chinese and wounding fifteen.

1887 • A revised edition of *Science and Health with Key to the Scriptures* by Christian Science founder Mary Baker Eddy quotes approvingly selections from Edwin Arnold's poetic rendition of the *Bhagavad Gita*. In later editions, references to Hinduism disappear.

1888 • *The Buddhist Ray*, America's first English-language Buddhist magazine, begins publication under the editorship of Philangi Dasa (Herman C. Vetterling).

1889 • The Reverend Soryu Kagai becomes the first Jodo Shinshu priest to arrive in Hawaii. Before returning to his Japanese home, he establishes a small Buddhist temple.

1893 • The World's Parliament of Religions, held at the Chicago World's Fair, provides a venue for Americans to learn about Asian religious traditions from Asian teachers. Buddhism, Hinduism, Confucianism, Jainism, Taoism, and Shinto are all represented.

• C. T. Strauss, a Jew from New York, becomes the first American formally to convert to Buddhism on U.S. soil when he takes the "Three Refuges" in Chicago just days after the Parliament.

1894 • Swami Vivekananda establishes the New York Vedanta Society.

• *The Gospel of Buddha* by Buddhist sympathizer Paul Carus presents Buddhism as a rationalist's faith with striking similarities to Christianity.

1897 • Zen popularizer D. T. Suzuki moves from Japan to La Salle, Illinois, to work at Open Court Publishing with Paul Carus.

• Marie de Souza Canavarro, in a ceremony at New Century Hall in New York City, becomes the first woman formally to profess

Buddhism in the United States. She then sets off for a three-year stay in Ceylon.

1898 • Young Men's Buddhist Association (Bukkyo Seinen Kai) emerges in San Francisco, and opens the first Buddhist temple in the continental United States.

1899 • Shuye Sonoda and Kakuryo Nishijima, Jodo Shinshu (True Pure Land) Buddhists from Japan, arrive in San Francisco as the first full-time Buddhist missionaries to the United States. They establish what will emerge as the Buddhist Mission of North America (BMNA) in 1914.

1900 • BMNA priests start the Dharma Sangha of Buddha for Caucasian converts and begin publishing *Beikoku Bukkyo* ("Buddhism in America") for Japanese immigrants.

• Hawaii becomes a U.S. territory.

1901 • *The Light of Dharma*, a sophisticated English-language Buddhist magazine, is published by Japanese Pure Land Buddhists in San Francisco.

1902 • Inventor Thomas Edison produces the first American film about India, a documentary called *Hindoo Fakir*.

1903 • Tsunetaro Kanzawa emigrates from Japan to San Francisco and begins preaching Tenrikyo, the Shinto-based "Religion of Heavenly Wisdom."

1904 • The North American Shinto Church is established in San Francisco. It will later move to Los Angeles.

1905 • Asiatic Exclusion League is formed for "the preservation of the Caucasian race upon American soil." Its constitution describes Asians as "unassimilable."

1906 • The San Francisco Vedanta Society builds the first Hindu temple in North America.

• Soyen Shaku's *Sermons of a Buddhist Abbot* becomes the first book published in English on Zen.

• Asian-Indian nationalists in New York establish the Pan Aryan Association and Indo-American Association in support of a free India.

1907 • Anti-Indian riot forces hundreds of Asian Indians working at lumber mills in Bellingham, Washington, to flee to Canada.

1907–8 • "Gentleman's Agreement" between United States and Japan limits the immigration of Japanese laborers.

1912 • Sikhs in northern California organize the Pacific Coast Khalsa Diwan Society in Holt, California. They then transform a small home in nearby

Stockton into America's first Sikh *gurdwara* (temple). A new gurdwara will be built on an adjacent lot in 1915.

- Swami Paramananda begins publishing a Vedantist magazine, *The Message of the East.*

1914   • Thousands of Indians leave the United States and Canada to spearhead an ill-fated rebellion in India.

1917   • U.S. Congress passes, over President Wilson's veto, the Immigration Act of 1917, which halts emigration from a "barred zone" in Asia that includes China and South and Southeast Asia (but not Japan and the Philippines).

1920   • Swami Paramahansa Yogananda, a "kriya yoga" teacher from the Yogoda Satsanga Society of India, arrives in Boston as a delegate to the International Congress of Religious Liberals.

1922   • In *Ozawa* v. *U.S.*, the U.S. Supreme Court decides that Japanese immigrants are not "free white persons" eligible for naturalization.

- Nyogen Senzaki, a student of Soyen Shaku who upon his arrival in the United States in 1905 had vowed to remain silent on Buddhist matters for seventeen years, delivers his first American lecture in San Francisco and establishes his "floating zendo."

1923   • In *U.S.* v. *Bhagat Singh Thind*, the Supreme Court rules that a "Hindu," while admittedly a "Caucasian," is not a "free white person" eligible for U.S. citizenship.

1924   • The Asian Exclusion Act imposes a national origins quota system that severely restricts immigration from Asia, Japan included.

- In the first Buddhist ordination ceremony in Hawaii, Bishop Yemyo Imamura ordains the Reverend Ernest Hunt a priest in the Hongwanji sect of the Jodo Shinshu tradition.

1927   • Katherine Mayo's *Mother India* is published. A caustic critique of the Indian people and their religions, it quickly becomes the most widely read book in America on India.

- W. Y. Evans-Wentz's *Tibetan Book of the Dead* introduces Americans to Tibetan Buddhism.

1929   • The first in a series of Fu Manchu movies establishes Dr. Fu Manchu, a Chinatown thug, as the super-villain of the silver screen.

1930   • For the first time, Nisei (second-generation Japanese Americans) outnumber the Issei (first-generation). The Nisei-dominated Japanese American Citizens League is formed in Seattle.

1931   • White actor Warner Oland debuts in "yellowface" in the title role in "Charlie Chan Carries On." Hollywood would eventually make over forty more movies about Chan and his "Confucius says" aphorisms.

- Sokei-an Shigetsu Sasaki, another student of Soyen Shaku, incorporates the Buddhist Society in America (later the First Zen Institute of America).

- *The Good Earth* by Sinophile Pearl Buck presents a positive portrait of Chinese peasant life. This bestseller will be made into a movie in 1937.

1932
- Dwight Goddard's *A Buddhist Bible* appears. It includes excerpts from the Taoist scripture the *Tao-te ching*.

- *Re-Thinking Missions*, the report of the "Layman's Inquiry" into Protestant missions supervised by Harvard professor William E. Hocking, signals a shift in missiology away from conquest and toward collaboration with other religions.

1934
- Followers of Buddha, a short-lived American experiment in Buddhist monasticism, is established by Dwight Goddard.

1935
- Swami Yogananda's Self-Realization Fellowship (SRF) is incorporated.

1941
- The Japanese attack on Pearl Harbor draws the United States into World War II.

1942
- President Franklin D. Roosevelt signs Executive Order 9066, authorizing the forced relocation of Japanese Americans to internment camps. Virtually every Japanese-American Buddhist is interned.

1943
- Chinese Exclusion Act of 1882 is repealed. Chinese are granted naturalization rights, but the immigration quota for "persons of Chinese ancestry" is set at only 105 per year.

1944
- Officials of the Buddhist Mission of North America gathered at the Topaz Relocation Center in Utah rename their organization the Buddhist Churches of America (BCA).

1945
- Americans drop the atomic bomb on Japan and World War II comes to an end.

1946
- The Luce-Celler Bill, by removing India from the Asiatic Barred Zone and granting Asian Indians naturalization rights, opens the door to one hundred immigrants from India annually.

- Swami Yogananda's *Autobiography of a Yogi* is published. It will become a countercultural hit in the sixties and seventies.

1947
- India and Pakistan become independent states.

1949
- Communist victory in China reawakens negative stereotypes of the Chinese, and shifts the center of out-migration from Canton to Hong Kong and Taiwan.

1952   • McCarran-Walter Act overturns 1790 legislation restricting citizenship to "free white persons." The immigration quota for Asia is set at 2,990 (versus a European quota of 149,667).

• "4' 33"" by Zen-influenced composer John Cage debuts. Musicians sit silently for four minutes and thirty-three seconds.

1953   • Celebrations of the centenary of the birth of Sarada Devi, the Holy Mother, signal a new openness in America's Vedanta Societies to devotional Hinduism.

1958   • Jack Kerouac's *Dharma Bums* signals the interest of the Beat Generation in Buddhism.

• Geshe Wangyal, a Mongolian teacher in the Gelug order of Tibetan Buddhism who came to New Jersey in 1955, incorporates the Lamaist Buddhist Monastery of America (now the Tibetan Buddhist Learning Center), the country's first Tibetan monastery.

1959   • Chinese troops put down a Tibetan revolt. Tens of thousands of Tibetans flee, including the Fourteenth Dalai Lama, the spiritual head of the Tibetan people, who goes into exile in India and makes the cover of *Time*.

• "Guru to the Stars" Maharishi Mahesh Yogi brings Transcendental Meditation to the United States.

• Civil rights leader the Reverend Martin Luther King, Jr., visits India.

1960   • The Nichiren Shoshu Academy (NSA) brings the Nichiren Buddhist practices of the Soka Gakkai ("Value Creation Society") of Japan to California.

1962   • San Francisco Zen Center incorporates under the direction of Soto Zen master Shunryu Suzuki Roshi.

1963   • Dom Aelred Graham's *Zen Catholicism* points to the interest of Catholic mystics in Zen techniques and Buddhist-Christian dialogue.

• Thich Quang Duc, a Vietnamese Buddhist monk, immolates himself in Saigon in a protest against the Vietnam war.

1964   • Robert Thurman becomes the first American to be ordained a Tibetan Buddhist monk.

1965   • The Immigration Act of 1965 puts an end to the national origins quota system which had severely restricted Asian immigration since 1924. The new "family reunification" policy opens the door to a second wave of Asian immigration and helps spark an eastward turn in American religion and culture.

• *Nostra Aetate*, a statement of the Second Vatican Council of the Roman Catholic Church on "The Relationship of the Church to Non-Christian

Religions," affirms that Catholicism "rejects nothing of what is true and holy" in Buddhism and Hinduism.

- Jazz great John Coltrane records *Om*, *First Meditations*, and *Meditations*, three albums that demonstrate the interest of African-American jazz musicians in Vedanta-style Hinduism, West African religious traditions, and Tibetan Buddhism.

1966
- Martial artist Bruce Lee, the Hong Kong-born martial artist who would later appear in a series of popular movies, debuts as Kato in the TV show "The Green Hornet."

- A. C. Bhaktivedanta Swami Prabhupada establishes the International Society for Krishna Consciousness (ISKCON).

- Theravada Buddhist monks from Sri Lanka establish the Buddhist Vihara Society in Washington, D.C.

- Jain immigrants organize America's first Jain center in New York City.

- The Jodo Shinshu-based Institute of Buddhist Studies is founded in Berkeley, California. It will affiliate in 1985 with the Graduate Theological Union.

- The Tassajara Zen Mountain Center, established by the San Francisco Zen Center in the Los Padres National Forest, becomes America's first formal Zen monastery. It is open to both men and women.

- Swami Satchidananda establishes the Integral Yoga Institute.

1967
- Hakuyu Taizan Maezumi Roshi, a Japan-born Rinzai Zen monk, founds the Zen Center of Los Angeles (ZCLA).

1968
- The Beatles visit India, where they study various forms of meditation, and *Life* magazine proclaims 1968 the "Year of the Guru."

- The Sino-American Buddhist Association, a Chinese Buddhist group, is founded in San Francisco under the leadership of Hsuan Hua.

1969
- Billed as "a teacher for the Aquarian Age," Yogi Bhajan establishes the Sikh-based Healthy, Happy, Holy Organization (3HO) in Los Angeles.

- Tarthang Tulku, a Tibetan monk of the Nyingmapa sect, arrives in Berkeley, California, and founds the Nyingma Meditation Center.

1971
- Thirteen-year-old "boy guru" Maharaj Ji organizes the Divine Light Mission (later Elan Vital). His followers are called "premies."

1972
- The Swaminarayan Mission and Fellowship, an American outgrowth of a devotional form of Hinduism popular in India's Gujarat state, is incorporated in New York. Devotees revere the nineteenth-century saint Sri Swaminarayan.

1973 • The Jain Center of Greater Boston is founded. Members will move into their own temple in 1981.

1974 • Chogyam Trungpa, a Tibetan monk of the Kargyupa sect, establishes the Naropa Institute in Boulder, Colorado. It will later become America's first Buddhist university.

• Followers of Swami Muktananda establish the Siddha Yoga Dham Associates (SYDA) Foundation.

1975 • Saigon falls to the North Vietnamese, prompting 130,000 Vietnamese refugees to emigrate to the United States.

• Joseph Goldstein, Jack Kornfield, Jacqueline Schwartz, and Sharon Salzberg—all Jewish-born Buddhists (Jubus)—open the Insight Meditation Society in Barre, Massachusetts, for the teaching and practice of Theravada-style *Vipassana* ("Insight") meditation.

1976 • Members of the Nichiren Shoshu Academy celebrate the bicentennial by organizing fife and drum corps and touring the country with a replica of the Liberty Bell.

1977 • America's first two major Hindu temples are dedicated: the Hindu Temple Society of North America (in Flushing, New York) and the Sri Venkateshwara Temple (outside Pittsburgh, Pennsylvania).

1978 • The Buddhist Peace Fellowship is established in an effort to promote "engaged Buddhism" in America.

1979 • Philip Glass writes the opera *Satyagraha*. Mahatma Gandhi is the main character.

• *Hinduism Today* begins publication in Honolulu.

1980 • The Buddhist Sangha Council of Southern California is established in an effort to foster a spirit of ecumenical cooperation among area Buddhists.

1981 • Bhagwan Shree Rajneesh, the controversial Indian guru best known for his fleet of Rolls-Royces, transfers his headquarters from Poona, India, to eastern Oregon.

• The Federation of Jain Associations in North America (JAINA) is established.

1982 • Benjamin Hoff's *The Tao of Pooh* appears.

1984 • "The Karate Kid" brings the image of the Asian holy man to the big screen. Sequels will follow in 1986 and 1989.

1987 • Shinto priests dedicate the Tsubaki Grand Shrine of America, the first traditional Shinto shrine on the U.S. mainland, in Stockton, California.

1988   • U.S. Congress issues an apology and $20,000 in reparations to each Japanese American interned in a World War II camp.

      • Hsi Lai Temple, the largest Buddhist temple in the western hemisphere, is completed in Hacienda Heights, California, at a cost of $25 million.

1990   • Japan-born composer Kitaro translates the *Kojiki*, the ancient Shinto "Record of Ancient Matters," into his distinctive, New-Age style.

1991   • Soka Gakkai International-USA (SGI-USA), a lay Buddhist movement, splits from the priestly Nichiren Shoshu Academy.

      • *Tricycle: The Buddhist Review* appears. It will boast 60,000 subscribers after five years.

1992   • Father Robert E. Kennedy, a Jesuit priest, is installed as a Zen teacher "empowered to teach and to transmit the dharma" at the New York Zen Community in Yonkers.

      • Alice Coltrane, an African-American guru also known as Swami Turiyasangitananda, opens a Hindu temple in Chatsworth, California. She is the widow of jazz artist John Coltrane.

1993   • The Parliament of World Religions is held in Chicago one hundred years after the first parliament was held at Chicago's 1893 World's Fair.

      • The Jain Society of Metropolitan Chicago opens the largest Jain center in North America.

      • *Little Buddha*, a film that tells the story of a Seattle boy identified as a reincarnation of a deceased Tibetan Buddhist master, opens in theaters.

1994   • The Beastie Boys release the song "Bodhisattva Vow."

      • The Milarepa Fund, devoted to fostering a nonviolent transition to a Free Tibet, is founded.

1996   • Vice President Al Gore visits Hsi Lai Temple, sparking a national controversy about Democratic Party fund-raising.

1997   • Pop icon Michael Jackson meditates in the lotus position on MTV.

      • The "Year of Tibet" in Hollywood. Two films on the Dalai Lama—*Seven Years in Tibet* and *Kundun*—premiere. Buddhism shares the cover of *Time* with actor Brad Pitt.

      • Thich Nhat Hanh, the popular Vietnamese Buddhist teacher, officially opens the Maple Forest Monastery (*Tu Vien Rung Phong*) in Hartland, Vermont.

FURTHER READING

ASIAN RELIGIONS

Ellwood, Robert S., and Richard Pilgrim. *Japanese Religion: A Cultural Perspective.* Englewood Cliffs, N.J.: Prentice-Hall, 1985.

Fenton, John Y., et al., eds. *Religions of Asia.* 1983. 3d ed. New York: St. Martin's Press, 1993.

Harvey, Peter B. *An Introduction to Buddhism: Teaching, History and Practices.* New York: Cambridge University Press, 1990.

Kitagawa, Joseph, ed. *The Religious Traditions of Asia.* New York: Macmillan, 1989.

Klostermaier, Klaus K. *A Survey of Hinduism.* 1989. 2d ed. Albany: State University of New York Press, 1994.

McLeod, W. H. *The Sikhs: History, Religion, and Society.* New York: Columbia University Press, 1989.

Oxtoby, Willard G. *World Religions: Eastern Traditions.* New York: Oxford, 1996.

Smith, Jonathan Z., ed. *The HarperCollins Dictionary of Religion.* San Francisco: HarperSanFrancisco, 1995.

Thompson, Laurence G. *Chinese Religion: An Introduction.* 1969. 5th ed. Belmont, Calif.: Wadsworth, 1996.

RELIGION IN THE UNITED STATES

Ahlstron, Sydney E. *A Religious History of the American People.* New Haven, Conn.: Yale University Press, 1972.

Albanese, Catherine L. *America: Religions and Religion.* 1981. 3rd ed. Belmont, Calif.: Wadsworth, 1998.

Butler, Jon, and Harry S. Stout. *Religion in American History: A Reader.* New York: Oxford University Press, 1998.

Gaustad, Edwin S., ed. *A Documentary History of Religion in America.* 1982–83. 2d ed. Grand Rapids: Eerdmans, 1993.

Hackett, David G. *Religion and American Culture: A Reader.* New York: Routledge, 1995.

Lippy, Charles H., and Peter W. Williams, eds. *Encyclopedia of the American Religious Experience.* New York: Scribner's, 1988.

Melton, J. Gordon. *The Encyclopedia of American Religions*. 1978. 5th ed. Detroit: Gale Research, 1996.

Queen, Edward L. II, Gardiner H. Shattuck, Jr., and Stephen R. Prothero. *The Encyclopedia of American Religious History*. New York: Facts on File, 1996.

Tweed, Thomas A., ed. *Retelling U.S. Religious History*. Berkeley: University of California Press, 1997.

Wuthnow, Robert. *The Restructuring of American Religion: Society and Faith since World War II*. Princeton, N.J.: Princeton University Press, 1988.

ASIAN RELIGIONS IN THE UNITED STATES

Eck, Diana, ed. *World Religions in Boston: A Guide to Communities and Resources*. Cambridge, Mass.: The Pluralism Project, Harvard University, n.d.

―――. *On Common Ground: World Religions in America*. CD-Rom. New York: Columbia University Press, 1997.

Ellwood, Robert S. *Alternative Altars: Unconventional and Eastern Spirituality in America*. Chicago: University of Chicago Press, 1979.

Ellwood, Robert S., and Harry Partin. *Religious and Spiritual Groups in Modern America*. 1973. 2d ed. Englewood Cliffs, N.J.: Prentice-Hall, 1988.

Jackson, Carl T. *The Oriental Religions and American Thought: Nineteenth Century Explorations*. Westport, Conn.: Greenwood Press, 1981.

Laderman, Gary. *Religions of Atlanta: Religious Diversity in the Centennial Olympic City*. Atlanta: Scholars Press, 1996.

Miller, Timothy, ed. *America's Alternative Religions*. Albany: State University of New York Press, 1995.

Neusner, Jacob, ed. *World Religions in America: An Introduction*. Louisville, KY.: Westminster/John Knox Press, 1994.

Richardson, E. Allen. *East Comes West: Asian Religions and Cultures in North America*. New York: Pilgrim, 1985.

Seager, Richard Hughes. *The World's Parliament of Religions: The East/West Encounter, Chicago, 1893*. Bloomington: Indiana University Press, 1995.

Tweed, Thomas A. "Asian Religions in the United States: Reflections on an Emerging Subfield." In Walter H. Conser Jr. and Sumner B. Twiss, eds. *Religious Diversity and American Religious History: Studies in Traditions and Cultures*. Athens: University of Georgia Press, 1997.

BUDDHISTS IN THE UNITED STATES

Boucher, Sandy. *Turning the Wheel: American Women Creating the New Buddhism*. 1988. Rev. ed. Boston: Beacon Press, 1993.

Buddhist Churches of America. *Buddhist Churches of America: Seventy-Five Year History, 1899–1974*. 2 vols. Chicago: Nobart, 1974.

Dresser, Marianne, ed. *Buddhist Women on the Edge: Contemporary Perspectives from the Western Frontier*. Berkeley, Calif.: North Atlantic Books, 1996.

Fields, Rick. *How the Swans Came to the Lake: A Narrative History of Buddhism in America.* 1981. 3d rev. ed. Boston: Shambhala, 1992.

Honpa Hongwanji Mission of Hawaii. *A Grateful Past, A Promising Future: Honpa Hongwanji Mission of Hawaii, 100 Year History, 1889–1989.* Honolulu: Honpa Hongwanji Mission of Hawaii, 1989.

Hunter, Louise H. *Buddhism in Hawaii: Its Impact on a Yankee Community.* Honolulu: University of Hawaii Press, 1971.

Kashima, Tetsuden. *Buddhism in America: The Social Organization of an Ethnic Religious Organization.* Westport, Conn.: Greenwood, 1981.

Morreale, Don. *Buddhist America: Centers, Retreats, Practices.* Santa Fe, N.M.: John Muir, 1988.

Numrich, Paul David. *Old Wisdom in the New World: Americanization in Two Immigrant Theravada Buddhist Temples.* Knoxville: University of Tennessee Press, 1996.

Prebish, Charles S. *American Buddhism.* North Scituate, Mass.: Duxbury, 1979.

Prebish, Charles S. and Kenneth K. Tanaka, eds. *The Faces of Buddhism in America.* Berkeley: University of California Press, 1998.

Prothero, Stephen R. *The White Buddhist: The Asian Odyssey of Henry Steel Olcott.* Bloomington: Indiana University Press, 1996.

Queen, Christopher and Duncan Williams, eds. *American Buddhism: Methods and Findings in Recent Scholarship.* Surrey, U.K.: Curzon Press, 1998.

Tweed, Thomas A. *The American Encounter with Buddhism, 1844–1912: Victorian Culture and the Limits of Dissent.* Bloomington and Indianapolis: Indiana University Press, 1992.

———. "Buddhists." In David Levinson and Melvin Ember, eds. *American Immigrant Cultures.* New York: Macmillan, 1997.

Tworkov, Helen. *Zen in America: Profiles of Five Teachers and the Search for an American Buddhism.* 1989. Rev. ed. New York: Kodansha, 1994.

Yu, Eui-Young. "The Growth of Korean Buddhism in the United States, with Special Reference to Southern California." *Pacific World* 4 (1988), 82–93.

HINDUS, SIKHS, AND JAINS IN THE UNITED STATES

Fenton, John Y. *South Asian Religions in the Americas: An Annotated Bibliography of Immigrant Religious Traditions.* Westport, Conn.: Greenwood, 1995.

———. *Transplanting Religious Traditions: Asian Indians in America.* New York: Praeger, 1988.

Jackson, Carl T. *Vedanta for the West: The Ramakrishna Movement in the United States.* Bloomington: Indiana University Press, 1994.

La Brack, Bruce. *The Sikhs of Northern California, 1904—1975.* New York: AMS Press, 1988.

Leonard, Karen Isaksen. *Making Ethnic Choices: California's Punjabi Mexican Americans.* Philadelphia: Temple University Press, 1992.

Williams, Raymond Brady, ed. *A Sacred Thread: Modern Transmission of Hindu Traditions in India and Abroad.* Chambersburg, Penn.: Anima, 1992.

————. *Religions of Immigrants from India and Pakistan: New Threads in the American Tapestry*. New York: Cambridge University Press, 1988.

ASIAN RELIGIONS IN THE AMERICAN IMAGINATION

Ahlstrom, Sydney E. *The American Protestant Encounter with World Religions*. Beloit, Wis.: Beloit College, 1962.

Denker, Ellen Paul. *After the Chinese Taste: China's Influence in America, 1730–1930*. Salem, Mass.: Peabody Museum of Salem, 1985.

Gelbund, Geri, and Geri De Paoli, *The Transparent Thread: Asian Philosophy in Recent American Art*. Philadelphia: University of Pennsylvania Press, 1990.

Hutchison, William R. *Errand to the World: American Protestant Thought and Foreign Missions*. Chicago: University of Chicago Press, 1987.

Isaacs, Harold R. *Scratches on Our Minds: American Views of China and India*. Armonk, N.Y.: M.E. Sharpe, 1980.

Johnson, Kent, and Craig Paulenich, eds. *Beneath a Single Moon: Buddhism in Contemporary American Poetry*. Boston: Shambhala, 1991.

Lancaster, Clay. *The Japanese Influence in America*. 1963. 2d ed. New York: Abbeville, 1983.

Lavan, Spencer. *Unitarians and India: A Study in Encounter and Response*. Boston: Beacon, 1977.

Lee, Josephine. *Performing Asian America: Race and Ethnicity on the Contemporary Stage*. Philadelphia: Temple University Press, 1997.

Lipsey, Roger. *An Art of Our Own: The Spiritual in Twentieth-Century Art*. Boston: Shambhala, 1997.

Miller, Stuart Creighton. *The Unwelcome Immigrant: The American Image of the Chinese, 1785–1882*. Berkeley and Los Angeles: University of California Press, 1969.

Tonkinson, Carole, ed. *Big Sky Mind: Buddhism and the Beat Generation*. New York: Riverhead, 1995.

Versluis, Arthur. *American Transcendentalism and Asian Religions*. New York: Oxford University Press, 1993.

Yang, Jeff, et al. *Eastern Standard Time: A Guide to Asian Influence on American Culture from Astro Boy to Zen Buddhism*. Boston and New York: Houghton Mifflin, 1997.

Yu, Beongcheon. *The Great Circle: American Writers and the Orient*. Detroit: Wayne State University Press, 1983.

ASIAN-AMERICAN HISTORY AND CULTURE

Armentrout, Eve L. "Chinese Traditional Religion in North America and Hawaii." *Chinese America, History and Perspectives* (1988): 131–47.

Chang, Sucheng. *Asian Americans: An Interpretive History*. Boston: Twayne, 1991.

————, ed. *Hmong Means Free: Life in Laos and America*. Philadelphia: Temple University Press, 1994.

Chin, Frank, et al., eds. *Aiiieeeee!: An Anthology of Asian American Writers*. 1974. New York: Mentor, 1991.

Daniels, Roger. *Asian America: Chinese and Japanese in the United States since 1850*. Seattle: University of Washington Press, 1988.

———. *Prisoners Without Trial: Japanese Americans in World War II*. New York: Hill and Wang, 1993.

Foner, Philip S., and Daniel Rosenberg, eds. *Racism, Dissent, and Asian Americans from 1840 to the Present: A Documentary History*. Westport, Conn.: Greenwood, 1993.

Freeman, James A. *Hearts of Sorrow: Vietnamese-American Lives*. Stanford, Calif.: Stanford University Press, 1989.

Higa, Karin M. *The View from Within: Japanese American Art from the Internment Camps, 1942–1945*. Seattle: University of Washington Press, 1994.

Jensen, Joan M. *Passage from India: Asian Indian Immigrants in North America*. New Haven, Conn.: Yale University Press, 1988.

Kim, Elaine H., et al., eds. *Making More Waves: New Writing by Asian American Women*. Boston: Beacon, 1997.

Kim, Hyung-chan, ed. *Asian Americans and the Supreme Court: A Documentary History*. New York: Greenwood, 1992.

O'Brien, David J., and Stephen S. Fugita. *The Japanese American Experience*. Bloomington: Indiana University Press, 1991.

Rutledge, Paul James. *The Vietnamese Experience in America*. Bloomington: Indiana University Press, 1992.

Takaki, Ronald. *Strangers from a Different Shore: A History of Asian Americans*. New York: Penguin, 1989.

Tsai, Shih-shan Henry. *The Chinese Experience in America*. Bloomington: Indiana University Press, 1986.

Wechsler, Jeffrey. *Asian Traditions/Modern Expressions: Asian American Artists and Abstraction, 1945–1970*. New York: Harry N. Abrams, 1997.

Yoo, David, ed. *Racial Spirits: Religion and Race in Asian American Communities*. Special issue of *Amerasia Journal* 22 (Spring 1996).

INDEX

Index

Index

Index

Index

political scandal, 331, 333
popular culture: Asian religions in, 1, 3, 7, 21, 225; celebrities and, 1, 10n.2; and Indian gurus, 225; Taoism in, 7, 225, 339–41; and Zen, 7, 225, 229. *See also* advertising, artifacts, film, internet, martial arts, music, sports, television
Prabhavananda, Swami, 187–90
Prabhupada, A. C. Bhaktivedanta Swami, 244–48
prajna, 17, 137, 265
Prebish, Charles, 277
prejudice, 7. *See also* anti-Chinese sentiments, law, nativism
Priestley, Joseph, 26, 44–48, 51
prisons, 381–82
Protestantism, 2, 26, 117, 127: and Baptists, 26, 33, 39–42, 57–58, 193, 215; British, 35, 229; and Buddhism, 134, 141, 232; Calvinist, 117; at Church for the Fellowship of All Peoples, 215; and Congregationalists, 4, 25, 26, 35, 58, 119–21; and Disciples of Christ, 10; and Episcopalians, 10, 187–88, 229; and evangelicals, 4, 187, 226, 376; and Federal Council of Churches, 212; among Koreans, 9; Lutheranism, 117; mainline, 226; and Methodists, 5, 117, 206, 209, 325–26, 365; and missions, 3–4, 7, 27, 35, 63, 123, 131, 193, 210, 225, 381; and Pentecostals, 353; and Presbyterians, 35, 127, 201; Puritanism, 92; and Quakers, 10, 200; and Salvation Army, 206; and Unitarians, 4, 26, 32, 45, 48, 51, 54, 92, 111, 114, 145, 300, 361
puja, 16, 76, 294, 297–98
Pure Land Buddhism, 18, 78, 203–8. *See also* Buddhist Churches of America, Jodo Shinshu

Quakers, 10, 200

race. See ethnicity
racism. *See* anti-Chinese sentiments, Chinese, ethnicity, Japanese, law
Radha, 64
radio, 87, 324–26
Rajneesh, Bhagwan Shree, 225
Ramakrishna, Sri, 130, 131, 147
Ramakrishna Mission, 4, 16, 86, 130, 187, 253
Rao, S. V. Rama, 299
Ratanasara, Havanpola, 320
Rauschenberg, Robert, 218, 346
rebirth: and Chinese Buddhism, 55; among Greeks, Romans, and Egyptians, 49; in Hinduism, 50, 305; in Hinduism and Buddhism, 40; and Jainism, 19; and Japanese Buddhism, 57; as not central to Jodo Shinshu, 327–38; Ralph Waldo Emerson on, 92; release from, 14, 17; and Sikhism, 19; summary of, 15; T. S. Eliot on, 106
refugees, 3, 8, 389. *See also* Cambodians, immigrants, Vietnamese
reincarnation. *See* rebirth
Reinhardt, Ad, 346
religion: of Asia, 2–3; classification of, 6, 9, 27, 54; and ethnic identity and national origin, 13–14; ethnic and universal, 115–18; legal definition of, 378–81; and spiritual unity, 256; as "ultimate concern," 379
Religion of the Samurai, 160
Rethinking Missions, 209
Rice, Clarence Edgar, 123
Ridenour, Fritz, 226, 376
ritual: bathing in the Ganges, 29, 30; on Bodhi Day, 169–70; Buddha's Birthday (Vesak), 167, 172, 223, 315–19; in Buddhist Churches of America, 172–77, 328; Buddhist ordination, 332; Chinese, 44, 55–56, 77; Christmas, 5; Confucian, 21, 71–72, 98; cremation, 141; of East India Marine Society (Salem), 51, 53;

every action as, 269–70; Halloween, 334; hook swinging, 3, 30, 45; Hindu wedding, 212, 295–97; Hindu temple, 16, 294, 297–98; ISKCON sankirtan, 383; Maha Kumbhabhishekam, 289, 294; New Year (Tet), 312, 390; of Nichiren Buddhists, 18, 281; pansil, 134, 141–43; Passover, 5, 369; puja, 16, 294, 297–98; Shinto, 20, 56, 316; Sikh, 19, 33, 251, 385; suttee (sati), 3, 29, 30–31, 47–48, 49; Tibetan Buddhist and Roman Catholic, 58–59. *See also* chanting, meditation, pilgrimage, zazen
Rockefeller, John D., 209
Roman Catholicism: Asian, 362; and Buddhism, 36, 58–59, 223–24, 226, 362–65, 398; and ethics, 308–9; among Filipinos, 9, 13; in Hawaii, 381; hostility toward, 58; images in, 132; Jack Kerouac and, 196; Marie Canavarro and, 151; and missions, 27; on non-Christian religions, 398; and Sikhism, 63; Thomas Merton and, 191, 362–65; Vietnamese, 13; at the World's Parliament of Religions Centennial, 371
Roosevelt, Franklin D., 29, 74, 160, 164–66, 187
Ross, Nancy Wilson, 219, 380
Roy, Ram Mohan, 112

Sadanaga, Masayasu, 224
Sahn, Seung, 376
Sai Baba, Sathya, 257–58
St. Denis, Ruth, 64
Sakurai, Keitoku, 154
Salem, 2, 26, 51, 155
Salisbury, Edward, 62, 110
samsara, 1, 15, 17, 18, 293
Samu, Sunim, 372–76
San Francisco: Angel Island in, 160; Bruce Lee in, 335–36; Buddhist Churches of America temples in, 204; Chinatown in, 70, 75, 207, 357; Chinese in, 27; Chinese temples in, 9, 75–78; Hindu temples in, 289; Japanese Buddhist missionaries in, 63; Japantown in, 204; Vedanta in, 395; Zen Buddhist temples in, 203, 205; Zen Center in, 4, 161, 261, 274
San Francisco Zen Center, 4, 161, 261, 274
sangha, 17, 125, 168
Sanskrit: Buddhism, 367; and chanting, 5; in the Laws of Manu, 97; mantras, 238–39; the teaching of, 26, 62; T. S. Eliot's study of, 106; translation of, 204; Walt Whitman on, 105
Sant devotional movement, 251
Sasaki, Ruth Fuller, 200–203
Sasaki, Shigetsu, 161, 200, 201, 229, 231
Satchidananda, Swami (Gurudev), 225, 253–56
sati. *See* suttee
scholars, 2, 26, 62, 106, 110
science: and Buddhism, 139, 144, 148–49; in Buddhism and Christianity, 368; and the Chinese divine monkey, 77; and cloning, 306; and Jainism, 310
Self-Realization Fellowship, 64, 161–62, 181–82, 184–85
Senzaki, Nyogen, 161, 166–68, 225
Sesso-roshi, Oda, 342
sexual misconduct, 264, 274
Shaivism, 16, 251
Shaktism, 16
Shankar, Ravi, 345, 347
Shankara, 15, 230
Shasta Abbey (Mt. Shasta, Calif.), 270, 272, 354
Shingon Buddhism, 154–56, 204, 207
Shinran, 172, 206, 327
Shinto, and Asian religions, 3; Christian missionaries on, 119; and the classification of religions, 27; interpretation of, 56–57; at a Stockton shrine, 361; summary of, 20–21; at the World's Parliament of Religions, 127. *See also* Japanese
Shiva, 15–16, 257

Index

Shridharani, Krishnalal, 178–81
shrines: Chinese, 8; ecumenical, 254; Hindu, 294; 326–27; home, 8, 22, 281, 289; Jodo Shinshu, 326–27; portable, 155; Shinto, 20, 21, 361
Siddha Yoga Dham Associates (SYDA) Foundation, 251
Sikh Religious Society of Chicago, 312
Sikhism: and Christian missionaries, 119; and Christianity, 34–35, 63; and the classification of religions, 27; and ethics, 171; Five Ks of, 19, 385; and Hinduism, 34; on the internet, 1, 249; interpretations of, 32–35; and Islam, 34; summary of, 19–20; and youth, 312–14. See also Asian Indians, Sikhs
Sikhs: in Boston, 9; in Chicago, 312–14; and community disputes, 224; convert, 161, 224, 248–51, 386; dress of, 5, 83–84, 249, 386; and immigration, 8, 82–86; increasing presence of, 2; intergenerational tensions among, 312–15; in Los Angeles, 20, 388; in New York, 20; and public schools, 226, 385–88; Punjabi, 9, 248; in Stockton, 6, 33, 82–83. See also Asian Indians, Sikhism
Simpson, Margaret, 251–53
Singh, Nihal, 82–86
Sivananda, Swami, 253
Sloan, Mersene, 212
Snow, Elson B., 203–8
Snyder, Gary, 181, 196, 197, 231, 342–45, 369
Soen, Sanim, 225
Soka Gakkai: 3, 18, 207, 224, 277, 281–83
Sokei-an. See Sasaki, Shigetsu
soldiers, 2, 7, 34, 96, 165, 203–4
Sonoda, Shuye, 63, 78, 79, 80–82
Soto Zen Temple (San Francisco), 232, 261
Soyen, Shaku, 64, 137–40, 149, 160, 166, 168, 191
Speer, William, 70
sports, 1, 7, 241, 339, 353–57
Sri Ganesha Temple (Flushing), 289, 291
Sri Ganesha Temple (Nashville), 6, 299–302
Sri Lakshmi Temple (Boston), 9
Sri Lanka, 9, 17, 133–34, 141, 153–54, 215, 303
Sri Lankans, 3, 13, 319, 322–23
Sri Venkateswara Temple (Pittsburgh), 6, 289, 294–98, 300
Stockton, 6, 33, 64, 65n.2, 82–83, 312, 325
Strauss, C. T., 134, 369
Stuart-roshi, Maurine, 225, 270
Subramuniyaswami, Satguru Sivaya, 303
Sufism, 354, 364
Sumedha, Lengala, 322–23
Supreme Court, United States, 378–85
suttee, 3, 29, 30–31, 47–48, 49
Suzuki, D. T.: and Alan Watts, 229, 231; and American intellectuals, 2; and the interpretation of Zen, 191–93; and John Cage, 219; and Paul Carus, 149; as popularizer of Zen, 161, 191, 224; reply to Christian critic, 137–40; and Ruth Fuller Sasaki, 200; and Soyen Shaku, 64, 138
Suzuki, Shunryu: and the acculturation of Buddhism, 4; biography of, 261; and the establishment of San Francisco Zen Center, 161, 232, 261; and Phil Jackson, 354–55; on posture in meditation, 262–64
Swedenborgianism, 117
sympathizers, 5, 11n.5, 62, 123, 148, 203, 285

Tagore, Rabindranath, 159, 162
Tai Chi, 22, 225
Taiwanese, 1, 6, 331–34, 363. See also Chinese
Tan, Amy, 3, 225, 357–60
Tanaka, Kenneth K., 325
Tantric Buddhism, 18, 346, 264. See also Shingon, Tibetan Buddhism

Taoism: Alan Watts on, 229–30; in Boston, 9; and Buddhism, 18, 202; and Chinese immigrants, 62, 75–77; and Confucianism, 21; and ethics, 371; interpretations of, 36, 55, 206, 229–30; as interpreted in Tao of Pooh, 7, 339–41; and Paul Carus, 148; popularization of, 1, 7, 339; and Shinto, 21; summary of, 21–22; and Tai Chi and Chi Kung, 22, 225; on television, 351; among Vietnamese, 13; at the World's Parliament of Religions, 127. See also Chinese
Tao-te ching, 22
Tassajara Zen Mountain Center (California), 261
television, 1, 335, 336, 351
Temple of the Queen of Heaven (San Francisco), 76
temples: Asian, 1; Buddhist, 10n.2; Buddhist and Hindu, 7; Chinese, 6, 8, 22, 61, 62, 73, 75–78, 331–34; Hindu, 16, 213, 289, 290–94, 299–303; Jain, 19, 309; Japanese, 123, 160–61; Korean Buddhist, 223; Sikh, 6, 82, 312; Taiwanese Buddhist, 331–35; Thai Buddhist, 223, 328; Theravada Buddhist, 322; Vietnamese Buddhist, 315–19; 389–91; at Yogaville, 254; Zen Buddhist, 204, 205. See also architecture, gurdwaras
Tendai Buddhism, 154
Tenrikyo, 395
Tet, 312, 390
Thailand, 9, 17, 364
Thai Youth Club (Chicago), 327
Thais, 3, 13, 223, 319, 328–30, 364
theism, 372. See also God, monotheism
Theosophical Society, 64, 133, 141, 143, 145, 151–53, 185, 191
therapy, 1, 7
Theravada Buddhism: at Dharma Vijaya, 322–24; and Dharmapala, 133; number of U.S. temples practicing, 322; summary of, 17; Thomas Merton's encounter with, 354; and Vipassana in U.S., 225, 274, 275–77; at Wat Dhammaram, 328. See also Burmese, Cambodians, Laotians, Sri Lankans, Thais
Thien An, Thich, 315, 320
Thoreau, Henry David, 19, 95–98, 196, 215, 342
Thurman, Howard, 215–18
Thurman, Robert, 225
Thurman, Sue Bailey, 215–18
Tibet, 18, 162, 320, 349, 350, 401
Tibetan Book of the Dead, 161
Tibetan Buddhism: and the Beastie Boys, 349–50; and the Buddhist Sangha Council of Southern California, 320; and celebrities, 10n.2; Chogyam Trungpa on, 264–68; the Dalai Lama and, 54, 58, 162, 268, 319–22, 345, 350, 363–65, 371; in film, 1, 351–53; and Jews, 369–71; and mantras, 18, 238, 239; and parallels with Roman Catholicism, 54–55, 58–59; and Philip Glass, 347; summary of, 18; and teachers in U.S., 225; Thomas Merton on, 362–65; titles in, 227n.2
Tibetans, 225, 320. See also Tibetan Buddhism
Ticanwalla, Yogi, 179
T'ien, 37. See also Chinese, Confucianism
Tillich, Paul, 379
Tobase, Hodo, 232
Topaz Relocation Center, 160
trade, Asian, 2, 20, 25–26, 44, 51–53, 103
Transcendental Meditation, 162, 224, 241–44
Transcendentalism, 62, 92–97, 98, 100, 111, 114
transcontinental railroad, 63, 98, 100, 101
transnationalism. See immigration, migration
travel, 3: in Asia, 103, 121, 224, 362; and Beat Buddhism, 196–200; in Burma, 274; in Japan, 7, 154–56, 200, 225, 270, 342; in India, 29–32, 49, 145, 187, 215–18, 235, 258, 345, 369; and mental maps, 5; and plans for itinerant monks, 193; in Sri Lanka, 141, 151, 153–54; in Tibet, 349–50. See also missionaries, pilgrimage, trade